A Survey of

Old Testament

Introduction

by Gleason Archer, Jr.

MOODY PRESS

Chicago

Grateful acknowledgment is given here for the photos taken or furnished by:

Dr. Gleason Archer: 237, 243, 384, 394, 404, 415, 418, 427, 439, 442, 444, 455, 460, 462, 463, 473, 474, 475, 540

Earl Hagar: 90, 123, 154, 178, 287, 294, 392, 454

Dr. Gary Hill: 280

Dr. John Rea: 288, 377

Sisters of Zion, Jerusalem: 288, 377

Charts designed by
Mlodok & Hanson Design–Chicago: 18, 26, 42, 68, 200, 346-347, 386

Maps are taken from: *The Moody Atlas of Bible Lands.* by Barry J. Beitzel. Chicago: Moody Press, 1985.

Pre-press production and graphics by H.E.L.P.S. (Hill Educational Language Pictorial System), a division of Discovery Bible Ministries Inc.

5   7   9   10   8   6   4

Printed in the United States of America

To
My wife, Sandra

Gleason L. Archer (B.A., M.A., Ph. D., Harvard University; B.D., Princeton Theological Seminary; L.L.B., Suffolk Law School) is professor emeritus of Old Testament and Semitic languages at Trinity Evangelical Divinity School. He continues to teach part time at Trinity in Deerfield, Illinois, and has served as a minister of the Evangelical Free Church of America since 1966.

He is the author of numerous books, including *Job: God's Answer to Undeserved Suffering* and *Old Testament Quotations in the New Testament,* and he co-wrote *A theological Wordbook of the Old Testament.* His instrumental work in the preparation of the Old Testament portion of the New American Standard Bible has gained wide acclaim and positioned him as a world-renowned scholar.

CONTENTS

PART ONE: GENERAL INTRODUCTION

PART TWO: SPECIAL INTRODUCTION

ILLUSTRATIONS

PREFACE TO FIRST EDITION

The purpose of this *Survey of Old Testament Introduction* is to furnish a simple and usable text for the instruction of college and seminary students who have had no previous training in Old Testament criticism. It is also designed to provide a general discussion of the field for ministers and other serious Bible students. Due to the necessity of conserving space, the author has made no attempt to discuss all the most recent books and articles in this field, but rather has contented himself with developing the most representative and influential views of the acknowledged leaders in the study of Old Testament introduction. An attempt has been made in the interest of clarity to confine the discussion to the main issues and to handle those issues in a way which the novice can understand and appreciate.

The reader will find that this book adheres to a consistently conservative or evangelical viewpoint. For this the author makes no apology, except to say that it is his personal conviction that only the orthodox view of the Bible does real justice to the testimony of the biblical text itself and truly squares with the evidence presented by all the relevant data. At the same time a consistent effort has been made to deal fairly with the differing views and theories of those adhering to a liberal or neoorthodox position, and to present their premises and conclusions in a way to be readily comprehended and fairly appraised by the reader.

PREFACE TO SECOND EDITION

No major changes have been introduced into this new edition, but an effort has been made to correct typographical errors or to clarify obscure wording here and there where ambiguities have been noted. Certain chapters have been amplified, however, and a few portions (notably in chap. 20) have been deleted in order to make way for an improved treatment of the subject matter. A selective use has been made of some of the more recent works dealing with Old Testament criticism which have appeared since 1963. I wish to express thanks to the many students and readers of the first edition who have contributed suggestions for the improvement of this volume.

Trinity Evangelical Divinity School, Deerfield, Illinois
September, 1973

PREFACE TO THIRD EDITION

After nearly three decades this *Survey of Old Testament Introduction* has proved to be helpful to many thousands of Bible students who train for ministry in the Lord's service, and who are in need of being adequately equipped to deal with the issues of authentic divine authority and inspiration involved in the Hebrew-Aramaic Scriptures of the Old Testament. When the first edition became available in 1965 there was little indication that it would become so widely used over so long a period of time as has proved to be the case. In 1974 a second edition proved to be timely, especially in view of increasing archaeological discoveries emanating from the Qumran Caves and Tell Mardikh. These two editions have been translated into Italian, Portuguese, French,

Chinese, Spanish, Korean and German, and are widely used all over the world in the preparation of pastors and Bible teachers on every continent of our globe. For this totally unexpected distribution of a fairly technical piece of scholarship we can only give God the glory.

It is now time to prepare an updated third edition of this work in order to inform a new generation of Bible students that the Bible continues to be demonstrable as the trustworthy and inerrant Word of God, despite all of the efforts of modern skeptics to undermine its credibility as authentic revelation from God. By any fair examination of the data which it contains, employing the rules of legal evidence and avoiding the pitfalls of humanistic subjectivism and circular reasoning, it is abundantly apparent that this most influential book in all of human history can only be understood by any unbiased investigator as being the inerrant revelation from God that Jesus of Nazareth affirmed to be the true status of the Hebrew Scriptures.

Most of the additional material in this third edition deals with more recent approaches and variations in modern Liberal scholarship of the twentieth century, in order that evangelical workers may be acquainted with the most prominent leaders in the antisupernaturalist camp, and come to terms with the radical biases of those who would appear to be learned scholars and therefore worthy of credence. This edition of our work will serve to bring out the basic fallacies of their attacks upon God's Word, and reassure the Church of the supernatural and utterly trustworthy authority of the Holy Scriptures. In addition we should point out that a good number of illustrations, maps and charts have been added in order to enhance the interest and usefulness of this work.

We can only rejoice in the amazing upsurge of evangelical scholarship that has taken place in some of the largest conservative training schools in our country since the first edition came upon the scene. We are looking for continued growth in the spread of the Gospel all over Planet Earth in these coming decades before the Lord returns. And we give Him all the glory for the multiplied thousands of Bible-believing pastors, missionaries and congregations who are preparing the way for His coming again. To this end the Third Edition of *Survey of Old Testament Introduction* is humbly and sincerely dedicated.

In closing I wish to express profound appreciation for the encouragement and assistance of Dr. Gary Hill, general editor of *The Discovery Bible* project, and the valued co-workers who have made possible the production of this enlarged addition. Notably and most especially, Mrs. Vicki Westerhoff has served as my manager and proofreader week by week and has made it possible for me to complete the project by the appointed deadline. Bernie Burke deserves the credit for the design and production of the book, Daniel Hill has managed the computerized photography, and Tom Volpert served as the D.I.G.A.R. specialist. For them all I give God the thanks and the glory for the achievement of this new format and all of its helpful pictorial additions.

Gleason L. Archer
Feb. 1994

ABBREVIATIONS

A	Codex Alexandrinus
AB	*Archaeology and the Bible*, G. A. Barton
ABH	*Archaeology and Bible History*, Joseph P. Free
ALQ	*Ancient Library of Qumran*. F. M. Cross
ANET	*Ancient Near Eastern Texts*, J. B. Pritchard (ed.)
AOT	*Archaeology and the Old Testament*, M. F. Unger
AOOT	*Ancient Orient and the Old Testament*, K. A. Kitchen
AP	*The Archaeology of Palestine*, W. F. Albright
ASOR	American Schools of Oriental Research
ASV	American Standard Version
B	Codex Vaticanus
BA	*Biblical Archaeologist*
BAM	*Our Bible and the Ancient Manuscripts*, Frederic Kenyon
BASOR	*Bulletin of the American Schools of Oriental Research*
BDB	*Brown, Driver, Briggs, Gesenius Hebrew-English Lexicon*
CBQ	*Catholic Biblical Quarterly*
CD	*Damascus Document* (from Cairo Genizah)
CSS	*Companion to Scripture Studies*, J. E. Steinmueller
CT	*Christianity Today*
CVSS	*The Christian Review of Science and Scripture*, B. Ramm
DJD	*Discoveries in the Judaean Desert of Jordan*
DSPS	*The Dead Sea Psalms Scroll*, J. A. Sanders
DSS	*Dead Sea Scrolls*, Millar Burrows
EA	*Die El-Amarna Tafeln*, J. Knudtzon
EBD	*Encyclopedia of Bible Difficulties*, G. L. Archer
EG	*Wortherbuch Der AEgyptischen Sprache*
FBM	*The Five Books of Moses*, O. T. Allis
GATE	*Grundriss für Alttestamentliche Einleitung*, Wilhelm Moeller
IBOT	*Introduction to the Books of the Old Testament*, W. O. E. Oesterley and T. H. Robinson
ICC	*International Critical Commentary*
IDB	*Interpreter's Dictionary of the Bible*
IEJ	*Israel Exploration Journal*
IGOT	*Introductory Guide to the Old Testament*, M. F. Unger
ILOT	*Introduction to the Literature of the Old Testament*, S. R. Driver
IOT	*Introduction to the Old Testament*
ISBE	*International Standard Bible Encyclopedia*
JAOS	*Journal for the Study of the Old Testament*
JBL	*Journal of Biblical Literature*
JNES	*Journal of Near Eastern Studies*
JSS	*Journal of Semitic Studies*
JTC	*Journal for Theology and Church*
KJV	King James Version
LAP	*Light from the Ancient Past*, J. Finegan

LXX	Septuagint Version of the Old Testament
MLDSS	*More Light on the Dead Sea Scrolls*, Millar Burrows
MT	Masoretic Text of the Old Testament (Hebrew)
NASB	New American Standard Bible
OHH	*An Outline of Hebrew History*, J. B. Payne
OTI	*Old Testament Introduction*, John H. Raven
OTMS	*Old Testament and Modern Study*, H. H. Rowley
PEQ	*Palestine Exploration Quarterly*
POT	*The Problem of the Old Testament*, James Orr
PTR	*Presbyterian Theological Review*
QHBT	*Qumran and the History of the Biblical Text*, F. Cross and S. Talmon
RB	*Revue Biblique*
RQ	*Revue de Qumran*
RSV	Revised Standard Version
SAC	*From the Stone Age to Christianity*, W. F. Albright
SIOT	*Scientific Investigation of the Old Testament*, Robert Dick Wilson
SIP	*Short Introduction to the Pentateuch*, G. C. Aalders
SWDS	*Scrolls from the Wilderness of the Dead Sea*, (Smithsonian Exhibit Catalogue, American Schools of Oriental Research, 1965)
TAT	*Der Text Des Alten Testaments*, E. Würthwein
TOT	*Text of the Old Testament*, E. Würthwein
VAB	*Vorasiatische Bibliothek*
VT	*Vetus Testamentum*
1QS	First Qumran Cave *Serekh* or *Rule of the Congregation*

1 INTRODUCTION

THE HOLY BIBLE is like no other book in all the world. It is the only book which presents itself as the written revelation of the one true God, intended for the salvation of man, and demonstrating its divine authority by many infallible proofs. Other religious documents, such as the Muslim Koran, may claim to be the very word of God, but they contain no such self-authenticating proofs as does the Bible (e.g., the phenomena of fulfilled prophecy). As the record of God's holy will for man, the Bible is of utmost importance to understand aright the true meaning of the revelations it contains. It will not do to construe the words of Scripture as if they were given in our modern age and addressed to present-day English-speaking peoples facing twentieth-century problems. To be sure, the Bible does convey God's message to us today, and is as relevant to us as it was to the Hebrews of ancient times. But the form in which that message was given was an ancient Hebrew form, and it was in the first instance addressed to people who faced the special issues and circumstances peculiar to their own day and age. We cannot properly understand the underlying and permanent principles contained in these ancient utterances of God unless we first of all take stock of the problems and challenges that confronted His people in the generation in which He spoke to them.

THE PURPOSE OF THE BIBLE

The Holy Bible comes to us as a set of directions, right from the hand of the Manufacturer who first invented and produced the human race. For any piece of machinery a purchaser must consult diligently every word of instruction as to how to put the machine or contrivance together, or else his result will be frustration and disaster. For such a marvelously constructed creation as man, with all of his spiritual and material components, the need of an authoritative book of directions is utterly necessary. Why are we here on Planet Earth? What makes us different from other biological species, and what is the purpose of our existence?

Basically there are two possible answers to this question, as set forth in the third chapter of Genesis, where Adam and Eve have enjoyed an ideal setting of safety and plenty in happy fellowship with the God who created them to be His children, engaged in His service and committed to His glory. The clear and evident purpose of their existence was to glorify God and enjoy Him forever. But since they were moral agents possessing a free will, it was necessary for them to be faced with an alternative purpose of life. This was persuasively presented to them by the serpentine agent of Satan, who suggested that God did not really love them for their own sakes and only wished to exploit them by forbidding access to the Tree of the Knowledge of Good and Evil. The Lord was accused of depriving of them of their basic right, which was to seek their own interests and assert their own just prerogatives. The life proposed by Satan was to live for themselves, to seek their own happiness and ascend to a godlike knowledge of good and evil. When Eve accepted this ego-centered principle for her life's purpose and persuaded Adam to join with her in this stand against God and His holy will, the love relationship between God and man was interrupted and profoundly altered by the Fall.

God had to seek Adam and Eve out as they vainly tried to hide in the bushes from His gaze and then direct them to confession and repentance, followed by expelling them from Eden, and subjecting them to labor and pain as they shifted to the more hostile environment of the world outside. But He was able to counter the triumph of Satan by the plan of redemption which was first intimated to Eve in Gen. 3:15, to declare to them that a messianic descendant of the woman would some day crush the head of the Satanic serpent and pay full atonement for their sin upon the altar of sacrifice. The skins with which their naked bodies were covered came from animals who had been slain, and Abel's later offering of a sheep upon the altar indicates quite clearly that Adam's family believed in and looked forward to, the redemption which the Lord Jesus achieved for them and all of their believing descendants upon the Hill of Calvary.

Sophisticated modern scholarship may dismiss this record in Genesis as childish myth, but the fact still remains that the two alternatives set before Eve must be chosen and answered by every member of the human race. Either we human beings are created for loving fellowship with God with the purpose of living for His glory, or else we replace Him with our own ego as the highest value in life. There is no other eligible choice left to us, for even a dedication to the welfare of others or of mankind or society in general can be valid only if we have indeed as a human race been given a special value as children of God. No such value is capable of confirmation or proof, once the authority and trustworthiness of the Bible has been rejected. Those who put themselves above God as the most important person in the universe become guilty of moral insanity and take no more benefit from the Book of directions which comes to us in the Holy Bible.

It should also be pointed out that modern intelligentsia who assert a knowledge of the purpose of life (intelligent self-interest) which surpasses that of the prophets and apostles of old, and of the Lord Jesus Himself, put themselves in a very awkward fideistic position. The Scripture confronts them with a pattern of prediction and fulfillment which is completely beyond mere human ability. None of us really knows what the future may bring; even the events of the morrow are hidden from us day by day. But the Bible is replete with short-range and long-range predictions that could not possibly have been foreknown by man apart from the inspiration of God. A selection of these predictions will be found in Excursus 1 at the end of this book. Suffice it to say that this evidence is so clear and irrefutable that no thinker can honestly say that he is intellectually respectable if he rejects the divine inspiration of the Holy Bible.

THE SCOPE OF INTRODUCTION

Old Testament introduction is the term applied to a systematic study of the ancient background against which the first thirty-nine books of the Bible are to be properly understood. It deals with matters of language, custom, historical situations, persons, places, and events alluded to in the various books of the Bible. In its larger scope it includes the following branches of study:

1. The languages in which the Old Testament was originally written, that is, Hebrew and Aramaic, along with those related Semitic languages (such as Arabic, Assyrian, Phoenician, Ugaritic, and Syriac) which help us understand the meaning of the words used in the biblical text.

2. The history of the Hebrew people and of those neighboring countries with which they had contact.

3. The religion and culture of these non-Hebrew nations, as they are revealed to us by ancient pagan authors and by the discoveries of modern archaeology.

4. The authorship of the several books of the Bible, since the question of who wrote the book has an important bearing upon its meaning and its reliability.

5. The date, or at least the approximate time, when each book was composed—since this often gives a clue as to what issues were confronting God's people when He spoke to them.

6. The historical situation and contemporary problems to which the inspired authors addressed themselves as spokesmen for God.

7. The original text of each book as it existed before slips of the pen or other copyists' errors may have crept into the form of the text which has been preserved to us. (This is known as textual criticism.)

8. The integrity of the text, that is, the question of whether each book was entirely written by the author claimed for it, or whether the writings of others have been combined with it.

9. The history of the transmission of the text, that is, the way in which each book was copied and handed on in the various manuscript families, and translated into the various ancient languages of the peoples to whom Judaism and Christianity came during subsequent centuries, until finally the Hebrew text itself (and its various translations into Greek, Latin, Syriac, etc.) was put into printed form after the invention of the printing press.

As a general rule, the first three divisions of introduction described above are dealt with in separate courses in language or history, while Old Testament introduction as an academic subject is restricted to the last six divisions. Furthermore, within introduction itself there are two main subdivisions: general introduction and special introduction.

CLASSIFICATION OF SEMITIC LANGUAGES
(According to Geographical Location)

	East Semitic	**South Semitic**	**Northwest Semitic**	
Primary	Akkadian	Arabic	Canaanite	Aramaic
Dialects	Babylonian	North Arabic	Eblaic	Old Aramaic
	Assyrian	South Arabic	Ugaritic	Biblical Aramaic
		Minean	Phoenician	Imperial Aramaic
		Hadramautian	Hebrew	Nabataean
		Qatabanean	Ammonite	Syriac
		Ethiopic	Moabite	
		Amharic		

General introduction deals with matters of the text (both in the original language in which it was composed and in the early versions into which it was first translated). It also considers the canon, that is, the question of which books are truly inspired and authoritative, and the approximate period in history when they were so recognized by the people of God. It gives an account of the origin and extent of the canon and the arrangement and preservation of the books that comprises it. Since the question of the date and authorship of the Pentateuch (the five books of Moses) is so deeply involved with the theory of the canon, it is usually included in the field of general introduction.

As for *special introduction*, it treats the individual books of the Old Testament one by one, giving an account of authorship, date, purpose, and integrity. It may also discuss the overall structure and basic message of each book, although a detailed treatment of its contents belongs more properly to a course in Bible survey than in introduction.

THE RELATIONSHIP OF THE OLD TESTAMENT TO THE NEW

The New Testament authors regarded the books of the Old Testament (the Law and the Prophets) as a single composite whole (the Scripture), ultimately authored by God Himself, although mediated through human authors who wrote down His truth under His infallible guidance (cf. Gal. 3:8; 2 Peter 1:20). The inspired apostles regarded the intention of the divine Author of the Hebrew Scriptures as the important thing; the intent of the human author was a merely subordinate matter. It could even happen that the human author of the Old Testament prophecy did not understand the full significance of what he was writing, although his actual words expressed the purpose of the divine Author who inspired him (see 1 Peter 1:10-11). The New Testament writers viewed the entire Hebrew Scriptures as a testimony to Jesus Christ, the perfect Man who fulfilled all the law; the Sacrifice and High Priest of the ritual ordinances; the Prophet, Priest, and King of whom the prophets foretold; and the Lover whom the poetical books described. They saw prophetic significance even in the historical events of the Old Testament record. Thus the crossing of the Red Sea prefigured Christian baptism (1 Cor. 10:1-2); Joshua's conquest of Canaan prefigured the spiritual rest into which Christians enter by faith (Heb. 3-4); and the calling of Israel out of Egypt foreshadowed the experience of the child Jesus (Matt. 2:15).

In general we may say that the Old Testament presented the preparation of which the New Testament was the fulfillment; it was the seed and plant of which the New Testament was the glorious fruit. Precisely because Jesus of Nazareth fulfilled what the Old Testament predicted, His life and deeds possessed absolute finality, rather than His being a mere religious sage like many others. For this reason also, the Gospel of Christ possesses divine validity which sets it apart from all man-made religions. The Old Testament demonstrates that Jesus and His Church were providential, the embodiment of the purpose of God; the New Testament proves that the Hebrew Scriptures constituted a coherent and integrated organism, focused upon a single great theme and exhibiting a single program of redemption.

The Semitic Family of Languages

Just as truly as the genius of the Greek language imposed its stamp upon the New Testament revelation and the terms in which its message was cast, even so was the genius of the Hebrew language determinative for the expression of the Old Testament message. It made a great deal of difference that Greek was precise in expressing time values, and that Hebrew laid chief emphasis upon mode of action rather than upon tenses. Adequate interpretation of the Old Testament revelation demands a thorough grasp of these peculiar traits of the Hebrew verb and of Hebrew syntax generally; otherwise much misunderstanding and wresting of the Scriptures will result.

To a very large extent, Hebrew shared these grammatical and syntactical characteristics with the rest of the Semitic languages. Therefore it is important to examine these related tongues and derive from them the light which they can throw upon Hebrew usage. Moreover, in the matter of vocabulary, the study of Comparative Semitics is of utmost significance. It often happens that a word which appears only once or twice in the Hebrew Bible is found quite commonly in some of the related languages, and can be interpreted with a high degree of accuracy by comparison with them.

The traditional classification of the various Semitic languages divides them, according to the geographical location of the nations speaking them, into north, south, east, and west. East Semitic includes but one main language, Akkadian, divided into the slightly differing dialects of Babylonian and Assyrian. South Semitic includes Arabic (subdivided into North Arabic, the classical, literary language; and South Arabic with its subdialects: Sabean, Minean, Qatabanian, and Hadramautian) and Ethiopic (or Geez) with its modern descendant, Amharic. Northwest-Semitic embraces both the Canaanite and the Aramaic dialects, which is usually divided into eastern and western branches (the eastern being the basis for the Syriac language of the Christian era, and the western being the basis for biblical Aramaic as found in Daniel and Ezra). West Semitic (often classed with Aramaic in what is called Northwest Semitic by modern scholars) is comprised of Ugaritic, Phoenician, and Canaanite (of which Hebrew and Moabite are dialects).

It should be added that the newly discovered Eblaic language from Tell Mardikh would seem to be basically Canaanite, in its vocabulary, but somewhat East Semitic in its morphology. Dating from the 24th century B.C., it is as old as the Akkadian of Sargon I of Agade. For a more extensive treatment of Ebla, see Excursus 2.

Non-Semitic tongues which contributed some terms in the Hebrew language include: (1) the basically Hamitic speech of Egypt (which was subjected to Semitic influence upon the Hamitic inhabitants of the Nile Valley; (2) Sumerian, the agglutinative speech of the earlier, non-Semitic race which conquered and civilized Lower Mesopotamia prior to the Babylonians; and (3) the Indo-Iranian Persian which appears in post-Exilic books like Daniel and Ezra, and is distantly related to Greek. Each of these contributed a small percentage of vocabulary to biblical Hebrew.

2 THE INSPIRATION OF THE OLD TESTAMENT

BEFORE COMMENCING a higher critical study of the Old Testament, it is appropriate for us to come to terms with the basic question of what kind of book it is. If it is merely a product of human genius, like many other documents upon which religions have been founded, then the data which it presents must be handled in one specific way. That is, these holy writings must be dealt with in purely literary terms, and naturalistic explanations must be found for every feature which appears to be supernatural (such as fulfilled prophecy). If, on the other hand, the thirty-nine books of the Old Testament are inspired by God, employing human instruments to record the truth He revealed to man, then the data must be handled in a quite different fashion. That is to say, everything which might appear to be inconsistent with that standard of accuracy and truth which divine inspiration presupposes[1] must be carefully investigated in order to arrive at a satisfactory reconciliation of apparent discrepancies. Thus the whole line of investigation is profoundly influenced by the premise with which we start.

EVIDENCE FOR THE UNIQUE INSPIRATION OF THE BIBLE This is not the place to enter into a thorough treatment of Christian evidences; that is the province of textbooks on apologetics. But it is appropriate to suggest here, at least in a cursory way, why it is reasonable and proper to start with the premise that the Old Testament is a collection of books inspired by God.

In the first place, there is significant unity which underlies the entire collection of thirty-nine books in the Old Testament, betraying an organic interconnection which carries through the many centuries during which it was being composed. These books exhibit a remarkable singleness of purpose and program, most rea-

---

1. There remains, of course, a third possibility: that God chose to reveal His truth through an imperfect revelation in which truth was mingled with error. But this would be a quite useless or unusable type of revelation, inasmuch as it would require infallible human judgment to discern the truth from the error. See the section under "Inerrancy of the Original Autographs" in this chapter.

sonably explained as the operation of a single mind, the mind of the divine Author Himself.[2] (A classic discussion of this aspect of Scripture is found in chap. 2 of James Orr's *Problem of the Old Testament* [POT]. Though he published this work in 1907 [New York: Scribner], Orr's line of argument has never been successfully refuted and is still valid today.)

Second, of all world religions, only the Hebrew-Christian offers a logically defensible epistemology (science of religious knowledge). The end result of four thousand years of human investigation and philosophic inquiry has, apart from the Bible itself, been hopeless disagreement and confusion in the whole area of religion. Some theorists have urged the manufacturing of a system of ethics and vague theism which they call a world religion. But the fact remains that the tensions between Christianity, Judaism, Hinduism, Buddhism, and Islam are just as sharp today as they ever have been, even though milder methods of propagation or protection are usually employed today than in earlier ages. They still give entirely different answers to the question, "What must I do to be saved?"

Contrast the situation which prevails in the realms of medicine and science. The many centuries of experimentation and research have resulted in general agreement among all civilized nations as to the basic laws of chemistry and physics. To be sure, the emergence of new data makes necessary the constant revision of the theories and conclusions which scientists publish from year to year; but by and large, the scientific world remains in substantial agreement the world over.

In the case of religion, however, which deals with questions of the greatest importance for mankind, there has appeared no consensus whatsoever. It often happens that two men who have been reared as brothers in the same home, have enjoyed the same educational advantages, and possess the same degree of intelligence, may hold views of religion which diametrically oppose each other. If it were possible for the tools of human reason and scientific research to lead to valid results in the realm of metaphysics, men of equal education and enlightenment would surely come to some measure of agreement (just as they do in philology or science). Nothing, however, could be further from the case so far as religion is concerned. We are scarcely any nearer to agreement today than our ancestors were four thousand years ago; perhaps even less so, for they had not yet invented atheistic naturalism at that early period. It logically follows that human investigation, even with the most careful and scientific methodology, can lead to nothing more

---

2. Of course it is possible to handle the Old Testament writings in an artificially dissectionist way, in the interests of a theory of diverse sources and conglomerate authorship. One who has espoused such theories is not obliged to interpret texts in the light of their overall context and setting, but he may always, by ingenious twists of interpretation, find disagreements and discrepancies between the sources. He may uncover divergent viewpoints and inconsistencies in any given work which would never occur as such to the mind of the unbiased reader who is simply reading the book to grasp its message. But even the doctrinaire dissectionist must finally acknowledge that in the form in which the Hebrew Scriptures have been preserved to us, there is very little difference, if any, between the concept of God and the covenant which appears in the latest portion of the Old Testament and that which is found in its earliest written sections. Nor can there be any doubt that from the standpoint of Christ and the New Testament apostles, the entire Old Testament represented a single unity that spoke as with a single voice—"the Holy Scripture."

solid than mere conjecture when it comes to the destiny of the soul and the meaning of life. Man by his own searching cannot find out God; at best he can only conjecture. A guilty defendant before the court can hardly be objective about himself.

How then can we know God or His will for our lives? Only if He reveals Himself to us! Unless He Himself tells us, we can never know for sure the answers to those questions which matter most to us as human beings. At this point it is important to observe that the Bible presents itself to us as the written revelation of God. This purports to be a book in which God gives us the answers to the great questions which concern our soul, and which all the wisdom and science of man are powerless to solve with any degree of certainty. The Bible asserts of itself that it is the special revelation from God; it must therefore be acknowledged as claiming to be the right kind of source from which to derive a trustworthy knowledge of religious truth.[3] It comes to us with the claim that the words are from God Himself: "Thus saith the Lord." If there be a God, and if He is concerned for our salvation, this is the only way (apart from direct revelation from God to each individual of each successive generation) that He could reliably impart this knowledge to us. It must be through a reliable written record such as the Bible purports to be.[4]

INERRANCY OF THE ORIGINAL AUTOGRAPHS

We must next ask ourselves the question, What kind of record is this Book going to be? One containing errors of various kinds, or one free from all error? If this written revelation contains mistakes, then it can hardly fulfill its intended purpose: to convey to man in a reliable way the will of God for his salvation. Why is this so? Because a demonstrated mistake in one part gives rise to the possibility that there may be mis-

---

3. To be sure, there are a few other religious scriptures which make the same claim for themselves, such as the Koran and the Book of Mormon. It must be conceded, however, that these two documents lack the credentials which authenticate the Bible as the true record of God's revelation. Most notably they lack the validation of prior prophecy and subsequent fulfillment, and the all-pervading presence of the divine-human Redeemer. The Book of Mormon is vitiated by many historical inconsistencies and inaccuracies, and the Koran (which is claimed to have been dictated from a heavenly archetype coeternal with Allah) exhibits not only the most startling historical inaccuracies but also the changing viewpoints of a human author (Muhammed) in the light of the current events of his own day. Nor is there any comparison between the Bible and these other books when it comes to the grandeur and sublimity of thought it conveys, or the power with which it penetrates the human soul with life-changing consequences. (For specific details, see Appendixes 2 and 3.)

4. What about oral tradition? May not the inerrant truth of God be handed down from mouth to mouth through successive generations? Yes, indeed, it may be, and undoubtedly portions of the Bible were preserved in this way for a good many years before finding their authoritative, written form. But oral tradition is necessarily fluid in character and in constant danger of corruption because of the subjective factor—the uncertain memory of the custodian of that tradition. The legacy of faith was handed down through the millennia from Adam to Moses in oral form, for the most part, but the final written form into which Moses cast it must have been especially superintended by the Holy Spirit in order to insure its divine trustworthiness. The Scriptures themselves lay the greatest emphasis upon their written state, and scarcely ever impute divine trustworthiness to mere oral tradition. While it was of course true that the words which Moses, the prophets, Jesus of Nazareth, and the apostles spoke were divinely authoritative from the moment they were uttered, yet there was no other way of accurately preserving them except by inscripturation (i.e., recording them in writing under the guidance of the Holy Spirit).

takes in other parts of the Bible. If the Bible turns out to be a mixture of truth and error, then it becomes a book like any other.

No doubt, there is truth in every other religious document known to man—the Koran, the Vedas, the Upanishads, the Analects, the Iliad, and the Odyssey—even though this truth may coexist with an abundance of error. What is to be done with books of this sort, books containing both truth and error? There is only one thing that can be done, and that is to subject them to the critical faculty of the human reason. Within proper limits, to be sure, the reasoning powers of man have a legitimate and necessary function in weighing the evidences presented by these documents, to see whether they are consistent with divine origin. Here it is a question of recognizing the identity of a purported revelation as to whether it is the Word of God. Human reason is competent to pass upon these evidences, applying the rule of self-contradiction and the other canons of logic, in order to determine whether the data of the texts themselves square with the claims of divine origin. (It has already been pointed out in footnote 3 that only the Bible, as opposed to other religious documents, contains decisive evidences of divine inspiration and authority.)

But it is a very different thing for human reason to attempt to pass judgment upon divine revelation as such, to determine its truth or falsity. For such judgments to be valid, they must proceed from a Judge who possesses a knowledge of metaphysical truth which is superior to that of the revelation itself. In other words, man must know more about God and the soul and spiritual values than the Bible itself knows, if he is to pass valid judgment on the truth of the Bible. But this is obviously not the case, as pointed out previously (pp. 22-23), and therefore man is totally dependent on divine revelation for this all-important knowledge. For this reason, if that revelation is to come in a usable and reliable form, not dependent on man's fallible judgment, it must come in an inerrant form. Otherwise it would depend ultimately on the authority of man for its validation, and, therefore, could not serve its purpose as a trustworthy disclosure of divine truth.

TEXTUAL TRANSMISSION NOT NECESSARILY INFALLIBLE

At this point we must make a distinction. Inerrancy (freedom from all error) is necessary only for the original manuscripts (autographs) of the biblical books. They must have been free from all mistakes, or else they could not have been truly inspired by the God of truth in whom is no darkness at all. God could never have inspired a human author of Scripture to write anything erroneous or false.[5] To say that God could

5. The question may be raised as to the infallibility of the sources from which the Scripture record (such as the genealogical tables in Genesis and Chronicles) may have been copied. If temple archives or palace records were consulted (as they probably were) and if these records were previously written down by uninspired men (as was probably the case), why can we not limit the inerrancy of Scripture to mere accuracy in copying out the human record, whether or not that record was free from mistake? In other words, could there not be inspired mistakes in the Scriptures?

We must answer this question with another: What essential difference is there between a fallible human record and a fallible human speaker? If the written words of men could be accepted into Scripture even though erroneous and mistaken, does it not follow that their spoken words could also be so

not use fallible man as an instrument of His infallible truth is as illogical as to insist that an artist can never produce a valid painting because his brush is capable of slipping.

But what about the text of the Bible as we now possess it? Is that text necessarily free from all mistakes of every kind? Not when it comes to copyists' errors, for we certainly do find discrepancies among the handwritten copies that have been preserved to us, even those which come from the earliest centuries. Some slips of the pen may have crept into the first copies made from the original manuscripts, and additional errors of a transmissional type could have found their way into the copies of copies. It is almost unavoidable that this should have been the case. No one alive can sit down and copy out the text of an entire book without a mistake of any kind. (Those who doubt this statement are invited to try it themselves!) It would take nothing short of a miracle to insure the inerrancy of a copy of an original manuscript.

Granted, then, that errors have crept into our texts as we now have them, how can they serve as a reliable medium for disclosing God's will? Are we not right back with the problem of books containing both truth and error? Not at all, for there is a great difference between a document which was wrong at the start and a document which was right at the start but was miscopied. One may read a letter from his friend or relative and find in it such common slips as *of* for *or*, or *and* for *an*, or *led* for *lead* and yet by a simple process of correction in the light of the context, he may easily arrive at the true sense intended by the writer. Only if the errors which have gotten into the copies are so serious as to pervert the sense altogether does the message fail in accurate communication. But if the letter came from a correspondent who was confused, mistaken, or deceitful, then the errors and misinformation it contains are beyond remedy and the reader is injured thereby.

An objection is raised in modern scholarly circles in regard to the faithfulness of the transmission of the original text of scripture which seems to be quite specious and illogical. In view of the unquestioning acceptance of so many of the earliest surviving copies of Greek and Latin classical authors, very seldom is any objection raised on the ground of their unreliability because they are late or because there are so few of them.[6] But, in the case of the Bible there are hundreds of witnesses to the text of the Old Tes-

accepted? Who can suppose that everything that Moses or Isaiah or Malachi spoke was free from all error? Was it not when they were uttering the Word of the Lord that their utterance was infallible? As God employed their oral communications to reveal His truth, safe-guarding them from error until they were recorded in written form, so also God could take erroneous human archives and guide the human author to avoid all their errors and record only what was in fact true. Whatever Scripture asserts to have been historically true, regardless of the intermediate source of the information, must be understood as trustworthy and reliable. It makes no essential difference whether the source was written or oral, whether it came from a fallible human hand or a fallible human mouth; in either case the Holy Spirit eliminated mistakes and insured the inscripturation only of truth. All the discrepancies which have come down to us in the Received Text of the Hebrew Scriptures are perfectly well accounted for by errors in later textual transmission. There is no need to resort to a theory of mistakes copied out in the original autographs, and to do so endangers the authoritativeness of Scripture as a whole.

6. For a fuller comparison note the early authors, dates, and number of extant documents which rarely receive the same criticism as the far better attested biblical MSS. (See charts on following pages.)

EXTRABIBLICAL HISTORIANS

Author	Date	Title of Work
Eusebius	Ca. A.D. 263-340	The Life of Constantine, Ecclesiastical History
Herodotus	Ca. A.D. 484-425	The Histories
Flavius Josephus	A.D. 37-97	Antiquities of the Jews, Bellum Judaicum
Philo of Alexandria	30 B.C.-A.D. 40	Allegories of the Sacred Law
Polybius	Ca. 203-120 B.C.	Histories
Strabo	Ca. 64 B.C.-A.D. 24	Geography
Suetonius	Ca. A.D. 69-140	The Twelve Caesars
Tacitus	Ca. A.D. 58-120	Germania, Historiae, Annals
Thucydides	Ca. 460-400 B.C.	The History of the Peloponnesian Wars
Xenophon	Ca. 430-355 B.C.	Anabasis, Cyropaedia, Hellenica, Memorabilia

tament and over 20,000 witnesses to the text of the New Testament in their original languages and therefore it is safe to say that no documents of ancient times have ever had such a full and impressive witness to the text as is found for the 66 books of the Bible. It is highly significant that these non-biblical texts are so cheerfully accepted even though, for example works of Tacitus, Lucretius, Catullus, and Aristotle have fewer than five extant copies each, and largely bear much later datings than many biblical texts. It is difficult to avoid the conclusion that the objection as to the trustworthiness of the text is hardly sincere, but rather it appears as special pleading on the basis of a hostile bias that is scarcely worthy of responsible scholarship. It should be added that this kind of concern for flawless accuracy has a certain bearing on related matters such as the standard of weights and measures which should prevail throughout a society. One can hardly purchase an absolutely perfect pound or an absolutely perfect foot measure in any store in America. But, we all understand that in the Bureau of Weights and Measures in Washington D.C. there is a perfect standard. Those measures and weights that can be purchased can be judged by reference to those in the Bureau of Weights and Measures for objective verification.

COMPARISON OF OTHER ANCIENT WRITINGS

AUTHOR	Earliest Copy	No. of Copies
Caesar	900 A.D.	10
Plato (Tetralogies)	900 A.D.	20
Tacitus (Annals)	1100 A.D.	20
also minor works	1000 A.D.	1
Pliny the Younger (History)	850 A.D.	7
Thucydides (History)	900 A.D.	8
Suetonius	950 A.D.	8
Herodotus (History)	900 A.D.	8
Sophocles	1000 A.D.	100
Catullus	1550 A.D.	3
Euripedes	1100 A.D.	9
Demosthenes	1100 A.D.	200
Aristotle	1100 A.D.	5
Aristophanes	900 A.D.	10

This brings up the question of the faithfulness of the transmission of the Bible text. There are numerous types of manuscript error which the textual critic may discover in the early manuscripts of the Old Testament. (These will be discussed in chap. 4). Are these of so serious a nature as to corrupt the message itself, or make it impossible to convey the true meaning? If they are, then God's purpose has been frustrated; He could not convey His revelation so that those of later generations could understand it aright. If He did not exercise a restraining influence over the scribes who wrote out the standard and authoritative copies of the Scriptures, then they corrupted and falsified the message. If the message was falsified, the whole purpose of bestowing a written revelation has come to naught; for such a corrupted Scripture would be a mere mixture of truth and error, necessarily subject to human judgment (rather than sitting in judgment upon man).

Do we have any objective evidence that errors of transmission have not been permitted by God to corrupt and pervert His revelation? Yes, we have, for a careful study of the variants (different readings) of the various earliest manuscripts reveals that none of them affects a single doctrine of Scripture. The system of spiritual truth contained in the standard Hebrew text of the Old Testament is not in the slightest altered or compromised by any of the variant readings found in the Hebrew manuscripts of earlier date found in the Dead Sea caves or anywhere else. All that is needed to verify this is to check the register of well-attested variants in Rudolf Kittel's edition of the Hebrew Bible or else the more recent *Biblia Hebraica Stuttgartensia*. It is very evident that the vast majority of them are so inconsequential as to leave the meaning of each clause doctrinally unaffected.

It should be clearly understood that in this respect, the Old Testament differs from all other pre-Christian works of literature of which we have any knowledge. To be sure, we do not possess ordinarily so many different manuscripts of pagan productions, coming from such widely separated eras, as we do in the case of the Old Testament. Strong confirmation of this type of copyist error is found in various pagan records that have been preserved to us for the purposes of comparison. For example, in the Behistun Rock inscription set up by Darius I, around 510 B.C., we find that line 38 gives the figure for the slain of the army of Frada as 55,243, with 6,572 prisoners – according to the Babylonian column. In a duplicate copy of this inscription found at Babylon itself, the number of prisoners was 6,973. But in the Aramaic translation of this inscription discovered at the Elephantine in Egypt, the number of prisoners was only 6,972 – precisely the same discrepancy as we have noted in the comparison of Ezra 2 and Nehemiah 7 (cf. F. W. König, *Relief und Inschrift des Königs Dareios I am Felsen von Bagistan* [Leiden: Brill, 1938], p. 48). Similarly in line 31 of the same inscription, the Babylonian column gives 2,045 as the number of slain in the rebellious army of Frawartish, along with 1,558 prisoners, whereas the Aramaic copy has over 1,575 as the prisoner count (ibid., p. 45). (For greater detail on the discrepancies between the three-language inscription of Darius I on the above mentioned Behistun Rock inscription [i.e., the Persian, Babylonian, and Elamite], and the Aramaic papyrus copy found in the Elephantine, consult F. W. König: ibid, pp. 36-57.) But where we do, for example in the *Egyptian Book of the Dead*, the variations are of a far more extensive and serious nature. Quite startling differences appear, for example, between chapter 15 contained in the Papyrus of Ani (written in the Eighteenth Dynasty) and the Turin Papyrus (from the Twenty-sixth Dynasty or later). Whole clauses are inserted or left out, and the sense in corresponding columns of text is in some cases altogether different. Apart from divine superintendence of the transmission of the Hebrew text, there is no particular reason why the same phenomenon of discrepancy and change would not appear between Hebrew manuscripts produced centuries apart. Even though the two copies of Isaiah discovered in Qumran Cave 1 near the Dead Sea in 1947 were a thousand years earlier than the oldest dated manuscript previously known (A.D. 980), they proved to be word for word identical with our standard Hebrew Bible in more than 95 percent of the text, but in 1QIs^b (ca. 75 B.C.) the preserved text is almost letter for letter identical with the Leningrad Manuscript. The five percent of variation consisted chiefly of obvious slips of the pen and variations in spelling. Even those Dead Sea fragments of Deuteronomy and Samuel which point to a different manuscript family from that which underlies our received Hebrew text do not indicate any differences in doctrine or teaching. They do not affect the message of revelation in the slightest.

THE DOCTRINE OF INSPIRATION AFFIRMED BY SCRIPTURE

Does the Bible assert infallibility for itself? It has sometimes been argued that the Scriptures do not even claim inerrancy for themselves. But careful investigation shows that whenever they discuss the subject, they do in fact assert absolute authority for themselves as the inerrant Word of God.

Matt. 5:18: "For verily I [Christ] say unto you, Till heaven and earth pass, one jot [the smallest letter in the Hebrew alphabet] or one tittle [a distinguishing projection in Hebrew letters] shall in no wise pass from the Law [the Old Testament], till all be fulfilled." This indicates that not only the thoughts conveyed by Scripture, but also the individual words themselves, as valid vehicles of those thoughts and as spelled out by individual letters, are possessed of infallible truth and will surely find their fulfillment and realization.

John 10:35: "The Scripture cannot be broken" carries the same implications as the preceding.

2 Tim. 3:16: "All Scripture is God-breathed[7] [*theopneustos*], and is profitable for doctrine." From New Testament usage it can easily be established that "Scripture" (*graphē*) refers to the whole canon of the thirty-nine books of the Old Testament as we have them today. 2 Peter 3:16 implies that Paul's New Testament epistles also enjoy the same status as inspired Scriptures (*graphai*).

Heb. 1:1-2: "God, who...spake...by the prophets, hath...spoken unto us by his

---

7. This word is really to be rendered "breathed out by God" rather than "breathed into by God." The emphasis is upon the divine origin of the inscripturated revelation itself rather than upon a special quality infused into the words of Scripture.

Son." This asserts the same infallibility for the writings of the Old Testament prophets as it attaches to the New Testament message of Christ Himself.

1 Peter 1:10-11: "Of which salvation the [Old Testament] prophets have inquired and searched diligently, who prophesied of the grace that should come unto you: searching what, or what manner of time the Spirit of Christ which was in them did signify, when it testified beforehand the sufferings of Christ, and the glory that should follow." The implication is that the Holy Spirit was in these Old Testament authors, and that He guided them into composing words of infallible truth sure of fulfillment, even though the human authors themselves might not fully know all that these divinely guided words actually signified. Because of verses like these, in interpreting Scripture we must seek to establish not merely the intention of the human author who wrote the words, but also (and more important) the intention of the divine Author who guided in the composition of those words.

2 Peter 1:21: "The prophecy [the Old Testament prophetic Scriptures] came not in old time by the will of man: but holy men of God spake as they were moved [carried along, as the wind bears along a sailing ship] by the Holy Ghost." In their speech (as committed to writing) these Old Testament authors who prophesied of Christ were supernaturally carried into inerrant truth, truth that is not to be subjected to mere "private interpretation" (v. 20).

All these passages add up to this doctrine of inspiration: that accuracy inheres in every part of the Old Testament as well as the New Testament, so that as a whole and in all its parts, the Bible is infallible as to truth and final as to authority. This accuracy extends even to matters of history and science as well as to theology and morals. Some scholars, such as Henry P. Smith and Charles A. Briggs, have attempted to draw a distinction between these two types of truth, and allow for error to inhere in matters of mere history or science. To this position there are two fatal objections. First, the New Testament makes no such distinction: the historicity of the literal Adam and Eve is implied in 1 Tim. 2:13-14 (otherwise Paul's comment would be quite irrelevant); as also in 1 Cor. 11:8-9, which clearly affirms that Eve was literally formed from a part of Adam's body, as Gen. 2:22 states; the literal historical experience of Jonah's three days in the stomach of the whale is absolutely essential if it is to serve as an analogy for Christ's three days in the tomb (Matt. 12:40). It is impossible to reject the historicity of these two often contested episodes without by implication rejecting the authority of the Christ of the Gospels and of the apostle Paul in the Epistles. As to the historicity of the flood and Noah's ark, compare Christ's own dictum in Matt. 24:38-39: "For as in the days that were before the flood they were eating and drinking...until the day that Noe [Noah] entered into the ark. And they knew not until the flood came, and took them all away." In Matt. 19:4-5 Jesus affirmed that the words of Gen. 2:24 were spoken by the Creator of Adam and Eve, who had just brought them together as husband and wife. In Mark 12:26 He clearly implies that God Himself had spoken to the historical Moses the very words of Ex. 3:6: "I am...the God of Abraham, the God of Isaac, and the God of Jacob." Note also that in Matt. 23:35 He put the historicity of Abel's murder upon the same plane as the murder of Zechariah, the son of Berachiah.

Second, it is not always possible to make a clean-cut separation between theology-ethics and history-science. There are crucial cases where both types of truth are involved, as in the case of the literal, historical Adam (upon whose fatherhood of the whole human race the whole theological argument of Rom. 5:14-19 depends). One cannot allow for error in history-science without also ending up with error in doctrine. (So also the Apostles' Creed: 1. Creation performed by a personal God, "Maker of heaven and earth," rather than through impersonal forces and mechanistic evolution. 2. God has a unique Son—Jesus. 3. Jesus was fathered by God the Holy Spirit and born of a virgin at a specific moment in history. 4. Jesus suffered under Pilate—crucified, died, and was buried. 5. The bodily resurrection of Christ on the third day.)

This brief survey of the views of Christ and His apostles serves to indicate that they regarded the Old Testament in its entirety as the inerrant record of God's revelation to man. In other words, the basic ground for the complete trustworthiness of Scripture is the trustworthiness of God Himself. When the Scripture speaks, it is God who speaks; unlike any other book ever written, the Word of God is "living and operative" (Heb. 4:12 says that the *logos* of God is *zōn* and *energēs*) and penetrates to the innermost being of man, sitting in judgment upon all human philosophies and reasonings with absolute and sovereign authority. Such a judgmental prerogative on the part of the Bible must presuppose its complete inerrancy, for if error inhered in the original text of Scripture on any level, it would inevitably be the object of man's judgment, rather than that authority which sits in judgment upon man.

In the last analysis, then, every man must settle for one of two alternatives: the inerrancy of Holy Scripture, or the inerrancy of his own personal judgment. If the Bible contains errors in the autographs, then it requires an infallible human judgment to distinguish validly between the false and the true in Scripture; it is necessary for every affirmation in the sacred text to receive endorsement from the human critic himself before it may be accepted as true. Since men disagree in their critical judgments, it requires absolute inerrancy on the part of each individual to render a valid judgment in each instance. Even the agnostic must assert for himself such infallibility of judgment, for he cannot logically assume an agnostic position unless he can affirm that he has surveyed all the evidence for the authority of Scripture and has come to a valid judgment that the evidence is insufficient to prove the divine authority of the Bible as the Word of God. These, then, are the only alternatives available to us as we confront the Scriptures: either they are inerrant, or else we are.[8]

THE INFALLIBLE PROOF OF FULFILLED PROPHECY

There is in holy Scripture a form of evidence which is discoverable in no other religious document known to man; that is the phenomenon of prediction and fulfillment

---

8. For a fuller discussion of the field of biblical trustworthiness and inspiration the reader is encouraged to consult G. L. Archer, *Encyclopedia of Bible Difficulties*, Zondervan, 1982, pp. 19-32.

according to an ordered plan followed by a God who is sovereign over history. No one could suppose that he would enjoy accuracy in fulfilling the predictions he might make concerning the future. Occasional human predictions might come to pass, but in the Scripture we have many hundreds of predictions which are revealed by God and which are later fulfilled in events of subsequent history.

None of us can be sure of what will happen to ourselves, or those in our immediate environment within the next twenty-four hours. Those who have attempted to predict future events have often been disappointed. In view of man's inability to foretell the future with any high degree of accuracy one is forced to the conclusion that the kind of fulfillments that are found in Scripture could only come from God Himself.

No scholar yet has been able to explain how the fifty-third chapter of Isaiah could have described so accurately what was to be the suffering of our Lord on Good Friday as the New Testament records. Similarly, the prediction of Isa. 49:6 was given at a time when Israel had suffered major defeats and losses through the oppression of her enemies and it was highly questionable whether any knowledge of the Hebrew religion would even be retained in future generations by any people. But Isa. 49:6 records the promise of God that the Servant of the Lord would bring to pass not only the regathering of the scattered people of Israel to their native land, but also that He would be a light unto the Gentiles unto the ends of the earth. Very clearly this refers to the events that followed the resurrection of Christ and the launching of the missionary enterprise that ultimately compelled even the empire of Rome to surrender to the Lordship of the Redeemer they had crucified. From there the message of the Gospel has gone out to every continent in the world so that there are large numbers of people who have been brought into a saving relationship to God through the proclamation of His atoning grace as promised in Isa. 49. There is no possible way to explain this kind of fulfillment on the basis of mere human literary activity or speculation. For further detail and examples of fulfillments the reader is encouraged to consult Excursus 1.

SUBBIBLICAL VIEWS OF INSPIRATION

Those who incline to a Neo-Orthodox approach in dealing with the inspiration of Scripture have usually (like H. H. Rowley of Manchester) set up the so-called "mind of Christ" as a standard for judging between doctrinal truth and error in the Bible. For example, they say that when Joshua and the Israelites slew the entire population of Jericho, this was due to their primitive or savage ideas of justice, rather than to the express commandment of God, as recorded in Deut. 20:16-18. Statements or judgments attributed to God in the Old Testament but which seem to be too severe for Christ's standard of meekness, patience, and love as contained in the New Testament, are to be rejected as mere human inventions concocted by Israel in their backward stage of religious development. The criterion of truth should be "the mind of Christ" as understood and approved by modern scholarship.

Nevertheless, investigation will show that many of Christ's statements recorded in the New Testament clash with this supposed "mind of Christ" in a most startling way. Note, for instance, Matt. 23:33: "Ye serpents, ye generation of vipers, how can ye escape the damnation of hell?" Again, Matt. 25:41: "Depart from me, ye cursed, into everlasting fire, prepared for the devil and his angels." We have no accredited record of what Christ's mind actually was other than the sayings recorded in the gospels. It is fatally inconsistent to set up a philosophic notion as to what the viewpoint of Christ actually was, on the basis of some of His recorded statements, and then to reject the authenticity of other statements recorded in the same source, simply because they conflict with modern preference. Such a procedure really amounts to imposing human judgment upon the written Word of God, and allowing only that portion of the Word to be true which the human mind endorses. But we have already seen that the human reason is an inadequate and discredited tool for attaining true religious knowledge. If the Bible is truly the Word of God, it must sit in judgment upon man; man is not competent to sit in judgment upon the Holy Bible. His reasoning powers are to be employed in the task of consistent interpretation of the message of the Bible, in order that he may be sure to understand what God means by the words of Scripture. But never may he pass judgment against the clear teachings of Scripture as established by exegesis; for if he does, he by implication rejects the authority of Scripture as a whole.

More typically Neo-Orthodox is the view which regards the Bible as something less than the written Word of God; the Bible is merely a *witness* to the Word of God. According to this view, the Word of God is a dynamic principle which comes into operation only when there is a living or "existential" encounter between the believer and God. God speaks with power to him from the pages of Holy Writ and establishes a personal relationship, rather than merely instilling propositional truth into his mind. (*Propositional* here refers to the kind of truth which may be stated in propositions, such as, "God is an eternal Spirit." Propositions may be grasped as mere objects of knowledge, like mathematical formulas; but divine truth, it is urged, can never be mastered by man's mind. Divine truth reaches man in an "I-Thou" encounter; it is like an electric current with both a positive pole and a negative pole as conditions for existence.) Since the biblical text was written by human authors, and all men are sinful and subject to error, therefore, it is claimed, there must be error in the biblical text itself. But, it is argued, the living God is able to speak even from this partially erroneous text and bring believers into vital relationship with Him in a saving encounter. Such a view of the Bible leaves ample room for all manner of scientific and historical errors, and for all the adverse judgments of rationalistic higher criticism against the authenticity of the writings of Moses, Isaiah, Daniel, and all the rest. All these findings may be (and undoubtedly are) true as an accurate account of how the Bible humanly originated. Nevertheless, God has appointed this error-studded Scripture to be a uniquely authoritative witness to His revelation, and He is able to use it in a dynamic way to "save" men.

Thus, in their zeal to sidestep the assaults of rationalistic higher criticism upon the trustworthiness of the biblical record, and to rescue the significance of the Christian message in the face of scientific objections to the supernatural, the theologians of the Neo-Orthodox movement have resorted to a paradoxical view of the nature of revelation itself. They hold the position that by its very nature, divine revelation cannot be inscripturated. As soon as it is imprisoned in words, especially words setting forth propositions about God and spiritual truth, then it becomes the object of men's minds and cognitive powers. It thus falls under the control of man, and finds itself imprisoned within the covers of the written word. Revelation therefore is not to be equated with revealed doctrines or propositions about theology; rather, it consists of a direct encounter between God and man, as one subject confronting another subject. Revelation thus bears an analogy to a personal encounter between human beings; they experience each other as personalities, rather than as a set of statistics or items of information on an identification card.

From this same viewpoint it may be urged that it is a matter of no consequence whether the accounts recorded in Scripture are accurate or not. The gospel record of the virgin birth, for example, or the bodily resurrection of Christ, may very well be unhistorical (since modern scientific theory leaves no room for such miraculous events), but this makes no particular difference. Through these pious legends of the early church, we may encounter God and the suprahistorical realities to which these stories point. To rely upon the infallible accuracy of the written record of the Bible is held to be an obstacle to true faith. The dogma of an infallible Scripture operates as an unhealthy crutch upon which to lean; true faith soars above the manifest errors of the Bible to the transcendental truth to which the Bible points—truth available to the believer only through a personal encounter with the living God.

But this Neo-Orthodox view is confronted with a host of logical difficulties. It puts the authority of Scripture on the basis of sheer unverifiable faith. How can we be sure that God has not spoken to us from the record of the Koran (which is demonstrably full of errors and anachronisms), or from the Egyptian Book of the Dead, or from the Hindu Vedas? Why only from the Bible? Objective verification is not only discarded as impossible, but the desire for it is condemned as reprehensibly earthbound and rationalistic. One must simply believe! Whom or what? Why, the Scripture, of course. But regrettably enough, the Scripture itself seems to be totally unaware of this Neo-Orthodox approach to religious knowledge. It positively bristles with propositional truths about God, truths which may be reduced to creedal statements which the human mind may intellectually grasp. Perhaps this may be explained away as a manifestation of the fallibility and frailty of the sinful men who wrote the Bible. But how does one get beyond the text of the Bible to the more rarefied, ineffable, suprahistorical, personal-encounter truth which is supposed to lie beyond? Why, by a direct encounter with God, of course! Yes, but whose direct encounter? Barth's? Brunner's? Niebuhr's? Tillich's? These giants of the Neo-Orthodox movement have many stark disagreements among themselves on matters theological. Some, like Barth, disagree even with themselves quite noticeably from decade to decade. It is hard to see how the eternal and unchanging truth of God can be validly interpreted in Barth's celebrated *Commentary on Romans,* when his views are modified so remarkably as they are from edition to edition of that work.

As a matter of fact, then, this Neo-Orthodox view of Scripture raises far more serious difficulties than it seeks to solve. It is virtually impossible for Crisis theologians to make any affirmations at all about God or faith or any other aspect of religious truth which do not ultimately rest upon the propositional statements of the written Word of God. For example, to quote from William Temple's dictum concerning Holy Scripture: "No single sentence can be quoted as having the authority of a distinct utterance of the all-holy God."[9] But how does Archbishop Temple know that there is a single God, rather than a host of gods, as pagan religions teach; or no God at all, as Marxism teaches? Only from the authority of the written Bible, or of a confessing church which demonstrably trusted in the infallible authority of that Bible. Again, how does he know that the one true God is "all-holy"? Only because the Scripture affirms Him to be so–a propositional affirmation! Remove the authority of the written record of divine revelation, and the statement of Temple or Brunner or any other religious teacher concerning religious truth is reduced to the status of a mere conjecture, completely devoid of authority, and resting upon the same questionable basis as any other human opinion.

How may we know that faith is an important and saving principle, as Neo-Orthodox teachers insist? Only because it is so taught in the written Word of God. Otherwise it may well be, as most of the non-Christian world believes, that salvation is achieved only by good works. Even the possibility of an encounter between God and man is only guaranteed to us by the affirmations of Scripture, and its numerous records of such encounters. Otherwise the whole "experience" of divine-human encounter may be a mere matter of hallucination and autosuggestion, devoid of metaphysical reality.

Thus it turns out that every religious affirmation of the adherents of this school is ultimately dependent upon the truthfulness of the written Word of God, the Hebrew-Christian Scriptures. If these are erroneous in any portion, then they may be erroneous in any other portion; no reliance can be placed in them at all, or indeed in any affirmation which Neo-Orthodox theologians have derived from them—and all their doctrinal statements about God, encounter, and faith have in fact been derived from them. In other words, if the authority of the Bible as written cannot be trusted, then no insight of crisis theology has any more value than a mere human opinion—unless perchance the theologian happens to enjoy in his own person the very attribute of infallibility which he denies to Scripture.

This brings us to the question of the peculiarity of Neo-Orthodox faith, the faith which soars to God without the fettering dogma of scriptural inerrancy. What is faith, but a trust in something or someone other than itself? In what or whom, then, is this exalted faith reposed? Ostensibly it is reposed in God, or in the insights derived from

9. William Temple, *Nature, Man and God* (London: Macmillan, 1953), p. 350.

Procedures for Handling Biblical Difficulties

1. Be fully persuaded an explanation or reconciliation exists.

2. Trust in the inerrancy of Scripture as originally written down.

3. Carefully study the context and framework of the verse to ascertain the original intent of the author.

4. Practice careful exegesis: determine author intent, study key words, note parallel passages.

5. Harmonize parallel passages.

6. Consult Bible commentaries, dictionaries, lexical sources, encyclopedias.

7. Check for a transmissional error in the original text.

8. Remember that the historical accuracy of the biblical text is unsurpassed; that the transmitted text of Scripture is supported by thousands of extant manuscripts some of which date back to the second century B.C.

religious experience as the believer encounters God, whether in the pages of Scripture or in some other context. But how are these insights to be adjudged in their validity? Since they cannot be verified by appeal to any objective authority whatever (whether the Scripture or an infallible human teacher or church), the believer cannot look to any authority except his own. He cannot even be sure that there is a God, if the Bible is not reliable as an objective witness; he can only trust in himself. In other words, this Neo-Orthodox type of faith must in the last analysis be faith in man, not in God; that is, the believer's faith is reposed in himself. Since the Bible cannot be trusted, nor any human authority either (since humanity implies fallibility), therefore the Neo-Orthodox believer can know nothing except his own opinion, and hope that this may turn out to be correct. Otherwise he is irretrievably lost. It is only a bit of self-deception for him to suppose that his faith rests in a God outside himself; lacking any objective authority whatever, he is at the mercy of his own subjective impressions and opinions. He can never be sure that his revelations are not mere hallucinations.

Dealing with Difficulties in the Bible

It must be admitted that the text of Scripture as transmitted to us contains occasional difficulties which appear to challenge the doctrine of biblical inerrancy. Some of these difficulties are relieved by a proper use of the science of textual criticism. Others, such as discrepancies in statistics or the spelling of names, call for an emending of text which goes beyond the available data of textual criticism. Still others present logical difficulties, such as the endorsement given in Judg. 11 to the apparent sacrifice of Jephthah's daughter, when Deut. 12:31 forbids all human sacrifice in Israel.

There are two possible methods of dealing with these problems: (1) one may hold in abeyance the biblical claims to infallibility until each individual difficulty is cleared up. Each time a new problem presents itself, the Bible becomes demoted to a suspect status until the matter is satisfactorily settled. Meanwhile, the believer is kept on the tenterhooks of painful suspense and anguish of soul until the Bible is again cleared of the charges against it. (2) One may, even in the face of apparent discrepancies, retain his faith in the infallibility of the biblical record and wait with patience for the vindication which later investigation will surely provide. Having been convinced that only divine origin explains the phenomena of Scripture, he may take his stand with Jesus of Nazareth upon the inerrancy of the written Word of God, and look forward to an eventual clearing up of all the problems that may arise.

Those who follow this second approach may perhaps be accused of illogical subjectivism, because they proceed on the basis of an *a priori* conviction. But this accusation is not well founded, for the Bible cannot be studied at all except upon the basis of one *a priori* or another. One must start with the prior assumption that the Bible is either a fallible record or an infallible one. There is no middle ground; one cannot remain in a state of neutral suspense and insist, "Just let the Bible speak for itself." We must first of all ascertain what kind of book this Bible is which does the speaking. Is it the infallible Word of God, or is it the error-prone product of man, having elements of divine truth intermingled with human mistakes? If it presents such data as to compel an acknowledgment that it can be only of divine origin—and it does present such data in abundance—then the only reasonable course is to take seriously its own assertions of infallibility. If the Scriptures constitute an authoritative self-disclosure of God, then any discrepancies which appear must be dealt with as only apparent, not real. When all the facts are in, the charges of error will prove to be unsubstantiated.

It should be pointed out that such a procedure is commonly followed in human relations without adverse criticism. For example, a husband who has come to the conviction that his wife is a faithful and virtuous woman will steadfastly refuse to become suspicious of her, even though she has been seen going out with some other man. Without jumping to adverse conclusions, he will simply await further information which will clear up the situation and satisfactorily explain her association with the man in question. It would be foolish and unworthy for him to abandon his conviction of her integrity until her action is vindicated. Only an initial presumption that she is inconstant and untrustworthy would justify such a reaction on his part.

Even so it is foolish and unworthy for one who has been convinced of the divine authority of the Bible to question its infallibility until each new allegation against it has been cleared up. Rather than being a scientific and objective procedure, as is sometimes asserted, such a policy involves only an illogical shifting from one *a priori* to another with weakminded vacillation. A genuine, outright contradiction in the Scriptures (especially if demonstrable for the original autographs) would be good cause for abandoning faith in the inerrancy of Scripture; but until such has been proved, or until some outright error in history or science has been demonstrated according to the laws of legal evidence, the believer in Scripture need never feel embarrassed about holding to the assumption that it is the inerrant Word of God. It is highly significant that no such mistake has ever yet been proved to the satisfaction of a court of law, although various attempts have been made to do so.[10]

10. Cf. Harry Rimmer, *That Lawsuit Against the Bible* (Grand Rapids: Eerdmans, 1940). For additional material on the subject of difficulties in the Bible, consult the spirited defense of biblical authority and inerrancy found in Wick Broomall, *Biblical Criticism* (Grand Rapids: Zondervan, 1957), pp. 11-84. For detailed handling of discrepancies in the Biblical narrative, see Gleason Archer, *Encyclopedia of Bible Difficulties* (Grand Rapids: Zondervan, 1964). For more general discussions of the inspiration of the Old Testament, see R. K. Harrison, *Introduction to the Old Testament* (Grand Rapids: Eerdmans, 1969), pp. 462-75; J. W. Montgomery, *Crisis in Lutheran Theology* (Grand Rapids: Eerdmans, 1967), pp. 15-44; M. H. Woudstra, "The Inspiration of the Old Testament" in *The Bible: The Living Word of God*, ed. Merrill C. Tenney (Grand Rapids: Zondervan, 1968), pp. 123-42.

PART ONE

GENERAL INTRODUCTION

3

THE HEBREW MANUSCRIPTS
AND THE EARLY VERSIONS

WE NO LONGER have access to infallible originals of the various books of the Hebrew Scriptures. The earliest copies which have been preserved to us are in some instances no closer than a thousand years to the time of original composition. Nevertheless they constitute our primary authority today as to the inspired Word of God, and all our copies and translations of the Holy Scriptures are necessarily dependent upon the earliest and best available manuscripts of the Hebrew and Aramaic originals. We must therefore review the written evidence upon which our modern printed editions of the Hebrew Bible are based, and have some idea of the large and varied body of evidence with which Old Testament textual criticism has to deal.

Of course the Hebrew manuscripts take priority in value, inasmuch as God's revelation first came to Israel in the Hebrew tongue, and there is far less likelihood of corruption in the copying out of manuscripts into the same language than when a translation into another tongue is involved. But in cases where scribal errors have crept into the Hebrew copies, it is quite possible that the early translations into Greek, Aramaic, or Latin might give us a clue to the original Hebrew word or phrase which has been garbled in the Hebrew manuscripts themselves. For this reason we must survey not only the earliest and best Hebrew manuscripts, but also the earliest and best copies of the ancient translations, or versions, as well.

THE PRE-CHRISTIAN MANUSCRIPTS

THE EARLIEST HEBREW MANUSCRIPTS

The pre-Christian manuscripts consist principally of the remarkable discoveries in the Dead Sea caves. Technically these are referred to as Qumran materials, since the various caves in which these discoveries were found are located near the canyon of the Wadi Qumran, along the northwest coast of the Dead Sea. The technical identification of these Dead Sea documents consists of the number specifying which of the caves was the scene of its discovery, followed by an abbreviation of the name of the book itself, plus a superior letter indicating the order in which this particular manuscript came to light, as over against other copies of the same book. For

Pre-Christian
Qumran Scrolls	300 B.C. A.D. 50	Varied Old Testament Texts

Post-Christian
British Museum Oriental	A.D. 850	Pentateuch
Codex Cairensis	A.D. 895	Former & latter prophets
Aleppo Codex	A.D. 900	Old Testament
Leningrad MS	A.D. 916	Latter prophets
Leningrad MS B-19A	A.D. 1010	Old Testament
Samaritan Pentateuch	*unavailable*	Pentateuch
Torah Finchasiye	A.D. 1204	Pentateuch

Printed Editions
Bologna Edition of Psalter	A.D. 1477	Psalms
Soncino Edition of Old Testament	A.D. 1488	Entire Old Testament
Second Bomberg Edition	A.D. 1525/26	Entire Old Testament

Greek Versions
Septuagint	250-150 B.C.	Torah
Aquila's Version	A.D. 130	Fragments
Symmachus' Version	A.D. 170	Entire Old Testament
Theodotion's Version	A.D. 180 or 190	Entire Old Testament

Aramaic Targums
Targum of Onkelos	A.D. 200	Tora
Targum of Jonathan be Uzziel	A.D. 300	Joshua to Kings Isaiah to Malachi
Targum of Pseudo-Jonathan	A.D. 650	Torah
Jerusalem Targum	A.D. 700	Torah

Latin Versions
Old Latin; Itala Version	A.D. 200	Fragments
Wurzburg Palimpsest Codex	A.D. 450	Torah, Prophets
Lyons Codex	A.D. 650	Genesis to Judges
Jerome's Vulgate	A.D. 390-404	Entire Old Testament

Syriac Versions
Peshitta Syriac Old Testament	A.D. 100-200	Entire Old Testament
Syriac Hexapla	A.D. 616	Entire Old Testament

example, the famous Dead Sea Isaiah Scroll—which still remains the only complete copy of a book of the Old Testament yet discovered and published—is technically referred to as lQIsᵃ, meaning: the first discovered (or most important) manuscript of Isaiah found in Cave 1 of Wadi Qumran. The so-called Hebrew University Scroll of Isaiah (although lQIsᵃ has also now passed into the possession of the Hebrew University, by way of purchase from St. Mark's Monastery) is technically known as lQIsᵇ.

In addition to the biblical fragments which have been published from Cave 1 and Cave 4, thousands of fragments have been recovered from Cave 4, with over 380 different manuscripts identified, of which perhaps 100 are from the Old Testament.[1] Cave 2 furnished more than 180 legible fragments (one-fourth of which were biblical). The biblical materials from Cave 3 (famous for its copper scroll containing an inventory of sacred treasure hidden for safekeeping) and Caves 5 and 6 are rather meager and of minor importance, partly because they did not contain material of great significance. Cave 7 has different ranges of MS fragments, all of which are copied out in the Greek language, even though some of them translate from Old Testament texts. For details see p. 42. There has been very little reported as yet concerning the contents of Caves 8, 9, and 10. As for Cave 11, it has yielded five relatively complete scrolls: a portion of Leviticus, a scroll of a selection of Psalms, an Aramaic Targum of Job, and a noncanonical Apocalypse of the New Jerusalem.[2]

Some of the major publications of the Qumran materials are: Millar Burrows (ed.), *The Dead Sea Scrolls of St. Mark's Monastery* (New Haven, Conn.: ASOR, 1950), containing the photographed text of lQIsᵃ and the Habakkuk Commentary, lQpHb; O. P. Barthelémy and J. T. Milik, *Discoveries in the Judean Desert*, vol. 1, *Qumran Cave* (Oxford: Clarendon, 1955), containing brief fragments from Genesis, Exodus, Leviticus, Deuteronomy, Judges, Samuel, Isaiah, Ezekiel, Psalms; Eleazar Sukenik, *ʾWṢR HMGYLWT HGNWZWT The Treasure of the Hidden Scrolls* (Jerusalem, 1954), containing the Hebrew University manuscript (MS) of Isaiah, lQIsᵇ. The following is a list of the published and unpublished biblical manuscripts of which public notice has been given in the scholarly journals.

1. The Dead Sea Scroll of Isaiah (lQIsᵃ)—the entire sixty-six chapters (150-100 B.C.). This important text belongs to the same manuscript family as the Masoretic Text (MT). Only occasionally does it favor a Septuagint (LXX) reading, and most of its deviations from the MT are the result of obvious scribal lapses, for the text was rather carelessly copied. Yet some of the proper names point to an earlier and more reliable vocalization than does the MT; for instance, 1QIsᵃ points to the vocalization *turtān* (cf. the Akkadian *turtannu*), which is certainly more reliable than the MT's *tartān* (in 20:1).[3]

1. See F. M. Cross in BASOR, no. 141 (Feb 1956), and in *The Ancient Library of Qumran* (rev. ed., Garden City, N.Y.: Doubleday, 1958), pp. 39-40.

2. Millar Burrows, MLDSS, pp. 14, 28-30. Cf. Appendix 4 for a more complete listing of the contents of the various individual caves.

3. Dewey Beegle discusses these vocalizations in BASOR, no. 123 (Oct 1951). For a discussion of textual variants in general, see Burrows in BASOR, no. 111 (Oct 1948), "Variant Readings in the Isaiah Manuscript."

2. The Habakkuk Commentary (lQpHb)—chapters 1 and 2 only, with commentary notes interspersed between verses (100-50 B.C.). Here again the Habakkuk text quoted stands in a very close relationship to the MT. The variants are fairly numerous, though minor in character, and often explicable as simple scribal errors. Very seldom does a variant find support in the LXX or other versions. Incidentally, the commentary (or *pesher*) is of a very special kind: it is usually concerned with how each verse has been fulfilled in recent (Hasmonean) history or by current events.[4]

3. The Hebrew University Isaiah Scroll (lQIs[b])—substantial portions of chapters 41-66 (copied ca. 50 B.C.). This has a far closer fidelity to the MT than 1QIs[a] does. It was published by E. L. Sukenik in 1948 and 1955 as *The Treasure of the Hidden Scrolls*, which also included the *Miḥāmah* and the *Hōdāyōt*.

4. 1Q Leviticus fragments—a few verses each of chapters 19-22 (copied perhaps fourth century B.C.—de Vaux, and Burrows guardedly agrees, whereas Cross prefers second century). They were published in Barthelémy, p. 51. Textually this MS is in remarkable agreement with the MT. It is written in paleo-Hebrew script.

5. 4Q Deuteronomy-B—32:41-43 written in hemistichs as poetry, not as prose. It favors the LXX as against the MT in three instances. It was published by Skehan in BASOR, no. 136 (Dec 1954); he suggests no date for this.

6. 4Q Samuel-A—1 Samuel 1 and 2—twenty-seven fragments (first century B.C.). This agrees with the LXX as against the MT in several places; in other places, it differs from both. It was published by Cross in BASOR, no. 132 (Dec. 1953). A photo is in QHBT 273 ("Qumran and the History of the Biblical Text").

7. 4Q Samuel-B—1 Samuel 16, 19, 21, 23 (225 B.C. or earlier). This is even more sparing in *matres lectionis* (vowel-indicating letters) than the MT. This text consistently agrees with the LXX as against the MT. It was published by Cross in JBL, no. 74 (Sept. 1955). It was republished in Cross & Talmon's *Qumran and the History of the Biblical Text* (Harvard U. Press, 1975), in the chapter entitled "The Oldest MSS from Qumran," pp. 147-76; transcriptions are on pp. 170-73 (F. M. Cross); photos are on p. 154. This cross-dates Item 7 as 4th century (QHBT 167).

8. 4Q Jeremiah-A—likewise archaic and for the same reason, according to Cross. ALQ, 187; translation only.

9. 4Q XII-A—(XII signifying a MS of the minor prophets). It is referred to by Cross in the above-mentioned article as a third-century B.C. cursive. (4QXII[C], according to Sanders.) Semitica 5 (1955) pp. 147-72 (M. Testuz).

10. 4Q Qoh[a]—a second century cursive text of Ecclesiastes, derived from a source at least third century or earlier, according to Cross. It was published by James Muilenberg, "A Qoheleth Scroll from Qumran," BASOR, no. 135 (Oct. 1954) pp. 20-28.

11. 4Q Exodus—a fragment of chapter 1 with a variant which favors the LXX (1:5 reads "seventy-five" instead of the MT's "seventy"). Compare Frank M. Cross, Jr., *The Ancient Library of Qumran* (New York: Doubleday, Anchor, 1961), pp. 184-85.

---

4. An excellent discussion of this "commentary" is found in F. F. Bruce, *Biblical Exegesis in Qumran Texts* (Grand Rapids: Eerdmans, 1959), pp. 7-17.

12. 4Q Paleo-Exodus[m]—portions of chapters 7, 29, 30, 32 (and perhaps others), written in Paleo-Hebrew script. This MS favors the Samaritan Pentateuch as against the MT in a significant number of instances. Compare P. J. Skehan, "Exodus in the Samaritan Recension from Qumran," JBL, no. 74 (1955), pages 182-87. (Photo in QHBT 275.)

13. 4Q Paleo-Exodus[l], copied perhaps 100 B.C., that conforms quite closely to the MT (QHBT 276).

14. 4Q Numbers—written in square Hebrew but with Samaritan-type expansions; for instance, after 27:23 comes an insert derived from Deuteronomy 3:21. But in other instances it agrees with the LXX as against the Samaritan and the MT (as in 35:21).

15. 4Q Deuteronomy-A—chapter 32 (Song of Moses). This MS inclines toward the LXX as against the MT at 32:43 (although it omits some of the LXX expansion here).[5]

16. 4Q Jeremiah[b]—supports the briefer text of Jeremiah reflected in the LXX (QHBT 276).

17. 7Q Daniel—a few fragments of Daniel in 2nd century handwriting, including the transition from Hebrew to Aramaic in 2:4. (J. Trever in RQ 19 [1965] 323-26 for plates.)

18. 11Q Psalms—a manuscript of Psalms from Cave 11, copied in the formal book-hand style of the Herodian period. The bottom third of each page has been lost. Thirty-three psalms have been preserved, including Ps. 151 of the LXX. Four separate fragments contain portions of four more psalms, thus making a total of thirty-seven. Represented are Pss. 93, 101-103, 105, 109, 118, 119, 121-130, 132-146, 148-151, although they do not always follow the sequence of the MT (e.g., Ps. 105 is followed by Pss. 146, 148, 121-130). There are also about six noncanonical poems (two of which are known in a Syriac translation) and one prose portion listing the number of psalms written by David (cf. BASOR, no. 165, pp. 13-15).[6] DJD (1965), J. A. Sanders. (4QDt2, according to Sanders) (QHBT 406).

From the foregoing descriptions it becomes apparent that the Qumran materials point to three or possibly four main manuscript families: (1) the proto-Masoretic, from which the consonantal text of our present-day Hebrew is derived; (2) the proto-Septuagintal, the Hebrew *Vorlage* (preceding model) of the original Greek translations that eventuated in the later Septuagint; (3) the proto-Samaritan, forming the basis for the later Samaritan text of the Hebrew Pentateuch (probably lacking the later Samaritan additions inserted in the interest of sectarian bias); (4) a neutral family, standing more or less midway among the conflicting traditions of the first three families.

However, it should be understood that the existence of these non-Masoretic manuscript families does not necessarily mean that the proto-Masoretic does not represent

---

5. Manuscripts 11-14 are discussed by Burrows in MLDSS. No. 14 is briefly discussed by Skehan in BASOR, no. 136, pp. 12-15 (Dec 1954). Translations have been published of "commentaries" or *peshārîm* from Cave 4 commenting on Nah., Ps. 37, Isa., and Hos. (as well as of the pseudepigraphical works "Blessings of the Patriarchs," the "Testimonies of the Twelve Patriarchs," and a *Florilegium* or *Anthology of Eschatological Midrashîm*). Cf. Johann Maier, *Die Texte vom Toten Meer*, 2 vols. (Basel, Switz: E. Reinhardt, 1960), 1:180-89; 2:162-67. See also Appendix 4.

6. As for the Hebrew manuscripts discovered by the excavators of Masada (cf. Yigael Yadin, *Masada* [New York: Random, 1966]), the most important were: (1) fragments of Pss. 81-85 completely agreeing

the purest textual tradition of all. Nothing in the new discoveries from the Qumran caves endangers the essential reliability and authority of our standard Hebrew Bible text, as represented for example in the Kittel editions of *Biblia Hebraica*. They do not indicate that the Septuagint is necessarily to be exalted to a more respected position than before as a witness to the original text, except perhaps in such books as 1 and 2 Samuel in which, for some reason, we have an unusually defective Hebrew text in the MT. Certainly we may expect increasing assistance from Qumran sources in regard to Samuel, and perhaps also in some portions of Deuteronomy (particularly in those instances where a New Testament author has quoted a verse according to the LXX wording rather than the MT's).[7]

EARLY TEXT VERSIONS

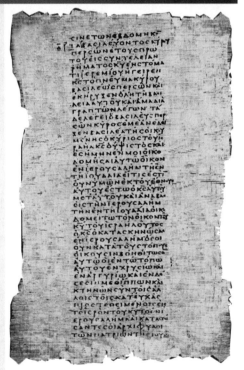

CODEX SINAITICUS (ESTHER 2 IN LXX)   CODEX VATICANUS (EZRA 1:1-2)

with the consonantal text of the MT; (2) fragments of Lev. slightly differing from the MT; (3) the Sabbath Scroll (a Qumran type of sectarian work); (4) a fragment of Ps. 150 on white leather; (5) fragments of Ecclesiasticus in a first-century A.D. hand, very close in wording to the eleventh-century text found in the Cairo Geniza (despite the claims of many modern scholars that the latter was a spurious retranslation from a Syriac version); (6) fragments of Lev. 8-12, identical with the MT; (7) fragments of the apocryphal Book of Jubilees; (8) fragments of Ezek. 37, and (9) fragments of Deut. 33-34, both of which were identical with the MT.

7. Donald E. Gowan: *Bridge Between the Testaments*, Pickwick Press, Pittsburgh, 1990, p. 221. In reference to the DC, 390 years after 587 B.C., which would be 197 B.C., would be the beginning of the

One further remark should be made concerning the consonantal MT. When it is compared with such examples of the proto-Masoretic tradition as 1QIsᵃ (which contains many "extra" *matres lectionis*), the MT obviously goes back to a pre-Maccabean recension of the Hebrew Bible and points to the activity of a standardizing revision committee under official auspices, who consulted all the earliest and best manuscripts then available (no doubt including the official copies in the temple archives) and produced a sort of resultant text much after the manner of Westcott and Hort or Eberhard Nestle in their New Testament editions. Unlike Westcott and Hort, however, the Jewish scholars never took the trouble to record the prior manuscripts from which they had worked, but simply discarded them altogether, (or consigned them to a storeroom) feeling that their new and official text met all practical needs.

When did this hypothetical committee do its work? Some have suggested the so-called Council of Jamnia in A.D. 90, but this hardly agrees with the evidence of texts like the Hebrew University Isaiah Scroll, which corresponds almost letter for letter with the MT and yet dates from about 50 B.C. A more likely supposition is that the standardization of the consonantal text of the Old Testament took place around 100 B.C.[8]

There remains just one more pre-Christian MS to list here, one which did not come from the Qumran caves:

19. Nash Papyrus—containing the Decalogue and the *shema'*, that is, Ex. 20:1-17 and Deut. 6:4-9 (dated by Cross at 100 B.C., by Albright at 50 B.C.). This text is close to the Masoretic tradition. It was purchased by W. L. Nash from an Egyptian antique dealer who stated that it was discovered in the *Fayyūm*. It has been published by W. F. Albright, "A Biblical Fragment from the Maccabean Age: the Nash Papyrus," JBL, no. 56 (1937), pp. 145-76. (Cf. Würthwein, TOT, pl.5.)

THE POST-CHRISTIAN MANUSCRIPTS

1. British Museum Oriental 4445—a copy of the Pentateuch, the consonantal text of which dates from about A.D. 850, vowel points being added a century later. (Most of Genesis and Deuteronomy are missing.)

2. Codex Cairensis (C)—containing the Former Prophets and the Latter Prophets, as copied out by Aaron ben Asher in A.D. 895. This manuscript was apparently seized by the Crusaders from Karaite Jews in Jerusalem in A.D. 1099, but finally ended up in

Hasidic movement 20 years later in 177 B.C. and the rise of Môreh Haṣṣâdîq ("the Teacher of Righteousness"). The so called "wicked priest" may have been one of the Hasmoneans, either Jonathan or, as Cross prefers, Simon Maccabeus (BAR, 3/77, pp. 31-32). On page 233 Gowan continues, "The desert community at Qumran began between 150 and 140 B.C. after an earlier flight to Damascus." (This book furnishes a very useful summary of the apocraphal and pseudepigraphical books of the Inter-testamental Era.)

8. Moshe Greenberg comes to a somewhat similar conclusion as a result of the Qumran data. He believes that the Jerusalem scribes began systematically correcting and editing the text of the Old Testament as early as the third century B.C., and that this project gained momentum under the Hasmonean (Maccabean) kings in the second century. While the standardized text may not have prevailed until after the fall of Jerusalem, it is fair to say that "the prevalence of the standard, not its creation, came after A.D. 70" (Quoted in Burrows, MLDSS, p. 161). F. M. Cross in QHBT 186 suggests that the *textus receptus* (of the MT) of the Pentateuch and the Former Prophets was the local text of the Babylonian Jewish community established between the 4th and 2nd centuries B.C.

the possession of the Karaites in Cairo. (Cf. Kittel, *Biblia Hebraica*, which specifies that Aaron was the copyist rather than Moses ben Asher, his father. Apparently it was finally transferred to Aleppo. (Cf. Ernst Würthwein, 4th ed., TOT, p. 34.)

3. The Aleppo Codex—containing the entire Old Testament and coming from the first half of the 10th century. Aaron ben Mosheh ben Asher added punctuation and Masora. Originally in Jerusalem, it later went to Cairo, thence to Aleppo. It has lost about one-fourth of its contents including almost all of the Torah, much of Canticles, Qoheleth, through Esther, Daniel and Ezra. It is now in Jerusalem (Würthwein TAT⁴ 34).

4. Leningrad MS of the latter prophets, dating from A.D. 916, according to most authorities. (Cf. Würthwein, 14:26, where it is called P.) This codex with Babylonian punctuation was discovered by Firkowitsch at Tschufutkale in Crimea.

5. Leningrad MS B-19A—the entire Old Testament, containing the Ben Asher Masoretic Text. Dated at A.D. 1010 as a faithful copy of an A.D. 980 MS (which has since been lost), this MS furnished the basis for Kittel's *Biblia Hebraica*, third edition (and all subsequent editions), which is the standard text for Hebrew scholarship today. Previous to 1929 the standard text had been the Ben Hayyim edition of 1525. (The model codex C of Ben Asher has until recently been jealously guarded by the Sephardic synagogue in Aleppo, and its custodians refused permission even to photograph it, much less permit its use in Kittel's *Biblia Hebraica*. After having been partially burned in an Arab riot, the Aleppo was finally acquired by the state of Israel in its damaged condition and it will very take its place beside the Leningrad MS as the basis for critical editions of the Hebrew Bible in the years to come.

6. The Samaritan Pentateuch. The earliest MSS of this version are still in Nablus, withheld by the Samaritan sectarians from publication. Pietro della Valle first discovered a form of this Samaritan text in Damascus, in 1616, and it was then published in the Paris Polyglot in 1645. (One interesting MS more recently discovered is the Torah Finchasiye, copied in A.D. 1204, and containing in parallel columns the Hebrew, an Aramaic Targum, and an Arabic translation, all written in Samaritan characters.) This Samaritan version contains about 6,000 variants from the MT, mostly mere differences in spelling. But in 1,900 instances, it agrees with the LXX as against the MT (e.g., particularly in the ages of the patriarchs). It also contains biased sectarian insertions, designed to show that Jehovah chose Mt. Gerizim rather than Zion, and Shechem rather than Jerusalem as His holy city. It shows a popularizing type of text, modernizing antique forms and simplifying difficult sentence constructions. In 1815, Wilhelm Gesenius condemned it as nearly worthless for textual criticism. In more recent times both Geiger and Kahle have argued that this judgment was unfair. Kenyon (BAM, pp. 49-50) gives a favorable judgment of its worth. The standard edition was edited by August von Gall (Giessen, Germany: A. Töpelmann, 1918). (It should be added that the Samaritans wrote in an alphabet quite different from square Hebrew but descended from the old paleo-Hebrew character.) No MS of the Samaritan Pentateuch is known to

be earlier than the tenth century A.D. (F. M. Cross's *Ancient Library of Qumran*, pp. 172-73,192-93, contains a good description and evaluation of the Samaritan text.)

MOST IMPORTANT EARLY
PRINTED EDITIONS OF THE HEBREW BIBLE

1. Bologna Edition of the Psalter, A.D. 1477.
2. Soncino Edition of Old Testament (vowel-pointed), 1488.
3. Second Bomberg Edition of Old Testament (text of Jacob ben Chayim, with Masora and Rabbinical notes, under patronage of Daniel Bomberg), 1525-26. This became the basis of all modern editions up to 1929.

THE EARLY VERSIONS OF THE OLD TESTAMENT
THE GREEK VERSIONS

1. The Septuagint—translated in Alexandria 250-150 B.C. The traditional account of the origin of this version is given in the Letter of Aristaeus to Philocrates, which originated between 130 and 100 B.C. Despite fabulous embellishments, the letter reflects an actual historical event, in which the Torah at least (if not more of the Old Testament) was cast into Greek for the convenience of Greek-speaking Jews who knew little Hebrew. Paul Kahle has inferred from this letter that there were already earlier translations of the Torah which were revised by a committee in the reign of Ptolemy II (rather than being a completely new translation made at that time). Yet Kahle doubts that there was, apart from the Torah, any single standard Old Greek version, but inclines to the view that it was the early church which assembled a standard text from various Old Greek versions already current. Yet P. de Lagarde (followed by A. Rahlfs) believes there actually was a standard, original LXX text for the whole Old Testament even from pre-Christian times, and he has used very careful methodology in preparing a critical text for publication. (Rahlfs' edition is the easiest one to obtain for study purposes today.) The following is a list of the most important manuscripts or manuscript fragments of the Septuagint.

a. Rylands Papyrus 458, containing portions of Deut. 23-28 (150 B.C.), has been preserved to us in a mummy wrapping. Kenyon (BAM, p. 63) states that it tends to favor A (Codex Alexandrinus) and *Theta* (Codex Washingtoniensis I, a sixth century MS) as against B (Codex Vaticanus).

b. From Qumran Four come the following cave fragments: a Leviticus fragment on papyrus which agrees well with the standard LXX text, but uses *IAO* instead of *kyrios* for "Jehovah"; another Leviticus fragment on leather which contains 26:2-16, with ten variations from the later LXX, and five other variants where the LXX MSS are themselves in disagreement; a Numbers fragment on leather, containing 3:3–4:14. In quite a few instances it uses a different Greek word from the LXX, but apparently for the same Hebrew word in the original. (These are all discussed by Burrows, MLDSS, pp. 136-37, and are apparently assigned by him to first century B.C.) D. Barthelémy reports (in "Chainon manquant de l'histoire de la Septante" [1952] in QHBT 128) that in August 1952, the Ta'amireh tribesmen discovered in a new cave (Wadi Khabra [QHBT 269] on Nahal Heber) of the Judean Desert a scroll from the Second Revolt (second half of the first century A.D.), in fragments, all from the Minor Prophets: Micah (4:3-7 transcribed on p. 129), Jonah, Nahum, Habakkuk (quote from Hab. 1:14–2:5, 13-15 on p. 134), Zephaniah, and Zechariah (from the end of the first century A.D.).

c. The Chester Beatty Papyri were found at Oxyrynchus in Egypt; #VI, ca. A.D. 150, is a papyrus codex containing portions of Numbers and Deuteronomy, tending to agree with A and *Theta* against B; #VII, ca. A.D. 230, contains portions of Isaiah with glosses in Fayyumic Coptic; #V, ca. A.D. 270, contains portions of Gen. (chaps. 8, 24, 25, 30-46); #IV, ca. A.D. 350, contains Gen. 9:1–44:22.

d. Papyrus 911, from Egypt, dated about the end of the third century A.D., written in a cursive uncial hand, contains fragments of *Genesis* 1-35, in a pre-Hexaplaric text showing affinities to MSS E and D (i.e., the Bodleian *Genesis* of the tenth century, at Oxford, and the Cotton Genesis of the fifth century, at the British Museum).

e. Freer Greek Manuscript V of the minor prophets (W) in Washington, comprising 33 papyrus leaves, dates from the second half of the third century A.D., written in an Egyptian hand, and containing a fairly complete text of all the prophets except Hosea. The text is of pre-Hexaplaric type, and among the uncial manuscripts it is somewhat closer to Q and Aleph than to the others. Yet it bears noteworthy affinities to such minuscule MSS as 407, 198, 233, 534, and 410—which likewise show a pre-Hexaplaric type of text.

f. Origen's *Hexapla,* was written about A.D. 240. Origen lived A.D. 185-254. Because of the many divergences in the MSS of the LXX then current, and because he had noticed that some portions of the Hebrew text were missing in the LXX, Origen determined to draw up a more satisfactory Greek Old Testament in the following way. He copied out six parallel columns (*hexapla* means sixfold) consisting of (1) the Hebrew original, (2) the Hebrew transliterated into Greek letters, (3) the literal Greek translation of Aquila, (TAT, 4th ed., p. 58), (4) the idiomatic Greek translation of Symmachus, (5) the Septuagint itself, and (6) the Greek translation of Theodotion. Where sections appeared in the LXX which were not in the Hebrew, he inserted an obelus (horizontal diacritical stroke) and closed with a metobelus (a stroke with a dot or short cross stroke). Where a portion in the Hebrew was not in the LXX, he inserted a Greek translation from one of the other columns, setting it off with an asteriscus (a cross with intervening dots) and a metobelus.

Origen's original *Hexapla* was apparently never copied out for publication; it was far too voluminous to be marketable. But the contents of the fifth column (the LXX plus additions) were later published by Eusebius and Pamphilus, carefully including the diacritical symbols. A copy of this has been preserved to us in the Codex Sarravianus (G), dating from the fourth or fifth century, and containing portions of Genesis through Judges. Another witness seems to be Codex Marchalianus (Q) from the sixth century, which contains portions of Isaiah through Malachi with Hexaplaric readings in the margin. (See Würthwein, TOT, p. 53.) No other considerable section has been preserved of this edition in Greek, but fortunately it was translated into Syriac by order of Bishop Paul of Tella in 616 (cf. see "Syriac Versions" below) and some MSS of this have been preserved, with the all-important diacritical marks appearing in the Syriac text.

g. The Hesychian Recension (a revision of the Septuagintal text made in Egypt by Bishop Hesychius, martyred in A.D. 311) does not survive in any early MSS except possibly Q, but it is thought to be preserved in a later form in minuscules 49, 68, and some others, and in the Coptic and Ethiopic versions generally, as well as in the Itala or "Old Latin."

h. The Lucianic Recension (made by Lucian of Samosata and Antioch, also martyred in A.D. 311) has likewise survived only in later MSS, notably Codex Venetus (N), an eighth-century MS containing portions of Exodus and Leviticus. Kahle feels that the appearance of some characteristically "Lucianic" readings in MSS prior to Lucian's lifetime—especially in certain Old Latin MSS—indicates the earlier existence of an "Ur-Lucian" text (*Handschriften aus der Höhle* [Stuttgart: W. Kohlhammer, 1951], p. 34).

i. Codex Vaticanus (B) (A.D. 325-350) is a magnificent MS which contains most of the New Testament as well as the Old Testament. This represents a pre-Origenic text (even though copied out later than the *Hexapla*) of the LXX. One book (Daniel), however, is not from the LXX but from Theodotion, (which is much closer to the Hebrew MT than the so-called LXX version of Daniel).

j. Codex Sinaiticus (Aleph) (ca. A.D. 375-400) is another splendid MS, which also contains the complete New Testament, although portions of the Old Testament are missing. In part it resembles the Vaticanus, and in part the Alexandrinus.

k. Codex Alexandrinus (A) (ca. A.D. 450) is also an important New Testament text. It shows some affinities to the Hexaplaric, although basically it is an Egyptian type of text.

The LXX varies greatly in quality and value from book to book. The Pentateuch was translated with greater accuracy, for the most part, than were the other books of the Old Testament, probably because it had to serve as a sort of Greek Targum at synagogue worship services for the Jewish congregations in Egypt. The former prophets (i.e., Joshua through 2 Kings) and Psalms are rendered with considerable fidelity to their Hebrew *Vorlage*, generally speaking. In the case of the latter prophets (Isaiah through Malachi), the tendency is more definitely toward paraphrase, and the more difficult Hebrew passages are often inexpertly handled. The remaining poetic books (apart from Psalms) show a similar tendency toward freedom in rendering.

In considering the value of the LXX for the textual emendation of any particular book, we must first of all study the character of the translation as a whole, so far as that particular book is concerned. If it seems to be quite paraphrastic in its translation technique, its usefulness for text amendment is very much less than if it tends, on the whole, to be quite literal. If, on the other hand, it makes consistently good sense throughout the book, and evidences a good grasp of Hebrew, it deserves respect. Yet it must be remembered that the LXX text has come down to us in various and divergent forms (such as to give rise to suspicions of a quite heterogeneous origin), and betrays a rather low standard of scribal fidelity in its own transmission. Greek scribes did not bind themselves to the same stringent rules of literal and meticulous accuracy as were embraced by the Jewish scribes of the period of the Sopherim (see chap. 4, section on "The Work of the Sopherim").

One significant example of the perils of reconstructing a Hebrew *Vorlage* on the basis of the LXX translation has come to light with the discovery of a sizable portion of the Hebrew original of Ecclesiasticus (The Wisdom of Jesus ben Sira) in the Apocrypha. Previous to this discovery (in 1897) textual critics had conjectured a number of emendations in the Greek text in order to bring it more closely in line with the presumed Hebrew original. But when this portion of the recovered Hebrew original was published (by Cowley and Neubauer), it was discovered that the Greek translator had dealt very freely with his original, and had in the interests of a more Hellenistic viewpoint taken considerable liberties (even though the Hebrew original had been composed by his own grandfather). Kenyon remarks: "The moral to be drawn from this discovery is consequently one of caution in assuming that variations (even considerable ones) in the Septuagint from the Masoretic Hebrew necessarily imply a different text. They *may* do so, no doubt; but we must be prepared to make considerable allowances for liberty of paraphrase and for actual mistakes, especially in the case of books which are likely to have been the latest to be translated."[9]

2. The later Greek versions

a. Aquila's Version was written by Aquila, who came from Pontus. He is said to have become a proselyte to Judaism, and a pupil of Rabbi *Aquiba*. His work was published about A.D. 130, apparently, and proved to be of a strictly literal character. He endeavored to adhere to one standard Greek equivalent for each Hebrew word, whether or not it made good sense in Greek in each context. (Thus he rendered the accusative particle *ʾeth* by the Greek preposition *syn*, "with," governing the accusative case instead of the usual dative.) Barthélemy suggests that Aquiba's version depended on the proto-Theodotion "kaige" recension of A.D. 30-50 (QHBT 270). Aquila's translation has survived only in quotations and fragments, especially from Kings and Psalms 90–103.[10]

b. Symmachus' Version (perhaps A.D. 170) rendered the Old Testament into good idiomatic Greek, although still adhering to high standards of accuracy. Symmachus

9. Kenyon, BAM, p. 95.

10. These fragments have been collected in Frederick Field's edition of the Hexaplaric fragments *Origenis Hexaplorum quae supersunt*, 1875. The Aquiba fragments found in the Cairo Geniza were published by F. C. Burkitt in 1897. Examples of Aquiba's translation are given in the introduction of Rahlfs' *Septuagint*, pp. viii-x. Barthélemy argues in "Les Devanciers d'Aquila" (supplement to VT 1963) for a proto-Theodotion *Recension* dating from A.D. 30-50. It includes the supplements to the LXX text of Jeremiah and Job which supplied the MT material formerly missing, as well as the Theod. text of Daniel □λ is consistently rendered by *kaíγe*. Possibly this recension was connected with the Targumist Jonathan ben Uzziel.

was an Ebionite, according to Jerome, although Epiphanius reports that he was a Samaritan convert to Judaism. Unfortunately there are only a few fragments which have survived; they are collected in Field's edition (see footnote 10).

c. Theodotion's Version (ca. A.D. 180 or 190) was actually not a fresh, new translation, but a revision of an earlier Greek version from probably A.D. 30-50, whether of the LXX or of some other is much disputed. The fact remains that readings of the "Theodotion" type are found in MSS earlier than Theodotion's time (e.g., in some New Testament quotations from the Old Testament, in the Epistle of Barnabas, and in the Epistles of Clement and Hermas). Kenyon and Kahle incline to the view that what Theodotion revised was a non-Septuagintal text.[11] In the case of Daniel, the Theodotion translation altogether displaced the original LXX version of that book, for the very good reason that Theodotion was faithful to the form of the Hebrew original current in the early Christian centuries. (The original LXX Daniel has been preserved only in a single late minuscule, MS 88, and in the recently discovered Chester Beatty Papyri IX-X.)

In our present century, George Lamsa, who came from an Aramaic speaking community in the Middle East, has advanced the theory that much of the New Testament was originally composed in Aramaic which was subsequently translated into the Greek New Testament that we now have. There is, however, no evidence to support this claim and it is not taken seriously by New Testament scholarship.

THE ARAMAIC TARGUMS

During the Babylonian Exile, the Jewish people began to forsake their ancestral Hebrew more and more for the Aramaic tongue, which had become the international language for diplomacy and commerce and the principal medium of communication between the Persian government and its subjects after the establishment of the Persian empire. As Jewish congregations became more uncertain of their Hebrew (although Hebrew never ceased to be studied and spoken by the learned class in Palestine right up to the second century A.D.), it became necessary for an interpreter to repeat to them in Aramaic the message which had just been read in the synagogue service from their Hebrew Bible. But this interpreter (*methurgemān*, Aramaic) would not limit himself always to mere translation, but would often (especially in the case of the prophets) explain the message by a paraphrase, designed to show in what way the utterance of the original was to be understood. After centuries of oral tradition, especially after the

---

11. In Rahlfs' edition of the Septuagint (1:xxvii) he states, "Theodotion did not provide an entirely new translation, but taking the LXX as his basis, he corrected it according to the original text." He then cites Isa. 25:8, where the LXX rendered *l-n-s-h* by *iskhysas*, and replaced the LXX's *katepien ho thanatos* ("death swallowed up") by *eis nikos* ("unto victory"). Also he points to Zech. 12:10, where LXX rendered *;-š-r-d-q-r-w* ("whom they pierced") by *anth' hōn katōrkhēsanto* ("against whom they danced in triumph"), as if from *r-q-d-w*, but Theodotion rendered it by *hon exekentēsan* ("whom they pierced through"). Of course 1 Cor. 15:54 follows *eis nikos*, but John 19:37 follows *exekentēsan*. Rahlfs then comments, "This conformity will not, however, as I have pointed out, justify the conclusion that there had existed an earlier Theodotion earlier than John or Paul. Cf. my *Über Theodotion-lesarten im N.T.* in ZNW 20 (1921) pp. 181-89.

banishment of the Jews from Palestine in A.D. 138, it seemed wise to commit this Aramaic paraphrase to writing as a *targum* (interpretation). This may have occurred as early as Rabbi Aqiba.

There was a tradition that the oral Targum began in Ezra's time (Neh. 8:7-8), but there is no evidence of a written Targum until A.D. 200 or thereabouts. An entirely different Targum of Job was discovered in 11Q dating back to 100 B.C. It is in fragmentary condition, but enough of it has been preserved to determine its distinctive characteristics. The value of the Targums for textual criticism is limited by the fact that their Hebrew *Vorlage* was very nearly the same as that of our "received text" (i.e., the second Bomberg edition). Only occasionally do they betray any divergences which are explicable only on the basis of a variant wording in their Hebrew original. Therefore their value is greater for the history of interpretation than for textual criticism as such.

1. The Targum of Onkelos on the Torah (coming from third century A.D., possibly as a recension of an earlier paraphrase) was produced by the Jewish scholarly circles in Babylon. (It is not quoted from by extant Palestinian writings any earlier than A.D. 1000.) Traditionally it was assigned to a certain Onkelos, who was supposed to be the same native of Pontus who composed the Aquila Greek translation (in other words, Onkelos equals Aquila). But the Eastern origin and the later time of composition militate against this tradition. At any rate, Onkelos, whoever he was, adheres very closely to the Hebrew original in almost every passage except in the poetic chapters of the Pentateuch.

2. The Targum of Jonathan ben Uzziel on the Prophets (i.e., Joshua to Kings, Isaiah to Malachi) was composed in the fourth century A.D., and likewise in Babylonian circles. It is far more paraphrastic and free in its rendering of the Hebrew text than in Onkelos.

3. The Targum of Pseudo-Jonathan on the Torah comes from about A.D. 650 and consists of a mixture of Onkelos with Midrashic materials.[12] It is of small critical value.

4. The Jerusalem Targum on the Torah comes from about A.D. 700. This too is of little critical value.

THE LATIN VERSIONS

1. The Old Latin or Itala Version (composed during the second century, completed about A.D. 200) was not a direct translation from the Hebrew but was merely a Latin translation from the Septuagint. Hence the Itala is of value only as a "daughter translation"; it helps only in ascertaining the earlier text of the LXX. This version, which existed in many and divergent forms, seems to have arisen in North Africa. Subsequent to the appearance of Jerome's translations, it fell into disuse and finally was abandoned, except in the case of the Psalter (as indicated in the next paragraph). It has survived only in fragments (apart from the psalms themselves), and these were collected and published by Sabatier in 1739. Among the manuscripts are the following.

a. Würzburg Palimpsest Codex, coming from about A.D. 450, contains fragments

---

12. See the paragraph on the *Midrash.* chap. 4. pp. 66–67.

of the Torah and prophets.

    b. Lyons Codex, from about A.D. 650, contains fragments from Genesis to Judges.

    2. Jerome's Vulgate (A.D. 390-404) began in 382 when Jerome was commissioned by Pope Damasus to revise the Itala with reference to the Greek Septuagint (for even though Jerome was already versed in Hebrew, Damasus did not at first intend anything so radical as a new Latin translation from the Hebrew original). About the same time that Jerome's translation of the Gospels was ready (for he was working with New Testament revision also), he produced his earliest Psalter, which became known as the Roman Psalter (because it was adopted for use at St. Peter's in Rome). It involved only a slight revision of the Itala, bringing it more closely into line with the LXX. Later (387-390), Jerome produced a second translation, known as the Gallican Psalter, on the basis of the fifth column of Origen's *Hexapla*. This was originally published with diacritical marks, but these were eventually dropped, and it became the standard translation of the Psalms for the Latin church from that day until this. But in the later years of Jerome's translation activity, he perfected his Hebrew by extended residence in Bethlehem, studying under Jewish rabbis. The result was his so-called Hebrew Psalter, which was a fresh and somewhat more accurate rendering from the Hebrew text then current in Palestine.[13] Between 390 and 404, Jerome produced the rest of the Old Testament (including the Apocrypha, although he questioned its canonicity). This received more or less official acceptance as the new, authoritative Latin Bible for the Western church. Over the subsequent centuries, it was published in parallel columns with the Itala (from whence it received some corruption). Finally, about the middle of the sixteenth century, the Council of Trent appointed a commission to produce an expurgated edition of the Vulgate, and this indirectly resulted in the Sixtine Edition, which was published in 1590, followed by a Clementine amended edition in 1592.

THE SYRIAC VERSIONS

    Contemporaneously with the formation of the Aramaic Targum of Onkelos, the Syrian Christians were beginning to produce a more or less standard translation of the Bible into their Eastern Aramaic dialect. (The Aramaic spoken by the Jews of Palestine and Babylon was of the Western type, and was written in the same square Hebrew characters as the Hebrew Scriptures themselves. But the Christian Aramaic speakers adopted a quite dissimilar alphabet of their own, bearing some superficial resemblances to Arabic script.) In the case of the New Testament translations, it is obvious that they have been derived from the Greek original; they even abound in Greek loanwords which have been taken over from the Greek text. It was not until later that the tradition sprang up among the Syrian Christians that their gospels were really the original from which the Greek was translated (on the specious ground that the mother tongue of Christ and the apostles was Aramaic).

---

13. A careful comparison of the Vulgate Psalter (a faithful rendering of the LXX Psalter) with Jerome's *Iuxta Hebraeos* fails to show a clear superiority on the part of the latter; quite frequently the Vulgate LXX rendering is more satisfactory for the Hebrew original.

1. The *Peshitta* (i.e., "the simple") Syriac Old Testament must have been composed in the second or third century A.D., since it was quoted already in fourth-century Syriac writings. At first the Old Testament portion was translated from the Hebrew original, but later it underwent some revision in order to make it conform more closely to the Septuagint. Therefore its textual witness is ambiguous and it must be used with care and discrimination for purposes of textual criticism. The *Peshitta* achieved an official status for the Syriac-speaking church when it was revised and published under the authority of Bishop Rabbula of Edessa (ca. A.D. 400). As to its contents, the *Peshitta* in its earliest form lacked the Apocrypha (indicating that it had been translated from the Hebrew canon rather than from the LXX). It also lacked Chronicles, although this was later added, in the form of a translation from the targum of Chronicles. Later still the greater part of the Apocrypha was added (except Tobit and 1 Esdras).

2. The Syriac Hexapla is the only other extant Old Testament translation. As explained above, it consisted of a translation of the fifth column of Origen's *Hexapla*, and was published under the sponsorship of Bishop Paul of Tella in A.D. 616. The extant portions of it were published in part by A. M. Ceriani and in part by P. de Lagarde. The Codex Mediolanensis, containing 2 Kings, Isaiah, the Minor Prophets, Lamentations, and the poetical books except for the Psalms, was published by H. Middeldorpf in Berlin, 1835.

In our present century, George Lamsa, who came from an Aramaic speaking community in the Middle East, has advanced the theory that much of the New Testament was originally composed in Aramaic which was subsequently translated into the Greek New Testament that we now have. There is, however, no evidence to support this claim and it is not taken seriously by New Testament scholarship.

OTHER VERSIONS

1. The first group of translations that are neither Greek nor Hebrew are the Coptic versions. Coptic was a vernacular descended from the language of the Egyptian hieroglyphs, although by Christian times it had borrowed many Greek words and was written in an adapted form of the Greek alphabet. Five or six distinct dialects of Coptic were spoken, but the Bible translations are mostly either in Sahidic (a southern dialect) or in Bohairic (spoken in Memphis and the Delta). Of the two, the Sahidic is earlier, going back possibly to the second century A.D., although the earliest extant manuscripts date from the fourth century. The Bohairic is later, and somewhat more of it has survived (although neither the Sahidic Old Testament nor the Bohairic is complete). They markedly differ from each other in diction and show every evidence of complete independence from each other. Yet both go back generally to the Hesychian Recension of the LXX. They were translated from the Greek, not directly from the Hebrew.

2. The Ethiopic Version was probably made in the fourth century, although the earliest extant MSS are from the thirteenth century. It also is a daughter translation, either from the LXX or (as others think) from the Coptic or Arabic.

3. Arabic translations never became standardized into one authoritative version, but most of them were made from the LXX. The Arabic translation of Saadia Gaon forms a notable exception; being a Jew, he translated directly from the Hebrew text (ca. 930).

4. The Armenian Version seems to have received its earliest form in the early fifth century. It shows some influence by the *Peshitta.*

5. Of the Gothic Version by Wulfilas (ca. A.D. 330), little remains of the Old Testament. The Codex Argenteus contains only a portion of Neh. 5-7 and nothing more.

THE POLYGLOTS

A word should be said about the great polyglots which began to appear about the time of the Reformation. The polyglots were elaborate and expensive printed editions in which the Hebrew text and all of the available ancient versions were printed in parallel columns.

1. The Complutensian Polyglot was the earliest (so named from Complutum, or Alcala, in Spain, where it was prepared). It came out under the auspices of Cardinal Ximenes and was published under the papal sanction in 1522 (although it had already been run off the press in 1514-1517). The Old Testament portion appeared in the first of its six volumes.

2. The Antwerp Polyglot (under the patronage of Philip II of Spain) came out in 1569-1572 in eight volumes. It added to the contents of the Complutensian Polyglot the Targum of Jonathan on the prophets and also a Targum on the Hagiographa.

3. The Paris Polyglot, which appeared in 1645, followed the text of the Antwerp Edition, but added also the Samaritan Pentateuch and Samaritan Aramaic Version, the Peshitta, and an Arabic version.

4. The London Polyglot added to all of this the Itala, an Ethiopic version of Psalms and Song of Solomon, and the Apocrypha (in Greek, Latin, Syriac, and Arabic), the Targum of Psuedo-Jonathan on the Pentateuch, and even a Persian version. It was edited in six volumes by Bishop Brian Walton in 1656-1657.

4. LOWER CRITICISM OF THE OLD TESTAMENT

IN CONTRADISTINCTION to higher criticism, which deals with questions of the authorship and integrity of the text of Bible books, the science of lower criticism (or textual criticism) is concerned with the task of restoring the original text on the basis of the various copies which have been preserved to us. It attempts to work through the evidence provided by the variants, or different readings, where the surviving manuscripts disagree with each other, and by the use of a scientific system, arrive at what was most probably the wording used by the original author.[1]

TYPES OF MANUSCRIPT ERROR

It is a well-known fact that certain characteristic types of error are apt to accompany the copying out of any written document. Sometimes the copyist would substitute a word of similar sound for the one used in the original (e.g., *whole* for *hole*, or *there* for *their*); he might inadvertently write the same word twice (e.g., *and and*); or he might switch the order of letters (e.g., *seige* instead of *siege*). The types of error which could be listed in this connection are very numerous indeed. They can usually be detected from the context itself, and the intelligent reader can easily tell what the copyist really meant to write.

But there are some types of scribal inadvertence which could be explained in any one of several different ways, and some standard method or system is needed to arrive at that correction which is most likely to have been the word or expression used in the original. In the transmission of the sacred text of Holy Scripture, we find that the same types of scribal slip as appear in secular works have crept into the copies of Bible books. As has already been suggested, it would take nothing short of a miracle to make possible an infallible copy of an infallible original. God has not seen fit to perform such miracles as the Scriptures have been handed down from copy to copy between the

---

1. For an excellent resource for additional study, see Jacob Weingreen: *An Introduction to the Critical Study of the Text of the Hebrew Bible* (Oxford Press, N.Y., 1981).

12 MOST COMMON MANUSCRIPT ERRORS

Haplography - Singular entry of a letter which should have been written twice.

Dittography - Writing twice what should have been written once.

Metathesis - Transposing of letters or words.

Fusion - Combining all or part of two words into a single word.

Fission - Division of a single word into two words.

Homophony - Substitution of one homonym for another.

Misreading similar letters - Confusion of one letter for another of similar shape.

Homoeoteleuton - Omission of an intervening passage due to having a similar ending (such as between two sentences).

Homoeoarkton - Omission of an intervening passage from the beginning of two similar sentences.

Accidental omission - Loss of a single word or letter.

Vowel misreading - Misreading vowel letters as consonants.

Vowel point variations - Misreading a weak vowel as an actual consonant or, a discrepancy in added vowel points giving a change in word meaning.

time of original composition and the invention of the printing press. There is no particular reason why He should have. Therefore we have to deal intelligently with the problems presented by transmissional errors and deal with them in as objective and systematic fashion as possible. This, then, is the special task of biblical lower criticism.

First of all it is necessary to analyze the various types of error which copyists were apt to commit, and observe the contexts in which such errors were most likely to occur. This is necessary preparation before proceeding to their correction. Some of the commonest classes of error are listed below, and are illustrated for the most part from the First Qumran Isaiah Scroll (1QIsᵃ).

1. Haplography—the writing of a letter, syllable, or word only once, when it should have been written more than once. For example, Isa. 26:3, *BᵉKāBāṬᵉḤuW* (or *BiṬᵉḤuW*), meaning "in thee they trusted" (or "in thee; trust ye"), instead of *BᵉKā BāṬuWaḤ BiṬᵉḤuW* ("trusting in thee; trust ye"). As written in consonants only (as of course all Hebrew was before A.D. 800), it would be merely the difference between the scroll's *BK BṬHW* and the MT's *BK BṬWḤ BṬḤW*. Such haplography has probably crept into the MT of Judg. 20:13, *BNYMN* ("Benjamin") being written for *BNY BNYMN* ("the children of Benjamin"). The latter reading has been preserved by the LXX, and indicates the original wording (as we can tell from the plural verb *'ābû* which goes with this noun, for a simple *BNYMN* would demand a singular verb). The accidental omission of a letter is also known as haplography even when no doubling

is called for. For example, the Isaiah Scroll reads *BḤZQT YD* ("with strength of hand") in Isaiah 8:11, instead of the MT's *BḤZQT HYD* ("with the strength of the hand").

2. Dittography—the writing twice of that which should have been written but once. For example, in Isa. 30:30, *HŠMY' HŠ MY'* ("cause to be heard cause to be heard") instead of the MT's simple *HŠMY'* ("cause to be heard"). Again, in Ezek. 48:16 the MT reads, *ḤMŠ, HMŠ M'WT* ("five five hundred") instead of the proper *ḤMŠM'WT* ("five hundred").

3. Metathesis—reversing the proper position of letters or words. For example, Isa. 32:19 *HY'R* ("the forest") instead of the MT's *H'YR* ("the city")—which alone makes good sense in the context. Again, in Ezek. 42:16 the MT consonantal text has *ḤMŠ'MWT QNYM* ("five cubits reeds") instead of the obvious *ḤMŠ M'WT QNYM* ("five hundred reeds")—the proper correction having been indicated by the Masoretes in their apparatus (see under "Masoretes," pp. 67-68).

4. Fusion—the combining of two separate words into one. Würthwein cites Amos 6:12 where *BBQRYM* ("with oxen") probably stands for an original *BBQR YM* ("with oxen the sea"—i.e., "Shall one plough the sea with oxen?"). Rypins cites Isa. 3:15 *MLKM* (according to the consonantal text of the MT), which would mean "their king"; but what the context calls for (and what the Masoretes amend to) is *MH LKM* ("What is the matter with you?"). In this connection note that Jerome, following the interpretation of the LXX, understood the term *L'Z'ZL* (for Azazel) in Lev. 16:8 as a case of fusion for *L'Z'ZL* ("for a goat of sending away"—which certainly makes excellent sense in the context, and does away with a bothersome proper name, Azazel, otherwise unknown in pre-Christian times).

5. Fission—the dividing up of a single word into two words. For example, in Isa. 2:20, the MT's *LḤPR PRWT* ("to a hole of rats") should be amended to the scroll's *LḤPRPRYM* ("to the shrew-mice"), as the LXX shows (which simply transcribed the word as *pharpharōth*, without attempting to translate it). Rypins cites the MT's *KY DRKYK* ("because thy ways") in Ezek. 7:4, arguing that it originally read *KDRKYK* ("according to thy ways"). Yet this last emendation lacks any strong support.

6. Homophony—the substitution of one homonym for another. For example, frequently we find *LW* ("to him") subsituted for *L'* ("not"). Thus in Isa. 9:3, both the MT and the scroll, read, *HRBYT HGWY L' HGDLT HŚMḤH* ("Thou hast multiplied the people; thou hast not multiplied the joy"), where far better sense is obtained from *HRBYT HGWY LW HGDLT HSMḤH* ("Thou hast increased the people, thou hast increased the joy for him"). The confusion arose from the fact that both *L'* ("not") and *LW* ("for him") were pronounced *lō*. The second reading is the one endorsed by the *qerê*.

7. Misreading of similar appearing letters. From 600 B.C. onward, *D* (*daleth*) and *R* (*rēsh*) resembled each other closely enough so that they were often confused, especial-

ly in proper names. Thus the "Dodanim" of Gen. 10:4 appears as "Rodanim" in 1 Chron. 1:7—which is thought by many to be the better reading, since it probably refers to the Rhodians. Again, W (*waw*) and Y (*yodh*) were written very similarly from 150 B.C. and onward, and even in the Isaiah Scroll they are often difficult to distinguish. Where the MT reads WD'W ("and know ye") the scroll has YD'W ("let them know") in Isa. 33:13. One interesting example of this occurs in Acts 7:43, which quotes the LXX spelling of Raiphan as the name of the idol, whereas the MT of Amos 5:26 (from which this was quoted) spells it *Chiun*. How could this confusion have arisen? In mere consonants *Chiun* appears as KYWN; *Raiphan* would be RYPN. However the fifth century B.C., as the Elephantine Papyri testify, the shape of K (𐤊) was very similar to R (𐤓), and W (𐤅) greatly resembled P(𐤐). In that period, then, a copy of Amos would have presented a name which could be read either as KYWN or as RYPN. (From the Akkadian *Kaiwanu*, the name of the god who presided over the planet Saturn, we gather that the MT has preserved the more original spelling in this case.) As for Stephen (whose speech is reported in Acts 7), the verse he quoted is recorded by Luke in the LXX version, which was the only form of the Old Testament accessible to his Greek-speaking readers.

8. Homoeoteleuton—the omission of an intervening passage because the copyist's eye had skipped from one ending to a second similar ending. *Homoeoteleuton* is Greek for "similar ending." An example of this in the scroll is found in Isa. 4:5 (all the words omitted being contained between the parentheses): WBR' YHWH...'NN (YWMM W'ŠN WNGH' LHBH LYLH KY 'L KL KBWD ḤPH WSKH THYH LṢL) YWMM MḤRB.[2] From this it will be observed that the eye of the scribe skipped from the first YWMM ("by day") to the second YWMM, resulting in the loss of thirteen words in between (cf. Ps. 145:13*b*) from the LXX.

9. Homoeoarkton—In 1 Sam. 14:41 the LXX has two occurrences of "O Lord God of Israel," with twenty-five words between them. The MT lacks all of these words and has only one "O Lord God of Israel." The only fair conclusion is that the MT dropped these words by homoeoteleuton (or homoeoarkton—similar beginning), rather than that the LXX inserted all these extra words from some unknown source. (Cf. Kittel's *Biblia Hebraica*, 12 ed., p. 426.)

10. Accidental omission of words in situations where no repetition is involved. One celebrated instance is 1 Sam. 13:1, where the MT reads, "Saul was...year(s) old when he began to reign." Unfortunately textual criticism does not help us, for both the LXX and the other versions have no numeral here. Apparently the correct number fell out so early in the history of the transmission of this particular text that it was already lost before the third century B.C.

2. The vowel-pointed text reads: וּבָרָא יְהוָֹה עַל כָּל־מְכוֹן הַר־צִיּוֹן וְעַל־מִקְרָאֶהָ עָנָן וְיוֹמָם

עָשָׁן וְנֹגַהּ אֵשׁ לֶהָבָה לָיְלָה כִּי עַל־כָּל־כָּבוֹד חֻפָּה׃

11. Misreading vowel letters as consonants. The Hebrew letters ' ('aleph), H (he), W (waw), and Y (yodh) were true consonants only, in the earlier stages of Hebrew writing. But gradually they came to be used to indicate the presence of certain vowels, and when so used, the ', H, W, or Y was not to be pronounced at all, but was simply a *mater lectionis* (indicating a pure-long vowel). In the Maccabean period we find that the use of these vowel letters greatly expanded, probably because the correct pronunciation of Hebrew was becoming uncertain to a people who were by now using Aramaic for all ordinary purposes. Most of the earlier Qumran MSS show this proliferation of *matres lectionis*. In the first century B.C. the Sopherim (see section on "Sopherim" in this chapter) reverted to the less encumbered spelling of the older period, and largely restricted the vowel letters to indicate "pure-long" vowels only (rather than "tone-long" or short vowels, as the second century B.C. scrolls often did). But occasionally some of the superfluous *matres lectionis* were preserved in cases where, if understood as true consonants, they made a substantial difference in meaning. An instance in point, according to Würthwein, is Amos 2:7 where the MT's *HŠPYM* (*haššō'apîm* ("who trample upon") has replaced the original *HŠPYM, haššā'apîm* (from the verb *šûp,* "crush").

12. Variants based on the vowel points only. It should be understood that the vowel points were not inserted by the Masoretes to make the consonantal text of the Hebrew Bible accurate by providing vowel sounds until after A.D. 600. In most cases we can assume that the oral tradition which was followed by the Masoretic scribes is correct unless there are strong indications in the context that suggest they were in error. One interesting example of this has to do with Ps. 2:9 where we have consonants that could indicate the verb "to shepherd" or the verb "to smash" depending on how we vowel them; i.e., *terō'ēm* from *rā'a'* ("smash") seems to be confirmed by the second half of the verse: "You will dash them to pieces like pottery." On the other hand, the LXX reads *poimaneis* ("You will rule"), implying the vowel pointing *tir'ēm* from *rā'ah.* This is confirmed by the word for "rod", which is *šēbet,* the regular word for the scepter of a king. It is highly significant that this verse is quoted in Rev. 2:27: "He will rule (or "pasture") them with an iron scepter; he will dash them to pieces like pottery."

Other interesting examples may be found in Isa. 9:6, Mic. 5:1, Ps. 22:9, and Ps. 19:2. A discussion of these may be found in EBD, pp. 41-42.

THE CANONS OF TEXTUAL CRITICISM

Certain standard criteria have been set up by textual critics to help in arriving at an intelligent choice among two or more competing variants. It often happens that two or more of these rules or "canons" apply in a given situation and tip the scale of preference in opposite directions. Thus, one of two readings may conform more perfectly to the known style and diction of the author, whereas the other may be the

Canons of Textual Criticism

The preferred reading is the one that...

- Is Older
- Is more difficult
- Is shorter
- Best explains variants
- Has the widest geographical support
- Conforms to the style and diction of the author
- Reflects no doctrinal bias

more difficult (Canon #6 vs. Canon #2). Or else the older reading (Canon #1) may at the same time be the longer reading (Canon #3). In such cases the rule of thumb is to give priority to the canons in the order of their listing below. But this method must be applied with great discrimination and with due consideration of all the special circumstances that might weaken the case for the particular variant which the prior canon might seem to favor. For example, a rigid application of Canon #1 would automatically give preference to the Dead Sea Scroll of Isaiah as over against the MT in every case of disagreement. But a careful study of the entire scroll indicates that the copyist followed far lower standards of scribal fidelity than those of the official recension on which the MT itself was based. Or again, a very old copy may in turn be derived from an earlier exemplar which had suffered gaps or wormholes, or the like. These would betray themselves through occasional loss of words or conjectures which markedly depart from other textual traditions. But with due respect to these special complicating factors, the canons listed below will serve as a reliable guide to the textual critic.

Canon #1: The older reading is to be preferred. As just indicated, the older manuscript is not necessarily the most carefully copied manuscript; this canon applies where the older manuscript is at least as reliable as the later, and equally free of oddities or peculiarities.[3] An example would be Isa. 61:1 from 1QIs[a] (2nd cent. B.C.) which appears in the first Qumran scroll which appears as *PQḤQWḤ* whereas the MT reads

---

3. In this connection note this excellent statement by Burrows, "It should not be necessary, but perhaps it is, to say again that an old reading is not necessarily a good one. The Qumran texts are full of variant readings which are demonstrably inferior to those of the traditional text. To put the same thing in another way, paradoxical but true, a pre-Masoretic reading is not necessarily older than a Masoretic

PQḤ-QWḤ. The MT is to be preferred as more reliable. The older MS is not necessarily the most carefully copied MS. This canon applies when the older MS is at least as reliable as the later MS and equally free of oddities or peculiarities.

The MT is to be preferred because it shows a doubling of the second and third radical which is common in Hebrew. The Qumran reading has the difficulty of presenting a pattern which is otherwise not known in Hebrew.

Canon #2: The more difficult reading (*lectio difficilior*) is to be preferred. This is because a scribe was more apt to simplify or clarify the wording of his original than he was to make it harder for his reading public to understand. If he left a rare word or difficult expression or irregular grammatical form, it must be because he found it that way in his model. This does not apply, of course, if the difficulty involved arose from ignorance or inadvertence on the part of the copyist himself. Nor does it apply if the difficult reading does not make sense at all, or utterly contradicts the author's meaning as expressed elsewhere. Isa. 53:3 in the MT reads *WYDW ḤLY*. The Isaiah scroll read *WYWD ḤWLY*. The Qumran reading would be more easily expected than that of the MT. The Qumran translates "one who is acquainted with illness," the passive participle. Although the MT is less likely to be expected, it is probably the original intent of the author because he would be less likely to change it from the Qumran form to the MT form than vice versa.

Canon #3: The shorter reading is to be preferred. This is because copyists were more apt to insert new material than they were to leave out any of the sacred text they had before them. In cases of haplography or homoeoteleuton, of course, this canon does not apply.

Canon #4: The reading which best explains all the variants is to be preferred. For example, Ps. 22:16 (Matt. 22:17) reads *K'RY YDY WRGLY*, which, as pointed by the Masoretes (*Kā' ᵃRiY*), means "*like the lion* my hands and my feet" ("they have pierced my hands and my feet," KJV). The Hebrew column in the Complutensian Polyglot reads *K'RW*, vocalized as *Ka'RuW*, which means "they have bored through." Which reading best explains the variants (in this case, the reading in the versions)? Probably the second reading, for the LXX, the *Peshitta*, the Vulgate, and even Jerome's Hebrew Psalter all read, "They have dug through" or "pierced." Symmachus rendered it as "seeking to bind" (which does not clearly favor either *K'RY* or *K'RW*).

Canon #5: The reading with the widest geographical support is to be preferred. Thus a reading favored by the LXX, the Itala, and the Coptic will not be as well attested as one in which the *Peshitta* and the Samaritan agree. This is because the Itala and Coptic are daughter translations of the LXX and all belong to the Alexandrian recen-

reading. The proto-Masoretic text existed at Qumran and elsewhere along with divergent texts; on the whole it is fair to say that it was the trunk and they were the branches that had sprung out of it. The greatest contribution of the Dead Sea Scrolls to textual criticism is still their demonstration of this fact" (MLDSS, p. 162).

sion, whereas the Peshitta and the Samaritan represent somewhat different textual traditions. Similarly, the likelihood is great that a variant attested by such diverse traditions as the Samaritan and the LXX is closer to the original than the MT reading. For example, in Num. 22:35, both the Samaritan and the LXX agree on *TŠMR LDBR* ("thou shalt be careful to say"), whereas the MT reads simply *TDBR* ("thou shalt speak"). Of course Canon #3 might seem to favor the MT here, but the presence of this same locution in widely separated traditions is hard to explain as a later insertion which by coincidence turned out to be the same.

Canon #6: The reading which most conforms to the style and diction of the author is to be preferred. This is a mere statement of likelihood, of course. But where two variants present themselves, each equally possible in the context, but one conforming to the author's usual way of expressing that type of thought, and the other sounding a bit different from the style he uses elsewhere, the former is to be preferred. Yet it should be added that textual critics of the slash-and-slice school have greatly overused this canon in a most inadmissible way, and have imposed upon passages that do not for some reason suit them a rather subjective and arbitrary judgment as to what the ancient author could or could not have said.

Canon #7: The reading which reflects no doctrinal bias is to be preferred. For example, we know from the Targums and from the LXX that later Jewish thought shied away from any humanlike representations of God, or from locutions which implied that He had a body, parts, or passions. A variant which tends to minimize this factor is known as an "antianthropomorphism." For example, in Isa. 1:12 we find in the consonantal text (the *kethib*) the word *LR'WT*, which would normally be pointed *LiRᵉ'oWT* ("to see"). But this would imply the possibility of man's beholding the face of God, and so for this reason (presumably) the Masoretes pointed the word *LēRā'oWT* ("to be seen, or to appear"), thus permitting the interpretation, "to appear before Me." This should normally have been spelled *LHR'WT*, if Isaiah really had intended to say "to appear." We do well, therefore, to explain the Masoretic pointing here as an antianthropomorphism and to prefer the *kethib* as the original reading.

SUMMARY OF TEXTUAL METHODS

In addition to the general rules given above, it would be well to summarize an excellent methodology proposed by Würthwein.[4]

1. Where the MT and the other witnesses offer the same text and it is an intelligible and sensible reading, it is inadmissible to reject this reading and resort to conjecture (as too many critics have done).

2. Where there is a genuine deviation from the MT on the part of the other witnesses (and the deviation is not simply a matter of translator's interpretation) and both

---

4. Ernst Würthwein, TOT(Grand Rapids: Eerdmans, 1979), IV: III-19

readings seem equally sensible, then the preference should normally be given to the MT (unless one of the canons intervenes to give clear preference to the other reading).

3. Where the text of the MT is doubtful or impossible because of factors of language or sense-in-context, and where at the same time other witnesses offer a satisfactory reading, then the latter should be given favorable consideration. Especially is this so if it can be seen how the MT reading might have been corrupted through some familiar scribal error. But if there is reason to believe that the ancient translator produced a clear reading only because he could not make out what the Hebrew text meant and guessed at its meaning and supplied what would be plausible in the context, then we have an obscurity which textual criticism cannot relieve except by conjecture. We must simply label it as obscure or corrupt.

4. Where neither the MT nor the other witnesses offer a possible or probable text, conjecture may legitimately be resorted to. But such a conjecture should try to restore a reading as close as possible to the corrupted one itself, with due consideration for the well-known causes of textual corruption (note "Types of Manuscript Error" above).[5]

5. In all textual-critical work, due regard must be given to the psychology of the scribe himself. We must always ask ourselves the question, How might this error—if error there be—have originated from his hand? Does this accord with his type or habit of mind as observed elsewhere in his work?

By means of this careful formula, Würthwein attempts to set up a method of objectivity and scientific procedure that will eliminate much of the reckless and ill-considered emendation which has too often passed for bona fide textual criticism.

THE WORK OF THE SOPHERIM, THE TALMUD, AND THE MASORETES

The *Sopherim* represented that order of "scribes" (for so the term signifies) which first had its rise under Ezra, the greatest scribe of them all. They formed a recognized guild of Bible-text custodians in Jesus' day. Their activity extended from 400 B.C. to A.D. 200, and their great achievement was to standardize a pure text of the Hebrew Scriptures (as pure as their manuscript sources permitted them). Presumably they had much to do with the hypothetical revision committee[6] and saw to it that all the copies of Scripture produced by their hands (and they were the official Bible publication society of that day) would conform to the standard text. At some unknown peri-

---

.5. At this point it would be well to call attention to an excellent observation quoted with approval by A. Bentzen, "We always run the risk of introducing a new error by conjecture... "conjectures generally are quite useless to the historian, because it is never justified to infer any conclusions from conjectures, at least without noting that the conclusion is another conjecture" (*Introduction to the Old Testament,* 1:97). This point is well taken, would that Bentzen himself had observed the wider implications of this principle for rationalist higher criticism. There too a conclusion based upon a mere conjecture (and what is there in the Documentary Theory which is free from conjecture?) is itself only another conjecture—and not, to use a hackneyed phrase, one of "the assured results of modern scholarship."
6. See chap. 3, p. 47.

Early Jewish Writings

Title	Type	Date	Purpose
Sopherim	Textual	400 B.C.-A.D. 200	Standardization of pure text
Midrash	Textual interpretation and commentary	100 B.C.-A.D. 300	Doctrinal and homiletical exposition
Tosefta	Addition or supplement	A.D. 100-500	Teachings and traditions of the Tannaim
Talmud	Textual instructions	A.D. 100-500	Contains the Mishnah and the Germarah
Mishnah	Repetitions, teaching	A.D. 200	Oral laws and traditions
Gemara	Commentary	A.D. 200-500	Supplement or expanded commentary on the Mishnah
Masoretes	Commentary	A.D. 500-950	Inserted vowel points - moderate textual criticism

od (perhaps in the first century B.C.) they hit upon the device of counting all the verses, words, and letters of each book in the Old Testament, and appending these figures at the end of the book concerned. This would enable any checker to tell whether he had a perfect copy before him, for he had only to count the verses, words and letters, and if they did not number to the right total, he would know there was an error. These statistics of the Sopherim have been included in the *Masora Finalis* of each book in the Masoretic Bible. It should be clearly understood that the Sopherim worked only with the consonantal text; they had nothing to do with the vowel points. Vowel points were not even invented until after A.D. 500.

One other contribution of the Sopherim consisted in the so-called *tiqqūnêsōpherîm*, or "decrees of the scribes," eighteen in number. Many of these were of an antianthropomorphic character (cf. Canon #7 above). For instance, in Gen. 18:22, "Jehovah stood yet" is altered to "Abraham stood yet." Or else they protect the dignity of God in an altered reading. Thus in the traditional text of 1 Sam. 3:13, the sons of Eli curse "God" (*'LHYM*), but this is changed to: "they curse" (or "bring a curse") "upon themselves" (*LHM*—the *aleph* and *yodh* being omitted). Still others of these emendations seem to have little point or justification.[7]

According to Jewish tradition, the term *Sopherim* is to be applied more exactly to the earliest group of scribes from the fifth century to third century B.C. (from Ezra to Antigonus of Socho). After them came the *Zugoth* (the pairs of textual scholars) from the second to first centuries B.C. (from Jose ben Joezer to Hillel). The third group were the *Tannaim* ("repeaters, or teachers"), from the death of Hillel to the death of Judah Hannasi after A.D. 200. The teachings of all three groups are found in the Mishnah, the Tosefta, the Baraithoth, and the Midrash. More than two hundred Tannaim are mentioned in these works, most of them being entitled either Rabbi or Rabban ("teacher").

The Jews preserved, at first by oral tradition and then in writing, an enormous amount of traditional interpretation of the Torah and other parts of the Old Testament, together with folklore embellishments, anecdotes, and homilies of various sorts. Much of this had to do with practical legal questions, or with intricate details of ritual, or the like. This mass of tradition has been preserved in two major collections, the Midrash and the Talmud, plus a minor one known as the Tosefta. They are now described in chronological order.

The *Midrash* (textual study, or text interpretation, from *dāraš*, to "search, investigate") was brought together between 100 B.C. and A.D. 300. It was a doctrinal and homiletical exposition of the Old Testament. Composed in both Hebrew sections and Aramaic sections, it provided a commentary on the written law (i.e., the Pentateuch).

---

7. These are all listed in C. D. Ginsburg's translation of Jacob ben Chayim's *Introduction to the Bomberg Bible* (1524-1525). Cf. Stanley Rypins, *The Book of Thirty Centuries*, p. 37.

It consisted of two parts: the *Halakah* ("procedure"), commenting on the Torah only; and the *Haggada* ("declaration," or "explanation"), commenting on the entire Old Testament, and including various proverbs, parables, and tales. These contain the earliest extant synagogue homilies. They have some importance for textual criticism in their numerous quotations of the Old Testament text, occasionally in a slightly different form from the MT.

The *Tosēfta* ("addition, or supplement") arose between A.D. 100 and 300. It consists of a collection of teachings and traditions of the Tannaim which were closely related to the Mishnah. According to tradition, it contains that part of the original Mishnah which Rabbi Aqiba (ca. A.D.100) omitted from his edition of the Mishnah, which was abbreviated in order to facilitate memorization.

The *Talmûd* ("instruction," from *limmēd*, "to teach") grew up between A.D. 100 and 500. It consists of two main divisions. The *Mishnah* ("repetition," or "teaching") was completed around A.D. 200. Composed in Hebrew, it contained a digest of all the oral laws (supposedly communicated by word of mouth from Moses to his seventy elders), traditions, and explanations of Scripture. It is divided into six orders (*sedārîm*): agriculture, feasts, women, civil and criminal law, sacrifices or holy things, and unclean things. These in turn are subdivided into sixty-three tractates (for the titles of which, see ISBE, p. 2905). The sages who contributed to the Mishnah were known as *Tannaim* (the latest order of Sopherim, as mentioned above). The second main division is the *Gemara* ("the matter that is learned," from *gemar*, "to complete, accomplish, or learn"). An Aramaic word, it indicates that it was composed in Aramaic rather than Hebrew. It consists of a supplement to be attached to each of the tractates by way of expanded commentary upon the Mishnah. It arose in two distinct forms, the Palestinian Gemara (ca. A.D. 200), and the much larger Babylonian Gemara (ca. A.D. 500). The sages who contributed to the Gemara were known as *Amoraim* ("speakers, explainers," from *'āmar*, "to speak").

The *Masoretes* were the scholars who between A.D. 500 and 950 gave the final form to the text of the Old Testament. They were so called because they preserved in writing the oral tradition (*masorah*) concerning the correct vowels and accents, and the number of occurrences of rare words of unusual spellings. They received the unpointed, consonantal text of the Sopherim and inserted the vowel points which gave to each word its exact pronunciation and grammatical form. They even engaged in a moderate amount of textual criticism. Wherever they suspected the word indicated by the consonantal text was erroneous, they corrected it in a very ingenious way. They left the actual consonants undisturbed, as they had received them from the Sopherim. But they inserted the vowel points which belonged to the new word which they were substituting for the old, and then they inserted the consonants of the new word itself in very small letters in the margin. For example, in Isa. 28:15 occurs the word cluster *KY—'BR*. As normally pointed, this would read *KiY—'āBaR* ("when it has passed over"), and this is therefore the reading of the *kethîb* (which is an Aramaic term meaning "the thing written", i.e., the word indicated by the consonants). But the Masoretes felt that an imperfect tense should follow *KiY* ("when") in this connection, and therefore inserted under *'BR* the vowels appropriate to *Ya'ªBōR* ("it passes over"); and then in the margin they wrote in small letters *Y'BR*, which indicates this *qerê* (an Aramaic term meaning "read!") variant. (The customary abbreviation for *kethîb* is *K*, and that for *qerê* is *Q*.)

Perhaps the most famous (and frequent) example of a *qerê* reading is the covenant name of God, Jehovah. This name is written with the four consonants *YHWH*, going back to an original pronunciation, *Yahweh*. The proper, original rendering of Jehovah, therefore, is *Yahweh* (or *Jahweh*, as the Germans write it). But the Jews as early as Nehemiah's time began to feel qualms about pronouncing the holy name, lest they bring upon themselves possible penal consequences under the third commandment. It therefore became accepted practice to substitute the title "Lord" (*'ªDōNāY*) for the name *Yahweh* whenever reading it aloud. To indicate this substitution, the Masoretes inserted the vowels of *'ªDōNāY* under the consonants of *JaHWeH*, resulting in the appearance of *JeHōWāH* or "Jehovah." Misunderstanding this *qerê*, European scholars of the Renaissance period (when Hebrew became avidly studied in Europe) supposed that the proper pronunciation of the name was "Jehovah"—and so it has come down to us today. It was actually *Yahweh* (this may be called the *kethîb* reading), but the mistake has become so sanctioned by usage that devout Christians generally are loath to accept any reversion to the pronunciation which was historically correct.

In addition to the insertion of vowel points and the indication of *qerê* readings, the Masoretes also busied themselves with accent marks. At first the accent marks were simpler and more sparingly used, but later they became more complicated, especially as the accentual system became perfected by the Tiberian School of Masoretes (Tiberias being the city mentioned in the Gospels as situated by the Sea of Galilee). The most celebrated of all the Masoretes were Moses ben Asher (with his learned son Aaron) and ben Naphtali. The standard text of the Hebrew Bible is based on a ben Asher text (the Leningrad Codex of the Old Testament).

At the side margins of the Masoretic MSS was placed the *Marginal Masorah*. This included not only the consonants of *qerê* readings (as described above), but also statistics as to how often various words and phrases appearing in that line of script occurred elsewhere in the Hebrew Scriptures. Or else they indicated how often they occurred elsewhere with that particular spelling or combination of words. The most frequent notation of this sort was a single *L* (*lamed*) with a dot over it, standing for *Lō* ("not") and indicating that this word or this spelling does not occur elsewhere in the Hebrew Scriptures. (This of course served notice on future copyists that any other occurrence of this unique word or spelling would be rejected as an error.)

At the bottom margin of the Masoretic MSS was the *Larger Masorah*, containing more information of this sort, often furnishing mnemonic devices whereby all the occurrences of infrequent words or phrases could be remembered. For example, at Gen. 1:1 the Masoretic note says with reference to the first word cluster (In-the-beginning—*bᵉrē'šît*): "The sign is: God establishes the righteous" (*ᵉlōhîm yā ḳîm haṣṣedek*). This indicates that in the first occurrence (Gen. 1:1) the next word after *bᵉrē'šît* is God; the second occurrence of *bᵉrē'šît* (Jer. 26:1) has the name of King Jehoiakim after it (for Jehoiakim, or *Yᵉhō-yāḳîm*, means "Yahweh establishes"); the third occurrence of *bᵉrē'šît* (Jer. 28:1) is followed by the name of Zedekiah (for Zedekiah, or *Ṣedeḳ-Yah*, means "Righteous is Yahweh"). Needless to say, this type of information is of marginal interest to most modern scholarship, and thus the Masoretic notations are not widely studied in non-Jewish circles.

The *Final Masorah* contains mostly statistics as to the number of verses, letters, and the like, occurring in the book, and indicates the middle word and the middle letter.

Two other features of the Masoretic recension deserve mention, because of their bearing upon textual criticism. There are fifteen dotted words ("*neqûdôt*") in the Old Testament text, and Jewish tradition has it that these were words which in the judgment of the scholars of the so-called Great Synagogue (apparently founded by Ezra) should be deleted, or at least marked as doubtful. For example, in Num. 3:39 the word "and Aaron" is dotted, inasmuch as Aaron himself was not one of those numbered in the census. The other device is that of suspended letters, that is, letters placed above the line. These occurred in four passages, where the Masoretes (following the decision of the Sopherim) suspected the genuineness of the letters so placed. Thus in Judg. 18:30 the original wording apparently was, "Jonathan the son of Gershom the son of Moses" (*MōšeH*, Hebrew); but to safeguard Moses' reputation, an extra *N* (*nun*) was inserted (although slightly above the line) so as to change the name from "Moses" to "Manasseh" (*MᵉNašeH*).[8]

In conclusion we should accord to the Masoretes the highest praise for their meticulous care in preserving so sedulously the consonantal text of the Sopherim which had been entrusted to them. They together with the Sopherim themselves gave the most diligent attention to accurate preservation of the Hebrew Scriptures

---

8. For a careful discussion of these, see S. Talmon's preface to "The Ten Nequdoth of the Torah" by Romain Butin, N.T. (Ktav Publishers, 1969), p. xxviii. This includes the evidence of the MS Neofiti I in the Vatican Library.

that has ever been devoted to any ancient literature, secular or religious, in the history of human civilization. So conscientious were they in their stewardship of the holy text that they did not even venture to make the most obvious corrections, so far as the consonants were concerned, but left their *Vorlage* (i.e., the older text from which the copy was made) exactly as it was handed down to them. Because of their faithfulness, we have today a form of the Hebrew text which in all essentials duplicates the recension which was considered authoritative in the days of Christ and the apostles, if not a century earlier. And this in turn, judging from Qumran evidence, goes back to an authoritative revision of the Old Testament text which was drawn up on the basis of the most reliable manuscripts available for collation from previous centuries. These bring us very close in all essentials to the original autographs themselves, and furnish us with an authentic record of God's revelation. As W. F. Albright has said, "We may rest assured that the consonantal text of the Hebrew Bible, though not infallible, has been preserved with an accuracy perhaps unparalleled in any other Near Eastern literature."[9]

9. Quoted in H. H. Rowley, OTMS, p. 25.

5 THE CANON OF THE OLD TESTAMENT

THE TERM canon is derived from a Greek word *kanōn*, which means "straight rod, or straight edge, or ruler." As applied to literature, canon has come to mean those writings which conform to the rule or standard of divine inspiration and authority. In the Hebrew Scriptures there are thirty-nine books which were considered by the Jewish community to be canonical. These are the same as those accepted by the apostolic church and by the Protestant churches since the days of the Reformation. The Roman church adds to these fourteen other books (or portions of books) which compose the Apocrypha, and consider these of equal authority with the rest. This raises the question, What makes a book of Scripture canonical? When were these various books composing the Old Testament considered or accepted as canonical by God's ancient people? We shall defer a consideration of the claims of the apocryphal books until a later part of this chapter. First let us consider the tripartite division of the Hebrew canon (Law, Prophets, Writings), and the explanations which have been offered for it.

THE CANON OF THE OLD TESTAMENT

The Masoretic edition of the Old Testament differs in certain particulars from the order of books followed in the Septuagint, and also from that of Protestant churches. The compilers of the Greek Version (LXX) observed a more or less topical arrangement, as follows.

The 5 books of law: Genesis, Exodus, Leviticus, Numbers, and Deuteronomy.

The 15 books of history: Joshua, Judges, Ruth, 1 and 2 Samuel, 1 and 2 Kings (generally these last four are named, 1, 2, 3, and 4 Kingdoms), 1 and 2 Chronicles, 1 and 2 Esdras (the first being apocryphal, the second being canonical Ezra), Nehemiah, Tobit, Judith, and Esther.

The 7 books of poetry and wisdom: Job, Psalms, Proverbs, Ecclesiastes, Song of Solomon, Wisdom of Solomon, and Wisdom of Sirach (Ecclesiasticus).

The 19 books of prophecy: the 12 Minor Prophets—Hosea, Amos, Micah, Joel, Obadiah, Jonah, Nahum, Habakkuk, Zephaniah, Haggai, Zechariah, and Malachi;[1] the

1. This order of the Minor Prophets in the Greek Septuagint was altered in the Latin Vulgate to the

7 Major Prophets—Isaiah, Jeremiah, Baruch, Lamentations, Epistle of Jeremiah, Ezekiel, and Daniel (including Susanna, Bel and the Dragon, and the Song of the Three Holy Children).

THE SUPPLEMENTAL BOOKS OF HISTORY: 1 AND 2 MACCABEES

In general the Latin Vulgate follows the same order as the Septuagint, except that 1 and 2 Esdras is Apocryphal equal our Ezra and Nehemiah, whereas the Apocryphal parts (3 and 4 Esdras) are placed after the New Testament books, as is also the Prayer of Manasseh. Also, in the Vulgate the Major Prophets are placed before the Minor Prophets. From this listing it will be apparent that the Protestant Bible follows the same topical order of arrangement as the Vulgate, except that all the Apocryphal parts (including the considerable additions to Esther) are omitted. In order, then, the Protestant Bible follows the Vulgate, but in content it follows the MT.

It should also be noted that in the Syriac Peshitta the original order of the books was: Pentateuch, Job, Joshua, Judges, Samuel, Kings, Chronicles, Psalms, Proverbs, Ecclesiastes, Ruth, Canticles, Esther, Ezra, Nehemiah, Isaiah, Twelve Minor Prophets, Jeremiah, Lamentations, Ezekiel, and Daniel.

The order of books in the Masoretic Text is as follows: the Torah (or Pentateuch); the prophets (*Nᵉbi'îm*) in the following order: Former Prophets—Joshua, Judges, (1 and 2) Samuel, and (1 and 2) Kings; Latter Prophets—Major Prophets: Isaiah, Jeremiah, and Ezekiel, and the twelve Minor Prophets (in the same order as in the English Bible); the Writings (*Kethûbîm*, Greek, *Hagiographa*, "Holy Writings"): Poetry and Wisdom— Psalms, Proverbs, and Job (but Leningrad Codex has Psalms, Job, and Proverbs); the Rolls or *Megilloth*—Song of Solomon, Ruth, Lamentations, Ecclesiastes, and Esther (but Leningrad: Ruth, Song, Ecclesiastes, Lamentations, Esther); Historical—Daniel, Ezra, Nehemiah, and 1 and 2 Chronicles.

It ought to be mentioned, however, that the order of the books composing the MT represents a later division (largely resorted to in order to facilitate discussion with Christian apologists who appealed to the Old Testament in their polemic against Judaism). The earlier division consisted of the same content as the thirty-nine books listed above, but arranged in only twenty-four books. This meant that 1 and 2 Samuel were counted as one book; likewise 1 and 2 Kings and 1 and 2 Chronicles. The twelve Minor Prophets were also counted as one book, (since they could all be contained quite easily in a single scroll) and Ezra and Nehemiah formed a single unit. Josephus, however, who wrote near the end of the first century A.D., gives evidence of a twenty-two book canon.[2] This apparently involved the inclusion of Ruth with Judges and of

order followed in modern Bible translations, with Joel coming after Hosea rather than after Micah. Even the present day Greek Orthodox editions of the LXX conforms to the Vulgate order.

2. The passage from Josephus reads as follows: "We have but twenty-two [books] containing the history of all time, books that are justly believed in; and of these, five are the books of Moses, which comprise the laws and earliest traditions from the creation of mankind down to his death. From the death of Moses to the reign of Artaxerxes King of Persia, the successor of Xerxes, the prophets who succeeded Moses wrote the history of the events that occurred in their own time, in thirteen books. The

Lamentations with Jeremiah. Yet essentially, whether thirty-nine books, or twenty-four, or twenty-two, the basic divisions of the Hebrew canon have remained the same. The reason Ruth and Lamentations were later separated from Judges and Jeremiah, respectively, is that they were used in the Jewish liturgical year, along with the three other units in the *Megilloth*. That is to say, Canticles (Song of Solomon) was read at Passover (in the first month); Ruth was read at Pentecost (in the third month); Lamentations was read on the ninth of Ab (fifth month); Ecclesiastes was read at the Feast of Tabernacles in the seventh month; and Esther was read at the Feast of Purim in the twelfth month. This accounts for the MT order in the *Megilloth*: Canticles, Ruth, Lamentations, Ecclesiastes, and Esther.

From what has just been said about the inclusion of Ruth in Judges and Lamentations in Jeremiah, it is apparent that the list of *Kethûbîm* was by no means fixed and rigid. If under the twenty-two book division of Josephus these two units (Ruth and Lamentations) of the *Kethûbîm* were earlier included under the prophets, then the third category of the Hebrew canon must have been smaller in the first century A.D. than the later MT division would indicate. Josephus refers to the third category as having only four books, which he describes as containing "hymns to God and precepts for the conduct of human life." This would seem to exclude Daniel from the third division and imply its inclusion among the prophets, since Daniel is neither hymnic nor preceptive. The same would be true of the historical books such as Ezra, Nehemiah, and Chronicles. The still earlier description of the third division by the prologue of Ecclesiasticus as "others who have followed in the steps of the Prophets" and "other books of our fathers" is too vague to serve as a basis for any deductions. But it is rather striking that the New Testament never specifies any other book besides the Psalms as comprising the third division of the Old Testament (Luke 24:44 speaks of the Law of Moses, and the Prophets, and the Psalms). Usually the Hebrew Scriptures are referred to simply as "the Law and the Prophets"; in one place even a passage from Psalms (Ps. 82) is spoken of as being written "in your law" (John 10:34). The Qumran Manual of Discipline and the Zadokite Document refer to the Scriptures simply as "Moses and the Prophets."[3] No deductions as to the books in the *Kethûbîm* may safely be drawn from, since the later book-order is obviously not pre-Christian in its origin.

THE ANTILEGOMENA

At this point a word must be said about the so-called *Antilegomena* ("the books spoken against"). The Mishnah mentions the existence of controversy in some Jewish

remaining four documents (Job, Psalms, Proverbs, Ecclesiastes) comprise hymns to God and practical precepts to men" (*Contra Apionem.* 1.8). Apparently these thirteen "prophets" were: Joshua, Judges Ruth, Samuel, Kings, Chronicles, Ezra, Nehemiah, Esther, Isaiah, Jeremiah-Lamentations, Ezekiel, Daniel, the twelve Minor Prophets, and possibly Song of Solomon. This means that the assignment of Chronicles, Esther, Ezra, Nehemiah, Daniel, and Song of Solomon to the third division of the Hebrew canon was later than the first century A.D. Hence any argument against the authenticity of Daniel based upon its final assignment to the *Kethûbîm* lacks validity.

3. Laird Harris, *Inspiration and Canonicity of the Bible*, p. 146.

circles during the second century A.D. relative to the canonicity of Canticles, Ecclesiastes, and Esther. Doubts were expressed by some during the same period as to the book of Proverbs. Ezekiel had also, according to the Gemara, been under discussion as to its authority until the objections to it were settled in A.D. 66. We are told that the disciples of Shammai in the first century B.C. contested the canonicity of Ecclesiastes, whereas the school of Hillel just as vigorously upheld it. The scholarly discussions held at Jamnia in A.D. 90[4] sustained the claims of both Ecclesiastes and Canticles to divine authority. These minority objections should not be misconstrued as having delayed the canonicity of the five books concerned, any more than Martin Luther's sixteenth-century objections to James and Esther delayed canonical recognition of these books.

To deal with the charges against these disputed books, we must take them up one by one. The criticism of Ecclesiastes was based upon its alleged pessimism, its supposed Epicureanism, and denial of the life to come. But thoughtful students of the book came to the conclusion that none of these charges was justified when the work was interpreted in the light of the author's special technique and purposes.[5]

The criticism of the Song of Solomon was based on the passages in it which speak of physical attractiveness in bold and enthusiastic imagery bordering on the erotic (if taken in a crassly literal way). But the allegorical interpretation of Hillel, who identified Solomon with Jehovah and the Shulamite with Israel, revealed spiritual dimensions in this truly beautiful production. Christian exegetes followed this lead in applying the figure of Solomon to Christ and the bride to the Church, and attained thereby richer insight into the love relationship between the Savior and His redeemed.

As for Esther, the objection was that the name of God does not appear in it. But this drawback (difficult though it is to explain) was more than offset by the remarkable manifestations of divine providence working through every dramatic circumstance in order to deliver the Jewish race from the greatest threat to its existence ever faced in their history.

In the case of Ezekiel, the problem it presented consisted in the disagreements of detail between the latter-day temple and ritual of the last ten chapters and those of the Mosaic tabernacle and Solomonic temple. But it was pointed out in rebuttal that these differences were found only in minor details and might pertain to a still future temple,

---

4. There is, incidentally, very little support for the supposition that there ever was an official synodical meeting at Jamnia, or Jabneh, either in A.D. 90 or at any other time. R. K. Harrison asserts: "As far as the facts of the situation are concerned, very little is known about the supposed Synod of Jamnia. After Jerusalem was destroyed by the forces of Titus in A.D. 70, Rabbi Johanan ben Zakkai obtained permission from the Romans to settle in Jamnia, where he purposed to carry on his literary activities. The location soon became an established center of Scriptural study, and from time to time certain discussions took place relating to the canonicity of specific O.T. books including Ezekiel, Esther, Canticles, Ecclesiastes and Proverbs. There can be little doubt that such conversations took place both before and after this period and it seems probable that nothing of a formal or binding nature was decided in these discussions, even though, as Rowley had indicated, the various debates helped to crystallize and establish the Jewish tradition in this regard more firmly than had been the case previously" Harrison, OTI, p. 278. (Cf. H. H. Rowley, *The Growth of the Old Testament*, p. 170; E. J. Young, in C. F. H. Henry's *Revelation and the Bible*, p. 160.)

5. These matters will be taken up in detail when the book is analyzed in chap. 35.

rather than to the second temple erected by Zerubbabel. In any event, it was to be confidently expected that Elijah upon his return to earth would clear up all these difficulties for the faithful.

The objections to Proverbs were not so serious, but centered rather in a few apparently contradictory precepts, such as 26:4-5: "Answer not a fool according to his folly. ... Answer a fool according to his folly."

ANCIENT WITNESSES TO THE MASORETIC CANON

How early was this twenty-two book canon of the Palestinian Jews? The earliest extant reference to the three main divisions of the Hebrew Scripture is to be found in the prologue to the apocryphal book Ecclesiasticus, composed ca. 190 B.C. in Hebrew by Jesus ben Sirach. The prologue itself was composed in Greek by the grandson of this author, who translated the entire work into Greek. In the prologue (dating from about 130 B.C.) we read, "Whereas many and great things have been delivered to us by the Law and the Prophets and by others that have followed their steps—my grandfather, Jesus, when he had much given himself to the reading of the Law and the Prophets and other books of our fathers, and had gotten therein good judgment, was drawn on also himself to write something pertaining to learning and wisdom." What is classified in the MT canon as the Kethûbîm ("the Writings or Hagiographa") is referred to here as (a) books by others who have followed in the steps of the prophets, (b) other books of our fathers. This shows that a tripartite division of some sort already existed in the second century B.C. Note also that 1 Maccabees, composed about the same time as the prologue, refers to two episodes in Daniel (1 Macc. 2:59-60, i.e., the deliverance of Daniel himself from the lions' den) and quotes expressly from the Psalms (e.g., 1 Macc. 7:17 quotes from Ps. 79:2-3); and both these books (apparently regarded as canonical) belong to the Kethûbîm. As for the New Testament, Luke 24:44 refers to the Old Testament as "the law of Moses, and the Prophets, and the Psalms." Not only the Psalms, but also Proverbs and Daniel are often referred to as the authoritative Word of God, and even Lamentations is alluded to in Matt. 5:35. Since these four books belong to the later list of Kethûbîm, there is no reasonable doubt that the third division of the Hebrew canon was put on a level with the first two as divinely inspired.

Next we come to Josephus of Jerusalem (A.D. 37-95), whose numeration of the Old Testament as consisting of twenty-two books has already been alluded to. In his Contra Apionem, he says, "We have not tens of thousands of books, discordant and conflicting, but only twenty-two containing the record of all time, which have been justly believed to be divine." After referring to the five books of Moses, thirteen books of the prophets, and the remaining books (which "embrace hymns to God and counsels for men for the conduct of life"), he makes this significant statement: "From Artaxerxes (the successor of Xerxes) until our time everything has been recorded, but has not been deemed worthy of like credit with what preceded, because the exact succession of the prophets ceased. But what faith we have placed in our own writings is evident by our conduct; for though so long a time has now passed, no one has dared to add anything to them, or to take anything from them, or to alter anything in them" (1.8).

Note three important features of this statement: (1) Josephus includes the same three divisions of the Hebrew Scriptures as does the MT (although restricting the third group to "hymns" and *hokmâ*), and he limits the number of canonical books in these three divisions to twenty-two.[6] (2) No more canonical writings have been composed since the reign of Artaxerxes, son of Xerxes (464-424 B.C.), that is, since the time of Malachi. (3) No additional material was ever included in the canonical twenty-two books during the centuries between (i.e., from 425 B.C. to A.D. 90). Rationalist higher critics emphatically deny the last two points, but they have to deal with the witness of such an early author as Josephus and explain how the knowledge of the allegedly post-Malachi date of sizable portions, such as Daniel, Ecclesiastes, Song of Solomon, and many of the psalms, had been kept from this learned Jew in the first century A.D. It is true that Josephus also alludes to apocryphal material (as from 1 Esdras and 1 Maccabees[7]); but in view of the statement quoted above, it is plain that he was using it merely as a historical source, not as divinely inspired books.

The oldest catalogue of the books of the Old Testament canon now in existence is the list of Bishop Melito of Sardis, written ca. A.D. 170. He states that he went to the Orient to investigate the number and order of the books of the Old Testament and came to the following result: "Five of Moses—Genesis, Exodus, Leviticus, Numbers, and Deuteronomy; Joshua, Judges, Ruth, four of Kingdoms, two of Chronicles, Psalms of David, Proverbs of Solomon (which is also Wisdom), Ecclesiastes, Canticles, Job; the Prophets—Isaiah, Jeremiah, and the Twelve in one book, Daniel, Ezekiel, Ezra." In this list note: (1) Lamentations is omitted, but was probably subsumed under Jeremiah; (2) Nehemiah likewise, but probably included with Ezra; (3) Esther is omitted altogether for some unknown reason; (4) with the possible exception of the term *Wisdom* (which conceivably could refer to the Wisdom of Solomon) no book of the Apocrypha is included.

In the third century A.D., Origen (who died in 254) left a catalogue of twenty-two books of the Old Testament which was preserved in Eusebius' *Ecclesiastical History* (6:25). This indicates the same list as that of the twenty-two book canon of Josephus (and of the MT). The only difference is that he apparently includes the Epistle of Jeremiah, being perhaps ignorant of the fact that it was never written in Hebrew.

Approximately contemporaneous with Origen was Tertullian (A.D. 160–250), the earliest of the Latin Fathers whose books are still extant. He states the number of canonical books as twenty-four. Hilary of Poitiers (A.D. 305-366) numbers them as twenty-two. Jerome (A.D. 340-420) both in the *Prologus Galeatus*[8] and elsewhere advo-

---

6. For an explanation of how this corresponds to the thirty-nine books in the Protestant canon, see footnote 1 above.

7. Cf. Henry B. Swete, *An Introduction to the Old Testament in Greek* 2d. ed. (Cambridge: U. Press, 1902), p. 378.

8. The pertinent quotation from the *Prologus Galeatus* is as follows (Archer's translation): "This prologue,

cated recognition of only the twenty-two books contained in the Hebrew, and the relegation of the apocryphal books to a secondary position.[9] Thus, in his *Commentary on Daniel* he cast doubt upon the canonicity of Susanna on the ground that a certain word play put into Daniel's mouth was derivable only from Greek and not from Hebrew (implication: the story must have been originally composed in Greek). Similarly also in connection with Bel and the Dragon he remarks: "This objection is easily solved by asserting that this particular story is not contained in the Hebrew of the book of Daniel. If, however, anyone should be able to prove that it belongs in the canon, then we should be obliged to seek out some other answer to this objection."[10]

THE QUESTION OF THE CANONICITY OF THE APOCRYPHA

Not only the Roman Catholic and Greek Orthodox communions contend for the canonicity of the fourteen apocryphal books (in whole or in part), but also Protestant scholars of liberal persuasion speak of an "Alexandrian Canon" as having equal claims to validity with those of the so-called Palestinian Canon (of twenty-two or thirty-nine books). The evidences appealed to for this contention deserve careful scrutiny.[11]

The first argument adduced in favor of the Apocrypha is that the early versions contained them. This, however, is only partially true. Certainly the Aramaic Targums did not recognize them. Not even the Syriac Peshitta in its earliest form contained a single apocryphal book; it was only later that some of them were added. We have just seen that Jerome, the great translator of the Scriptures into Latin, did not recognize the Apocrypha as being of equal authority with the books of the Hebrew canon. A more careful investigation of this claim narrows down the authority of the Apocrypha as resting upon only *one* ancient version, the Septuagint, and those later translations (such as the Itala, the Coptic and Ethiopic, and later Syriac) which were derived from it. Even in the case of the Septuagint, the apocryphal books maintain a rather uncertain existence. The Codex Vaticanus (B) lacks 1 and 2 Maccabees (canonical, according to Rome), but includes 1 Esdras (noncanonical, according to Rome). The Sinaiticus

---

like a helmeted vanguard (*principium*) of the Scriptures, can apply to all the books which we have translated from Hebrew into Latin, so that we can know whatever is apart from these must be placed among the Apocrypha. Therefore the Wisdom commonly entitled Solomon's, the book of Jesus the son of Sirach, and Judith and Tobias and The Shepherd [presumably the Shepherd of Hermas] are not in the canon. I discovered the First Book of Maccabees is Hebrew; the Second is Greek, as can be tested by its very wording." In Jerome's *Preface to the Books of Solomon* he mentions finding Ecclesiasticus in Hebrew, but states his conviction that the Wisdom of Solomon was originally composed in Greek rather than Hebrew, since it shows a Hellenic type of eloquence. "And so," he goes on, "just as the church reads Judith and Tobias and Maccabees (in public worship) but does not receive them into the canonical Scriptures, so let it read these two books also for the edification of the people, not for the establishing of the authority of the doctrines of the church."

9. Cf. Robert H. Pfeiffer, *Introduction to the Old Testament*, p. 69.

10. Gleason L. Archer (trans.), *Jerome's Commentary on Daniel* (Grand Rapids: Baker, 1958), p. 155, 157.

11. G. D. Young, in his chapter on the Apocrypha in *Revelation and the Bible* (ed. Carl F. H. Henry), gives one of the most recent conservative treatments of this subject. R. L. Harris's, *Inspiration and Canonicity of the Bible*, chap. 6, is very helpful also. But perhaps the most adequate discussion is found in Unger, IGOT, pp. 81-114.

(Aleph) omits Baruch (canonical, according to Rome), but includes 4 Maccabees (non-canonical according to Rome). The Alexandrinus (A) contains three "noncanonical" Apocrypha: 1 Esdras and 3 and 4 Maccabees. Thus it turns out that even the three earliest MSS or the LXX show considerable uncertainty as to which books constitute the list of Apocrypha, and that the fourteen accepted by the Roman church are by no means substantiated by the testimony of the great uncials of the fourth and fifth centuries.

It is urged by protagonists of the Apocrypha that the presence of apocryphal books in the LXX indicates the existence of a so-called Alexandrian Canon, which included these fourteen extra books. But it is by no means certain that all the books in the LXX were considered canonical even by the Alexandrian Jews themselves. Quite decisive against this is the evidence of the writings of Philo of Alexandria (who lived in the first century A.D.). Although he quotes frequently from the canonical books of the "Palestinian Canon," he never once quotes from any of the apocryphal books. This is impossible to reconcile with the theory of a larger Alexandrian Canon, unless perchance some Alexandrian Jews did not accept this Alexandrian Canon, while others did.

Secondly, it is reliably reported that Aquila's Greek Version[12] was accepted by the Alexandrian Jews in the second century A.D., even though it did not contain the Apocrypha. A reasonable deduction from these evidences would be that (as Jerome himself put it) the Alexandrian Jews chose to include in their edition of the Old Testament both the books they recognized as canonical and also the books which were "ecclesiastical" (i.e., considered valuable and edifying though not inerrant).

Additional support for this supposition (that subcanonical works may be preserved and utilized along with canonical) has recently been found in the discoveries of Qumran Cave 4. There in the heartland of Palestine, where surely the Palestinian Canon should have been authoritative, at least two apocryphal books are represented—Ecclesiasticus and Tobit. One fragment of Tobit appears on a scrap of papyrus, another on leather; there is also a leather fragment in Hebrew. Several fragments of Ecclesiasticus were also discovered there, and so far as they go, at least, agree quite exactly with the eleventh-century MS of Ecclesiasticus found in the Cairo Geniza back in the 1890s (cf. Burrows, MLDSS, pp. 177-78). For that matter, the Fourth Qumran Cave has also yielded pseudepigraphical works like the Testament of Levi in Aramaic, the Testament of Levi in Hebrew, and the book of Enoch (fragments from ten different MSS!). Surely no one could seriously contend that the straightlaced Qumran sectarians considered all these apocryphal and pseudepigraphical works canonical simply because they possessed copies of them.

Appeal is often made to the fact that the New Testament usually employs the LXX translation in its quotations from the Old Testament. Therefore, since the LXX did contain the Apocrypha, the New Testament apostles must have recognized the authority of the entire LXX as it was then constituted. Moreover it is a fact, it is urged, that

12. Cf. chap. 3, p. 52.

appeal is occasionally made to works outside the Palestinian Canon. Wildeboer[13] and Torrey[14] have collected all possible instances of such quotations or allusions to apocryphal works, including several which are only suspected.

But all this line of argument is really irrelevant to the issue at hand, since none of these sources is even alleged to be from the fourteen books of the Roman Apocrypha. In most cases these works which are supposed to have been quoted from have long since disappeared—works such as Apocalypse of Elias and (apart from a Latin fragment) Assumption of Moses. Only in one instance, the quotation from Enoch 1:9 in Jude 14-16, has the source quoted from survived.[15] There are quotations from pagan Greek authors too in the New Testament. In Acts 17:28 Paul quotes from Aratus' *Phaenomena*, line 5; in 1 Cor. 15:33 he quotes from Menander's comedy, *Thais*. Surely no one would suppose that such quotations as these establish the canonicity of either Aratus or Menander. On the contrary, the testimony of the New Testament is most decisive against the canonicity of the fourteen books of the Apocrypha. Virtually all the thirty-nine books of the Old Testament are quoted from as divinely authoritative, or are at least alluded to.[16] While it has just been pointed out that mere quotation does not necessarily establish canonicity, nevertheless it is inconceivable that the New Testament authors could have considered the fourteen books of the Roman Catholic Apocrypha canonical and never once quoted from or alluded to any of them.

The second chief argument in favor of the Apocrypha is that the church Fathers quote from these books as authoritative. It would be more correct to say that *some* of the early Christian writers appear to do so, while others take a clear-cut stand against their canonicity. Among those in favor are the writers of 1 Clement and Epistle of Barnabas, and most notably Jerome's younger contemporary, Augustine of Hippo. Yet we must qualify this advocacy as only apparent, or at least presumptive, for we have already seen that Jude could quote Enoch as containing a true account of one ancient episode without necessarily endorsing the whole book of Enoch as canonical. As for Augustine, his attitude was rather uncritical and inconsistent. On the one hand, he threw his influence at the Council of Carthage (A.D. 397) in favor of including the entire fourteen as canonical; on the other hand, when an appeal was made by an antagonist to a passage in 2 Maccabees to settle an argument, Augustine replied that his cause must be weak if he had to resort to a book not in the same category as those received and accepted by the Jews.[17]

The ambiguous advocacy of the Apocrypha on the part of Augustine is more than offset by the contrary position of the revered Athanasius (who died in A.D. 365), so

---

13. Gerrit Wildeboer, *Origin of the Canon of the Old Testament*, trans. B. W. Bacon (London: Luzac, 1895).

14. Charles C. Torrey, *The Apocryphal Literature* (New Haven, Conn.: Yale U.,1945).

15. Complete only in the Ethiopic, some portions in Greek, and Qumran Cave 4 fragments in Hebrew and Aramaic.

16. The exceptions, as revealed in the quotation list at the end of Nestle's *Greek New Testament*, are Ruth, Ezra, Ecclesiastes, and Canticles. Yet, Rom. 8:20 seems to reflect Eccl. 1:2.

17. G. D. Young, in *Revelation and the Bible*, p. 176.

highly regarded by both East and West as the champion of Trinitarian orthodoxy. In his Thirty-ninth Letter he discussed the "particular books and their number, which are accepted by the church." In paragraph 4 he says, "There are, then, of the Old Testament twenty-two books in number," and he proceeds to enumerate the same books as are found in the MT in approximately the same order as in the Protestant Bible. In paragraphs 6 and 7 he states that the extrabiblical books (i.e., the fourteen of the Apocrypha) are "not included in the canon," but merely "appointed to be read." Nevertheless the Eastern Church later showed a tendency to concur with the Western in the acceptance of the Apocrypha (second Trullan Council at Constantinople in A.D. 692). Even so, there were many who had misgivings about some of the fourteen, and at last in Jerusalem in 1672 the Greek Church narrowed down the number of canonical Apocrypha to four: Wisdom, Ecclesiasticus, Tobit, and Judith.

TESTS OF CANONICITY

First we may consider certain inadequate tests which have been proposed in recent times.

1. J. G. Eichhorn (1780) considered age to be the test for canonicity. All books believed to have been composed after Malachi's time were excluded from consideration. But this theory does not account for the numerous older works like the Book of Jashar (Josh. 10:13; 2 Sam. 1:18) and the Book of the Wars of Jehovah (Num. 21:14) which were not accounted authoritative.

2. F. Hitzig (ca. 1850) made the Hebrew language the Jewish test of canonicity. But this does not explain why Ecclesiasticus, Tobit, and 1 Maccabees were rejected even though they were composed in Hebrew. It also raises questions as to the acceptability of the Aramaic chapters of Daniel and Ezra.

3. G. Wildeboer[18] makes conformity to the Torah the test of canonicity for the later books. But later on in his discussion he introduces many other criteria which render this worthless: (a) canonical books had to be written in Hebrew or Aramaic; and they either had to (b) treat ancient history (like Ruth or Chronicles), or (c) speak of the establishment of a new order of things (Ezra, Nehemiah), or (d) be assigned to a famous person of ancient times, such as Solomon, Samuel, Daniel, or (perhaps) Job, or (e) be in complete harmony with the national sentiment of people and scribes (Esther). Here indeed we have a bewildering profusion of tests. As for Wildeboer's original criterion, how can we be sure that the Words of Nathan the prophet (referred to in 2 Chron. 9:29) or Isaiah's Acts of Uzziah (2 Chron. 26:22) or Jeremiah's Lamentation for Josiah (2 Chron. 35:25) were not in conformity to the Torah, at least as much so as their other words or writings which have been preserved in the canon? As for (e), many of the pseudepigraphical works, like Enoch, Lamech and the Testament of the Twelve Patriarchs, the Testament of Adam, and several others, were assigned to famous men of old, and it is not absolutely certain that none of them was originally composed in Aramaic (if not in Hebrew).

18. Wildeboer, p. 97.

The only true test of canonicity which remains is the testimony of God the Holy Spirit to the authority of His own Word. This testimony found a response of recognition, faith, and submission in the hearts of God's people who walked in covenant fellowship with Him. As E. J. Young puts it, "To these and other proposed criteria we must reply with a negative. The canonical books of the Old Testament were divinely revealed and their authors were holy men who spoke as they were borne of the Holy Ghost. In His good providence God brought it about that His people should recognize and receive His Word. How He planted this conviction in their hearts with respect to the identity of His Word we may not be able fully to understand or explain. We may, however, follow our Lord, who placed the *imprimatur* of His infallible authority upon the books of the Old Testament."[19]

We may go further than this and point out that in the nature of the case we could hardly expect any other valid criteria than this. If canonicity is a quality somehow imparted to the books of Scripture by any kind of human decision, as Liberal scholars unquestioningly assume (and as even the Roman Church implies by her self-contradictory affirmation: "The Church is the mother of the Scripture"), then perhaps a set of mechanical tests could be set up to determine which writings to accept as authoritative and which to reject. But if, on the other hand, a sovereign God has taken the initiative in revelation and in the production of an inspired record of that revelation through human agents, it must simply be a matter of recognition of the quality already inherent by divine act in the books so inspired. When a child recognizes his own parent from a multitude of other adults at some public gathering, he does not impart any new quality of parenthood by such an act; he simply recognizes a relationship which already exists. So also with lists of authoritative books drawn up by ecclesiastical synods or councils. They did not impart canonicity to a single page of Scripture; they sim-

TEST OF CANONICITY

The only true test of canonicity is the testimony of God the Holy Spirit to the authority of His own Word.

19. E. J. Young, "The Canon of the Old Testament," in *Revelation and the Bible*, p. 168.

ply acknowledged the divine inspiration of religious documents which were inherently canonical from the time they were first composed, and formally rejected other books for which canonicity had been falsely claimed.

LIBERAL THEORIES AS TO THE ORIGIN OF THE CANON

The foregoing survey has furnished a proper basis on which to evaluate the standard higher critical account of the evolution of the Hebrew canon. Those who do not take seriously the Bible's own claim to be the uniquely inspired revelation of God's will must necessarily cast about for some more rationalistic, down-to-earth explanation of the origin of these books. Because of antisupernaturalistic presuppositions, they must be true to their own philosophical principles in rejecting all biblical data which testify to direct revelation from God. For example, the Pentateuch affirms with great frequency, "Jehovah said unto Moses, 'Speak unto the children of Israel and say unto them—'" But scholars who do not believe that God could ever speak personally and intelligibly to Moses (or any other man) must reject all such biblical statements as legendary. The notice that Moses wrote out a copy of the Torah and laid it up before the ark of the covenant (Deut. 31:9, 26) must be ruled out of court. The same is true of the numerous references to a written law of Moses in Joshua (e.g., 1:8, and also 8:32, which affirms that Joshua had the Torah inscribed on stone stelae for public convenience). Only those references to a reading of the Torah which accord with rationalist presuppositions are to be taken as historical. The Development Hypothesis (cf. chaps. 11 and 12) and the Documentary Theory of the Pentateuch are explained in detail further on, but for the present a brief summary of the critical theory of the canon must suffice.

Liberal scholarship explains the threefold division of the Hebrew canon (i.e., Torah, Prophets, and *Kethûbîm*) as resulting from three separate stages in the composition of the various books themselves. That is to say, the Torah arose in successive accretions starting at 850 B.C. (the earliest written document), combined with a later document between 750 and 650; then in 621, at the time of Josiah's reform, Deuteronomy became the first unit of the Pentateuch to achieve canonicity, being formally accepted by both king and people (2 Kings 23). During the Babylonian Exile (587-539 B.C.), the ritual and priestly sections were written up by Levitical authors under the inspiration of Ezekiel, and their activity continued down to the time of Ezra (who was one of their number). Nehemiah 8:1-8 contains a record of the first public reading of the entire Torah as "the book of the Law of Moses" (some parts of which had been just newly finished—according to the Documentarians—and all of which was at least five hundred years later than the death of Moses). Ezra's public was somehow convinced that these five books of mixed and spurious parentage were indeed the product of Moses' pen and contained the authoritative Word of God. Thus they imparted canonization to the first division of the Old Testament, the Torah, in 444 B.C.

So far as the second division, the Prophets, is concerned, these were gradua¹' assembled into an authoritative list between 300 and 200 B.C. It could not have beeι much earlier than that, because (according to higher critical theory) certain parts of Isaiah, Joel, Zechariah and others were not written until the third century B.C. (Some scholars, like Duhm, insisted that certain portions of Isaiah were not composed until the second or first century B.C.) Hence the second division achieved canonical status under unknown circumstances at a place unknown at a time unknown, but approximately 200 B.C.[20]

As for the third division, the *Kethûbîm* or writings, they were not collected (and most of them were not even written) until well after the collection of the prophets had begun. Since Daniel, on grounds of literary criticism, was composed around 168 B.C., the *Kethûbîm* could not have been assembled much before 150 B.C., since a couple of decades at least were necessary for a book to achieve canonical stature. Preliminary or tentative canonization of this third group of books was doubtless achieved between 150 and 100 B.C., but final ratification was deferred until the hypothetical Council of Jamnia in A.D. 90.

Such is the usual account of the formation of circles today. Granted their presuppositions and critical methodology, it is perhaps reasonable enough. If, however, their datings of portions of the Old Testament which they have assigned to post-fifth-century times can be shown to be ill founded (as the succeeding chapters attempt to do), then this whole theory of the canon must be abandoned in favor of that account which is presented by the Scripture itself. The biblical authors indicate very clearly, whenever the matter comes up that the various books of the Bible were canonical from the moment of their inception, by virtue of the divine authority ("Thus saith the Lord") behind them, and the books received immediate recognition and acceptance by the faithful as soon as they were made aware of the writings.

As to the Torah, we are told in Deut. 31:9 that an authoritative copy of it was laid up before the ark not long before Moses' death in 1405 B.C. We are not told anywhere at what time the three sections of the prophets (Former Prophets, Major Prophets, and Minor Prophets) were assembled into a single main division. If Malachi was the latest book in this group, canonization of the whole could hardly have taken place until about 400 B.C. The criterion for what books belonged to the prophets may have been their authorship. They were all composed by the authoritative interpreters of the law who belonged to the prophetic order (according to Deut. 18), and either transmitted their messages directly from God, or else composed an account of Israel's history according to God's perspective (Judges, Samuel, and Kings).

As for the third division, the Writings, it is obvious that all inspired books which did not belong to either of the first two groups were put here. All they had in common was that they were not composed by human authors who belonged to the prophetic order. Thus Daniel's memoirs were assigned to the *Kethûbîm* by the later rabbis because he was a civil servant and did not belong to the prophetic order. It is true that he like David and Solomon possessed a prophetic gift, but none of these were formerly

20. Pfeiffer, p. 15.

anointed as prophets of Jehovah. The same nonprophetic status characterized the unnamed authors of Job and Esther, as well as Governor Nehemiah and Ezra the scribe. (We have already seen that Lamentations, which was the composition of Jeremiah, originally was included among the prophets.) But there can be no question of time sequence, so far as the second and third groups are concerned. Much of the material of the *Kethûbîm* was written before the earliest of the writing prophets. The units of each division were formed more or less contemporaneously, and they were assigned later to each group, the prophets and the writings, on the basis of authorship. While we have no actual notice as to who composed Joshua, Judges, Samuel, or Kings, the viewpoint of the authors—as even Liberal critics are swift to agree—is consistently a prophetic one.

6 HISTORY OF THE DOCUMENTARY THEORY OF THE PENTATEUCH

UNTIL THE RISE of deistic philosophy in the eighteenth century, the Christian church had always taken at face value the claims of the Pentateuch to have been composed by the historic Moses of the fifteenth century B.C. A few Jewish scholars, such as the pantheistic Spanish Jew, Benedict Spinoza (a name derived from *espinoso*: "spiny, thorny"), had suggested the possibility of later authorship of at least parts of the Torah, but these conjectures had been largely ignored by European scholarship, until the deistic movement created a more favorable attitude for historical skepticism and the rejection of the supernatural. (Spinoza in 1670 had expressed the view in his *Tracatus Theologico-Politicus* that the Pentateuch could hardly have been written by Moses, since he is referred to in the third person, *he*, rather than by the first, *I*; nor could he have recorded his own death, as is done in Deut. 34.[1] Spinoza therefore proposed Ezra as the final composer of the Torah. (Although this suggestion was largely ignored in his own generation, it constituted a remarkable anticipation of the final formulation of the Documentary Hypothesis by Graf, Kuenen, and Wellhausen in the latter half of the nineteenth century.)

EARLY DEVELOPMENTS

The Documentary Hypothesis—the theory that the Pentateuch was a compilation of selections from several different written documents composed at different places and times over a period of five centuries, long after Moses—had its beginning with Jean Astruc, a French physician who became interested in the literary analysis of Genesis. He was intrigued by the way in

---

1. This argument based on the use of the third person is very weak. Many well-known ancient authors, such as Xenophon and Julius Caesar, referred to themselves in their own historical narratives in the third person almost exclusively. As to the obituary notice in Deut. 34, it does not even purport to have been written by Moses, and was undoubtedly added by Joshua or some other near contemporary. But this in no way renders doubtful the Mosaic authorship of the rest of Deuteronomy which does claim to have been his compostion. Even the higher critics do this in their own writings. Cf. O. Eissfeldt (*The Old Testament, An Introduction*, Ackroyd translation, 1965, p. 169). "Eissfeldt, to obviate the confusion which can so easily arise from the use of the sigla J[1] and J[2]... "introduced 4 siglum L..." Note that in Edward

Qumran

QUMRAN CAVE 4, THE SITE OF THE MAIN LIBRARY AT QUMRAN, WAS VANDALIZED BY THE ROMAN LEGIONNAIRES IN A.D. 68. CAVE 4 PRODUCED FRAGMENTS OF 38 OLD TESTAMENT BOOKS (EXCLUDING ESTHER) WHICH CONFIRMS THAT THE HEBREW CANON USED BY JESUS WAS THE SAME AS THE ONE THAT WE HAVE TODAY.

which God was referred to only as Elohim (God) in Genesis 1 and mostly as Jehovah (or Yahweh) in Gen. 2. In his *Conjectures Concerning the Original Memoranda Which It Appears Moses Used to Compose the Book of Genesis* (1753), he tried to account for this phenomenon by the supposition that Moses used two different written sources which gave two different accounts of creation. He contended that in composing these two chapters, Moses quoted one author who knew of God only by the name of Elohim (presumably the earlier writer) and another author who referred to Him only as Jehovah.[2] While Astruc's proposal found little immediate favor, it set forth a criterion of source division which before long met with a response from a scholarly world (which was similarly involved in the dissection of Homer's epics into many different sources) and furnished the first basic assumption of the Documentary Hypothesis, the criterion of divine names.

The next stage came with the *Einleitung in das alte Testament* (*Introduction to the Old Testament*) of Johann Gottfried Eichhorn,[3] published in 1780-1783. He divided

Chiera's "They Wrote on Clay," p. vi refers to the untimely death of Professor Chiera. Does this posthumous publication cast any doubt on Chiera's authorship? George Cameron prepared it for publication (Free ABH 120).

2. This explanation, of course, ignored the fact that Gen. 1 presents God as Creator and Sovereign over all nature, hence only Elohim was appropriate; whereas Gen. 2 presents Him as a covenant God to Adam and Eve, hence Jehovah only was appropriate, except where the compound title Jehovah Elohim occurs. It is interesting to observe that rationalist twentieth-century scholars such as Ivan Engnell revert to the same reason for the choice of divine name in the Torah that was recognized prior to the rise of the Documentary Hypothesis. Cf. chap. 9, pp. 128-31.

3. Cf. chap. 9, pp. 131ff.

the entire book of Genesis, plus the first two chapters of Exodus (up to Moses' interview with God at the burning bush) between the Jahwist and the Elohist (J and E). He attempted to correlate the supposedly divergent "parallel accounts" and "doublets" (e.g., the "two accounts" of the Flood) with these two "sources" and isolate the characteristic traits of each. He at first attributed to Moses the editorial work of combining these "pre-Mosaic" written materials, but in later editions of his *Einleitung* he at last yielded to the growingly popular view that the Pentateuch was written after the time of Moses. Thus was the J-E division extended to much of the Pentateuch.

The third stage came with the contribution of Willem Martin Lebrecht De Wette concerning Deuteronomy. In his *Dissertation Critico-Exegetica* [4] (1805) and his *Beitraege zur Einleitung* (1806), he set forth the view that none of the Pentateuch came from a period earlier than the time of David. But as for Deuteronomy, it bore all the earmarks of being the book of the law which was found by the high priest Hilkiah in the Jerusalem temple at the time of King Josiah's reform, according to 2 Kings 22. Both the king and the priest were united in the purpose to abolish all worship and sacrifice to Jehovah outside the capital city. Centralization of worship would contribute to closer political unification of all parts of the kingdom, and it would insure that all revenues from the pious would pour into the coffers of the Jerusalem priesthood. Therefore this book was concocted to serve the governmental campaign, and its discovery was then staged at the psychological moment. This pinpointed the date of composition as 621 B.C. (the date of Josiah's reformation) or shortly before. Thus arose document D (as it came to be called), entirely separate in origin from J or E, and framed to support governmental policy by means of its references (see chap. 12) to the "city which Jehovah shall choose." This made the roster of "sources" for the Pentateuch include three documents: E (the earliest), J, and the late seventh-century document D.

Strictly speaking, however, De Wette did not belong to the Documentary School, but rather to the Fragmentary Theorists. The Fragmentary Theory of the origin of the Pentateuch was first propounded in 1792 (*Introduction to the Pentateuch and Joshua*) by a Scottish Roman Catholic priest named Alexander Geddes. Geddes held that the Torah was composed in the Solomonic era from many separate fragments, some of which were as old as Moses, or even older and then were fitted into a historical context.

Geddes' views were adopted by Johann Vater (*Kommentar über den Pentateuch*, 1802), who analyzed the book of Genesis alone into no less than thirty-nine fragments (which of course involved the division of E into diverse elements). While some fragments dated from the Mosaic age, the final combination and arrangement did not take place until the time of the Babylonian Exile (587-538 B.C.). The compelling reason for this later date derives from these passages in the Torah (i.e., Lev. 26:27-45 and Deut. 28:58-63) which predict the Babylonian captivity and the later restoration from Exile.

---

4. The full translated title of DeWette's Ph.D. thesis was, "A critical, exegetical dissertation in which it is shown that Deuteronomy, different from the earlier books of the Pentateuch, is the work of some later author."

Even the predictions contained in Gen. 49 would imply a later fulfillment after the prediction had been fulfilled. It should be noted, however, that Deut. 28:64-68 was not actually fulfilled until the first and second revolt of the Jews against the Roman powers, which resulted in the Jews being scattered throughout the Mediteranean and the Near East. (Cf. Chap. 18, pp. 281-82) De Wette fell in line with this type of source analysis, alleging that the historical records of Judges, Samuel, and Kings did not betray the existence of Pentateuchal legislation (since the laws of Moses were consistently ignored as if non-existent).[5] Therefore there could not have been any such laws until the later Jewish monarchy.[6]

There were no major changes in the development of the Documentary Hypothesis between De Wette and Hupfeld. During this intervening period, certain other theories of Pentateuchal composition found able advocates. The Supplementary Theory, advocated by Ewald, Bleek, and Delitzsch, assumed the existence of one basic document or body of tradition (E) which underlay all the rest and which dated from about 1050 – 950 B.C., i.e., from the time of Saul, David, and Solomon. But this earlier material acquired additions and supplements by the later author of J, who left the earlier E material largely unaltered as he incorporated it with his own.

Heinrich Ewald (of Göttingen and Tübingen) in his *Komposition der Genesis* (*The Composition of Genesis*, 1823) stressed that the essential basis of Genesis was very early, even if not quite Mosaic. He discounted Eichhorn's use of repetitions and headings in the Hebrew text to prove diverse authorship, for he pointed out that early Arabic works (the unity of whose authorship was unquestioned) employed similar techniques as characteristic traits of Semitic style. In his *Geschichte Israels* (*The History of Israel*, 1840), he expressed the view that Moses personally composed the Decalogue (Ex. 20) and a few of the oldest laws. Genesis 14 and Num. 33 were also of very ancient origin. But these earlier materials were supplemented by a Book of Covenants, composed by an anonymous Judean in the period of the Judges. In the time of Solomon came a Book of Origins written by an anonymous Levite, containing much of the material of document E. A third supplement came in the ninth century (the time of Elijah) in the form of a biography of Moses. Later still came a prophetic narrator, and lastly a Judean from the time of Uzziah (middle eighth century) who introduced the name "Yahweh" in numerous places and reworked the whole corpus as final editor. This 1840 work of Ewald's actually involved a departure from the Supplementary Theory to the Crystallization Theory, a modification which regarded each successive contributor to the Mosaic corpus as reworking the entire body of materials, rather than simply adding his own isolated contributions here and there. Thus by successive layers of molecules, a sort of literary "crystal" was built up. (Other advocates of the Crystallization Theory were August Knobel [1861] and Eberhard Schrader [1869], who simplified the growth process somewhat in their treatments of the Pentateuch.)

5. Cf. chap. 12, pp. 165-69, for a refutation of this claim.
6. For discussion of G. T. Manley's findings in regard to this false claim, see pp. 275, 277.

The second Supplementarist mentioned above was Friederich Bleek, who in 1822 came out with an extension of literary source analysis to the book of Joshua, thus giving rise to the term *Hexateuch* ("six volume") as the form in which the Mosaic tradition found its final written form, rather than in any mere five-volume Pentateuch. In 1836 he published his observations on Genesis, in which he granted that some passages in it were genuinely Mosaic. The first considerable supplementation came in the time of the United Monarchy (tenth century) when an anonymous compiler brought together the earliest form of Genesis. A second important redaction came in the period of King Josiah (approximately 630 or 620 B.C.) by the anonymous compiler of the book of Deuteronomy, who incorporated Joshua also to form the Hexateuch.[7] Bleek later published a complete Old Testament introduction, the second edition of which (appearing in 1865) was soon translated into English (1869). In this work he took a stand against some of the most unwarranted extremes of the literary criticism then in vogue; yet he made many unwise and unjustified concessions to the whole Documentarian approach.

As for Franz Delitzsch, the third Supplementarist scholar mentioned above, he was far more conservative in tendency than were Ewald and Bleek. In his commentary on Genesis, appearing in 1852, he advanced the view that all portions of the Pentateuch attributed by the text itself to Mosaic authorship were genuinely his. The remaining laws represented authentic Mosaic tradition, but were not codified by the priests until after the conquest of Canaan. The non-Mosaic parts of document E were probably composed by Eleazar (the third son of Aaron), who incorporated the book of the covenant (Ex. 20:23–23:33). A still later hand supplemented this work, including Deuteronomy with it. Delitzsch produced a series of excellent commentaries on most of the books of the Old Testament (some of them in collaboration with Karl Friedrich Keil, a pupil of Hengstenberg's). In the latter part of his career (1880), Delitzsch shifted to a modified form of the regnant Documentary Hypothesis. (Incidentally, Franz Delitzsch is not to be confused with his son, Friedrich Delitzsch, who distinguished himself particularly in the field of Assyriology, and who held somewhat more liberal views of Old Testament criticism than did his father.)

Mention was made in the previous paragraph of Ernst Wilhelm Hengstenberg, the leader of the conservative wing of German biblical scholarship. He was a very able defender of the Mosaic authorship of all five books of Moses, and he skillfully refuted the standard arguments for diverse sources which had been purveyed in scholarly circles since the days of Astruc and Eichhorn. His most influential work was translated into English in 1847 as *The Genuineness of the Pentateuch*, and it did much to bolster the conservative position. As has already been mentioned, he exerted a profound influence upon Friedrich Keil, who became the foremost conservative Old Testament scholar in the German-speaking world during the latter half of the nineteenth century. In America the Princeton Seminary scholars Joseph Addison Alexander and

---

7. For a discussion of the difficulties besetting this theory of a Hexateuch, see chap. 19, p. 287-88.

William Henry Green vigorously upheld the same viewpoint, and subjected the Documentarian School to devastating criticism which has never been successfully rebutted by those of Liberal persuasion.

In 1853 appeared the epoch-making work of Hermann Hupfeld, *Die Quellen der Genesis* (*The Sources of Genesis*). His contribution to the discussion resulted in what has been termed the "Copernican revolution in the history of the Documentary Theory." In the first place he subjected document E to a thorough reexamination, and distinguished in it two distinct sources: one (E²) consisting of those rather considerable portions of the Elohist which greatly resembled J in style, vocabulary, and type of subject matter, and which occasionally seemed to contain allusions to material also found in (the presumably later) J. Indeed, if it were not for the divine name (Elohim), it would be very difficult to tell such passages from J. (It should be observed that the admission of the existence of such passages as these dangerously undermined the soundness of using the divine names Elohim and Jahweh as a valid criterion for source division.) Hupfeld therefore segregated such portions (beginning at Gen. 20) from the rest of the E corpus, which latter he adjudged to be the earliest and called the "Grundschrift" ("basic document") and designated as E¹. This E¹ document roughly corresponds with what later criticism renamed P, or the Priestly Code. The later E² (which later came to be designated simply as E) was still a bit earlier than J (the Jahwist). D (the Deuteronomic work) was of course the latest (dating from Josiah's time). Therefore the correct order of the "documents" was for Hupfeld as follows: PEJD.

It should be mentioned here that Hupfeld was not the first to originate this idea of E division, but was preceded by Karl David Ilgen of Jena, who in 1798 published a work setting forth the view that Genesis was made up of seventeen different documents, among the authors of which were two Elohists and one Jahwist. This work, however, was a product of the Fragmentary School and did not carry very wide or lasting influence.

Hupfeld's *Quellen* also emphasized the continuity of the supposed documents E¹, E², and J, and tried to demonstrate that when segregated by themselves, the sections of Genesis assigned to each of the three made good sense and could stand in their own right as separate works.[8] But most noteworthy of all was Hupfeld's emphasis upon a hypothetical redactor (i.e., a final editor) who rearranged and supplemented the whole corpus of Genesis through Numbers and who accounted for all the instances where J passages came up with words or phrases supposedly characteristic of E, and vice versa. In other words, wherever the theory ran into trouble with the facts or ran counter to the actual data of the text itself, the bungling hand of R (the alleged anonymous redactor) was brought in to save the situation.

Hupfeld's contributions provoked new interest in the Documentary Theory among scholarly circles. Particular attention was devoted to document E¹, Hupfeld's *Grundschrift*. First of all appeared the discussion of Karl Heinrich Graf in 1866. Like his

---

8. This ingenious attempt at verification is capable of easy refutation, however, as is mentioned in chap. 9, pp. 128-29.

teacher, Eduard Reuss, Graf believed that this Priestly Code in the Pentateuch contained legislation which was of later origin than Deuteronomy itself (621 B.C.), for the reason that D shows no acquaintance with the legal portions of P (the Priestly Code), although it does reflect the laws of J and E.[9] Hence we are to regard the legislation of P as dating from the time of the Exile (587-539 B.C.). The historical portions of P, however, were undoubtedly very early. Thus the order of the "documents" with Graf turned out to be: historical —P, E, J, D, and legal — P. He felt that E was supplemented by J, and then in Josiah's time E[J] was redacted by the author of D.

But P was not destined to remain long in the split condition in which Graf had left it. A Dutch scholar, Abraham Kuenen, in his *De Godsdienst van Israel* (*The Religion of Israel,* 1869) argued very forcefully for the unity of P, insisting that the historical portions of this "document" could not legitimately be separated from the legal. And since Graf had proved the exilic or post-exilic origin of the priestly legislation, therefore the entire P document had to be late. This meant that what Hupfeld had determined to be the earliest portion of the Pentateuch (his *Grundschrift*) turned out to be altogether the latest portion of all, which received its final definitive form when Ezra assembled the entire Pentateuchal corpus in time for the public Bible reading ceremony mentioned in Neh. 8. The new order of the "documents" was now: J, E, D, and P. J was the basic document of the Torah (largely because of J's "anthropomorphic" presentation of God, which was thought to reflect an earlier stage in the evolution of Israel's religion), and E was incorporated into it afterward. D was added next in Josiah's time, just before the end of the Jewish monarchy. During the ministry of Ezekiel in the exilic period, the Holiness Code (H), consisting of Lev. 17–26, was formulated as the earliest portion of P; the rest of P originated in the late sixth century and the first half of the fifth century—nearly a thousand years after the death of Moses, in the time of Ezra.

After the work of Hupfeld, Graf, and Kuenen, the stage was set for the definitive formulation of the newer Documentary Theory by Julius Wellhausen, whose most important contributions were *Die Komposition des Hexateuchs* (*The Composition of the Hexateuch*), which appeared in 1876, and *Prolegomena zur Geschichte Israels* (*Introduction to the History of Israel*), which came out in 1878 (Berlin: Druck & Verlag von G. Reimer). Although Wellhausen contributed no innovations to speak of, he restated the Documentary Theory with great skill and persuasiveness, supporting the JEDP sequence upon an evolutionary basis. This was the age in which Charles Darwin's *Origin of Species* was capturing the allegiance of the scholarly and scientific world, and the theory of development from primitive animism to sophisticated monotheism as set forth by Wellhausen and his followers fitted admirably into Hegelian dialecticism (a prevalent school in contemporary philosophy) and Darwinian evolutionism. The age was ripe for the Documentary Theory, and Wellhausen's name became attached to it as the classic exponent of it. The impact of his writings soon made itself felt

---

9. See chap. 12, pp. 169-71, for a refutation of this claim.

throughout Germany (claiming such luminaries as Kautzsch, Smend, Giesebrecht, Budde, Stade, and Cornill) and found increasing acceptance in both Great Britain and America.

In England it was William Robertson Smith (*The Old Testament in the Jewish Church*, 1881) who first interpreted Wellhausianism to the public. Samuel R. Driver gave it the classic formulation for the English-speaking world (*Introduction to the Literature of the Old Testament*, 1891), although he was personally of somewhat more conservative theological convictions than the architects of the Documentary Theory had been. The same is true of George Adam Smith, who counted himself an Evangelical in theology and yet devoted his skilled pen to a popularization of the Documentarian type of approach to the Old Testament prophets (notably Isaiah and the Minor Prophets, for which he wrote the exposition in the *Expositor's Bible* edited by W. R. Nicoll). In the United States the most notable champion of the new school was Charles Augustus Briggs of Union Seminary (*The Higher Criticism of the Hexateuch* [New York: Scribner's, 1893]), seconded by his able collaborator, Henry Preserved Smith.

As we shall see in the next chapter, the twentieth century has witnessed a vigorous reaction against Wellhausen and the Documentary Hypothesis, and general confidence in it has been somewhat undermined, even in Liberal circles. Nevertheless, no other systematic account of the origin and development of the Pentateuch has yet been formulated so lucidly and convincingly as to command the general adherence of the scholarly world. For want of a better theory, therefore, most nonconservative institutions continue to teach the Wellhausian theory, at least in its general outlines, as if nothing had happened in Old Testament scholarship since the year 1880.[10] In England, W. O. E. Oesterley and T. H. Robinson's *Introduction to the Books of the Old Testament* (London: SPCK, 1934) was basically Wellhausian, although some uncertainties are expressed concerning the comparative dating of the "documents" (J-E may have been contemporaneous with D, and H may have been a bit earlier than D). In American Julius A. Bewer's *Literature of the Old Testament* (New York: Longmans, 1922) and Robert H. Pfeiffer's *Introduction to the Old Testament* (1948) adhered quite loyally to classic Wellhausianism (although Pfeiffer isolated a new document, S, a pessimistic Edomite source, and also dated the Ten Commandments as later than D, rather than constituting a part of E).

In Germany itself the influence of Form Criticism (which will be discussed in the next chapter) has resulted in an attempt to synthesize the Form Critical approach of Gunkel and Gressman with the Documentarianism of Wellhausen. This synthesis appears most strongly in the work of Otto Eissfeldt (*Einleitung in das Alte Testament*,

---

10. Illustrative of this attitude is this quotation from a foremost British scholar, H. H. Rowley, "That it [the Graf-Wellhausen theory] is widely rejected in whole or in part is doubtless true, but there is no view to put in its place that would not be more widely and emphatically rejected....The Graf-Wellhausen view is only a working hypothesis, which can be abandoned with alacrity when a more satisfying view is found, but which cannot with profit be abandoned until then" (*The Growth of the Old Testament* [New York: Longmans, 1950], p. 46).

1934, English ed. *The Old Testament, an Introduction* [New York: Harper & Row, 1965]). In Scandinavia, Aage Bentzen of Copenhagen (*Introduction to the Old Testament*, 1948) holds mainly to the type of synthesis which Eissfeldt had attempted; but his earlier compatriot, Johannes Pedersen, as well as Sigmund Mowinckel of Oslo and Ivan Engnell of Uppsala, Sweden, inclines far more definitely toward a form-critical or history-of-tradition approach than to Wellhausian source criticism. In England and the United States, however, the rule of Wellhausen continues more or less supreme in most nonconservative schools, and makes its influence felt in many of the more or less conservative schools of the old-line denominations. Therefore we must treat the Documentary Theory as still a live issue today, even though Liberal scholarship on the European continent has administered well-nigh fatal blows to nearly all its foundations.

DESCRIPTION OF THE FOUR DOCUMENTS OF THE DOCUMENTARY HYPOTHESIS

J—written about 850 B.C.[11] by an unknown writer in the Southern Kingdom of Judah. He was especially interested in personal biography, characterized by vivid delineation of character. He often portrayed or referred to God in anthropomorphic terms (i.e., as if He possessed the body, parts, and passions of a human being[12]). He also had a prophet-like interest in ethical and theological reflection, but little interest in sacrifice or ritual.

E—written about 750 B.C. by an unknown writer in the Northern Kingdom of Israel. He was more objective than J in his narrative style and was less consciously tinged with ethical and theological reflection. He tended rather to dwell upon concrete particulars (or the origins of names or customs of particular importance to Israelite culture). In Genesis, E shows an interest in ritual and worship, and he represents God as communicating through dreams and visions (rather than through direct anthropomorphic contact, after the fashion of J). In Exodus through Numbers, E exalts Moses as a unique miracle worker, with whom God could communicate in anthropomorphic guise.

About 650 B.C. an unknown redactor combined J and E into a single document: J-E.

D—composed, possibly under the direction of the high priest Hilkiah, as an official program for the party of reform sponsored by King Josiah in the revival of 621 B.C. Its object was to compel all the subjects of the kingdom of Judah to abandon their local sanctuaries on the "high places" and bring all their sacrifices and religious contributions to the temple in Jerusalem. This document was strongly under the influence of the prophetic movement, particularly of Jeremiah. Members of this same Deuteronomic school later reworked the historical accounts recorded in Joshua, Judges, Samuel, and Kings.

---

11. The dates suggested are those proposed in S. R. Driver's ILOT, pp. 111-23.
12. For a discussion of the abundant anthropomorphisms in document P, see K. A. Kitchen, AOOT, p. 118.

P—composed in various stages, all the way from Ezekiel, with his Holiness Code (Lev. 17–26) ca. 570 B.C. (known as H), to Ezra, "the ready scribe in the law of Moses" under whose guidance the latest priestly sections were added to the Torah. P is concerned with a systematic account of the origins and institutions of the Israelite theocracy. It shows a particular interest in origins, in genealogical lists, and details of sacrifice and ritual.

SUMMARY OF THE DIALECTICAL DEVELOPMENT OF THE DOCUMENTARY HYPOTHESIS

1. Astruc said that different divine names point to different sources—J and E division; this idea was extended more thoroughly by Eichhorn (E earlier than J).

2. De Wette defined D as a manufacture of Josiah's time (621 B.C.).

3. Hupfeld divided up E into the earlier E^1 (or P) and the later E^2 (which more closely resembles J). His order of documents was PEJD.

4. Graf thought that the legal portions of P were Exilic, latest of all, even though historical portions may be early. His order of documents was: P^{1}EJD^2

5. Kuenen felt that historical portions of P must be as late as the legal. He gave as the order of documents: PEJD.

6. Wellhausen gave the Documentary Theory its classic expression, working out the JEDP sequence upon a systematic evolutionary pattern.

Observe the contradictions and reversals which characterize the development of this Documentary Theory. (1) Different divine name points to different author (Astruc, Eichhorn), each with his own circle of interest, style, and vocabulary. (2) Same divine name (Elohim), nevertheless employed by different authors (Hupfeld); whereas some E passages really do not greatly differ from J in circle of interest, style, or vocabulary. (3) That Elohist (P) which most differs from J in interest and style, must be the earliest (Jahweh being a later name for God than Elohim). (4) No, on the contrary, this P must be latest instead of earliest (for this fits in better with Evolutionary Theory about the development of Hebrew religion from the primitive polytheistic to the priest-ridden monotheistic.) (5) J of course is later than E (all the critics up to Graf); but no, J is really earlier than E (Kuenen and Wellhausen).

The most thoroughgoing refutation of the Wellhausen hypothesis to appear at the end of the nineteenth century in America was furnished by William Henry Green of Princeton, in his *Unity of the Book of Genesis* (New York: Scribner, 1895) and *Higher Criticism of the Pentateuch* (New York: Scribner, 1896). With great erudition and skill he showed how inadequately the hypothesis explained the actual data of the biblical text, and upon what illogical and self-contradictory bases the critical criteria rested.

A general discussion of the fallacies in the Documentary Theory which render it logically untenable will be found in chapter 8. The various criteria used by the Documentarians to prove diverse authorship will be discussed more in detail in chapters 9 and 10. Refutation of specific arguments dealing with particular books in the Pentateuch will be found in the chapters (14-18) which deal with those books.

7 HIGHER CRITICISM OF THE PENTATEUCH IN THE TWENTIETH CENTURY

PERHAPS THE MOST helpful way to present the trends of Old Testament scholarship between 1890 and 1950 is to arrange the effect of their contributions upon the structure of the Graf-Wellhausen Hypothesis. Hence the order followed will be topical rather than strictly chronological.

As we have already indicated, much of modern scholarship has remained loyal to the methods of Documentary analysis, and their innovations have been limited more or less to isolating a few more "Documents" beyond the time-honored four, JEDP. Thus, for example, Otto Eissfeldt in his *Hexateuchsynopse* (1922) thought he discerned within J a Lay Source (L)—more or less equivalent to Julius Smend's J^1 (*Die Erzählung des Hexateuchs auf ihre Quellen untersucht*, 1912). This L (*Laienschrift* as Eissfeldt called it) reflected a nomadic, Rechabite ideal (cf. the reference to Rechab in 2 Kings 10 and the Rechabite ideal in Jer. 35:1-19), which was completely hostile to the Canaanite way of life. He concluded that L arose in the time of Elijah (ca. 860 B.C.) and found its way into Judges and Samuel as well.

Somewhat similar to L was the new document K (for Kenite). This dealt mostly with certain details in the life of Moses, or described relations between the Israelites and the Kenites. It was isolated by Julius Morgenstern (*The Oldest Document of the Hexateuch*, 1927), and identified by him as the basis for the reforms of King Asa (ca. 890 B.C.) as recorded in 1 Kings 15:9-15. Even Robert H. Pfeiffer (as already mentioned) announced in his *Introduction to the Old Testament* the discovery of a document S (for Mount Seir, the most prominent landmark in Edom) which appeared in the J and E sections of Gen. 1-11 and also in the J and E portions of Gen. 14-38. This supposedly appeared in the reign of Solomon (ca. 950 B.C.), but later additions (made from 600 to 400 B.C.) composed an S^2. Thus we have as a result of the industry of the post-Wellhausians the additional letters K, L, and S, largely drawn off from J or E.

For the most part, however, the trend of twentieth-century scholarship has been toward the repudiation of the Graf-Wellhausen theory, either in whole or in part. In order to sort out these attacks and arrange them in a systematic fashion, we may imagine the Documentary Hypothesis in the form of a beautiful Grecian portico supported by five pillars: (1) the criterion of divine names (Jahweh and Elohim) as an indication of diverse authorship; (2) the origin of J, E, and P as separate written documents, composed at different periods of time; (3) the priority of J to E in time of composition; (4) the separate origin of E as distinct from J; (5) the origin of D in the reign of Josiah (621 B.C.). Let us consider the criticisms leveled at each of these pillars in the above-mentioned order.

AGAINST THE VALIDITY OF DIVINE NAMES AS A CRITERION OF SOURCE

As early as 1893 August Klostermann (*Der Pentateuch*) rejected the inerrancy of the Masoretic Hebrew text in the transmission of the divine names, and criticized their use as a means of identifying documentary sources. But the first scholar to make a thoroughgoing investigation of the relationship of the MT to the LXX was Johannes Dahse in his "Textkritische Bedenken gegen den Ausgangspunkt der Pentateuchkritik" ("Textual-critical Doubts About the Initial Premise of Pentateuchal Criticism") in a 1903 issue of the *Archiv für Religionswissenschaft*. Here he showed that the LXX has a non-corresponding name (i.e., *theos* for *Yahweh* or *kyrios* for *Elohim*) in no less than 180 instances. This means that the MT is not sufficiently inerrant in the textual transmission of the names to serve as the basis for such subtle and precise source division as the Documentarians have attempted. (This appeal to the LXX was all the more damaging because of the high prestige that version enjoyed as over against the MT in matters of textual emendation. Because the Documentarians themselves had been using it so freely for correction of the Hebrew text, it was more than embarrassing for them to be exposed as naively assuming the inerrancy of the transmission of the divine names in the Hebrew Torah.)

In England, a Jewish attorney named Harold M. Wiener began a series of studies in 1909 which dealt with this same troublesome discrepancy between the LXX and the MT. He argued that this uncertainty as to the correct name in so many different passages rendered the use of names impractical and unsafe for the purposes of source division. Wiener also discussed the alleged discrepancies between the various laws of the Pentateuchal legislation, showing that these so-called disagreements were capable of easy reconciliation and required no diversity of authorship.[1] While he conceded the presence of some non-Mosaic elements, he insisted upon the essential Mosaicity of the Pentateuch.

---

1. In connection with the alleged contradictions between Pentateuchal laws as indicating diversity of authorship, compare the situation in the *Code of Hammurabi*. K. A. Kitchen comments, "Thus, it is easy to group social laws and cult-regulations into small collections on the basis of their content or form and postulate their gradual accretion in the present books, with the practical elimination of Moses. One may do this equally to the Hammurabi laws (on content), and postulate there a hypothetical process of accretion of laws into groups on themes prior to conflation in Hammurabi's so-called 'code.' But this does not eliminate Hammurabi from 'authorship' of his code. His laws are known from a monument of his own time in his own name; therefore any accretions of laws in his collection occurred before his work. Furthermore there are apparent contradictions or discrepancies in the Hammurabi 'code' that are 'no less glaring than those which serve as the basis for analyzing strata in the Bible' (M. Greenberg, *Yehezkel Kaufmann Jubilee Volume*, 1960, p. 6). These obviously have no bearing on the historical fact of Hammurabi having incorporated them in his collection" (AOOT, p. 134; see also p. 148).

The eminent successor of Kuenen at the University of Leiden, B. D. Eerdmans, also admitted that the force of this argument derived from Septuagintal data, and definitely asserted the impossibility of using the divine names as a clue to separate documents (*Altestamentliche Studien*, vol. 1, *Die Komposition der Genesis*, 1908). In this same work he attacked Wellhausian source division from an entirely different approach, that of comparative religions. He felt he could trace a primitive polytheistic background behind many of the sagas in Genesis, indicating a far greater antiquity in origin than either an 850 B.C. J or a 750 B.C. E. Even the ritual elements embodied in P were much older than the final codification of the laws themselves, because they reflected ideas belonging to a very early stage of religious development. The codifying priests included provisions of such antiquity that they themselves no longer fully understood their significance.

According to Eerdmans, the Mosaic era should be recognized as the time when much of the Levitical ritual had its origin, rather than in the Exilic or post-exilic age (as the Documentarians had supposed). Moreover, from the standpoint of literary criticism, the fundamental unity of the Genesis sagas was flagrantly violated by the artificial source division practiced by the Graf-Wellhausen school. Eerdmans therefore withdrew from the Documentary School altogether and denied the validity of the Graf-Kuenen-Wellhausen theory in the preface of the above-mentioned work.[2] He felt that the earliest written unit in the Pentateuch was a polytheistic Book of Adam (commencing at Gen. 5:1) which originated sometime before 700 B.C. (although of course the oral tradition upon which it was based was many centuries older). Later there was united with this another polytheistic work which he called an Israel recension. But after the "discovery" of Deuteronomy, these earlier writings were re-edited according to a monotheistic reinterpretation, and after the Exile this entire work received some further expansions. In this alternative to the Graf-Wellhausen theory, we see a revival of the old supplementary approach, combined with an exaggerated dependence upon comparative religion techniques. But at least Eerdmans showed how flimsy were the "assured results" of Wellhausen scholarship under the impact of a fresh investigation of the data of the Hebrew text. The revered triad of J, E, and P was no longer so secure upon its pedestal.

The attack of Sigmund Mowinckel, a Norwegian scholar, against the J-E source division was from a different standpoint, that of Form Criticism (see next section). In two articles published in the *Zeitschrift für Altertumswissenschaft* (1930) he denied the independence of the J and E traditions from each other, and denied also that E was of North Israelite origin. He asserted that E was simply a religious adaptation of J from the standpoint of a Judahite school. The stories of ancient times contained in E always depend upon the narratives contained in J, and E quite often employs Jahweh as a name for God. In this connection he denied that Ex. 3:14 represented a promul-

2. See also his *Altestamentliche Studien*, vols. 2-4, 1908-1914.

gation of Jahweh as a new name for God, but on the contrary it presupposed that Jahweh was already known to the Hebrews. (He shows from Josh. 24:2-4, an E passage, that the author knew that Abraham had lived in Mesopotamia, even though all of this account in Gen. 11 had been assigned to J.) Mowinckel concluded that E was really not an author at all, but an oral tradition which continued the same body of material as that which found an earlier written form in J. E then signifies a long drawn-out process between the period when J found written form and the final inscripturation of the E material after the fall of the Jewish monarchy.[3]

W. F. Albright expresses skepticism concerning the reliability of the divine-names criterion, saying, "The discovery of relatively wide limits of textual variation antedating the third century B.C. makes the minute analysis of the Pentateuch which became fashionable after Wellhausen completely absurd. While it is quite true that there is less evidence of recensional differences in the Pentateuch than there is, for example, in Samuel-Kings, there is already more than enough to warn against elaborate hypothetical analyses and against finding different 'sources' and 'documents' whenever there appears to be any flaw or inconsistency in the received text. Such a subjective approach to literary-historical problems was always suspect and has now become irrational."[4] (While Albright remains basically Documentarian in his acceptance of J, E, and P as separate written sources, he feels that they must be identified by other criteria than the use of Yahweh or Elohim alone, and that their history was somewhat more complicated than Wellhausen supposed. Cf. Albright, p. 34.)

AGAINST THE ORIGIN OF J, E, AND P AS SEPARATE DOCUMENTS

Hermann Gunkel was associated with Hugo Gressmann as a founder of the new school of *Formgeschichte* (Form Criticism). (In New Testament criticism this approach assumed that during a period of oral tradition, A.D. 30-60, stories and sayings circulated as separate units in Christian circles. Gradually these became altered and embellished according to the theological views current in each circle, as the discerning critic can discover as he seeks to get back to the original nonmiraculous and unembellished kernel of each of these units. (Unfortunately for this method, however, the opinions and tastes of the critic himself inevitably influence his procedure in a very subjective way.) Gunkel's most important contributions in the field of Pentateuchal criticism were *Die Sagen der Genesis* (*The Sagas of Genesis*), 1901; a fifty-page contribution to Hinneberg's *Die Kultur der Gegenwart* entitled "Die altisraelitische Literatur" ("The Ancient Israelite Literature") published in 1906; and his 1911 work, *Die Schriften des Alten Testaments*.

Form Criticism, according to his formulation of it, maintains: (1) no accurate literary history is possible for the older period (attempts to reconstruct the sequence of

---

3. Mowinckel, *The Two Sources of the Pre-Deuteronomic Primeval History in Genesis 1–11* (Oslo, Norway, 1937). Aage Bentzen has a good discussion of Mowinckel's approach in his *Introduction to the Old Testament*, 2:48.

4. Albright, *Yahweh and the Gods of Canaan* (Garden City, N.Y.: Doubleday, 1968), p. 29.

the development of written documents have broken down under the impact of contrary data from the texts themselves, and we really know nothing for certain about these hypothetical documents of the Graf-Wellhausen hypothesis); (2) the only practical approach to the Pentateuchal literature is the synthetic creative (rather than the analytic critical of the Documentarians), whereby we must define the various types of categories or genres (*Gattungen*) to which the original material belonged in its oral stage, and then follow through the probable course of the development of each of these oral units until the final written form which they assumed in the exilic period or thereafter[5] (note how completely this approach erases the fine distinctions which Wellhausen had drawn between J, E, and P); and (3) as a practitioner of the methods of the *religionsgeschichtliche Schule* (comparative religionist school), Gunkel paid strict attention to the parallel phenomena of the religion and literature of ancient Israel's pagan neighbors, where the development of these *Gattungen* (literary genres) could be more clearly discerned and illustrated. In the light of the Egyptian and Mesopotamian materials it was possible, he felt, to ascertain with fair precision the *Sitz im Leben* (life situation) of each example of these different types and see through what process they evolved in their subsequent history. Thus, Genesis was really a compilation of sagas, for the most part, and all these were handed down in a fairly fluid oral form until final reduction to written form at a late period.

It will be observed that this *Formgeschichte* approach throws the JEP analysis into discard as an artificial and unhistorical attempt at analysis by men who simply did not understand how ancient literature like the Torah originated. Insofar as it demonstrates the artificiality of the Wellhausian source analysis, Gunkel's treatment of the Pentateuch represents a certain gain, from the Conservative viewpoint. He should likewise be credited for recognizing the great antiquity of much of the oral tradition material which lay behind the text of the Torah.

But Gunkel's assumption that the books of Moses found a final written form only as late as the Exile seems to ignore the cumulative evidence that the Hebrews were a highly literate people from the time of Moses onward. To be sure, the earliest scrap of written Hebrew thus far discovered by archaeology is the schoolboy's exercise known as the Gezer Calendar (ca. 925 B.C.), but nearly all of Israel's neighbors were recording all types of literature in written form for many centuries before that period, and even the underprivileged Semitic laborers at the turquoise mines in the Sinai Peninsula were scrawling their alphabetic inscriptions as early as 1500 B.C., if not earlier. Even up at the northernmost tip of the Canaanite area, at Ugarit, the contemporaries of Moses were recording their pagan scriptures in alphabetic characters. It requires an

---

5. "The idea of a unilinear evolution from smaller, 'primitive,' literary units to larger, more complex entities (and of growth of a work by gradual accretion) is a fallacy from the mid-third-millennium B.C. onwards, as far as ancient Oriental literature is concerned....Thus, among Sumerian literature of ca. 1800 B.C., Kramer mentions (in *Bible and the Ancient Near East*, pp. 255, 257, etc.) nine epic tales that vary in length from about 100 up to 600 lines; scores of hymns (of four different types) ranging from less than fifty to over 500 lines in length, several laments for Dumuzi (Tammuz) varying from less than fifty to over 200 lines," Kitchen, p. 131. Kitchen then goes on to cite other examples from Middle Kingdom and New Kingdom Egyptian literature.

excessive credulity to believe that the Hebrews alone were so backward that they did not know how to reduce to writing their most important legal and religious institutions until after 600 B.C. The Pentateuchal record itself abounds in references to writing, and portrays Moses as a man of letters. Even a common term for "officer," repeatedly used in Ex. 5 (a J passage) and elsewhere in the Pentateuch, is the Hebrew *shōṭēr*, which is derived from the same root as the common Babylonian verb "to write" (*shaṭāru*). Therefore this feature in Gunkel's theory seems to be beset with insuperable difficulty in view of this textual evidence. Furthermore, the fact that Deuteronomy follows a form that was discontinued after 1200 B.C.—the Hittite type of the suzerainty treaty—is proof positive that it could not have been composed after 1200, when suzerainty treaty forms followed a different pattern (no historical prologue, divine witness between the stipulations and the curses, the series of blessings for covenant keeping). Failure to defer to this clear evidence means that the late-date theory goes counter to the evidence of comparative literature and therefore must surrender the claim to be "scientific."

It should be pointed out, moreover, that the comparative literature of the ancient Near East serves to render highly questionable some of the basic presuppositions of Form Criticism. Thus, the doctrinaire premise of the *Gattungsforschung* methodology is to look for small fragments and scattered utterances as being the original form which the oral tradition took at the very beginning. But in so early an Egyptian work as the *Admonitions of Ipuwer* (now dated at 2200 B.C.), we find long and extended tirades, rather than the short, disconnected apothegms which Form Criticism would lead us to expect. In the Babylonian oracles also (as Sidney Smith points out in *Isaiah XL-LV*, [Toronto: Oxford, 1944], pp. 6-16) occur long connected passages. Kitchen says in *The New Bible Dictionary*, the practitioners of *Formgeschichte* "have failed entirely to distinguish between the complementary functions of written transmission (i.e., down through time) and oral dissemination (i.e., making it known over a wide area to contemporaries), and have confused the two as 'oral tradition,' wrongly overstressing the oral element in Near Eastern transmission."[6]

In 1924, Max Löhr published the first of his series on "Investigations of the Problem of the Hexateuch" entitled *Der Priestercodex in der Genesis* (*The Priestly Code in Genesis*). By means of minute exegetical study of the so-called P passages in Genesis, he showed that no independent existence of such a source could be established. Its material was so inextricably involved in the J and E sections, that it could never have stood alone. Löhr even went on to reject the Graf-Wellhausen analysis altogether, and came to the conclusion that the Pentateuch in general was composed by Ezra and his assistants in Babylon, drawing upon a heterogeneous store of written materials from the pre-exilic period. These materials included sacrificial laws and other ritual directions, religious and secular narratives of various sorts, and sundry prophecies and genealogical lists. But these prior written materials were incapable of identification with any large, specific documents such as Wellhausen's J and E.

---

6. Kitchen, *The New Bible Dictionary* (Grand Rapids: Eerdmans, 1962), p. 349b.

In 1931 Johannes Pedersen of Copenhagen came out with a radical critique of the Documentary Theory entitled *Die Auffassung vom Alten Testament* (*The Concept of the Old Testament*). In this work he rejected Wellhausian Source Criticism as inadequate to describe the culture of the ancient Hebrews. He made four specific points.

1. In such J and E stories as the communications between Jahweh and Abraham, the cycle connected with Sodom, the Jacob and Esau narrative, the Tamar and Judah episode—all accounts of this sort are of very ancient origin, even though they did not receive their present written form until after the Exile. (This meant that J and E components of this category were both much more ancient than the 850 B.C. and 750 B.C. dates of the Documentarians, and also much later, i.e., contemporaneous with the Priestly contributions.)

2. It must be said that in general, J and E cannot be maintained as separate narratives without artificially imposing an Occidental viewpoint upon the ancient Semitic narrative techniques and doing violence to Israelite psychology.

3. In document D it is impossible to make out a clear distinction (as the Documentarians had attempted to do) between older and newer elements. On the contrary, the anti-Canaanite bias which pervades Deuteronomy shows it to be the product of post-exilic conditions (for only after the return could such a self-contained Israelite community have arisen such as D depicts). This means that we must abandon the older date of Josiah's reign for the composition of Deuteronomy.

4. As to document P, it shows post-exilic composition clearly enough from its schematic arrangement and its style of diction; but on the other hand it contains many legal regulations which point to pre-exilic conditions. Particularly is this true of the social laws. In other words, all the "sources" in the Torah are both pre-exilic and post-exilic. We cannot make out the 850 B.C. J document and the 750 B.C. E document which Wellhausen tried to isolate in the Mosaic material. We can only conjecture that the earliest nucleus of the Torah was the Moses saga and the Passover legend contained in Ex. 1-15.

In 1945, in Uppsala, Sweden, appeared a work by Ivan Engnell called *Gamla testamentet, en traditionshistorisk inledning* (*The Old Testament, a Traditio-historical Introduction*), which more or less followed the line which Pedersen had taken. Engnell boldly condemned the Wellhausian fabric of criticism as representing a modern, anachronistic book view, a purely artificial interpretation in modern categories which do not apply to ancient Semitic material. He asserted that an adequate treatment of this Hebrew literature required a radical break with that whole approach. He then made the following points.

1. There never were any parallel, continuous documents of prior origin from which the Torah was finally composed in its post-exilic form.

2. The evidence of the LXX text shows the unsoundness of the criterion of divine names for Source Division; and even as they have been marked off by Wellhausen, these supposed sources are by no means consistent in their use of the names for God.

We must understand that the true explanation for the usage of these names is to be found in the context in which they occur, for it is the context that determines which name is most appropriate, as Conservative scholars have always maintained.

3. Rather than being of Judahite origin, Deuteronomy more strongly suggests North Israelite background. It is most unlikely that D could ever have been concocted in the Jerusalem temple, in view of the prominence it gives to Mt. Gerizim rather than Mt. Zion.

4. The only safe division that can be made of the Pentateuchal material is (a) a P-work extending from Genesis through Numbers and evidencing characteristics which point to a P-type school of tradition; and (b) a D-work (Deuteronomy through 2 Kings) which shows a different style of treatment and points to a definite D circle of traditionists. The legal material in Exodus through Numbers originated from the oracle-giving and judicial functions of the various local sanctuaries, where along with oral tradition some early written traditions were cultivated. Genesis is made up of an Abraham cycle, a Jacob cycle, and a Joseph complex. Gunkel's analyses of the individual stories and legend cycles are trustworthy. These were originally cultic legends connected with different sanctuaries. Doubtless, the book of the covenant (Ex. 20:23–23:19) was one such collection; Ex. 34:17-26 (the so-called ritual Decalogue) was another; and the Holiness Code (Lev. 17–26) represents still another complex. P represents a southern tradition, whereas the Deuteronomic work (Deuteronomy through 2 Kings) represents a northern tradition,[7] although the final form imposed on it reflects the viewpoint of those who wished the cultus to be centralized in Jerusalem.

5. Oral tradition played a major role in all this until the final reduction to writing. We must therefore reckon, not with written sources and redactors, but with units of oral tradition, circles of tradition, and schools within these traditionist circles. Continuous written documents would necessarily have exhibited consistent differences of style and purely linguistic constants which would occur only in the document concerned. But as it is, no consistent distinctives of this sort can be made out, and those which the Documentarians claim to have discovered can be maintained only by question-begging devices such as redactors and glosses and later emendations. (This of course implied that the elaborate word lists and tables such as are drawn up in Driver's ILOT must be discarded as unsound.)

Another interesting writer who perhaps could be listed in this group is Wilhelm Moeller, who was originally a convinced adherent of the Wellhausen school. But after a careful reexamination of the evidence, he became impressed with the inadequacy of the Documentary Hypothesis in the light of the actual data. His first attack was published in 1899 in German under the title of *Historico-critical Considerations in Opposition to the Graf-Wellhausen Hypothesis by a Former Adherent*. A more powerful onslaught appeared in 1912: *Wider den Bann der Quellenscheidung* (*Against the Spell of Source Divi-*

---

7. Cf. the command to set up an altar and to inscribe the text of the Torah upon stone stelae on Mt. Ebal in Deut. 27:1-8.

sion). Here he demonstrated the weakness of the arguments for the Documentary Hypothesis and cogently argued the case for the unity of the Pentateuch. In his 1925 work, *Rückbeziehungen des fünften Buches Mosis auf die vier ersten Bücher* (*Backward References of the Fifth Book of Moses to the First Four Books*), he showed that Deuteronomy contains numerous references to Genesis through Numbers which presuppose their existence prior to the composition of Deuteronomy and their availability to the author himself. But perhaps Moeller should not be listed with these other critics, since his investigations led him back to the position of the historic Christian church in regard to the authorship of the Pentateuch, and he thereby became an adherent of the Conservative cause. All the others, of course, were (or are) Liberals.

Yehezkel Kaufmann of Hebrew University in the 1940s and 1950s reexamined the assumption of the Wellhausen school that P omitted all mention of the centralization of the sanctuary because it took this centralization for granted. He found this to be utterly unwarranted circular reasoning and argued that monotheism characterized Israel's religion from the beginning. (Cf. his *Religion of Israel* [Chicago: U. of Chicago, 1960], p. 205, quoted in this text on p. 110.) Yet he still accepted the four documents as separate entities, even though the priority of D to much of P could no longer be sustained.

AGAINST THE PRIORITY OF J TO E

In his 1920 work entitled *Deuteronomy and the Decalogue*, R. H. Kennett advanced the argument that E was really the earliest of the written documents rather than J, and was composed about 650 B.C. for the mixed or hybrid population of North Israel (subsequent to the deportation of the ten tribes in 722 B.C.). J was written a few decades later, down in the Hebron area as a sort of counterblast to Josiah's reforms (with his insistence on the sole legitimacy of the Jerusalem temple); its date was about 615 B.C. This J was probably the document referred to by Jeremiah 8:8, "But, behold, the false pen of the scribes hath wrought falsely."[8]

It goes without saying that the views of Pedersen (see p. 105) belong also in this division, for if all the materials of the Pentateuch are post-exilic in their final written form, there can be no more talk of the priority of J to E. The same is true of Engnell (see pp. 105-6). If all of Genesis was made up of legend cycles preserved at the various local sanctuaries, and if all of Exodus through Numbers belongs to a P school of tradition, then there is no room for a J prior to E, nor indeed for any separate written J and E at all.

AGAINST THE INDEPENDENT EXISTENCE OF E AS A DOCUMENT LATER THAN J

Paul Volz and Wilhelm Rudolph cooperated in 1933 in the publication of a study entitled *Der Elohist als Erzähler: ein Irrweg der Pentateuchkritik?* (*The Elohist as a Narrator: A Mistake in Pentateuchal Criticism?*). After a careful reexamination of the E pas-

---

8. Kennett's views on Deuteronomy are discussed on p. 110.

sages, these scholars drew the conclusion that there were really no good grounds for making out a separate, coherent E source. They were simply parts of J or supplements to it. Volz proposed to do away with separate J and E sources and return to something comparable to the old Supplement Hypothesis. In Genesis we have only a single story writer (J), and E was no more than a later editor of this J work who may possibly have inserted a few sections of his own. As for P, no stories at all emanate from him; he was only the recorder of legislation and the composer of doctrinal sections such as Genesis 1 and 17.

The contribution of Mowinckel (pp. 101-2) may be referred to here. E was to him no separate document from J, but simply a Judahite religious adaptation of the Jehovistic material. E was more of a process than a document. Likewise, Pedersen's approach (p. 105) involved a complete denial of the separate existence of J and E. Both represent oral material going back to the earliest time, and together they received written form after the exile.

Against the Josianic Date for Deuteronomy

Ever since De Wette's identification of Deuteronomy as the book of the law which was discovered by Hilkiah in the temple and read aloud to King Josiah in 621 B.C., the Josianic date for D was considered one of the surest of the "assured results of modern scholarship" by the whole Wellhausen school. As Wellhausen himself declared in his *Prolegomena*: "About the origin of Deuteronomy there is still less dispute; in all circles where appreciation of scientific results can be looked for at all, it is recognized that it was composed in the same age as that in which it was discovered, and that it was made the rule of Josiah's reformation, which took place about a generation before the destruction of Jerusalem by the Chaldeans."[9]

Against the background of this confidence, it is interesting to compare the treatment of the Josianic date (so pivotal to the whole Documentary Hypothesis) accorded by the twentieth-century critics from 1919 onward. Some of these insurgents shifted the date of D's origin to a much earlier period than 621 B.C., while others preferred to transfer it to the post-exilic age. But both groups were unanimous in condemning the Josianic date as altogether unthinkable in view of the data of the text itself and of the historical conditions known to have prevailed at that time.

Critics Preferring an Earlier Date for Deuteronomy

In 1919, Martin Kegel produced his *Die Kultusreformation des Josias* (*Josiah's Reformation of the Cultus*) in which he gave his grounds for considering the 621 date unsound for D. Since even those influential leaders (such as the priesthood of the high places and the pro-idolatrous nobility) did not raise the issue of the genuineness of Deuteronomy as an authentic work of the great lawgiver Moses (even though they

---

9. Wellhausen, *Prolegomena*, trans. J. Sutherland Black and Allen Menzies *(Edinburgh:* A.&C. Black, 1885), p. 9. (In this connection it should be noted that 2 Kings 22:13 implies that Josiah believed it was a book known to his ancestors: "Our fathers have not listened to the words of this book.")

had every incentive to challenge its authenticity), it follows that D must have been a very ancient book indeed by Josiah's time, and must have been known as such. (Kegel was even inclined to doubt the identification of the discovered book of the law with Deuteronomy alone; he felt that the evidence pointed toward the inclusion of all the other parts of the Pentateuch which were already in writing.) Furthermore, the oft-repeated assertion that the main purpose of Josiah's reform was to enforce worship at the central sanctuary (the Jerusalem temple) was not at all borne out by the evidence of 2 Kings and 2 Chronicles; they show that his chief concern was the cleansing of Jehovah worship from idolatry.

In 1924, Adam C. Welch of Edinburgh pointed out that a "law of the single sanctuary" would have been quite impractical for the seventh century B.C., for it did not reflect conditions which prevailed at that time. Furthermore, he showed that many of the legal regulations in D were much too primitive in character to fit in with the late Jewish monarchy.[10] Rather than showing a Judahite origin, some of the laws indicated a North Israelite origin. It was therefore far more justifiable to look to the age of Solomon (tenth century B.C.) as the time when the main core, at least, of the Deuteronomic legislation was written down. One insertion only was definitely assignable to Josiah's time, and that was Deut. 12:1-7 which made the central sanctuary mandatory (a passage which was used by Josiah to sanction his reform program). But the primary purpose of the book in its original form was to purify the cultus at all the various local sanctuaries and thus to combat the contaminating influence of Canaanite theology and practice.

Other more recent writers who favored a pre-Josianic date for Deuteronomy include R. Brinker (*The Influence of Sanctuaries in Early Israel*, pp.189ff.), who argued that the essentially Mosaic legislation of Deuteronomy was later supplemented by priests in the various local sanctuaries; but its main thrust was opposition to Canaanite idolatry. Gerhard von Rad suggested that Deuteronomy arose among circles of rural Levites and must have been completed by 701 B.C. (*Studies in Deuteronomy*, 1953, p. 66). A. Westphal felt that it dated from the early part of Hezekiah's reign. Both Albright (*The Biblical Period from Abraham to Ezra*, 1963, p. 45) and Eissfeldt dated Deut. 32 (the "Song of Moses") to the time of Samuel, citing MS fragments from 4Q.

In the following decade a series of articles was issued from the pen of Edward Robertson in the *Bulletin of John Rylands Library*, in 1936, 1941, 1942, and 1944, in which he defended the thesis that at the time of conquest, the Hebrews must have entered Palestine as an organized community possessing a nucleus of law, including the Decalogue and the Book of the Covenant (Ex. 20–23). After their settlement in Canaan, they split up into various religious communes, each with its own special sanctuary. These various local traditions of Mosaic law were combined by Samuel (cf. 1 Sam. 10:25) on the threshold of the establishment of the United Monarchy. This background satisfactorily accounts for the diverse elements and inconsistencies of the background material of the Tetrateuch. As for Deuteronomy, it was composed shortly

10. Welch, *The Code of Deuteronomy* (New York: George H. Doran, 1924).

thereafter, about 1000 B.C., in order to cement together the new political unity. This work then was lost and not rediscovered until the reign of Josiah.

During the 1940s and 1950s, Yehezkel Kaufmann of Jerusalem argued for the priority of P to D, saying, "Only in D and related literature is there a clear and unmistakable influence of the centralization idea. In the time of Hezekiah the idea began to gain favor; Josiah drew its ultimate conclusions. Thereafter Judaism was enthralled by the image of the central sanctuary and chosen city. It is incredible that a priestly law which evolved at this time should pass over this dominant idea in silence. It has been shown above that there is no trace whatever of D's centralization idea in P; P must therefore have been composed before the age of Hezekiah."[11] This meant that P had to be dated early in the eighth century or before, rather than being a product of the exilic or post-exilic age. Kaufmann was convinced that monotheism characterized Israel's religion from the very first, and that the tabernacle was an authentic, historic shrine employed in the days of Moses. "The idea that the tent is a reflex of the Second Temple is a baseless contention of modern criticism."[12]

CRITICS PREFERRING A LATER DATE FOR DEUTERONOMY

R. H. Kennett's work on *Deuteronomy and the Decalogue* has already been referred to (p. 107).[13] It was his thesis that the legislation of D presupposes not only J and E, but also H (which according to the Wellhausen scheme did not arise until 570 B.C. under Ezekiel's influence). Particularly is this true of Deut. 12. The inference is, then, that D must have been late exilic at the very earliest. (According to Kennett, the order of the documents was EJHDP, i.e., E—650 B.C., J—615 B.C., H—570 B.C., D—500 B.C., P—450 B.C. Contrast this with Wellhausen's EJHDP.)

In 1922 Gustav Hölscher produced his *Komposition and Ursprung des Deuteronomiums* (*The Composition and Origin of Deuteronomy*). In this work Hölscher quite decisively denied that D could have constituted the book of the law which Hilkiah found. The characteristic legislation of Deuteronomy does not at all conform to the contemporary conditions prevalent in Josiah's time. For example, the enforcement of a single sanctuary law would have been utterly impractical idealism before the tragedy of the fall of Jerusalem and the restoration of the exiles from Babylon to make a new beginning in the land. During the centuries preceding the exile, how could even a visionary reformer seriously expect that whole communities in Israel which had embraced the worship of false gods or the worship of Jehovah with images could be put to the sword by the central government (as Deut. 13 and 17 required)? Kings and Chronicles testified to the fact that almost every municipality in Judah was infected with this idolatry, not excluding Jerusalem itself.

It would never have occurred to a lawmaker after the population of Israel had settled down along the whole tract of Palestine, all the way from Dan to Beersheba, to

---

11. Kaufmann, "The Religion of Israel," p. 205.
12. Ibid, p. 183.
13. Kennett, *Deuteronomy and the Decalogue* (Cambridge: U. Press, 1920).

enact a provision that all the male inhabitants had to forsake their homes and farms for days or weeks at a time no less than three times a year, just to participate in religious rites at some central sanctuary. The only sensible conclusion to draw is that Deuteronomy was drawn up when the Jewish remnant under Zerubbabel and Jeshua had newly resettled the land. (At this point it would be appropriate to suggest that if Deuteronomy does so clearly point to a time when the Hebrews had newly settled the land and were still grouped closely together, these specifications admirably accord with the time and setting the book of Deuteronomy gives for itself [1:1-4], that is, when Israel was all assembled on the plains of Moab just prior to the conquest [ca. 1400 B.C.]. But Hölscher does not even discuss this possibility.)

With this conclusion of Hölscher's, Johannes Pedersen (cf. p. 105) was in general agreement. He felt that the pervasive anti-Canaanite bias in Deuteronomy pointed to the antiforeign spirit which prevailed in the age of Zerubbabel and Nehemiah. (But Pedersen likewise failed to consider the possibility that such an anti-Canaanite spirit characterized the age of Moses and Joshua, when the whole corrupt culture of the Canaanites lay under the condemnation of God.)[14]

How shall we characterize the trend of twentieth-century scholarship in its treatment of Pentateuchal criticism and of the Wellhausen hypothesis? At the very least it must be regarded as a period of reaction against the neat, tight structure erected by the Documentary Theory of the nineteenth century. Almost every supporting pillar has been shaken and shattered by a generation of scholars who were brought up on the Graf-Wellhausen system and yet have found it inadequate to explain the data of the Pentateuch. At the same time it must be recognized that for the most part, even those scholars who have repudiated Wellhausen have shown no tendency to embrace a more conservative view of the origin of the books of Moses. They have undermined the defenses and torn down the bastions which buttressed the Documentary Hypothesis, but they have gravitated quite definitely into an even more implausible position than that occupied by their predecessors: despite the analogy of Israel's pagan neighbors and contemporaries (who embodied their religious beliefs in written scriptures long before Moses' time), the Hebrews never got around to inscripturating the records of their faith until 500 B.C. or later. It requires a tremendous willingness to believe the unlikely for an investigator to come up with a conclusion like that.

We close with an apt quotation from H. F. Hahn, "This review of activity in the field of Old Testament criticism during the last quarter-century has revealed a chaos of conflicting trends, ending in contradictory results, which create an impression of ineffectiveness in this type of research. The conclusion seems unavoidable that the higher criticism has long since passed the age of constructive achievement."[15]

It is of great importance to biblical scholarship that students of higher criticism be accurately informed as to the contribution and distinctive emphasis of each mod-

---

14. A discussion of the evidence for the Mosaic authorship of Deuteronomy may be found in chap. 18.

15. H. F. Hahn, *Old Testament in Modern Research*, p. 41.

ern critic so that he understands his presuppositions and his line of evidence and logic so as to be able to explain this to an inquirer even though he doesn't accept it as sound theology. It is important to have a mastery of the contributions of Liberal or Negative Criticism in order to respond intelligently in dealing with their errors. This facilitates effectiveness in discussion or confrontation with those who have been trained in the school of Negative Criticism. Otherwise a defender of the historical Christian position may be taken as imperfectly informed in his theological training and scholarship. A good conservative scholar must be able to analyze accurately and fairly the positions taken by Rationalist scholars before he can successfully refute them. Therefore, we have prepared an excursus with a more detailed discussion of some of the more recent scholars who carry on the tradition of the Documentary Hypothesis or *Formgeschichte* so we may be well-informed as to what and why these scholars believe as they do. This enables the evangelical student to understand the fallacies of those approaches when dealing with the data that bears upon the subject at hand. In this way a student of conservative conviction may find himself on much more advantageous footing than would be the case if he simply ignored and rejected without serious refutation those liberal views and conclusions which he understands to be false. See Excursus 3.

KEYS TO IDENTIFY LIBERAL CRITICISM

1. Employs circular reasoning

2. Textual evidence is devalued in favor of Hegelian dialectic

3. Assumes lower literary standard for Hebrew authors than contemporaries

4. Gives pagan documents prior credibility over Scripture

5. Assumes a purely human origin for Israel's religion

6. Artificially concocted "discrepancies" are manipulated as proof text for biblical error

7. Espouses literary duplication or repetition as demonstrating diverse authorship

8. Claims "scientific reliability" for dating of documents according to a theory of evolution

9. Assumes a superior knowledge of ancient history over original authors who lived 2000 plus years closer to the events which they record

8 THE AUTHORSHIP OF THE PENTATEUCH

CHAPTERS 6 AND 7 have traced the development of the theories of Liberal scholarship as to the authorship of the Pentateuch. Beginning with the triumph of deism in the 1790s and continuing through the age of Hegelian dialecticism and Darwinian evolutionism in the nineteenth century, the verdict has been against Mosaic authorship. The earliest written portions of the literary hodgepodge known as the books of Moses did not antedate the ninth or eighth century B.C. In the present century some concessions have been made by various scholars as to possible Mosaicity of certain ancient strands of oral tradition, but so far as the written form is concerned, the tendency has been to make the whole Pentateuch post-exilic. By and large, however, Mosaic authorship has not even been a live option for twentieth-century Liberal scholarship; that battle was fought and won back in the early 1800s, and it was principally the architects of the Documentary Theory who deserved the credit for banishing Moses into the illiterate mists of oral tradition. On the basis of the brief description of the rise of the Documentary Hypothesis given in the two preceding chapters, we are in a position to indicate, at least in cursory fashion, the most obvious weaknesses and fallacies which have vitiated the whole Wellhausian approach from its very inception.

WEAKNESSES AND FALLACIES OF THE WELLHAUSIAN THEORY

1. The Documentary Theory has been characterized by a subtle species of circular reasoning; it tends to posit its conclusion (the Bible is no supernatural revelation) as its underlying premise (there can be no such thing as supernatural revelation). That premise, of course, was an article of faith with all Western intelligentsia back in the eighteenth century Enlightenment (Encyclopédistes in France, die Aufklärung movement in Germany); it was implicit in the prevailing philosophy of deism. Unfortunately, however, it rendered impossible any fair consideration of the evidences presented by the Scripture of supernatural revelation. Furthermore, it made it absolutely obligatory to find rationalistic, humanistic explanations of every miraculous or God-manifesting feature or episode in the text of Scripture. But this attempt to deal objectively with literary data

from an antisupernaturalistic bias was foredoomed to failure. It is like the attempt of persons who are color blind to judge the masterpieces of Turner or Gainsborough. The first fallacy, then, was *petitio principii* (begging the question).[1]

2. The Wellhausen theory was allegedly based upon the evidence of the text itself, and yet the evidence of the text is consistently evaded whenever it happens to go counter to the theory. For example, the Documentarians insisted, "The historical books of the Old Testament show no recognition of the existence of P legislation or a written Mosaic code until after the exile." When in reply to this claim numerous references to the Mosaic law and P provisions were discovered in the historical books, the reply was made, "Oh well, all those references were later insertions made by priestly scribes who reworked these books after the exile." This means that the same body of evidence which is relied upon to prove the theory is rejected when it conflicts with the theory. Or to put it in another way, whenever the theory is opposed by the very data it is supposed to explain, the troubleshooting team of Redactor and Interpolator, Inc. is called to the rescue. Elusive tactics like these hardly beget justifiable confidence in the soundness of the result.

3. The Documentarians assume that Hebrew authors differ from any other writers known in the history of literature in that they alone were incapable of using more than one name for God; more than one style of writing, no matter what the difference in subject matter; or more than one of several possible synonyms for a single idea; or even more than one theme-type or circle of interest. According to these theorists (to use an illustration from English literature), a single author like Milton could not possibly have written merry poems such as *L'Allegro*, lofty epic poetry such as *Paradise Lost*, and scintillating prose essays such as *Areopagitica*. If he had been an ancient Hebrew, at least, he would have been speedily carved up into the ABC multiple-source hypothesis! The whole structure of source division has been erected upon exclusivist assumptions demonstrable for the literature of no other nation or period.[2]

4. Subjective bias was shown in the treatment of the Hebrew Scriptures as archaeological evidence. All too frequently the tendency has been to regard any biblical statement as unreliable and suspect, though the very antiquity of the Old Testament (even by the critics' own dating) should commend it for consideration as an archaeological document. In case of any discrepancy with a pagan document, even one of a later age, the heathen source has been automatically given the preference as a historical witness. Where there happens to be no corroborative evidence at hand from non-Israelite sources or archaeological discoveries of some sort, the biblical statement is not to be trusted unless it happens to fall in with the theory. It makes no difference

---

1. "The supposed consistency of criteria over a large body of writing is contrived and deceptive (especially on vocabulary, for example), and will hold for 'style' only if one in the first place picks out everything of a particular kind, then proclaims it as all belonging to one document separate from the rest, and finally appeals to its remarkable consistency—a consistency obtained by deliberate selection in the first place, and hence attained by circular reasoning. 'P' owes its existence mainly to this kind of procedure," K. A. Kitchen, AOOT, pp. 115-16.

2. For a critique of this artificial methodology from the standpoint of a classical scholar, cf. chap. 9, p. 139-40, and the reference to Dornseiff.

how many biblical notices, rejected as unhistorical by nineteenth-century pundits, have been confirmed by later archaeological evidence (such as the historicity of Belshazzar, the Hittites, and the Horites), the same attitude of skeptical prejudice toward the Bible has persisted, without any logical justification. (It would be naive to suppose that pagan Egyptian, Babylonian, and Assyrian records—in contrast to the Hebrew Scriptures with their lofty ethical standards—were free from propagandistic *Tendenz* or party bias.) It is to the credit of W. F. Albright that much of his scholarly endeavor was directed toward rehabilitating the reputation of the Old Testament as a reliable record of the past. In numerous books and articles, he showed again and again that the biblical record has been vindicated against its critics by recent archaeological discovery.

5. The Wellhausen school started with the pure assumption (which they have hardly bothered to demonstrate) that Israel's religion was of merely human origin like any other religion, and that it was to be explained as a mere product of evolution. It made no difference to them that no other religion known (apart from offshoots of the Hebrew faith) has ever eventuated in genuine monotheism; the Israelites too *must* have begun with animism and crude polytheism just like all the other ancient cultures. The overwhelming contrary evidence from Genesis to Malachi that the Israelite religion was monotheistic from start to finish has been evaded in the interests of a preconceived dogma—that there can be no such thing as a supernaturally revealed religion.[3] Therefore all the straightforward accounts in Genesis and the rest of the Torah relating the experiences of Abraham, Isaac, Jacob, and Moses have been subjected to a cynical re-analysis intended to show that a monotheistic veneer has been applied to those old polytheistic worthies by so-called Deuteronomists or the late priestly school.[4]

6. Whenever by ingenious manipulation of the text a "discrepancy" can be made out by interpreting a passage out of context, no reconciling explanation is to be accepted, but the supposed discrepancy must be exploited to "prove" diversity of sources. (Cf. Pfeiffer's imagined discrepancy [IOT, p. 328] between the "two accounts" of the slaying of Sisera. Judges 5:25-27 is alleged to represent Jael as having slain him with her hammer and tent peg while he was drinking milk; Judg. 4:21 says she did it while he was asleep. Actually, 5:25-27 does not state that he was drinking at the moment of impact; but it would be useless to point this out to Pfeiffer, for he has already divided up the "discrepant accounts" between J and E.)

7. Although other ancient Semitic literatures show multiplied instances of repetition and duplication by the same author in their narrative technique, Hebrew literature alone cannot show any such repetitions or duplications without betraying

---

3. Cf. Kaufmann's critique of the assumption that Israel began with polytheism and idolatry before it evolved into monolotry and monotheism, p. 107.
4. An excellent refutation of this comparative religionist approach comes from G. E. Wright in his *Old Testament Against Its Environment* (1950). Although a moderate advocate of the Documentary Theory, he was convinced by archaeological data that the Hebrews were truly unique in their early espousal of monotheism and clung to it despite the opposition of idol-worshiping neighbors.

diverse authorship.[5] It is instructive to study the sectarian literature from the Qumran caves and see how long the Israelites continued to employ repetition for purposes of emphasis. For example, compare Plate I and Plate IV of the *Manual of Disciplines*[6] where the requirements for entering the monastic community are set forth in such a way as to invite the attention of the Documentarian source divider. The same would be true for Ugaritic epics such as *Keret* and Homer's *Iliad* and the *Odyssey*. Compare the extensive use of repetition in the chancery style of Daniel who wrote as a lawyer or civil servant who employed the style of precise repetition found in statutory law today.

8. With highly questionable self-confidence, the Wellhausen school has assumed that modern European critics, who have no other ancient Hebrew literature with which to compare (for the biblical period, at least), can with scientific reliability fix the date of composition of each document. They also assume that they can freely amend the text by substituting more common words for the rare or unusual words preserved in the MT but which they do not understand or do not expect in the given context. As foreigners living in an entirely different age and culture, they have felt themselves competent to discard or reshuffle phrases or even entire verses whenever their Occidental concepts of consistency or style have been offended.

9. They have also assumed that scholars living more than 3,400 years after the event can (largely on the basis of philosophical theories) more reliably reconstruct the way things really happened than could the ancient authors themselves (who were removed from the events in question by no more than 600 or 1000 years, even by the critics' own dating).

To sum up, it is very doubtful whether the Wellhausen hypothesis is entitled to the status of scientific respectability. There is so much of special pleading, circular reasoning, questionable deductions from unsubstantiated premises, that it is absolutely certain that its methodology would never stand up in a court of law. Scarcely any of the laws of evidence respected in legal proceedings are honored by the architects of this Documentary Theory. Any attorney who attempted to interpret a will or statute or deed of conveyance in the bizarre and irresponsible fashion of the Source Critics of the Pentateuch would find his case thrown out of court without delay. Compare for example this statement by Judge William Dixon of Pasadena, California, relative to a proposed constitution for a new church merger in the United Church of Christ: "It is elementary that in the interpretation of a written contract all of the writing must be read together and every part interpreted with reference to the whole, so that each provision therein will be effective for its general purpose."[7] Surely this principle has a relevance even for the non-legal portions of the works of Moses. Had it been followed in Pentateuchal analysis, the JEDP hypothesis would have been an impossibility.

---

5. See reference in chap. 6, p. 92, to Ewald's comparison of Hebrew narrative techniques and those of the Arabs.
6. Millar Burrows, DSS, pp. 371, 376.
7. Cf. William Dixon, in *Pilgrim Frontier* (June 1960), p. 4.

POSITIVE EVIDENCES OF MOSAIC AUTHORSHIP

When all the data of the Pentateuchal text have been carefully considered, and all the evidence, both internal and external, has been fairly weighed, the impression is all but irresistible that Mosaic authorship is the one theory which best accords with the surviving historical data. For the purposes of a convenient survey, and without elaborate demonstration or illustration at this point, we shall list the various areas of evidence which point to this conclusion.

THE WITNESS OF THE SCRIPTURES TO MOSES' AUTHORSHIP

1. The Pentateuch itself testifies to Moses as having composed it. We find these explicit statements (ASV): Exodus 17:14: "And Jehovah said unto Moses, Write this for a memorial in a book...that I will utterly blot out the remembrance of Amalek." Exodus 24:4: "And Moses wrote all the words of Jehovah"; and verse 7: "And he took the book of the covenant, and read in the audience of the people." Exodus 34:27: "And Jehovah said unto Moses, Write thou these words: for after the tenor of these words I have made a covenant with thee and with Israel." Numbers 33:l-2: "These are the journeys of the children of Israel....And Moses wrote their goings out according to their journeys." Deuteronomy 31:9: "And Moses wrote this law, and delivered it unto the priests"; and verse 11: "When all Israel is come to appear before Jehovah thy God...thou shalt read this law before all Israel in their hearing." It is interesting to observe that Wellhausen, in his *Prolegomena*, nowhere (according to the index to the English edition, at least) discusses any of these five explicit references in the Torah to Moses' writing of these portions of the Pentateuch. Where passages are found that conflict with Wellhausen's theory, he simply passes them over in silence. Apparently he never even entertained the possibility of Moses contributing a single word to the Pentateuch; certainly not the Ten Commandments nor Moses' fashioning of the brazen serpent in Num. 21:9 (*Prolegomena*, p. 439), which for Wellhausen proved Moses was idolatrous.

2. In other Old Testament books we find such references as these: Joshua 1:8: "This book of the law shall not depart out of thy mouth, but thou shalt meditate thereon...that thou mayest observe to do according to all that is written therein." (In v. 7 this was described as "the law which Moses my servant commanded thee.") Joshua 8:31: "As it is written in the book of the law of Moses, an altar of unhewn stones—" (i.e., Ex. 20:25). In verse 32: "And he [Joshua] wrote there upon the stones a copy of the law of Moses." First Kings 2:3: "And keep the charge of Jehovah...according to that which is written in the law of Moses" (David being the speaker here). Second Kings 14:6 (referring to King Amaziah): "But the children of the murderers he put not to death; according to that which is written in the book of the law of Moses, as Jehovah commanded" (quoting Deut. 24:16). (The date of this episode was ca. 796 B.C.) Second Kings 21:8 (referring to the reign of Manasseh, 696-642 B.C.): "If only they will observe to do...according to all the law that my servant Moses commanded them." Other references are found in the Old Testament record from the time of Josi-

ah onward (when, of course, Deuteronomy had been published, and possibly also JE, according to the Wellhausen hypothesis). The authorship of the Torah is always attributed personally to Moses. Such references are: Ezra 6:18; Neh. 13:1; Dan. 9:11-13; Mal. 4:4.

3. The New Testament also strongly affirms Mosaic authorship. Apart from the numerous references to the Torah as "Moses," we select the following quotations which emphasize the personality of the historical Moses. Matthew 19:8: "Moses for your hardness of heart suffered you to put away your wives." John 5:46-47: "For if ye believed Moses, ye would believe me; for he wrote of me. But if ye believe not his writings, how shall ye believe my words?" John 7:19: "Did not Moses give you the law, and yet none of you doeth the law?" Acts 3:22: "Moses indeed said, A prophet shall the Lord God raise up unto you" (quoting from Deut. 18 :15). Romans 10:5: "For Moses writeth that the man that doeth the righteousness" (quoting Lev. 18:5). It is hard to see how anyone can embrace the Documentary Theory (that Moses wrote not a word of the law) without attributing either falsehood or error to Christ and the apostles. Mark 12:26 states that God uttered to the historical Moses the words of Ex. 3:6.

OTHER INTERNAL EVIDENCES

But now we pass from the direct statements of Scripture itself concerning Mosaic authorship of the Pentateuch to another line of evidence which is more indirect, but nonetheless almost as compelling. The most objective method of dating the composition of any written document is to examine its internal evidences. That is to say, by taking note of the incidental or casual allusions to contemporary historical events, to current issues, geographical or climatic conditions, to the prevalent flora and fauna, and to indications of eyewitness participation, it is possible to come to a very accurate estimate of the place and date of composition. Judging therefore by the internal evidences of the Pentateuchal text, we are driven to the conclusion that the author must have been originally a resident of Egypt (not of Palestine), a contemporary eyewitness of the Exodus and the wilderness wandering, and possessed of a very high degree of education, learning, and literary skill. No one else conforms to these qualifications as closely as Moses the son of Amram. We submit a brief summary of these evidences.

1. Eyewitness details appear in the account of the Exodus which suggest an actual participant in the events, but which would be altogether beyond the ken of an author who lived centuries after the event. For example, in Ex. 15:27 the narrator recalls the exact number of fountains (twelve) and of palm trees (seventy) at Elim. Numbers 11:7-8 gives the appearance and taste of the manna with which Jehovah fed Israel (no doubt for the benefit of coming generations in conquered Canaan, where Moses knew no manna would fall).

2. The author of Genesis and Exodus shows a thorough acquaintance with Egypt, as one would expect of a participant in the Exodus. He is familiar with Egyptian names, such as *Ōn* as the native name (hieroglyphic *'wnw*) for Heliopolis; Pithom for

Pr-;tm ("The House of Atum"—a god); Potiphera', for P;-d'-p;-R' ("The Bowman of Ra'"
or the "sun-god"); Asenath for Ns-N't ("The Favorite of Neith"—a goddess), Joseph's
wife; Moses for Mw-s;[8] ("Water-son"), or possibly a short form of Thutmose of
Ahmose (since Egyptian subjects were often named after the reigning Pharaoh); the
special title of honor bestowed on Joseph by Pharaoh: Zaphenathpa'nēaḥ (Gen.
41:45), which probably represents the Egyptian 𓏏𓆓𓏏𓈖𓄿𓊪𓋹𓂝𓈖𓐍 df; nt; p ;'nḫ is
the way it would have been in hieroglyphic Egyptian —"Nourisher of the land of the
Living One [Pharaoh]." (This explanation by Sayce and Yahuda, similar to that of
Lieblein, accounts perfectly for all the Hebrew consonants: ṢPNTP'NḤ. Furthermore,
names compounded with this same df; are known to have been common in Joseph's
period.[9] The interpretation favored by Mallon, Steindorff, Barton, and Albright: ḏd p;
nṯr' w·f 'nḫ—"The god speaks, he lives"—involves major deviations from the Hebrew
consonants and does not make as good sense in the context of the situation.)[10]

He also uses a greater percentage of Egyptian words than elsewhere in the Old
Testament. For examples: the expression 'abrēk (Gen 41:43—translated, "bow the
knee") is apparently the Egyptian ' b rk ("O heart, bow down!"), although many other
explanations have been offered for this;[11] weights and measures, such as zeret ("a
span") from drt—"hand"; 'ephah (tenth of a homer) from 'pt; hīn (about five quarts
volume) from hnw; gōme' ("papyrus") from ḳmyt; qemaḥ ("flour") from ḳmḥw (a type
of bread); šēš ("fine linen") from sšr ("linen"); yeōr ("Nile, river") from 'trw—"river"
(which becomes eioor in Coptic).[12]

One of the most ambitious modern works discussing the Egyptian background of

---

8. The traditional Arabic pronunciation, Musā, certainly favors Mw-s; ("Son of water").

9. For example, in the fourteenth dynasty (a century and a half after Joseph's time) we meet with three
royal names containing this same term, df;w: Mr-df;-R' (#186 in Ernest A. T. W. Budge's King-List), Nb-
df;w-R' I (#188) and Nb-df;w-R' II (#190). That p; 'nḫ ("the Living One") was used to refer to the
Pharaoh is attested by the name of the twenty-first dynasty prince, P;y'nḫ son of King Ḥr-Ḥr s;-'mn
(#328 in Budge's list). Budge, The Book of the Kings of Egypt (London: K. Paul, Trench, Trubner, 1908).

10. Albright points to the names of members of Aaron's family as decisive evidence of authentic Egyptian connection (H. C. Alleman and E. E. Flack, Old Testament Commentary, p. 141. Thus, Phinehas is p;
Nḥsy ("The Nubian"); Hophni is probably from ḥfn(r) ("tadpole"); Pashhur from pš (or Pšš.t) Ḥr ("The
portion of Horus"); Merari is probably from mrry ("continually beloved"). But at the same time,
Albright feels that the Egyptian names like Potiphar and Zaphenath-paaneah come from a later period
than the Twelfth Dynasty or Hyksos period (when Joseph would have had his career in Egypt). If his
identifications are accepted, it must be conceded that the Egyptian definite article p; which appears in
these two words would hardly be expected before the eighteenth dynasty (the time of Moses). But we
have already indicated that Joseph's Egyptian title is to be otherwise construed, retaining only the p;,
in front of 'nḫ, and pointing to the Pharaoh as "that Living One"—a genuine demonstrative use of p;
which would be admissible for twelfth dynasty. The etymology of Potiphar was probably Pḏty pri was
probably "A Bowman Champion" 𓊪𓂧𓏏𓏭𓊪𓂋𓇌 .

11. R. K. Harrison suggests that this meant, "Pay heed!" (Old Testament Times [Grand Rapids: Zondervan, 1957]), p. 96.

12. These examples have been carefully selected so as to avoid two common pitfalls into which some
writers have fallen in their discussion of Egyptian loanwords in the Torah. First, they have inadvertently
slipped in legitimate loanwords from Egyptian, but which do not occur in surviving Egyptian documents until the post-Mosaic books of the Old Testament. Secondly, they have included words from
Egyptian which were actually borrowed by Egyptian from Semitic dialects (mostly during the Hyksos
period or thereafter). Furthermore they have cited words possessed in common by Egyptian and
Hebrew, but which came in both languages from prehistoric times and involved no borrowing from

the portion of the Pentateuch which deals with Joseph and Moses in Egypt is Abraham S. Yahuda's *Language of the Pentateuch in Its Relationship to Egyptian.* Not confining himself to mere loanwords, Yahuda discusses a large number of idioms and turns of speech which are characteristically Egyptian in origin, even though translated into Hebrew. Thus in the strange expression of Gen. 41:40 which the KJV renders, "According unto thy word shall all my people be ruled," but which literally says, "According to thy utterance all my people shall kiss" (*nāšaq,* Hebrew)—Yahuda finds a clarification in the Egyptian use of *sn* ("to kiss") which is used before "food" to indicate eating the food. The titles of the court officials, the polite language used in the interviews with Pharaoh, and the like, are all shown to be true to Egyptian usage.[13]

Another writer, Garrow Duncan, devotes several pages to a demonstration of the minute accuracy and authentic local coloring of the author of the Torah. He remarks, "Thus we cannot but admit that the writer of these two narratives [i.e., of Joseph and of the Exodus]...was thoroughly well acquainted with the Egyptian language, customs, belief, court life, etiquette and officialdom; and not only so, but the readers must have been just as familiar with things Egyptian."[14]

Some eminent Egyptologists of Wellhausian persuasion have appealed to Egyptian evidence to prove a late date for the Hebrew narrative. For example, Georg Steindorff (*Aufenthalt Israels,* p. 15) has argued that a more contemporary author would

either direction (e.g., such a word as Egyptian *ḥsb*—"reckon", Hebrew *ḥāšaḇ*—"reckon, think," and which exists in Arabic, Ethiopic, and Aramaic as well). A fairly complete listing of all Hebrew words having an Egyptian relationship in any of these abovementioned categories may be found in Erman and Grapow's *Wörterbuch der Aegyptischen Sprache,* 6:243-44.

13. Yahuda, *The Language of the Pentateuch* (New York: Oxford, 1933). It should be added that Yahuda, while very well versed in both Hebrew and Egyptian, leaves himself open to criticism in the matter of methodology. All too often he is content to point to a resemblance between Egyptian usage and that of Moses, without going on to clinch his case by showing that this usage occurs most characteristically in the Pentateuch rather than in post-Mosaic books of the Old Testament, and that it does not occur in cognate Semitic languages. Thus, he adduces the Hebrew *lipnē Par'ōh* ("in the presence of Pharaoh") as a translation of Egyptian *m ḥr ḥm.f* ("in the presence of his majesty"); but he does not deal with the somewhat similar idiom in Aramaic *(qᵉdom malkā* — "in the presence of the king"). It is true, however, that only Hebrew and Egyptian use the word *face* (Hebrew *Pānim,* Egyptian *ḥr*) in expressing this idiom. Again, he refers (p. 21) to the king's entrusting his signet to Joseph as his vizier; but he does not go on to prove (as he really should) that this was never done by sovereigns in other ancient countries as well. Moreover, some of his Egyptian etymologies require a little more proof than he gives, e.g., that *'ḥ;w* ("time") really was derived from *'ḥ'* ("to stand") —hence "the standing," meaning the term of life. This he connects with the Hebrew *he'mîd* "cause to stand" or ("to raise up"), which is used with reference to Pharaoh in Exodus 9:16. The logical connection of all this is a bit tenuous, to say the least. Yet in general it should be recognized that an ample number of pertinent examples are included in Yahuda's discussion to establish his thesis: "A close intimacy between Hebrews and Egyptians prevailed in no other period than that of Israel's sojourn in Egypt; it is only in the Egyptian epoch of Israel that Hebrew would gradually have begun to develop into a literary language, until it reached the perfection which we encounter in the Pentateuch" (p. xxxii).

14. J. Garrow Duncan, *New Light on Hebrew Origins* [London: Macmillan, 1936], p. 176. (See also pp. 73-179). Duncan's lectures were delivered at Glasgow University. Nevertheless, he is to be regarded as a well-read student rather than as an independent scholar. He leaned quite heavily upon Yahuda in this book, for he apparently lacked Yahuda's thorough training in Egyptian. Some of Duncan's sources were antiquated, it would seem, for he refers (p. 107) to the common title *;my-r* ("overseer") as *mer* (a pronunciation largely abandoned by 1910). However, his argument is in the main well supported and he certainly advocates a Mosaic date with cumulative evidence which is impossible to explain away.

surely have known and mentioned the names of these various Egyptian kings. But Yahuda furnishes a plausible explanation for the fact that the Hebrew records do not mention the names of the Pharaohs until the time of Solomon and thereafter.[15] While the Israelites resided in Egypt, they simply followed the usual custom of New Kingdom Egyptian official language by referring to the king simply as *pr-';* ("Pharaoh,—Great House") while refraining from mentioning his personal name in proximity to that particular title (however often they may have mentioned it in connection with other royal titles). Hence instead of being an evidence of lateness, this conformity to Eighteenth Dynasty Egyptian usage turns out to be strong evidence of an authentic Mosaic date of composition.

ROSETTA STONE

THE ROSETTA STONE WAS DISCOVERED NEAR THE VILLAGE OF ROSETTA, EGYPT IN 1779. WRITTEN ABOUT 200 B.C., ITS TRI–LINGUAL INSCRIPTION (HIEROGLYPHICS, DEMOTIC EGYPTIAN, GREEK) MADE POSSIBLE THE DECIPHERMENT OF EGYPTIAN HIEROGLYPHICS. JEAN CHAMPOLLIAN BEGAN ITS TRANSLATION IN 1822. (COURTESY OF THE BRITISH MUSEUM)

On the other hand, it should be noted that in the later period, for example in the tenth century, the name of the king of Egypt is given in the Old Testament without the title of Pharaoh preceding it—still conforming to Egyptian usage. An example is the reference to Shishak (Sheshonq, in Egyptian) in 1 Kings 11:40. Not until the late seventh century and early sixth century does the Hebrew historiographer depart from correct Egyptian usage enough to append to the title Pharaoh the actual name of the king (e.g., Pharaoh-Neco in 2 Kings 23:29 and Pharaoh-Hophra in Jer. 44:30).

3. The author of the Torah shows a consistently foreign or extra-Palestinian viewpoint so far as Canaan is concerned. The seasons and the weather referred to in the narrative are Egyptian, not Palestinian. (Cf. the reference to crop sequence in connection with the plague of hail, Ex. 9:31-32. Delitzsch states that this information pinpointed the incident as occurring late in January or early in February.)[16]

The flora and fauna referred to are Egyptian or Sinaitic, never distinctively Palestinian. Thus, the shittim or acacia tree is indigenous to Egypt and the Sinai Peninsula, but not to Palestine (except on the lower shore of the Dead Sea);[17] it is a distinctive

15. Yahuda, p. 48.

16. Keil and Delitzsch, *Biblical Commentary on the Old Testament*, vol. 1, *The Pentateuch* (Grant Rapids: Eerdmans, l963), pp. 492-93

17. E. W. G. Masterman, "Plant Zones in the Holy Land," ISBE, p. 508*b.*

desert tree. Out of this material the wood for the tabernacle furniture was to be made. The skins to be used as the outer covering of the tabernacle were to be skins (Ex. 25:5; 36:19), the *taḥash* being a dugong which is found in seas adjacent to Egypt and Sinai but foreign to Palestine.[18] The lists of clean and unclean birds and animals contained in Lev. 11 and Deut. 14 include some which are peculiar to Sinai (such as the pygarg or *dishōn* of Deut. 14:5 and the ostrich of Lev. 11:16), but none of which are peculiar to Canaan. The wild ox or antelope (*te'ō*, Hebrew) of Deut. 14:5 is a native of Upper Egypt and Arabia but not of Palestine. (Yet it has been reported in Syria, according to *The Westminster Dictionary of the Bible*, p. 30a.) In this connection the coney, hyrax, or rock badger (*shāphān*, Hebrew) of Lev. 11:5 has often been cited as peculiar to Sinai and Arabia. This is, however, disputed by H. B. Tristram, who claims to have found them as far north as North Galilee and Phoenicia.[19] In all these specific instances, of course, it should be remembered that the distribution of animals tends to become restricted in the course of time. Thus, lions were fairly abundant in the Near East in ancient times, but are in the present day restricted to India and Africa (although a few lions have been spotted in the Palestinian Ghor). Bears were also dangerous predators in O.T. times (cf. 1 Sam. 17:34; 2 Kings 2:24; Amos 5:19).

Both Egypt and Sinai are very familiar to the author from the standpoint of geography. The narrative of the Exodus route is filled with authentic local references which have been verified by modern archaeology. But the geography of Palestine is comparatively unknown except by patriarchal tradition (in the Genesis narratives). Even in Gen. 13, when the author wishes to convey to his audience some notion of the lush verdure of the Jordan plain, he compares it to "the land of Egypt as thou goest unto Zoar" (v. 10), referring to a locality near Mendes, midway between Busiris and Tanis in the Delta. (Cf. Budge, *Egyptian Dictionary*, 2:1058, which refers to it as a fortress in the Delta, a district near Mendes.) Obviously the audience for which Genesis was written knew what it was like in Egypt but were unfamiliar with the appearance of the Jordan Valley. Similar is the reference to Shalem (ASV marg.), "a city of Shechem, which is in the land of Canaan" (Gen. 33:18)—a type of reference impossible to explain if the writer had lived in a post-exilic generation, after Israel had already been settled in the land of Canaan for nine centuries or more with Shechem as one of the most prominent cities north of Jerusalem. After Joshua's conquest of Canaan, what Hebrew reader would have to be told that Shechem was in the land of Canaan? In general, the author of the Pentateuch seems to regard Palestine as a new, comparatively unknown territory into which the Israelites are going to enter at a future time.

4. The atmosphere of Exodus through Numbers is unmistakably that of the

---

18. See Joseph P. Free, ABH, p. 106. The *taḥash* has been also identified as a porpoise or dolphin (Koehler-Baumg. Lexicon, p. 1026a). See also G. S. Cansdale, *Animals of Bible Lands* (Paternoster, 1970), pp. 138-39. The *dishōn*—*Addax nasomaculatus*, a desert antelope midway between oryx and hartebeest with horns 36 inches long; Wildox—Desert Oryx, ibid, pp. 84-85; Coney—Hyrax, ibid, p. 130.

19. Cf. Tristram's *Natural History of the Bible* (London: SPCK, 1867), p. 77.

THE WILDERNESS OF ZIN, IN THE SOUTHERN SECTION OF THE SINAI PENINSULA, IS WHERE THE ISRAELITES SPENT MOST OF THE 38 YEARS IN THEIR WILDERNESS WANDERINGS.

desert, not of an agricultural people settled in their ancestral possessions for nearly a thousand years (as Wellhausen supposed). The tremendous emphasis upon a tabernacle or large tent as the place of worship is altogether out of place for authors living centuries after the cedar-timbered temple of Solomon had been built (a temple which differed from the appointments of the tabernacle in several important details). But it would be altogether relevant for a nomadic people constantly on the march through the desert. The materials of which it was to be made are most carefully specified over a large number of chapters. Its central location in the midst of the encampment and the exact location of the twelve tribes on the four sides of it (Num. 2:1-31) have a perfect appropriateness to the generation of Moses, but none whatsoever to any later generation. The references to the desert crop up everywhere. For example, the scapegoat is to be sent off into the desert (Lev. 16:10). Sanitary instructions are given for desert life (Deut. 23:12-13). The exact order of march is specified in Num. 10:14-20 in a way that would have significance only while the entire population of Israel was concentrated into one large group and was in a process of migration.

5. Particularly in the book of Genesis there are references to archaic customs which are demonstrable for the second millennium B.C., but which did not continue during the first millennium. Notably in the legal documents discovered at Nuzi and dating from the fifteenth century, we discover references to the custom of begetting legitimate children by handmaidens (as Abraham did with Hagar); to the validity of

an oral, deathbed will (like Isaac's to Jacob); to the importance of the possession of the family teraphim for the claiming of inheritance rights (which gives point to Rachel's theft of Laban's teraphim in Gen. 31). From other sources comes confirmation of the historical accuracy of the transaction in Gen. 23 whereby Abraham purchased the cave of Machpelah.[20]

6. There are significant archaisms in language, as well. For example, the word for the pronoun "she" is frequently spelled *HW'* instead of the regular *HY'*. There are only three occurences of this spelling *h-w* ; for *h-y-'* in the rest of the O.T. (1 Kings 17:15, Isa. 30:31, Job 31:11). We also meet with *N'R* instead of the feminine form *N'RH* for "young girl." Occasionally (i.e., twice in Genesis) *HLZH* (*hallāzeh*) appears for the demonstrative "that" instead of *hallāz*, the form used in Judges, Samuel, and thereafter. The verb for "laugh" is spelled *ŚḤQ* (in Genesis and Exodus) instead of *ŚḤQ*; "lamb" is *KŚB* instead of the later *KBŚ* (*kebeś*). By some scholars it has been argued that there is too little difference between the Hebrew of the Torah and that of eighth-century authors like Amos, to allow for the passage of over five centuries. Two factors must be borne in mind here.

First, the possible changes in pronunciation and form are greatly obscured by the unvoweled, consonantal alphabet in which the Old Testament was preserved until Masoretic times. After all, even Old English would not look so very different from Elizabethan English if both were written in consonants only! Second, the central importance of the Torah in the education of post-Mosaic youth must have exerted as decisive an influence upon the Hebrew they used as the Qur'an has had upon thirteen centuries of literary Arabic (which even today is still the same language essentially as that of Muhammed in A.D. 620). In both cases the ancient document was taken as a unique divine revelation and an all-comprehensive constitution upon which the entire culture was built. Such a situation makes for extreme conservatism in the development of the literary language.

As for the objection that the Mosiac period was too early for the use of the definite article *ha-* (since other Semitic languages did not develop a word for "the" as early as that), this is easily explained from Israel's exposure to Egyptian influence. It was precisely during the Eighteenth Dynasty in Egypt that the definite article (*p;, t;, n;*) began to make its appearance even in literary texts, although sporadic occurrences appear even in Twelfth Dynasty texts such as the *Eloquent Peasant*.[21] Undoubtedly this reflected the customary usage in colloquial Egyptian during the age of Moses, and the Hebrews could hardly fail to have felt the need for a similar article in their own language. It is therefore not surprising to find full-fledged use of the article in the prose sections of the Torah (although the poetic passages used it very sparingly indeed—as was true of later Hebrew poetry).

All these features (1-6) are easily reconcilable with Mosaic authorship; they are virtually impossible to harmonize with the Wellhausen theory of stage-by-stage com-

---

20. See chap. 13, p. 180.
21. See A. H. Gardiner's *Egyptian Grammar* (New York: Oxford, 1927), par. 112.

position from the ninth to the fifth centuries. The laws of evidence would seem to demand a rejection of the Documentary Hypothesis as clearly inadequate to account for the actual data of the Pentateuchal text.

7. There is a most remarkable unity of arrangement which underlies the entire Pentateuch and links it together into a progressive whole, even though successive stages in revelation (during Moses' writing career of four decades) result in a certain amount of overlapping and restatement. By implication even the Documentarians are forced to concede this unity by resorting to a hypothetical redactor to explain the orderliness and harmony of arrangement evident in the final form of the Torah as it has come down to us.[22]

MOSES' QUALIFICATIONS

From all that has been recorded concerning Moses himself, it is evident that he had every qualification to be the author of just such a work as the Pentateuch. He had the education and background for authorship, since he received from his ancestors that wealth of oral law which originated from the Mesopotamian cultures back in the time of Abraham (hence the remarkable resemblances to the eighteenth century *Code of Hammurabi*), and from his tutors in the Egyptian court he received training in those branches of learning in which Eighteenth Dynasty Egypt excelled the rest of the ancient world. From his forebears he would naturally have received an accurate oral tradition of the career of the patriarchs and those revelations which God had vouchsafed to them. He would have a personal knowledge of the climate, agriculture, and geography of Egypt and the Sinai Peninsula such as the author of the Pentateuch so patently displays. He would have had every incentive to compose this monumental work, since he was the founding father of the commonwealth of Israel, and it was upon these moral and religious foundations that his nation was to fulfill its destiny. He certainly had plenty of time and leisure during the slow, tiresome forty years of wandering in the Sinai desert to compose a book several times the size of the Torah. Moreover, he had just come from a culture in which the art of writing was so widely cultivated that even the toilet articles employed by the women in the household contained an appropriate inscription. Writing in both hieroglyphic and hieratic characters was so widely prevalent in the Egypt of Moses' day that it seems absolutely incredible that he would have committed none of his records to writing (as even the twentieth-century critics contend), when he had the grandest and most significant matters to record which are to be found in all of human literature. At a time when

22. A typical concession as to the remarkable unity of the Pentateuchal legislation is found in these words of Eduard Riehm: "Most of the laws of the middle books of the Pentateuch form essentially a homogeneous whole. They do not indeed all come from one hand, and have not been written at one and the same time....However, they are all ruled by the same principles and ideas, have the same setting, the like form of representation, and the same mode of expression. A multitude of definite terms appear again and again. In manifold ways also the laws refer to one another. Apart from isolated subordinate differences, they agree with one another, and so supplement each other as to give the impression of a single whole, worked out with a marvelous consistency in its details" (*Einleitung in das Alte Testament*), 1:202.

even the unschooled Semitic slaves employed at the Egyptian turquoise mines in Serabit el-Khadim were incising their records on the walls of their tunnels, it is quite unreasonable to suppose that a leader of Moses' background and education was too illiterate to commit a single word to writing. Thus it turns out that the modern theories which reject Mosaic authorship put more of a strain upon human credulity than can reasonably be borne.

9 VARIATIONS AND DOUBLETS AS CRITERIA FOR SOURCE DIVISION

THE VARIATION BETWEEN YAHWEH AND ELOHIM

AS WE HAVE ALREADY SEEN in our review of the history of the Documentary Hypothesis (chap. 6), the basic criterion for source division followed by the pioneers of this critical school was the occurrence of "Jehovah" (*Yahweh*) and "God" (*Elohim*) as favorite or preferred names for God in Genesis. The argument was that the prevalence of Elohim in Gen. 1 marked it as originating from an author (E or P) who referred to God only by that term, and never employed any other title than this. Correspondingly the preponderance of Yahweh in Gen. 2 marked it as coming from a different author (J), who knew God only as Yahweh. It is necessary for us to examine the credibility of this diverse Source Theory as an adequate explanation for the distribution of these divine titles in Genesis and the rest of the Torah.

From the standpoint of comparative religions, it is doubtful whether the religious literature of any of Israel's pagan neighbors ever referred to a paramount god by a single name. In Babylonia, the Sumerian counterparts were alternated with the Akkadian names: Bel was also Enlil and Nunamnir (*Prologue of Lipit-Ishtar Code*); Anum was Ilum, Sin was Nanna, Ea was Enki, Utu was Shamash, and Ishtar was Inanna or Telitum (cf. *Prologue to Hammurabi's Code*). At Ugarit, Baal was also called Aliyan,[1] El was Latpan, and Kothar-wa-Khasis ("the artificer god") was Hayyin (cf. Aqhat, ANET, p. 151). In Egypt, Osiris (the judge of the dead and lord of the netherworld) was also Wennefer, Neb-Abḏu, and Khentamentiu (cf. the Ikhernofret Stela in the Berlin Museum);[2] his son Horus was also Re-Harakhti, and so on throughout the Egyptian pantheon. In Greece, the king-god Zeus was known also as Kroniōn and Olympios, Athena was Pallas, Apollo was Phoebus and Pythius—titles which appear in paral-

---

1. Note also that in the Hadad Tablet from Ugarit, Baal is used interchangeably with Hadad, (G. R. Driver, *Canaanite Myths and Legends*, pp. 70-72).
2. Cf. ANET[3], pp. 329-30; Ikhernofret was a treasury official under Senwosret III in Dynasty XII, (ca. 1950 B.C.)

lelism in Homer's epics without requiring any theory of diverse sources. At the time of Astruc and Eichhorn, of course, the Semitic and Egyptian data were virtually unknown; otherwise it is impossible that any theory of source division based on divine names could ever have arisen. But now that these facts are well known in the twentieth century, it is hard to see how anyone can take seriously the terms *Yahwist* or *Elohist* any longer. In connection with the Ebla tablets (BA 5/76, p. 48), Pettinato points out that previous to the reign of King Ebrium (ca. 2330 B.C.), we meet names like Mi-ka-il and En-na-il. From his time on, they appear as Mi-ka-ya and En-na-ya. He remarks, "This amply demonstrates that at Ebla at least *'Ya'* had the same value as *'Il'* and points to a specific deity." (C. Wilson, *Secrets of a Forgotten City*, p. 111.)

A most impressive parallel to the irregular distribution of the two divine names in the Torah is furnished by the sacred scriptures of the Muslims, the Koran. No one can question the unity of authorship of the Koran, and yet we meet with a similar phenomenon in this Arabic text. The name *Allahu* corresponds to *Elōhîm*, and *Rabbu* ("lord") is equivalent to the *Adonay* (Lord) which the later Jews used in referring to Yahweh. In some suras (chapters) of the Koran, we find the two terms intermingled, but in others only the one or the other appears. For example, in the following suras the name Rabbu never occurs: 4, 9, 24, 33, 48, 49, 57, 58, 59, 61, 62, 63, 64, 86, 88, 95, 101, 102, 103, 104, 107, 109, 111, 112. On the other hand, the following suras never use the name Allahu: 15, 32, 54, 55, 56, 68, 75, 78, 83, 87, 89, 92, 93, 94, 99, 100, 105, 106, 108, 113, 114. Here we have indisputable evidence that ancient Semitic literature was capable of selective use of divine names even though composed by the same author.

One remarkable feature of the Wellhausian source division is the occasional appearance of the wrong name in the "Jehovistic" and "Elohistic" portions of the Pentateuch. Early in the development of this multiple-document theory, an effort was made to bolster the case for diversity of authorship by drawing up lists of near synonyms which were supposed to occur only in the one "source" or the other. (For example, of the two words for "female slave," *šiphḥâ* was assigned exclusively to J and *'āmah* to E,[3] in Gen. 33, Driver assigned the passage to J because of its use of *šiphâ*, even though *Elōhîm* appears throughout. Likewise the name *Sinai* was assigned to J and P, the name *Horeb* was reserved for E and D.)

Despite the effort to keep these "characteristic words" and their appropriate divine names in their separate watertight compartments, occasional leaks have

---

3. In regard to this assignment of *'amah* to E and *šiphâ* to J, it should be noted that Gen. 20, the first considerable portion of E appearing in Genesis, uses *šiphâ* in verse 14 (the alleged J word), and *ʾamâ* in verse 17. In order to salvage the situation, critics like Holzinger in his commentary on Genesis are constrained to delete *šiphâ* from verse 14 on the ground that "E does not use the word." (Cf. G. C. Aalders, SIP, p. 39.) He does the same thing to *šiphâ* in Gen. 30:18, another E passage, with the assertion, "This word in the text of E cannot be original." Here we have a striking example of circular reasoning. Because this word occurs in J passages it must have been used only by J—but wherever it was used in E sections it must be a J insertion, or a blunder by a later redactor. By this methodology one can prove anything one likes, so far as vocabulary is concerned. But it should hardly masquerade as a scientific handling of the textual evidence.

occurred, so to speak. Thus we discover that Elohim occurs in such passages as Gen. 3:1-5 (where the serpent thus refers to God); Gen. 16:13 (where Hagar calls the name of Jehovah: "Thou art an *El* that sees"); Gen. 32:28-29 (Jacob at Peniel is said to have striven with Elohim—a very anthropomorphic motif—and received the name *Yisra-El*, or Israel). On the other hand, Yahweh occurs in such E passages as Gen. 22:11 (where the angel of Jehovah restrains Abraham from plunging the knife into Isaac) and verse 14 (where Abraham calls the place "Jehovah-jireh"); Gen. 28:17-22 (where Jacob makes a vow, saying, "Jehovah will be my God"). Yahweh also occurs in such passages as Gen. 7:16; 14:22; and 17:1. Despite all the vigilance of the Source Critics with their scissors and paste, a few slips like these have occurred, even though the general practice was to slice a verse in two where the compound name Yahweh-Elohîm occurs (e.g., Gen. 2:4; where 4*a* is assigned to P and 4*b* to J), rather than allow the "wrong" name to appear and thus embarrass the theory. (Yahweh-Elohîm occurs eleven times in Gen. 2: Yahweh never stands alone!)

It has already been pointed out[4] that serious objection was raised against using the names as a criterion for source division on the ground of the numerous discrepancies which occur between the name appearing in the MT and that employed in the corresponding LXX translation. This threw doubt upon the soundness of any process of separation which depended so completely upon the infallibility of the MT in the transmission of Yahweh and Elohim, when inaccuracy was charged against it by those same critics in practically all the rest of the Torah. The actual data of the Hebrew documents themselves do not well sustain the old Astruc theory that a different name necessarily indicates a different author.

What explanation does account for the distribution of Yahweh and Elohim throughout the Torah? A careful study of the etymology and usage of the two names indicates that the name chosen depended upon the context of the situation. Elohim (which is apparently derived from a root meaning "powerful, strong, or foremost") is used to refer to God as the Almighty Creator of the universe and Lord over nature and mankind in general. Hence only Elohim is appropriate in Gen. 1, since the subject dealt with there is creation. Yahweh, on the other hand, is the covenant name of God, which is reserved for situations in which some covenant engagement of God is involved. Thus in Gen. 2 this name is very frequently used, because the subject matter is God's gracious dealing with Adam and Eve under the covenant of works. In Gen. 3 it is the serpent, as the agent or embodiment of Satan, who stands in no covenant relationship with God, and hence refers to Him as Elohim—an example which Eve also follows as long as she is talking with the serpent. But it is *Jehovah* God who calls out to Adam (3:9) and reproves Eve (3:13), and who also, as covenant-keeping God of the repentant couple, lays a curse upon the serpent (3:14).

This distinction between the two names of God was clearly perceived and defined by Rabbi Jehuda Hallevi as long ago as the twelfth century A.D., when he defined Elo-

---

4. See chap. 7, p. 100.

him as the divine name in general, whereas *Adonay* (or Yahweh) specified the God of
revelation and covenant. Even Kuenen felt constrained to concede: "The original distinction between Jahweh and Elohim very often accounts for the use of one of these
appellations in preference to the other."[5] A little later he comments: "The history of
critical investigation has shown that far too much weight has often been laid on
agreement in the use of the divine names....It is well, therefore, to utter a warning
against laying an exaggerated stress on this one phenomenon."[6] An admission like
this would seem to indicate qualms as to the validity of the most fundamental of all
the criteria for source division, even on the part of a principal architect of the Documentary Hypothesis.

Although the Documentarians belong to a school of thought that scornfully
rejects any attempt to establish Christian doctrines by proof texts, they have occasionally become stalwart champions of the proof text method themselves; that is,
insisting on a literal interpretation of the words of a single verse or two quite irrespec-
tive of context or of the analogy of scriptural teaching elsewhere. In no instance is
this more striking than in their treatment of Exodus 6:2-3: "I am Yahweh: and I
appeared unto Abraham, unto Isaac, and unto Jacob, as El Shaddai; but by my name
Yahweh I was not known (*lônôda'tî*) to them." This is pressed to mean that according
to this author (E), the name *Jehovah* was first revealed to Moses. (J, however, did not
know about this later tradition and mistakenly assumed that *Jehovah* was appropriate
for the pre-Mosaic narrative as well.) But this in point of fact involves a very superficial analysis of the Hebrew verb *to know* (*yāda'*), and of the implications in Hebrew of
knowing a person's *name*. That it could not be meant in a baldly literal sense is shown
by the absurdity of supposing that the entire ten plagues were necessary to convince
the Egyptians (Ex.14:4: "And the Egyptians shall know that I am Jehovah") that the
God of the Hebrews was named Yahweh. Obviously both in Ex. 6:7, "Ye shall know
that I am Jehovah your God, who bringeth you out from under the burdens of the
Egyptians," and in 14:4 the implication is that they shall witness God's covenant
faithfulness in delivering His people and destroying or punishing their foes.[7] They
will thus come to know Him by experience as Jehovah, the covenant God. The
expression "to know that I am Jehovah" occurs at least twenty-six times in the Old
Testament, and in every instance it conveys this same idea. Hebrew usage therefore
indicates clearly enough that Ex. 6:3 teaches that God, who in earlier generations had
revealed Himself as El Shaddai (God Almighty) by deeds of power and mercy, would
now in Moses' generation reveal Himself as the covenant-keeping Jehovah by His
marvelous deliverance of the whole nation of Israel. As Orr points out, the "name"
(*shēm*, Hebrew) denotes the revelation side of God's being.[8]

5. Abraham Kuenen, *Hexateuch* (1886), p. 56.
6. Ibid, p. 61.
7. Cf. also Exodus 10:2, "I made a mockery of the Egyptians, and how I performed My signs among
them; that you may know that I am YHWH."
8. James Orr, POT, p. 225. At this point a word should be said about the etymological significance of

It is quite significant that in recent years even some of the leading Liberal scholars in Europe have surrendered the traditional Wellhausian exegesis of Exodus 6:3. Thus Ivan Engnell says, "The different divine names have different ideological associations and therewith different import. Thus, Yahweh is readily used when it is a question of Israel's national God, indicated as such over against foreign gods, and where the history of the patriarchs is concerned, while on the other hand Elohim, 'God,' gives more expression to a 'theological' and abstract-cosmic picture of God in larger and more moving contexts....So then, it is the traditionist, *the same* traditionist, who varies in the use of the divine names, not the 'documents'."[9] So also Sigmund Mowinckel: "It is not E's view that Yahweh is here revealing a hitherto unknown name to Moses. Yahweh is not telling his name to one who does not know it. Moses asks for some 'control' evidence that his countrymen may know, when he returns to them, that it is really the God of their fathers that has sent him...the whole conversation presupposes that the Israelites knew the name already.[10]

OTHER VARIATIONS IN DICTION AND STYLE

It has already been suggested that from the earliest days of the Documentary Hypothesis, in the time of Astruc and Eichhorn, an effort was made to bolster the theory of separate sources by drawing up lists of distinctive words which were alleged to

the name *Yahweh*. It is usually inferred from Ex. 3:14 that it meant, "He is." "I am that I am" is the Hebrew *'ehyeh 'ᵃšêr 'ehyeh*, which comes from the verb *hayah* ("to become or be"). From the Aramaic equivalent, *hᵃwa'*, we may infer that the Hebrew verb was originally pronounced *hawah*. Therefore in Moses' day *'ehyeh* may have been pronounced *'ᵃhweh*. If Moses, then, went down to Egypt and declared of God "He is" (rather than adhering to the first person "I am") he would have said *Yahweh*. But if *Yahweh* means "He is," are we to understand this as an affirmation of God's eternal existence? (So even Orr interprets it: "The Self-Existent One"; the French version construes it as *l'Éternel*.)

There are two objections to this: the verb *hayah* never expresses mere ontological existence but rather the notion of "happen, become, enter into a new condition or state or relationship"; and the name *Yahweh* is never used in contexts which affirm God's eternal existence as such, but rather (as we have seen) in a convenantal context. This accords perfectly with the characteristic affirmation of the covenant: "I shall be—*'ehyeh*—their God and they shall be—*yihyū*—my people." Thus in Ex. 6:7: "I *will be* to you a God; and ye shall know that I am Jehovah"; i.e., He is (the covenant God of His covenant people).

Other suggestions have been made, however, which deny the interpretation "He is" in either sense. W. F. Albright (SAC, p. 16) and D. N. Freedman (in JBL 2:79 [1960]: 151-56) construe Yahweh as a *hiphil* form, *yahyeh*: "He causes to be." This they derive from the phrase *Yahweh Sabaoth* ("Lord of Hosts," KJV), which they understand to have meant originally: "He causes hosts to come into existence." This would accord better with the *a*-vowel in *Yahweh* than would the above-mentioned explanation, "He is" (which theoretically ought to have been *yihweh* rather than *yahweh*). But a well-nigh fatal objection to this interpretation is found in the fact that *Yahweh* is never actually used in the Old Testament to emphasize God's role as Creator, but rather as God of the covenant. Moreover, this particular verb never occurs in the *hiphil* anywhere in the Old Testament.

Still others have denied any connection at all with the verb to be (*hāyāh*), feeling that it would hardly have existed in an earlier form, *hāwah*. Theophile J. Meek of Toronto (*Hebrew Origins* [New York: Harper & Row, 1960], p. 116) insists that it comes from a verb existing in Arabic as *hawâ* ("to blow".) Therefore "He blows" would be the name of a storm-god of the Sinai desert. This of course imputes a polytheistic origin to Israel's religion, and utterly fails to account for the covenantal frame of reference exhibited by the name *Yahweh* as actually used in the Old Testament.

9. Engnell, quoted in OTMS, p. 66.

10. Mowinckel, quoted in OTMS, p. 54.

have been used only by J or E, as the case might be, and not only by the other source. Examples have been given earlier in this chapter; for instance, the synonyms for "female slave" (*šiphâ* and *'āmâ*, assigned to J and E respectively) and the variant geographical terms Horeb (E or D) and Sinai (J or P). Yet these lists seem to have been made out by very dubious, question-begging methods which tend to vitiate the whole procedure. These methods are as follows.[11]

1. The various types of subject matter have been strictly segregated and parceled out to the various "sources" on a compartmentalized basis. Thus, vivid biographical narrative has all been assigned to J, etiological legends are usually attributed to E, and statistics or genealogical lists or ritual prescriptions to P. Naturally each type of subject matter tends toward a specialized vocabulary, and this would account for the preference for certain words or idioms in one genre as over against another. The style and vocabulary employed in a newspaper editorial are apt to differ quite markedly from those of a sports write-up, even though the same author may have composed them both. One could draw up similar lists of specialized terms appearing in Milton's essay *Areopagitica* as over against his tractate on divorce; yet they were both by the same author.

2. In selecting characteristic words for each list, the critics have been forced to resort to interpolations in order to explain the occurrence of a P word in a J passage, or a J word in an E passage. It is necessary, for example, to assign to P all of the occurrences of "and Aaron" in Ex. 8, even the J passages such as verses 1-4 and 8-15. This is because of the critical dogma that Aaron was an unhistorical personage not invented until the time of the composition of the Priestly Code. Similarly, when Padan-aram (a P name) occurs in Gen. 31:18 (an E section) the second half of verse 18 is awarded to P, leaving the rest of verses 4-45 to E (thus salvaging the dictum that Padan-aram occurs only in P, as over against the name Aram-naharaim, which is employed by J, E and D). But this is just a question-begging procedure. The initial contention was that the Hebrew text itself could only be accounted for by diverse sources using specialized vocabulary; but wherever the Hebrew text embarrasses the theory by coming up with the "wrong" word, that offending word must straightway be dealt with as an interpolation from another "source." By such methods as these, it would be possible to take any literary composition ever written and divide it up into diverse sources, explaining away all inconvenient discrepancies as mere interpolations.

The Documentarians have also assumed without proof that ancient Hebrew authors were incapable of variety in their modes of expression; variety in the biblical text can only be explained by diversity of authorship. Yet it is well known that in the literature of other nations, the accomplished writer was very apt to employ variety of phrase in order to avoid monotony. This is particularly apparent in parallelistic poetry, such as Gen. 30:23-24: "And she conceived, and bore a son: and said, 'Elohim has

---

11. See K. A. Kitchen, AOOT, p. 124, which lists five different Egyptian words for "boat" in the Kamose Stela, and two words for "envoy" in an inscription of Ashurbanipal.

taken away my reproach';[12] and she called his name Joseph (*yôsēph*), saying, 'May Jehovah add (*yôsēph*) to me another son.' "While this statement of Rachel's is not poetry in the technical sense, it partakes of the parallelistic flavor of poetic style. It is obvious from the wordplay—*yôsēph, yôsēph*—that this verse is a single unit. Yet because of the artificial criterion followed by Wellhausians, they feel constrained to parcel out the first clause to E and the second to J.

A similar example is in Gen. 21:1–2: (*a*) "And Jehovah visited Sarah as He had said," (*b*) and "Jehovah did to Sarah as He had spoken." (*c*) "And Sarah conceived, and bore Abraham a son in his old age," (*d*) "at the set time of which Elohim had spoken to him." Under the constraint of their theory, the critics have assigned (*a*) and (*c*) to J, and (*b*) and (*d*) to P. Yet the fact that even (*b*) contains Jehovah occasions them considerable embarrassment, since a P passage prior to Exodus 6:3 should read "Elohim." (The LXX here reads *Kyrios*, or the equivalent of Jehovah, in all three instances!)

It should also be recognized that variety may be used by a single author for the sake of emphasis or vividness. For example, in the Exodus account of Pharaoh's refusal to release the Israelite population, three different verbs are used to refer to his obstinacy in the face of the ten plagues: *ḥāzaq* ("become strong or bold") or *ḥizzēq* ("to make strong or bold"), *hiqšâ* ("make hard"), and *hikbîd* ("make heavy or insensible"). The critics assign the first to P and E, the second to P alone, and the third to J. But actually these are used with a fine discrimination by the Hebrew author to describe the progressive hardening of the king's heart, first as a result of his own willful refusal, and then as a result of God's judicial blinding of His stubborn foe. Thus in Ex. 7:13 (a P verse), we read that Pharaoh's heart "became bold" (*ḥāzaq*); the next verse, 14, quotes Jehovah as remarking on the new condition of Pharaoh's heart as being "heavy" or "stubborn" (*kābēd*), which is a very natural sequence psychologically. This alternation between *ḥāzaq* and *hikbîd* (Pharaoh's voluntary response and God's judicial hardening of his heart) continues throughout the narrative (Ex. 7-9) according to a deliberate plan on the part of the author. Critics have completely overlooked this in their artificial parceling up between P and J.

In other cases the variety of phrasing may be employed to emphasize or amplify some statement of particular importance. Thus, in the death notices of women such as Deborah, Rebekah's nurse (Gen. 35:8), or Rachel (35:19), it is described in simple terms: "She died and was buried." But in the case of the patriarchs, such as Abraham (Gen. 25:8), Isaac (35:29), and Jacob (49:33), the formula is more solemn and elaborate: "He gave up the ghost (*gāwa'*) and died, and was gathered to his people, and his sons buried him." Yet the Documentarians, ignoring this obvious distinction, assign the obituaries of the women to E and the patriarchal obituaries to P, after a mechanical and artificial type of dissection. On the other hand, they leave many other passages undisturbed, even though they show precisely similar variety in the wording;

---

12. That is to say, the imperfect *qal* of *'āsaph*, ("to take away") is *yō'sēph*, which sounded the same as the jussive *hiphil* of *yāsaph*, ("to add"). This would certainly have been regarded as a word play by a Hebrew listener, even though it was actually the perfect *qal* of *'āsaph* which occurred in Gen. 30:23.

for example, verses like Ex. 1:7: "And the children of Israel were fruitful, and increased abundantly, and multiplied, and waxed exceeding mighty; and the land was filled with them"—all of which is assigned to P; or chapters like Gen. 24, with its four different designations of Rebekah (damsel, woman, virgin, and maiden)—all assigned to J (cf. Allis, FBM, pp. 63-64).

The critics have always regarded the longer form of the pronoun "I" (*'ānōkī*) as earlier in usage than the shorter form (*'anî*), and therefore a criterion for Source Division. Hence the formula "I am Jehovah" (*'ānōkī Yahweh*) in Ex. 20:2, 5 is assigned to J-E, and its occurrence in Deut. 5:6, 9 would presumably be a repetition from this earlier (J-E) tradition. Actually, however, the choice between *'anî* and *'ānōkī* is partly governed by convention or cliché; the usual phrasing for "I am Jehovah" is *'anî Yahweh*, and it occurs also in J (Gen. 28:13; Ex. 7:17), even in contexts that freely employ *'ānōkī* for "I." The argument of the critics based on the high preponderance of *'anî* in an exilic author like Ezekiel overlooks the fact that sixty of its occurrences in Ezekiel (as well as nearly fifty in P) consist in this same stereotyped expression, *'anî* Yahweh (cf. Allis, FBM, p. 65). But the whole argument has more recently been rendered ridiculous by the discovery of both forms of the first person singular pronoun almost side by side in the fifteenth-century Ugaritic inscriptions.[13] This is a striking instance of how untrustworthy are the lines of argument used to buttress the Documentary Theory. Post-Wellhausian archaeological discovery overthrows the "assured results" of Wellhausian scholarship and demonstrates the unreliability of deductions based upon ignorance.

Supposed Doublets and Parallel Accounts

From the earliest days of the Documentary Theory, a principal line of argument resorted to for proving the existence of Diverse Sources in the Pentateuch has been the asserted existence of doublets and parallel accounts. The two creation accounts, the differing strands in the flood narrative, the three namings of Isaac, and the like, have assertedly resulted from a clumsy combination of diverse traditions of the same event. Some later editor or redactor has allegedly gathered these all together in such a way as to leave many of the discrepancies still in the text, making possible a scientific disassembling of the parts by a discerning critic. This type of analytic dissection has its principal appeal to those who are already committed to the theory of multiple authorship. Those who come to the text with an open mind fail to note any such divergences as they read it through.

1. In the case of the supposed pair of creation accounts, Gen. 1 stemming from P in exilic or post-exilic times, and Gen. 2 from J in the ninth century, it should be observed that Gen. 2 does not even purport to be an account of the creation of the world. It has only to do with the creation of Adam and the environment (Eden) in which he was set. Many scholars feel that Gen. 2:4: "These are the generations (*tôlᵉdôt*) of the heavens and of the earth in the day that Yahweh Elohim made earth

---

13. See Cyrus H. Gordon, *Ugaritic Handbook*, sec. 49 (Rome: Pontificio Instituto Biblico, 1947): 2:15-21.

and heaven," constitutes the heading of the section which ensues (even though the two names for God compel source critics to parcel the verse up between J and P). But *tôlᵉdôt* nowhere else expresses the idea of creation. In the nine other occurrences of this formula ("these are the generations") found in the Torah, it always introduces an ensuing account of the offspring of an ancestor through the successive generations descended from him. It may therefore well be that we have in Gen. 2 an account of the offspring of heaven and earth (in this case, principally Adam and Eve) after the initial creation has already taken place. (Conceivably in this instance, however, it may refer back to Gen. 1).

There is, however, an element of recapitulation involved here, for the creation of the human race is related all over again (cf. Gen. 2:7 and 1:26-27). But actually this technique of recapitulation was widely practiced in ancient Semitic literature. The author would first introduce his account with a short statement summarizing the whole transaction, and then he would follow it up with a more detailed and circumstantial account when dealing with matters of special importance. To the author of Gen. 1–2, the human race was obviously the crowning, or climactic, product of creation, and it was only to be expected that he would devote a more extensive treatment to Adam after he had placed him in his historical setting (the sixth creative day). It is a mistake to suppose that Gen. 2 indicates the creation of the animal order as taking place after the origin of man. It only states that the particular individuals brought before Adam for naming had been especially fashioned by God for this purpose. (It does not imply that there were no animals anywhere else in the world prior to this time). Or else, as Aalders suggests (SIP, p. 44), the word *formed yāṣaph* (in Gen. 2:19) can equally well be translated "had formed" (since the Hebrew perfect tense does double duty for both past tense and past perfect). This would mean that God brought before Adam every beast and fowl which He had *previously* formed out of the earth. Lastly, the obvious fact should be noted that no genuine creation account even in pagan religions, would ever omit mention of the creation of the sun, moon, stars, earth, and seas, as Gen. 2 does. Such omissions eliminate all possibility of this chapter's being properly classified as a real cosmogony, in the light of ancient Near Eastern comparative literature.

Kenneth Kitchen observes in this connection,

> It is often claimed that Genesis 1 and 2 contain two different creation narratives. In point of fact, however, the strictly complementary nature of the 'two' accounts is plain enough: Genesis 1 mentions the creation of man as the last of a series, and without any details, whereas in Genesis 2 man is the centre of interest and more specific details are given about him and his setting. There is no incompatible duplication here at all. Failure to recognize the complementary nature of the subject-distinction between a skeleton outline of all creation on the one hand, and the concentration in detail on man and his immediate environment on the other, borders on obscurantism.

He then goes on to cite the varied styles in ancient Near Eastern monumental texts which could not have had any textual prehistory, such as the Karnak Poetical Stela in honor of Thutmose III, the Gebel Barkal Stela, and various royal inscriptions from Urartu, which show a pattern of general praise of the prowess of the ruler, followed by a detailed account of specific victories. He concludes by observing:

What is absurd when applied to monumental Near Eastern texts that had no prehistory of hands and redactors should not be imposed on Gen. 1 and 2, as is done by uncritical perpetuation of a nineteenth-century systematization of speculations by eighteenth-century dilettantes lacking, as they did, all knowledge of the forms and usages of Ancient Oriental literature.[14]

2. As to the diverse flood narratives (Gen. 6–8 being parceled out between J and P), it should be observed that the unbiased reader is unable to detect any diverse elements in these three chapters as they stand in the MT, and that divergences are made possible only by an artificial process of dissection. It is only an unproved assumption to insist, as Wellhausen did, that the general command to take two of every species into the ark (P) is incompatible with the exceptional provision to take seven pairs of every "clean" species (J). To the ordinary reader, the basis for the distinction is plain enough, and by no means involves irreconcilable viewpoints. The same thing is true concerning the number of days during which the flood lasted. It is contended that J makes out the flood to be forty days in length (Gen. 7:12, 17; 8:6—plus two more weeks for the sending out of the dove), where P makes it 150 days (Gen. 7:24). But a consecutive reading of the whole narrative makes it apparent that the author put the length of the downpour itself at forty days, whereas the prevalence of the water level above the highest portions of the land surface endured for 150 days (for 7:24 does not say that it rained during that entire period).

Allis points out (FBM, pp. 95-97) that only in the three major points of emphasis in the flood narrative is it possible to make out "parallel accounts," namely: the sinfulness of man as the cause of the flood; the destruction of all flesh as the purpose of the flood; the rescuing of a representative remnant of man and beast from the destruction of the flood. These three elements are stressed by the characteristic Hebrew device of restatement in slightly different terms after suitable intervals in between. But outside these three elements it is almost impossible to make out parallel accounts which do

14. Kitchen, AOOT, pp. 116-17. Compare further the analogy brought out by Kitchen in the 2300 B.C. biography of General Uni, which contains (*a*) flowing narrative style (as in J and E passages) in sections where he describes his career of service for the state, (*b*) stereotyped refrains recording Pharaoh's official recognition of his achievements (cf. the P style), (*c*) the victory paean chanted by his troops during their return from Palestine (a special H or hymnic source)—yet all are accepted as unmistakably unitary in authorship and free from later insertions (*New Bible Dictionary*, ed. J. D. Douglas [London: Inter-Varsity, 1962], p. 349). It should be added that exactly the same phenomenon occurs in the celebrated "Israel Stela" of Merneptah. The first two-thirds of that inscription is a panegyric in honor of the king for all his marvelous attributes and achievements, and then in the remainder gives an account of his invasion of Canaan and defeat of the Israelites. Wellhausen would surely have attributed the two sections to a Source A and a Source B, except for the absurdity of so treating an intact royal stela from the 19th Dynasty in the thirteenth century B.C.

not depend upon each other for missing details. For example, according to the critical analysis, J makes reference to the ark without any explanation as to its construction. Only P records the entering of Noah and his family into the ark (Gen. 7:13-16a), except that J states Jehovah shut them in the ark (even though the author of J apparently does not state how they got in there). Only J knows about the sending forth of the birds for reconnoitering purposes (8:6-12); P says nothing about it.

It is fair to say, therefore, that the actual data of the text are easily reconcilable with unity of authorship, but furnish serious obstacles to division into two divergent sources. It is also peculiar, if the Genesis flood narrative is made up of two strata separated by nearly four centuries in origin, that the Babylonian account of the flood (found in the Gilgamesh Epic) includes both J elements and P elements in its version of the episode. Thus, it speaks of the measurements of the ark (a P element), and of the sending forth of the birds (a detail from J), and of the offering up of a sacrifice of thanksgiving after the flood was over (likewise from J). The Babylonian parallels make the conclusion almost unavoidable that both the J portion and the P portion of Gen. 6–8 are of equal antiquity, and go back ultimately to the same oral tradition as did the Utnapishtim episode in the Gilgamesh Epic. The Babylonian account in turn shows noteworthy dependence upon a centuries-older Sumerian account.[15]

Other alleged doublets in Genesis may be discussed more briefly. There are said to be three accounts of the naming of Isaac (Gen. 17:17—P; 18:12—J; and 21:6—E). But there is no particular reason why both Abraham and Sarah should not have laughed with incredulity, as each in turn heard the prediction of his birth, and then at last laughed with joy.

4. As for the two accounts of Joseph's abduction to Egypt—the J account that the Ishmaelites bought him (Gen. 37:25), and the E account that the Midianites took him (37:28)—this duality of names simply points to a fact well known to the author's contemporaries, that the Midianites were accounted a subtribe of the Ishmaelites. In Judg. 8:24 we read concerning the kings of Midian, Zebah, and Zalmunna, and their followers: "For they had golden earrings, because they were Ishmaelites." Originally, to be sure, Midian was descended from Abraham by Keturah (Gen. 25:2), but the Ishmaelite tribes and Keturah tribes seem to have become interrelated in north Arabia because of their common descent from Abraham.[16]

5. The two episodes where Abraham passed off Sarah as his sister, before Pharaoh (Gen. 12:10 -20), and before Abimelech of Gerar (Gen. 20:1-18), are alleged to be variant forms of the same original legend. But the supposition that men never make the same mistake twice, or yield to the same temptation more than once, is, to say the least, naïve, especially when we consider the fact that Abraham came out financially better off on both occasions.

15. J. B. Pritchard, ed. ANET, pp. 42-44.

16. Kitchen points to analogies in the use of variant names for the same people in a single passage in such Egyptian documents as the Stela of Sebekkhu (ca. 1850 B.C.) where the enemies confronting the Egyptians are variously styled *Mntyw-Sst* ("Asiatic Bedouin"), *Rtnw ḥst* ("vile Palestinians"), and '*mw* ("Asiatics"), *New Bible Dictionary*, p. 657.

6. As for the episode in Gen. 26:6 -11 where Isaac resorted to the same subterfuge in regard to his wife Rebekah, and did so moreover at Gerar at a time when an Abimelech was king of the Philistines, it is to be conceded that there are remarkable points of resemblance with the E account in Gen. 20 (where Abraham and Sarah are involved). But before we resort to the Wellhausian explanation of a garbled version of the same tradition (Gen. 26 being attributed to J), we must satisfy ourselves on these three points: first, that sons never repeat the bad example of their parents; second, that the inhabitants of Gerar must necessarily have improved their sexual morals by the time Isaac settled among them; third, that Philistine dynasties never handed on the same name from ruler to ruler (i.e., Abimelech I, Abimelech II, etc.), even though this was demonstrably the practice in Egypt (whose Dyn. XII showed such a series as Amenemhat I, II, and III, and also Senwosret I, II, and III) and in Phoenicia (where a succession of Hirams or Ahirams ruled at Tyre and Byblos). It ought to be pointed out, incidentally, that both the Egyptian adventure of Abraham in Gen. 12 (where he denied that Sarah was his wife) and the Gerar episode of Isaac (Gen. 26) are attributed to J by the Documentarians. Here, then, is an instance where a doublet does not indicate necessarily a difference in source. The same is true of Jacob's second visit to Bethel (when he reaffirms the name Bethel a second time); E records this second visit (Gen. 35:1-8) as distinct from the first (Gen. 28:18-22). Here again is a "parallel account" which is conceded even by the critics to stem from the same source.

7. There are two accounts of the flight of Hagar from Abraham's home. The one in Gen. 16:4-14 is attributed to J (relating how she fled before Ishmael was born) and the E account, Gen. 21:9-21, relates how she fled again when Ishmael was already a young lad. But considering the tensions existing between Sarah and Hagar over the years, was it not reasonable for two such incidents to occur at different times and under dissimilar circumstances? Does not history abound in such repeated episodes in the lives of other important personages, such as Bishop Athanasius and his three banishments (in A.D. 335, 339, and 356)? (Would not the same type of divisive literary criticism have to parcel out these three banishments to three different "sources" whose several traditions have later been combined by a redactor?)

8. As for the two namings of the well at Beersheba, the first time under Abraham in Gen. 21:31 (attributed to E), and the second time under Isaac in Gen. 26:33 (attributed to J), there is no compelling necessity for regarding these as variant traditions of the same original episode. Considering the nomadic habits of Abraham and his immediate descendants, it is altogether likely that the hostile inhabitants of the locality would have stopped up the well after the Hebrew sheikh had moved away. Upon Isaac's return to the old familiar rangeland would it not be quite natural for him to open the well again and piously revive the old name which his father had given to it? Would it not be expedient for him also to confirm his right to the well by a renewed treaty (confirmed by a *shibʿâ*, "oath") with the current ruler of the land? (Here it should be observed that the word *shibʿâ* is but the feminine form of the word *sheba'* in the name *Beersheba*; they both mean "oath.")

Hebrew Style One Answer to Doublets

Part of the answer to the theory of doublets may be found in the nature of Hebrew literary style. O. T. Allis has pointed out that there are three traits of Hebrew style which are well known to have been practiced by individual Hebrew authors but which can easily be exploited by modern division-minded critics for dissection into hypothetical "sources." These three traits are paratactic sentence structure, repetition of elements of major importance, and poetic parallelism.[17] A few words of explanation are appropriate at this point.

1. Paratactic sentence structure refers to the characteristic technique of Hebrew rhetoric by which subordinate or interdependent ideas are linked together by the simple connective *and* (*we*-, Hebrew). For example, in Gen. 1:14, where the idea expressed in an Indo-European language would employ a purpose clause, "Let there be lights in the firmament of heaven *in order* to serve as signs and seasons," the Hebrew author says: "Let there be lights in the firmament of heaven...*and* they shall be for signs, and seasons." Or again, Isa. 6:7 literally reads, "Lo, this has touched thy lips; *and* thine iniquity is taken away, and thy sin is being atoned for." But what Isaiah meant to convey here was, "Lo, this has touched thy lips *in order that* thine iniquity may be removed and thy sin be atoned for." This same Hebrew particle (*we*) and may be used to convey the temporal idea of "when," or the circumstantial idea of "while," or the consequential idea of "then," or the epexegetic idea of "even" or "that is to say." The versatility of *we*- is universally conceded by Hebrew grammarians. But a dissection-minded critic may easily carve up these component elements of a Mosaic sentence on the supposition that fragments of diverse sources have been clumsily glued together by a later redactor who simply used an *and* to link them together. If a Hebrew author had written his material in classical Greek, for example, or in Latin, much of this divisive analysis of the Wellhausian school would have been well-nigh impossible, for in those languages subordinate conjunctions or participles are customarily employed to express the same ideas as Hebrew expresses in paratactic form.

2. The second trait is the tendency to repeat in slightly varied form those elements of the narrative which are of especial importance. One example of this technique has already been given in connection with the flood narrative. It was there pointed out how the repetition of the three major points of emphasis has furnished divisionists with their only convenient material for dissection, whereas the rest of the account shows no evidence whatsoever of multiple sources. Somewhat similar is the series of chapters recounting the ten plagues (Ex. 7–11). In some cases a plague is fully described in five characteristic parts: threat, command, execution, supplication for removal, and cessation. For Source Critics it is a perfectly simple matter (although purely artificial) to parcel these out among hypothetical authors. Thus the threat and cessation are given to J, while the command and execution are assigned to P. But in the case of the less grievous plagues, the description is briefer and they have to be distributed more or less intact to one source. Hence the plagues of lice and of boils are

17. Allis, FBM, p. 94.

assigned to P without anything left over for J or E. By this arbitrary arrangement, J knows only of seven plagues, P comes up with only five, and E with only four (plus a fifth which is only threatened but never carried out). Consequently no two of these sources agree as to the number or nature of the plagues, and each of them needs the information contained in the others in order to complete the series of ten.

3. A third characteristic of Hebrew style which lends itself to artificial source division is poetic parallelism. Parallelism is the term given to the balanced structure of paired clauses which is employed so extensively in Hebrew verse, such as Ps. 24:1: "The earth is Jehovah's and the fullness thereof; the world, and they that dwell therein." As can be seen from this example, corresponding synonyms are employed in the two members of the parallelism: "earth" corresponds to "world," and "fullness" corresponds to "they that dwell therein."

Careful examination of the alleged doublets and parallel accounts—so stressed by Kuenen and Wellhausen as criteria for source division— tends to show that these phenomena are capable of a far more natural and unforced explanation of the basis of single authorship than is possible on the theory of multiple sources. The JEDP hypothesis does not really square with all the evidence, and it treats much of its allegedly supporting data in a way that would never be admissible in a court of law. Moreover, the methodology of this type of literary criticism is all the more suspect because it proves to be so facile an instrument for dividing up even compositions which are universally acknowledged to be of single authorship.

Green gave an excellent illustration on this in his "documentarian" analysis of the parable of the prodigal son in Luke 15.[18] In this parody of Wellhausen's technique, he points out that source A and source B agree that there were two sons, one of whom received a portion of his father's property, and was subsequently reduced to penury through his own extravagance. But only A distinguishes the sons as elder and younger; B makes no mention of their relative ages. In A the younger obtained his share of the inheritance by solicitation, while his father retained the rest for himself; according to B the father divided up the inheritance between the two sons on his own initiative. A states that the prodigal remained in his father's neighborhood and reduced himself to penury by riotous living; in B he went to a distant country and spent all his property, but did not indulge in any unseemly excesses. Green carries this through exactly in the manner of S. R. Driver, complete with characteristic A words and B words which have been inserted in the wrong place by a bungling redactor. Green then proceeds to do the same thing with the parable of the good Samaritan. Being thoroughly versed in the methodology of the Wellhausian school he handles his material as if he were an accredited member of the guild, and thus demonstrates its artificiality.

---

18. William Henry Green, *Higher Criticism of the Pentateuch*, pp. 119-22.

10 LATE WORDS AND ARAMAISMS AS CRITERIA FOR SOURCE DIVISION

ONE OF THE MOST IMPOSING CRITERIA resorted to by divisive criticism, in demonstrating the lateness of certain portions of the Pentateuch, consists in listing words occurring in the text which are seldom used otherwise in extant Hebrew literature, except in the post-Christian writings of the Talmud and Midrash. This method gives a most plausible impression of scientific objectivity and carries great weight with those who have heard only one side of the story. There is another side, however, which must also be considered by the thoughtful observer, and which robs this argument of much of its force. Briefly stated, the argument runs as follows: If a word occurring less than three or four times in the Old Testament recurs only in later Hebrew literature (the Talmud and Midrash), then the word is of late origin, and the Old Testament passage must be of late composition. Employing this criterion it has been possible for critics to bolster their contention that the Priestly Code (P) is of exilic or post-exilic origin, and also to separate large portions of Isaiah and other post-Mosaic books as later insertions from the Persian period or even from the Greek.

During the second decade of the twentieth century, Robert Dick Wilson of Princeton took the trouble to make an exhaustive tabulation of all the so-called rare words in the Hebrew Scriptures, and he later published the resultant statistics.[1] Surprisingly enough, it turned out that such rare words occur in every book of the Old Testament and in almost every chapter. If this criterion is trustworthy, then *all* the books of the Old Testament are late and none are early. Compare the following figures, bearing in mind that the higher the percentage of "rare words" which recur in the same sense in the Talmud, the later in composition the Old Testament book must be—if this criterion is valid. The number of rare words (i.e., words occurring five times or less) is given in one column and the percentage of these appearing in the Talmud in the next column.

1. Robert Dick Wilson, SIOT, p. 135.

RARE WORDS

Critics	Dates	Occurrences	Talmud
Document P	550-450 B.C.	192	53.1%
Document D	621 B.C.	154	53.2%
Document H	570-550 B.C.	48	50.0%
Document E	750 B.C.	119	48.7%
Document J	850 B.C.	162	44.4%
Jeremiah	620-580 B.C.	278	32.1%
Isaiah 1-39	740-680 B.C.	121	22.3%
Isaiah 40-66	550-300 B.C.	62	25.8%
Daniel	168 B.C.	47	29.8%

From these statistics it is apparent that the latest of all, the book of Daniel (according to higher critical dating), has the third lowest percentage of the nine cited (i.e., 29.8 percent), and that J (the earliest of them all) has a far higher percentage of rare words recurring in the Talmud, i.e., 44.4 percent. Document E, allegedly earlier by two or three centuries than P, scores less than 5 percent below P; whereas D (supposedly more than a century earlier than P) totals up to just about the same percentage as P. From these figures it becomes apparent that the whole approach is unsound and the argument invalid. Post-exilic Ezra 1-6 comes up with only 16.7 percent, even though it is dated 450-370 B.C. by critics; Malachi (430 B.C.) also ranks low, with 23.1 percent—as over against the 850 B.C. "Jehovist" with its 44.4 percent. We must therefore abandon this type of investigation altogether, for it leads only to absurd results.

Why are these "rare words" so inconclusive as a time indicator? Principally because of the insufficiency of the data. We today possess in the Bible only a tiny fraction of all the literary output of the ancient Hebrews. There are a good three thousand words in the Old Testament which occur less than six times; fifteen hundred of them occur but once (*hapax legomena*). But this by no means indicates that they were uncommon in all other levels of Hebrew communication apart from the Bible itself. Mere fortuity may account for their infrequency in the Scriptures, just as some very common English words happen to occur only once in the English Bible, such as "invasion" (1 Sam. 30:14), "jumping" (Nah. 3:2) and "lance" (Jer. 50:42). Every new discovery of ancient Canaanite and Aramaic inscriptions brings to light words which had hitherto been known only from documents centuries later in origin. D. W. Thomas of Cambridge refers "to the re-emergence in late literature of words which themselves are very ancient, and which may or may not be, through pure accident, attested in earlier documents. Hebrew itself offers many interesting examples of this. If, for example, we had only Ben Sira (*Ecclesiasticus*), should we not be tempted to argue that the word 'swḥ ("reservoir") in 50:3, not occurring elsewhere in Hebrew, is a late word? Yet it is to be found on the Moabite Stone (11.9, 23)! Since the ninth century B.C. this old Semitic word lay hid until it turned up again seven hundred years later in Ben Sira."[2] Here we may add that it occurs no less than four times in the copper scroll of Qumran Cave 3 dated the first century A.D.[3]

ARAMAISMS AS A CRITERION FOR LATENESS

The architects of the Documentary Hypothesis assumed that the presence of an Aramaic word in a biblical text was an indication of post-exilic origin. It was not until the Babylonian captivity that the Jews began to abandon their ancestral Hebrew and adopt the more widely spoken Aramaic language, which was used in commerce and international correspondence throughout a large portion of the Persian empire from the Tigris to the Nile. By Ezra's time (according to Neh. 8:8), the Hebrew Torah required interpreters for the congregation to understand its import, and very likely this explanation was given in Aramaic, which was now the household speech of the Jewish populace. Prior to the Exile, however, only the well-educated nobility and civil servants understood Aramaic, as we may gather from the incident in 701 B.C. when the Assyrian Rabshakeh was urged to keep his remarks in Aramaic, lest the Jewish soldiers nearby might understand his Hebrew (2 Kings 18:26). Consequently it is unthinkable, argued the Wellhausians, that any authentic pre-exilic Hebrew would have contained Aramaisms.

But this assumption of the preservation of Hebrew and Aramaic in watertight compartments prior to the captivity has been quite discredited by more recent archaeological discoveries. For instance, the inscription of King Zakir of Hamath composed about 820 B.C. (Lidzbarski's *Ephemeris für Semitische Epigraphik* 3:3) shows a most remarkable admixture of Canaanite (or Hebrew) in its Aramaic text. For example, it uses the Hebrew 'š for "man" rather than the usual Aramaic 'nš; it employs the Hebrew ns' for "lift up" rather than the Aramaic nṭl. Likewise also the Panammu Inscription from the first half of the eighth century, composed in the north Syrian principality of Ya'udi, shows the same intrusion of Hebrew or Canaanite forms; for example, 'nk instead of 'n for "I," ntn instead of yhb for "give," šm instead of tm' for "there," and yšb instead of ytb for "sit, dwell."

It should be noted that these Hebraisms in Aramaic cannot be accounted for as

---

2. Thomas, *The Recovery of the Ancient Hebrew Language,* p. 18.

3. J. M. Allegro, *Treasure of the Copper Scroll* (Boston: Routledge & Kegan, 1960), p. 30. Cf. Kitchen, AOOT, pp. 142-44, listing Egyptian words in the Pyramid Texts (Dyn. V) which do not reappear in extant literature until the Ptolemaic period (Dyn. XXXII). (By the "late work criterion" these Pyramid texts would have to be dated 300 B.C.!) He notes that *ketem* ("gold"), listed by Brown-Driver-Briggs' Lexicon (BDB) as "late," traces back to Sumerian (ca. 2000 B.C.); *Kārōz* ("herald") and *kᵉraz* ("proclaim") in biblical Aramaic, which used to be classed as a borrowing from Greek *kēryx* ("herald"), seems to be derived from a Hurrian *kirenzi* in a Nuzi document ca. 1500 B.C.; *ḥemer,* a word for "wine" which used to be classed as late in biblical Hebrew and Aramaic, has been attested in Ugaritic and in eighteenth century Mari texts. As for *qibbēl,* ("receive"), which Eissfeldt cited to prove that Prov. 19:20 was "late," Kitchen points out that this word occurred in a Tell Amarna letter (ca. 1390 B.C.) from the king of Shechem to Pharaoh (AOOT, p. 145).

peculiarities of Jewish Aramaic, since these inscriptions were composed by non-Jews in regions fairly remote from Palestine. That this intermingling of Canaanite and Aramaic was of very early origin is indicated by the Ugaritic literature of fifteenth century Ras Shamrah. Ugaritic was a dialect of West Semitic closely related to Hebrew, and yet as early as the time of Moses we find such an intrusion of Aramaisms as to give some scholars grounds for arguing that Ugaritic was basically an Aramaic dialect which had absorbed many Canaanisms.

The Genesis record makes it clear that Aramaic influences were at work in Hebrew from its earliest stages. After his long sojourn in Aramaic-speaking Haran, Abraham and all his household must have been very fluent in that language before they migrated to Canaan and gradually adopted the tongue of its inhabitants. Isaac's bride, Rebekah, came to him from Aramaic-speaking Padan-aram; likewise both of Jacob's wives, Leah and Rachel. When Jacob's uncle Laban overtook him at Gilead, we are told in Gen. 31:47 that Laban called the witness cairn *Yegar-śāhᵉdūtā* ("the heap of witness"), whereas Jacob called it by the same thing in Canaanite: *Gal'ēd* ("Gilead"). In the period between the Conquest and the reign of Saul (1400 -1010 B.C.) the contacts with Aramaic-speaking peoples were doubtless minimal, but with the extension of Hebrew power under David and Solomon to the borders of Hamath and the west bank of the Euphrates, there must have been a rich exchange of cultural influences and linguistic contacts with Aramaic speaking Damascus, Hadrach, Zobah, and Hamath. These would have been particularly noticeable in the dialect of the northern Hebrew tribes contiguous to these Syrian principalities.[4] During the United Monarchy, there would very naturally have been a broadening of Hebrew vocabulary to include Aramaic and North Israelite terms or grammatical traits, particularly in the language of poetry. Hence the comparative frequency of Aramaisms in some of the later Davidic psalms and in Ecclesiastes and Song of Solomon.

These considerations furnish a good basis for concluding, first, that the presence of an Aramaism is no decisive evidence for assigning a post-exilic date to a biblical document in which it occurs; second, that the literary genre makes a difference as to the frequency with which Aramaisms may occur in a given text. Of course if in narrative prose there is a consistent and sustained Aramaic influence at work, extending even to idioms and grammatical formations, then it may be validly deduced that the Hebrew author was equally at home in Aramaic. Yet such a situation is demonstrable only in books which purport to be exilic or post-exilic, such as the Hebrew section of Daniel, Ezra, Nehemiah, and (to a certain extent) in Esther. (Interestingly enough, no such Aramaic influence is demonstrable for post-exilic prophets, such as Haggai, Zechariah, and

4. A. Hurwitz points out that Aramaic existed in various dialects, some of which exerted an early influence on Israel and the Hebrew language. On p. 236 he says: "It is quite possible that the Aramaic which exerted its influence upon Job—and which perhaps was the original language of the book—was Early Aramaic, rather than the Aramaic of the Persian period. Such a consideration must also be taken into account in studying the Book of Proverbs; namely, that the Aramaisms of this book are not necessarily those of late Biblical Hebrew. The possibility remains that the proverbs may have passed from nation to nation in Early Aramaic, their original language and style" ("The Chronological Significance of 'Aramaisms' in Biblical Hebrew" in *Israel Exploration Journal*, 18:4 [1968], pp. 234-40).

Malachi. For some reason they adhered to a relatively pure Hebrew diction, despite the prevalence of Aramaic in their day. They were probably so steeped in the language of the Torah that they were consciously biased in favor of Mosaic purity as they spoke in the name of the Lord.)

On the other hand, it should be emphasized that Documentarian critics have tended to exaggerate the Aramaic elements discoverable in the Hebrew Scriptures. A great number of Hebrew words which they have classified as Aramaisms turn out, on closer examination, to have a very good claim to the status of authentic Hebrew words, or else to be derivable from Phoenician, Babylonian, or Arabic dialects, rather than from Aramaic. For example, many critics have carelessly assumed that Hebrew nouns ending in -ôn are necessarily Aramaic because the -ān ending is so common in Aramaic. Yet the fact of the matter is that this ending is also found with fair frequency in Babylonian and Arabic, and further proof is necessary to demonstrate that it could not have been native in Hebrew from Canaanite times;[5] and that it was derivable only from Aramaic and not from Babylonian (Akkadian) or Arabic. Of the sixty-three nouns ending in -ôn or -ān in the Pentateuch (and which are therefore asserted to be Aramaic) the Aramaic Targum of Onkelos renders only twelve by the same nouns ending in -n; it renders the remaining fifty-one by other nouns entirely (and most of them without any ending in -n). At the same time, in the entire Targum of the Torah, Onkelos exhibits only sixty-three nouns in -n, whereas the Hebrew original itself has the same number, sixty-three. This seems to be rather tenuous evidence for the proposition that -n is indigenous only to Aramaic and necessarily an Aramaism in Hebrew! (Cf. Wilson, SIOT, pp. 147-48.)

In Kautzsch's *Die Aramäismen im Alten Testament* he listed about 350 words in the Hebrew Old Testament as being certainly, probably, or possibly of Aramaic origin. Concerning these 350 words, R. D. Wilson reports that 100 of them have never (as of 1926) been found in any Aramaic document, and of the remaining 250, a good 135 have never been found in an Aramaic document earlier than the second century A.D. Of the remaining 115 which have been found in documents from before that time, 75 are found in Babylonian, Arabic, Phoenician, or Ethiopic (as well as in Hebrew and Aramaic)—which leaves the question open as to who borrowed from whom (or were they all derived from the same parent Semitic language?). (Cf. SIOT, pp. 155, 156.) Wilson goes on to point out that 50 out of Kautzsch's 350 "Aramaic" words are found in the Pentateuch; but of these 50 words, only 24 are employed by Onkelos in his Aramaic Targum of the Torah. It would be natural to expect that authentic Aramaic words would be eagerly embraced for the translation into Aramaic, but it turns out that less than half of them were. To be sure, some of these so-called Aramaic words might have become obsolete by the time of Onkelos, but a 54 percent loss is well beyond the normal rate

---

5. It has been established with absolute certainty from Egyptian evidence that the -n ending did exist in the Canaanite language prior to the Israelite conquest. In recording his conquests in Palestine the Egyptian Thutmose III lists no less that seventeen cities ending with -n (1475-1450 B.C.). In the Tell el-Amarna Letters (1400-1370 B.C.) there are twenty-six cities mentioned with names terminating in -n. There is no possibility of Aramaic borrowing here!

of vocabulary change in the course of six centuries or so. Moreover, the roots of 16 out of these 24 words in Onkelos occur also in Babylonian or Arabic.

Considerable doubt must therefore attach to the great majority of these 350 "Aramaisms" listed by Kautszch.[6] In most cases these words occur in Hebrew books older by seven centuries than their earliest occurrence in extant Aramaic documents. To be sure there is a regrettable paucity of Aramaic materials from the pre-Christian centuries, but the classification of Hebrew words as Aramaisms ought to be established upon more solid grounds than mere scholarly conjecture. When we remember that critics have on the basis of Aramaisms assigned about 1500 verses of pre-exilic literature to a post-exilic date, it is reasonable to demand written documentation to verify the Aramaic status of these words. To be sure, there are some linguistic tests by which a genuine Aramaism can be distinguished in Hebrew, even apart from such documentation. That is to say, if the word in question contains one of seven telltale consonants, and if that same root exists in other Semitic languages, it is usually possible to tell whether a word is authentically Aramaic and borrowed by the Hebrew author as a loanword.

The significant consonants are listed below in Arabic (which usually preserves the most primitive Semitic pronunciation), Hebrew, and Aramaic, with a sample word to illustrate each shift. The meaning of the word is given at the commencement of the row. (*Ḏ* represents the sound of *th* in *this*; *š* is *sh* in *she*; *ṯ* is *th* in *thing*; *ẓ* is a deep-throated *z* sound which is close to a *th* in *this*; *ṣ* is an intense *s* that is close to a *ts* in quality; *ṭ* is a deep-throated *t* sound made slightly back of the position of ordinary *t*; d is a deep-throated sound resembling *d* followed by voiced th in a -*dth* combination; ' is a sort of grunt or snarl which is made deep in the throat as the throat muscles are tightened up; *ḥ* is a deep-throated *kh* sound like *ch* in *Loch Lomond*.)

COMPARISON OF PRONUNCIATIONS

	Arabic	Hebrew	Aramaic
(1) "to sacrifice"	*ḏabaḥa*	*zābaḥ*	*dᵉbaḥ*
(2) "to break"	*ṯabara*	*šābar*	*tᵉbar*
(3) "to look at, guard"	*naẓara*	*nāṣar*	*neṭar*
(4) "land, country"	*'ardun*	*'ereṣ*	*ᵃraʿ*

---

6. In Bauer-Leander's *Historische Grammatik der Hebraischen Sprache des Alten Testaments*, vol. 1, sec. 2, we meet this significant statement (translated): "Since we have only an inadequate knowledge of Hebrew vocabulary, owing to the meager extent of the literature of the Old Testament, it would be rash (*voreilig*) to regard immediately as Aramaic all words which only appear in later writings; after all they might just happen not to be instanced in the earlier writings. They can only be recognized as such with perfect assurance when their phonetic state shows them to be Aramaic. But in many cases there is no solid basis for judgment." It should be understood that neither Aramaic nor Syriac was vowel-pointed prior to 700 A.D. and so there is no way of firm assurance as to their "phonetic state."

From this simplified chart it is apparent how a Hebrew word containing one of these four significant consonants can be detected as an Aramaic borrowing. Thus if a word which ought to show a *z* turns up with a *d* instead (1), or instead of a šit appears with a *t* (2), or instead of a ṣit shows a *ṭ* or ' (3) (4), then it may be borrowed from Aramaic. Wilson (SIOT, p. 142) calculates that there are eighteen roots in biblical Hebrew which also occur both in Arabic and Aramaic with consonant shift (1), eighteen with consonant shift (2), nine with (3), and eleven with (4). Yet of all these fifty-six instances, Wilson finds only five which pass the consonant-shift test for an Aramaism: *nādar* "to vow," *'ātar* "to abound," *ṭillēl* "to cover" (Neh. 3:15), *bᵉrōt* "fir tree" (Song 1:17), and *mᵉdibat* "causing to flow" (Lev. 26:16)—although Wilson argues that even this word really comes from a root *dā'ab* "to be weak" (and therefore it would not come under consonant shift #1). Only four or five roots may easily be accounted for on the grounds of intercultural relations, and there is no need to resort to post-exilic dating for the four which occur in pre-exilic books.

We close this discussion with this brief quotation from M. H. Segal's *Grammar of Mishnaic Hebrew*, "It has been the fashion among writers on the subject to brand as an Aramaism any infrequent Hebrew word which happens to be found more or less frequently in Aramaic dialects. Most of these Aramaisms are as native in Hebrew as they are in Aramaic. Many of them are also found in other Semitic languages."[7] Note also that Norman Snaith found only three or four of the alleged forty-one Aramaisms in Job to be demonstrably genuine Aramaisms which are absent from earlier books of the Hebrew Bible.[8] He states, "We hold that if a root is found elsewhere than in Aramaic, and if the transformation rules concerning the consonants are observed, then the word is not an Aramaism. It is, we maintain, a rare word which has been retained in the memory of the literary writers, those who were wise men in Israel, those who had pretensions to culture and who were aware of the literature of the other countries of the Fertile Crescent."[9]

---

7. Segal, *Grammar of the Mishnaic Hebrew* (New York: Oxford U. 1927), p. 8.
8. Obviously Snaith assumes that *Job* is a late book in the O.T. canon. But the internal evidence in Job is irreconcilable with a late dating.
9. Snaith, *The Book of Job* (Naperville, Ill.: Allenson, 1968), p. 104.

11 WELLHAUSEN'S RECONSTRUCTION OF HEBREW HISTORY IN THE PREPROPHETIC AND PROPHETIC PERIOD

IN ORDER TO SUPPLEMENT the rather brief indications of chapter 6 as to the reinterpretation of Hebrew religious history developed by the Documentarians in the nineteenth century, it will be appropriate here to examine it in somewhat greater detail and to analyze its weaknesses. This discussion will be divided into two chapters for convenience' sake; the treatment of the Priestly Period will be deferred until chapter 12.

It will be recalled that the Wellhausen school regarded the 850 B.C. J and 750 B.C. E as the earliest written portions of the Pentateuch. These represented the earlier phase of the prophetic period (apart from the oral prophets who went back to Samuel's time). From the time of the Judges, of Moses, and of the patriarchs, we have, according to this theory, only garbled traditions handed down by word of mouth over a period of many centuries, and which were finally committed to writing in J and E. How were these oral traditions to be sifted scientifically so as to separate the original fact from legendary or slanted accretions? The Documentarians found a ready method for this in the methodology of Hegelian philosophy and Darwinian evolutionism which were then at the very height of fashion in philosophical circles.

As A. Noordtzy of Utrecht pointed out in "The Old Testament Problem,"[1] the nineteenth century was dominated by an anthropocentric viewpoint. Man came to be regarded as an end in himself, and God existed only as a means to be used for man's benefit. The idea of evolution had captured the thinking of that day, and was thought to furnish the best key to the understanding of history as well as of nature. Religion was discussed only from the standpoint of its subjective benefits to man. All possibility of special revelation from a personal God was discounted, and the religious side of man was to be explained by a natural process of development as a mere expression of his cultural activity. Since a study of comparative religions showed a

1. Noordtzy, translated in *Bibliotheca Sacra*, vols. 98-99, nos. 388-90, 1940-41.

consistent pattern of progress, as they thought, from primitive animism or fetishism to polydemonism, then to polytheism, monolatry, and finally monotheism, they concluded that Israel's religion must have developed along similar lines. The present form of the Hebrew text of the Torah does not testify to anything but a monotheistic viewpoint, but this is to be explained as the reworking of the ancient traditions by the priestly school of the post-exilic period, who imposed their fully evolved monotheistic viewpoint upon them. Even J and E belonged to an age dominated by the monotheism of the eighth-century prophets (notably Amos in the vanguard of these), and the original animism and polytheism of the patriarchs were thus veneered over to conform to the later theology. But a keen-scented practitioner of comparative religions could nevertheless ferret out some of the traces of the more primitive belief by sloughing off all the monotheistic accretions. Proceeding upon the assumption that Israel's religion must have been of natural origin, not supernatural, these nineteenth-century analysts (such as E. B. Taylor, Schultze, and W. Robertson Smith) exploited every slightest detail in the ancient record which might be reinterpreted to indicate a submonotheistic faith.[2]

Much dependence was laid upon the supposed analogy of the development of the religion of non-Israelite nations in the ancient Near East. In Egypt, for example, by a process of syncretism (explaining a group of similar gods as only manifestations or phases of the one basic god) the Egyptians ascended from the exuberant polytheism of an earlier age to a higher stage very close to monolatry by the Eighteenth Dynasty, when Amon-Re' was exalted as the supreme deity of whom all lesser gods were but secondary phases. This in turn paved the way for the quasi-monotheism of King Akhnaton (1387-1366 B.C.), which represented the high point in Egyptian religion.[3] In Baby-

2. In this connection it should be observed that some eminent anthropologists of the present century dissent from the evolutionistic assumption of original animism and polytheism, and find significant evidence of a purer form of religion in man's earliest stages. For example, Wilhelm Schmidt in Der Ursprung der Gottesidee (1912-1936) has demonstrated by dint of painstaking anthropological research that in some primitive cultures at least, there was an original monotheism which has greatly degenerated in subsequent ages, leaving its traces in the notion of supreme beings and "high" gods to bear witness to it in widely scattered areas of human population. Albright (SAC, pp. 170-71) refers to these researches as quite conclusive, remarking, "There can no longer be any doubt that Fr. Schmidt has successfully disproved the simple evolutionary progression first set up by the Positivist Comte, fetishism-polytheism-monotheism, or Taylor's animism-polytheism-monotheism."

T. J. Meek refers to the argument developed by Lagrange and Langdon that the Sumerian god An or Anum (later defined as the sky-god) was originally regarded as the one and only god, because only his name is preceded by no determinative sign for god (whereas the names of all other deities are preceded by the star sign which spells the name An itself). But as the Sumerians later fell away into polytheism, they thought of their new gods as simply forms or manifestations of the one true god, An, and only later conceived of them as entirely independent deities. Similarly Lagrange and Langdon argued that the Semites also had but one god, Ilu or El (a good Hebrew term for God), who later became defined as merely the sky-god, whereas each of the new gods added to the pantheon was another El or god. But all of this is more or less conjectural, Meek feels, because in the earliest stage of writing, both Sumerians and Akkadians wrote their god names without the An- or Ilu- determinative (Hebrew Origins, pp. 188-90).

3. Actually, of course, the theory that the king of Egypt was the incarnation of the sun-god, and was therefore himself a god, continued in force even in Akhnaton's case, and that too after his religious reforms. From this standpoint, therefore, it is not quite accurate to speak of his theological position as "true monotheism," although it came very close to it.

KING TUT'S THRONE

THE BACK OF KING TUT'S THRONE DEPICTS THE KING AND HIS QUEEN UNDER ATON (THE SUN DISK) (CA. 1360 B.C.)

lon we find a supposedly similar development in the elevation of the god Marduk to supremacy, subsuming all other deities under him. In Greece the colorful polytheism of Homer gave way in later centuries to the monotheistic philosophies of Xenophanes and Plato (who so often referred to *ho theos*, "the god"). Progress toward monotheism, then, was simply part of a general evolutionary process through which Israel must have passed, like any other ancient nation.

The fact remains, however, that the actual data of comparative religions render this argument from analogy altogether untenable. It is an incontestable fact of history that no other nation (apart from those influenced by the Hebrew faith) ever did develop a true monotheistic religion which commanded the general allegiance of its people. Isolated figures may be pointed out like Akhnaton and Xenophanes (both of whom also spoke of "gods" in the plural number), but it remains incontrovertible that neither the Egyptians nor the Babylonians nor the Greeks ever embraced a monotheistic faith on a national basis. Right down to the days of Christ and the apostles, the inhabitants of those lands and of all other nations of which we have any knowledge were firmly committed to a belief in many gods and goddesses, composing a pantheon of celestial government. They believed in sky-gods, water-gods, tree-gods, earth-gods, and all the rest, just about as their forefathers had thousands of years before. While the philosophic schools may have reduced the gods to one impersonal essence (such as the Stoics), or denied the existence of God altogether (such as the Epicureans), or simply occupied the middle ground of agnosticism, the great masses of their countrymen still clung to a belief in the ancestral deities, along with an assortment of foreign gods (including those which were imported from Egypt and Asia) to give their religion a dash of exotic color.

This is the verdict of history: only Israel appeared with a monotheistic religion on a national basis. This is a fact that demands a reasonable explanation in face of the utter contrast which the Hebrew nation presented to all its ancient neighbors. It does not reduce the difficulty to hypothecate a polytheistic origin for Israel's religion, for this only accentuates the problem of explaining how in Israel—and only in Israel—

HISTORICAL HIGH PLACE

ALTAR OF BAAL DISCOVERED AT PETRA

BAAL WAS THE MOST PROMINENT CANAANITE DEITY. THIS FERTILITY GOD'S SACRIFICIAL RITES WERE PERFORMED AT HIGH PLACES SUCH AS THIS.

polytheism gave way to monotheism. (Since both the Christian faith and the Islamic religion developed directly from Hebrew monotheism, they furnish no exception to the uniqueness of Israel's religion.) So far as this writer is aware, there is no other reasonable explanation of this fact except that which is given by the Old Testament itself, that Israel derived this monotheistic faith by direct revelation from God. It was no product of the natural Hebrew "genius for religion" (as is often asserted), for the Scripture record witnesses rather to the natural Hebrew genius for irreligion and apostasy. It attests the readiness of the ancient Israelites to adopt the polytheism of their heathen neighbors and forsake their covenant relationship with Jehovah. At least until the time of the Exile (587 B.C.), the Hebrew Scriptures themselves affirm that the ten northern tribes first, and then the two tribes of the Southern Kingdom, were constantly straying off into the worship of degenerate foreign deities and attempting to break away from God's revealed Word. The fact that they did not permanently fall away is uniformly represented as being due to the hindering power of God's grace and of His continued message to them through the prophets.

THE PREPROPHETIC PERIOD ACCORDING TO WELLHAUSEN

Following the guiding principles of comparative religions, it was possible for the architects of the Documentary Hypothesis to "discover" traces of lower religion in the faith of primitive Israel. Animism, for example, shimmers through the account of Jacob's sleeping on a stone pillow at Bethel (Gen. 28:18); of course this stone was actually a cult object, somewhat like the sacred Black Stone of the Kaabah in Mecca. Stone worship must also lie behind the account of the cairn erected by Jacob and Laban in Gilead (Gen. 31:47). Did not the idolatrous Canaanites set up a stone pillar beside their altars on the high places, in the belief that the local Baal would reside in that stone, and sally forth to feast upon their sacrifices? The fact that idolatrous Israelites followed the same practice when they took over the high places from the Canaanites testifies to their adherence to stone worship even in the last stages of the Divided Monarchy.

As for tree worship, even the idealized figure of Abraham, if he ever really existed (and some critics, like Nöldeke, were prepared to question this), had faith in sacred trees. Witness the reference to his sojourning by the "terebinth of Moreh" in Gen. 12:6. (*Mōreh* in this case would signify teacher, from *hōrah*, to "teach," because the devout could hear the tree speak to them by the rustling of its leaves—just like the oaks of Zeus at Dodona.) Later on we find him setting up his headquarters by the "oaks of Mamre" in Gen. 14:13; he must have worshiped these trees also. In post-Mosaic times we have the significant instance of the prophetess Deborah, who made her headquarters by a sacred palm tree (Judg. 4:5). Other traces of animism are found in the legislation attributed to Moses. For example, Ex. 20:25 provides that any altar erected to Yahweh must be made of unhewn stone. Why unhewn? To avoid the possibility of engraving cult symbols on the altar (as we might naturally infer after a command against graven images), or was it to obviate offending the *daemon* who was superstitiously supposed to inhabit the stone in its natural, unhewn state? To comparative religionists, of course, only the latter explanation would commend itself. Likewise also in the injunction in Lev. 19:9 to avoid mowing or gleaning the corners of the wheat field, the original reason was to avoid giving offense to the vegetable spirit who was believed to reside in the standing grain; the ostensible reason given in P (to afford a little free grain for the destitute of the community) was a later refinement.

As for idolatry, the Documentary reconstruction of Hebrew history could find abundant evidence that the religion of early Israel was both idolatrous and polytheistic. We may feel certain, according to these critics, that the worship of the golden calf (Ex. 32) was endorsed by Moses (especially if we regard the image as a cultic representation of Yahweh Himself). Otherwise there would have been an energetic protest made in 930 B.C. when Jeroboam I of Israel set up the calf images at Bethel and Dan—a measure to which he never would have resorted had there been any written Mosaic law forbidding idolatry. It was only later, under the influence of the new monotheistic prophetic school of the E period (and later on with the Priestly School, of course), that the original tradition was so altered as to make Moses disapprove of this calf worship, and the later invented figure of Aaron is charged with responsibility for having fashioned it in the first place. It is alleged that Elijah failed to utter any condemnation of these calves of Jeroboam (ca. 860-850 B.C.), showing that he was not scandalized by Jehovah worship carried on with the aid of images (but see 1 Kings 18:18, "I have not troubled Israel, but you and your father's house, in that you have forsaken the commandments of the Lord and have followed Baalim," whose worship always involved praying to the idol of Baal). But otherwise, since we have virtually no record of Elijah's preaching preserved to us, this is a very questionable assertion to make. We certainly do have a record of an outright condemnation of the image and altar of Jeroboam at Bethel by an anonymous Jewish prophet of an earlier generation than Elijah's, according to 1 Kings 13. It is claimed that not even Amos himself condemned the calves.[4] Yet this assertion runs counter to the condemnation of the Ephraimite cultus found in Amos 3:14, "On the day that I punish Israel's transgres-

---

4. W. R. Smith, quoted in *Prophets of Israel*, Moses Buttenweiser (New York: Macmillan, 1894) p. 175.

THE HORNED ALTAR. A STONE ALTAR WITH "HORNS" (VERTICAL CORNER PROJECTIONS) FOUND AT BEERSHEBA IN 1973. WHEN REASSEMBLED, IT STOOD 157 CM. HIGH. CONSTRUCTED OF ASHLAR BRICKS, THIS ALTAR WAS LIKELY TORN DOWN DURING HEZEKIAH'S REFORM.

sions, I will also punish the altars of Bethel; The horns of the altar will be cut off" (NASB). As for the brazen serpent of Moses (Num. 21:8-9), preserved until Hezekiah's time in the national sanctuary (cf. 2 Kings 18:4), the Wellhausen school felt confident that this was a perfectly respected idol of the serpent-god, patron of the tribe of Levi,[5] until the eighth century, when the prophetic monotheistic party gained dominance in Judah, and Hezekiah had it destroyed. But this is mere conjecture devoid of any objective evidence.

The same critics feel certain that infant sacrifice was sanctioned by the primitive faith of early Israel. The provision of Ex. 22:29 (J-E) that a firstborn son must be redeemed by a special offering presupposes that originally firstborn sons were sacrificed on the altar, just like the firstlings of the livestock. Not until the time of D (it is claimed) was a clear distinction made between the two. (Yet compare Ex. 13:1-2, a P passage, where no clearer distinction is made between firstborn sons and firstlings than in Ex. 22:29.) The perfectly reasonable principle enunciated by the Hebrew text, that God challenged a special propriety in the firstborn because of His having protected all the Hebrew firstborn during the night of the Passover, is ignored completely as a mere "priestly" rationalization.

Early Israel, according to these critics, had no written laws at all (even though the Sumerians, Babylonians, Assyrians, and Hittites codified their laws as early as the time of Moses or earlier), and the oldest legislation preserved to us in the Torah is the so-

5. Meek, pp. 122-23.

called ritual decalogue of J, in Ex. 34:11-26. Aside from the fact that this passage begins without any introductory formula as a decalogue, and that it really contains not ten commandments but eight, it remains extremely unlikely that the fundamental written law of the Hebrew people (as late as 850 B.C.) should omit all sanctions against murder, adultery, larceny, fraud, and dishonor to parents. Yet, none of these offenses is mentioned in this so-called decalogue. It should be observed that stringent provisions on nearly all these subjects were codified in the Babylonian *Code of Hammurabi* (ca. 1750 B.C.) as well as in the Hittite and Sumerian codes. Chapter 125 of the Egyptian *Book of the Dead* lists virtually all these crimes in the negative confessions which the deceased was expected to make before the assembled judgment-gods of the netherworld. Is it credible that only the Hebrews were too backward to condemn such sins, when those pagan neighbors with whom they were most closely associated had written condemnation of them in their legal and religious literature for nearly fifteen hundred years previously? (The main nucleus of the *Book of the Dead* was at least that early.) This would seem to put too great a strain upon the credulity of even the most partisan devotees of scientific naturalism if they were to pay any attention at all to such flimsy arguments based upon mere Hegelian dialetic.

The Documentarians discerned in the preprophetic period a development from the grosser polytheism of the patriarchal period to a sort of monolatry whereby the Hebrew tribes came increasingly to devote their loyalty to Yahweh alone, as being their own national god. The plural background of this god was, of course, betrayed by the plural state of their commonest word for "God," namely *Elôhîm*, with its plural *-îm* ending. (Actually this is more properly to be regarded as the plural of majesty.[6]) In the period of the Judges, we find Jephthah negotiating with the Ammonites in these terms (Judg. 11:24): "Will you not possess what Chemosh your god gives you to possess? And all that Yahweh our God has dispossessed before us, we will possess." (But it is quite obvious from the situation that Jephthah is not speaking as a theologian but as a foreign diplomat, negotiating with them in terms which they could understand as he appealed to their sense of fair play.) Even King David is thought to have conceded the existence of other gods in 1 Sam. 26:19: "They have driven me out this day that I should have no share in the heritage of Jehovah, saying, Go, serve other gods." (But this expression was simply the ancient equivalent of "serving under another flag"; even the monotheistic Deuteronomist uses this type of language: "Jehovah will bring thee...unto a nation that thou hast not known, thou nor thy

---

6. Cf. the comment of Gesenius-Kautzsch-Cowley, *Hebrew Grammar* (Oxford: Clarendon 1966), sec. 124g: "*The pluralis excellentiae or maiestatis,* as has been remarked above is properly a variety of the abstract plural, since it sums up the several characteristics belonging to the idea, besides possessing the secondary sense of an intensification of the original idea....So especially *Elôhîm,* "Godhead, God" (to be distinguished from the numerical plural *gods,* Ex. 12:12, etc.). The supposition that *Elôhîm* is to be regarded as merely a remnant of earlier polytheistic views (i.e., as originally only a numerical plural) is at least highly improbable, and moreover would not explain the analogous plurals." The next section cites as other examples *qᵉdôshîm,* "the Most Holy" (only of Yahweh), Hos. 12:10, Prov. 9:10, 30:3, *ᵃdônîm* ("lordship, Lord"); Cf. Isa. 19:4 (where *ᵃdônîm* is accompanied by a singular adjective *qāsheh*— "cruel"), and *bᵃ'ālîm*—"lord, master" (of slaves, cattle, or inanimate things, e.g., Ex. 21:29; Isa. 1:3).

fathers; and there shalt thou serve other gods, wood and stone" [Deut. 28:36]. Here the service of foreign gods simply refers to servitude in a land dominated by a false heathen religion.)

The Wellhausians also insist that Hos. 3:4, "For the children of Israel shall abide many years without king, and without prince, and without sacrifice, and without [cultic] pillar, and without ephod or teraphim," implies that the idolatrous pillars and the teraphim (household gods) were regarded by Hosea as legitimate, since the king and sacrifice, and so forth, were coupled with them in this clause. On the contrary, however, careful attention to context shows that everything cultic which is listed in this verse is regarded by the author as illegitimate and under the condemnation of God: the unsanctioned Israelite dynasty (cf. Hos. 8:4, "They have set up kings, but not by me"), the non-Levitical priesthood, the unacceptable sacrifice not offered at the Jerusalem altar, and all the rest. No legitimacy is implied in this verse, after all, for the next verse states that in the latter day the Israelites will return to their true God and to David, their proper king, and worship in all purity and holiness — as they were not then doing.

Such are the textual bases for the higher critical reconstruction of the religious history of Israel prior to the rise of the writing prophets. These arguments turn out to afford very tenuous support for the theory of primitivism and polytheism in the post-Abrahamic period, and all their alleged proof texts are capable of a far different interpretation which better accords with the rest of the evidence.

THE PROPHETIC PERIOD ACCORDING TO WELLHAUSEN

Beginning with Amos, who is considered by the critics of this school to have been the earliest of the writing prophets, a revolutionary new change of direction is supposed to have taken place in the religious thinking of Israel. This creative thinker from the hill country of rural Judea came with an epoch-making new idea, the idea of monotheism: there is no God but Yahweh Himself, and all the gods of the heathen are imaginary! Those who followed Amos, men like Hosea, Isaiah, and Micah, enthusiastically embraced this new emphasis on monotheism and contributed to its ultimate triumph in the religion of Israel. In Jeremiah's time this movement produced its classic manifesto in the book of Deuteronomy, in which the uniqueness and supremacy of Jehovah were proclaimed with prophetic fervor and then attributed to the venerable figure of Moses. In many respects, according to these critics, this prophetic period (760-587 B.C.) represents the highest and purest achievement of the religion of Israel. As interpreted and expurgated by nineteenth-century Liberalism, these Hebrew prophets pretty largely hewed to the line of the Liberal gospel, with its emphasis upon social justice and salvation by good works or noble character. From this standpoint the postprophetic movement initiated by Ezekiel and the Priestly School represented a retrogression into ritualism and formalism and emphasis upon such priestly functions as atoning sacrifices.

In this connection it is interesting (perhaps even amusing) to read this vivid description of the radical change between the preprophetic period and the age of the prophets, as expressed by Lewis Browne: The prophets of the eighth century "transformed a jealous demon who roared and belched fire from the crater of a volcano into a transcendent spirit of love. They took a bloody and remorseless protector of a desert people, and without realizing it, changed him into the merciful Father of all mankind. In fine, they destroyed Yahweh and created God!"[7] This is surely a masterpiece of misstatement and misrepresentation, shot through with fallacies from beginning to end, but it illustrates the perverted notion of Hebrew religion taught in many quarters today as a popularization of the Wellhausen hypothesis. Suffice it to say that there is surely no parallel to this to be found anywhere else in human history, that neither the introducers of a radically new concept of God nor those to whom they introduced it realized that there was anything new about it. Both the prophets themselves and their audiences seemed to labor under the impression that it was the God of Moses whose message they were transmitting. They claimed to be summoning their countrymen to return once more to the ancestral God of the patriarchs, to the God of Mount Sinai and the Exodus (cf. Hos. 11:1; 12:9, 13; Amos 2:10; 9:7; Mic. 6:4; 7:15), not to any new, watered-down deity capable of nothing but sweetness and light. Lewis Browne would be well advised to reread Isa. 24, 34, and 63, if he supposes that any of the thunder and smoke was removed from God's judicial wrath by the innovating prophets of the newer, more enlightened age.

In order to demonstrate this opposition to sacrifice as having been indeed the emphasis of the prophets, the architects of the Development Hypothesis felt that they had only to cite a few proof texts and to interpret them in their own special way (out of context). Thus it was possible to show that the great prophets of the eighth and seventh centuries rejected any system of blood sacrifice as a valid way of access to God, even denying that it had any Mosaic validity. There were four favorite passages which they used for this purpose.

Amos 5:21-26: "I hate, I despise your feasts, and I will take no delight in your solemn assemblies. Yea, though ye offer me your burnt-offerings and meal-offerings, I will not accept them…But let justice roll down as waters and righteousness as a mighty stream. Did ye bring unto me sacrifices and offerings in the wilderness forty years, O house of Israel? Yea, ye have borne the tabernacle of your king [Sakkuth your king, RSV] and the shrine of your images [Kaiwan your star-god, RSV], the star of your god, which ye made to yourselves." (Actually the tense of "borne" can be rendered: "Ye were bearing," or even—although this is against the context—"Ye will bear.") The Documentarians interpret this question to imply the answer: "No, we never did bring God sacrifices and offerings during the Exodus wanderings." Much more reasonably Amos' question may be taken at face value to mean: "Did you offer sacrifices to Me at that time? Yes, you did, but what impure and unacceptable sacrifices they were (just like those you offer Me in this corrupt generation), for you also carried on the clan-

7. Browne, *This Believing World* (New York: Macmillan, 1926), p. 236.

destine worship of idols, even in the days of Moses!" This surely is the interpretation which best accords with the stream of the argument which Amos is developing in this chapter.

Micah 6:6-8: "Wherewith shall I come before Jehovah?...Shall I come before him with burnt-offerings, with calves a year old? Will Jehovah be pleased with thousands of rams?...He hath showed thee, O man, what is good; and what doth Jehovah require of thee, but to do justly, and to love kindness, and to walk humbly with thy God?" This is construed to mean that Micah rejects the principle of sacrifice altogether, and that God desires only a virtuous life to satisfy His requirements for salvation. But this is to foist a modern Liberal notion upon the teaching of the ancient prophet. It is obvious from the context that Micah was dealing with the problem of religious formalism accompanied by an ungodly and immoral life on the part of the Jewish worshiper. Even the most lavish and extravagant offerings upon the altar cannot make up for the lack of heart submission and of a sincere purpose to obey the will of God in matters of practical ethics. Acceptable worship must proceed from a surrendered life. There is no rejection of the sacrificial cultus as such, but only as a hypocritical substitute for true godliness.

Isaiah 1:11-17 is another prophetic utterance along the same line: "What unto me is the multitude of your sacrifices? saith Jehovah: I have had enough of the burnt-offerings of rams, and the fat of fed beasts....Wash you, make you clean; put away the evil of your doings from before mine eyes; cease to do evil; learn to do well; seek justice, relieve the oppressed, judge the fatherless, plead for the widow." This is interpreted by Wellhausians to be a plea to do away with the ceremonialism of blood sacrifices and get down to the business of performing meritorious good works, thus earning their salvation (just as good Liberals of our modern age are expected to do). But that this exegesis falls wide of the mark is sufficiently indicated by the statement in verse 15: "And when ye spread forth your hands, I will hide mine eyes from you; yea, when ye make many prayers, I will not hear: your hands are full of blood." If the previous remarks amounted to a rejection of blood sacrifice *as such*, then it must logically follow here that prayer also is being rejected *as such*, since the same type of expression is used in both cases. But not even the most enlightened modern Liberal would like to think that the prophet Isaiah was opposed to prayer; if only from the standpoint of subjective therapy, prayer must be regarded as both beneficial and praiseworthy. All parties would acknowledge that the prophet is not denying the validity of prayer, but only the prayer of bloody-handed, unrepentant miscreants who mock God by the very prayers they mouth. In other words, acceptable worship must be based upon a true and living faith as it finds expression in a God-fearing life. Hence it follows that the same principle governs in Isaiah's deprecatory remarks about sacrifices and feast days. By no means does he deny that they were ordained of God in the law of Moses.

Jeremiah 7:22-23: "For I spake not unto your fathers, nor commanded them in the day that I brought them out of the land of Egypt, concerning burnt-offerings or sacrifices: but this thing I commanded them, saying, Hearken unto my voice, and I will be your God, and ye shall be my people; and walk ye in all the way that I command you, that it may be well with you." What could be more obvious, asks the critic, than that Jeremiah here is denying (ca. 600 B.C.) that God had ever spoken to Moses about the sacrificial cultus? Obviously the material of P could not yet have been composed by that time, but only centuries later, as an addendum to J, E, and D, otherwise Jeremiah would never have made a statement like that. But if we analyze what the prophet is actually saying in this passage, we find that the words quoted come from Ex. 19, before even the first installment of the law was revealed to Moses by God, even before the promulgation of the Ten Commandments in Ex. 20. It certainly was true that "in the day that I brought them out of the land of Egypt" God had not yet said anything to the Israelites about sacrifice or burnt offering. (Even the Passover lamb involved no altar, according to Ex. 12.) He first closed with them on the basis of a covenant engagement requiring absolute and unconditional obedience as a condition of the covenant. It was only afterward that the provisions concerning sacrifice were outlined to Moses. The point was that Jeremiah's contemporaries had been substituting ritual ceremonies for genuine piety, and they needed to be reminded that historically God's first summons to Israel had been for absolute obedience to His moral law before He ever gave them a provision for sins in the atoning blood of the altar of sacrifice. Incidentally, it is instructive to note Jeremiah's cordial approval of the sacrificial system elsewhere in his prophecy: 17:19-27, concerning hallowing the Sabbath; 31:14, God will satiate the priests with fatness; 33:11,18, the Levitical priests shall "never lack a man before Me to offer burnt offerings, to burn grain offerings, and to prepare sacrifices continually."

Thus the Documentarian critics assigned virtually all cultic regulations to the Priestly School of the post-exilic period. But they regarded certain of the noncultic legal provisions of the Torah as originating with E or J-E, notably the book of the covenant (Ex. 21-23). This body of law was supposed to have evolved from the experience of Israel in the land of Canaan over a period of four or five centuries after the conquest. This code did not suggest the unique legitimacy of one central sanctuary. On the contrary, it sanctioned any number of local sanctuaries, according to Ex. 20:24: "An altar of earth shalt thou make unto me, and shalt sacrifice thereon thy burnt-offerings...in every place where I record my name I will come unto thee and I will bless thee." Closer examination, however, shows that this passage is not referring to the possibility of multiple sanctuaries at all, but only to the type of altar to be used for God's worship, prior to the fashioning of the bronze altar for the tabernacle. Not until later (as is recorded in Ex. 40) was the tabernacle completed and the divinely prescribed altar dedicated. No doubt also it was to serve as a principle to follow in situations where resort to the altar at the central sanctuary was impractical (as for example where Elijah built his altar on Mount Carmel, 1 Kings 18:31). Allis (FBM, p. 173) suggests that the words of Ex. 20:24 translated, "in every place where I record my name," might be better rendered, "in all of the place" (*b*ᵉ*kol-hammāqōm*), that is, in all of Palestine. (Properly speaking, "in every place" would be *b*ᵉ*kol māqōm*, without the definite article *ha-*.) The idea then would be that in all of the Holy Land, where God will cause His name to be remembered, He will come to His worshipers and bless them.

In general, the Documentarians insist that the historical fact that many local sanctuaries were maintained in Israel prior to Josiah's reign is proof positive that there could have been no Mosaic laws in existence forbidding them. Had there been such laws, they would of course have been obeyed. But this reasoning is vitiated by the undeniable fact that even after the reform of Josiah in 621 B.C., idolatrous high places continued to be maintained in Judah (cf. Ezek. 6:3).[8] The critics acknowledge that "Mosaic" laws forbidding all other sanctuaries besides the local one were solemnly adopted in the reign of Josiah. Yet in the time of Zedekiah, Josiah's third successor, the high places were still in operation. In this case the Wellhausians themselves must acknowledge that this law was broken even after its enactment. If so, why may this not have been the case in preceding centuries as well, that local sanctuaries were maintained even after the temple of Solomon had been dedicated? In general we may say that the argument that laws could not have existed simply because they were ignored, is altogether too naïve. On such a basis one would have to deny that there are any laws against robbery or adultery in existence in modern America!

So far as the Mosaic prohibition of local sanctuaries is concerned, it ought to be pointed out that not even Deuteronomy prohibits the erection of local altars to Yahweh until such time as God shall have indicated His choice of a holy capital city in which alone it would be permissible to present sacrifice. In Deut. 12:10-11, the regulation is made that after the Lord has given His people rest from all their enemies round about—which did not take place until the reign of David—then God would choose a special place for worship to which all Israel should resort for cultic purposes. Hence there is no contradiction at all between E (in Ex. 20:24) and D (in Deut. 12:10-11). Moreover, it should be observed that wherever the idolatrous high places, or even Jehovah-worshiping high places are referred to in the Hebrew record after the consecration of Solomon's temple, they are always spoken of as deviations from the Mosaic law, and the successive kings of Judah are often judged as to their character by whether or not they removed the "high places." On the other hand, even J offers considerable difficulty to the theory that no centrality of worship was cherished as an ideal at the time of the Exodus, for in Ex. 23:17 it is required that all Israelite males "appear before Jehovah" three times a year (that is, at the three great feasts of Passover, Pentecost, and Tabernacles). There would hardly be any point to this provision if all that was required was to put in an appearance at one's own local shrine. Thus even the earliest stratum of the Pentateuch (according to the JEDP hypothesis) implies a central point of worship as prescribed by Jehovah.

In this connection it should be noted that the Wellhausen School tends to dismiss the Mosaic tabernacle as a figment of the imagination of the Priestly School.

---

8. Ezekiel 6:3, "I will bring a sword upon you and I will destroy your high places." Also cf. Ezek. 16:39, "I shall also give you into the hands of your lovers, and they will tear down your shrines, demolish your high places, strip you of your clothing, take away your jewels, and leave you naked and bare."

There never was any such structure as the tabernacle, they feel, but it was invented by the Priestly School to furnish a Mosaic sanction for the Jerusalem temple. In the interests of this theory, therefore, all references to the tabernacle are automatically assigned to P in the Pentateuch, and also those passages where reference is made to the tabernacle in Joshua, Judges, and Samuel. Having thus by definition assigned all mention of the tabernacle to the Priestly School, it becomes possible for these critics to come up with the triumphant conclusion that no pre-exilic work ever makes any mention of the tabernacle. But this of course is a mere question-begging procedure, rather than an objective handling of the evidence.

Further embarrassment is furnished to this theory (that there was no central sanctuary regulation until Josiah's time) by the positive indications of the record of pre-Josianic times contained in Kings. Certainly the dedicatory prayer of Solomon (cf. especially 1 Kings 8:29-30) implies the unique validity of this temple and its altar, as if already in Solomon's time it was the only lawful and proper place of worship for believing Israel. After his accession in 931 B.C., Jeroboam found it necessary to restrain his subjects of the northern ten tribes from going down to Jerusalem to worship by resorting to the erection of a rival sanctuary in Bethel containing a golden calf (1 Kings 12:26-28). This concern of Jereboam's presupposes the previously unique status of the Jerusalem temple as the central sanctuary in Solomon's time, for it is unlikely that there had been a multiplicity of local sanctuaries practicing idolatry during the Divided Monarchy when not a single idolatrous cult object has yet been found in Israelite strata from this period (Aalders, *A Short Introduction to the Pentateuch* [London: Tyndale], 1949, p. 81). As for the period of Hezekiah, a good century before Josiah's reform, the Hebrew record declares that he enforced the unique claim of the Jerusalem temple by forcibly suppressing all sacrifice and worship at the local high places throughout his domain. It is very difficult to dispose of this reform under Hezekiah as a fictitious prototype of the Josianic revival, as some critics attempt to do. The record of Sennacherib's attempt to capture Jerusalem by threats and negotiation is very circumstantial and convincing as to its historicity. In the course of his parley with the Jewish envoy, the Assyrian commander, Rabshakeh, seeks to discourage the defenders of Jerusalem from looking to Jehovah for deliverance, saying: "But if ye say unto me, We trust in Jehovah our God; is not that he, whose high places and whose altars Hezekiah hath taken away, and hath said unto Judah and to Jerusalem, Ye shall worship before this altar in Jerusalem?" (2 Kings 18:22). This incidental reference to Hezekiah's enforcement of the unique claim of the Jerusalem temple is corroborative testimony of a very high order. It is hard to explain this away as a "priestly" embellishment, since the critics do not otherwise contest the authenticity of this account of Sennacherib's invasion.[9]

At this point we should mention some of the major difficulties standing in the way of dating the legal provisions of J-E and D between 850 and 600 B.C. As George

---

9. Driver, ILOT, p. 187, implausibly attributes this account to a writer living in the next generation after Isaiah, or within three decades after the episode took place in 701 B.C.

Mendenhall points out: "It is hard to conceive of a law code which could be more at variance from what we know of Canaanite culture than the Covenant Code (Ex. 21-23—J-E)....The Canaanite cities were predominantly commercial, rigidly stratified in social structure....The Covenant Code shows no social stratification, for the slaves mentioned are not members of the community, with the single exception of the daughter who is sold as an *amah* or slave-wife (who is herself strongly protected by law)....The laws of the Covenant Code reflect the customs, morality and religious obligations of the Israelite community (or perhaps some specific Israelite community of the North) before the monarchy...since it exhibits just that mixture of case law and apodictic law (technique and policy respectively) which we find in covenants from the Hittite sources and in Mesopotamian codes as well, any study which assumes that it is a later, artificial composite from originally independent literary sources may be assigned rather to rational ingenuity than to historical fact."[10] At the same time Mendenhall reasons that the Pentateuchal laws must have originated subsequently to the Conquest since they have in view a sedentary population rather than a desert nomad society. But this argument overlooks the obvious and announced purpose of the Mosaic code: it was to serve for Israel's guidance *after* it had conquered and settled the promised land, not while it was on the march through the Sinai wilderness.

As to the familiar argument of the Documentarians that the Mosaic law could not have been in existence during the preprophetic era since it is never referred to in the (carefully expurgated) documents J and E,[11] Mendenhall has another interesting observation to make. The written law codes of the ancient Semites, he says, were of little importance in actual court procedures. Thus in the thousands of Old Babylonian legal documents subsequent to the inscribing of Hammurabi's Code, not once is that code explicitly referred to. "If, as we believe, the same was true in Israel, the lack of references to the codified law in the prophets and historical works proves nothing at all concerning the existence of a law code" (such as the book of the covenant, Ex. 21-23).[12] Here, then, the argument from silence is demonstrably false, since the same reasoning would disprove the prior existence of Hammurabi's Code as well, even though that code has been preserved to us from Hammurabi's own time.

Last, it ought to be pointed out that neither J nor E betrays the slightest inkling of an awareness of the existence of a monarchy in Israel. Nowhere is there any suggestion whatsoever that the twelve tribes were to be under the rule of a king, and the only prophetic indication that there would be such a thing as a human sovereign over Israel is found in Gen. 49:10 (J): "The scepter shall not depart from Judah, nor the ruler's staff from between his feet." This seems very hard to reconcile with the supposition that the nation had existed as a monarchy for three centuries before J

---

10. Mendenhall, *Law and Covenant in Israel* (Pittsburgh: Biblical Colloquium, 1955).

11. Compare the passages cited on p. 117 referring to the law of Moses, and also those from Amos discussed on pp. 344-45.

12. Mendenhall, pp. 11-12.

found written form. Even D devotes only a few verses for the direction of a possible future king over Israel (Deut. 17:14-20), and even there gives the impression that the appointment of a king is a remote eventuality in the future. Stranger yet, the assertedly post-exilic document P betrays no consciousness whatever of the institution of royalty.[13] This seems impossible to reconcile with the supposition that the chosen line of David had reigned for more than four centuries in the holy city of Jerusalem. Surely any author manufacturing a Mosaic warrant for the institutions of the priesthood would have attributed to the great lawgiver a very strong and explicit sanction for the kingship as well. It is hardly conceivable that any patriotic Jewish author, who believed in the divine authorization of the Davidic dynasty, could have passed it over in complete silence. All the legal codes of other ancient Near Eastern nations ruled over by monarchs have much to say concerning the duties and prerogatives of their kings. The only reasonable explanation for the fact that P and E are completely silent concerning Hebrew royalty is that there was not yet any king over Israel when they were written. The isolated predictions in J and D lead to a similar conclusion; if composed during the monarchical period, as the Documentarians assert, regulations involving royalty would necessarily have been woven throughout the fabric of these "documents."

---

13. About the only suggestion of monarchy in Israel to be found is the statement in Gen. 36:31: "And these are the kings that reigned in the land of Edom, before there reigned any king over the children of Israel." But here again the appointment of a Hebrew king is regarded as a mere possibility, at best a remote future eventuality that would furnish a fulfillment of the promise made to Abraham in Gen. 17:6 (P): "And kings shall come out of thee." In view of the fact that only the secondary line of Esau had achieved royal status, it was appropriate for a covenant-conscious author in the fifteenth century to note the fact that the posterity of Jacob had not yet attained to that dignity.

12

WELLHAUSEN'S RECONSTRUCTION OF HEBREW HISTORY IN THE PRIESTLY PERIOD

ACCORDING TO THE WELLHAUSEN HYPOTHESIS, the decline and fall of the Jewish monarchy, with the subsequent deportation of the Israelites into captivity, compelled them to surrender political aspirations and look to their religious institutions as a basis for continuing existence as a nation. For this reason the professional priesthood of the tribe of Levi assumed increasing importance, and the ritual practices were elaborated into the form in which they were finally codified in Document P. Prior to the Exile, according to this theory, there had been no really standardized regulations binding upon all the faithful, but worship and sacrifice were conducted according to simple and flexible patterns. While this sounded all very well according to Evolutionary Theory, there were some nineteenth-century researchers in the field of comparative religions who had misgivings. Even so staunch a Wellhausen supporter as W. Robertson Smith felt that Wellhausen was mistaken in supposing that an anxious care to fulfill ritual requirements was post-exilic only.[1] On the contrary, it existed among all the Semites from the earliest stages of their cultural development. Rather than the antithetical epochs of the Wellhausian (Hegelian) doctrine, Smith felt that there was a continuous development through successive periods. For example, Smith believed that the atonement and communion type of sacrifice was early, because based upon the clan type of society; but that the meal offering and heave offering were later, because they were based upon a stage in society when property rights were recognized.[2]

According to the Documentary Theory, there was a clear line of development in the restriction of the priesthood to the family of Aaron. At first the priesthood was open to all Israelites ("And ye shall be unto me a kingdom of priests," Ex. 19:6, a J-E verse). Actually this statement in Ex. 19:6 refers to the role of Israel as God's covenant nation over against all the Gentile, heathen nations, who needed the mediatorship of the Hebrew people if they were ever going to learn of the one true God. Besides, there

---

1. Smith, *The Religion of the Semites.*
2. See H. F. Hahn, *The Old Testament in Modern Research*, pp. 49-51.

is a great difference between the statement: "Ye are a kingdom of priests" and the statement: "Any Israelite is eligible for the priesthood." It is asserted that J-E does not even restrict the priesthood to the tribe of Levi. This, of course, is true, for by definition all references to the priesthood are automatically assigned to P even when they occur in the midst of a J or E passage. But certainly the Documentarians are unable to point to a single passage in the Pentateuch *subsequent* to Aaron's ordination in Lev. 8 that permits any non-Levite to become a priest. (Not even the Torah itself implies that the priesthood was restricted to Levi *prior to* Aaron's consecration.)

The next stage, according to Wellhausen, was represented by Deuteronomy (assertedly forged in 621 B.C.), which restricts the priesthood to the tribe of Levi in general, although not to the family of Aaron in particular. Any Levite may become a priest, according to D, and it was not until the time of the Priestly Code (550-450 B.C.) that this honor was confined to the descendants of Aaron alone. Yet actually it can be demonstrated that D was quite aware of a distinction between the family of Aaron and the rest of the Levites. For example, in Deut. 27:12-14 it was ordained that the tribe of Levi stand with five other tribes on the slope of Mount Gerizim, while the other six tribes stand over against Mount Ebal. But in the valley between the two groups a select group of Levites was to stand, that is, "the priests the Levites" (cf. v. 9), and they were the ones who were to recite a distinctive series of divine curses. It is difficult to avoid the inference that this select group in the valley were Aaronic priests. Likewise in 1 Kings 8:4, a passage attributed by Driver to a Deuteronomistic compiler (ILOT, p. 181), there is a distinction implied between the priests and the Levites: "And they brought up the ark of Jehovah...even these [holy vessels] did the priests and the Levites bring up." (Kuenen felt constrained on dogmatic grounds to snip this verse out of its Deuteronomic context and assign it to P.)

The first stage of restriction of the priesthood came with the latter part of Ezekiel's ministry, it is claimed. For Ezekiel (44:7-16) was the first one to assign an inferior status to all Levites not of the family of Zadok (a contemporary of David descended from Aaron). But the context makes it clear that the special status of the family of Zadok was due to the fact that during the apostasy of the seventh and early sixth centuries, only this division of Aaron's posterity steadfastly refused to cooperate with the idolatrous policies of the Jewish government. It is difficult to see, moreover, how this narrowing down of the priesthood to the descendants of Zadok alone furnished a basis for the extension of sacerdotal status to the whole posterity of Aaron. Nevertheless, according to the Development Hypothesis, this is precisely what happened. From the earlier stage of accessibility to the whole tribe, the priesthood was narrowed down to one small subclan of the descendants of Aaron, and finally thrown open to all Aaronids without distinction. The logical progression here is difficult to see.

At any rate according to this theory, the final stage was the supremacy of the family of Aaron within the tribe of Levi, a development which took place during the Babylonian Exile. This theory is usually bolstered by the contention that Aaron himself was a fictitious character who had no place in the original traditions of Moses and the Exodus. But in order to sustain this contention it was necessary for these critics to deal with many J passages in which Aaron's name appeared (e.g., Ex. 4:14-16, 27-30), at least thirteen occurrences. Each of these had to be lifted out of the J context and branded as P insertions. By this procedure it became possible to come out triumphantly with the dictum: "Aaron is never mentioned in J." Also the deferral of the high-priestly office to the time of the Exile is somewhat embarrassed by the prominence of certain high priests mentioned in pre-exilic Jewish history, men like Jehoiada (2 Kings 12:9), Hilkiah (2 Kings 22:4, 8), and Seraiah (2 Kings 25:18).

The contention that the rise of the priestly school was accompanied by an exaltation of the family of Aaron led quite naturally to the corollary that it was precisely in this same period (550-450 B.C.) that ritual came to the forefront in Judah. Hence the numerous passages in Exodus, Leviticus, and Numbers which deal with matters of ritual and sacrifice are to be regarded as belonging to the latest portion of the Torah, and the technical terms of sacrifice come largely from the vocabulary of the Exilic Period. But as we have already pointed out at the beginning of this chapter, W. R. Smith dissented from the view that in the earlier stages of religion there was little concern for ritual requirements. He felt that the testimony of comparative religions pointed to the contrary, and that even quite primitive peoples lay great emphasis upon following pre-scribed procedure in offering sacrifice and other cultic observances. But this is no longer a mere matter of opinion, for with the unearthing of the extensive Ugaritic literature from Ras Shamra (dating back to 1400 B.C. or earlier), it has been discovered that many of the technical terms of sacrifice branded by Wellhausen as exilic turn up in this early period. Even in so remote a corner of the Canaanite-speaking world as Ugarit we find such P terms as *ishsheh* ("offering made by fire"), "whole burnt offering" (*kālîl*), "peace offerings" (*sh^elāmîm*), and probably *āshām* ("guilt offering").[3] It is hard to avoid the conclusion that these terms were already current in Palestine at the time of Moses and the conquest, and that the whole line of reasoning which made out the terminology of the Levitical cultus to be late is devoid of foundation.[4]

In order to support a late date for the Priestly Code it is usually asserted that none of its provisions or ordinances is mentioned in any of the pre-exilic literature; the pre-exilic authors seem to be quite ignorant of them. Therefore, it is urged, the material contained in document P must have been composed after the fall of Jerusalem (587 B.C.). Driver says, "The pre-exilic period shows no indications of P being in operation"

3. Cyrus H. Gordon denies that Ugaritic *aṭm* has any relation to the Hebrew *'āšām*. It occurs in Text 27:7-9 in fragmentary lines which Gordon leaves untranslated. Text 45:7 likewise has "(....) lgd aṭm," but this too is fragmentary. However, since Gordon offers no translation at all for either of these texts, it would seem to be going beyond the evidence to deny that *aṭm* might correspond to *'āšām*. Strangely enough, Gordon omits the word altogether from the glossary of his 1955 *Ugaritic Manual*, even though that glossary is supposed to contain all the complete words of the Ugaritic texts, whether or not their meaning is known.

4. John Gray questions examples given by T. H. Gaster, but he goes on to contribute other examples: Ugaritic *d-b-ḥ* is the Hebrew *zabah* ("to sacrifice at the altar"); *m-t-n* is the Hebrew *mattan*, ("gift [offered to God"]); *n-d-r* is Hebrew *neder* ("vow"): *š-q-r-b* is equivalent to Hebrew *hiqrîb* ("present an offering"). (Ugaritic uses a *shaphel* for Hebrew *hiphil*.) *Š-'-l-y* is therefore equivalent to the Hebrew *he^elah* ("offer up on the altar"). *Legacy of Canaan*, 2d. rev. ed. (Leiden, Netherlands: E. J. Brill, 1965), pp. 195-99.

(ILOT, p. 136). Again, "Nor is the legislation of P presupposed in Deuteronomy" (p. 137). These assertions, however, are not supported by the textual evidence. The pre-exilic historical books in general, and Deuteronomy in particular, do in fact refer to Levitical legislation as already in being and as binding upon the conscience of Israel.

In the first place, it is significant how even Driver himself is compelled to qualify the sweeping generalizations just quoted when he discusses Deut. 14:3-20: "Here is a long passage virtually identical in Deuteronomy and Leviticus [i.e., Lev. 11:2-23, concerning clean and unclean animals]; and that it is borrowed by D from P— or at least from a priestly collection of *tôrôth*—rather than conversely, appears from certain features of style which connect it with P and not with Deuteronomy.... If so, however, one part of P was in existence when Deuteronomy was written" (ILOT, pp. 137-38). But actually this is not the only such section in Deuteronomy. Deuteronomy 15:1 refers to the year of release, just as it was ordained in Lev. 25:2-7. Moreover Deut. 23:9-10 implies a knowledge of those laws of ceremonial impurity which are contained in Lev. 15:16. Deuteronomy 24:8, "Take heed in the plague of leprosy, that thou observe diligently and do according to all that the priests the Levites shall teach you: as I commanded them, so shall ye observe to do." This expressly affirms the existence of a Mosaic law of leprosy which had been given to the priests (as in Lev. 13 and 14). Other references in Deuteronomy which point explicitly to P laws pertain to Lev. 11, 13-15, 17-19, and Num. 18:20-24. If these are really old laws (as Driver suggests) which existed prior to the codification of P, then (as Orr points out in POT, p. 315), "These old laws must have been so extremely like those we possess in Leviticus that it is hardly worth disputing about the differences, and the argument against the pre-exilian existence of the Levitical law goes for nothing."

But it is not only in Deuteronomy that these references to P legislation appear. In the 755 B.C. text of Amos 2:11-12, we read: "And I raised up of your sons for prophets, and of your young men for Nazarites....But ye gave the Nazarites wine to drink." This passage implies a knowledge of Num. 6:1-21 (P), the only place in the Old Testament where the order of Nazarites is established; the prohibition against their drinking wine is found in Num. 6:3 (P). Again, in Amos 4:5 condemnation is voiced of those who "offer a sacrifice...of that which is leavened," which certainly alludes to the provision found in Lev. 2:11 (P), where the use of leaven in sacrifice was forbidden. Such characteristic P terms as *burnt offering, meal offering,* and *peace offering,* all occur in Amos 5:22 (cf. Lev. 7:11-14; 8:1-32). Likewise we meet with *free will offering* ($n^e d\bar{a}b\bar{a}h$) in Amos 4:5 (cf. Lev. 7:16-18; 22:18; Num. 15:3—all P passages), and *solemn assembly* ($^{a}\d{s}\bar{a}r\bar{a}h$) in Amos 5:21 (Lev. 23:36; Num. 29:35).

The only reasonable inference from all these references (including those also which allude to Deuteronomy) is that already in 755 B.C. there was a written body of law, including both P and D, and labeled by the prophet himself as the Torah of Yahweh (Amos 2:4), and accepted by his public as an authentic and authoritative body of legislation binding upon them.[5] Nor is there the slightest hint or suggestion that either

5. See chap. 22, pp. 354-55.

Amos himself or any other representatives of the Prophetic School were attempting any innovation or promulgating any new teaching in theology or in the cult. Pfeiffer and Eissfeldt have attempted to evade the impact of this evidence from Amos by asserting that all such allusions to the Torah are later insertions. But surely this is a counsel of desperation which contrasts markedly with the confident assertion of Graf, Kuenen, and Wellhausen, that no traces of P legislation are to be found in any pre-exilic Hebrew literature. This was an argument allegedly based upon the evidence of the biblical text itself. When therefore the text itself refutes the claim, there is no reasonable alternative but to withdraw it as unfounded. Nor is this kind of evidence confined to Amos, for it is also found in Hosea. Compare Hos. 8:11-12: "For Ephraim has multiplied altars for sinning....I wrote for him the ten thousand things of my law; but they are accounted as a strange thing." It is difficult to see in this expression, "ten thousand things of my law," a mere reference to J and E, in which the legislative element is quite negligible.

It should be borne in mind in this connection that a customary method for ascertaining the date when a document was written is to take stock of all references to contemporary conditions, social and political, which it contains; particularly the incidental allusions (for these are apt to betray the true date of even spurious works which pretend to have been written earlier than they really were). Applying this investigative method to the "Priestly Code," we find that the internal evidence points with almost overwhelming conclusiveness to a date long before the Babylonian Exile; it is impossible to square many features of P with what we know of post-exilic conditions. For example:

1. The tabernacle of Exodus and Leviticus (regarded by Wellhausen as mere fiction, projected back to Moses' time to furnish a warrant for the temple at Jerusalem) had but one table of shewbread (whereas Solomon's temple had ten), and only one lampstand (Solomon's had ten), and measured only ten cubits by thirty (whereas the temple was twenty by sixty). The dimensions represent a 200 percent increase, whereas the articles of furniture were multiplied 1000 percent.

2. Note also that this allegedly fictitious tabernacle was stated by P to have been dedicated on the first of Nisan (Ex. 40:2), whereas the post-exilic temple of Zerubbabel was dedicated on the third of Adar (Ezra 6:15) and the temple of Solomon some time in the month of Ethanim, or Tishri (1 Kings 8:2).

3. The post-exilic temple apparently lacked the Ark of the Covenant and its two Tables of the Decalogue (for no mention is made of them after the fall of Jerusalem in 587 B.C.), and yet they figured very prominently in P's tabernacle.

4. The post-exilic priesthood is never referred to as possessing the Urim and Thummim, or as wearing an ephod, in any purportedly post-exilic record (although they may perhaps have done so).

5. Very striking is the contrast between P with its single fast (the Day of Atonement) and the three or four major fasts observed by the post-exilic Jews (cf. Zech. 8:19). Certainly any exilic or post-exilic priests, seeking to manufacture Mosaic sanc-

tions for all their cherished contemporary rites and institutions, would not have failed to include some sort of warrant for at least some of the extra fasts.

6. As regards the celebration of the Passover, P (Ex. 12:7, 46) permits the eating of the Passover meal in private homes—a license hardly compatible with a monopolistic priesthood—rather than insisting upon its celebration at the central sanctuary (as Deut. 16:5-12 ordains). Apparently, the Ex. 12 provision had in view Israel's nomadic existence prior to the Conquest, whereas Deuteronomy looked forward to conditions prevailing in Palestine after its conquest and settlement.

7. As for the cities of refuge, mentioned so prominently in P (Num. 35:9-14), they are never mentioned as such in the post-exilic records. Furthermore, most of them were situated well outside the boundaries of the Persian province of Judea in Ezra's time.

8. Elements in the Jewish ritual and temple service which figured very prominently in the post-exilic period receive no mention whatsoever in this allegedly priest-inspired document, P. Thus, we find no reference whatsoever to (1) the Levitical guild of temple singers; (2) the scribes, of which Ezra himself was the acknowledged leader; (3) the temple servants known as the Nethinîm; (4) the employment of musical instruments. It is impossible to explain how a professional priestly group, manufacturing a spurious law of Moses for the purpose of justifying and enforcing their claims to special authority, could have failed to include Mosaic sanctions for any of these items. Nor, for that matter, is it explicable how J and E and D could have failed to mention items (1), (3), and (4), if they were in fact composed later than the reign of Solomon (970-931 B.C.), under whom the temple singers, Nethinîm, and musical instruments were intimately involved in the temple cultus. It is therefore difficult to account for this astonishing silence about matters of peculiarly priestly interest, except upon the basis that P was in fact composed before Solomon's time.[6]

9. In this connection it ought to be pointed out that the holy city of Jerusalem is never mentioned in the Mosaic legislation. There is a reference to Melchizedek, king of *Salem*, in Gen. 14; Mount Moriah is named as the scene of Isaac's near-sacrifice; and "the mountain of thine inheritance" is a phrase appearing in Ex. 15:17. But never once is Jerusalem referred to as such in the Torah. How is it possible that after five hundred years of existence as the religious and political capital of the Jewish commonwealth, the assorted contributors to document P neglected to include any slightest sanction for the holy city? Not even by later interpolations (such as apparently crept into the Samaritan text of the Torah to establish the sanctity of their holy Mount Gerizim) were Zion and Jerusalem certified as the uniquely acceptable place in which to offer sacrifice according to either P or J or E. Even Deuteronomy leaves the "place Jehovah shall choose" (12:5, 14; 16:16) altogether anonymous, though it would have been very easy for a seventh-century author to insert at least the name of Jerusalem, even if he hesitated to disturb the illusion of Mosaic origin by specifying its future importance. A large

---

6. Cf. Yehezkel Kaufmann, *The Religion of Israel*, pp. 175-200, for a more detailed discussion of the antiquity of the Priestly Code, which he believes to be much earlier than Deuteronomy.

number of other Palestinian cities are referred to by name in document D, but never Jerusalem.

10. Lastly it should be pointed out that one of the most frequent and characteristic titles of God employed by the post-exilic prophets and authors is never once found in the entire Pentateuch. This title is Jehovah of Hosts (*Yahweh Ṣebā'ôt*), which occurs sixty-seven times in Isaiah (in sixty-six chapters), eighty-three times in Jeremiah (in fifty-two chapters), thirteen times in Haggai (in two chapters), fifty-one times in Zechariah (fourteen chapters), and twenty-five times in Malachi (three or four chapters). This indicates a mounting frequency or popularity for this title culminating in the three post-exilic prophets: Haggai (6.5 times per chapter), Zechariah (3.5 times per chapter), and Malachi (6 to 8 times per chapter). It is well-nigh impossible to explain how *Yahweh Ṣebā'ôt* could fail to appear in document P, if in fact it was composed after the exile. (While it is true that Ezekiel does not use this title either, the Documentary Theory attributes strong Ezekiel influence only to H, i.e., Lev. 17-26, and dates the rest of P as arising between 550 and 450 B.C.) No other title for God approaches the frequency with which this one was used by the very prophets in whose generation this Priestly Code was supposedly being composed. (At the same time it should be recognized that the narrative authors, Ezra and Nehemiah, do not employ this expression except in Chronicles. For some reason it was not much used by the Jews dwelling in Babylonia.) It occurred eleven times in 1 and 2 Samuel, six times in Kings, but not once in the entire Pentateuch. The most natural inference to draw from these data is that *Yahweh Ṣebā'ôt* did not come into vogue as a title for God until after the period of the Judges, and that P, along with J, E, and D, was composed before the age of the Judges began.

13 ARCHAEOLOGICAL EVIDENCE FOR THE ANTIQUITY OF THE PENTATEUCH

IT WAS ONLY NATURAL that the Wellhausen Hypothesis should base its judgments concerning the historicity of the Old Testament record upon the data of archaeology then available in the nineteenth century. Yet those data were regrettably meager during the formative period of the Documentary Theory, and it was possible on the basis of the ignorance which then prevailed to discount many statements in Scripture which had not yet found archaeological confirmation.

For example, at that time it was assumed that writing was relatively unknown in Palestine during the Mosaic period, and that no part of the Pentateuch could, therefore, have found, for example, a written form until the tenth or ninth centuries B.C. The references to the Hittites, for example, were treated with incredulity and condemned as mere fiction on the part of the late authors of the Torah; the same was true of the Horites and even the historicity of Sargon II (722-705 B.C.), since no extrabiblical references to him had yet been discovered. The existence of such a king as Belshazzar (in the book of Daniel) was ruled out of possibility because no Greek author had mentioned him, and the biblical record could be presumed to be wrong. But since the days of Hupfeld, Graf, and Kuenen, archaeological discovery has confirmed the use of alphabetic writing in the Canaanite-speaking cultures before 1500 B.C., and has contributed large numbers of documents to demonstrate the existence and major importance of both the Hittites and Horites (or Hurrians, as they are more commonly known), and also cuneiform tablets containing the name of Belshazzar, as viceroy under Nabonidus.

Thus it has come about that in case after case after case where alleged historical inaccuracy was pointed to as proof of late and spurious authorship of the biblical documents, the Hebrew record has been vindicated by the results of recent excavation, and the condemnatory judgments of the Documentarian Theorists have been proved without foundation. W. F. Albright, esteemed the foremost archaeologist of his generation, and a man who was himself brought up on the Wellhausen theory, had this to say in 1941: "Archaeological and inscriptional data have established the historicity of innumerable passages and statements of the Old Testament; the number of such cases is many times greater than those where the reverse has been proved or has been made probable."[1] Further on in the same article he said, "Wellhausen still ranks in our eyes as the greatest Biblical scholar of the nineteenth century. But his standpoint is anti-

WORLD EMPIRES OF THE BIBLE	
EMPIRE	**DATE**
Assyria	740-612 B.C.
Babylonia	612-539 B.C.
Medo-Persia	539-331 B.C.
Macedonia	332-301 B.C.
Diadochi	301-63 B.C.
Rome	189 B.C.-A.D. 476
The Eastern Roman Empire continued until A.D. 1453	

quated and his picture of the early evolution of Israel is sadly distorted." A more recent author, John Elder, states: "It is not too much to say that it was the rise of the science of archaeology that broke the deadlock between historians and the orthodox Christian. Little by little, one city after another, one civilization after another, one culture after another, whose memories were enshrined only in the Bible, were restored to their proper places in ancient history by the studies of archaeologists....Contemporary records of Biblical events have been unearthed and the uniqueness of Biblical revelation has been emphasized by contrast and comparison to newly discovered religions of ancient peoples. Nowhere has archaeological discovery refuted the Bible as history."[2] J. A. Thompson affirms, "Finally, it is perfectly true to say that biblical archaeology has done a great deal to correct the impression that was abroad at the close of the last century and in the early part of this century, that Biblical history was of doubtful trustworthiness in many places. If one impression stands out more clearly than another today, it is that on all hands the over-all historicity of the Old Testament tradition is admitted."[3]

This chapter cannot do justice to so extensive a subject as the entire field of biblical archaeology, but can only bring out a few of the best-known and most significant discoveries of the post-Wellhausen era. Standard works on this subject are: Albright,

1. "Japheth in the Tents of Shem," in *The American Scholar*, 42:692-94 (1941), p. 181.
2. Elder, *Prophets, Idols and Diggers* (New York: Bobbs Merrill, 1960), p. 16, a book endorsed by an editorial board consisting of American Liberal clergymen.
3. J. A. Thompson, *Archaeology* (Grand Rapids: Eerdmans, 1959), p. 13.

W. F., *The Archaeology of Palestine*; Barton, G. A., *Archaeology and the Bible*, a work consisting largely in translations of ancient pagan documents having a relevance for the Old Testament; Finegan, J., *Light from the Ancient Past*, which contains more extensive discussion and less actual translation; Free, J. P., *Archaeology and Bible History*, a conservative treatment of the field on a semi-popular level; Price, I. M., et al., *The Monuments and the Old Testament* (Philadelphia: Judson, 1958), an extensive revision of an older work, which surveys the field on a semipopular level from a moderately Liberal standpoint; Pritchard, J. B. (ed.), *Ancient Near Eastern Texts*, which is now the standard translation for almost all the ancient documents and literature having a bearing upon the Bible; Thomas, D. W. (ed.), *Documents from Old Testament Times* (New York: Harper & Row, 1958), containing an excellent anthology of ancient non-biblical texts in translation, with introductions and notes; Unger, M. F., *Archaeology and the Old Testament*, contains a somewhat more thorough and up-to-date discussion from the conservative standpoint than Free's *Archaeology and Bible History*.

In the following pages an attempt is made to group some of the foremost discoveries affecting erroneous criticisms leveled against the historical accuracy of the Pentateuch by adherents of the Documentary School. Each of these ill-founded allegations is followed by a list of archaeological data tending to refute it. No attempt is made to discuss these various discoveries in detail, but a brief summary is given of their importance relative to the allegation concerned.

ILL-FOUNDED ALLEGATIONS

ALLEGATION: The art of writing was virtually unknown in Israel prior to the establishment of the Davidic monarchy; therefore there could have been no written records going back to the time of Moses.

REFUTATION: (1) The earliest Hebrew document thus far discovered is the Gezer Calendar, written about 925 B.C. (found by Macalister in the 1900s). But since it is obviously a mere schoolboy's exercise, it demonstrates that the art of writing was so well known and widely practiced in Israel during the tenth century that even the children were being taught this skill in the provinces.

(2) The Ugaritic or Ras Shamra Tablets (discovered by Schaeffer in 1929) date from about 1400 B.C. They are written in a thirty-letter alphabet and couched in a language more closely related to Hebrew than to any other known Semitic dialect. They principally consist of religious epic poetry referring to such deities as El, Baal, Anath, Asherat, and Mot, and exhibit the depraved polytheism which characterized the Canaanites at the time of the Israelite conquest. As already pointed out in chapter 12, they feature several cultic terms which were falsely alleged by Wellhausen to be post-exilic P inventions. This surely establishes the fact that these technical terms for sacrifice were the common property of the whole Canaanite area nearly a thousand years before they were supposed to have arisen according to the Documentary Hypothesis.

They also furnish many parallels to poetic clichés and characteristic expressions found both in the poetic portions of the Pentateuch and in the Psalms. They refer to Baal's home as being situated "on the mountain of his inheritance," which comes very close to Ex. 15:17 with its phrase, "the mountain of thine inheritance" (understood by the critics as a reference to Mount Zion, and therefore post-Davidic).[4] Even some of the poetic forms and parallelisms in these Ugaritic epics show a close resemblance to Hebrew poetry. Compare, for example, the tricolonic parallelism used in the song of Miriam (Ex. 15:7, 8) and in some of the Psalms (e.g., Ps. 92:9), which reflects a style characteristic of the Ugaritic poems. Some of the rare and dubious words of the Hebrew poetry occur also in the Ras Shamra documents, which have therefore shed light upon their meaning. (Cf. Albright, AP, pp. 231-33.)[5]

(3) Even earlier than the Ras Shamra literature was the assortment of alphabetic inscriptions found at the turquoise mines of Serabit el-Khadim (the ancient Dophkah), dating from 1500 B.C. at the very latest. These hieroglyphic inscriptions (discovered by Petrie in 1904) exhibit an alphabetic system which furnishes the ancestry for the letters of the Phoenician alphabet. Obviously the authors of these inscriptions were Semitic miners in the employ of Egypt. The natural inference is that already by that time writing was so widely diffused among the Semites of the pre-Mosaic age that even the lowest classes of society could read and write. (Some have suggested that these were Hyksos slaves, as Albright conjectures, who were compelled to work in these mines after they were expelled from Egypt.) It is interesting to observe that more recently potsherds have been discovered at Hazor inscribed in this same Sinaitic script (Y. Yadin, et al.: Hazor I [1958], Hazor II [1960]), which suggests that the knowledge of writing in this alphabetic script was extended throughout Palestine in Moses' time.

ALLEGATION: The Genesis accounts of the career of Abraham and his descendants are untrustworthy and often unhistorical. Nöldeke even went so far as to deny the historical existence of Abraham altogether.

REFUTATION: The twentieth century has brought abundant confirmation of the biblical record through the following archaeological discoveries.

(1) The city of Ur in Southern Sumeria was thoroughly excavated by Leonard Woolley (1922-1934), and it proved to be a large and flourishing city which enjoyed

---

4. An epithet of Baal in 1 Aqhat 43-44 is r-k-b '-r-p-t (probably vocalized as rākib 'urpāti) meaning "Rider of the Clouds"; this appears in Ps. 68:5 as r-k-b b- '-r-b-w-t (rōkēb bā 'ᵃrābôt) as a description of Yahweh (a phrase formerly misinterpreted as "Rider in the Deserts"). Cf. Cyrus Gordon, Ugaritic Manual, p. 179b.

5. Tiamat in Ugaritic: Tᵉhôm, goddess of chaos, was overthrown by Marduk, in 14/13 cc. B.C., referred to in Ebla, 2400 B.C., as ti'amat, which like the Hebrew is used as a term for "deep, ocean abyss" (K. A. Kitchen: The Bible and Archaeology, p. 26). It is also to be noted that the name of the goddess of "chaos" and "the deep," Tiamat, seems to be cognate with the term for "abyss" or "great deep." Tᵉhôm occurs in Gen. 1:2; however, it should be understood that the probabilities are great that Tᵉhôm, as a masculine, meaning "abyss," originated earlier than the name given to the supposed goddess of the deep, and therefore this scarcely implies any borrowing of pagan material in order to explain the appearance of Tᵉhôm in the Hebrew Bible.

an advanced civilization around 2000 B.C., which would have been precisely Abraham's period. The average middle-class citizens lived in well-appointed houses containing from ten to twenty rooms. Schools were maintained for the education of the young, for schoolboy tablets have been discovered which attest their training in reading, writing, arithmetic, and religion (Free, ABH, pp. 49-50). There has been some question in recent years as to whether it was the Sumerian Ur that was referred to, but the evidence for a more northerly city of the same name is still meager, and at any rate could not have been called "Ur of the Chaldees" (*UR KASDÎM*).

(2) The name *Abram* has been discovered in tablets dating from the sixteenth century B.C. Thus, an Akkadian tablet dated 1554 B.C., or the eleventh year of Amisadugga of Babylon (Barton, AB, p. 344), records the hiring of an ox by a farmer named Abarama. Two other tablets refer to this same man as Abamrama.[6]

(3) As for Abraham's career in Palestine, the excavations at Shechem and Bethel show that they were inhabited in Abraham's time. A ninth-century writer might well have represented the patriarch as stopping at cities which were not standing in the twentieth century B.C., although they may have become famous later.

(4) The older scholars criticized Gen. 13 as unhistorical, on the ground that the Jordan valley was relatively uninhabited in Abraham's time. But Nelson Glueck has in recent decades uncovered more than seventy sites in the Jordan valley, some of them as ancient as 3000 B.C.[7]

(5) Genesis 14 was rejected by Nöldeke on the grounds that (*a*) the names of the Mesopotamian kings were fictional, (*b*) there was no such extensive travel from Mesopotamia to Palestine in Abraham's day, and (*c*) there was no such line of march east of the Jordan River. But as to (*a*) the likelihood of a Chedorlaomer, king of Elam, more recent discovery has shown that an Elamite dynasty did indeed establish a temporary over-lordship in Sumer and Akkad, and that some of these kings had names beginning with "Kudur" ("servant"), and that there was an Elamite goddess named Lagamar. Thus, a king Kudur-lagamar may well have participated in this invasion. It is stated in one tablet (Barton, AB, p. 349) that a king named Kudur-Mabug had a son named Eri-aku (or else his name could be read Arad-Sin, "Servant of the moon-god"), and that he was king of Larsa—very close to "Arioch king of Ellasar" (Gen. 14:1). The Mari Tablets also attest the currency of the name Ariyuk. (So Albright in Rowley,

---

6. Following an older chronology, Barton dates the first tablet at 1965 B.C.; but according to P. E. Van der Meer's date in *The Ancient Chronology of Western Asia and Egypt* (Leiden, Netherlands: E. J. Brill, 1947), Ammiṣaduqa began his reign in 1565.

7. Note that the Ebla documents refer to *Si-da-mu,* Sodom; *E-ma-ra,* Gommorrah; *Si-ba-iy-um,* Zeboiim; *Ad-ma,* Admah; *Be-la,* Bela or Zoar. C. A. Wilson (*That Incredible Book: The Bible*) identifies (with Bryant G. Wood in *Bible & Spade,* "Have Sodom and Gomorrah Been Found?") Sodom with Khanazir (at the extreme south end of the Ghor), Gomorrah with Feifa, Zoar with Safi, Admah with Numeira, and Zeboiim with Bab edh-Dhra—each on a spur overlooking a wadi, enclosed by a stone wall, with a tower at the end and located next to a perennial spring (p. 63). Apparently an earthquake disturbed the granite bituminous oil basin beneath all these cities, shooting up sulphur and bitumen into the air releasing natural gases that were ignited. Strata high on the side of Mt. Usdum were welded together by great heat, with deposits or formations of marl (p. 65).

OTMS, p. 6.) A Babylonian wagon contract dating from a time shortly after Hammurabi stipulates that the wagon hired must not be driven to the coast of the Mediterranean (indicating that wagons could indeed be driven to Palestine in those days). (Cf. Barton, AB, p. 347.)

The net result of all this archaeological confirmation of the agreement of Gen. 14 with conditions existing in that period has been to convince Gunkel, Albright, and many others, that this episode rests upon authentic tradition perhaps going back to the twentieth century B.C. Albright concludes, "In spite of our failure hitherto to fix the historical horizon of this chapter, we may be certain that its contents are very ancient. There are several words and expressions found nowhere else in the Bible and now known to belong to the second millennium. The names of the towns in Transjordania are also known to be very ancient."[8] It should be pointed out, however, that the earlier identification of "Amraphel king of Shinar" with the celebrated Hammurabi of Babylon is now no longer tenable, for it is now known that he lived in the eighteenth century, whereas Abraham belonged to the twentieth or twenty-first century (according to the biblical record). This revised date for Hammurabi's reign (ca. 1792-1750 B.C., according to Rowton) has been established on the basis of diplomatic correspondence discovered at Mari between Zimri-Lim, the last king of Mari, and Hammurabi himself.[9] Since the time of Zimri-Lim has been fixed

A BABYLONIAN BOUNDARY STONE
BOUNDARY STONES WERE IN USE IN THE THIRD MILLENNIUM B.C. IN MESOPOTAMIA AND WERE VERY COMMON FROM THE SECOND MILLENNIUM B.C. ONWARD. SUCH STONES FROM BABYLON WERE BOULDERS WITH INSCRIPTIONS STATING THE TITLE–DEED TO THE LAND, DIMENSIONS OF THE GROUND, AND A CURSE TO ANY PERSON INJURING OR REMOVING THE LANDMARK.

from other synchronisms, the later date for the famous lawgiver seems firmly grounded.

(6) The Mari Tablets were discovered by Parrot at Tell Hariri on the middle Euphrates in 1933. These twenty thousand tablets were written in Akkadian during

8. H. C. Alleman and E. E. Flack (eds.), *Old Testament Commentary*, p. 14.
9. See BASOR, no. 88 (Dec. 1942): 28-361.

the eighteenth century B.C., and confirm the existence of the city of Nakhur (which could have been so named after Abraham's brother, Nahor, according to Gen. 24:10; cf. 11:27). They also refer to the name Ariyuk (Arioch) as current in the early second millennium. They even mention the Habiru (which is probably the Akkadian form of the Canaanite term '*Ibrîym* or *Hebrew*), a designation first applied to Abraham in the Genesis record, but which from the cuneiform evidence, seems to have referred to certain groups of warlike "wanderers" or "people from the other side" (based on the assumption that the root of the name was derived from the verb '*ābar*, "cross over, pass through"), who may or may not have been ethnically related to each other. It is interesting to note that one of the names occurring in these documents from Mari is Banu-Yamina (note the similarity to *Benjamin*), a tribe of fierce nomads. The early occurrence of this word gives a background for its appearance in later Hebrew history.

(7) The Nuzu or Nuzi Tablets, found by Chiera and Speiser at Nuzi (near Kirkuk) on the Tigris in 1925, date from the fifteenth century, and betray a strong, Hurrian influence in the type of Akkadian used in the several thousand tablets discovered. They serve to confirm the historicity of many of the customs and usages practiced by Abraham and the other patriarchs prior to the Egyptian sojourn. (*a*) Abraham's reference to his servant Eliezer as "son of his house" in Gen. 15:2 (prior to the birth of Ishmael and Isaac) indicated that he had adopted him as his legal heir. God's rejection of this arrangement (Gen. 15:4) might have occasioned Abraham embarrassment had it not been customary (as Nuzi texts show) to set aside the claims of an adopted son if a natural heir was subsequently born into the family. (*b*) The legitimacy of selling one's birthright (as Esau sold his to Jacob in Gen. 25:33) was established at Nuzi, for in one case an older brother was validly recompensed by a payment of three sheep for selling to his younger brother the rights of primogeniture.[10] (*c*) The binding character of a deathbed will, such as was elicited from Isaac by Jacob, is attested by a case where a man named Tarmiya established his right to a woman he had married by proving that his father on his deathbed orally bestowed her on him. This was sufficient to win the lawsuit brought against him by his brothers. (*d*) A plausible motive for Rachel's theft of her father's teraphim (Gen. 31) is supplied by a Nuzi record of a case where a man was able in court to claim the estate of his father-in-law because he possessed the family teraphim (or household gods).[11] H. H. Rowley comes to this conclusion regarding the patriarchal narratives in Genesis; "Their accurate reflection of social conditions in the patriarchal age and in some parts of the Mesopotamia from which the patriarchs are said to have come, many centuries before the present documents were composed, is striking."[12]

10. See C. H. Gordon in *The Biblical Archaeologist* 3 (1940): 5.
11. Cf. Gordon in *Revue Biblique* 44 (1935): 35.
12. Rowley, in *Bulletin of the John Rylands Library*, 32 (Sept. 1949): 76. Note also the comments of J. A. Thompson, "The fact that there are so many links with the world of the first part of the second millennium B.C. is inexplicable if the stories of the Patriarchs are only the inventions of later days. It would seem impossible for the Israelites of those centuries to have access to such information as we now find beneath the earth on thousands of baked clay tablets. The fact that the Bible customs are so close to

(8) The Hittite Legal Code (discovered by Winckler at Ḫattušaš or Boghaz-köy 1906-1912 and dating from about 1300 B.C.) illuminates the transaction recorded in Gen. 23 where Abraham purchased the cave of Machpelah from Ephron the Hittite. Hittite law explains the reluctance of Abraham to buy the entire parcel, and his preference for acquiring only the cave itself and the territory immediately adjacent. The law required the owner of an entire tract to perform the duties of *ilku* or feudal service, a responsibility which doubtless included pagan religious observances. As a Jehovah-worshiper, Abraham was alert enough to prefer avoiding this involvement by purchasing only a fraction of the parcel, thus leaving Ephron responsible to perform *ilku* as original owner of the tract. As Manfred Lehmann brings out,[13] the account in Gen. 23 exhibits such an intimate knowledge of Hittite procedure as to make it certain that the episode antedated the destruction of the Hittite power in the thirteenth century B.C.

(9) It was the contention of many archaeologists, Albright included, that the references to camels as included in Abraham's holdings in livestock (Gen. 12:16) and as employed by his servant who conducted the courtship of Rebekah (Gen. 24:10, 14, 19-20) were anachronistic embellishments coming from later centuries. Likewise the mention of camels as employed by the slave traders who purchased Joseph on their way down to Egypt (Gen. 37:25). This deduction was drawn from a lack of clear extrabiblical reference to camels prior to the twelfth century in any of the archaeological discoveries made before 1950. But like so many arguments from silence, this contention must be abandoned as discredited by subsequent findings. Kenneth Kitchen points out (AOOT, p. 79) that even apart from a probable (but disputed) eighteenth-century allusion to camels in a fodder list from Tell Atshana (as attested by W. G. Lambert in BASOR, no. 160 [Dec. 1960]: 42-43), there is undoubtedly a reference to the domestication of camels in some of the lexical lists from the Old Babylonian period (2000-1700 B.C.). An early Sumerian text from Nippur alludes to camel's milk (cf. *Chicago Assyrian Dictionary* [1960]: 7:2*b*). Back in the twenty-fifth century B.C., the bones of a camel were interred under a house at Mari (André Parrot, in *Syria* 32 [1955]: 323). Similar discoveries have been made in Palestinian sites in levels dating from 2000 B.C. onward. From Byblos in Phoenicia comes an incomplete camel figurine dating from the nineteenth or eighteenth century (Roland de Vaux, in *Revue Biblique*, 56 [1949]: 9). More recent discovery has further shown this negative judgment to be unjustified. (Cf. R. J. Forbes, *Studies in Ancient Technology*, vol. 2 [Brill, 1965], chap. 4, pp. 194-213; "The Coming of the Camel," p. 197). Forbes cites an early Dynastic limestone vessel shaped like a recumbent pack camel; also discovered are pottery camels' heads from Hierakonpolis and Abydos in the Egyptian First Dynasty (p. 198). Also included is a figurine of a recumbent camel at Byblos during

---

the contemporary customs is a strong argument either for written records, or for reliable oral traditions. We are compelled to conclude that the narratives of Genesis 12-50 have a solid historical basis." *Archaeology & the Old Testament*, p. 31.

13. BASOR, no. 129 (Feb. 1953): 18.

the Middle Kingdom Period (p. 203). Oppenheim found at Gozan (Tell Halaf) an orthostat of an armed camel rider which was dated 3000 B.C. or at least early 3rd millennium. A small camel figurine discovered at Megiddo closely resembles Dynasty I types. Middle Kingdom camel bones were found at Gezer (p. 209). The Akkadian term for male camel, *ibulu/udra/uduru*; for female camel, *udrate*; for dromedary, *gammalu*: (E-G v:116.10) in Coptic (*jamūl*). (The Sumerian term was *ANŠE A-ABBA:* "an ass of the sea-lands or dromedary"). Once again the Old Testament record has been vindicated as a completely trustworthy and historical account, despite the temporary lack of archaeological confirmation.

ALLEGATION: The legislation of the Priestly Code represents a late, post-exilic stage in the development of Israel's religion; laws of this sort could never have been devised until the fifth century B.C.

REFUTATION: (1) The Babylonian *Code of Hammurabi* (C. H.), discovered by de Morgan and Scheil at Susa in 1901, shows numerous similarities to the provisions in Exodus, Leviticus, and Numbers, relative to the punishment of crimes and the imposition of damages for torts and breaches of contract. Many of these similar laws are included by Wellhausen in document P. Generally speaking, the resemblances are found in the Israelite *mišpāṭîm* (civil laws of customary origin, generally having an "if—then—" type of structure). For example, (*a*) Lev. 19:23-25 provides that after an orchard is planted, the cultivator of it may not eat of its fruit until the fifth year. *Code of Hammurabi* #60 stipulates that the tenant farmer who has planted an orchard may not eat of its fruit until the fifth year (at which time he must let the owner of the property take the better half of the crop). (*b*) Leviticus 20:10 provides the death penalty for both the adulterer and the adulteress. C. H. #129 provides that both parties to adultery are to be drowned, unless a pardon is secured from the king, or unless the wife is pardoned by her husband. (*c*) Numbers 5:11-28 describes a procedure for determining the guilt or innocence of a wife who has been suspected by her husband of infidelity: she is to drink a potion of "bitter water" upon which a curse has been invoked if she is guilty. C. H. #132 provides that a wife suspected of adultery (although not apprehended in the act) shall be cast into the river to see whether she will sink (if guilty) or float (if innocent). (*d*) Leviticus 20:12 requires the death penalty for both parties when a man commits adultery with his daughter-in-law. C. H. #155 exacts capital punishment only of the father-in-law in such a case, presumably on the ground that the woman would not dare to refuse the head of the household. (*e*) Leviticus 24:19-20 fixes the damages for mayhem as the same injury to be inflicted on the offender (an eye for an eye, tooth for a tooth). C. H. #196, 197, 200 all require the same penalty where both parties are of the same social class, but only monetary damages where the injured party is of a lower class.

The resemblances are so striking as to demonstrate that laws of the P type are by no means too advanced for the age of Moses, since they found a fairly close correspondence with the legal systems prevailing in Babylonia centuries before his time.[14] It can hardly be objected that the Israelites were too primitive to be governed by laws such as these back in Moses' time, since according to their own explicit record they had been living in the midst of one of the most advanced civilizations of ancient times for over four hundred years, and would naturally have entertained more advanced concepts of jurisprudence than tribes indigenous to the desert. It might be expected that Egyptian regulations would have exerted a more profound influence upon the Hebrew code than did the Babylonian (which could only have survived as an oral tradition from Abrahamic days). But since no law codes have ever yet been discovered in Egypt (Pritchard, ANET, p. 212), it is impossible to assess the Egyptian element one way or the other. It should be understood, of course, that the differences between the Torah and the *Code of Hammurabi* are far more striking than the resemblances. But the differences proceed largely from the entirely different religious ideology to which each of the two cultures adhered.

Most numerous, however, are the resemblances between the Babylonian code and the Book of the Covenant contained in Ex. 21–23. Compare, for example, Ex. 21:2-11 with C. H. #117 (poor debtors are to be bondslaves for three years and released on the fourth year); Ex. 21:15 with #195 (If a son has struck his father, his hand shall be cut off. They shall cut off his hand); Ex. 21:16 with #14 (If an *awēlum* has stolen the young son of another *awēlum*, he shall be put to death); Ex. 21:22-25 with #209-213; Ex. 21:28-36 with #250-252; Ex. 22:7-9 with #120; Ex. 22:9 with #267; Ex. 23:1-3 with #1-4. This evidence of course establishes the possibility of a Mosaic date for these regulations, rather than the 800 B.C. period assigned to them by the Documentary School. The same is true of those provisions which show an affinity to the Deuteronomic legislation (Deut. 19:16-21 and #1; Deut. 22:23-27 and #130), which is not a mere restatement of laws in Exodus through Numbers. The legislation of eighteenth-century Babylon establishes the possible antiquity of these allegedly Josianic (seventh century) provisions of document D.

(2) The fifteenth-century Ras Shamra Tablets, as before pointed out,[15] furnish a goodly number of technical terms for sacrifice which Wellhausen had declared to be of fifth-century origin (*offering made by fire, peace offering, sin offering, trespass offering*, and possibly even *t^enūpah, heave offering*—cf. Koehler-Baumgartner, p. 1034*a*).[16] In addition to cultic terms we find mention of the rite of boiling a kid in its mother's milk as an acceptable way to approach a god (Gordon, Text 52:14). This gives point to the prohibition of this superstitious heathen practice in Ex. 23:19; 34:26; and Deut. 14:21.

14. Cf. the quotation from Mendenhall on p. 158 pointing to a pre-monarchy setting for the Covenant Code (Ex. 21-23).

15. See chap. 12, p. 167.

16. Sacrificial terms in the Pentateuch set forth as original terms given to Moses, but which are attested as to early origin by the Ras Shamra tablets.

šqrb'(š'ly: equivalent to Hebrew-*hiqrîb* - "to bring near, present an offering")

iššeh - fire offering	*š^elāmîm* - fellowship offering	*āšām* - guilt offering
kālîl - whole burnt offering	*zebaḥ* - blood sacrifice	*mattān* - gift offering
neder - votive offering		

EGYPTIAN BOOK OF THE DEAD

A JUDGMENT SCENE FROM THE PAPYRUS OF ANI, ROYAL SCRIBE AND GOVERNOR OF GRAINERIES.

Concerning this whole question of the late date assigned by critics to the Mosaic legislation, Millar Burrows of Yale had this to say: "Scholars have sometimes supposed that the social and moral level of the laws attributed to Moses was too high for such an early age. The standards represented by the ancient law codes of the Babylonians, Assyrians and Hittites, as well as the high ideals found in the *Egyptian Book of the Dead*, and the early wisdom literature of the Egyptians, have effectively refuted this assumption."[17]

Another important line of evidence has been found in the remarkable analogy between the structure of second-millennium suzerainty treaties and the structure of Deuteronomy, and legal portions of Exodus as well. (For more specific details, see chap. 18 on Deuteronomy.) Albright states that this presentation of the Covenant undertaking between Yahweh and Israel "preserves a clear pattern which in no fewer than eight distinct points reflects the characteristic structures of Syro-Anatolian treaties of the 14th and 13th centuries B.C., which had been preserved in the Hittite archives at Boghazköy. The structure of half a dozen Assyrian, Aramaic and Phoenician treaties which we know from the 8th cent. B.C. and later is quite different."[18]

ALLEGATION: The whole account of the Hebrew conquest of Transjordan and Palestine as recorded in Numbers and Joshua is grossly unhistorical and out of harmony with conditions prevailing in the late second millennium.[19]

17. Burrows, *What Mean These Stones?* (New Haven, Conn.: ASOR, 1941), p. 56.

18. Albright, SAC, p. 16.

19. As J. A. Thompson states in *Archaeology and the Old Testament*, p. 24, "It would not be surprising, therefore, if laws and customs found in the northern areas were paralleled in Palestine, for the simple reason that they were brought to the new land by the Patriarchs and preserved there through regular contact with their former homeland. The result of this discovery has been that whereas it was commonly held at the close of the last century and at the beginning of this one that these stories in Gene-

MAJOR ARCHAEOLOGICAL PERIODS

Archaeological Period	Dates	Biblical Period
Pottery	5000 B.C.	Pre-Abraham
Chalcolithic	4000-3200 B.C.	Pre-Abraham
Early Bronze	3200-2100 B.C.	Pre-Abraham
Middle Bronze	2100-1500 B.C.	Abraham to Moses
Late Bronze	1500-1200 B.C.	Moses to Judges
Iron Age I	1200-970 B.C.	Judges to Solomon
Iron Age II	970-600 B.C.	Divided Kingdom
Iron Age III	600-330 B.C.	To end of the Old Testament
Hellenistic I	330-165 B.C.	Inter-testamental
Hellenistic II	165-63 B.C.	Inter-testamental (Maccabean)
Roman	63 B.C.- A.D. 330	New Testament

* There is substantial debate regarding the dating of LB and IAI. For a full discussion cf. J. J. Bimson, *Redating the Exodus and Conquest*, JSOT, Sheffield, Almond Press, 1978.

REFUTATION: (1) The Egyptian Execration Texts of the Twelfth Dynasty serve to confirm the historicity of the political situation in Palestine as portrayed in the Pentateuch and in Joshua. These consist of two groups: a collection of inscribed bowls found by Sethe in 1926 (now in the Berlin Museum) dating from about 1920 B.C.; and a group of inscribed statuettes found by Posener in 1940 (now in the Brussels Museum) dating from about 1820 B.C. These objects were inscribed with the names of tributary cities and states in Palestine which were bound by oath to be loyal to Egypt. Their apparent purpose was voodooistic; that is, if the people represented by these names should violate their oaths, the jars or statuettes were to be smashed, so as to bring a curse upon the rebels themselves. The significant factor is that the inscriptions in the second group indicate a perceptible decrease in tbe number of tribal units and an increase in the number of city-states in the land of Palestine—the situation reflected in the book of Joshua.[20]

(2) The Tell el-Amarna Tablets, discovered at Tell el-Amarna (ancient Akhetaten) in 1887, and dating from 1400-1370 B.C., consist of a file of correspondence written in Akkadian cuneiform to the Egyptian court by Palestinian and Syrian princelings.

sis were artificial stories composed in the days of the Kings, it is now clear that we are here dealing with the genuine society of the earliest part of the second millennium B.C. The comment of W. F. Albright in this connection is typical of many now being made: 'So many corroborations of details have been discovered in recent years that most competent scholars have given up the old critical theory according to which the stories of the patriarchs are mostly retrojections from the time of the dual monarchy, 9th-8th centuries B.C.' "

20. Cf. Albright, AP, p. 83. In this connection Albright also observes that a rare word for "henchmen" occurring in Gen. 14:14 *h^enîkîm*—has proved to be derived from the Egyptian *hnkw* ("henchmen" "trained servants," KJV), which appears in these Execration Texts—cf. Rowley, OTMS, p. 6.

These letters contain for the most part alarming reports of the depredations of fierce invaders and urgent requests for Egyptian troops to help repel these dangerous incursions. They also report a condition of chaotic disunity among the various petty kings of Canaan, and a tendency to forsake their allegiance to Egypt in favor of an alliance with the invading Ḫabiru'Apiru (as Albright and Mendenhall transcribe the name). The towns mentioned by a correspondent from Megiddo as having fallen to the invaders are all in the region of Arad in the south, which was the first territory invaded by the Israelites, according to Num. 21:1-3. Other cities listed as already fallen are those recorded in Joshua as having been captured early in the Israelite conquest: Gezer, Ashkelon, and Lachish. There are no letters at all from Jericho, Beersheba, Bethel, or Gibeon, which were the first to fall before Joshua's troops. More details concerning the Amarna correspondence will be given in chapter 19, but from what has been already indicated it is safe to say that these tablets record the Hebrew conquest of Canaan in 1400-1380 B.C. from the standpoint of the Canaanites themselves.

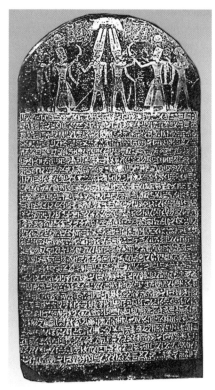

(3) The "Israel" Stela of King Merneptah, found by Petrie at Thebes in 1896, dates from 1229 B.C., and contains the only extant Egyptian reference to the Hebrew nation as "Israel." In this encomium of praise to the Egyptian king (son of Rameses the Great) a list of nations and localities is given toward the close of the inscription, with the declaration that they were conquered or pillaged by Merneptah's irresistible troops. This list includes the land of the Hittites, Canaan itself, Ashkelon in Philistia, Gezer near the Valley of Aijalon, Yanoam up at the northern tip of Palestine (near Laish-Dan), Israel (with an ethnic determinative rather than a local city determinative), and the land of the Horites. Obviously, if Merneptah found Israelites in possession of portions of Palestine even up toward the northern frontier, the Israelite conquest must already have taken place substantially before 1229 B.C.[21] Since this Palestinian campaign is dated in

ISRAEL STELA OF MERNEPTAH. ON TOP OF THIS GRANITE STELA ARE TWO REPRESENTATIONS OF THE GOD AMUN-RE, FLANKED BY MUT AND KHONSU. THE 28 LINES OF HIEROGLYPHIC TEXT SPECIFICALLY MENTION ISRAEL. (FROM THEBES; 1208 B.C., HT. 318 CM. CAIRO MUSEUM.)

21. Concerning the date of the Exodus, compare the archaeological findings referred to on pp. 241ff.

the fifth regnal year of Merneptah, he could not have been the pharaoh of the Exodus, as the older exponents of the "late date theory" used to maintain. (The only way to avoid this conclusion is to allege, contrary to the Genesis record itself, that some Israelites never migrated to Egypt with the rest of the family of Jacob.) It would obviously be difflcult for Merneptah to have been the pharaoh who permitted the Israelites to flee from Egypt, and then after their forty years of wilderness wandering and several more years of conquest, to find them settled in Palestine by his fifth year! [22]

It is worthy of note that in recent years Cyrus Gordon has assembled impressive evidence from comparative literature of the ancient Near East and early Greece to show that the basic criteria for source division by the Wellhausen school are totally invalid for non-Israelite literature. Just as the Homeric account of the shield of Achilles fashioned by Haephestus in the *Iliad* described it as depicting on the surface various scenes of the activities of war and peace in ancient Hellenic society, so also the author of the Pentateuch brought together a panorama of the varied aspects of second millennium Hebrew society, war and peace, cultic regulations and civil or criminal law, and all that made up the life of that people. There is absolutely no need of hypothecating a different author to account for each of these varied elements. Gordon also points to the Standard of Ur (a mosaic of lapis lazuli and shell inlaid in a wooden base ca. 2500 B.C.); this likewise furnished a comprehensive view of Sumerian life, illustrated by themes of war and peace. (Cf. Gordon, "The Minoan Bridge," in *Christianity Today* [March 15, 1963], p. 6; R. K. Harrison, *Old Testament Times*, pp. 41, 50.)

Many other archaeological discoveries tending to verify the accuracy of the biblical record will be described in subsequent chapters, in which their evidence bears upon special details relevant to particular books in the Old Testament. It is because of the cumulative impact of all these findings that archaeologists like W. F. Albright have felt constrained to concede the essential accuracy of the Pentateuch. Albright puts it this way: "The contents of our Pentateuch are, in general, very much older than the date at which they were finally edited; new discoveries continue to confirm the historical accuracy or the literary antiquity of detail after detail in it....It is, accordingly, sheer hyper-criticism to deny the substantially Mosaic character of the Pentateuchal tradition" (AP, p. 224). In an earlier article ("Archaeology Confronts Biblical Criticism") he affirmed that the assumption that pious fraud and pseudepigraphy were common in Israel "is without parallel in the pre-Hellenistic Orient." On the contrary, he states, we find there a superstitious veneration for both written word and oral tradition.

Discoveries at Ebla

In 1964 an archaeological expedition was launched by the University of Rome to examine a prominent hill, located about 44 miles south of Aleppo, known as Tell

---

22. Cf. Merneptah's Israel Stela, discussed on p. 244.

Mardikh, (under the leadership of Paolo Matthiae). It turned out to have been occupied as early as 3500 B.C. It was not definitely identified as the city of Ebla (mentioned in the *Code of Hammurabi*) until the discovery of a dedication of a statue to "King Ibbiṭ-Lim, king of Ebla." This exciting discovery led to intensified excavation that yielded to the investigators an entire library in 1974. The first portion of this library consisted of 42 tablets in Akkadian cuneiform discovered on a palace floor located on the acropolis. In the following year 14,000 more tablets or tablet fragments were unearthed, many of them still arranged in library order, even though they had fallen to the floor after their wooden shelves were consumed by fire. Apparently the city was stormed and put to the torch in the reign of Naram Sin, king of Akkad, in 2250 B.C.

It was at this juncture that Giovanni Pettinato, a foremost Sumerologist, was summoned to analyze and translate this immense collection of cuneiform tablets dating back to centuries before the birth of Abraham (the earliest of them dated as early as 2500 B.C.). Pettinato soon made the astonishing discovery that certain of the documents were finished off not only by the customary Sumerian formula of *dub-gar* ("tablet written"), but others by a senseless pair of signs reading *gal-balag*, which could also be read as *ik-tub*. Read like this it meant "he wrote" in a language neither Sumerian nor Akkadian, but quite evidently using the verb *kataba*, which is extensively employed in Arabic, Phoenician, Ugaritic, and Hebrew meaning "wrote." Since the morphology of the verb was similar to Akkadian (a so-called *iprus* form), it appeared that the native inhabitants actually spoke a tongue having morphological similarities to Akkadian, but with a vocabulary very definitely Canaanite. This was abundantly confirmed when a large number of lexical texts were brought to light. These consisted of lists of words in Sumerian which were paired with the Eblaite equivalents. This demonstrated that written records were kept in this portion of Syria by a people who spoke a language closely related to Canaanite, even though using a verbal morphology closer to Akkadian. It would appear to have been a dialect spoken by Amorites or some closely related ethnic group, having a greater affinity to Canaanite than to Aramaic, which was apparently the predominating tongue at Padan-Aram back in Laban's time (cf. Gen. 31:47). Amazingly enough, many of the names of kings and leading men in Ebla bore a remarkable resemblance to names that were later used by the Hebrews themselves. Among these were *Ibrium* (biblical Eber), *Ish-ma-il* (Ishmael), *Ish-ra-il* (Israel), *Na-khur* (Nahor) and *Mi-ka-il* (Michael). Commercial and political relations were maintained with cities like Dor, Hazor, Megiddo, Shalem (Jerusalem), Gaza, and Ashtaroth (cf. Ashtaroth-Qarnaim).

City I dated back to 3500 B.C., but its greatest prosperity occurred in the period of City II, datable to 2400-2250 B.C., under the leadership of kings like Igrish-Ḥalam, Irkab-Damu, Ar-Ennum (a contemporary of King Sargon of Agade), Ebrium, Ibbi-Sippish and Dubaḥa-Ada (who had the misfortune of being conquered by Naram-Sin of Agade, who plundered Ebla in 2250 and put it to the torch. It was not long before Ebla was rebuilt after this catastrophe, about 2000 B.C. (City III), but it never regained

ARCHAEOLOGICAL EVIDENCES TO THE OLD TESTAMENT

EVIDENCE	DATES	CULTURE	SIGNIFICANCE
EBLA	2350–1600 B.C.	EBLAIC SUMERIAN	EARLY ADVANCED CIVILIZATION & WRITTEN LANGUAGE – LARGE LIBRARY
CITY OF UR (DYNASTY III)	2000 B.C.	SUMERIAN	EARLY ADVANCED CIVILIZATION
CODE OF HAMMURABI	1700 B.C. (ROWTON)	AKKADIAN	PARALLELS MOSAIC CODE
EGYPTIAN EXECRATION TEXTS OF DYNASTY XII	1900 B.C.	EGYPTIAN HIEROGLYPHIC	EGYPTIAN CLAIMS TO SOVEREIGNTY OVER CANAANITE CITIES
MARI TABLETS	1700 B.C.	HURRIAN	DOCUMENTATION OF NAKHUR, HABIRU; PATRIARCHAL CUSTOMS
INSCRIPTIONS FROM TURQUOISE MINES OF SERABIT EL–KHADIM	1500 B.C.	PROTO–PHOENICIAN	EARLY PICTOGRAPHIC ALPHABETIC
RAS SHAMRA TABLETS	1400 B.C.	UGARITIC	EPIC POETRY STYLES EARLY SACRIFICIAL TERMS
NUZI TABLETS	1400 B.C.	HURRIAN	CONFIRM HISTORICITY OF PATRIARCHAL CUSTOMS IN GENESIS
HITTITE LEGAL CODE	1300 B.C.	HITTITE	PATRIARCHAL SUZERAINTY TREATY; PATRIARCHAL CUSTOMS
TELL EL–AMARNA TABLETS	1400 B.C.	AKKADIAN CUNEIFORM	REFERENCES TO HEBREW CONQUEST OF CANAAN
MERNEPTAH STELA	1220 B.C.	EGYPTIAN	MENTION OF NAME "ISRAEL"
GEZER CALENDAR	925 B.C.	HEBREW	WRITING PREVALENT
BLACK OBELISK OF SHALMANESER III	840 B.C.	AKKADIAN	CONFIRMATION OF ISRAEL'S KING JEHU
MOABITE STONE	840 B.C.	MOABITE	HISTORICITY OF 2 KINGS 3 AND OMRI
SILOAM INSCRIPTION	702 B.C.	HEBREW	HEZEKIAH'S WATER DIVERSION TUNNEL
SARGON'S INSCRIPTION	720 B.C.	AKKADIAN	SARGON'S VICTORY OVER SAMARIA
NEO–BABYLONIAN CHRONICLE	600 B.C.	AKKADIAN	RECORD OF NEBUCHADNEZZAR'S INVASION OF PALESTINE
ELEPHANTINE PAPYRI	420 B.C.	ARAMAIC	IMPERIAL ARAMAIC OF THE TIME OF DANIEL & EZRA
TAYLER PRISM OF SENNACHERIB	685 B.C.	AKKADIAN	SENNECHERIB'S ADVANCE AGAINST JUDAH IN 701
LACHISH OSTRACA	CA. 588 B.C.	HEBREW	CHALDEAN INVASION OF JUDAH
NABONIDUS CHRONICLE	550 B.C.	NEO–BABYLONIAN AKKADIAN	RECORDS BELSHAZZAR AS SECONDARY RULER OF BABYLON
BEHISTUN ROCK	500 B.C.	OLD PERSIAN, ELAMITE, AKKADIAN	NON–BIBLICAL REFERENCE TO PERSIAN CONQUEST OF BABYLON UNDER DARIUS
CYRUS CYLINDER	500 B.C.	OLD PERSIAN	CYRUS'S VICTORY AND DECREE PERMITTING FREEDOM OF WORSHIP

its former power, and was eventually sacked by the Hittites in 1600 B.C., about the same time that they pillaged Babylon itself.

Among the cities with which Ebla maintained trade relations were *Si-da-mu-ki* [23] (apparently Sodom) or *Sa-dam-ki,* and *Sa-bi-im* (equivalent to Zeboiim). This is attested in Pettinato's *Archives of Ebla* (Doubleday, 1981, p. 287). These two cities of the Pentapolis of the Plain, where Lot made his home prior to the destruction meted out by the Lord according to Gen. 19, were formerly dismissed by Wellhausen and the Documentarians as merely legendary rather than historical. Therefore their attestation by contemporary records going back to the time of Abraham comes as another refutation of the skepticism of the Wellhausen School of scholarship.

Additional information about the Ebla Tablets may be found in Excursus 2 in the latter part of this book.

---

23. The ending *-Ki* in these names was simply a determinative for a geographical name and was not pronounced aloud. Thus *Sidamu-Ki* would have been read as *Sidamu* (equivalent to Hebrew *S^edōm*).

PART TWO
SPECIAL INTRODUCTION

14 GENESIS

THE TITLE *Genesis* ("beginning," Greek) was applied to this book by the Septuagint. The Hebrew title consists of the first word or two in the book, *bᵉrē'šît* ("in the beginning"). The main theme or subject matter consists of origins: the origin of the created world, of the human race, of the various nations of earth, and then particularly of the covenant family which composes the redeemed people of God.

As for the authorship of the book, it contains no explicit record as to who composed it. According to tradition, however, the author was Moses himself, and a specific ordinance like circumcision on the eighth day, which is first introduced and explained in Gen. 17:12 (as well as in Ex. 12:48 and Lev. 12:3), is referred to in the New Testament (John 7:23) as part of the law of Moses. In support of this tradition is the circumstance that precisely the information needed to make the book of Exodus intelligible is supplied by the book of Genesis. It is in Genesis that the promises to Abraham, Isaac, and Jacob are spelled out, the promises so frequently referred to in the other books of the Torah as being fulfilled by the momentous events of the Exodus and the Conquest of Canaan. Moreover, the fact that Ex. 1:1 begins with the word *and* (Hebrew) suggests that it was intended to follow some preceding book.

An additional consideration is found in the requirements of the situation confronting Moses as he sought to write out a constitution for the theocracy of Jehovah shortly to be established in the Promised Land. It was absolutely essential to national unity for the Israelite people to have an accurate record of their own national origin in Abraham and God's covenantal dealing with him and his seed. While materials which the author used for the composition of this book no doubt came to him from five to six centuries before his time, prior to Jacob's migration into Egypt, nevertheless Moses seems to have served as a Spirit-guided compiler and interpreter of the pre-existent material which had come to him from his forebears in oral and written form.

OUTLINE OF GENESIS

I. Beginning of mankind, 1:1–11:32

A. Creation of the world, 1:1–2:3
B. Place of man in the world, 2:4–25
C. Entry of sin and the resultant fall, 3:1–4:26 (Covenant of grace instituted)

D. Antediluvian races and patriarchs (Adam to Noah), 5:1-32
E. Sinfulness of the world purged by the flood, 6:1–9:29
F. Posterity of Noah and the early races of the Near East, 10:1–11:32

II. Life of Abraham, 12:1–25:18

A. Abram's call, and his acceptance of the covenant by faith, 12:1–14:24
B. Renewal and confirmation of the covenant, 15:1–17:27
C. Deliverance of Lot from Sodom, 18:1–19:38
D. Abraham and Abimelech, 20:1-18
E. Birth and marriage of Isaac, the son of promise, 21:1–24:67
F. Posterity of Abraham, 25:1-18

III. Life of Isaac and his family, 25:19–26:35

A. Birth of Esau and Jacob, 25:19-28
B. Sale of Esau's birthright to Jacob, 25:29-34
C. Isaac and Abimelech II, 26:1-16
D. Dispute at Beersheba, 26:17-33
E. Esau's marriages, 26:34-35

IV. Life of Jacob, 27:1–37:1

A. Jacob in his father's home, 27:1-46
B. Jacob's exile and journey, 28:1-22
C. Jacob with Laban in Syria, 29:1–33:15
D. Jacob's return to the promised land, 33:16–35:20
E. Posterity of Jacob and Esau, 35:21–37:1

V. Life of Joseph, 37:2–50:26

A. Joseph's boyhood, 37:2-36
B. Judah and Tamar, 38:1-30
C. Joseph's promotion in Egypt, 39:1–41:57
D. Joseph and his brothers, 42:1–45:15
E. Joseph's reception of Jacob in Egypt, 45:16–47:26
F. Jacob's last days and final prophecies, 47:27–50:14
G. Joseph's assurance to his brothers of complete forgiveness, 50:15-26

It will be observed from this outline how carefully and systematically the entire patriarchal period has been dealt with by the author of Genesis. The guiding principle throughout the narrative is the covenant of grace, and God's gracious dealings with true believers from the time of Adam onward. First there is the selective process whereby the covenant fellowship is narrowed down by stages to a single individual, Abraham; then the elective principle widens to include a large family, that of Jacob. Thus the stage is set for the nurturing of an entire nation in the favored refuge of Goshen in Egypt.

Two considerations reinforce this impression of single authorship in Genesis. The first is the significant use of the term *tôledôt* ("generations, offspring, descendants") to introduce most of the main sections indicated in the outline above. Thus, it occurs at 2:4; 5:1; 10:1; 11:10; 11:27; 25:12; 36:1. Usually what follows *tôledôt* is a genealogical list, although it may be a review of the development of that which has already been originated (as in the case of 2:4: "These are the generations of the heavens and of the earth when they were created"). In this last passage, it should be emphasized that *tôledôt* nearly always prefaces a list or account which is about to follow; it hardly serves as a terminal postscript to a list or account which has just been given. This means (as Aalders, SIP, p. 44, and Moeller, GATE, p. 15, point out) that the assignment of Gen. 2:4a to "P" (whose creation account has just been given in Gen. 1) is not justified according to the usage of this term *tôledôt* in other passages. It could well serve as an introduction to the account of Adam and Eve in Eden, which is given in the rest of Gen. 2 (a J passage).

The second unitary consideration is found in the technique of the author in dealing with ancestral figures who are not of the chosen line. Moeller (GATE, p. 15) points out that Cain's genealogy (4:17-24) is given before that of Seth (4:25-26); those of Japheth and Ham (10:1-4 and 10:6-8) are given before that of Shem (10:21-22), even though Ham was presumably the youngest of the three brothers. The genealogies of Lot (19:29-30) and Ishmael (25:12-15) appear before that of Isaac (25:19). So also Esau's descendants (36:1-10) are listed before those of Jacob (37:2). The author's motive in each case seems to dispose more briefly of the non-elect branches of the human line before taking up the genealogy of those patriarchs who had a genuine faith in Jehovah. Such systematic treatment hardly accords with a theory of heterogeneous and awkwardly combined sources posited by the Wellhausen theory.

PAGAN CONCEPTS OF THE ORIGIN OF THE WORLD Contrary to earlier experts, who regarded the Genesis account as derived from pagan sources, Heidel, Lambert and Millard[1] reject the idea that Gen. 1–2 had any close relation at all to the Babylonian Enuma Elish (K. A. Kitchen, *The Bible and Archaeology*, p. 27). Enuma Elish assumes the eternity of pre-existent matter out of which arose a pair of creator gods by forces that are not explained, which somehow began the creative process. This really doesn't deal with the question of how creation did take place. If we have primeval matter, which is obviously destructible through nuclear fission, it is difficult to believe it was there from the very beginning or even before any beginning. Furthermore, matter has been found to possess a very elaborate structure, with atomic components of intricate complexity. This can only be understood as the product of intelligent design. To say that the creation epics of any of the ancient neighbors of Israel had any bearing on the

---

1. Lambert and Millard: "Atramhasis, The Babylonian Story of the Flood," pp. 16-25, "Old Babylonian Epic of Atramhasis," dated ca. 2000 B.C.

creation record as presented in the Old Testament is to miss the whole point of the stark contrast between creation ex nihilo and the assumption of the eternity of physical matter.

Only in the Bible does it state that God created everything *ex nihilo*. The pagan cultures imply that there never was a time when matter did not exist. The conclusion that the material universe was created by nothing or emerged from nothing is logically impossible and puts the atheist in a position of total irrationality. As R. C. Sproul so adeptly states, "The modern view is far more miraculous than the biblical view. It suggests that nothing created something. More than that, it holds that nothing created everything—quite a feat indeed."[2]

GENESIS 1 AND MODERN SCIENTIFIC EVIDENCE

THE SIX CREATIVE DAYS AND THE AGE OF THE WORLD

From a superficial reading of Genesis 1, the impression would seem to be that the entire creative process took place in six twenty-four-hour days. If this was the true intent of the Hebrew author (a questionable deduction, as will be presently shown), this seems to run counter to modern scientific research, which indicates that the planet Earth was created several billion years ago. In the nineteenth century the chief evidence for this extreme antiquity (which was then, however, computed to be far less than is the case today) was found in the rate at which sediment is deposited by water action in modern times. In the Gulf of Mexico, sedimentary layers are deposited at the rate of a few inches a year; yet, successive layers of deposit as thick as 28,000 feet have been found, thus indicating the passage of well over 100,000 years in time. This, of course, is valid only upon a uniformitarian hypothesis, that is, that natural forces have been operating through the processes of erosion, sedimentation, and magmatic (or volcanic) action in just the same manner and at the same rate, throughout all preceding ages as they do now. (Uniformitarianism has been vigorously challenged by many authorities on account of the evidence of violent twisting and tilting and thermodynamic metamorphism exhibited in many mountainous, or once mountainous, regions.[3] The appearance of fossils, many of them left by species of animals no longer

---

2. R. C. Sproul, *The Holiness of God* (Wheaton, Ill.: Tyndale, 1985), p. 21.

3. An impressive array of evidences tending to disprove the assumptions of uniformitarianism has been collected by Harold W. Clark in his *New Diluvialism* (Angwin, Calif.: Science Publications, 1946). Uniformitarianism teaches that all geologic processes in past ages proceeded in approximately the same way and at the same rate as they do today. He points out: (1) the lower sedimentary deposits in the region of the Gulf of Mexico show evidence of immense volumes of water sweeping northwestward across a shallow sea; whereas the higher strata show a reversal of currents, with great waves carrying sand, gravel, and clay southwestward across the deeper sediments. These currents were of such vast extent as to sweep heavy materials forward for several hundred miles. There is simply no such tremendous water action known anywhere in the world today. (2) The immense forces which formed the great mountain chains of the Alps, the Andes, and the Rockies cannot be remotely paralleled by any phenomenon observable today. These mountain systems were developed along lines of ancient seas, which were long and narrow and apparently quite shallow at first, but then burdened with thousands of feet of rapidly deposited sediment. Then came rapid movements of uplift accompanied by the erosive action of terrific streams of water which carved out the present mountain peaks. (3) Accompanying

surviving, in these sedimentary strata served as a sort of geological time clock which strengthened the impression of a very great age for the earth. Most of the fossils represented genera which had disappeared long before the more recent strata had been deposited, and which therefore could not have been suddenly destroyed in a single catastrophe such as Noah's flood. (Especially the numerous fossil species of plant and animal living in the sea would remain unaffected by the flood, unless of course the sudden intermingling of salt water with fresh would account for their extinction.)

The more recently expanded knowledge of nuclear physics has brought into play another type of evidence which seems to confirm the great antiquity of the earth, that is, the decay of radioactive minerals. According to the calculations of physicists, uranium 238 over a period of four and one-half billion years will decay through sixteen intermediate stages (thorium 234, etc.) to lead 206, which is a stable mineral and will not further decompose through radioactivity. Rubidium 87 takes sixty billion years to decay into strontium 87. By computing the proportion of the "daughter" product to the parent radioactive deposit it is possible to estimate the age of the specimen in question, assuming the validity of the uniformitarian approach in geochronology.

The most recent geochronologists have perfected techniques which they think eliminate to a large extent the possible factors of error (such as the presence of the "daughter" mineral at the time when the radioactive isotope itself was deposited, or else the leaching out of portions of the specimen by underground water action). They tend to use two or three different radioactive isotopes when present in the same deposit, and thus can check the accuracy of the results computed from each decayed specimen. Better known to the general public is the carbon 14 method. All plants and animals receive into their tissues a certain amount of carbon 14 (a product of the decomposition of nitrogen under the impact of cosmic rays in the upper atmosphere). After the plant or animal dies, it can absorb no more of this carbon 14, and that which it already contains in its system gradually breaks down by radioactivity to form nitrogen 14. This process takes place rather quickly, however, over a period of only 5,580 years, and hence is quite useless for any deposits 30,000 years old or older.[4]

these upward movements were tremendous lateral pressures of inconceivable force. Thus, the whole middle and eastern portion of the Rocky Mountains has been thrust violently westward, producing a series of gigantic folds which in some cases broke in two and thrust one range across the top of another one for great distances. The Alps in Switzerland have been so violently overturned that geological experts have been almost baffled to interpret the strata. One point that seems beyond dispute is that terrific forces surpassing anything now known (and therefore impossible to estimate as to length of time) have disturbed the earth's surface on a scale and at a rate altogether different from what is observable today. Estimates of time based upon present-day geologic processes are therefore quite valueless (pp. 12-13).

4. Cf. Herbert Feely in *Journal of the American Scientific Affiliation* (Sep. 1955), pp. 47-48. Note also that some bristlecone pines live up to 4,000 years, as datable from tree rings. Recent laboratory experiments have shown that disintegration rates on growth rings older than 1000 B.C. are faster than the present C[14] rate; estimated at 750 years younger from dates between 5100 and 4810 B.C. and 100 years younger from dates between 1499 and 1000 B.C., the discrepancy in rate may be due to changes in cosmic ray intensity or changes in the equilibrium between the atmosphere and the volume of ocean water. The deviation may partly be due to the volume of ocean water, or partly to the Ice Age rhythms that were influenced by solar wind patterns (*Encyclopedia Brittanica*, 1971 *Yearbook of Science*, pp. 392-93).

Can such an enormous time interval (five billion years or more, according to some estimates—made, of course, on uniformitarian assumptions) be reconciled with the six creative days of Genesis 1? This all depends upon the significance of the Hebrew word *yôm* ("day"). There are three alternative theories currently advocated by biblical scholars concerning these "days."

1. The word *yôm* represents a literal, twenty-four-hour day, and Gen. 1:3–2:3 gives us a record of an exact week in which God completely restored from chaos a creation (recorded in Gen. 1:1) which had suffered a cosmic catastrophe (possibly at the time Satan and his angels were cast out of God's presence). Support for this interpretation has assertedly been found in Isa. 45:18 where God is stated not to have created the earth "void" (*bōhû*, Hebrew, being the same as the "void" of Gen. 1:2). Therefore Genesis 1:1 must indicate a complete and perfect creation prior to the chaotic state mentioned in Gen. 1:2, for this is the only possible deduction from Isa. 45:18 when so interpreted. (Yet this interpretation encounters the difficulty that *bōhû* in v. 19 clearly means "in vain.") It should be noted in this connection that the verb "was" (*hāyᵉtâ* in Gen. 1:2) may quite possibly be rendered "became" and be thus construed to mean: "And the earth became formless and void."[5] Only a cosmic catastrophe could account for the introduction of chaotic confusion into the original perfection of God's creation. This interpretation certainly seems to be exegetically tenable, but it encounters at least two major difficulties. (*a*) It means that the whole magnificent achievement of the original creation is dismissed with the bare statement in Gen. 1:1, "In the beginning God created the heaven and the earth." All attention is then devoted to a reconstruction of a recently disturbed world order, and events that took place five or six thousand years ago. (*b*) It means also that the inspired Book of Origins has nothing to say about the order of the creative process, or indeed about anything that pertains to geology. There is no more any need to harmonize geology and Genesis, for they deal—according to this interpretation—with entirely different subject matter.

Perhaps it should be added that advocates of this theory have often embellished it with highly questionable speculations concerning the original status of Satan as presiding over the worship of Jehovah in a pre-catastrophe Eden beautified with gem-laden trees (equating the "prince of Tyre" in Ezek. 28 with Satan himself). Jeremiah 4:23-26 has also been fitted into this catastrophe theory on the ground that it contains the expression *tōhû wabōhû* ("without form and void") found in Gen. 1:2. So construed, it

---

5. Properly speaking this verb *hāyâ* never has the meaning of static being like the copular verb "to be." Its basic notion is that of becoming or emerging as such and such, or of coming into being. It may signify "was" only in a derivative way from the idea of becoming or of coming into the observer's view as such and such. Even the five examples of *hāyâ* as "be, exist" cited in Gesenius-Buhl's *Lexicon* (p. 178*b*) are capable of being interpreted nascently or by way of an occurrence. For example, Job 1:1: "There *was* a man named Job" implies more the notion of occurrence rather than of static being. Sometimes a distinction is attempted along the following lines: *hāyâ* means "become" only when it is followed by the preposition *lᵉ*; otherwise there is no explicit idea of becoming. But this distinction will not stand up under analysis. In Gen. 3:20 the proper rendering is: "And Adam called the name of his wife Eve because she *became* the mother of all living." No *lᵉ* follows the verb in this case. So also in Gen. 4:20: "Jabal *became* the father of tent dwellers." Therefore there can be no grammatical objection raised to translating Gen. 1:2: "And the earth *became* a wasteness and desolation."

indicates that prior to the catastrophe there must have been cities and men who were destroyed some time between Gen. 1:1 and 1:2 (even though Jer. 4:23-26 apparently sets forth a prophetic scene of a catastrophe which is yet to come).[6]

2. *Yôm* represents a revelational day. That is, in six literal days (or possibly in a vision which represented to Moses the whole drama of creation in six visionary days). God described to His prophet the mystery of how He had brought creation into being, and the stages by which He did so. These stages did not necessarily represent strictly chronological sequence (since the making of the heavenly bodies is delayed until the fourth day, after the creation of vegetation which requires sunlight to exist). They are only in part chronological, and in part topical. That is to say, the various stages or phases of creation are introduced in a logical order, as they bear upon the human observer living on the earth. It is therefore more logical to describe first the earth's surface upon which the observer must stand, before introducing the sun and moon which are to shine upon the earth and regulate the seasons.[7]

This interpretation is perhaps tenable without surrendering the inerrancy of the Bible record. But it encounters several serious difficulties, chief among which is the complete absence of any hint or suggestion in the text of Genesis 1 that a mere vision is being described. It reads like perfectly straightforward history: In the beginning God created heaven and earth: on the first "day" He created light; on the second day He separated the waters into the upper and the lower, and so on. Second, it would seem highly improbable that it would require an entire twenty-four-hour period to convey to Moses the three verses pertaining to the creation of light. Third, since the initial creation spoken of in Gen. 1:1 is not apparently included in the first revelational "day," the question arises whether it was included in this supposed vision granted Moses, or whether this was communicated in some nonvisionary manner. At any rate, if Genesis 1 was really only a vision (representing, of course, the actual events of primeval history) then almost any other apparently historical account in Scripture could be interpreted as a vision—especially if it relates to transactions not naturally observable to a human investigator or historian.

3. *Yôm* represents a geologic age or stage in the creative process. This was the explanation resorted to by nineteenth-century geologists who respected the authority of the Bible, notably J. W. Dawson (e.g., *The Origin of the World According to Revelation and Science*, 1877) and James Dana (*Manual of Geology*, 1875). According to this view the term *yôm* does not necessarily signify a literal twenty-four-hour day, but is simply equivalent to "stage." It has often been asserted that *yôm* could not bear this meaning, but could only have implied a literal day to the Hebrew mind according to Hebrew usage. Nevertheless, on the basis of internal evidence, it is this writer's conviction that *yôm* in Gen. 1 could not have been intended by the Hebrew author to mean a literal twenty-four-hour day.

6. See Bernard Ramm's CVSS, pp. 195-210, for a fuller treatment.

7. Exponents of this view include J. H. Kurtz, *Bible and Astronomy*, 3d ed., 1857; and P. J. Wiseman, *Creation Revealed in Six Days*, 1948. It is the explanation favored by Ramm, CVSS, pp. 218-27.

THREE THEORIES OF CREATIVE DAYS (Yôm)

1. Literal Day

2. Revelational Day

3. Geological Day

In the first place, *yôm* is apparently used in Gen. 2:4 to refer to the whole creative process just described in Gen. 1 as taking up six days: "These are the generations of the heavens and the earth in the *day* that Jehovah God made earth and heaven." Since the stages in creating heaven and earth have just been described, it is legitimate to infer that the "day" here must refer to the whole process from day one through day six. In the second place, Gen. 1:27 states that after creating all the land animals on the sixth day, God created man, both male and female. Then, in the more detailed treatment of Gen. 2, we are told that God created Adam first, gave him the responsibility of tending the Garden of Eden for some time until He observed him to be lonely. He then granted him the fellowship of all the beasts and animals of earth, with opportunity to bestow names upon them all. Some undetermined period after that, God observed that Adam was still lonely and finally fashioned a human wife for him by means of a rib removed from him during a "deep sleep." Then at last he brought Eve before Adam and presented her to him as his new life partner. Who can imagine that all of these transactions could possibly have taken place in 120 minutes of the sixth day (or even within twenty-four hours, for that matter)? And yet Gen. 1:27 states that both Adam and Eve were created at the very end of the final day of creation. Obviously the "days" of chapter 1 are intended to represent stages of unspecified length, not literal twenty-four-hour days.

As for the objection that the "days" of Gen. 1 are represented as consisting of an "evening" and a "morning," and therefore must be understood as literal, it may be replied that the formula "evening and morning" serves only to indicate that the term *day*, albeit symbolical for a geological stage, is used in the sense of a twenty-four-hour cycle rather than "day" in contrast to "night" (as, for example, *day* is used in 1:5*a*). In this connection it should be pointed out the New Testament references to Christ's entombment as lasting "three days and three nights" are to be explained as equivalent to "during a period of three twenty-four-hour days," rather than implying a literal three (daylight) days and three nights. In other words, Jesus died about 3:00 P.M. on Friday (a portion of the first twenty-four-hour day), remained in the tomb on Saturday, and rose early on Sunday (or during a third twenty-four-hour day). From the appearance of this expression in Gen. 1, "the evening and the morning," as the Hebrew way of indicating a twenty-four-hour day, it was a logical procedure to speak of three such days as "three days and three nights." (Thus we avoid the difficulties encountered by those who hold to a Wednesday theory of the crucifixion in the face of insurmountable evidence that it occurred on Friday.)

The day-age theory, then, accounts for the six creative days as indicating the broad outlines of the creative work of God in fashioning the earth and its inhabitants up until the appearance of Adam and Eve. Modern geologists agree with Genesis 1 in the following particulars: (*a*) The earth began in a confused and chaotic form, which sub-

8. Cf. D. Dewar, "The Earliest Known Animals," *The Journal of the Transactions of the Victoria Institute* 80: 22-29.

sequently gave way to a more orderly state. (*b*) The proper conditions for the maintenance of life were brought into being: the separation of the thick vapor surrounding
the earth into clouds above and rivers and seas below, with the evaporation-precipita-
tion cycle, and also with the increasing penetration of the sunlight (for the previous
creation of the sun is suggested by the first command: "Let there be light") to the surface of the earth. (*c*) The separation of land from sea (or the emergence of dry land
above the receding water level) preceded the appearance of life upon the soil. (*d*) Vegetable life had already made its appearance before the first emergence of animal life in
the Cambrian period. As a matter of fact, all the invertebrate phyla appear contemporaneously with remarkable suddenness in the Cambrian strata, with no indication in
any of the pre-Cambrian deposits as to how these various phyla, classes, and orders
(represented by no less than 5,000 species) may have developed.[8] (*e*) Both Genesis and
geology agree that the simpler forms appeared first and the more complex later. (*f*)
Both agree that mankind appeared as the latest and highest product of the creative
process.

Thus in its broad outlines, the sequence set forth in the Hebrew account is in harmony with that indicated by the data of geology. It is true that the mention of the
fashioning of the sun, moon, and stars on the fourth creative day does not correspond
with the quite conclusive evidence that the planet earth appeared subsequently to the
creation of the sun. But inasmuch as the creation of light on the first "day" indicates
the priority of the sun even in the Mosaic account, we are to understand on exegetical
grounds that the emphasis on the fourth day was not the original creation of the heavenly bodies as such, but rather their becoming available for the purpose of regulating
time and the cycles of the rotation and revolution of earth and moon. The specific
verb for "create *ex nihilo*" (*bārā'*) is not used in Gen. 1:16, but rather the more general
term, *make* (*'āsâ*).[9] The fair inference is that a dense vapor encompassing the earth had
hitherto precluded this possibility, even though suffIcient diffused light may have previously penetrated to support the growth of plant life. (Note that the Hebrew of Gen.
1:14 may be rendered, "Let luminaries in the firmament of heaven be for the purpose
of separating between day and night, in order that they may be for signs.")

Advocates of the literal-day theory have often pointed to the sanction of Ex. 20:11
for confirmation of literalness of the days. In confirming the sanctity of the Sabbath,
Jehovah states: "For in six days Jehovah made heaven and earth...and rested on the
seventh day." But this does not necessarily presuppose literal, twenty-four hour days,

---

9. The verb *bārā'* is used for creation *ex nihilo* in Gen. 1:1 and in most other passages where it appears.
In a weakened sense it may refer to the production of something new or unprecedented, such as a
wonderful deed of power which God performs in the arena of history (Ex. 34:10; Num. 16:30; Jer.
31:22; Isa. 45:7, 8; 48:7). But always it is God who is the subject of *bārā'*, never man; and when it takes
an object of the thing created, it never indicates any preexistent material out of which it is made. (In
Arabic, however, a related form, *bārā'*, means "to form or fashion by cutting." A Phoenician cognate,
bōrē means something like "cutter" or "engraver." Yet Arabic also has a *bārā'a* ("create"), Aramaic has
b°rā ("create") and Akkadian *barū* ("make, create"), and Sabaean [a dialect of Old South Arabic] has a
b-r-' meaning "found, build." But the determining factor in Hebrew is the actual usage in those contexts of the Old Testament where the word occurs.)

for the seventh day is explicitly hallowed in terms of the completion of the work of creation. For this purpose of memorial observance, the only possible way in which the seventh age (the age of completion, according to the day-age theory) could be hallowed would be a literal seventh day of a seven-day week.[10] It would certainly be impractical to devote an entire geologic age to the commemoration of a geologic age!

BIBLICAL CREATIONISM AND MODERN EVOLUTIONISM

More fundamental an issue than the length of the creative days is the question of the fact of divine creation as over against such competing theories of origin as Darwinian evolution. As formulated by Charles Darwin in his *Origin of Species* (1859), evolution sought to explain the origin of biological species by natural selection rather than by God's design. That is to say, the process by which plants and animals developed was not governed by any divine intelligence according to teleological principles, but rather according to a completely mechanical principle: the survival of the fittest. As the reproductive cycle progresses, taught Darwin, the following generation shows slight variations from the generation preceding. Over a long period of time, after hundreds and thousands of generations, some of these variations become more or less fixed characteristics which are passed on to the descendants. These new characteristics contribute to the formation of varieties or subspecies, and finally to the emergence of new species. Those characteristics which enabled their possessors to compete more successfully in the ceaseless struggle with their environment insured their survival. But those who developed peculiarities which gave them no advantage, but only disadvantage, in coping with their competitors, naturally tended to die off. Hence only those that were fittest to survive were perpetuated and became a successful species. Thus the lower and simpler gradually became more advanced and complex, until finally Homo sapiens appeared as the climactic product of natural selection—presumably because man is the most fitted for survival and can most successfully cope with his environment.

As to the most fundamental question of all, the origin of matter itself, and the related question as to the origin of the earliest form of life to appear in the primeval ooze, Darwin had no answer to give, except possibly a deistic one (which dismisses God as a mere First Cause, who simply started the mechanism going and then completely removed Himself from the scene). "Therefore I should infer from analogy," he says in one passage, "that probably all the organic beings which have ever lived upon this earth have descended from one primordial form into which life was first breathed by the Creator." Therefore there is nothing completely atheistic about Darwin's formulation of evolution so far as the origin of matter is concerned (even though many of his followers have decided for the eternal existence of matter rather than concede the existence of God). Yet there remained no objective basis at all for the moral law or for

---

10. Additional scriptural analogies to the use of a day to represent or commemorate a year or longer time unit are found in Lev. 23:42-43 where the week represents 40 years of wandering in the wilderness, and Ezek. 4:4-5 where God Himself says that each day represents an entire year. It would certainly be impractical to devote an entire geological age to the commemoration of a geologic age!

spiritual values beyond materialistic considerations of survival, the survival of "the fittest." Furthermore, the Darwinian theory left no room for any meaningful divine activity in the process of "creation"; except for the supplying of primeval raw material, there really was no creation but only development according to natural selection. But we must ask who or what determined the selective process? And what or who determined fitness?! This represented almost a total contradiction of Gen. 1.

Space will not permit a detailed or adequate treatment of the theory of evolution in a book of this sort (even if its author had the equipment to handle it with competence). But it will perhaps be sufficient to point out a few areas in which Darwin's theory does not seem to square with the evidence, and where it betrays such serious inadequacies as to relegate it increasingly to the status of a mere passing phenomenon in the history of scientific thought. We shall treat these weaknesses under the following four headings.

1. From the standpoint of genetics (the science of heredity), the basic assumptions of natural selection run quite contrary to the evidence. Many decades of painstaking research have demonstrated that while it is true that individuals within a species do vary slightly from one another, it is not true that these variations are specifically inheritable by the next generation. The extensive experiments of Gregor J. Mendel showed that the range of variation possible within a species was strictly limited and afforded no progress whatsoever toward the development of a new species. Thus the individuals of a race of pure-bred tall peas might vary slightly in height, but the progeny of the tall ones was not on the average taller than the progeny of the short ones. It is true that by selective breeding, certain characteristics possible within a single species may be emphasized to form a special strain (as in the case of the many different types of dog), but there is a strictly limited circle of possibilities beyond which no breeder can go. He is powerless, in other words, to develop a new species. Mendel's work proved conclusively that the "chance variations" by which Darwin had set so much store are quite predictable and cannot possibly contribute to the formation of new species.

The same verdict must be pronounced on Jean Baptiste de Lamarck's theory of the inheritability of acquired characteristics (a theory to which Darwin occasionally appealed when mere natural selection seemed inadequate to account for a set of facts). Despite the enormous number of experiments undertaken to prove Lamarckian "use inheritance" (as it is called), the end result has been altogether negative. Characteristics acquired by special effort on the part of a parent are not passed on to his children, for the simple reason that there is no possible way in which these acquired characteristics (such as a special athletic proficiency) can affect his genes. All of heredity (on the non-spiritual side, at least) seems to depend upon the chemistry of the genes themselves. So far as the form or structure of animals is concerned, there is not a single claim to have established the theory of use inheritance which has not subsequently been discredited.[11]

11. Cf. Robert E. D. Clark, *Darwin: Before and After* (Chicago: Moody, 1967).

It should be added that while evidence is lacking for the inheritability of individual variations, there are sudden changes or mutations which occasionally take place in the history of a species. For example, a new variety of plants when isolated in small colonies, as on a mountainside, may result from a sudden mutation (involving a slight alteration in the genes themselves). Yet the fact remains that even though thousands of mutations have been closely studied, not a single clear example has been demonstrated whereby a mutation has made an animal more complicated or brought any new structure into existence. No progress whatsoever has been made since Darwin's time in solving any of the fundamental problems of evolution. In a review of M. J. D. White's *Animal Cytology and Evolution* (1954), I. Manton remarked: "The fundamental causes of evolution on the grand scale, as it has occurred through geological time and in the fashioning of the great groups of animals and plants, cannot yet be described or explained."[12]

2. Darwin's argument from the data of embryology has proved quite fallacious. He reasoned that in the development of the fetus in the womb it recapitulates its entire evolutionary past, as the fertilized ovum enlarges and produces more and more complicated organs and members. The visceral pouches in the human embryo, for example, were essentially the same organ as the gills of a fish, and therefore point back to man's emergence from a form of fish life. But this line of reasoning conveniently overlooks the undeniable fact that these structures never function as gills at any stage in embryonic life. Indeed, it is hard to see how the recapitulation theory can be squared with the actual sequence of development within the fetus. For example, the respiratory surface does not develop until very late in the formation of the embryo in the womb; yet it is inconceivable that in any prehuman stage the putative ancestor of man could have survived without any respiratory mechanism at all. Again, the size of the head in an embryo is simply enormous in proportion to the rest of the body, and yet the head of all the alleged prehuman ancestors was relatively small in proportion to the rest. Nor is it true that simple organs in the fetus slowly become more complicated. The eye, for example, results from the final fitting together of several different parts which appear to be formed separately at first and then are combined according to a predetermined pattern for which there is no ascertainable physical cause.

It's true enough, to be sure, that the embryos of all mammals develop from single-celled ova which appear to be quite identical, and that during the earlier stages this close resemblance continues. But does this fact require a theory that all mammals developed from the same common, pre-mammalian ancestors? A far more obvious and plausible explanation is that in the development of any embryo from its initial stage as a one-celled ovum, its simpler parts must be formed before the more complicated parts can be developed. We can hardly expect fine adjustments and complicated organs to come into being before the main structure to which they are to be attached. But to explain the earlier similarities of form by common ancestral origin is as implau-

12. I. Manton, in *Nature* 157 (1946): 713.

sible (as Clark pungently puts it) as to imagine that raindrops are derived from pebbles because both are round. "The connection is real enough, but it is a mathematical connection, inherent in the nature of the universe, and is not due to any direct connection between the objects."[13]

It is safe to say that there is no datum from embryology which does not betray the operation of deliberate design and purpose by an all-wise Creator, rather than the mechanical operation of natural selection. Very occasionally in the growth of an embryo the mechanism of growth seems to malfunction. Then it is found that a totally new mechanism may take over and produce the desired structure. Sometimes two or three of these "double assurance" mechanisms are called into play in order to insure the proper development of the fetus; yet inexplicably enough, they go into action when needed. But since such malfunctions are exceedingly rare, it is almost impossible to account for them by any principle of the "survival of the fittest." It looks much more like the intervention of a divine intelligence. This, of course, is not to deny that some fetuses do develop improperly and turn out to be defective specimens which can scarcely survive or perform any useful function. In the case of human beings, the results can be quite tragic and difficult to explain. But on Darwinian presuppositions it is impossible to explain even the sense of pathos engendered by this example of dysteleology.[14] The consistent Darwinian can only shrug his shoulders and remark, "It is only surprising that there aren't more of these." For to the Darwinian there is no answer beyond mechanistic natural selection and the "survival of the fittest."

3. Natural selection is unable to explain innumerable instances of adaptation in which there was evidently no transitional stage. Natural selection would lead us to expect that ants and termites learned to associate together in colonies because they found from experience that this increased their chances of survival. But there are no fossil evidences whatever of either ants or termites prior to their organized life together in colonies. Or, to take an anatomical example, we have to consider how any supposed transitional stages toward the development of the organ of sight could possibly have conferred any advantage in the battle for survival until the eye had actually been fully formed. If the animal had possessed (in its transitional phase) a mere patch of skin especially sensitive to light, and then the process of natural selection had been brought to bear upon its successive mutations, how would anything short of actual sight have fitted the creature to survive more successfully than competitors who lacked such light-sensitive patches? And yet the Darwinian hypothesis necessarily implies that at every stage of the development of new and more complicated organisms, even before

13. Clark, pp. 171-72.

14. The term *dysteleology* applies to cases where the teleology (or intelligent purpose) is hard to see. It refers to instances where something seems to have gone wrong, such as misshapen or monstrous births, or long and excruciatingly painful fatal illness endured by people of godly convictions and exemplary life. It may even be applied to devastating plagues like the medieval Black Death, or widely destructive floods, or earthquakes. Cases like these are very difficult to reconcile with the all-wise purpose of a loving and omnipotent God. Hence the term *dysteleology* (apparent absence of intelligent purpose).

they were at all usable, the animal so developing must have enjoyed thereby some specific advantage over its competitors. As for the much-cited example of the growth cycle of the frog, the principle of natural selection is of only limited help. That is, it might conceivably explain why tadpoles learned to swim, feed, and run away from their enemies more efficiently than less capable ancestors. But how does it throw any light upon why they finally turned into frogs? Can it seriously be contended that frogs are more fitted to survival than fish are? Clearly some more sophisticated explanation must be found than mere mechanistic natural selection.

In short, the Darwinian theory accounts for the data of biology far less adequately than does the sublimely simple affirmation of Genesis 1, that all species of plant and animal came into being in response to the creative will of an omnipotent and all-wise God, and that their development has in every stage been governed by His design. All the structural resemblances (such as the skeletal resemblances so relied upon to indicate a genetic relationship between man and the lower orders of vertebrates) may be satisfactorily accounted for by a directive force operating from without (or from above), rather than by mechanical forces operating from within living tissue as such. Even the phenomenon of apparently useless vestigial parts, such as the coccyx at the end of the human spine, does not demonstrate an ancestry tracing back to tail-bearing simians. Such vestiges only attest a general or basic plan followed by the creative force (or the divine intelligence) which fashioned the various vertebrate phyla.

A similar carry-over of engineering design is traceable in the year-by-year development of the modern automobile, from the 1901 Ford sedan (let us say) to the 1994 model. In some cases vestigial remains (like the retention of a crank opening at the base of the radiator for many years after self-starters had been introduced) marked the evolution of this make of car. The same thing is true of the "portholes" of the Buick models between the 1940s and 1950s (until the final token vestige of the 1957 model). But it can hardly be said that the earlier models made themselves more advanced or more complicated; this was the work of the designers and engineers who produced the new model for each successive year. There is nothing in the data of geology, or of biology in general, to indicate any essential difference in the procedure followed by the Creator Himself. Once the model, or species, had been set up, it then was ready for mass production through the built-in system of procreation and reproduction with which all animals are endowed—each species being controlled within Mendelian limits by its own particular set of genes.

4. The modern abandonment of the Darwinian theory of gradual differentiation as the mechanism by which all classes and orders of life have evolved has led to the substitution of a new type of evolution (the quantum theory of emergent evolution) which commands the allegiance of most foremost scientists today. But emergent evolution involves factors of sudden mutation or change so radical as to put it into the category of a mere philosophical credo incapable of verification by laboratory methods

or of explanation on strictly mechanistic principles. In Darwin's generation it was confidently expected that more extended geological and biological research in subsequent decades would uncover the transitional forms of life which would bridge the gap between the various orders and phyla. But most twentieth-century scientists have completely despaired of this search.

Austin H. Clark (*The New Evolution* [1930], p. 189), for example, remarked on "the entire lack of any intermediates between the major groups of animals—as, for instance, between the backboned animals or vertebrates, the echinoderms, the mollusks and the arthropods." He went on to say, "If we are willing to accept the facts, we must believe that there never were such intermediates, or in other words, that these major groups have from the very first borne the same relationship to each other that they have today." Similarly G. G. Simpson pointed out that each of the thirty-two known orders of mammals appeared quite suddenly in the paleontological record. He stated, "The earliest and most primitive known members of every order already have the basic ordinal characters, and in no case is an approximately continuous sequence from one order to another known."[15]

Clark, Simpson, and their modern colleagues have therefore taken refuge in the theory of emergent evolution, which affirms that dramatic new forms arise by mere chance, or by some kind of creative response to new environmental factors which cannot be further analyzed or rationally described. But can such an explanation (which really is no explanation but only an appeal for faith) be considered a more reasonable alternative than the creative act of a superior intelligence? As Carl Henry puts it: "Supposition of abrupt emergence falls outside the field of scientific analysis just as fully as the appeal to supernatural creative forces."[16]

Despite the foregoing considerations, however (or perhaps in ignorance of them), there are many committed Christians who are prepared to accept the theory of evolution upon a theistic basis. That is to say, they profess adherence to the mechanistic process of natural selection (according to Darwin's formulation), or even to the newer emergent theory of evolution; but they nevertheless insist that matter was not eternal (as nontheists must suppose), but that it was created by God *ex nihilo*. Furthermore, they regard the whole mechanism of the evolutionary process as devised and controlled by God, rather than by some mysterious force which cannot be entirely accounted for by science.

To those who hold this position it should be pointed out that historically the whole theory was elaborated in an effort to explain the development of life along purely natural mechanical principles, without the necessity of any divine influence whatever. Darwin and his colleagues made the most determined efforts to overthrow the argument for God's existence based upon the evidence of design in nature, and exploited

15. Clark, *The New Evolution* (New Haven, Conn.: Yale U., 1930), p. 189; Simpson, *Tempo and Mode in Evolution* (New York: Columbia U., 1944), p. 106.
16. Quoted in *Evolution and Christian Thought Today*, ed. R. Mixter (Grand Rapids: Eerdmans, 1959), p. 211.

every conceivable instance of dysteleology and purposelessness which they could discover. They pointed to the fact that out of the many thousands of eggs laid by a mother fish a very small percentage ever survive to maturity, and that only a very few seeds deposited by fruitbearing trees ever live to produce new trees. (Thus the food supply afforded to other creatures by this overabundance of roe and fruit was conveniently ignored.) A consistent effort was made to explain the universe without God. For this reason, Darwinian evolution became the official philosophy of the leading atheistic movements of the twentieth century (such as the purest form of Nazism and of Marxist socialism). Darwin's concession that a higher power may have provided the original raw material and vital impulse which started evolution at the beginning was nevertheless a complete negation of Hebrew-Christian revelation. It inevitably led to the result that moral and religious conceptions discoverable in mankind result from a mere fortuitous combination of molecules and have no counterpart in spiritual reality.

Evolution as a philosophy of world view really involves an outright denial of spiritual reality even as it rejects the existence of a personal God. All of its leading exponents have said as much in no uncertain terms. Ernst Haeckel's *Riddle of the Universe* (1929) employed the evolutionary thesis to disprove supernatural religion and became thereby one of the major influences for atheism in the twentieth century. G. G. Simpson declared that a wholehearted acceptance of evolution is inconsistent with belief in the activity of God in the universe.[17] Charles Darwin himself, during an interview with a newspaper reporter soon after the publication of the *Origin of Species*, simply shrugged his shoulders at the whole moral issue. When asked if it was not true that his book had shown every criminal how to justify his ways, he simply dubbed the accusation "a good squib" and let the matter drop.[18] In view of such factors as these, it seems a very dubious procedure for a convinced Christian who means to be loyal to the authority of Scripture to acknowledge himself an evolutionist, except in a most restricted sense—in fact, in a sense utterly unacceptable to Darwin and all his followers. For a Christian, there is no alternative to identifying natural selection with divine selection, whether in a direct or an indirect sense.

THE ANTIQUITY OF THE HUMAN RACE

Since the first discoveries of the fossils and artifacts of prehistoric man back in the 1850s, the antiquity of the human race has provided a problem of reconciliation with the Genesis record. According to modern estimates the so-called Swanscombe man (found in Kent, England), the Pithecanthropus (found in Java) and the Sinanthropus (found in Peking, China) lived anywhere from 200,000 to 500,000 years ago. All of them show marked differences from Homo sapiens, to be sure, and some paleanthropologists have conceded that "the cranial and dental differences...appear to be as well

17. Simpson, *The Meaning of Evolution* (Baltimore: Williams & Wilkins, 1949), p. 230.
18. Cf. Clark, p. 96.

marked as those which are commonly accepted as justifying a genetic distinction between the gorilla and the chimpanzee."[19]

As for the Neanderthal man, commonly dated from 50,000 to 100,000 years ago, the same writer says: "The skeletal differences from *Homo sapiens* are of much the same order as those which have been accepted as valid evidence of specific distinction in other groups of primates."[20] These early anthropoids cannot be dismissed as mere apes in their mentality, for their remains are accompanied by stone implements, such as arrowheads and ax heads; and charred remains indicate strongly the use of fire for cooking purposes. Especially in the case of the Neanderthal deposits, there seems to be evidence of burial with adjacent implements as if there was some sort of belief in life after death (necessitating the use of such implements—or their spiritual counterpart— by the deceased). Some crude statuettes have likewise been discovered which may possibly have had cultic purposes, and some of the remarkable paintings discovered in some of the caves may have been of Neanderthal origin (although most were perhaps from a later age). The radiocarbon analysis of the more recent find indicates strongly an age of at least 50,000 years. The fluorine content of the bones of the *Pithecanthropus erectus* indicates that they were contemporaneous with the surrounding deposit in which they were found. The Zinjanthropus of Tanganyika is dated by the potassium-argon process as 1,750,000 years old, according to a report by L. S. B. Leakey.[21]

It is theoretically possible, of course, that later research may prove that all of these chronological estimates were based upon faulty methodology, and it may conceivably be that these earlier anthropoids will have to be dated as much more recent.[22] On the other hand, it is most unlikely that they can be brought within the time span indicated by the genealogical lists of Gen. 5 and 10. Either we must regard these lists as having no significance whatever as time indicators,[23] or else we must reject these earlier humanlike species as being descended from Adam at all.

Buswell states: "There is nothing in the Bible to indicate how long ago man was created."[24] This appears to be an overstatement, for even allowing the numerous gaps in the chronological tables given in Gen. 5 and Gen. 10 it is altogether unreasonable to suppose that a hundred times as many generations are omitted in these tables as are included in them. (And yet this is what a 200,000 B.C. date for Adam would amount to.) In the genealogy of the Lord Jesus given in Matt. 1:2-17 there are only seven possible links missing as against a total of forty-two given (during the 2000 years between Abraham and Christ), or a ratio of one to six. This is slender ground upon which to build a theory that 1,980 generations were omitted from the list between Adam and

19. LeGros Clark, *The Fossil Evidences for Human Evolution* (Chicago: U. Chicago, 1955), p. 106.
20. Ibid., p. 60.
21. Leakey, in *National Geographic* (Oct. 1961).
22. Cf. chap. 15, n. 12.
23. This has been implied by B. B. Warfield, *On the Antiquity and Unity of the Human Race*, PTR (1911)—a judgment in which J. O. Buswell III concurs in Mixter, p. 181.
24. Ibid.

Abraham, and only nineteen or twenty were given. It therefore seems a dubious option for one who holds to the accuracy of the Genesis record to accept a date of 200,000 B.C. for Adam.

The *Westminster Dictionary of the Bible* lists three possibilities for the genealogies of Gen. 5 and 10.

1. If they represent literal generations without any gaps, the total from Adam to the Flood comes out to 1,656 years, and the total from the Flood to the birth of Abraham about 290 years. This makes up a grand total of 1,946 years from Adam to Abraham. This interpretation is dubious, however, since no such grand total (long date) is given in the text itself, and since the grouping into ten predeluge and ten postdeluge generations is suspiciously similar to the schematized fourteen, fourteen, fourteen of Matt. 1 (where demonstrably there are six or seven links missing). Moreover, Luke 3:36 indicates that a Cainan, son of Arphaxad, is missing in Gen. 10:24 (which states that Arphaxad was the "father" of Shelach, the son of Cainan according to Luke 3).

2. The genealogies record only the most prominent members of the ancestry of Abraham, omitting an undetermined number of links (although presumably not as many links as actually are named in the lists concerned). A variation of this view would construe the formula "A begat B" as meaning either B himself or some unnamed ancestor of B (perfectly allowable in Hebrew parlance, since grandfathers are occasionally said to have begotten their grandsons; at least Bilhah's grandsons are spoken of as her sons in 1 Chron. 7:13). The ages of the patriarchs who lived several centuries (even 900 years or more) would be understood as the actual lifetime of the individuals named. This view would allow for a time span of possibly five or six thousand years between Adam and Abraham—depending upon how many links are omitted.

Incidentally, there is some question whether Abraham was really Terah's oldest son, even though he was mentioned first in Gen. 11:26, where Terah is stated to have begotten all three sons when he was seventy—or at least he began fatherhood at that age. In Gen. 11:27 it is stated that Terah begat Abraham, Nahor and Haran (who was apparently the eldest of the three sons). But since Terah died at the age of 205 according to 11:32, Abraham could not have been born until his father was 130, *if* he was only seventy-five at Terah's decease—as suggested by 12:4. (While there is nothing in Gen. 11 or 12 that states positively that Terah had died before Abraham left Haran, this is made quite explicit in Acts 7:4.)

3. Or else the names listed in Genesis 5 represent an individual and his direct line by primogeniture—an interpretation which makes possible adding the entire lifetime figures almost end to end, thus coming out to a grand total of 8,227 years between the birth of Adam and the flood. For example, when Adam is said to have lived 930 years, this really means that Adam and his direct line were at the head of affairs for 930 years. At the end of this time they were superseded by the family of Seth, which remained in control through Seth's main line for 912 years (Gen. 5:8). Thus it would not have been until 1,842 years after Adam's birth that the family of Enosh took over the leadership—

and so on. One difficulty with this theory, however, is that Seth is the oldest surviving son of Adam to be mentioned, apart from the exiled Cain, and it is difficult to imagine by what other son Adam's direct line would have descended before the allegedly collateral line of Seth took over.

On the whole, then, the second interpretation seems the most tenable of the three. (The first interpretation, of course, leaves insufficient room to account even for the attested history of Egypt, which doubtless goes back to at least 3500 years B.C., and that, too, necessarily after the flood.)

To revert to the problem of the Pithecanthropus, the Swanscombe man, the Neanderthal and all the rest (possibly even the Cro-Magnon man, who is apparently to be classed as *Homo sapiens*, but whose remains seem to date back at least to 20,000 B.C.), it seems best to regard these races as all prior to Adam's time, and not involved in the Adamic covenant. We must leave the question open, in view of the cultural remains, whether these pre-Adamite creatures had souls (or, to use the trichotomic terminology, spirits). But the clear implication of Gen. 1:26 is that God was creating a qualitatively different being when he made Adam (for note that the word rendered "man" in Gen. 1:26-27 is the Hebrew *'Adam*), a being who was uniquely fashioned in the image of God. Only Adam and his descendants were infused with the breath of God and a spiritual nature corresponding to God Himself.[25] Romans 5:12-21 demands that all mankind subsequent to Adam's time, at least, must have been literally descended from him, since he entered into covenant relationship with God as the representative of the entire race of man. This indicates that there could have been no true genetic relationship between Adam (the first man created in the image of God) and the pre-Adamite races. However close the skeletal structure of the Cro-Magnon man (for example) may have been to Homo sapiens, this factor is scarcely relevant to the principal question of whether these cave men possessed a truly human soul or personality. They may have been exterminated by God for unknown reasons prior to the creation of the original parent of the present human race. Adam, then, was the first man created in the spiritual image of God, according to Gen. 1:26-27, and there is no evidence from science to disprove it.[26]

After these preliminary questions relating to the confrontation between the first chapter of Genesis and modern science, we are now in a position to proceed with the study of the remainder of the book in the chapter following.

---

25. In his remarkable volume entitled *Human Destiny*, the French scientist Lecomte du Noüy insists that evolution was a response to the divine will. Man arises from within the evolutionary process, and at a certain moment, perhaps the Cro-Magnon age (30,000 B.C.), man became truly man by a mutation—a mutation in which God breathed into him "free will," and a capacity to choose between good and evil, i.e., a conscience.

26. Further helpful discussion of these matters will be found in E. J. Young's chapter "Are the Scriptures Inerrant?" in *The Bible: the Living Word of Revelation*, ed. M. C. Tenney (Grand Rapids: Zondervan, 1968), pp. 105-10.

15 GENESIS (CONTINUED)

IT IS THE PURPOSE of this chapter to discuss the various passages in Genesis about which particular question has been raised, other than the matters pertaining to natural origin which have aleady been handled in the previous chapter. In each case the passage to be treated has been used as the basis of a charge of inaccuracy and unreliability leveled at the book as a whole.

THE HISTORICITY OF ADAM AND THE FALL

As to the relationship of Gen. 2 to Gen. 1, it has already been pointed out[1] that the use of the divine names (*Elohîm* and *Yahweh*) is quite reconcilable with unity of authorship. Since *Elohîm* ("God") was the appropriate title for noncovenantal contexts, Moses (assuming that he was the author of the whole book) could very well have employed it exclusively for the creation account of chapter 1, and then shifted to *Yahweh* (*Elohîm* (for the most part) in chapter 2, where he dealt with the covenant of works set up between God and Adam.

Questions have been raised as to how seriously we are to take this whole narrative about Adam and Eve (and the serpent in the Garden of Eden) as literal history. Many prefer to regard it as a mere myth or fable (*suprahistory*, to use the neo-orthodox term) in which the moral downfall of man is described by a fictitious episode designed to illustrate it. (Yet insofar as man is a fallen creature, a moral agent with an innate sense of guilt, the myth allegedly reflects a sublime truth, even though no such isolated episode actually took place.) No decisive objections, however, have ever been raised against the historicity of Adam and Eve either on historical, scientific, or philosophical grounds. The protest has been based essentially upon subjective concepts of improbability.

From the standpoint of logic, it is virtually impossible to accept the authority of Rom. 5 ("By one man sin entered into the world....By one man's offense death reigned by one....By one man's disobedience many were made sinners") without inferring that the entire human race must have descended from a single father. In Rom. 5, Adam is contrasted with Christ. If therefore Christ was a historical individual, Adam himself must have been historical (or else the inspired apostle was in error). Again, Paul takes

---

1. Chap. 9, pp. 129-30.

the details of Gen. 2 and of the temptation and fall in Gen. 3 as literal history. In 1 Tim. 2:13-14 he says: "For Adam was first formed, then Eve. And Adam was not deceived, but the woman being deceived was in the transgression." There can be no question that the New Testament authors accepted the literal historicity of Adam and Eve. The origin of the human race is necessarily a matter of revelation by God, since no written records could extend back to a time prior to the invention of writing. Conceivably the true account of man's origin could have been handed down by oral tradition (and perhaps it was so handed down until Moses' time). But apart from revelation, written down as inspired Scripture, there could be no assurance as to which of the bewildering variety of legends of man's origin known to the many different cultures of earth was the true and reliable account. Here the inspired record tells of a literal Adam and Eve, and gives no indication whatever that the account is intended to be mythical.[2] In this connection note that Luke 3:38 traces the ancestry of Jesus back to Enos, to Seth, and finally to Adam himself (who must therefore have been as historic an individual as Seth and Enos). It was certainly taken as historical by Christ and the apostles.

Some recent writers, such as Alan Richardson, have compared the narrative material in Gen. 1-11 to the parables of the New Testament. "A parable is a story which may or may not be literally true (no one asks whether the good Samaritan ever literally happened); but it conveys a meaning beyond itself. It implies that beyond the words of the story which our outward ears have heard there is a meaning which only our spiritual hearing can detect."[3] But this comparison with New Testament parables involves the presumption that the author of Genesis intended the narrative of chapters 1-11 to be a mere analogy or comparison to illustrate some theological truth, and did not mean for his readers to get the impression that these episodes narrated ever took place in actual history. The characteristic introduction to Jesus' parables was: "The kingdom of God is like—." Always there is some doctrinal or ethical teaching which is being explained to the listener, and an illustration is resorted to in order to make the point clear. But the narratives and genealogical lists of Gen. 1-11 have no such framework. Nowhere is it stated that the beginning of the world or of mankind was *like* anything analogous. A parable is never to be explained in terms of itself; it always involves an analogy drawn from something else. Just as it would never have been said, "The kingdom of God is like the kingdom of God," so it could never have been intended to imply, "The beginning of the human race was like the beginning of the human race," or "The universal flood was like the universal flood." Hence the parabolic element is completely missing here, and Richardson's interpretation is scarcely tenable.

---

2. Possibly the mention of a talking serpent (Gen. 3:1, 4-5) might suggest a myth. But both the context itself and other references in Scripture (cf. Rev. 20:2, "that old serpent, which is the Devil, and Satan") make it clear that the serpent was a mere guise through which the Satanic tempter spoke to them. In this reptile Satan had a fitting and appropriate vehicle by which to make his approach. Similarly, Balaam's ass (Num. 22:28) was the vehicle through which Jehovah spoke to His disobedient servant.

3. Richardson, *Genesis I-XI* (London: SCM, 1953), p. 28.

NOAH'S ARK AND THE FLOOD

As to the great deluge of Gen. 6-8, some discussion has already been devoted to the specious grounds upon which Wellhausen dissected this account into J and P.[4] There it was shown that the entire section consisted of one tightly knit, homogeneous narrative.

The larger question raised by nineteenth century scholarship was whether such an event as a world-wide flood ever took place. The comparative lack of geologic evidence for a worldwide cataclysm has given rise to doubts as to the universality of the flood. It is alleged that no characteristic or uniform flood-type deposits have been discovered in the sites excavated in the Mesopotamian Valley. The thick flood stratum found by Leonard Woolley at Ur dates from early fourth millennium (ca. 3800 B.C.), but only one other flood stratum from that period has thus far been discovered, that found by Stephen Langdon at Kish (a much shallower deposit, incidentally). The other flood deposits, discovered at Kish, Shuruppak, Uruk, and (possibly) Lagash, represent an inundation of a thousand years later, judging from the archaeological remains and stratigraphical sequence.[5] While the excavations may not in all cases have penetrated low enough to reach the 3800 B.C. level in some of the above mentioned, in Kish, at least, the dig went down to apparently undisturbed virgin soil right below the 2800 B.C. level.

It is of course true that these few deep excavations are by themselves insufficient for any firm conclusions. But they have led most archaeologists to question the possibility of a general deluge over a more than local area—at least within the period investigated in the excavations themselves—and even staunch conservative apologists as listed by Ramm[6] have defended the theory of a flood restricted to the cradle of the human race in Mesopotamia (or possibly extending up to the Caspian basin).

George F. Wright seems to incline to the possibility that it may have been limited to the Euphrates valley, provided the human race was then restricted to this area and was thus totally destroyed. Yet he also refers to geological evidence for the flood in Egypt, Palestine, Sicily, France, and England (possibly even North America).[7] The Jamieson, Fausset, and Brown Commentary (JFB) indicates that the Hebrew text does not necessarily imply a universal flood. L. M. Davies also conceded that the flood was not necessarily universal, although he pointed to such distant phenomena as the frozen mammoths of Siberia as evidence for a very extensive and sudden inundation. (Unfortunately, however, for this correlation, the latest of the Siberian mammoths is conjectured by paleontologists to be earlier than 30,000 B.C.) J. W. Dawson denies that the Hebrew author had in mind a literally universal flood.[8]

4. Chap. 9, pp. 136-37.

5. Cf. Andre Parrot, *The Flood and Noah's Ark* (New York: Philosophical Library, 1955), p. 52.

6. B. Ramm, CVSS, pp. 238-47.

7. Wright, in ISBE: 2:821-26, has an excellent summary of the corroborating evidence of the Genesis account.

8. Yet in the one-volume reprint of JFB by Zondervan, p. 22, we read concerning Gen. 7:20: "fifteen cubits upward...and the mountains were covered." "The language is not consistent with the theory of a partial deluge." See Davies, *Journal of the Transactions of the Victoria Institute* (1930): 62:62-95; see also Dawson, *The Meeting Place of Geology and History* (New York: Revell, 1894), p. 151.

In explanation of this assertion, it needs to be pointed out that the Hebrew *'ereṣ*, translated consistently as "earth" in our English Bibles, is also the word used for "land" (e.g., the *land* of Israel, the *land* of Egypt). There is another term, *tēbēl*, which means the whole expanse of the earth, or the world as a whole. Nowhere does *tēbēl* occur in this account, but only *'ereṣ*, in all the statements which sound quite universal in the English Bible (e.g., 7:4, 10, 17, 18, 19). Thus, Gen. 6:17c can be rendered: "Everything that is in the *land* shall die"—that is, in whatever geographical region is involved in the context and situation. If this interpretation be allowed, then the mountains whose summits were submerged by the flood would have been the relatively lower mountains of the region surrounding Mesopotamia, rather than including the mighty Himalayas (such as Mount Everest with its nearly six miles in height). Correspondingly, the word *ground* (*'ᵃdāmāh*) which occurs in the ASV of 7:4 ("earth," KJV) can be understood as the soil surface of the same area covered by the *'ereṣ* of the other verses. But the phrase "under the whole heaven" in 7:19 ("and all the high mountains that were under the whole heaven," ASV) may not be so easily disposed of. It is doubtful whether anywhere else in the Hebrew Scriptures this expression "the whole heaven" can be interpreted to indicate a mere geographical region. For this reason most careful exegetes, like Franz Delitzsch in the last century[9] and more recently H. C. Leupold,[10] have not conceded the exegetical possibility of interpreting Gen. 7 as describing a merely local flood.

Formidable scientific problems are raised by a universal flood, according to Ramm's summary.[11] (1) According to the best estimates, to cover the highest Himalayas would require eight times more water than our planet now possesses. (2) The withdrawal of so great a quantity of water constitutes an almost insuperable problem, for there would be no place to which it could *drain off*. (Ramm so interprets the verb *shākak* in Gen. 8:1—yet the lexicons render it "decrease," "abate" ["assuaged," KJV and ASV] rather than "drain off.") The mechanics of this abatement of water would certainly be difficult, for the atmosphere could not possibly hold that much water in evaporated form, and it is doubtful if any underground cavities in the earth could receive more than a small fraction of this additional volume of water. (3) Scarcely any plant life could have survived submersion under salt water for over a year, and the mingling of ocean water with the rain must have resulted in a lethal saline concentration, even though the mixture would have been considerably diluted. Practically all marine life would have perished, except those comparatively few organisms which can withstand tremendous pressure, for 90 percent of present marine life is found in the first fifty fathoms, and many of these species cannot survive distant migration from their native feeding grounds. Presumably the fresh water fish would have died, even though the salinity might have been high enough to support saltwater fish. (4) Certain

9. Delitzsch, *Pentateuch* (Grand Rapids: Eerdmans, 1949), 1:146.
10. Leupold, *Exposition of Genesis*, vol. 1 (Grand Rapids: Baker, 1950).
11. Ramm, CVSS, 244-46.

areas of the earth's surface show definite evidence of no submersion. For example, in Auvergne, France, there are reportedly cones of loose scoria and ashes from volcanoes thousands of years older than the flood, and yet they show no signs of having been washed or disturbed by flood waters.

Perhaps difficulties (1) and (3) can be accounted for by special creative or recreative acts of God. (But why then the concern for the preservation of the land animals in the ark, if re-creation was so readily available?) But (2) would seem to call for a good deal of uncreation or complete annihilation of aqueous matter—which appears highly improbable. Difficulty (4) seems to defy explanation, unless the volcanoes involved were really of post-Noahic origin, and the criteria for dating them earlier turn out to be erroneous. Or else perhaps the scoria and ashes may not have been so easily disturbed by water action as the argument assumes, or else they may have been covered over by later strata before the Flood.

It cannot be maintained, however, that even a local flood will solve all these scientific difficulties. Gen. 7:19 states most explicitly that all the water level rose well above "all the high mountains that were under the whole heaven." Assuming that the mountains involved were merely local (a difficult interpretation to make out from the text), at the very least the peaks of Mount Ararat itself were covered, since the ark came to rest where the higher peak (over 17,000 feet high) would be visible. The unavoidable inference would be that the water level rose more than 17,000 feet above the present sea level. This creates difficulties almost as grave for the local flood theory as those which that theory is supposed to avoid. How could the level have been that high at Ararat without being the same height over the rest of the world? Only during a very temporary surge, such as that of a tidal wave, can water fail to seek its own level. To suppose a 17,000-foot level in Armenia simultaneous with an uninundated Auvergne in France would be to propound a more incredible miracle than anything implied by the traditional understanding of a universal flood.

The only possible solution, apparently, would be found in the supposition that the height of Ararat was much lower than at present. It is very difficult to date reliably a major upward thrust of the mountain-making variety, and hence it is quite possible that even in the few millennia which have followed the flood, the great mountain ranges have attained far higher elevation than they did before Noah's time. Thus the recent uplift of the Sierra Nevada range in California is the only reasonable explanation of the dying out of the bristle-cone pine tree, thousands of years old, on their eastern slopes which (to judge from the width of the season rings in their trunks) apparently flourished during an earlier period when rainfall from the landward breezes from the Pacific shore was fairly plentiful. Since this species is still dying out under conditions created by increased elevation of the westernmost peaks (resulting in the cutting off of winds from the Pacific), this must have been of recent occurrence (*The National Geographic* [March 1958], pp. 355-68). But such a supposition could be applicable not only to the Ararat range but also to the Himalayas and the Cordilleras as well, and it would alleviate somewhat the problem of water supply for a universal flood.

A very interesting line of evidence has been furnished by some exponents of diluvialism in the various ossiferous fissures which have been discovered in widely separate locations in both hemispheres. A. M. Rehwinkel, for example, in his *Flood* (1951), describes these great fissures, some of them in hills of considerable height, and anywhere from 140 to 300 feet in depth, containing the most heterogeneous mammal remains. Since no skeleton is complete, the inference is that none of these animals fell into these fissures while still alive. Nor is there any evidence of weathering in these bones, nor of being rolled by streams. They must have been deposited under water, since they were cemented together by calcite. Notably in one such deposit in the Saar Valley region were found the remains of bears, wolves, and oxen, as well as many small animals; others have been located on the Island of Cerigo or Kythera (off the southeastern tip of the Peloponnesus), in the Rock of Gibraltar, and near Odessa on the Black Sea. This last named site was excavated in 1847 and produced about 4,500 bones of bears, hyenas, horses, boars, mammoths, rhinoceros, aurochs, deer, and many small creatures. In Malta a fissure was discovered in which along with these heterogeneous remains were found huge blocks of stone which could only have been carried there by violent water action. At Agate Springs in Nebraska, a similar discovery was made in 1876. In a ten-acre area were the remains of at least a thousand animals who apparently had died instantly in great numbers.

All these finds certainly point to a sudden catastrophe involving the breaking up of the earth surface into enormous cracks, into which were poured the corpses of great numbers of animals who were suddenly overwhelmed in a flood. Whether or not the fluorine dating and carbon 14 tests would indicate a sufficiently recent date to identify this catastrophe with Noah's flood is another matter. In the case of extinct species such as the mammoth, the question of the true date of their extinction is of pivotal importance. Some scientific grounds for bringing this event closer to our own time would have to be found before these data (assembled by George McCready Price and repeated by Rehwinkel) can be associated with the biblical episode. It is possible that uniformitarian presuppositions with regard to the fluorine test and carbon 14 will some day be shown invalid by the discovery of new evidence.[12]

At this point it should be mentioned that some writers have raised the question of whether in point of fact the flood resulted in the destruction of the entire human race (apart from the family of Noah). The list of descendants in the respective lines of Ham, Shem, and Japheth as recorded in Gen. 10 does not permit any easy identification with the remoter races who lived in the lower reaches of Africa, Far East Asia, Australia, and the Americas. Particularly in the case of Australia, with its peculiar fauna indicating a

---

12. At this point a word of caution should be given concerning the reliability of carbon 14 dating. As J. C. Whitcomb pointed out at the annual meeting of the Evangelical Theological Society (Dec. 28, 1959), some of the scientists themselves have questions about the trustworthiness of the results. A British archaeologist, Stuart Piggott, reported that two radiocarbon tests on a sample of charcoal indicated a date of 2620-2630 B.C. for the construction of the Henge of Durrington Walls. But absolutely com-

long period of separation from the Eurasian continent, the difficulty of assigning either the human or the subhuman population with the passengers in the ark has been felt to be acute. Perhaps, then, these scholars suggest, we are to see in the family of Noah only the ancestors of the nations more immediately surrounding the Holy Land, that is, the peoples of the Near and Middle East, and of the Mediterranean coastlands.

This suggestion encounters at least three formidable difficulties, in the light of the biblical evidence. The first is that the divine purpose, as indicated in the flood narrative, was to destroy the entire human race. Thus in Gen. 6:7 we read: "And the Lord [Jehovah] said, I will destroy man [hā'ādām] whom I have created from the face of the earth; both man, and beast, and the creeping thing, and the fowls of the air; for it repenteth me that I have made them." So also verse 17: "And, behold, I, even I, do bring a flood of waters upon the earth, to destroy all flesh, wherein is the breath of life, from under heaven; and everything that is in the earth shall die." Even if we hold in abeyance the admissibility of translating 'ereṣ here as "land" rather than "earth," it seems quite evident that a total destruction of the human race was involved.

Second, it is made abundantly evident in the Genesis account that the reason for sending the flood was the sinful condition of mankind. Gen. 6:5 reads: "And Jehovah saw that the wickedness of man was great in the earth, and that every imagination of the thoughts of his heart was only evil continually." Again, in verse 11: "The earth also was corrupt [wattishshāḥēt] before God, and the earth was filled with violence [ḥāmās —"injurious wrongdoing"]. It hardly seems likely that the ancestors of the Australians and Far Eastern peoples presented such a stark contrast in morals to the Middle Eastern nations that God saw fit to exempt them from the judgment of the flood. The Scripture clearly includes all mankind in the verdict of guilty (e.g., Rom. 3:19, "That every mouth may be stopped, and all the world may be guilty ["accountable," RSV] before God"). This is a basic premise of the New Testament gospel. No ground for dif-

pelling archaeological evidences called for a date approximately a thousand years later. Piggott concluded that the radiocarbon date is "archaeologically inacceptable" (Antiquity, 33:132 [Dec. 1959], 289). In this same issue, the editor of the journal remarks, "It is very important to realize that doubts about the archaeological acceptability of radiocarbon dates is not obscurantism....It is an attempt to evaluate all the available evidence, physical and non-physical. We certainly need reassurance beyond all reasonable doubt at the present moment that scientists know all about the variables involved, that Elsasser, Ney and Winckler are wrong in supposing that there was variation in the intensity of cosmic-ray formation, and that others are wrong in supposing that there were fluctuations in the original C-14 content." (Ibid., p. 239.)

Laurence Kulp in Scientific Monthly (75 [Nov 1952], 261) admits that "there are two basic assumptions in the carbon 14 method. (1) One is that the carbon 14 concentration in the carbon dioxide cycle is constant. (2) The other is that the cosmic ray flux has been essentially constant—at least on a scale of centuries." Whitcomb points out that there are still other unproved assumptions: (3) the constancy of the rate of decay of carbon 14 atoms; (4) dead organic matter is not later altered in its carbon content by any biological or nonbiological activity; (5) the carbon dioxide content of the ocean and atmosphere has been constant throughout the ages; (6) the huge reservoir of oceanic carbon has not changed in amount throughout the last 50,000 years; (7) the rate of formation and the rate of decay of radiocarbon atoms have been kept in perfect and constant equilibrium throughout the same period. It is highly significant that W. F. Albright in an interview reported in Christianity Today went so far as to say: "Carbon 14 is almost totally useless in dating bones which contain a minimum of carbon" (Jan. 18 [1963], p. 4).

ferentiating between the nations closer to Palestine and those more remote from it can possibly be made out on the basis of superior morality.

Third, we have the unequivocal corroboration of the New Testament that the destruction of the human race at the time of the flood was total and universal. In 2 Peter 3:6 we read: "The world that then was, being overflowed with water, perished." Compare 2 Peter 2:5: God "spared not the old world, but saved Noah the eighth person, a preacher of righteousness, bringing in the flood upon the world of the ungodly." Christ Himself remarked, according to Matt. 24:38-39, concerning the days of Noah: "For as in the days that were before the flood they were eating and drinking, marrying and giving in marriage, until the day that Noah entered into the ark, and knew not until the flood came, and took them all [hapantas] away; so shall also the coming of the Son of man be." While the word all may not always be used in a completely universal sense in Scripture, it is consistently used to apply to the whole number of individuals involved in the situation under discussion. Certainly all men since Adam have been sinners; therefore even in Noah's day all must have been included in the destruction of the great deluge.[13]

One very important line of evidence has yet to be mentioned, and that is the remarkable prevalence of oral and written traditions concerning the flood which have persisted among the most diverse peoples of earth. The Sumerians, Babylonians, and Assyrians of Mesopotamia might well be expected to cherish a similar tradition to that of the Hebrews, since they lived so close to the presumed seat of antediluvian civilization. Possibly the Egyptian legend reported in Plato's *Timaeus*, and Manetho's version (in which only Toth was saved from the flood) would be explicable from their geographical proximity to the Fertile Crescent. The Greek tradition of Deucalion and Pyrrha (so charmingly related in Ovid's *Metamorphoses*) might have been a borrowing from the Near East. The same could be true of the Noah tradition in Apamea (Asia Minor) which inspired a representation of the ark on some of their coins.[14]

But what shall we say of the legend of Manu preserved among the Hindus (according to which Manu and seven others were saved in a ship from a worldwide flood); or of Fah-he among the Chinese (who understood that he was the only survivor, along with his wife, three sons, and three daughters); or of Nu-u among the Hawaiians; or of Tezpi among the Mexican Indians; or of Manabozho among the Algonquins? All of these agree that all mankind was destroyed by a great flood (usually represented as worldwide) as a result of divine displeasure at human sin, and that a single man with his family or a very few friends survived the catastrophe by means of a ship or raft or large canoe of some sort.

Not all the primitive flood traditions include the saving agency of an ark. Among

---

13. For a more detailed refutation of the theory of a partial destruction of the antediluvian race, see J. C. Whitcomb and H. M. Morris, *The Genesis Flood*, pp. 44-48.

14. Cf. B. V. Head, *Historia Nummorum* (Oxford, 1911), p. 667, with a photograph of Noah (Greek NΩE) and his wife emerging from a rectangular chest. The coin was minted in late 2d century A.D., recording an early tradition that the ark came to rest on Mt. Celaenae overlooking Apamea.

some, such as the aborigines of the Andaman Islands in the Bay of Bengal, and the Battaks of Sumatra, it was a very high mountain top which furnished the vital refuge for the lone survivor. But otherwise the main outlines of the legend follow the basic structure of the Genesis account. The Kurnai (a tribe of Australian aborigines), the Fiji Islanders, the natives of Polynesia, Micronesia, New Guinea, New Zealand, New Hebrides, the ancient Celts of Wales, the tribesmen of Lake Caudie in the Sudan, the Hottentots, and the Greenlanders, all have their traditions of a universally destructive deluge which wiped out the entire human race except for one or two survivors. The most complete collection of these flood legends from all over the world is contained in Richard Andree's German work *Die Flutsagen Ethnographisch Betrachet* (1891). In English perhaps the most comprehensive report is found in James Frazer's *Folklore in the Old Testament* (vol. 1, 1918). Whether or not the worldwide prevalence of these traditions is reconcilable with a local-flood theory, at least it emphasizes the inclusion of all human races in the descendants of Noah, rather than excepting some of the populations of Africa, India, China, and America (as Ramm seems to imply).[15]

Often the Genesis account has been criticized as implausible because of the insufficient capacity of the ark according to the dimensions given. But on the basis of a cubit of twenty-four inches (although it may have been as much as four inches shorter) the ark would have been 600 feet long, 100 feet wide, and 60 feet deep. Assuming a box-like construction (altogether probable in view of its peculiar purpose), its capacity would then have been 3,600,000 cubic feet, or room enough for 2000 cattle cars (each of which carries 18 to 20 cattle, or 60 to 80 hogs, or 80 to 100 sheep). At the present time there are only 290 main species of land animal larger than sheep in size; there are 757 more species ranging in size from sheep to rats, and there are 1,358 smaller than rats. Two of each of these species would fit very comfortably into the cubic capacity of the ark, and leave plenty of room for fodder. There are, of course, manifold problems connected with maintaining such a large number of animals over so many months (especially if they maintained their normal eating habits), but none of them is insuperable. Perhaps it should be remarked at this point that a mere local flood, only coextensive with the human race in the Mesopotamian or Aral-Caspian depressions, is hard to reconcile with the divine insistence (cf. Gen. 6:19-20) upon the preservation of representatives of all the various kinds of animal. There are very few species today which are confined to that particular region, and so it is difficult to see why the animals in the surrounding, nonflooded areas would not have been able to repopulate the devastated region without hindrance, once the waters had receded. Hence, it would have been pointless to include them in the ark, unless the flood was indeed worldwide.

In an early Sumerian record discovered at Nippur is the earlier Sumerian account of the Flood, which records the event which, although broken after 37 lines, relates the address of a deity to his fellow gods apparently stating that this deity would save mankind from destruction. Subsequent to that, man will build cities and temples to

15. Ramm, CVSS, pp. 239-40.

the gods. After another break of 37 lines it states that kingship was lowered from heaven to earth and five cities were founded. These must have had a great deal to do with the decision of the gods to destroy mankind. In the next readable portion of this account we find that some of the gods are dissatisfied over this cruel decision. Ziusudra, the Sumarian equivalent of Noah, is now introduced as a pious and god-fearing king who is concerned to receive divine revelations in dreams or incantations while standing by a wall. Ziusudra hears the voice of a god informing him of the decision made by the assembly to send a flood to "destroy the seed of mankind." Apparently the text continued with detailed instructions to Ziusudra how to build a giant boat to save himself from destruction. But, 40 lines later, when the text again becomes legible, the flood had come upon earth with all violence for seven days and nights. After that the sun-god, Utu, came forth bringing his precious light to earth. Ziusudra prostrates himself before him and offers sacrifice. The poem closes with the narrative that portrays the deification of Ziusudra for his remarkable service in saving the human race. This was published by Arno Poebel in PBS, v, 1914 (ANET², pp. 42-44).

According to the Gilgamesh Epic, which contains the Babylonian account of the deluge,[16] it was after an assembly of gods had decreed the flood, that the god Ea betrayed this plan to a man named Utnapishtim of Shuruppak (a city on the Euphrates). Making up a lie (at Ea's suggestion) to lull the rest of the population into security, Utnapishtim built his unwieldy, cube-shaped ark (120 cubits in each dimension), and upon a signal (prearranged with the sun-god Shamash), he closed the door on himself, his family, his helmsman Puzur-Amurri, and all the animals in the six decks of his ship, and the deluge came. It lasted for two weeks (as contrasted with the one year and seventeen days of the Genesis account), and was of such violence in rain and wind that even the gods cowered in fear (the goddess Ishtar even shedding tears of regret at the destruction of mankind). After landing on the mountain of Nisir (in the Zagros Range northeast of Babylon), the ark held fast, and Utnapishtim sent out (a) a dove, (b) a swallow, and (c) a raven, the last of which did not return. He then disembarked and offered sacrifice to the gods, all of whom were by this time were so famished for lack of offerings that they came swooping down on the altar like a swarm of hungry flies (tab. XI. 1. 161). Enlil (or Bel) came up afterward, very angry that Utnapishtim had escaped death, but Ea successfully appealed to his sense of justice and reconciled Enlil to what had happened. Enlil thereupon promoted Utnapishtim and his wife to divine immortality. The resemblances to the Genesis narrative are such as to suggest a common origin in ancient oral tradition, but the differences are too great to permit a possibility of borrowing by the one from the other. The stark contrast between the passion-driven, quarrelsome, greedy gods of the Babylonian pantheon and the majestic holiness of Jehovah is most striking and significant. Likewise the utter implausibility of a cube-shaped ark and an inundation of the entire

---

16. Anet³, p. 93

world by a mere fourteen-day downpour stand in opposition to the seaworthy dimensions and the gradual sinking of the waters in the biblical record.

THE TABLE OF NATIONS IN GENESIS 10

From the standpoint of linguistic relationships there appear to be some marked discrepancies between the historical affinities among the Near Eastern nations and those indicated by the genealogical tables of Gen. 10. For example, Canaan is said to be descended from Ham (v. 6), and yet the Canaanites of 2000 B.C. were speaking a West Semitic dialect (of which Hebrew itself is a subdivision). It must be borne in mind, however, that language is not necessarily decisive for ethnic relationship, for Germanic Visigoths ended up speaking Spanish in Spain, the Ostrogoths Italian in Italy, the Germanic Franks adopted French in France, and the French-speaking Normans finally took up English in England. Correspondingly the Hamitic tribes which conquered Palestine in the third millennium B.C. may have succumbed to the influence of Semitic-speaking neighbors, regardless of what their original tongue may have been. It should moreover be noted that this assignment of the Canaanites to the posterity of Ham can only be accounted for on the basis of an accurate historical tradition preserved to the Hebrews of Moses' day. Otherwise they would have had every motivation to assign the Canaanites to Shem, since they spoke a Semitic language at least as early as the days of Abraham and Jacob (cf. Gen. 31:47).

Another problem is presented by the appearance of Sheba as a descendant both of Ham (v. 7) and of Shem (v. 28). In all probability the Sabaeans were originally Hamitic, but continual intermixture with Semitic neighbors in South Arabia finally altered their ethnic complexion to make them predominantly Semitic. Thus both the relationship of verse 7 and that of verse 28 would be correct.

As for Cush, verses 8-10 indicate he was the father of Nimrod of Babylonia, and yet his name became associated with Ethiopia (cf. Isa. 11:11; Ezek. 30:4, ASV marg.), a country known to the Egyptians as *K;š* (and may have been vocalized as *Kūsh*). Verse 6 refers to him as a son of Ham, which of course agrees with an African location. On the other hand, the Al Amran tribe of Arabia calls the region of Zebid in Yemen by the name Kūsh. There was also an important city near Babylon named Kish, from which Nimrod may have come. Putting all these evidences together, Unger (AOT, p. 83) suggests that the original home of the Hamitic Cushites was in Lower Mesopotamia, where Nimrod raised them to great power. From there the Cushites may well have extended their power to the Yemenite region of Arabia, and then crossed the Red Sea to invade "Ethiopia" (an area now occupied by the Republic of Sudan) and imposed their name upon that entire district. This would be no more unlikely than the colonization of Carthaginia by Phoenician settlers or the conquest of French Normandy, Saxon England, and Muslim Sicily by the Normans from Norway. Earlier examples would be the settlement and conquest of Sicily and southern Italy by the Greeks in the seventh and sixth centuries B.C. Some authorities draw into the discussion the little‾

known Kushu tribe mentioned in Middle Kingdom Egyptian inscriptions as inhabiting the borders of Syria and Palestine. But it is not clear how these could have engendered all the nations of Gen. 10:7 (most of which inhabited the Arabian Peninsula), or furnished the background for Nimrod, unless of course they actually represented settlements from the original Kushites of Lower Babylonia.

In view of the foregoing, it seems that A. H. Sayce was overhasty in surrendering the genetic reliability of Gen. 10 and interpreting it as merely a description of geographical relationships at a time when Canaan was under Egyptian domination (and hence would have been regarded as Hamitic, since Egypt or Mizraim was descended from Ham).[17] Even G. E. Wright (in the *Westminster Atlas*) concedes that this list is arranged on the whole from a racial point of view.

Some of the more interesting correspondences between the names of this chapter and the forms which they assume in Akkadian inscriptions are here listed. Of the descendants of Japheth, Gomer is identified with the Gimirriya or Gimirrai (known to the Greeks as Cimmerians), who came down from above the Caucasus Range and invaded Asia Minor, settling in Cappadocia. Madai was the ancestor of the Medes, and Javan of the Greeks (the name seems to have been preserved in the Ionians). Tubal's descendants were the Tabali, who fought Tiglath-pileser I around 1100 B.C., and the race of Meshech were the Mushke who warred with Shalmaneser III in the ninth century. Both lived in eastern Asia Minor. There is no extant record of the descendants of Magog. As for Tiras, he seems to have fathered the Tursenoi or Tyrrhenians, a Pelasgian race who at first inhabited the Aegean region.

Ashkenaz, of the line of Gomer, is identified with the Ashkuz or Scythians, who invaded the Near East from the North (via the Caucasus) and were formidable antagonists of the Assyrians, the Persians, and the Greeks. Little is known of Riphath, and Togarmah is tentatively identified with Tegarama in Southwestern Armenia. Elishah, of the line of Javan, is Alashia, now usually identified with Cyprus (cf. *Westminster Atlas*), as is also Kittim (a name preserved in Citium on the southern coast of that island). Tarshish has been associated with localities in Sardinia (where the name has been found on inscriptions) and also with Spain. Dodanim is perhaps to be connected with the Dardanians of the region around Troy in northwest Asia Minor; the Dardana are apparently equivalent to the Dardanians. But most scholars prefer the spelling Rodanim which occurs in the parallel passage in 1 Chron. 1:7 (ASV), apparently referring to the people of the island of Rhodes.

Cush has already been discussed. Mizraim ("The Two Districts") refers to Egypt; Phut is to be identified with Puta (referred to by Darius I) in Cyrenaica.[18] A distinction should be drawn between Ludim (v. 13), ancestor of the Lybians (if the true original reading, as Albright thinks, was Lubim), and Lud (v. 22), progenitor of the Lydians of Asia Minor. The classification of Elam as Semitic (v. 22) has been challenged on linguis-

---

17. Sayce, *The Higher Criticism and the Verdict of the Monuments* (London: SPCK, 1894).

18. Details concerning the rest of the descendants of Ham may be found in the most recent Bible dictionaries and in Unger's AOT, pp. 85-94.

tic grounds, since Elamite or Susian was a language non-Semitic in character. But as we have already seen, language is no infallible indicator of ethnic relationship, and there was besides, an early penetration of Semitic-speaking conquerors into Elam in the ascendancy of Sargon of Agade (ca. 2200 B.C.).

Concerning the descendants of Shem, Unger (AOT, pp. 97-99) lists all the available information, which is unfortunately meager enough. But as to the tribal descendants of Aram and Joktan (in Arabia), Albright has this interesting comment: "The most significant thing about the names of the tribal descendants of Aram and Joktan is that nearly all the names are archaic, not hitherto having been found in the inscriptions of the first millennium from Assyria and South Arabia. Moreover, several of the names belong to types known as personal names only in the early second millennium, though they may have continued as tribal names for many centuries thereafter."[19]

THE TOWER OF BABEL AND THE CONFUSION OF TONGUES

Genesis 11 informs us that initially the descendants of Noah used the same language and constituted a single culture which developed into a form of humanism that led them to emphasize a unity of polity and worship which was to be perpetuated by the erection of an enormous skyscraper that would serve as the capital of their domain. Because of the arrogance which underlay this project God saw fit to bring it to a halt and used the means of bringing them into a state of confusion because of their inability to speak any longer in the same language.

Chapter 10 of Genesis deals with the descendants of Ham, Shem, and Japheth as they began to repopulate the earth. There is no real indication in this chapter as to the languages they spoke, and so it is reasonable to assume that they all spoke about the same tongue as long as they were grouped together in the region of Mesopotamia. Ronald Youngblood in the *NIV Study Bible* suggests that the confusion of tongues episode may well have preceded the emergence of the various languages mentioned in chapter 10. This might be a possible inference were it not for Gen. 11:1, which plainly states that the whole human race at that time had one language only, even though they respected their ancestral division. Other recent evangelical commentators (such as Kyle Yates in *Wycliffe Bible Commentary* (1962); likewise H. L. Ellison in *The New Layman's Bible Commentary* (1979), D. F. Payne in The *International Bible Commentary* (1986), including even some of the older commentaries like Jamieson, Fausset and Brown, seem to assume that the confusion of languages at Babel occurred after the spread of nations in the Middle East.

The motivation for God's intervention at this point is very clear and understandable. The desire to remain in international harmony was perhaps reasonable at that juncture, but unfortunately it involved an effort to maintain One World unity upon a humanistic basis. The enormous tower they planned to erect would serve as a sort of

19. In Alleman-Flack, *Old Testament Commentary*, p. 139.

United Nations headquarters that would keep all of Noah's descendants politically correct, as it were, without any meaningful regard to the supremacy of God. They purposed to "make a great name" for themselves (v. 4), using the latest architectural techniques emerging from the invention of hard-baked bricks. Their mindset showed a certain approximation to modern-day attitudes that assume that man can get along very nicely without God and successfully solve all their personal and societal problems simply by working together.

God's response to this challenge was swift and decisive. The result of human self-pride is mutual

THE GREAT ZIGGURAT AT UR, LITERALLY, "THE HILL OF HEAVEN," WAS DISCOVERED AT THE RUINS OF UR. MORE THAN 4,000 YEARS OLD, THIS TEMPLE TO THE MOON GOD WAS BUILT AS A SERIES OF STEPPED PLATFORMS WITH THE HOUSE OF THE GOD ON TOP. ITS STRUCTURE PROBABLY RESEMBLED THE TOWER OF BABEL. THE ZIGGURAT IS 200 FEET LONG, 100 FEET ACROSS, AND 250–300 FEET HIGH.

alienation. Because of sin we become so egoistic that we can no longer understand each other, nor do we even care to do so. They suddenly found themselves unable to comprehend what their fellow-workers were trying to say to them, especially if they came from a different family line. Thus they lost their ability to work together and had to abandon their great building project. It was only natural that they should migrate from the Plain of Shinar (or Mesopotamia) and begin to populate the rest of Asia, Europe, Africa, and so on, during the centuries preceding the call of Abraham. Once again, even as before the Flood, the human race had failed to keep in covenant relationship with the God who created them in His own image. Only a very few had remained loyal to the faith of Noah.

As for 11:9, which seems to furnish an etymology for the name Babel, it should be understood that this was the kind of wordplay which occurs in Scripture from time to time. For example, Abigail said to David in 1 Sam. 25:25 concerning her boorish husband, Nabal: "He is just like his name—his name is Fool (*Nābāl*), and folly goes with him." It is however quite likely that his parents would never have purposely named their baby boy "Fool," but rather something more positive. Arabic has the name *Nabbālun*, which means "Bowman," and so it is quite likely that that meaning was what they intended. It is in Hebrew that *nābāl* means "fool," but not in the language of their neighbors just south of Judah. Here then we have a hidden meaning derived from Babel (Akkadian *Bab–ili,* "Gate of God"), and brought out of *bābal,* which means "confuse." Jastrow's *Dictionary of Talmudic Hebrew,* p. 173, lists the *pilpel* stem *balbēl* as an intensive with the same meaning of confusion, "mix up, confuse." Needless to say, there is a significant similarity between Babel and *balbēl.*

Thus it is a mistake to categorize this account as a late fanciful story without historical foundation. It is important to note in recent times the testimony for this event is to be found in the Sumerian culture as early as the Third Dynasty of Ur.[20] Robert T. Boyd reports the discovery of a ten by five foot stela erected by King Ur-Nammu which says concerning a certain ziggurat: "The erection of this tower highly offended all the gods. In a night they threw down what man had built and impeded their progress. They were scattered abroad and their speech was strange" (*Tells, Tombs and Treasures* [Grand Rapids: Baker, 1969], p. 78).

ABRAHAM AND GENESIS 14

The archaeological confirmation of the historical trustworthiness of the Genesis account of Abraham's life has already been reviewed in chapter 13 (pp. 171-75). There it was shown: (1) that the name *Abram* appears in cuneiform records of the first half of the second millennium B.C.; (2) that both Ur and Haran were flourishing cities in the twenty-first century B.C.; (3) that Shechem and Bethel (if Beitin is correctly identified as Bethel) were inhabited during that period, and likewise that the Jordan Valley was highly populated; (4) that the names of the invading kings listed in Gen. 14 were appropriate to that age, and travel from Mesopotamia to Palestine was quite extensive, and Elamite power (suggested by the Elamite name Chedorlaomer) was in the ascendancy at approximately the same time. (As for the Sodom-Gomorrah Pentapolis, Ebla records refer to each as contemporary cities back in 2300 B.C., cf. p. 170 n. 5); (5) We noted that Abraham's negotiations in purchasing the cave of Machpelah conformed to Hittite law practiced in the second millennium. Unger (AOT, p. 107) and J. B. Payne[21] date the birth of Abraham in the twenty-second century, and his migration to Palestine in the twenty-first (more precisely estimated by Payne as 2091, although Unger implies a few years later), during the period of the Third Dynasty of Ur (2070-1960).

Since the name of Hammurabi was so long associated with that of Abraham, on the ground of his supposed identity with Amraphel king of Shinar (Gen. 14:1), it is well to indicate the most recent lines of evidence for 1770 B.C. as the midpoint in Hammurabi's career. In an article in the *Journal of Near Eastern Studies* (April 1958, p. 97), M. B. Rowton lists the data as follows: (1) A piece of charcoal from a building in Nippur constructed several years before or after the accession of Ibi-Sin (a king of the Third Dynasty of Ur who preceded Hammurabi by 235 years) yielded the radiocarbon date of 1992 B.C. plus-or-minus 106. This would mean a date for Hammurabi of 1757 plus-or-minus 106 (Rowton's dates for Hammurabi are 1792-50; cf. IDB ii517 in 1958,

---

20. S. N. Kramer in JAOS, March 1968, "*The Babel of Tongues: A Sumerian Version,*" p. 217, a fragment of 27 lines from "The Golden Age": records "Once upon a time there was no snake, no scorpion, hyena or lion..." (1.145): "the whole universe, the people in unison, [spoke] to Enlil in one tongue....All the world worshipped one God, Enlil, and spoke to him in the one and same tongue." Kramer comments: "Our new piece puts it beyond all doubt that the Sumerians believed that there was a time when all mankind spoke one and the same language, and that it was Enki, the Sumerian god of wisdom who confounded their speech." The reasons for confusing their language are not stated in the fragment.

21. Payne, OHH, p. 35.

JNES 4/58, p. 111). (2) Reed mats from the ziggurat (or stage tower) of Ur-Nammu, founder of the Third Dynasty of Ur, erected in Uruk (or else possibly in the reign of his successor, Shulgi), yielded the radiocarbon date of 1868 plus-or-minus 133. This would place the accession of Hammurabi in 1581 plus-or-minus 133. (3) The observation records kept for the planet Venus in the reign of Ammizaduqa of Babylon (the fourth in succession after Hammurabi) allow for three possible dates for Hammurabi's accession: 1848, 1792, and 1728. Of these, Rowton favors the second, 1792, on the basis of a statement by Tiglath-pileser I (whose dates are 1112-1074, according to P. E. van der Meer) that he had renovated a temple of Anu and Adad 701 years after it was built by Shamshi-Adad I, a contemporary of Hammurabi. This would suggest a date of 1813 for the period of Hammurabi. These evidences tend to confirm the synchronism of Zimri-Lim and Hammurabi mentioned in chapter 13 (p. 172), and establish the dates of his reign during the eighteenth century (ca. 1792-1750)—far too late for Abraham. The reference to "Dan" in 14:14 has been taken as evidence of a post-Mosaic date for Genesis. But this name appears at least as early as Dynasty II (LD III, 211, 4) in Egyptian as Matu Dan-nu-na (VAB II b 24) 211, (cf. Harris 76.7)—Burchardt, M: "Die Altkanuäixhe Fremdwuörteru und Eigennamen im Aegyptischen," Leipzig, 1909 II, p. 60.

JACOB AND LABAN, GENESIS 31

It is interesting to observe in the case of Jacob, who had gone to work for Laban in the Mesopotamian area by Padan-aram (Gen. 29:16-30), that there are parallels in the Nuzi documents to the obligation which was laid upon Jacob to work for 7 years in order to earn the right to marry Laban's daughter. The Nuzi documents record that it was common for a man to work for a specified length of time prior to receiving his wife from her father.

Furthermore, it is significant that there is a prohibition laid upon Jacob against marrying outside of the family. Laban says to Jacob in Gen. 31:50, "If thou shalt afflict my daughters, or if thou shalt take other wives beside my daughters, no man is with us; see God is witness between me and you." This prohibition, as stated by Laban, is again attested by a similar Nuzi custom in which it was forbidden that a man should take another wife beside the one he originally labored to obtain. Thus we see again that Nuzi documentation of the contemporary customs of the Patriarchal period illustrates the reliability of the biblical record and illumines the practices common to that day.

JOSEPH AND THE HYKSOS

A tradition at least as old as the time of Josephus (ca. A.D. 90) states that a Hyksos dynasty was ruling Egypt at the time Joseph rose to power as prime minister (or vizier) in Pharaoh's court. The Hyksos (a corruption of the Egyptian ḥeḳa'u ḥaswet, or "rulers of foreign lands") were a somewhat heterogeneous horde of Asiatic invaders, largely of Semitic background, who gradually infiltrated northern Egypt at first, and then took over the supreme power with an irresistible progress which carried them well into southern Egypt. Capturing Memphis, they made it their capital (along with Tanis or Avaris in the Delta), and established the Fifteenth and Sixteenth Dynasties. Manetho (ca. 250 B.C.) estimated their domination as lasting 500 years. But more recent evidence indicates that their rule was hardly more than 150 years.[22] They probably began filtering into Egypt about 1900 B.C. and finally gained control by 1730.[23]

According to the biblical chronology (assuming the correctness of a 1445 B.C. date for the Exodus and adding a 430-year sojourn in Egypt), the probable date of Jacob's migration into Egypt during Joseph's premiership was about 1875 B.C. This represents anywhere from 94 to 140 years before the rise of the Hyksos, and puts Joseph back in the period of the Twelfth Dynasty. Obviously these factors exclude the possibility that Josephus' tradition was reliable. It is perfectly true that a bond of sympathy might have existed between the Hyksos and the Hebrews because of their Canaanite language and Asiatic origin. The name of

SENWORSET III,
PROBABLE PHAROAH THAT JOSEPH ENCOUNTERED IN EGYPT.

one of the earliest rulers as reported by Manetho was Salitis, which bears a striking similarity to the Semitic *shalliṭ* ("ruler"). Semitic names were attached to a significant number of cities in northern Egypt, like Succoth (Ex. 12:37), Baal-zephon (Ex. 14:2), Migdol (Ex. 14:2), and various others. (Baal was apparently equated by them with the Egyptian Sutekh or Seth, the storm-god, and was adopted as patron god of the Hyksos dynasties. Hence the place name Baal-zephon, "Lord of the North.") Nevertheless there are clear indications in the text of Genesis, and also in Ex. 1, that the Pharaoh who welcomed Joseph was a native Egyptian and not a Semitic foreigner.

In the first place, the reigning Egyptian dynasty shows a nationalistic contempt for Asiatic foreigners. When Joseph receives his brothers in his banquet room, he is compelled to seat them by themselves, rather than as guests at his table. Genesis 43:32 states: "The Egyptians might not eat bread with the Hebrews; for that is an abomination unto the Egyptians." This could never have been said of Hyksos rulers, for the base of their power was Syria and Palestine, from which they had migrated, and in which they apparently retained power all during their period of ascendancy in Egypt. Their attitude toward other Semitic immigrants and visitors to Egypt could only have been cordial, rather than characterized by the race prejudice suggested in this verse.

In the second place, it is quite obvious that the sentiment of the Egyptian government in Joseph's time was strongly averse to shepherds. Genesis 46:34 states: "For

---

22. Cf. R. M. Engberg, *The Hyksos Reconsidered* (Chicago: U. Chicago, 1939).
23. Unger reckons the Hyksos domination as 1176-1570 B.C. (AOT, p. 84).

every shepherd is an abomination unto the Egyptians." While this has been abundantly verified from the Egyptian monuments (which frequently depict cattle but never
sheep on their bas-reliefs), it could scarcely have been true of the Hyksos, who were
known to the later Egyptians as the "Shepherd-Kings" (indeed Manetho so translates
the name Hyksos itself, although erroneously).[24] Hence it was a native dynasty which
was on the throne.[25] It was therefore necessary for the sons of Jacob to stress their possession of cattle and omit mention of their herds of sheep if they were to make a favorable impression before Pharaoh (Gen. 46:31-34).

Third, as John Rea has pointed out, the first chapter of Exodus presents an array of
data almost irreconcilable with the usual supposition that the "new king who knew
not Joseph" was an Egyptian of the Eighteenth or Nineteenth Dynasty.[26] Before considering these evidences, it would be well to note that at the very commencement of the
Eighteenth Dynasty, Ahmose drove out all the Hyksos population from Egypt (except
for that which was put to the sword), pursuing them even to their southern Palestinian
fortress of Sharuhen. If, then, the Israelites were friends and allies of the Hyksos (as is
usually assumed), it is hard to see why they were not expelled with them. On what
basis did the nationalistic Egyptians under King Ahmose make a distinction between

---

24. Manetho, as quoted by Josephus, connected the element *hyk-* with an Egyptian word for "king,"
and *sos* with a word for "shepherd." It is obvious that *hyk* represents the Egyptian *h-k-'*, (meaning
"chief, lord, ruler"), which is represented by the hieroglyphic character for shepherd's crook. As for
the *sos*, Manetho followed a late popular etymology which connected this element with *s-ʃ-s.w* a
word for "shepherds" or "bedouin" which is as early as the Eighteenth Dynasty (Erman-Grapow
4:412), but which was not used by the Hyksos themselves nor by the contemporary Egyptians in des-
ignating their race. Rather, the true etymology of "Hyksos" is *"h-k-;.w kh-;-s.wt'"* or "rulers of foreign
lands" (so George Steindorff-Keith Seele, *When Egypt Ruled the East* [Chicago: U. Chicago, 1953], p.
24). It has been objected that the Egyptian inscriptions speak of the Hyksos only as *ℰ;m.w*, or "Asiatics," and hence Manetho was completely mistaken in his use of this designation. But the justification
for the historicity of this title has been established by its appearance in the Eighteenth Dynasty
inscriptions such as that of Thutmose III in Medinet Habu, where Thutmose is spoken of as *h-wʃ -hqʃ
wkhʃ st* ("the smiter of the Hyksos"—or, "Rulers of Foreign Lands"—who attacked him). (Cf. Erman-
Grapow 3:171 and entry #29 in the *Belegstellen*.) The fact, however, that there was no element of
"shepherd" in the title *Hyksos*, makes it necessary to look for further evidence to establish the probability that they were more favorably disposed to sheep raising than were the native Egyptians themselves. But it is conceivable that the popular etymology recorded by Manetho originated not merely
from the similarity in sound between the Late Egyptian pronunciation of the words for "shepherds"
and "foreign lands," but also from the historically based tradition that the Hyksos actually did
engage in extensive sheep raising.

25. It should be added, however, that this attitude of disapproval toward sheep did not entail an
absolute prohibition of sheep raising even by reputable Egyptians during the Middle Kingdom. Sheep
are never included as acceptable offerings upon the altars to the gods or to deceased ancestors (the
funerary formula on the monuments is always bread, beer, oxen, and fowl), yet an occasional mention
of flocks of sheep is included in some of the funerary biographies (e.g., that of the Twelfth Dynasty
steward Montu-wosre, who speaks of himself as an overseer of oxen, donkeys, goats, sheep, and
swine, cf. W. C. Hayes, *The Scepter of Egypt* [1953], 1:299). Yet apart from the hieroglyphic symbol of
the word for "ruler" (*hq;*), which resembles a shepherd's crook (although it might have been used for
cattle as well as sheep), there is little or no evidence for styling the Egyptian king as "the good shepherd of his people," as J. A. Wilson does in chap. 6 of his *Burden of Egypt* (1951). He offers no substanti-
ation for this title in that chapter which he has so named.

26. Rea, "The Time of the Oppression and the Exodus," in *Bulletin of the Evangelical Theological Society*
(Summer 1930), pp. 58-69.

the Hyksos and the Hebrews? Is it not obvious that the Israelites must have been antagonistic to the Hyksos and favorable in their attitude toward the Egyptians during the long period of Hyksos occupation?

Fourth, the statement of the Pharaoh reported in Ex. 1:8-10 is quite pointless in the mouth of a native Egyptian. It would have been the grossest exaggeration to assert that the Israelites were more numerous than the Egyptians, but it was quite possible that they could become more numerous than the warrior caste of the Hyksos themselves. As for the king's apprehension that they might join up with enemies of the government in time of war, it is difficult to see what non-Egyptians they might have leagued with, surrounded as they were by Egyptians in the isolated pocket of Goshen. But if the speaker in this case was a Hyksos, there would be some point to an apprehension that they might make common cause with the Egyptians, who after all had been so cordial to them for Joseph's sake. The probability is that the "new king who knew not Joseph" was of the Hyksos dynasty, and it was he who put the Hebrews to work as slaves at his building projects. (It would then appear that there was a policy of

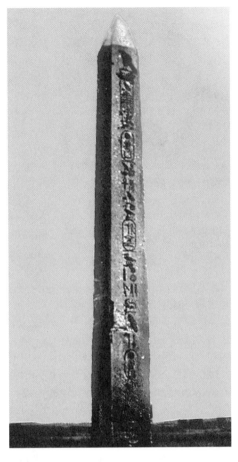

OBELISK FROM HELIOPOLIS

THIS OBELISK WAS ERECTED BY SESOSTRIS (1971–1928 B.C.) IN HELIOPOLIS, THE CENTER FOR WORSHIP OF THE SUN GOD RE.

oppression and enslavement a few decades after the expulsion of the Hyksos by the native Egyptian successor to Ahmose. Possibly this later phase is introduced at Ex. 1:15 along with the command to the midwives to practice infanticide.)

Fifth, in connection with this last detail, we have the evidence of the city of Raamses, mentioned in Ex. 1:11. As the narrative is related in the Hebrew text, this forced labor at Raamses (previously thought to be Tanis or Zoan, but, more likely shown to be Qantîr, 12 miles south of Tanis) took place before the birth of Moses (which is not mentioned until the next chapter). But if the exodus took place around 1290 (as most modern scholars suppose), and if Moses was eighty at that time, his birth took place in 1370, or a good sixty years before a Nineteenth Dynasty Rameses ever sat on the throne of

THE HYKSOS WERE A MIXED GROUP, INCLUDING MANY SEMITES. THEY WERE DRIVEN OUT OF EGYPT AROUND THE YEAR 1570 B.C. THE NEW KINGDOM OF EGYPT BEGAN AT THIS TIME.

Egypt. Therefore it could not have been at a city named after Rameses II (1299-1232 B.C.) that the Israelites worked (prior to the birth of Moses). Furthermore, it is doubtful whether the city of Tanis (or Zoan or Avaris, as it is variously called) could have been built during the Eighteenth Dynasty. G. E. Wright is quite positive in his report in his *Biblical Archaeology*: "After much digging at Tanis by the archaeologists Marriette, Petrie and Montet, not a single object of the Egyptian Eighteenth Dynasty has been found there.[27] The reason that Tanis was identified as the city of Raamses stemmed from the abundance of cornerstones and monuments bearing his name located at that site. But, further investigation revealed that many of these building units fit exactly into sockets or bases that were discovered in Qantîr. This indicates that the removal of the Ramesside materal took place at a later time in order to relocate the capital of that part of Egypt. But, originally the structures which were transported to Tanis had been erected in Qantîr (cf. Jack Finegan, *Light From the Ancient Past* [Princeton: Princeton U., 1976], p. 115). The city was destroyed by Pharaoh Amenhotep (1570-1546), and was probably not reoccupied before the fourteenth century."[28] Wright assumes that this evidence points to a thirteenth-century date for the building of the store city of Raamses, but this seems precluded by the fact that this activity was carried on before Moses was ever born, perhaps a long time before. The only possibility left (assuming the accuracy of the Hebrew record) is that it was the Hyksos who compelled the Israelites to task work at Pithom and Raamses, and not the early Eighteenth Dynasty monarchs.

This, of course, raises the question how Tanis could ever have been called Raamses two or three hundred years before the accession of Rameses himself. But there is some ground for believing that Rameses is a name which could have been in vogue back in the Hyksos period. Note that Gen. 47:11 speaks of "the land of Raamses" as the general area of Goshen, where Joseph settled his relatives. This would indicate that the name was current long before Moses' time. It is highly significant that Seti I, the father of Rameses II, was named after Seth, the patron god of the Hyksos dynasties, the god who was so abhorred by the Egyptian Eighteenth Dynasty. Albright came to this conclusion: "The Ramesside house actually traced its ancestry back to a Hyksos king whose era was fixed 400 years before the date commemorated in the '400-year Stela' of Tanis. The great-grandfather of Rameses II evidently came from an old Tanite family, very

---

27. It should be noted, however, that serious doubt exists whether Tanis has been correctly identifiied with the ancient Zoan or Avaris. John Van Seters in *The Hyksos, A New Investigation* (New Haven, Conn.: Yale U., 1966), pp. 100-147 furnishes the strongest evidence that the true location was Qantîr, 30 miles south of Tanis on the Pelusiac branch of the Nile.

28. Wright, *Biblical Archaeology* (Philadelphia: Westminster, 1957), p. 60.

possibly of Hyksos origin, since his name was Sethos (Suta)....Rameses II established his capital and residency at Tanis, which he named 'House of Rameses' and where he built a great temple of the old Tanite, later Hyksos, god Seth (pronounced at that time *Sûtekh*)."[29] As Rea points out, "If the Ramesside dynasty may be traced back to the Hyksos rulers, and if the dynastic name Seti or Sethos is a Hyksos name, then it is equally possible that the name Ramese or Raamses was a Hyksos name, or at least was used by them in Lower Egypt, where few records from that period have been found."[30] It might be added that the name Rameses (Egyptian *Ra' -messu* or *Ra' -mesesu*) literally means, "Begotten of Ra." The sun-god *Ra'* or *Re'* (as it is variously vocalized) was highly honored by the Hyksos as well as by the Egyptians themselves, for many of their royal names end with his name.

It has been asserted that the mention of Joseph in Gen. 41:43 as parading down the streets of the capital in Pharaoh's chariot points to the period of the Hyksos, since the extensive use of chariots in warfare was not known in Egypt prior to their invasion. Up until now there have been no Egyptian bas-reliefs or murals discovered which represent the chariot prior to the Eighteenth Dynasty. Nevertheless the two-wheeled chariot was used in Mesopotamia as early as the early third millennium.[31] (Cf. *Encyclopedia Britannica*, 1969 ed., 5:287.) *The New Bible Dictionary* (p. 204) shows a drawing of a copper model of a chariot drawn by four onagers from the Early Dynastic Period (ca. 2500 B.C.) from Tell Agrab. This article states: "Heavy wheeled vehicles drawn by asses were used for war and ceremonial in southern Mesopotamia in the third millennium B.C." Since monuments from Ur witness to the use of the chariot there, the fact that Byblos in Phoenicia was under the domination of Ur during the twentieth century (its ruler being called by the Sumerian title *ensi*) takes on special significance. During the Middle Kingdom (Joseph's period) the power of Egypt was once again extended to Byblos, and it is difficult to imagine how the discovery of the Mesopotamian chariot could have been kept from the Egyptians themselves. We do not need to infer that the chariot was widely used as a branch of the armed forces during the Twelfth Dynasty, but it remains quite conceivable, and even likely, that the king himself might have had ceremonial chariots constructed for official occasions at this early period. Its usefulness in warfare may not have been appreciated until after the Hyksos invasions, but it could hardly have been unknown to Egypt in the nineteenth century B.C.

29. Albright, SAC, p. 223.
30. Rea, p. 63.
31. Cf. a 300 B.C. copper miniature of a charioteer with four horses (or onagers) from Sumeria. J. A. Thompson, *The Bible and Archaeology* (Grand Rapids: Eerdmans, 1960), p. 28.

- ● important city mentioned in Egyptian sources during the patriarchal age
- ○ city in Egyptian sources (uncertain location)
- ● city mentioned in patriarchal narratives
- ○ city in patriarchal narratives (uncertain location)

Mediterranean Sea

Sea of Galilee

Acco
Rehob
Achshaph
Shimon

Joseph sold into slavery —Gen 37:17f

Beth-shan
Beth-haggan
Pella

Migdal
Dothan

Jacob comes to be called Israel —Gen 32:28

Simeon & Levi avenge rape of Dinah —Gen 34:25f

Temporary residence of Jacob upon return from Mesopotamia —Gen 33:17

Zarethan
Succoth
Mahanaim
Penuel

Burial spot of Joseph —Josh 24:32
Shechem

Aphek

Jacob builds an altar upon return from Mesopotamia—Gen 35:1f

Jacob dreams of a ladder —Gen 28:1f

Reunion of Jacob & Esau —Gen 33:1f

Lod

Burial of Rachel —Gen 35:16; 48:7; cf. 1Sam 10:2; Jer 31:15

Bethel

Abraham intends to sacrifice Isaac —Gen 22:2f

Timnah
Salem (Mt. Moriah)

Judah seduced by Tamar —Gen 38:14, 21
Enaim

Bethlehem

Ashkelon

Reunion of Jacob & Isaac after more than twenty years —Gen 35:27

Permanent residence of Jacob upon return from Mesopotamia —Gen 35:27; 37:14f

Abraham deceives the Abimelech about Sarah's identity —Gen 20:1f

Mamre/Hebron

Dead Sea

Kiriathaim

Isaac deceives the Abimelech about Rebekah's identity —Gen 26:6f

Eglon

Patriarchal burial plot for Abraham, Sarah, Isaac, Rebekah, Jacob, Leah —Gen 23:17; 25:9; 35:27; 49:29-31; 50:13

Gerar

Possible location of Sodom and Gomorrah —Gen 19:24f

God assures Jacob that he should go to Egypt—Gen 46:1f

Jacob & Rebekah deceive Isaac concerning birthright —Gen 27:5f

Beersheba

© 1994 The Moody Bible Institute of Chicago

PATRIARCHAL PERIOD

16 EXODUS

THE HEBREW TITLE of Exodus is W^eēlleh sh^emōt ("And these are the names of"), or more simply, sh^emōt ("the names of"), derived from the opening words of Ex. 1:1. The Septuagint title, *Exodos* ("exit, departure"), is the origin of the Vulgate's term *Exodus*. The theme of the book is the commencement of Israel as a covenant nation. It relates how God fulfilled His ancient promise to Abraham by multiplying his descendants into a great nation, redeeming them from the land of bondage, and renewing the covenant of grace with them on a national basis. At the foot of the holy mountain, He bestows on them the promises of the covenant and provides them with a rule of conduct by which they may lead a holy life, and also with a sanctuary in which they may make offerings for sin and renew fellowship with Him on the basis of forgiving grace.

OUTLINE FOR EXODUS

I. Training of God's man for God's task, 1:1–4:31

A. Moses' background: tyrannical persecution, 1:1-22
B. His adoption and early education, the first forty years, 2:1-14
C. His character disciplined, the second forty years, 2:15-25
D. His call from God at Horeb, 3:1–4:31

II. Triumphant grace: God's people delivered from bondage, 5:1–18:27

A. God's triumph over the world power through the ten plagues, 5:1–11:10
B. Six types of salvation, 12:1–18:27
    1. Passover: Calvary symbolized and appropriated, 12:1–13:22
    2. Red Sea crossing: the plunge of faith (baptism), 14:1–15:27
    3. Manna from heaven: the bread of life (Eucharist), 16:1-36
    4. The cleft rock: the water of life, 17:1-7
    5. Rephidim: foretaste of victory over the world, 17:8-16
    6. Appointment of elders: organization for religious fellowship, 18:1-27

III. Seal of holiness, 19:1–31:18

A. Covenant promise: absolute submission to God's revealed will, as "a holy nation, a peculiar people," 19:1-25
B. Basic principles of a holy life under the covenant; the Decalogue, 20:1-26
C. Holy living in one's conduct toward others (Book of the Covenant); the three great festivals, 21:1–23:33
D. Holy living in worship and fellowship with God (the types of priesthood, sacrifice, and the tabernacle furniture), 24:1–31:18

IV. Failure of the flesh and repentance for sin, 32:1–33:23

A. Rebellion, apostasy, idolatry: fellowship broken with God, 32:1-35
B. Repentance, chastisement, and intercession by Moses the mediator, 33:1-23

V. God's provision for sin: continuing forgiveness through sacrifice, 34:1–40:38

A. Reaffirmation of the covenant of grace and God's warnings against idolatry, 34:1-35
B. Means of grace to prevent backsliding: Sabbath and Tabernacle, 35:1-19
C. Congregation's pledge to carry out God's plan, 35:20–39:43
D. Forms of worship accepted and hallowed by the Lord, 40:1-38

From this outline it is apparent that the book was composed and arranged by a single mind, and that it was not a clumsy patchwork of three different sources assembled over a period of four centuries, as the Documentary Hypothesis asserts. The logical order in the arrangement of each part and the consistent adherence to the great central theme bespeak the skill of a single, highly gifted author.

THE EARLY HISTORY OF MOSES

Several matters pertaining to the book of Exodus have already been discussed in earlier chapters. The probable identification of the "pharaoh who knew not Joseph" with the Hyksos dynasty has been explained at the close of chapter 15. If this hypothesis is accepted, it would be most reasonable to see in Ex. 1:15-22 a reference to resumed persecution under Amenhotep I (1559-1539 B.C) and Thutmose I (1539-1514 B.C), in whose reigns the growing antiforeign sentiment of the Egyptian populace finally turned against the Hebrews (even though they too had been oppressed by the hated Hyksos). During the reign of Thutmose I, then, Moses was born (about 1527), and received from the princess who adopted him (perhaps Hatshepsut) the name Moses "son of the water," Egyptian; "drawing out," Hebrew). As to this Egyptian etymology *mw-sȝ* or "water-son," it is true that usually a possessive idea is expressed in Egyptian by "A of B," or in this case, "*sȝmw*." But in the case of proper names, the Egyptians also reversed the order occasionally, as in *The Tale of Sinuhe*, where Enshi, son of Amu, is referred to as "Amu-sa; Enshi." Or again, in the *Tale of the Eloquent Peasant* (likewise a Middle Kingdom work), Rensi the son of Meru is called "Meru-sa; Rensi." As for the often suggested etymology of "Mose" for Moses, understood as a shortened form of Ra'mosse (Rameses) or Thutmose ("begotten of Thoth"), this would be a perfectly acceptable alternative if it were not for Ex. 2:10, which implies that the name which the princess bestowed on the baby had some relevance, even in Egyptian, to the circumstances of his discovery at the riverbank. Of course there remains the possibility[1] that the true antecedent of "she" in Ex. 2:10 was not the Egyptian princess but rather the mother of Moses, who had been hired to be the baby's nurse. This would eliminate all need for an Egyptian etymology. But this would also presuppose that Moses' mother had not already named him at his circumcision, and that it was the mother who had drawn him out of the water rather than the princess, and lastly that it was the mother who had the prerogative of naming him, rather than his new royal fostermother. These three assumptions seem rather difficult to maintain in the light of all the circumstances, and so it is best to abide by the Egyptian etymology suggested above.

THE HATSHEPSUT STELA FOUND AT KARNAK

QUEEN HATSHEPSUT (1501–1482 B.C.) WAS THE REAL RULER OF EGYPT DURING THE REIGN OF THUTMOSE II AND THE FIRST 16 YEARS OF THUTMOSE III.

THE LENGTH OF THE SOJOURN IN EGYPT

As to the length of the sojourn of the Israelites in Egypt, the clear statement of the Hebrew text of Ex. 12:40 is that it totaled 430 years from the migration of Jacob's family until the Exodus itself. But since the LXX here reads that the 430 years included the sojourn of Abraham and his descendants in Canaan as well as Egypt, some have preferred this variant to the reading of the Masoretic Text. This would result in an Egyptian sojourn of about 215 years, and would bring Joseph's career squarely into the Hyksos period. But there are several considerations which render the 215-year interval very unlikely.

In the first place, a prediction was made to Abraham in Gen. 15:16 that after oppression in a foreign land, his descendants would return to Canaan "in the fourth generation." This follows shortly after verse 13, which states that the foreign oppressors "shall afflict them four hundred years." It is evident that in Abraham's case, a generation was computed at one hundred years, and this was appropriate enough in view

---

1. Favored by Kitchen in *The New Bible Dictionary*, p. 851.

of the fact that Abraham was precisely one hundred when he became the father of Isaac. At least four centuries, then, and not a mere 215 years, would mark the Israelite sojourn in the foreign land.

Second, although many of the family lines of prominent figures in the Exodus generation are indicated by only three or four links (e.g., Levi, Kohath, Amram, Moses, according to Ex. 6:16-20), there are some which feature as many as ten generations. Kitchen (AOOT, 54-57) points out that conformable to general ancient Near Eastern practice, "Ex. 6:16-20 is not a full genealogy, but only gives the tribe (Levi), clan (Kohath), and family group (Amran by Jochabed) to which Moses and Aaron belonged and not their actual parents.[2] The Amramites are shown as being already numerous at the Exodus (cf. Num. 3:27-28), so Amram must be considered as having lived much earlier." In 1 Chron. 7:25 there are no less than nine or ten generations listed between Joseph and Joshua (Ephraim—Rephah—Resheph—Telah—Tahan—Ladan—Ammihud—Elishama—Nun—Joshua). Ten generations can hardly be reconciled with a mere 215 years (especially considering the longer life span of pre-Exodus Israelites), but it fits in very plausibly with an interval of 430 years. Similarly, Bezaleel is in the seventh generation from Jacob (1 Chron. 2:1, 4, 5, 9, 18-21), Elishama is in the ninth generation from Jacob (Num. 1:10), and Nahshon, prince of Judah, is in the sixth generation after Jacob (1 Chron. 2:1, 4, 5, 9, 10). Compare also the genealogy of Ezra as set forth in Ezra 7:1-5 which indicates no less than seventeen generation links between Ezra and Aaron. If Ezra is dated at 457 B.C., seventeen generations would readily take us back to the 15th century, the time of Aaron.

Third, the increase from seventy or seventy-five persons[3] in the immigrant family of Jacob to a nation of more than two million souls (judging from the 603,550 men-at-arms mentioned in Num. 2:32) militates against a mere 215-year sojourn. If there were indeed only four generations,[4] then the rate of multiplication would necessarily have been astronomic. Even if seven generations should be crammed into the 215 years, there would have had to be an average of four surviving sons per father. But if the sojourn lasted 430 years, then the desired multiplication would result from an average of three sons and three daughters to every married couple during the first six genera-

---

2. Cf. EBD, vol. 3, p. 111. D. N. Freedman in "The Bible and the Ancient Near East" (G. E. Wright, ed. [London, 1961), states, "Exodus 6 lists a person's family by tribe, clan, and family group, which is a common ancient Near Eastern practice. In Egyptian royal geneologies several links are omitted between Raamses II and the kings of Dynasty XXI in the Berlin geneology published by Borchart (cf. Kitchen, AOOT, pp. 54-55). Observe Num. 3:27-28 in which the combined total of the Amramites, Izharites, Hebronites, and Uzzielites came to 8600—all of whom descended from Kohath, totalling 1/4 of 8600 male descendants.

3. The Hebrew text of Gen. 46:26-27 and Ex. 1:5 gives the figure as seventy, but the LXX gives it as seventy-five (so Stephen's speech in Acts 7:14). As Delitzsch explains it (Pentateuch, 1:370, n. 1), the variation is due to Septuagintal inclusion of the three grandsons and two great-grandsons of Joseph mentioned in Num. 26. These five names are actually inserted by the LXX into the text right after Gen. 46:20 (Mekhir, Galaad, Soutalaam, Taam, and Edom [Son of Soutalaam] according to the Greek spelling).

4. H. H. Rowley so insists in his forty-seven-page article, "Israel's Sojourn in Egypt," in Bulletin of John Rylands Library, 22:1.

tions, and an average of two sons and two daughters in the last four generations. At this rate, by the tenth generation there would be (according to Delitzsch, *Pentateuch*, 2:30) 478,224 sons above twenty by the four-hundredth year of the sojourn, while 125,326 males of military age would still be left over from the ninth generation. These together, then, would total 603,550 men–at–arms.

THE DATE OF THE EXODUS

According to 1 Kings 6:1 the temple of Solomon was begun in the fourth year of his reign (i.e., 966 or shortly thereafter), which was the four hundred and eightieth year after the Exodus.[5] This would give the exact date for the Exodus as 1445 B.C., in the third year of Amenhotep II (1447-1421). There may have been a few years more or less, if the figure of 480 was only meant to be a round number. This would mean that the Israelite conquest of Canaan would have commenced with the destruction of Jericho around 1405 (allowing for the forty years in the wilderness). This latter date has been confirmed by John Garstang's excavations at the site of Jericho, Tell es-Sultan, from 1930 to 1936. On archaeological grounds he dated the Late-Bronze level (City D) at 1400 B.C.

Further confirmation of this date is found in the statement of Jephthah recorded in Judg. 11:26, where he reminds the Ammonite invaders that the Israelites have been too long in possession of the contested land of Gilead for the Ammonites to challenge their legal right to hold it: "While Israel dwelt in Heshbon and its towns, and in Aroer and its towns...three hundred years; wherefore did ye not recover them within that time?" (ASV). Since Jephthah's period was admittedly earlier than the time of King Saul (whose reign began around 1050 B.C.), this certainly pushes the Israelite conquest back to 1400 B.C.

Still further confirmation is found in Paul's comment in Acts 13:19-20, which according to the earliest reading (as preserved in Nestle's text) states: "And when he [God] had destroyed seven nations in the land of Canaan, he gave them their land for an inheritance, for about four hundred and fifty years: and after these things [i.e., after the division of the land] he gave them judges until Samuel the prophet." (This is the rendering of the RSV; the KJV follows a later, untrustworthy reading here.) In other words, the interval includes the Exodus itself (when the Hebrews left Egypt to take possession of Canaan, Ex. 20:12), the Israelite conquest under Joshua, and the career of Samuel down to the date of David's capture of Jerusalem ca. 995. (Cf. Deut. 12:10, which states that the choice of a holy city for Jehovah's sanctuary will be revealed after "He giveth you rest from all your enemies"—including apparently, the Jebusites in Jerusalem.) This means that the 450 years of Acts 13 includes the period from 1445 to

5. The year 966 is J. B. Payne's date for the commencement of the Temple. Albright computes it at 958 (BASOR [Dec. 1945] 1:7), E. R. Thiele at 967 (*Mysterious Numbers of the Hebrew Kings* [Grand Rapids: Eerdmans, 1951], p. 254), and Begrich at 962. Unger personally prefers 961 (AOT, p. 141) and thus puts the Exodus at 1441. In the subsequent discussion, the writer uses the 966 date.

THE UNITED MONARCHY OF DAVID AND SOLOMON.

© 1994 The Moody Bible Institute of Chicago

995 B.C. It goes without saying that a materially later date for the Exodus would be utterly irreconcilable with Acts 13:19.

But notwithstanding this consistent testimony of Scripture to the 1445 date (or an approximation thereof), the preponderance of scholarly opinion today is in favor of a considerably later date, the most favored one at present being 1290 B.C., or about ten years after Rameses II began to reign. A still later date, ca. 1225, is favored by a diminishing number of authorities (such as H. H. Rowley), but in the earlier decades of the twentieth century it found support even from conservatives like M. G. Kyle in ISBE (who dated the fifth year of Merneptah about 1250 B.C.) and J. D. Davis (who dated the fifth year in his *Dictionary of the Bible*, 4th ed., as 1320).

J. Finegan lists five major arguments in support of the 1290 date: (1) the discrepancies between the Amarna Letters and the Hebrew record (in Joshua, Judges, Samuel); (2) the apparent absence of an agricultural civilization in Edom, Moab, and Ammon during the fourteenth century; (3) the impossibility of reconciling a 430-year sojourn with a Hyksos date for Joseph's career; (4) the lack of evidence that Thutmose III did any building in the Delta region; (5) the mention of the city of Raamses in Ex. 1:11.[6] These will be dealt with one by one.

As to (1), Finegan points to the fact that the letters from King Abdi-Ḫepa of Canaanite Jerusalem in the Amarna correspondence[7] indicate that his city was in imminent danger of capture by the Ḫabiru; yet 2 Sam. 5:6-9 shows that the Israelites did not capture Jerusalem until David's reign. Hence the Ḫabiru could not have been the Israelites, but an earlier, non-Israelite force of invaders. But the fallacy in this argument is obvious. The armies of Joshua did indeed menace Jerusalem, for they routed the Jerusalemite troops (together with their allies from Hebron, Jarmuth, Lachish, and Eglon) at the battle of Gibeon, and their king, Adoni-zedek, was subsequently flushed out of hiding and put to death (Josh. 10). But neither the letters of Abdi-Ḫepa nor the Hebrew account in Joshua states that the city itself was captured or destroyed. Not until after Joshua's death, apparently, did the army of Judah storm Jerusalem and put it to the torch (Judg. 1:8), and even then they did not permanently dispossess the Jebusites (Judg. 1:21).

As to (2), Finegan refers to the surveys of Nelson Glueck in the Transjordanian region, which failed to uncover any evidence of urban civilization or fortifications between 1900 and 1300 B.C. This means that there could have been no strong Edomite kingdom to oppose the Israelite advance up the east bank of the Dead Sea (cf. Num. 20:14-21) back in 1405 B.C. Nor would there have been any strong Moabite-Midianite coalition to face under King Balak (Num. 22-25), nor any armies of Sihon and Og to crush (Num. 21). But Glueck's investigations were largely in the nature of surface exploration, and could hardly have been called thorough. Moreover, there has come to light more recently a new line of evidence which seems to belie his deductions. In the

6. Finegan, LAP, pp. 106-8.
7. See chap.13, p. 179.

Biblical Archaeologist for February 1953, G. Lankester Harding reported the discovery of an ancient tomb in Amman (BA XVI, no. 7: "Archaeological News from Jordan") containing numerous artifacts (including black pricked ware, button-base vases, oil flasks, scarabs, and toggle pins) dating from about 1600 B.C. In Harding's *Antiquities of Jordan* (1959) he also speaks of characteristic Middle Bronze pottery and other objects found at Naur and Mount Nebo. A sixteenth century tomb was discovered at Pella in 1967 (ASOR newsletter, Dec. 1967). A Late Bronze Age temple was uncovered under a runway at the Amman airport in 1955 (CT, 22 Dec. 1971, p. 26). Franken's excavations at Deir Alla and those of Siegfried Horn at Heshbon have shown that the pottery of Transjordan was quite dissimilar from that produced on the west bank of the Jordan at the same period.[8] Yamauchi suggests that Glueck mistakenly assumed the homogeneity of pottery from both regions and thus may have introduced confusion into his interpretation of the data (ibid. See H. J. Franken and W. J. A. Power [VT, xxi 71, pp. 119-23]; "Glueck's Exploration in Eastern Palestine in the Light of Recent Evidence"). J. Bimson states, "I am forced to conclude, therefore, that there is no reason to date the Conquest in the 12th century B.C. Evidence from et-Tell does not support such a date, since it is not clear that there was a deliberate destruction of the Iron Age village at that time" (*Redating the Exodus and Conquest*, p. 65). Further excavation will no doubt uncover more products of this intermediate period and demonstrate once again the fallacy of hasty conclusions on the basis of superficial investigations.

As to (3), the difficulty of reconciling the viziership of Joseph with the Hyksos period in Egypt (since Joseph's career must have fallen in the first half of the nineteenth century according to the early date theory, and the Hyksos rule did not begin until 1730 or so), this discrepancy is freely admitted. But as has been already pointed out, the internal evidence of Ex. 1 points to the Hyksos dynasty as furnishing the "new king who knew not Joseph," and the Twelfth Dynasty as being the probable time of Joseph's career.[9] Therefore the point taken raises no difficulty whatsoever to a 1445 date for the Exodus.

As to (4), the lack of evidence of building activity in the Delta during the reign of Thutmose III (1501-1447), there are several significant indications from archaeological discovery which point in a more positive direction. It is a well-known fact that Thutmose III erected two red granite obelisks in front of the temple of Ra' in Heliopolis (situated at the base of the Delta); one of them now stands in London and the other in New York City. Since he describes himself in them as "Lord of Heliopolis," it is fair to assume that he did conduct building operations in that city. Moreover, a scarab from the Eighteenth Dynasty refers to the birth of Amenhotep II (Thutmose's son) as having taken place in Memphis (twenty-three miles below Heliopolis). This raises a strong pre-

8. Cf. also "Jordan" (1981, Summer, Fall), pp. 22-26, which locates the city of Sahab, 12 kilometers southwest of Amman, and comments: "This last Late Bronze town in Jordan is important because it revises all theories about a gap in occupation between the 18th and 12th centuries B.C. Previously it was thought that there were no major settlements in the Jordan during that period. But the discovery of a large wall and therefore an important city, refutes that theory" (p. 26).
9. Cf. pp. 224-25.

OBELISK OF THUTMOSE III

THUTMOSE III WAS PERHAPS THE GREATEST MILITARY CONQUEROR IN EGYPTIAN HISTORY AND A PROLIFIC BUILDER. HE EMPLOYED THOUSANDS OF CAPTIVES TO BUILD THIS OBELISK.

sumption that Thutmose maintained his headquarters there from time to time, at least, and probably did so for the purpose of strengthening his fortifications and staging preparations for his numerous Asiatic campaigns. It is inconceivable that he could have made fourteen or more campaigns in Syria if he had not built extensive barracks, depots, and other structures to accommodate his troops. The land of Goshen with its large reservoir of manpower must have often been commandeered for these construction projects. Even as far south as Thebes, the tomb of his vizier Rekhmire shows Semitic slaves hard at work making and transporting bricks.

As for Amenhotep II, discoveries at Bubastis (the Pi-beseth of Ezek. 30:17) uncovered by Naville in 1887-1889 included a red granite slab representing Amenhotep in worship before Amon-Ra', "he who dwells in Perwennefer." This calls to mind the close relationship which Amenhotep bore to the naval dockyard at Perwennefer near Memphis, over which his father had appointed him a commandant in his youth. W. C. Hayes concludes that he maintained large estates at Perwennefer, and resided there for extended periods of time.[10] In one inscription (ANET, p. 244) he speaks of riding from the royal stables in Memphis to visit the Sphinx at Gizeh. All this points to frequent royal residence in the Delta during the reign of Thutmose III (the pharaoh of the oppression) and Amenhotep II (the pharaoh of the Exodus)—conformable to the early date theory.

In regard to (5), the appeal to the treasure city of Raamses in Ex. 1:11, we have seen that there is no possibility of reconciling the Mosaic narrative as it now stands, with a 1290 date.[11] This labor upon the city of Raamses must have been carried on prior to the birth of Moses, unless the Ex. 1:15 account is out of chronological sequence and the name "Raamses" was an anachronism (and the strength of this whole argument is that this name was *not* an anachronism). Yet between 1300, the approximate date of the accession of Rameses II to the throne, and the year 1290 there is no room for the eighty years of Moses' life prior to the event of the Exodus itself. Therefore the 1290 date cannot be seriously considered as a theory reconcilable with the accuracy of the Hebrew account. Actually the prime advocates of this view do not,

---

10. Hayes, *The Scepter of Egypt* (Cambridge, Mass.: Harvard U., 1959), 2:141.
11. Chap. 15, pp. 231-32.

as a rule, hold to the reliability of the Mosaic narrative, but (as in the case of Meek and Albright) deny that the Joseph tribes (Ephraim and Manasseh) ever sojourned in Egypt, but rather the Levites alone, or possibly the tribe of Judah also.[12]

On the strength of the Israel stela of Merneptah[13] the adherents of the 1290 date have rightly urged that the Israelites must already have been settled in Palestine at least by 1229 B.C., and that this makes it very difficult to hold the older theory that Merneptah (1234-1225) was the pharaoh of the Exodus. It is a necessary inference from the Merneptah stela that Israel was already in Palestine, dwelling among the Hittites, Ashkelon, Gezer, and the Horites (11. 26ff.). Kyle's suggestion (in the ISBE article on the Exodus) that "Israel is laid waste, his seed is not" refers to the program of killing off the male babies of Israel eighty years before, while still enslaved in Egypt, is hardly worth serious consideration.

The presence of the Hebrew nation in Palestine by 1229 (or the fifth year of Merneptah) carries with it certain significant consequences. If the scriptural record of forty years' wandering in the wilderness be correct, then the Israelites could not possibly have left Egypt after 1269 B.C., or in the thirtieth year (approximately) of Rameses II. The Hebrew text implies that Moses was absent in Midian and Horeb at least thirty years, more probably forty. Compare Ex. 7:7, which states that he was eighty at the time of the Exodus, and Acts 7:23, which states that he was about forty when he slew the Egyptian. In other words, Rameses II could barely have ascended the throne when this incident took place and Moses had to flee from Egypt; more likely it would have occurred before Rameses' accession. But the clear implication of Ex. 4:19 ("Go, return into Egypt; for all the men are dead which sought thy life") is that the king who sought Moses' life had but recently died. The whole tenor of the narrative in Ex. 2 leads us to expect that it was the pharaoh of 1:22 who after "many days" passed away in 2:23. Whether this was the case, there is the greatest improbability that Merneptah's raid would have met with success against the triumphant Israelites under General Joshua in 1229 just as they were first entering the promised land. It is far more likely that the Egyptian expedition would have taken place after the initial phase of the conquest was over. This would push the Exodus back at least to the 1290 date, and make it utterly hopeless for Rameses II (who reigned from about 1300 to 1234) to serve as the "pharaoh of the oppression." Moses could not have spent forty years in exile dur-

---

12. Rowley in "Israel's Sojourn" (see n. 4 in this chapter), has this instructive comment to make: "The most notable feature of Albright's view appears to be its complete skepticism as to the historical value of the Israelite traditions." He goes on to point out that these traditions link Yahwism most definitely with Moses, they connect the ark with Moses. The Ephraimite Joshua is an attendant in the tabernacle; the Ephraimite Samuel serves in the Shiloh sanctuary, an Ephraimite shrine. This is hardly intelligible upon the theory that Moses was really a Judahite leader. Besides this, the biblical tradition makes the whole descent into Egypt turn upon Joseph, and yet Albright's theory denies that the Joseph tribes were ever in Egypt. It also disregards completely the statement made by Exodus that Moses was eighty years old at the time of the migration from Egypt, and makes the whole story of Moses' early life "sheer and ungrounded fabrication." He concludes by saying, "Not only does Albright's theory exaggerate the untrustworthiness of the Bible, but it renders it diffcult to see how traditions so perverse could have arisen" (pp. 272, 275).

13. Discussed in chap. 13, pp. 185-86.

ing the ten years between 1300 and 1290; yet it was evidently that same king who had sought Moses' life who "after many days" had died.

No other known pharaoh fulfills all the specifications besides Thutmose III. He alone, besides Rameses II, was on the throne long enough (fifty-four years, including the twenty-one years of Hatshepsut's regency) to have been reigning at the time of Moses' flight from Egypt, and to pass away not long before Moses' call at the burning bush, thirty or forty years later. In character he was ambitious and energetic, launching no less than seventeen military campaigns in nineteen years, and engaging in numerous building projects for which he used a large slave-labor task force. His son, Amenhotep II, who doubtless hoped to equal his father's military prowess, seems to have suffered some serious reverse in his military resources, for he was unable to carry out any invasions or extensive military operations after his fifth year (1445 B.C.) until the modest campaign of his ninth year (according to Memphis stela, at least—the chronology of this reign is a bit confused[14]). This relative feebleness of his war effort (by comparison with that of his father) would well accord with a catastrophic loss of the flower of his chariotry in the waters of the Red Sea during their vain pursuit of the fleeing Israelites.

In further confirmation of Amenhotep II as the pharaoh of the Exodus we have the "Dream Stela" of Thutmose IV (1421-1412), his son and successor. Although Adolf Erman demonstrated quite convincingly that the inscription itself comes from a later period (*Sitzungsberichte der königlichen preussischen Akademie der Wissenschaften*, 1904), nevertheless there can be little doubt that it represents faithfully the substance and much of the actual wording of an authentic inscription set up by Thutmose himself in the fifteenth century. Apparently the older stela had been seriously damaged and was copied (as well as its condition would allow) in a later century, when once again the sand was removed from the Sphinx at Gizeh. In this text the god Har-em-akht ("Horus in the horizon"), in whose honor the Sphinx was thought to be made, appears to young Thutmose in a dream while the latter was a mere prince in his father's household. He promises him the throne of Egypt upon the implied condition that he will remove the sand from the Sphinx.[15] It is quite obvious that if Thutmose IV had at that time been the oldest son of his father, Amenhotep II, there would have been no need for a divine promise that he should some day become king. He would naturally have succeeded to

---

14. John A. Wilson confesses in his footnote: "The translator finds it impossible to reconcile the dates in these several stelae [i.e., the Memphis stela and the Karnak stela, both of which were hacked up under Akhnaton and later repaired in the Nineteenth Dynasty]. The Memphis stela places the first campaign [into Asia] in Amenhotep II's seventh year, the second in his ninth year. The Amada stela below is dated in his third year, to record a celebration in Egypt after the return from the first campaign! Further, it is understood that Amenhotep was coregent with his father, Thutmose III, for a minimum of one year and up to a possible eleven years. A possible reconciliation would be that the seventh year after the coregency began in the third year of the sole reign" (ANET, p. 245). Thus Wilson equates the "seventh year" in the Memphis stela with 1440 B.C., but he later equates "year nine" in the same inscription with 1440 B.C., and also "year three" in the Amada stela he declares to be 1440 B.C. It does not aopear how three entirely different years, the third, the seventh, and the ninth, could all equal 1440 B.C. At best, then, the evidence from the various inscriptions of Amenhotep II is of an ambiguous character!

15. The translation of this inscription is given in ANET, p. 449.

SPHINX OF THUTMOSE IV

THIS FAMOUS MONUMENT AT GIZAH HAS, BETWEEN THE PAWS AND CLOSE TO THE BREAST, THE FAMOUS
DREAM STELA OF THUTMOSE IV, RECORDING HOW HE CLEARED IT OF SAND OVER 3,000 YEARS AGO.

the throne if he simply survived his father. It is a necessary inference, therefore, that the
oldest son of Amenhotep must have later predeceased his father, thus leaving the succession to his younger brother Thutmose IV. This well accords with the record in Ex.
12:29 that the eldest son of pharaoh died at the time of the tenth plague.

But even more conclusive than this is the situation in Goshen during the reign of
Thutmose III as compared to that which existed under Rameses II. In the time of
Rameses, some of his main building activity was right in the region of Wadi Tumilat,
or Goshen, and this meant that Egyptians must have been living all around this region
and in the midst of it as well. But the details of the plagues of flies, of hail, and of darkness (Ex. 8:22; 9:25-26; 10:23) make it clear enough that Goshen was at the time of the
Exodus inhabited almost exclusively by the Hebrews, and plagues which befell the rest
of Egypt made no appearance at all in Goshen. So far as we can tell from the archaeological evidence presently at hand, there were no Egyptians living there during the
reign of Thutmose.

We come now to a consideration of the date when the Late Bronze or Canaanite
city of Jericho (City D in Garstang's survey) met with destruction. John Garstang, who
did the most extensive excavation at this celebrated site, came to the conclusion that
this destruction took place around 1400 B.C. In the burial grounds belonging to this

level, Garstang found numerous scarabs, but none of them later than two bearing the name of Amenhotep III (1412-1376). Moreover out of more than 150,000 fragments of pottery found within the city itself, only one piece was found which was of the Mycenean type.[16] Yet Mycenean ware began to be imported into Palestine in increasing abundance from 1400 onward. The archaeological criteria for the reign of Amenhotep's successor, Amenhotep IV or Akhnaton (1376-1362), are distinctive, plentiful, and well established; but the Jericho evidence did not include a single fragment characteristic of his reign.[17]

Garstang also described the outer walls of this city as having been constructed of large, heavy stone, and observed that they had toppled outward, as if by a violent earthquake. There is considerable doubt, however, as to whether those walls belonged to this Late Bronze city or to an earlier one, for more recent excavation by Kathleen Kenyon[18] indicates the presence of Middle Bronze sherds in the earth fill between the inner and outer layer of this rampart. Yet there is no reason why a wall built in the Middle Bronze II period might not still have been in use by Late Bronze times, ca. 1400 B.C.

Although many have objected to Garstang's early date for the destruction of Jericho, their objections have largely been influenced by subjective preference for a later date (a preference partially based upon the time of the destruction of Lachish, Bethel, and Debir in the thirteenth century). In reply to such criticisms, Garstang wrote in the preface (p. xiv) to his 1948 *Story of Jericho:* "We are aware that varying opinions have appeared in print which conflict with our interpretation of the date of the fall of Jericho about 1400 B.C. Few such opinions are based on first-hand knowledge of the scientific results of our excavations; while many of them are devoid of logical reasoning, or are based upon preconceptions as to the date of the Exodus. No commentator has yet produced from the results of our excavations, which have been fully published in the *Liverpool Annals of Archaeology*, any evidence that City IV remained in being after the reign of Amenhotep III....We see no need therefore to discuss the date as though it were a matter for debate."

One specious objection which is sometimes raised to the 1400 date for the fall of Jericho is derived from the mention of iron implements found in it, according to Josh. 6:24. The argument runs as follows: 1400 falls within the Late Bronze Age; since iron was used in Jericho, its fall must have occurred during the Iron Age (which began in the thirteenth century). But it does not necessarily follow that iron was unknown during the Late Bronze Age; it might simply be that it was in such short supply that bronze had to be used by most people in most places. This is borne out by the fact that Josh. 6:24 speaks of the iron "vessels" in the same breath with articles of gold and silver; therefore we may legitimately infer at that time iron may have been scarce and expensive. Actually we know that iron was well known as early as Sumerian times, and

---

16. John Garstang, *The Story of Jericho*, p. 122.
17. Ibid., p. 249.
18. Kenyon, *Digging up Jericho* (New York: Praeger, 1957), pp. 46, 170, 181.

THE LOCATION OF ARCHAEOLOGICAL SITES THAT HAVE BEEN EXCAVATED UP UNTIL 1983.

the Semitic word for "iron" (*barzel*, Hebrew; *parzillu*, Akkadian) may even have been of Sumerian origin, since the Sumerian spelling for the word is *na*AN.BAR.[19] This indicates a knowledge and use of iron in the Mesopotamian Valley at least as early as the twentieth century B.C. Furthermore, iron objects have actually been found at Tell Asmar dating from about 2500 B.C.,[20] and also at Dorah in northwestern Turkey from about the same period there was discovered an iron-bladed sword with an obsidian hilt.[21]

Perhaps the most serious difficulty with the 1445 theory is to be found in the dates which are presently assigned to the destruction of some of the other cities which Joshua's forces are said to have captured, such as Lachish (Josh. 10:32), and Debir (Josh. 10:38). At Lachish (Tell ed-Duweir), the Late Bronze city seems to have been leveled in the reign of Merneptah (1234-1225), for there was found there not only a scarab of Rameses II but also some receipt ostraca with the notation, "Year four." The style of script is believed to be characteristic of Merneptah's time, and this might therefore indicate the date 1230 B.C., although this inference is scarcely compelling.

As for Debir or Kirjath-sepher, identified with Tell Beit Mirsim, a scarab was found of Amenhotep III (1412-1376),[22] Finegan (LAP, p. 140) cites no other evidence than this for his assumption that the layer of ashes upon the Late Bronze layer represents a destruction shortly before 1200 B.C. As for the destruction of Ai, described in Joshua 8, this was explained by Albright and his followers as a confusion with Bethel, since on archaeological grounds the site of Ai (Et-Tell) is said not to have been occupied at all between 2200 B.C. and a brief village settlement sometime between 1200 and 1000 B.C. (Finegan, LAP, pp. 136-37). But Bethel, a mile and a half away, was destroyed by a tremendous conflagration some time in the thirteenth century, and the fact that Joshua makes no mention of the capture of Bethel lends color to the belief that it was confused with Ai.

There are several observations to be made concerning these three sites. In the first place, Josh. 10:32 says nothing about the physical destruction of the city of Lachish. (Tell el-Hesi, wrongly identified by Petrie and Bliss with Lachish, has now been tentatively equated with Eglon; therefore its destruction-level is irrelevant to the date of the Exodus [ASOR Newsletter, April 1970, p. 3—J. E. Worrell]); Josh. 10:32 only speaks of the slaughter of its inhabitants. The devastation dating from 1230 B.C. may represent a later assault in the time of the Judges after the depopulated city had been reoccupied upon the departure of Joshua's troops. The same observation also applies to the destruction of Debir; Josh. 10:38 says nothing about leveling the walls or putting the city to the torch. Moreover, the evidence cited by Finegan seems to confirm the early

19. Cf. Deimel's *Šumerisches Lexikon*, Heft 2, where this term is cited from an inscription listed as Ebeling, KARI, 185, 3, 1.
20. Cf. "Oriental Institute Communications" No. 17, newsletter of the American Schools of Oriental Research, pp. 59-61.
21. See *Illustrated London News* (Nov. 28, 1959), p. 754.
22. Moshe Kochabi's survev of Judea in 1968 uncovered further evidence that Albright's identifcation of Tell Beit Mirsim with ancient Debir will have to be abandoned in favor of Rabud. Cf. E. Yamauchi's "Stones, Scripts and Scholars," in *Christianity Today* (Feb. 14, 1969), pp. 432-31.

date theory as much as the 1290 date, since Amenhotep III was on the throne during the 1400 entry of Canaan by the Israelites. As for the question of Ai, the identification with Bethel seems more tenuous, for Bethel was a hallowed and well–known religious center to the Hebrews from the time of Jacob onward, and it is most unlikely that they would ever have confused its location with that of Ai. In fact, this theory is quite untenable in view of Josh. 7:2, which states explicitly that Ai was on the east side of Bethel. The ancient historian would hardly have confused Bethel with an Ai which did not then exist as an inhabited site in the fourteenth or thirteenth century. If "Ai" was really Bethel, then what was the "Bethel" mentioned in Josh. 7:2? It is more reasonable to assume that Et-Tell is not the true site of Ai, and that we must look to further exploration to discover the true location.[23] The date of Bethel's destruction is therefore quite irrelevant to the dating of the Exodus.[24]

One final problem attaching to the early date theory of the Exodus has to do with the complete silence of Judges concerning the Palestinian expeditions of Seti I and Rameses II. If these invasions actually took place and the territory of Canaan was actu-

23. J. Simons in the *Archaeological Digest* (published by the *American Journal of Archaeology,* July-Sept. 1947), p. 311, objects that Et-Tell cannot be identifiied with the biblical Ai for four reasons. (1) Et-Tell is not very close to Beitin (or Bethel), whereas Josh. 12:9 states that it was "beside Bethel" (*miṣṣad Beyth-'El*). (2) Et-Tell is a large site, whereas Josh. 7:3 implies that it was a small community inhabited by few people. (3) Et-Tell was not an exposed ruin in the post-conquest period, whereas Josh. 8:28 indicates that Ai was a ruin during that era. (4) Joshua 8:11 refers to a broad valley running to the north of Ai, yet there is no such valley north of Et-Tell. As for Hazor, Y. Yadin concluded that the destruction-layer of level IA in the Lower City (dated in the second half of the thirteenth century) was the Joshua attack, but more likely it was that of Barak and Deborah (or Seti I). Bruce Waltke, in *Bib Sac* 120 (Jan.-Mar. 72), no. 513, indicates an earlier destruction level in "Palestinian Artifactual Evidence Supporting the Early Date of the Exodus." The destruction of Stratum II is ca. 1400 B.C. was marked by a a violent conflagration; so also in the *Bulletin of Near Eastern Archaeological Society,* 1972, pp. 2-21 (same article). Page 14: Yadin's suggestion that of the three destruction levels at Hazor (ca. 1400, ca. 1300, ca. 1230) it was 1230 (after which the tell was unoccupied) is untenable because three or four generations after Joshua, Deborah and Barak dealt with a strong and powerful Hazor. Furthermore, it should be noted that the record of Joshua's free and unhindered movement through the entire territory of Palestine from the Shephelah to Hazor and the highlands of the North could hardly be reconciled with the period of Rameses II. It is scarcely conceivable that that Pharaoh would have permitted such a freedom to Hebrew invaders if he controlled the coastal plain and the valley of Jezreel. But the fumbling, ineffective Palestinian policies of Amenhotep III and Akhnaton furnish a most advantageous setting for Joshua.

24. It is not even certain that Beitin has been correctly identified as the site of Bethel. Eusebius stated that Bethel lay twelve Roman miles north of Jerusalem (the location of Bireh), but Beitin is substantially more distant than that. Nor does Beitin lie on the main northerly road out of Jerusalem, as Eusebius implied for Bethel. Moreover there is no mountain between Beitin and Et-Tell, as Gen. 12:8 specifies, but only a small hill to the northwest of Et-Tell. (But between Bireh and a tell lying to the southeast a mile and a half away there is a substantial hill called Eṭ-Ṭawil.) There is, besides, no broad valley running to the north of Beitin (as Josh. 8:11 indicates for Bethel and Ai), but only a small, narrow one. Neither Beitin nor Et-Tell shows evidence of having been inhabited at the right period for either the early date or the late date Exodus theory. Moreover, Ai lay to the west of Michmash, whereas Et-Tell is to the north of it. Finally, there is no *'arabah* ("steppe, plain") or *môrād* ("downward slope") in the direction of Jericho beginning in the vicinity of Beitin, and yet there was such a feature near the biblical Bethel and Ai (Josh. 7:5). It should be added that until the mid-nineteenth century, there was no tradition whatever that Beitin was to be equated with Bethel. All of these matters are discussed by David Livingston, "The Location of Bethel and Ai Reconsidered" in *Westminster Theological Journal* (Nov. 1970), pp. 20-44.

ally subjected to the Egyptian power after the Israelite conquest had taken place, why are the Egyptians not mentioned along with all the other oppressors? If lesser powers like the Moabites, Ammonites, North Canaanites, and Philistines were mentioned, why were the Egyptians completely omitted during the interval between 1370 and 1050 (when Saul began to reign)? But if the Exodus actually took place in 1290 and the Conquest in 1250, there would be no silence to explain away, for the Israelites would not have entered upon the scene until after Rameses' conquests, the year 1279 marking the signing of his famous nonaggression pact with the Hittites.

In reply to this persuasive argument, it should first of all be pointed out that neither the 1290 date nor the 1230 date accounts for the failure of Judges to mention the invasion of Merneptah aforementioned (see p. 244). The same is true of the expeditions of Rameses III (1204-1172 B.C.) in Palestine. Yet this noteworthy monarch of the Twentieth Dynasty boasts in his inscriptions of having reduced both the Tjeker (Palestinians) and the Philistines to ashes (ANET, p. 262), and his bas-reliefs show him on his victorious progress to Djahi (the Phoenician coastline) to do further exploits. Monuments from his reign were discovered in the excavation of Beth-shan, at the eastern end of the plain of Esdraelon. How are we to explain this complete silence about Rameses III? Certainly not by the late date theory of the Exodus; for even according to that method of reckoning, the reign of Rameses III would have occurred in the time of the Judges. The only possible inference is that the Hebrew record did not see fit to mention these Egyptian invasions which took place after the Conquest. But if this was indisputably true of the incursions of two pharaohs (Merneptah and Rameses III), why may it not have been true of the two others (Seti I and Rameses II)? Also it is possible that the Hebrews did not mention the Egyptians because the two had little or no contact. The Egyptians were most active along the coastal plain of the Mediterranean, which the Hebrews seldom held. Primarily the Hebrews occupied the hills of Judea, Samaria, and Galilee.

Second, it is possible to work out a fairly satisfactory synchronism between the Egyptian history of the Nineteenth Dynasty and the earlier period of the judges. Garstang has advanced the interesting theory that the periods of "rest" referred to in Judges were times of Egyptian supremacy, but that the Hebrew historian purposely avoided mentioning the Egyptians as such because of an inveterate antipathy to a nation which had so cruelly oppressed his ancestors in Goshen. Periods of oppression, then, came when Egyptian power in Canaan was weak and the tribes of the area became restive, oppressing Israel.

On this view (which is essentially embraced by Unger and Payne) the oppression by Cushan-Rishathaim of Aram-of-the-Two-Rivers represented a Hittite advance (the Hittites having subdued North Mesopotamia by that time), which took place during the reign of Tutankhamen (Unger) or Amenhotep III (Payne). The eighty years' peace following the assassination of Eglon by Ehud (Judg. 3:12-30) coincided in part with the pacification of the land by Seti I in 1318, followed by the long reign of Rameses II. The quiet period ensuing upon Barak's victory over Sisera (ca. 1223-1183 according to Payne) may have been facilitated by the strong rule of Rameses III (1204-1172). Garstang suggests that the "hornet" which is to drive out the Canaanites before the Hebrews (according to Ex. 23:28; Deut. 7:20; Josh. 24:12) is a covert reference to the Egyptian power, since the bee or hornet was the symbol of pharaoh as king of Lower Egypt in the hieroglyphic spelling of that title (*bỵty* in Egyptian). This is somewhat dubious, however, on exegetical grounds. But the fact remains that the early date theory does permit easy synchronism between the periods in Judges and the known sequence of events in Egyptian history. (The late date theory, on the other hand, makes complete nonsense of the chronology of the book of Judges.) An additional factor which favors a 1445 Exodus is found in the Amarna Letters.[25]

THE COVENANT AND THE DECALOGUE

In Ex. 19:3-8 the covenant with Abraham and his seed (Gen. 12, 15, 17) was renewed with his descendants, now that they had become a great nation. At the foot of the holy mountain, Israel permanently committed itself to be of the Lord's people, and a holy (set-apart-for-Him) people, whose national goal—unlike the self-seeking of all other nations—was to be sincere and to give complete obedience to His will, walking in fellowship with Him, and making Him the object of their highest loyalty and love. "All that Jehovah hath spoken we will do" (v. 8). Anything less than this would have amounted to a purposeful withholding of complete obedience. It certainly was not intended (as some have supposed) to be a choice in favor of self-justification by performance of the deeds of the law. Grace reigned supreme in this Sinaitic covenant just as truly as it did in the Abrahamic. The whole body of the law which was revealed

MT. SINAI: THE TRADITIONAL LOCATION WHERE GOD GAVE MOSES THE TEN COMMANDMENTS.

25. Cf. chap. 13, pp. 184-85, and the discussion at some length in chap. 19.

to Moses and his people from this point on was a testament of grace, although mediated through a different economy from that of the Gospel (in which the Antitype superseded all the Old Testament types which had pointed toward Him). Hence the apostles apply exactly the same affirmation of royal priesthood to New Testament Christians as to Old Testament Israel (1 Peter 2:9 is an adaptation of Ex. 19:5-6). It was only the misunderstanding and misinterpretation of the law—as a system of merit-earning and self-justification—which is rejected in Romans 3 and Galatians 3 (and related passages).

As for the Decalogue (Ex. 20:1-17), the whole basis of its sanctions is stated to be God's act of redemption by grace ("I am Jehovah thy God, who brought thee out of... bondage"). The most solemn warnings against disobedience (the product of unbelief and rejection of God) are coupled with the most lavish promises of grace ("and showing lovingkindness unto thousands of them that love me and keep my commandments," ASV). While the distinctive element of love (for no heathen ever professed to love his god with his whole heart) is made more explicit in Deuteronomy than in the other books of the Torah, it is nevertheless an underlying presupposition in them all: the love of God for the believer and the believer's love for God. Yet the emphasis is constantly laid upon a holy life as the necessary and inevitable product of a true and living faith, even though a holy life has per se no saving virtue.

In regard to the wording of the first commandment ("Thou shalt have no other gods before Me"), it has often been alleged by the Wellhausen school that this dictum insists only on an exclusive worship of Jehovah (monolatry) rather than an outright affirmation of monotheism. There is, according to this interpretation, no denial of the existence of other gods; it is simply that Israel is to be exclusively loyal to its own national god. But this construction of the words is quite unwarranted; there would hardly be any other way of expressing the thought that Israel is to worship the one true God alone, and not to serve any other deities of their own devising (though, of course, such deities could exist only in their imagination). It is a sufficient refutation of this monolatrous interpretation to point to the analogy of Ps. 96:4-5: "For great is Jehovah, and greatly to be praised: he is to be feared above all gods"—surely an affirmation of monolatry according to Wellhausian interpretation; but the author goes on to affirm pure monotheism: "For all the gods of the peoples are idols, (elîlîm—"things of nought"); but Jehovah made the heavens" (ASV). This passage alone (and others could be cited) demonstrates conclusively that the mention of "gods" in the plural implied no admission of the actual existence of heathen gods in the first commandment.

There are certain variations between the form of the Ten Commandments in Ex. 20 and that given in Deut. 5. In Deut. 5:15 an additional motivation is given for hallowing the Sabbath (kindness to one's bondslaves, even as the Lord had compassion on captive Israel), and the wife is mentioned before the house rather than after it, in the tenth commandment. Since Deut. 5 occurs in the midst of a hortatory discourse addressed by Moses to the people, whereas Ex. 20 purports to be a record of the direct address of God to Israel, it is fair to conclude that the latter represents the accurate and original wording. In Deut. 5 the preacher inserts an explanatory interpolation (likewise under divine inspiration) which enforces the sanction of the fourth commandment more urgently upon the conscience of the people. Note that the variation of order between "wife" and "house" destroys the basis for the artificial distinction drawn by the Roman church between not coveting the neighbor's property (ninth commandment) and the neighbor's wife (tenth commandment). The fact that the order is immaterial—whether "house—wife" or "wife—house"—shows that all of Ex. 20:17 was intended as a single commandment. (The consequence, of course, is that the Romanist attempt to combine the first commandment with the second must fail, since that would result in only nine commandments.)

THE SPIRITUAL SIGNIFICANCE OF THE TABERNACLE

A considerable portion of Exodus (chaps. 25-28, 30, 35-40) is devoted to the design of the tabernacle and of the various articles of furniture which it was to contain. Each of these articles possessed a typical meaning which had a bearing upon the redemptive work of the Lord Jesus Christ. Proceeding from the outermost parts to the inner sanctum, we find the following significant features: (1) The outer hangings of the court (*ḥāṣēr*) enclosed a perimeter measuring fifty by one hundred cubits. This court was designed to separate Israel as a holy possession of God and keep it distinct from the Gentiles. This same principle was rigorously observed in the later temples, both that of Solomon and that of Herod (in which was found a Greek inscription threatening the death penalty to any Gentile who should venture beyond the barrier into the inner court). (2) The tabernacle itself was a large tent (*'ōhel*) measuring ten by thirty cubits (the cubit being a little over a foot and a half) and curtained off into two sections, the holy place and the holy of holies. (3) In the court outside of the tabernacle and situated in front of its curtain door (*māsāk*) or "outer veil" were placed the "great" altar or altar of burnt offering (*mizbaḥ ōlâh*) covered with bronze, on which all the offerings were presented, both the blood sacrifices (*zᵉbāḥîm*) and the grain offering (*minḥâ*), which is rendered "meat-offering" in the KJV but consisted of everything except meat (in the modern sense of flesh). (4) Between the brazen altar and the entrance curtain stood the laver (*kiyyôr*), a large wash basin made of bronze, in which priests had to wash their hands and their feet before entering the holy place. This probably typified the cleansing power of Christ's blood as represented and sealed to believers by baptism.

The tabernacle consisted of two compartments. (5) The holy place (*qōdesh*), measuring twenty by ten cubits, contained three sacred objects. (6) On the north or right side, was the table of "shewbread" (*shûlḥān wᵉleḥem pānîm*—table and bread of the Presence) on which were laid out twelve fresh loaves of fine flour every Sabbath. It undoubtedly typified Christ as the bread of life, and symbolized Israel also (the twelve tribes) as the people of God presented before him as a living sacrifice. (7) On the south or left side, stood the lampstand or "candlestick" (*mᵉnôrah*) with its seven oil lamps, typifying Christ as the light of the world, who by His Holy Spirit performs the perfect work of God (symbolized by the number seven), enabling His people to shine forth a light of testimony to the world (cf. Zech. 4). (8) On the west was located the small golden altar, the altar of incense (*mizbaḥ miqṭār*), used only for the offering of incense in front of the inner curtain (*pārōket*) which separated the holy place from the Holy of Holies. This golden altar probably typified the effectual prayer of Christ the Intercessor, and symbolized also the prayers of the saints (cf. Rev. 8:3). (9) The inner curtain (*pārōket*) typified the veil of Christ's flesh (cf. Heb. 10:20) which had to be rent (as it was at the hour Christ died, Matt. 27:51) if the barrier was to be removed which separated God from His people.

(10) Within the holy of holies (*qōdesh qodāšîm*), measuring ten by ten cubits, there was only (11) the ark of the covenant (*'arōn habberît*), consisting of a chest 2.5 by 1.5 cubits, covered by a lid of solid gold wrought into the shape of two cherubim facing each other with outstretched wings and looking downward at the surface of the lid. (12) This lid was called the "propitiatory"(*kappōret*, from *kippēr*, to propitiate or to atone), rendered by the KJV as "mercy seat," and upon it the high priest sprinkled the blood of the sin offering on the Day of Atonement, thus typifying Christ's atonement (Heb. 9:12) in the very presence of God. The ark thus represented the presence of God in the midst of His people; it was His footstool as He sat "enthroned between the cherubim" (Ex. 25:22; Ps. 80:1). Placed in front of the ark were the golden pot of manna and the rod of Aaron which had blossomed (Ex. 16:33; Num. 17:10). Apparently they were at a later time placed inside it (Heb. 9:4). But certainly the ark contained the two tablets of the Ten Commandments, symbolizing the gracious covenant and the law. These were the only objects left within the ark by the time of Samuel (1 Sam. 6:19), or at least by the time of Solomon (1 Kings 8:9).

17 LEVITICUS AND NUMBERS

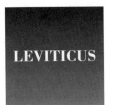

LEVITICUS

THE HEBREW BIBLE gives to the book of Leviticus the name *Wayyiqrā'* ("And He called"), the first word of 1:1. The LXX title *Leuitikon* means that which pertains to the Levites, and serves to indicate the central theme of the book. The chief emphasis of this compendium of priestly regulations is laid upon the holiness of Israel as a nation set apart for the service and glory of God. It deals particularly with the proper presentation of sacrifices and the maintenance of a clear distinction between that which is clean and that which is unclean.

OUTLINE OF LEVITICUS

I. Law of sacrifices, 1:1–7:38

A. Burnt offering, 1:1-17
B. Meal offering, 2:1-16
C. Peace offerings, 3:1-17
D. Sin offering for "inadvertent" sins, 4:1–5:13
E. Trespass offering, 5:14–6:7
F. Continual burnt offering and the offerings of priests, 6:8-23
G. Disposition of the victim in a sin offering, a trespass offering, and peace offerings, 6:24–7:27
H. Wave offering and the heave offering, 7:28-38

II. Consecration of the priests, 8:1–10:20

A. Consecration of Aaron and his sons, 8:1-36
B. Aaron as high priest, 9:1-24
C. Judgment upon Nadab and Abihu for disobedience, 10:1-20

III. Separation from defilement, 11:1–15:33

A. Clean and unclean foods, 11:1-47
B. Purification of mothers after childbirth, 12:1-8
C. Regulations governing leprosy, 13:1–14:57
D. Purification from bodily secretions, 15:1-33

IV. Day of atonement, 16:1-34

V. Place of sacrifice and the sanctity of blood, 17:1-16

VI. Practical Holiness: laws against unchastity, uncleanness, and idolatry, 18:1–20:27

VII. Priestly holiness and priestly duties, 21:1–22:33

VIII. Holy convocations: Sabbath, Passover, Unleavened Bread, Pentecost, Trumpets, Atonement, Tabernacles, 23:1-44

IX. Symbols of consecration; penalties for desecration, 24:1-23

X. Sabbatical year and year of Jubilee, 25:1-55

XI. Blessings of obedience, curses upon disobedience, 26:1-46

XII. Payment of vows and tithes, 27:1-34

UNDERLYING PRINCIPLES IN THE LEVITICAL LEGISLATION

No other book in the Bible affirms divine inspiration so frequently as Leviticus. Under the heading of the verb *to speak (dibbēr)* alone, the concordance lists no less than thirty-eight occurrences of the statement that Jehovah spoke to Moses or to Aaron. Nothing could be clearer than that this entire sacrificial system was no invention of the Hebrew people (either in Moses' day or in the course of later centuries) but a direct revelation of God. Otherwise no affirmation of divine origin is to be trusted for any statement in the rest of Scripture. While there may be some general resemblances or analogies which can be pointed out between these Levitical regulations and the cultus practiced by other ancient Semites, there is a complete absence of the degrading and superstitious elements characterizing the worship of the idolatrous nations during the Old Testament age.

A remarkable authentication of the divine origin of this Mosaic code is to be found in the semiprophetic twenty-sixth chapter. Here there is a preview of the subsequent history of Israel, with its progressive decline from faith to apostasy, and a clear intimation of the Babylonian Exile (vv. 32-39) and the subsequent restoration (vv. 40-45). It is not to be wondered at if antisupernaturalist critics felt under compulsion to date the origin of Leviticus as exilic (document H) and post-exilic (document P). No other course is open to one who on philosophical grounds denies the possibility of supernatural divine prediction.

There are at least five basic principles which operate throughout this book.

PRINCIPLES OF LEVITICAL LEGISLATION

Principle	Scripture
Maintain holiness	Lev. 19:2; 20:7; 20:26; 21:6
Maintain access to God by substitutionary atonement	Lev. 4, 16
Must worship according to God's ordination	Lev. 26, 27
Must remain sexually pure	Lev. 18
Abstain from commingling the holy and the profane	Lev. 13, 14
Religious year to be dominated by the number of seven (Sabbath, etc.)	Lev. 23, 24

1. As a unique people of God, redeemed Israel is *(a)* to keep holy, that is, to set themselves apart from the unconverted world unto the service and worship of the one true God; *(b)* to maintain access to God on the basis of the substitutionary atonement, by means of the shedding of the blood of the sacrifice, as an innocent life is substituted for the forfeited life of the guilty.

2. Since this access to God is made possible by grace alone, the believer must come before God only in the specific way which God has appointed. Hence all regulations as to ritual and sacrifice must originate with God rather than with man. (Anything invented by man might be thought to establish some kind of self-justifying personal merit.)

3. As a holy people spiritually wedded to Yahweh, Israel must rigorously abstain from all sexual unchastity, all violation of the marriage bond, and from contact with corruption and decay (in connection with corpses or defiling disease). These provisions are to be understood as giving expression to a fundamental attitude of a holy love toward God and man. The second great commandment as defined by the Lord Jesus (Matt. 22:39) was derived from Lev. 19:18: "Thou shalt love thy neighbor as thyself." The basic principle underlying monogamy is contained in Lev. 18:18,[1] for the term *sister* in that verse may also imply "another woman."

4. Nothing corrupt or liable to speedy decay may be presented as an offering to God. This excludes leaven, milk (which quickly sours), honey (which ferments), swine (associated by the heathen with the worship of the gods of the netherworld), and clothing made of a mixture of differing materials (such as wool and flax), which typified a commingling of the holy and the profane.

5. The religious year is dominated by the sacred number seven (symbolizing the

---

1. So states John Murray, *Principles of Conduct* (Grand Rapids: Eerdmans, 1957), pp. 253-56.

THE SEVEN FEASTS

FEAST	DATE	SYMBOLIC OF	SCRIPTURE
Passover (pesaḥ)	Abib 14	The death of Christ Our Sacrificial Lamb	Lev. 23:5 Deut. 16:1-8
Unleavened Bread (Maṣṣôt)	Abib 15-22	Life separated from sin	Lev. 23:6-8 Deut. 16:8
Wave-sheaf (ʿômer)	Abib 16	Resurrection of Christ Pentecost	Lev. 23:11
First fruits (Feast of Weeks) (ḥag shᵉbûʿôt)	Ziv 5	Coming of the Holy Spirit upon the Church	Ex. 34:22 Lev. 23:15-16 Deut. 16:9-12
Trumpets (yôm tᵉrûʿâ)	Tishri 1	Rapture or Second Coming of Christ	Num. 28:11-15 Num. 29:1-6
Day of Atonement (yôm kippûr)	Tishri 10	Pardon of God's people cf. Zechariah 12:10-14	Lev. 16:1-34 Ex. 30:10-30 Num. 29:7-11
Tabernacles (sūkkôt)	Tishri 15-22	Fellowship of God's people dwelling together in peace. Prophetic of the entire Millennial Kingdom the celebration of the completion of the Harvest	Lev. 23:34-42 Num. 29:12 Deut. 16:13-17

(Wavesheaf, First fruits, and Tabernacles) in thanksgiving to God, their Provider.

perfect work of God). Hence *(a)* every seventh day is a holy sabbath; *(b)* every seventh year is a Sabbath year of rest for the crop-bearing land; *(c)* after seven sevens of years the fiftieth year is to be hallowed as a jubilee, in which all mortgaged lands are to be returned to the original family; *(d)* Passover is held at the end of the second heptad of Abib, on the evening of the fourteenth; *(e)* the Feast of Unleavened Bread is celebrated for the next seven days; *(f)* the Feast of Pentecost is celebrated after seven sevens of days following the offering of the wave-sheaf (hence on the "fiftieth" day); *(g)* the seventh month, Tishri, is especially sanctified by three holy observances: the Feast of Trumpets, the Day of Atonement, and the Feast of Tabernacles; *(h)* the Feast of Tabernacles is celebrated seven days (fifteenth to twenty-second of Tishri), plus an eighth day for the final convocation.

With the discovery of other ancient law codes, such as the *Code of Hammurabi*, the fragments of the Sumerian laws of Lipit-Ishtar of Isin (about 1875 B.C., according to Kramer in ANET, p. 159), those of Bilalama, king of Eshnunna (about 1940 B.C., according to ANET, pp. 161, 217), it becomes increasingly apparent that some of the so-called P laws were strikingly similar to provisions enacted in the early second millennium, well before the age of Moses. Driver tried to salvage a post-exilic date for P by assigning these resemblances exclusively to H (for most of them are found in Lev. 17-26), and suggesting that Ezekiel included some very ancient materials in compiling his "holiness code." This, of course, tends to undermine the whole basis for dating H in the time of Ezekiel.

With the recent publication of legal documents from the north Canaanite city of Ugarit, still further resemblances have been coming to light, even in the matter of technical terminology. J. J. Rabinowitz has noted in Ugaritic conveyances of land (written in Akkadian) the formula *ṣamid adi dariti* ("joined in perpetuity"), and he remarks that it strikingly parallels the technical Hebrew expression in Lev. 25:23, 30, *liṣᵉmîtût* ("in perpetuity"). The words in question are cognate in the two languages, or else the Hebrew has borrowed an ancient Akkadian term. Rabinowitz remarks: "I do not profess to know what precisely is the significance of the above parallelism. It does seem to me, however, that it speaks volumes against those who would assign a late date to the sections of Leviticus relating to the year of jubilee (e.g., Pfeiffer, IOT, p. 240)."[2] (The discovery of characteristic P terms for sacrifice in the fifteenth-century Ugaritic tablets has already been discussed in chap. 13, pp. 175-176.)

THE THREE MAIN FESTIVALS OF THE HEBREW YEAR (LEV. 23)

A. The Passover (*pesaḥ*) and Unleavened bread (*maṣṣōt*) (vv. 4-5)

    1. Passover: on evening of fourteenth of Abib (the first month)

        a) Purpose: to commemorate Israel's deliverance from Egyptian bondage.

        b) Ritual: lamb slain, its blood to be sprinkled with hyssop on the lintel of the front door, and then roasted and consumed by the offerer with his family (Deut. 16:5-6 specified that after God chose a holy city, as capital the public Passover should be celebrated there).

        c) Typical significance: Christ's crucifixion (1 Cor. 5:7)

    2. Feast of Unleavened Bread: fifteenth to twenty-second of Abib (v. 6)

        a) Purpose: to commemorate the hardships of the hurried flight from Egypt. Absence of leaven symbolized sincere consecration to God

        b) Ritual: offering of the first fruits of wave-sheaf on the second day (i.e., the sixteenth of Abib); this consisted of barley, the earliest crop in the year (typifying the resurrection of Christ); also a prescribed burnt offering presented with the sheaf; a holy convocation (v. 7) on the fifteenth and twenty-second, both of which count as Sabbaths and require additional burnt offerings (two bullocks,

2. Rabinowitz in *Vetus Testamentum* 8 (Jan. 1958): 95.

The Six Types of Blood Sacrifice

Name	Purpose	Victim	God's Portion	Priest's Portion	Offerer's Portion
BURNT OFFERING (*'ōlah*)	TO PROPITIATE FOR SIN IN GENERAL, *ORIGINAL SIN*; A MEANS OF APPROACH BY UNHOLY PEOPLE TO HOLY GOD	MALE, UNBLEMISHED: OX/ SHEEP/ GOAT/ DOVE (ACCORDING TO WEALTH)	ENTIRE ANIMAL (HENCE CALLED *kālîl*, WHOLE BURNT OFFERING)	NOTHING	NOTHING
SIN OFFERING (*ḥaṭṭa't*)	TO ATONE FOR SPECIFIC TRANSGRESSIONS WHERE NO RESTITUTION WAS POSSIBLE	PRIEST OR CONGREGATION: *BULLOCK* RULER: *HE-GOAT* COMMONER: *SHE-GOAT*	FATTY PORTIONS (FAT COVERING INWARDS; KIDNEYS, LIVER, CAUL)	ALL THE REMAINDER (HAD TO BE EATEN WITHIN COURT OF TABERNACLE)	NOTHING
TRESSPASS OFFERING (*'āshām*)	TO ATONE FOR SPECIFIC TRANSGRESSIONS WHERE RESTITUTION WAS POSSIBLE, DAMAGES COMPUTED AT SIX-FIFTHS PAYABLE IN ADVANCE. LEGAL *SATISFACTION*	RAM (ONLY)	SAME AS ABOVE	SAME AS ABOVE	NOTHING
PEACE OFFERING (*shᵉlāmîm*) 1. THANK OFFERING (*tō^wdah*)	FELLOWSHIP WITH GOD; A *COMMUNION MEAL*. FOR UNEXPECTED BLESSING OR DELIVERANCE ALREADY GRANTED	UNBLEMISHED MALE OR FEMALE *OX/SHEEP/GOAT*	FATTY PORTIONS	1. WAVE OFFERING; BREAST—TO HIGH PRIEST 2. HEAVE OFFERING; RIGHT FORELEG—TO OFFICIATING PRIEST (TO BE EATEN IN ANY CLEAN PLACE)	REMAINDER (EATEN IN COURT, THE SAME DAY)
2. VOTIVE OFFERING (*Neder*)	FOR BLESSING OR DELIVER-ANCE ALREADY GRANTED, WHEN A VOW HAD BEEN MADE IN SUPPORT OF THE PETITION	UNBLEMISHED MALE OR FEMALE *OX/SHEEP/GOAT*	SAME AS ABOVE		REMAINDER (EATEN IN COURT, THE SAME DAY)
3. FREEWILL OFFERING (*nᵉdābāh*)	TO EXPRESS GENERAL THANKFULNESS AND LOVE TOWARD GOD, WITHOUT REGARD TO SPECIFIC BLESSINGS	MALE OR FEMALE *OX/SHEEP/GOAT* (MINOR IMPERFECTIONS PERMITTED)	SAME AS ABOVE	SAME AS ABOVE	REMAINDER (EATEN IN COURT, FIRST OR SECOND DAY)

one ram, seven lambs) and a sin offering (one goat); unleavened bread only to be eaten during this entire week.

B. Pentecost or the Feast of Weeks (*sheḇû'ôṯ*): sixth of Sivan (third month), or forty-nine days after the offering of the firstfruits on the second day of Unleavened Bread

1. Purpose: to dedicate to God the firstfruits of the wheat harvest.

2. Ritual: a holy convocation (counting as a Sabbath); wave offering of two loaves of leavened wheat flour; burnt offering (seven lambs, one bullock, two rams); sin offering (he-goat); and peace offering (two male lambs); an additional burnt offering and sin offering at the convocation itself (Num. 28:27).

3. Typical significance: the descent of the Spirit on the New Testament church (Acts 2).

C. Feast of Tabernacles or Booths (*sukkôṯ*): fifteenth to twenty-second of Tishri (seventh month)

1. Purpose: to commemorate the wilderness wandering and to rejoice in the completion of all the harvests (grain, fruit tree, vintage).

2. Ritual: convocations on fifteenth and twenty-second (both counting as Sabbaths); burnt offering (from thirteen to seven bullocks, day by day; two rams, fourteen lambs) and sin offering (one goat) (Num. 29); celebrants to live in booths, celebrating the week with fruits: the *ethrog* or citron in one hand, and the *lulab* or cluster of branches in the other (consisting of palms and willows).

3. Typical significance: apparently to foreshadow peace and prosperity of the coming millennial kingdom (cf. Zech. 14:16).

The basic principle underlying all the blood sacrifices (*zeḇāḥîm*) was atonement *(kippûr)* by the substitution of an innocent life for the guilty. In token of this substitution, the offerer laid his hand upon the victim's head, thus identifying himself with it as his representative. To signify his acceptance of the just penalty of death, the offerer himself slew his victim and then turned it over to the priest for the completion of the ceremony. The priest usually sprinkled or smeared a portion of the blood upon the altar.

The chart on the previous page indicates the distinction between the various types of sacrifice and presents in a schematic form the system set forth in the first seven chapters of Leviticus.

NUMBERS

The Hebrew title for this book is *Bemiḏbār* ("in the wilderness of"), taken from the first verse: "And Jehovah spake unto Moses in the wilderness of Sinai" (ASV). The LXX labels it *Arithmoi*, or Numbers, because of the prominence of census figures in this book. And yet the Hebrew title is quite appropriate to its general theme: Israel under God's training in the wilderness. Historical narrative occupies a larger proportion of this book than is the case in Leviticus or Deuteronomy, and the period of years

involved is far greater (forty years of discipline) than in the other books of the Pentateuch (excluding Genesis).

OUTLINE OF NUMBERS

I. Preparation for the journey from Sinai, 1:1–10:10

A. Numbering the army and assigning positions for the march, 1:1–2:34
B. Levites numbered and duties described, 3:1–4:49
C. Excluding defilement from the camp: laws of leprosy; restitution for
   damages; trial of accused adulteress, 5:1-31
D. Nazarites (type of wholly dedicated life); the Aaronic benediction, 6:1-27
E. Treasures dedicated to the tabernacle by the Twelve Tribes, 7:1-89
F. The Levites sanctified and installed in office, 8:1-26
G. The first annual Passover observed, 9:1-14
H. Following the pillar of cloud; the trumpet signals, 9:15–10:10

II. From Sinai to Kadesh-barnea, 10:11–14:45

A. First stage of the journey: the march begins, 10:11-36
B. First and second murmurings at Taberah and Kibroth-hattaavah (after
   feasting on quails); seventy elders prophesy, 11:1-35
C. Judgment upon Aaron and Miriam for rebelling against Moses; Miriam's
   leprosy cured, 12:1-16
D. The great rebellion at Kadesh-barnea after the adverse report of the ten
   spies, 13:1–14:45

III. From Kadesh-barnea to the plains of Moab, 15:1–21:35

A. Laws concerning meal offerings and sin offerings; death for blasphemy
   and Sabbath-breaking; the garment fringes, 15:1-41
B. Rebellion of Korah and validation of Aaronic priesthood, 16:1–17:13
C. Relationship of Levites to priests; offerings and tithes their only portion in
   Canaan, 18:1-32
D. The water of purification for uncleanness, 19:1-22
E. Death of Miriam; second smiting of the rock; Edom bars passage; death of
   Aaron, 20:1-29
F. Seventh murmuring and the brazen serpent; arrival at Moab, 21:1-20
G. First permanent conquests: defeat of Sihon and Og, 21:21-35

IV. Encounter with the Moabites and Balaam, 22:1–25:18

A. Balak hires Balaam, 22:1-41
B. Balaam's triple blessing and prediction of Israel's triumph, 23:1–24:25
C. The sin of Baal-peor, 25:1-18

V. Preparations for entering Canaan, 26:1–36:13

A. Arrangements for conquest and tribal apportionment of the land, 26:1–27:23

B. Laws concerning sacrifices and vows, 28:1–30:16

C. Vengeance on the Midianites, 31:1-54

D. Apportionment of Transjordan to Reuben, Gad, and Manasseh, 32:1-42

E. Summary of journeys from Egypt to Moab, 33:1-56

F. Plans for division of Canaan, 34:1–36:13

R. K. Harrison comments concerning the Hebrew text, "The text of Numbers has not been as well preserved as that of Leviticus, although there is comparatively little in the way of actual corruption. In Numbers 21:14 something appears to have dropped out of the Hebrew, while in Numbers 21:18 Mattanah is probably not a place name, as in the RSV, but rather a noun derived form the root *nathan*, and meaning 'gift.' Some difficulties of translation also exist in connection with Numbers 21:30 and 23:10" (R. K. Harrison, *Old Testament Introduction*, p. 634).

UNDERLYING PRINCIPLES

The spiritual lesson enforced throughout the book is that God's people can move forward only so far as they trust His promises and lean upon His strength. The tragedy of Kadesh-barnea was the unavoidable consequence of unbelief; only true believers can enter into God's rest. Without faith they can only die uselessly in the wilderness (cf. Heb. 3:7-19). The purpose of the census prior to the failure at Kadesh (Num. 1-4) and of the census of the later generation at the plains of Moab (Num. 26) was to show that they were not kept out of Canaan by their insufficient numbers. It was not the size of their army that mattered, but only the size of their faith. Although no more numerous than their fathers, the younger generation was able to conquer the Canaanites because they were willing to trust God all the way and to obey His marching orders (in a way that their fathers failed to do at Kadesh-barnea).

CREDIBILITY OF THE CENSUS FIGURES

Rationalist critics have always rejected the statistics of Numbers as implausibly high, and have usually dismissed them as the fabrication of the Priestly School. This, of course, is based upon the dubious proposition that the unusual is tantamount to the impossible. There has been a tendency among some of the more recent scholars to explain the statistics of the Hebrew text by reinterpreting the word for "thousand" (*'eleph*) as simply equivalent to family or clan. It is true that there is an *'eleph* which means family or clan (Judg. 6:15; 1 Sam. 10:19, etc.); but it is very clear from the numeration chapters (Num. 1-4; 26) that *'eleph* is intended in the sense of "thousand," for the smaller unit below this *'eleph* is *mē'āt*, "hundreds" (so Num. 1:21, 23, 25, etc.). The most that a "family" could contribute to the national army would be four or five men on the average, and it would be absurd to suppose that "hundreds" would be mentioned as the next lower numerical unit after an average contingent of five men each.

Actually, the advocates of this view that '*eleph* equals "family contingent"[3] assume that these passages in Numbers were taken from ancient fragmentary records of an old census (possibly from David's time or even earlier), misunderstood and reworked by later traditionists, or by the priestly editors themselves. These latter contributors, then, would be responsible for the lower figures (hundreds, tens, and digits) tacked on after the original numerations of "families." But even this unlikely hypothesis lacks plausibility in the light of the surrounding circumstances. Assuming that the total of 603,550 given in Num. 1:46 represents an original 603 families averaging five men each, how can it be supposed that a male population of 3,015 could have put the king of Egypt in fear because of their overwhelming numbers? Yet Pharaoh is made to say in Ex. 1:9, "Behold, the people of Israel are more and mightier than we." But usually the advocates of this view (Mendenhall included) understand '*eleph* in the sense of "family complex" or "clan," or as Martin Noth suggests,[4] "troop" or "military unit," and increase the contribution to fifty rather than a mere five. And yet even this treatment would result in a total fighting force of only 30,150, scarcely a formidable contingent in the midst of the highly populated Delta of Egypt.[5] Furthermore, even a J passage like Ex. 12:37 gives the same total in round numbers as Num. 1:46 (i.e., 600,000), and the same is true of Num. 11:21, a J-E section. Further corroboration is given by the total amount of ransom money—at the rate of a half shekel apiece—recorded in Ex. 38:25 as 100 talents, 1775 shekels. Since there were 3000 shekels to the talent, this comes out to exactly 603,550 contributors. It is therefore safe to say that no objective handling of the textual evidence can possibly sustain the thesis that '*eleph* in Numbers signifies anything less than a literal thousand.[6]

An objection has also been raised about Ex. 1:15 which mentions only two midwives, Shiphrah and Puah, as serving the needs of the entire Hebrew community in Goshen back in the days before Moses' birth. Even if the population had not reached the two million mark by their time, surely more than two midwives would be required

---

3. Such as G. Mendenhall in JBL (1958), pp. 52-66.

4. For further details see M. Noth, *Numbers: A Commentary*, (Philadelphia: Westminster Press, 1968), pp. 21-23.

5. In the Eighteenth Dynasty the Delta region of Lower Egypt was divided into twenty nomes, or administrative districts, whereas all the rest of the kingdom down to the First Cataract numbered only twenty-two. Thus it would be fair to infer that anywhere from one third to one half of the entire population of Egypt resided in the Delta. This does not mean, however, that all of this extensive territory was as well settled as it became in later times (some districts now contain 2000 inhabitants per square mile). Some of it was marshy and wild and used largely for cattle grazing even until Ptolemaic times. Nevertheless the population of Lower Egypt in the Eighteenth Dynasty must have numbered several million.

6. In the expression '*alᵉphê Yisrā'ēl*, ("the thousands of Israel"), found in Num. 1:16; 10:4, 36, the term probably refers to the tribes, according to Gesenius-Buhl *Lexicon*, p. 44*b*. It should also be noted that Numbers 26 yields a total of 601,703 males between 20 to 50 years of age, exclusive of the 23,000 Levites.

for a population of well over a million and a half. While this contention is certainly valid, so far as it goes, how could anyone suppose that an Elohist living around 750 B.C. imagined that two midwives would have sufficed for all the multitude in Goshen? Obviously the role of the two women named in Ex. 1:15 was that of superintendents or overseers over the whole obstetrical guild. Egyptian documents from that period indicate clearly that nearly every craft, skill, or profession was managed by an overseer (*imy-r*) who was responsible to the government. There is every reason to suppose that the bureaucratic regime of the Eighteenth Dynasty would have invested one or two midwives with responsibility for all the rest.

But if it be conceded that the census lists in Numbers furnish no evidence for a smaller figure than 600,000 men of military age, can such a huge number of migrants (possibly totalling 2,500,000 when the women and children were included) be thought to have survived for forty years in the Sinai desert? Even granting that the Sinai Peninsula was less arid than in modern times (for it then supported large and powerful tribes like the Amalekites of Ex. 17:8), it would be obviously impossible for such an enormous host with all their flocks and herds to be sustained in this unculti-vated wilderness. In answer to this rationalistic objection it should be noted that the entire narrative of the Israelite migration frankly concedes that this was a physical impossibility, from the natural standpoint. It emphasizes in every conceivable way— and so does the later Hebrew literature which recalls the history of Moses (Ps. 78:24; Neh. 9:20, etc.)—that the sustaining of this great multitude was a miraculous, super-natural work of God. The supply of food came from manna (Ex. 16:35), and the water came from the cleft rock (Ex. 17:6), and that too in such abundance as to supply the entire host. This is recorded as a sheer miracle, in terms as forthright and plain as any miracle in Scripture. To reject it on rationalistic grounds is to impose upon the Bible a philosophical prejudice against miracles, as such, which can never come to terms with the Scripture as the Word of God.

It has been argued by some that it would have taken the entire day for a multitude of two and a half million to get into formation for a line of march, and thus would have been unable to progress a single mile before night closed in upon them. Hence they could not have performed the journeys attributed to them in Numbers 33 and elsewhere. But actually the length of time required to fall into marching formation depends entirely upon the width and disposition of the columns themselves. It is not necessary to assume that they kept within the limits of a highway, for example, since they were moving over largely uninhabited range land. The four main divisions of approximately 500,000 each (cf. Num. 10:14-20) might just as well have formed their ranks simultaneously and completed preparations to march within four hours (from 6:00 to 10:00 A.M., for example) and then have completed a good ten miles in four hours before setting up camp again (which in turn might have occupied four hours between 2:00 and 6:00 P.M.).

It has also been objected to the credibility of the record in Numbers that the number of firstborn given in Num. 3:43 is much too low for a male population of over 600,000. There must have been far more than 22,273 firstborn sons in so great a company, unless indeed the families had numbered forty or more males apiece. But this argument, as Delitzsch points out (*Pentateuch*, 3:9-13), is founded upon the false assumption that the law (Num. 3:46-47) which required the sanctification of firstborn males was intended to operate retroactively. Nothing in the context suggests that any more are involved than those who were born between the event of the Exodus itself and this episode (thirteen months later) when the census was being taken. On the basis of 603,550 males, the probable number of males between twenty and thirty years of age would be about 190,000, more or less. This would yield an average number of new marriages per year of about 19,000. From this number of marriages, many of which would allow for two gestation periods in eighteen months, a figure in excess of 22,000 male births would hardly be excessive.

Others have objected that the supply of quails furnished to the Israelite host according to Num. 11:31 is absolutely incredible. A quantity of quail piled up over such an area for a depth of two cubits would result in about 70,000 bushels of quail per Israelite per meal. This, however, is a total misunderstanding of what the Hebrew text says. It does not state that the quail comprised a heap of bodies two cubits deep; it only indicates that the quail were deflected downward by a driving wind to a height of two cubits (about three feet) above the surface of the ground, where they could be easily knocked down by the meat-hungry Israelites. (The preposition 'al before the phrase "the face of the earth" may just as well be translated "above" as "upon" in a context where horizontal motion is involved.)

There are several other arguments of this character (cf., ISBE, 4:2168-69), but none of them stand up under analysis any better than do those which have just been treated.[7] Many other critical attacks upon the book depend entirely upon the acceptance of Wellhausian presuppositions for their cogency. Only by question-begging techniques of dissection, for example, is it possible to make out any inconsistencies in the account of the rebellion of Korah, Dathan, and Abiram in Num. 16. (Korah is assigned to P, and Dathan and Abiram to J-E.)

Finally, a word should be said about a much cited "proof text" appealed to by Documentarian Critics to disprove Mosaic authorship. It is argued that Moses could never have written Num. 12:3 about himself ("Now Moses was very meek, above all the men that were upon the face of the earth"). If Moses was truly that humble, how could he have written such a laudatory judgment concerning himself? A good answer to this is found in the *New Bible Commentary*: "Writing under the inspiration of the Holy Spirit, Moses did not hesitate to record his own sins and weaknesses in the clearest of language. It would be contrary to the remarkable objectivity of the Bible if he did not also record his strongest point, his meekness....[The contents of this verse] are necessary to

---

7. See T. Whitelaw's rebuttal in the ISBE article mentioned, and the appropriate sections of Delitzsch's *Commentary*.

a true understanding of this chapter."[8] Delitzsch comments, "It is simply a statement which was indispensable to a full and correct understanding of all the circumstances, and which was made quite objectively, with reference to the character which Moses had not given to himself but had acquired through the grace of God, and which he never falsified from the very time of his calling until the time of his death." He then goes on to quote the comment of Calmet: "As he praises himself here without pride, so he will blame himself elsewhere with humility" (*Pentateuch*, 3:77).

THE ORACLES OF BALAAM

Chapters 22-24 of Numbers record the vain attempt of King Balak of Moab to bring about the defeat and downfall of the Israelite host as they occupied his territory under the leadership of Moses. Realizing that he could not hope to overcome them by the military forces at his disposal, even with the help of the Midianite troops who were allied with him, he decided to resort to sorcery or magic. He knew of the reputation of a prophet named Balaam, who lived in Pethor near the bank of the Euphrates (Num. 22:5) and who had an impressive record as a servant of Yahweh, the God of Israel. By repeated appeals through his official agents Balak at length induced the reluctant seer to come to his aid and pronounce a potent curse upon the Hebrew forces that would insure their defeat. Balak promised Balaam great wealth and high honors if he would comply. But Balaam soon found that he was in trouble with God over his decision to cooperate with Moab, and after a confrontation with a threatening angel, perceived at first by his donkey (who actually spoke up in human language in reply to Balaam's angry reproach), he continued his way toward the plains of Moab with a firm commitment to utter only what Yahweh put into his mouth, whether or not it pleased the king who had hired him (22:35).

As it turned out, even though Balak took his guest to three different hills from where he could look down upon the Israelite encampment, Balaam found himself powerless to speak anything but words of promise and blessing in regard to the people of Moses—much to Balak's disgust. His reaction in 24:15-20 was to make even more explicit the coming conquest of Edom and Amalek that Israel would achieve. And then, in verses 22-24 he also predicted the Assyrian conquest of the Hebrews in later generations, and even the invasions of the Greeks and possibly also the Romans, referred to as the people from "Kittim."

As might be expected, the Documentarian scholars regard these passages as concocted no earlier than the eighth century B.C., and connect them with J or E. Robert Pfeiffer even questions the connection of Num. 23 with Balaam at all, until the time of the "Redactor" who injected them into the tradition which later grew up around his name (Pfeiffer, IOT, p. 279). Supernatural features like a talking donkey and a correct prediction of Israel's future would hardly find acceptance with any rationalist, and so this conjecture is only to be expected.

---

8. *New Bible Commentary*, ed. F. Davidson, A. M. Stibbs, and E. F. Kevan, p. 177*b*.

But it is interesting to observe that an extra-biblical witness about Balaam was discovered at Tell Deir 'Alla, known in Hebrew history as the Valley of Succoth, located not far from the junction of the Jabbok where it joins the Jordan River. In the ruins of an Iron Age II temple at that site some inscribed plaster fragments made reference to *Bl'm br B'r* ("Balaam son of Beor") who is referred to as *ḥōzēh 'ᵉlōhîm* ("seer of the gods"). Baruch Levine comments: "This fact alone, quite apart from the intriguing character of the text as a whole, enhances the realism of Biblical poetry and historiography. An epic figure known only from the Hebrew Bible (and from post-biblical interpretive literature) was, in fact, renowned in the Jordan Valley during the pre-exilic biblical period." (Cf. J. Hoftijzer and G. van der Kooij in "Aramaic Texts from Deir 'Alla," Leiden, 1976.) This kind of evidence furnishes impressive proof that "unlikely" narratives from the Mosaic period may have had a wider support than the Hebrew record among the pagan contemporaries of the Hebrews themselves.

18 DEUTERONOMY

THE HEBREW NAME of Deuteronomy is *'ēlleh haddᵉbārîm* ("these are the words") or more briefly, *Dᵉbārîm* ("words")—taken from the opening line of 1:1. The LXX called it by the more descriptive term *Deuteronomion* ("second law-giving"), because it consists mostly of a restatement of laws contained in Exodus, Leviticus, and Numbers. In the closing months of his earthly career, Moses addressed the assembled congregation of Israel and impressed upon them their peculiar privileges and obligations as the covenant people of Jehovah. Looking forward to the conquest of Canaan, he set forth the divinely ordained constitution of the new theocracy to be established in the land of promise. He laid the responsibility for the preservation of this theocracy upon the conscience of each individual citizen and worshiper.

OUTLINE OF DEUTERONOMY

I. First discourse: historical prologue, 1:1–4:49

A. God's gracious guidance from Horeb to Moab, 1:1–3:29
B. The new generation admonished to cherish the law, 4:1-40
C. Appointment of the Transjordanian cities of refuge, 4:41-43
D. Historical setting of this discourse, 4:44-49

II. Second discourse: laws by which Israel is to live, 5:1–26:19

A. Basic commandments, 5:1–11:32
 1. The Decalogue and the love of God to be taught to posterity, 5:1–6:25
 2. Steadfast obedience and constant grateful remembrance of God's dealings, 7:1–11:32
B. Statutes of worship and a holy life, 12:1–16:22
 1. Genuine worship and needful safeguards against idolatry, 12:1–13:18
 2. Rules about food, the Sabbaths, and the feast days, 14:1– 16:22
C. Judgments: the treatment of specific offenses, 17:1–26:19
 1. Death for idolatry; appellate procedure; the responsibilities of a king, 17:1-20

2. Penalties for witchcraft and false prophecy; the prophetic order and the Messiah-Prophet, 18:1-22
3. Cities of refuge for accidental homicides; penalties for fraud and perjury, 19:1-21
4. Rules of battle and siege, 20:1-20
5. Care of the deceased; captive wives; inheritance and family discipline; removal of the corpse from the gallows, 21:1-23
6. Concerning lost property; no masquerading as opposite sex; no mingling of seeds or yoking of diverse animals, 22:1-12
7. Laws concerning marriage, chastity, care of the body, cleanliness, 22:13–24:5
8. Laws concerning economic and social justice, 24:6–25:19
9. Laws of stewardship, offerings, and tithes, 26:1-19

III. Third discourse: warning and prediction, 27:1–31:30

A. The law to be inscribed and its sanctions recited at Mount Ebal, 27:1-26
B. Conditions for blessing and chastisement of the nation (prediction of future judgments upon Israel), 28:1-68
C. Review of God's benefactions; exhortations to faithfulness, 29:1-30:20
D. Written law entrusted to the leaders of Israel, 31:1-30

IV. Song of Moses: Israel's responsibility to the covenant, 32:1-43

V. Final charge and farewell, 32:44–33:29

A. Moses' last exhortation, 32:44-47
B. Moses warned of approaching death, 32:48-52
C. Moses' final blessing upon Israel, tribe by tribe, 33:1-29

VI. Death of Moses and his obituary, 34:1-12

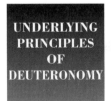

UNDERLYING PRINCIPLES OF DEUTERONOMY

As already indicated, Deuteronomy consists of a restatement and summary of the Law in a compendious form for the guidance of the Israelite nation as a whole. But much of this summary is couched in homiletical or sermonic terms. That is, Moses is not simply explaining what the laws of God are, but he is earnestly enjoining them upon the consciences of his people, and urging them to take with utmost seriousness God's call to a holy life. Certain characteristic emphases or leading thoughts dominate the various discourses. Among these are the following.

1. The spirituality of God (4:12, 15, 16) and His uniqueness and unity are set forth (4:35, 39; 6:4; 7:9; 10:17).

2. God's relationship to His people under the covenant is one of personal love

PRINCIPLES OF DEUTERONOMY

Spirituality of God	4:12, 15, 16
Uniqueness & Unity of God	4:35, 39; 6:4; 7:9; 10:17
Relationship of love between God and His covenant people	4:37; 7:13; 33:3
Love for God the dynamic principle of the believer's life	6:5; 7:8; 10:12, 15 11:1, 13, 22; 13:3; 19:9 30:6, 16, 20
Idolotry to be totally shunned	6:14, 15; 7:4; 8:19, 20 11:16, 17, 20; 13:2-12 30:17-18
Live as a holy people	7:6; 26:19; 28:9
Faithfulness rewarded; violation punished	Chaps. 28-30
Retain and obey the revealed truth from God "Remember and forget not"	9:7

rather than of merit-earning legalism (4:37; 7:13; 33:3).

3. For the believer the basic requirement is love for God, and this love is to be the dynamic principle for his life (6:5; 7:8; 10:12, 15; 11:1, 13, 22; 13:3; 19:9; 30:6, 16, 20).

4. Israel's greatest peril is idolatry, which is to be resisted and suppressed with uncompromising severity (6:14, 15; 7:4; 8:19, 20; 11:16, 17, 20; 13:2-12; 30:17, 18).

5. Because of their close relation to the holy One, the Israelites must live as a holy people (7:6; 26:19; 28:9). This holiness entails abstinence from unclean foods, safeguarded by restricting sacrificial worship to a chosen central sanctuary; it finds expression in love toward the neighbor and charity to the poor and underprivileged (widows, orphans, Levites, and foreigners).

6. Faithfulness to the covenant is to be rewarded by material benefits; violation and disregard of the covenant will be punished by material disaster, loss and ultimate exile (chaps. 28–30).

7. The characteristic admonition is: "Remember, and forget not!" Rather than embarking on some quest for "new truth" to replace the old, Israel is to retain and to obey the revealed truth which it has once and for all received from the absolute and unchanging Source of truth.

In general the Hebrew text of Deuteronomy has been well transmitted with few difficulties. But in Deut. 32:43 it appears that the LXX worked from a longer Hebrew *Vorlage* than the MT, and interestingly enough, Rom. 15:10 quotes from a clause which appears in the LXX insertion. Another Old Testament quotation also appears in Heb. 1:6, yet in this case the source may have been Ps. 95:7, which contains the same wording as the LXX in Deut. 32:43 (R. K. Harrison, *Old Testament Introduction*, p. 662).

THE MOSAIC AUTHORSHIP OF DEUTERONOMY

Considerable discussion has already been devoted to the higher criticism of Deuteronomy in chapter 7 (pp. 105-108). There it was pointed out that the 621 B.C. date assigned by the Documentarians to the composition of this book was found unsatisfactory by many rationalistic critics since the time of Wellhausen. These twentieth-century scholars have come to the conclusion that De Wette's theory of the origin of Deuteronomy in the reign of Josiah simply does not square with the internal evidence furnished by the text itself. The legislation it contains could never have arisen under the conditions which prevailed in the late seventh century B.C. The social, economic, and historical situation reflected by this book is quite different from that of Josiah's time. While none of these scholars could on philosophic grounds entertain the possibility of actual Mosaic authorship, their critique of Wellhausen's doctrinaire position has certainly left the date of Deuteronomic composition up in the air. Some have argued for a postexilic period, and others for a much earlier date. (Welch suggested the reign of Solomon, and Robertson the reign of David.) But they have at least agreed in condemning 621 B.C. as quite impossible for the composition of this last book in the Pentateuch.[1]

In the last two decades, however, considerable study has been directed toward the structure of the suzerainty treaties drawn up between vassal kings and their imperial overlords in the days of the Hittite ascendancy, in the latter half of the second millennium. As Meredith Kline points out, the typical suzerainty treaty of the Hittite period consisted of the following parts: (1) preamble (Deut. 1:1-5); (2) historical prologue (Deut. 1:6–4:49); (3) the stipulations or main provisions of the treaty (Deut. 5-26); (4) curses and blessings, or covenant-ratification (Deut. 27-30); (5) arrangements for succession, or continuation of the covenant (with invocation of witnesses and disposition of the text, and the periodic reading of the treaty before the public—cf. Deut. 31:33).[2] As contrasted with the second millennium treaties, those of the first millennium tend to vary in the order of the sections above specified, and they generally lacked section 2 (the historical prologue), or the blessings for covenant-faithfulness in section 4. G. E. Mendenhall remarks that it has been established that Deuteronomy conforms to the treaty structure of the second millennium, and hence this "covenant type is even more important as a starting point, because it cannot be proven to have survived the downfall of the great empires of the second millennium B.C. The older form of the covenant was no longer widely known after the United Monarchy."[3]

---

1. R. K. Harrison rightly points out that the command to build an altar on Mt. Ebal, up in North Israel (Deut. 27:1-8), precludes a date in Josiah's reign, or indeed at any period in Judah after 931 B.C. (IOT, p. 221).

2. Kline, *Treaty of the Great King* (Grand Rapids: Eerdmans, 1963), p. 28.

3. Mendenhall, "Covenant Forms in Israelite Tradition" in *Biblical Archaeologist* 17:3 (May 1954):50-76. Compare also Lasor, Hubbard, and Bush, *Old Testament Survey*, Eerdmans, 1982, p. 59, "Note that it is in the genre of the suzerain-vassal treaty form, whose comparison with the Mosaic covenant has been so fruitful, that one finds precisely this combination of history (in the historical prologue) and law (in the stipulations). Surely the correlation between this striking feature of the Pentateuch's form and the structure of one of its most important constituents, the Mosaic covenant, cannot be accidental!"

On Conservative presuppositions, it is possible to establish a very strong case for the Mosaic authorship of Deuteronomy. By the test of agreement with known historical conditions and by careful literary analysis, it is not difficult to show that only the pre-Davidic period can successfully be reconciled with the data of the Hebrew text. It can be shown by a fair handling of the evidence: (*a*) that Deuteronomy must have been written prior to the rise of the writing prophets in the eighth century B.C.; (*b*) that it also antedates the division of the Hebrew monarchy into Judah and Israel in 931 B.C.; (*c*) that it best agrees with a period near the conquest under Joshua. A very able reexamination of this evidence has been produced by the late G. T. Manley, demonstrating with most compelling logic that the data of the text itself preclude a post-Mosaic origin.[4] A few of the most significant arguments he advances will be found briefly summarized in the ensuing paragraphs of this chapter.

But before examining this positive evidence, it would be well to rebut some of the standard "proofs" of post-Mosaic authorship based upon allegedly "telltale" phrases or turns of expression found in the text itself. The first of these is "as at this day" (*kayyôwm hazzeh*), which occurs for example in 2:30. This phrase has been interpreted to mean that a great period of time has elapsed since the days of Moses, doubtless many centuries. But on what basis must this lapse of time be assumed? In virtually every instance where this phrase occurs, it fits in perfectly with the situation which would have existed in the closing days of Moses as he addressed the assembled host of Israel on the plains of Moab. Looking back over the vista of forty years (the period of the wilderness wanderings), it would have been altogether appropriate for him to add that the consequences of the episode or transaction mentioned still persisted until this closing year of his life. No real difficulty is presented by any of the six occurrences of this phrase: 2:30, the permanency of Sihon's conquest; 4:20, the continuance of Israel as the covenant nation; 4:38, "as at this day" refers to their imminent conquest of Canaan as their inheritance; 8:18 is prospective, for the hope is that God's favor in the future may continue as it is right now in Moses' time; 10:15 refers to the permanency of God's choice of Israel as His people; 29:28 has a prophetic perspective as it predicts a future judgment upon the disobedient nation.

A second "telltale" phrase is "beyond the Jordan," when it refers to the region east of the Jordan valley (as for example in 1:1). It is urged that if this work has really been composed in Moab, "on the other side of the Jordan" (*'ēber hayyardēn*) could only refer to Canaan proper. The fact that it demonstrably does refer to the eastern region of Gilead, Reuben, and Gad is said to prove that the author must have lived in Judah or Israel proper. But this is not the only possible inference by any means. As a matter of fact, *'ēber hayyardēn* occasionally refers to the region west of Jordan as well, in at least three other passages (3:20, 25; 11:30).[5] This would indicate an author residing in the

---

4. Manley, *Deuteronomy—the Book of the Law.*

5. Harrison finds only six cases in Deuteronomy where "beyond the Jordan" refers to the east side: Deut. 1:1, 5; 4:41 (twice), 47, and 49. He notes that Joshua 9:1 uses it to refer to the west side, even though in this case the narrator is admittedly on the west side (IOT, p. 637). We find the same usage in Josh. 22:7.

east, such as Moses in the plains of Moab. How are these variant uses of the phrase to be reconciled? By taking '*ēber hayyardēn* as a proper noun like *Transjordania*—a name attached to the land back in patriarchal times or earlier by the Palestinian population and adopted even by the inhabitants of the Transjordan region itself. Observe that during the British mandate over this territory (subsequent to World War I) the area was known as "Transjordania" even to those who lived in it, though "Transjordania" means "On the other side of Jordan." In New Testament times the lower part of this region, at least, was known as "Peraea" (The Other-side Land) even to its own inhabitants. It is a reasonable supposition that the term '*ēber hayyardēn* had become a standard designation for the territory to the east of Jericho regardless of where the speaker happened to be. In those three instances, however, where the phrase refers to Canaanland west of the Jordan, we are to understand this as used in its literal and obvious sense rather than as a geographical name.

So far as this writer is aware, there are no expressions in the text of Deuteronomy which are not perfectly reconcilable with Mosaic authorship. Only chapter 34 is demonstrably post-Mosaic, since it contains a short account of Moses' decease. But this does not endanger in the slightest the Mosaic authenticity of the other thirty-three chapters, for the closing chapter furnishes only that type of obituary which is often appended to the final work of great men of letters. An author's final work is often published posthumously (provided he has been writing up to the time of his death). Since Joshua is recorded to have been a faithful and zealous custodian of the Torah, Moses' literary achievement, it is quite unthinkable that he would have published it without appending such a notice of the decease of his great predecessor.[6]

EVIDENCE FOR THE PRIORITY OF DEUTERONOMY TO THE EIGHTH-CENTURY PROPHETS

The most characteristic title for God in Deuteronomy is "Yahweh thy God." If the book was composed in the seventh century or thereafter, it might be expected to reflect the theological terminology of the great prophets like Amos, Hosea, Isaiah, and Micah, who formulated classic Hebrew theology in the previous century. At the very least a Josianic work should have reflected the divine titles most in vogue during the ministry of Jeremiah, Josiah's contemporary. But the actual statistics show quite the contrary: (1) Hosea employs "Yahweh their God" only four times, as against fifteen occurrences of *Elōhîm* (God) alone and thirty-five occurrences of *Yahweh* alone. (2) Isaiah 1-35 employs "Yahweh their God" only three times, as over against very frequent occurrences of "Yahweh of hosts" and "the holy One of Israel." (3) Jeremiah characteristically uses the title "LORD of Hosts" (or Yahweh of hosts—Heb.) and seldom

---

6. Interestingly enough the same phenomenon occurs in the terminal writings of some of the modern higher critics themselves. For example, at the end of Roland de Vaux's *Archaeology and Dead Sea Scrolls*. published by Oxford in 1973 there is a brief comment by Kathleen Kenyon: "It is sad that Roland deVaux did not live to see the translation of his *Schweich Lectures appear*." But obviously this does not prove that de Vaux was not the real author of the rest of the book.

employs the Deuteronomic formula. The same is true with the post-exilic prophets Haggai, Zechariah, and Malachi. If, therefore, Deuteronomy was composed in the time of Josiah just before the Exile, or in the time of Ezra after the Exile (as Hoelscher and Kennett have argued), it is very difficult to account for its employment of a divine title which was not in vogue in either of those two periods. Especially is this true of the title "Yahweh the God of your fathers," which occurs frequently enough in Deuteronomy but never appears in either the pre-exilic or post-exilic prophets; yet it is to be found in Ex. 3:6 ("I am the God of thy father, the God of Abraham, the God of Isaac, and the God of Jacob") and an adaptation of it also in Ex. 15:2 and 18:4.

It was contended by the Wellhausen school that Deuteronomy shows a knowledge of the history and legislation contained in J and E, but not that of P.[7] Manley proceeds to show by comparative tables that this supposed ignorance of P is not borne out in actual fact. He asks the question, "If the Deuteronomic code were an 'expansion' of that in J–E, why should more than three-quarters of it have been omitted? Have burglary and theft ceased? Would not the laws protecting a slave (Ex. 21:22ff., 26ff.) have made a special appeal to an author who elsewhere is so concerned to protect the weak? Again, why should these old laws in Table B [this refers to a set of laws relating to idolatry, false witness, rights of the firstborn, etc., bearing some resemblance to provisions in the Hammurabic Code, but not discoverable in J-E at all], similar in type to the others, have remained so long unrecorded?...We are forced to the conclusion that the legislation of Deuteronomy is not an 'expansion' of the covenant code. Neither can it be attributed, as some scholars have maintained, to the old Canaanite civil law. There are marked differences between the Deuteronomic laws and those found in the Ras Shamra Tablets;...this suggests that [the Deuteronomic code] was fixed before the settlement in Canaan, and there are signs of strong reaction against Canaanite influence."[8] Again, in the case of leprosy, Deut. 24:8 tells the people "to take heed...and do all that the priests the Levites shall teach you; as I commanded them." Plainly, these words assume that the priestly law was already in existence, yet it is found only in P (Lev. 13-14). How can it be said that the author of Deuteronomy knew nothing about P?

Of course it could be argued that P has simply borrowed from D, but it should be remembered that much of the ground for dating D before P was based on the contention that D contained nothing distinctively priestly. If therefore it turns out that D does in fact contain substantial material otherwise peculiar to P, the basis for dating D earlier than P falls to the ground. (This of course has been recognized by those who insist that D also is post-exilic; but it leaves the point difficult to establish what book of the law it was that Hilkiah found in the temple in 621 B.C., if not even D was in existence at that time!)

In addition to the objections to Josianic dating raised by the critics mentioned in

7. Cf. Driver in ICC on Deut. 14.
8. Manley, p. 80.

chapter 7 (p. 105), we should observe how incongruent Deut. 16:21-22[9] is with the conditions existing during the reign of Josiah. Here we have a law which contemplates the making of more than one altar to Yahweh (a natural possibility prior to the erection of the temple), and therefore, like Deut. 27:1-8, creates a real difficulty for those who understand D to have been composed for the promotion of Josiah's program (i.e., that all valid worship must be carried on in the one center at Jerusalem). Note also that the special objects of Josiah's reform, the K*mārîm (the idol priests), the bāmôt (high places with their temples or shrines), and the bronze horses dedicated to the sun-god— all these receive no mention whatsoever in Deuteronomy. The state of affairs contemplated, then, in the book of Moses simply cannot be squared with the known historical conditions of the seventh century B.C.

EVIDENCE FOR THE PRIORITY OF DEUTERONOMY TO THE DIVISION OF THE MONARCHY

The text of Deuteronomy contains many references to the sinister nature of Canaanite influence upon the purity of Israel's religion. All the Canaanite shrines are to be completely demolished, and no trace is to be left of altar, asherah, or pillar. All the cultic practices pertaining to their pagan faith are to be sedulously avoided, such as boiling a kid in its mother's milk, or shaving the beard, or gashing the flesh in devotion to some heathen deity. These numerous provisions against the survival of Canaanite customs or shrines suggest a danger which still threatens the author's generation. It certainly seems as if it is a future menace to be dealt with, rather than an element of corruption that has already endured for centuries.

Of pivotal significance is the manner in which the Israelite tribes are referred to. If Deuteronomy had been composed subsequent to the schism of 931 B.C., it is hardly conceivable that no reference or allusion to this breach should have found its way into the text, yet as a matter of fact, where these tribes are mentioned they are represented as separate entities but all included in the single nation of Israel (cf. 1:13, 15; 5:23; 12:5, 14; 29:10; 31:28). The author of these passages betrays no awareness whatsoever of the cleavage between Judah and Ephraim.

EVIDENCE FOR THE COMPOSITION OF DEUTERONOMY PRIOR TO THE CONQUEST

In the earlier chapters of Deuteronomy particularly, there are numerous appeals to the hearers to recall past episodes and conditions which are within the memory of those who are being addressed. The memory of the Egyptian bondage is especially vivid. Six times the phrase occurs, "the house of bondage"; five times we read, "Remember that thou wast a bondman in the land of Egypt"; five times the formula appears, "through a mighty hand and by a stretched out arm." This last phrase, by the

---

9. Deut. 16:21-22 states, "You shall not plant for yourself an Ashērah of any kind of tree beside the altar of the Lord your God, which you shall make for yourself." In connection with Deut. 27:5 note also that an altar of unhewn stones was required for worship on Mt. Ebal.

way, occurs also in Ex. 6:1 (a J-E passage) and in Ex. 6:6 (a P passage), and is analogous to an expression which often occurs in Old Egyptian texts describing scenes of battle.[10]

Any theory of the origin of Deuteronomy must take account of the fact that the land of Canaan to the west of the Jordan is always viewed from the outside so far as the author's standpoint is concerned. Whether from the southern border or from the east and the Moabite highlands, the viewpoint is always that of a newcomer contemplating invasion, never that of an inhabitant who already dwells within its borders. Border cities such as Eshcol (1:24) and Gaza (2:23) are named, rather than such central locations as Hebron; and when the limits of the land of promise are indicated, they are described by such terms as "the mount of the Amorites" and "Lebanon" (1:7), not by the later terminology "from Dan to Beersheba," which would have been used after the Danite migration.

So far as the legislation is concerned, we have already observed a certain substratum of fundamental law which the Mosaic provisions contained in common with the Hammurabic Code, yet the contrasts between the two are even more significant than the similarities. For example, the Babylonian code makes a sharp class distinction between the free man (*awēlum*) and the semifree (*mushkēnum*), as well as the slave (*wardum*). In Deuteronomy there is virtually no class distinction, and social conditions correspond to those of a far more rural and agricultural community than was the case in Babylon (or in Israel of David's era). More significant still, Mosaic legislation had a deeply religious tone. The statutes of judgment were said to be those of Yahweh their God, and the Israelites were to observe them with all their heart and soul. Of the 346 verses which make up Deut. 12-26, more than half are moral and religious in character, while 93 of them are taken up with specific commands related to the approaching settlement in the land. It should be noted that the exhortations, warnings, and promises of blessing which are so characteristic of Deuteronomy are completely lacking in the Babylonian code. Note also that in the text of Hammurabi we find a strictly impersonal style such as would be usual for a sophisticated legal system pertaining to a more urbanized society. In Deuteronomy, however, we seem to be listening to an old and honored leader speaking to the people whom he has personally guided through many years, and reminding them of the experiences they have shared together.

We know enough about the Babylonia of Hammurabi's period to recognize that these were in fact the conditions when those laws were promulgated after centuries of monarchic rule. In the later years of the Hebrew monarchy, the conditions in Palestine must have approximated those in Babylon, for by that time trade and industry were well developed and class distinctions were strongly marked. Trades and crafts were regulated on a commercial basis, with money fines specified to indemnify property owners who suffered injury or loss. In Deuteronomy, however, we find no laws providing compensation for loss caused by careless builders or for injury to health due to incompetent physicians. This legislation is suited rather to a simple, agricultural people

---

10. Cf. A. S. Yahuda, *Language of the Pentateuch*, p. 68.

A CANAANITE SACRIFICIAL ALTAR OF LIMESTONE FROM MEGIDDO (10–9 C. B.C.) HT. 21 IN. THE STRATEGIC IMPORTANCE OF THIS CITY (ITS SIZE, STRENGTH AND WATER SUPPLY) HAS BEEN ARCHAEOLOGICALLY CONFIRMED. THE HEATHEN ALTAR DATES TO 2800 B.C.

deeply interested in their cattle; food and raiment are the chief concerns.

Lastly we revert once more to the incompatibility of Josiah's time with the type of legislation found in Deuteronomy regarding the preservation of Israel's faith. Deut. 13:1-18 and 17:2-5 decree the death penalty for apostasy or for inciting others to forsake the nation's covenant with Yahweh. It is hard to conceive of such laws being planned or revived during the time of Manasseh (Josiah's grandfather). There is no actual mention of them in connection with Josiah's reform. Even Driver is forced to the conclusion that "the time when they could have been enforced had long passed away; they had consequently only an ideal value" (*Deuteronomy*, in ICC, p. xxxii). But, as H. M. Wiener has pointed out, idealists may perhaps propose a lofty standard on a general basis, but they scarcely go so far as to lay down a specific procedure for handling the violations of the ideal. Yet in both these passages, a very definite procedure is prescribed, and that in chapter 13 particularly presupposes primitive conditions. The lawgiver here evidently relies upon the cooperation of the nation as a whole to carry out the sanction of this law, even if it entails civil warfare. Deut. 12:2-4 enjoins the destruction of all the Canaanite shrines "on every high hill and under every green tree," with all of their "pillars" and "asherim." Apparently the author regarded this destruction as both practical and possible in his time. He insisted that the land must be cleared of these idolatrous symbols before acceptable worship could be offered to Yahweh. Such an attitude would be quite inconceivable in the seventh century B.C., or indeed in earlier centuries subsequent to the time of Solomon, when idolatrous cults had penetrated to every level of Israelite society. Even the record of the book of Judges, pertaining to a time prior to the establishment of the monarchy, implies the existence of these Deuteronomic provisions. Thus the action of Gideon (Judg. 6:25-32) in destroying the altar and precinct of Baal suggests that he knew of some such injunction, and his father's defense of this deed implies that he supposed his son was doing the right thing.

Despite the efforts of Kennett and Hoelscher to find an appropriate historical setting in the post-exilic period of Ezra and Nehemiah, it is far easier to harmonize the historical and social conditions presupposed by Deuteronomy with what must have been the case in the time of the original conquest rather than in the period of the restoration. In Ezra's time, the Canaanites and Amorites were an all but forgotten memory, and the new Jewish commonwealth was threatened by such foreigners as the Ammonites, Philistines, and various other peoples who had little if any ethnic relationship to the original inhabitants of Canaan. Moreover, the confident tone of the author of Deuteronomy, who looks forward to irresistible conquest of the entire territory from Dan to Beersheba, is incapable of reconciliation with the discouraging and limited circumstances which confronted the tiny Persian province of Judea after the return from Babylon. In Deuteronomy we discover an attitude of glowing optimism which finds expression in the series of blessings appropriate to a people of the Lord about to settle in a new land in which no opposition can stand before them. It is a land which has been well cultivated and productive of fruits, and able to support its inhabitants on a most generous scale. This can scarcely be reconciled with the stripped and devastated land bereft of inhabitants, bare of fortifications, denuded of vineyards and fruit orchards, which confronted the returning immigrants from Babylon. Here again, then, the test of internal evidence points quite unmistakably to the time of the conquest, around 1400 B.C., rather than to any of the dates suggested by modern criticism.

Before taking our leave of Deuteronomy, a final comment should be made concerning the remarkable predictions embodied in chapter 28, beginning with verse 49. The Documentarians have interpreted these to refer to the invasions of Assyrian and Chaldean oppressors, and hence have insisted that that passage itself could not have been composed until the time of Josiah or the Exile. But a closer examination of the details reveals the inadequacy of this explanation, even from a rationalistic standpoint. It is quite clear in the light of subsequent history that only the Roman invasions of A.D. 70 and A.D. 135 satisfy the terms of this prophecy. Consider the following factors: (1) The invaders are to come "from the end of the earth" (v. 49)—far more appropriate to Rome than to Babylon. (2) Their language will be utterly alien to Hebrew—far truer of Latin than of Babylonian, a kindred Semitic tongue (v. 49). (3) The Jews are to be scattered among the nations, from one end of the earth to the other (v. 64)—which did not take place at the Chaldean conquest by any manner of means. (4) There is no suggestion whatever that there will be a return to Palestine by a remnant—as there was within a few decades of Nebuchadnezzar's death. (5) The captive Jews are to be conveyed to Egypt in huge numbers by ship, and prove to be a glut on the slave market—a development which never took place in connection with the Chaldean conquest, but which was literally fulfilled after Jerusalem fell to the legions of Titus in A.D. 70. (Josephus indicates that 97,000 prisoners were taken at the fall of Jerusalem, and many of them ended up in the Egyptian mines.)[11] The conclusion is irresistible that this prediction could only have come by supernatural revelation, and that its fulfillment took place centuries later than the Wellhausian date for the latest stratum of the Pentateuch.

RELIGIOUS OBSERVANCES

OBSERVANCE	SIGNIFICANCE (or purpose)	SCRIPTURE
Sabbath (*sabbaṯ šabbāṯôn*)	Day of rest in celebration of God's completed work of creation	Ex. 20:8-11 Ex. 31:12-17 Lev. 23:11-12
Sabbatic Year	Rest for the land agriculturally; Renunciation of debts	Ex. 23:10-11 Lev. 25:2-7
Year of Jubilee (*šanaṯ yôbēl*)	Rest for the land; Reversion of property	Lev. 25:8-16 Lev. 27:16-25
New Moon (*r'ōs ḥôdeš*)	Monthly offering for atonement	Num. 10:10 Num. 28:1-15

THE THEORY OF A DEUTERONOMIC SCHOOL

Ever since the days of Wilhelm De Wette (1805) it has become axiomatic for adherents to the Documentary Hypothesis to date the formation of the book of Deuteronomy in official public form as coming from the time of King Josiah in 621 B.C., a good 800 years after the death of the purported author. We have already discussed the indefensible nature of this hypothesis in the light of internal and external evidence. But inasmuch as scholars trained in the Wellhausen approach shield themselves from giving any honest consideration of the difficulties precluding the adoption of this theory, they naturally extend the implications of a Josianic date to all of the historical books and of prophets like Jeremiah as the members of a "Deuteronomic School." It is only natural, therefore, that a modern myth should arise under the title of "The Deuteronomist." This term presumably refers to the author or authors of the canonical book of Deuteronomy, but this Deuteronomic tradition seems to have permeated the thinking and outlook of various prophets and historians who were active during the seventh and sixth century B.C.

---

11. Josephus, *Wars of the Jews*, 6. 9.

The proof adduced for the origin of Deuteronomy in the time of Josiah is deduced from references and phrases of a Deuteronomic character which are found in the writings of these various authors. The logic is that if Deuteronomy is quoted in the seventh century, it must have originated in that same period. But from the standpoint of legal evidence this argument proves to be patently fallacious. It is only natural that in the writings of speakers and authors brought up in a given religious or literary tradition extending back to earlier times, such an authoritative scripture would be quoted or alluded to by authors who became active several centuries later. Who can doubt that the Quran originated with Mohammed in the early seventh century A.D.? Yet by the Documentarian logic, almost any period in subsequent Islamic history would exhibit fully as much awareness of the teachings and pronouncements of the Quran as the Josianic authors made of Deuteronomy or the other books of the Torah. One might as well allege that the Bible originated in the Elizabethan era, because it is so much alluded to or quoted from in the days of Shakespeare and Milton or the Puritan divines. In other words, we are dealing with a complete *non sequitur* which would never stand up in a court of law.

19 JOSHUA, JUDGES, AND RUTH

JOSHUA

APPROPRIATELY ENOUGH, this book is named after its principal character, Joshua, who dominates the scene from start to finish. His name in the longer Hebrew form appears as *Yᵉhōshûᵃ* (יהושע); in the Septuagint *Yēsūs*, or "Jesus." The narrative records the history of Israel from the passage of Joshua's army over the river Jordan to Joshua's final retirement and farewell speech. The theme of the book concerns the irresistible power of God's people in overcoming the world and taking permanent possession of their promised inheritance, provided only they maintain a perfect trust in God's strength and permit no sin of disobedience to break their covenant relationship with Him.

OUTLINE OF JOSHUA

I. Conquest of the land, 1:1–12:24

A. Joshua's divine commission, 1:1-9
B. Preparations to cross the Jordan; the spies rescued through Rahab, 1:10–2:24
C. The crossing of the Jordan River, 3:1–4:24
D. Circumcision at Gilgal, 5:1-15
E. Capture of Jericho, the assurance of victory, 6:1–27
F. Failure at Ai; the putting away of sin; the ultimate triumph, 7:1–8:29
G. The altar at Mount Ebal; the solemn reading of the law, 8:30-35
H. The alliance with the crafty Gibeonites (the first entanglement with the world), 9:1-27
I. Conquest of southern Canaan; the battle of Gibeon, 10:1-43
J. Conquest of northern Canaan, 11:1-15
K. Summary of Joshua's campaigns, 11:16–12:24

II. Dividing of the inheritance, 13:1–22:34

A. Joshua's instructions concerning the division, 13:1-7
B. Assignment to the eastern tribes, 13:8-33
C. Assignment to the western tribes, 14:1–19:51

D. Appointment of the cities of refuge, 20:1-9

E. Appointment of the Levitical cities, 21:1-45

F. Eastern tribes dismissed to their homes in Transjordan, 22:1-34

III. Joshua's final charge to Israel, 23:1–24:33

As R. K. Harrison observes, "The Hebrew text of the book of Joshua is in quite good condition, and seldom requires emendation. The LXX version indicates attempts to expand the Hebrew through the addition of words and phrases. Certain LXX manuscripts such as *Codex Vaticanus* exhibit wide variations, and may possibly represent an independent textual tradition from that of the MT. The Lucianic recension of the LXX appears to have been corrected by reference to Palestinian Hebrew sources" (R. K. Harrison, *Old Testament Introduction*, p. 678).

AUTHORSHIP AND DATE

It is reasonable to deduce that this book was largely composed by Joshua himself. Intimate biographical details are given from the very first chapter that only Joshua himself could have known (although of course he could have later imparted them to others). Joshua 24:26 records that the general himself wrote out his own farewell charge as quoted in the first twenty-five verses of the chapter. Earlier in the book (5:1, 6) we find passages in the first person plural, such as, "Jehovah had dried up the waters of the Jordan from before the children of Israel, until we were passed over." Such language as this certainly points to the work of an eyewitness who participated in the events himself.[1]

Other references point to a very early date of composition, even if not precisely within the lifetime of Joshua. Canaanite cities are mentioned by their archaic names; for example, Baalah for Kirjath-jearim (15:9), Kirjath-sannah for Debir (15:49) and Kirjath-arba for Hebron (15:13). Moreover, according to 13:4-6 and 19:28, Sidon was the most important city of Phoenicia, thus indicating a period before the twelfth century B.C. (when Tyre began to attain the ascendancy). According to 9:27, the Gibeonites "unto this day" were still "hewers of wood and drawers of water" around the tabernacle, even as Joshua had appointed them. This could no longer have been said in the reign of Saul, if we may trust the indication of 2 Sam. 21:1-9, that some of the Gibeonites had been massacred and their special status changed by King Saul. Certainly the references to Jerusalem (such as 18:16, 28) show very clearly that at the time of writing it was inhabited by the Jebusites and had not yet been captured by the Hebrews under King David.

On the other hand, there is evidence of later editorial work in the inclusion of

---

1. Note, however, that the *Kethib* '-B-R-N-W was altered by the Masoretic *Qerē* to '-B-R-M (which changes the reading "we passed over" to "their passing over"). This latter conforms to the interpretation of the Septuagint, the Latin Vulgate, and other versions. Even some Hebrew manuscripts have this reading. Yet no ancient witness exists to delete or alter the *L-N-W* ("to us") after "to give" in v. 6, and therefore the MT reading ("we passed over") would seem to be more likely in 5:1.

THE "POOL OF GIBEON" IS A CYLINDRICAL PIT APPROXIMATELY 37 FT. WIDE AND 35 FT. DEEP. IT HAS STAIRS DESCENDING TO THE BOTTOM OF THE PIT, WHERE ADDITIONAL STEPS LEAD TO A WATER CHAMBER 45 FT. BELOW.

events which could not have occurred until after Joshua's death. Not only do we have the notice of his decease (24:29-30) and the generalization that "Israel served the Lord all the days of Joshua, and all the days of the elders who lived after Joshua" (24:31), but we also find reference to Othniel's capture of Kirjath-arba (15:13-17; Judg. 1:9-13) and the migration of a portion of the Danite tribe to the extreme north of Israel (19:47; cf. Judg. 18:27-29). Taking all this evidence together, it seems to point to substantial composition of Joshua by the man after whom the book was named, and supplementary material (also inspired) very likely by Eleazar or his son Phinehas.

As we have already seen (chap. 6, p. 89), rationalist critics of the Wellhausen school have attempted to include Joshua with the five books of the Pentateuch, calling the whole collection the Hexateuch. They consider the basic material to come from J and E, but with considerable editorial work and redaction by the "Deuteronomic School." Later editorial work is thought to have been contributed by a redactor of the priestly school, who made his major insertions in chapters 13-21. But it should be pointed out that the biblical evidence makes it very difficult to hold that the Pentateuch never had any separate existence apart from Joshua.

The most significant evidence is found in the fact that only the Pentateuch was held by the Samaritan sect to be canonical. We know from the Samaritan form of the

Pentateuchal text that these northern sectarians even in post-exilic times considered themselves to be heirs of the Israelite ten tribes. Many of the deviations from the Masoretic Text of the five books of Moses consist of additions which make it explicit that God had chosen Mount Gerizim in the Ephraimite territory to be the place for His holy sanctuary, rather than the southern center of Jerusalem. Obviously the motivation for this is nationalistic propaganda, but the book of Joshua contains many elements which would have commended it to Samaritan nationalism. For example, it makes prominent mention of Shechem in Ephraim as an important center and a city of refuge. Its chief hero is an Ephraimite general, Joshua the son of Nun. It contains a record of the solemn reading of the law by the whole congregation of Israel between Mount Ebal and Mount Gerizim. Therefore the only possible explanation for the failure of the Samaritans to include *Joshua* in their authoritative canon was that it was not actually a part of the Mosaic Torah. The Torah must, therefore, have existed as a separate Pentateuch at the time of the Samaritan schism in the late 6th century B.C.

THE PLAIN OF JEZREEL (ESDRAELON) IS THE LARGEST VALLEY IN ISRAEL, CUTTING SOUTH-EASTWARD BETWEEN THE MOUNTAINS OF GALILEE TO THE NORTH AND THE MOUNTAINS OF SAMARIA TO THE SOUTH. THE JEZREEL VALLEY IS VERY FERTILE, BUT AT TIMES, IT BECAME QUITE MARSHY DUE TO THE FLOW OF THE RIVER KISHON THROUGH IT, ESPECIALLY IN THE WINTER. THIS VALLEY, AS THE VALLEY OF MEGIDDO, IS THE PREDICTED SITE OF THE BATTLE OF ARMAGEDDON (REV. 16:16).

THE TELL EL-AMARNA CORRESPONDENCE

In 1887 an accidental discovery led to the unearthing of an entire file of ancient diplomatic correspondence at the site of the ancient Akhetaton (Tell el-Amarna), the newly built capital of King Amenhotep IV (Akhnaton). These letters were written on clay tablets in Babylonian cuneiform, which was the accepted language for international correspondence during the Egyptian Eighteenth Dynasty. A preliminary examination of the contents of these tablets convinced C. R. Conder that they represented a Canaanite version of the sequence of events connected with the conquest of Canaan by the armies of Joshua. In 1890 he brought this correspondence to the attention of the public in the *Palestine Exploration Quarterly,* in an article entitled "Monumental Notice of Hebrew Victories." In the same year, H. Zimmern categorically affirmed that in the Amarna correspondence we have nothing less than a contemporary record of the Hebrew invasion of Canaan (in the *Zeitschrift des deutschen Palästinavereins*). These early investigators pointed out the frequent occurrence of the name "Ḫabiru" in the communications from King 'Abdi-Ḫepa of Jerusalem, who reported to the pharaoh with the greatest alarm that these invaders were carrying everything before them. Further study of the tablets convinced H. Winckler that marauding armies associated with the cuneiform characters SA.GAZ were to be equated with the Ḫabiru. Very frequent references to these SA.GAZ people are to be found in the communications of Canaanite princelings all the way up to Sidon in Phoenicia.

Later discoveries at Mari and Nuzi, as well as at Babylon, revealed the fact that Ḫabiru figured in the history of the Mesopotamian valley as early as the beginning of the second millennium B.C. They are referred to in the Sumerian inscriptions of Rim-Sin of Larsa and in Akkadian texts from Hammurabi's Babylon and Zimri-Lim's Mari, as well as of Warad-Sin and Rim-Sin of the Elamite dynasty. Often the name is preceded by the determinative meaning "warrior." Hittite and Old Babylonian texts indicate that contingents of the SA.GAZ received regular rations from the state, manned royal garrisons, and worshiped gods who were invoked in state treaties. The Hittite texts from Boghazköi furnish evidence that the Ḫabiru and the SA.GAZ are the one and the same people, for each form of the name appears in parallel columns of bilingual texts, and the gods of the SA.GAZ are there referred to as the gods of the Ḫabiri. In the Mari correspondence they appear as mercenary troops in the employ of leaders like Yapaḫ-Adad (cf. ANET, p. 483).

It is not certain how the characters SA.GAZ were pronounced, whether as Ḫabiru or by some such term as Ḫabbatu ("plunderer, robber") as is given in the ancient dictionaries. Many scholars have conjectured that SA.GAZ represented an appellative or descriptive term rather than the name of any particular tribe or people; whereas Ḫabiru referred to a definite ethnic group. Others, however, have rejected an ethnic significance even for Ḫabiru because of the great diversity in types of names which are attributed to individuals listed as Ḫabiri. Many of those from Old Babylonian sources and those at Nuzi are Akkadian Semitic names, but those from Alalakh are mostly non-Semitic.

In the light of the foregoing evidence, it may reasonably be questioned whether the Ḫabiru were a definite, homogeneous race, or whether the name was attached to migratory groups of people who possessed no real property and were not attached to the soil like the general populace of the land in which they happened to reside. Thus they may have been a group somewhat akin to the gypsies of modern times whose racial background is shrouded in mystery, but whose common characteristic is that they never settle down in one place, preferring to wander from region to region as they may find a living. This at least is the theory advanced by Moshe Greenberg in his monograph entitled, "the Ḫab/piru" (New Haven, Conn.: American Oriental Society, 1955). He thus would account for their appearance as mercenaries in the employ of foreign governments or as dependents who hired themselves out as serfs or slaves. Apparently the etymology for the name Ḫabiru points to the basic significance of "one who passes over" or "one who passes through (the land)," coming from the verb *'ābar* ("to pass through").

It is open to question, however, whether the term Ḫabiru necessarily connoted inferior social status. Meredith Kline points out that in some cases, as at Alalakh, the Ḫabiri are found at the head of city administration as government officials, or else as chariot-owning *maryannu* (the highest of the warrior castes).[2] Peace treaties were made with them, which would hardly have been effected with a mere dependent or servile populace. Kline personally regards the Ḫabiri as a more or less homogeneous ethnic stock of warrior tribes, who sold their services as mercenaries, and in some cases (like the Goths of the late Roman empire) settled down to become landowners and officials. In some instances, as at Alalakh, they became so culturally integrated with the people among whom they lived that they even adopted the non-Semitic personal names prevalent in that locality. He feels that they were largely allied with the Hurrian or Mitannian governments, and thus respected by them, even though they were feared and shunned in many non-Hurrian regions. Kline does not believe that they can successfully be linked with the Israelite Hebrews either ethnically, religiously, or culturally.[3] But this conclusion hardly does justice to the data of the Amarna Letters.

Discoveries at Ugarit make it evident that Ḫabiru were the same people referred to as the 'Apiru in Egyptian records. A text published by Virolleaud contains a list of towns subject to provide corvèe labor for the king of Ugarit; and this bilingual text shows on the Akkadian side, "Aleppo of the SA.GAZ" (Ḫal-bi [lu-mes SAG-GAZ]), and on the Ugaritic side, reads: "Aleppo of the 'Apirim" (Ḫlb 'prm). Apparently it was possible by dialectic modification to pronounce the middle *b* of Ḫabiru or 'Abiru as a *p*, for so it appeared in Ugaritic and also in Egyptian. Hence the Ḫabiru were "people from the other side," or "migrants," and this term may have been applied to those of diverse national origin. It is only in the Hebrew records that we find the name in the form *'ibrî* (Hebrew) used to refer to a single racial stock, namely the descendants of Abraham, "the Hebrew." Thus Abraham may have been called "the Ḫabiru" by the Canaanites because of his mode of life and because he was a foreigner; but then his descendants retained this designation in honor of their ancestor and transmuted it into an ethnic term. Such an interpretation of the name Ḫabiru and its apparent equivalent, SA.GAZ, leaves room for the possibility that some non-Israelite peoples were involved in the convulsive movements of Joshua's time, and participated in the invasions of the northerly regions at least.

2. Kline, in *Westminster Theology Review* 12: 1: 1-24.
3. Ibid.,12:2: 170-84.

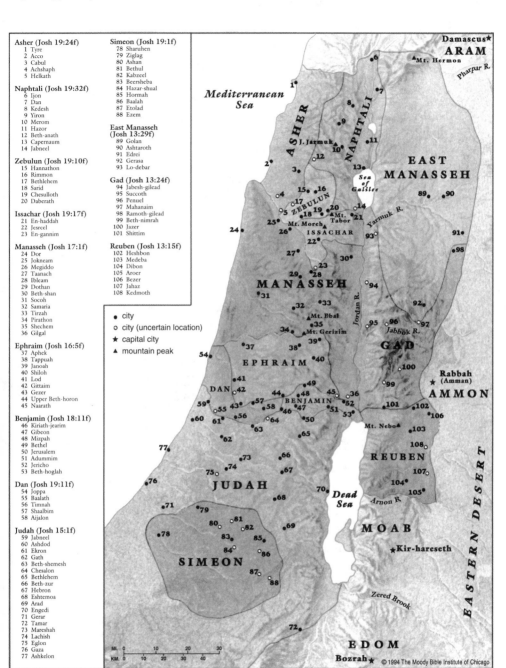

Asher (Josh 19:24f)
1 Tyre
2 Acco
3 Cabul
4 Achshaph
5 Helkath

Naphtali (Josh 19:32f)
6 Ijon
7 Dan
8 Kedesh
9 Yiron
10 Merom
11 Hazor
12 Beth-anath
13 Capernaum
14 Jabneel

Zebulun (Josh 19:10f)
15 Hannathon
16 Rimmon
17 Bethlehem
18 Sarid
19 Chesulloth
20 Daberath

Issachar (Josh 19:17f)
21 En-haddah
22 Jesreel
23 En-gannim

Manasseh (Josh 17:1f)
24 Dor
25 Jokneam
26 Megiddo
27 Taanach
28 Ibleam
29 Dothan
30 Beth-shan
31 Socoh
32 Samaria
33 Tirzah
34 Pirathon
35 Shechem
36 Gilgal

Ephraim (Josh 16:5f)
37 Aphek
38 Tappuah
39 Janoah
40 Shiloh
41 Lod
42 Gittaim
43 Gezer
44 Upper Beth-horon
45 Naarath

Benjamin (Josh 18:11f)
46 Kiriath-jearim
47 Gibeon
48 Mizpah
49 Bethel
50 Jerusalem
51 Adummim
52 Jericho
53 Beth-hoglah

Dan (Josh 19:11f)
54 Joppa
55 Baalath
56 Timnah
57 Shaalbim
58 Aijalon

Judah (Josh 15:1f)
59 Jabneel
60 Ashdod
61 Ekron
62 Gath
63 Beth-shemesh
64 Chesalon
65 Bethlehem
66 Beth-zur
67 Hebron
68 Eshtemoa
69 Arad
70 Engedi
71 Gerar
72 Tamar
73 Mareshah
74 Lachish
75 Eglon
76 Gaza
77 Ashkelon

Simeon (Josh 19:1f)
78 Sharuhen
79 Ziglag
80 Ashan
81 Bethul
82 Kabzeel
83 Beersheba
84 Hazar-shual
85 Hormah
86 Baalah
87 Etolad
88 Ezem

East Manasseh (Josh 13:29f)
89 Golan
90 Ashtaroth
91 Edrei
92 Gerasa
93 Lo-debar

Gad (Josh 13:24f)
94 Jabesh-gilead
95 Succoth
96 Penuel
97 Mahanaim
98 Ramoth-gilead
99 Beth-nimrah
100 Jazer
101 Shittim

Reuben (Josh 13:15f)
102 Heshbon
103 Medeba
104 Dibon
105 Aroer
106 Bezer
107 Jahaz
108 Kedmoth

• city
○ city (uncertain location)
★ capital city
▲ mountain peak

© 1994 The Moody Bible Institute of Chicago

THE BOUNDARIES OF THE LANDS DISTRIBUTED TO THE TWELVE TRIBES AFTER JOSHUA'S CONQUEST OF CANAAN.

Moshe Greenberg and many of his predecessors have rejected this identification of the Ḫabiru (SA.GAZ) with the Israelite invasion, both because of the diversity of names appearing in some of the Mesopotamian records, and also because of the reported activity of the SA.GAZ in Syria and Phoenicia. The objection is based on the ground that there is no allusion to any such northerly military operations in the Hebrew records. In answer to this it ought to be pointed out that there is nothing in Joshua to discourage the belief that the northernmost tribes, such as Asher and Naphtali, who settled right next to the Phoenician territory, may have conducted expeditions against Tyre, Sidon, and even Byblos (from which city most of the Phoenician correspondence is derived). Joshua does not pretend to list all the military operations into which the individual tribes entered after the major united campaigns had come to a close. This, then, is hardly a decisive objection to the identification of Ḫabiru with Hebrews. Other objections raised by Greenberg include the consideration that according to the Amarna correspondence it was possible for individuals or even a whole town to become Ḫabiri by deserting the Egyptian side.

For example, in the letter numbered 185 in the Mercer edition (J. A. Knudtzon, *Die El-Amarna Tafeln* [Leipzig: Hinrich, 1908-15], hereafter EA, 111:44), Rib-Addi declares that the inhabitants of Lachish have "become Ḫabiri." Even an Egyptian such as Amanḫatbi (Amenhotep) of Tushulti could escape reprisal for his misdeeds by fleeing to the SA.GAZ (EA 95:63). But it should be pointed out that these terms of expression do not necessarily signify the attainment of full citizenship, so to speak, in the ranks of the Ḫabiri, but may simply be a way of indicating a change of allegiance or the formation of a new alliance. Joshua records how the Gibeonite or Hivite league effected a treaty of peace with the conquering Israelites, although of course they did it by stratagem. There can be little doubt that other Canaanite communities made terms with the irresistible invaders in order to avoid total destruction. The Canaanite principalities which maintained the conflict against Israel were of course bitterly resentful of those who had gone over to their side, and they may well have referred to this maneuver as "becoming a Ḫabiru."

Greenberg also makes the observation that the SA.GAZ seem to have operated in relatively small, unrelated groups here and there throughout the land of Canaan, and thus do not present in any sense the same picture as the narrative in the book of Joshua, where we have great bodies of troops from all twelve tribes operating under a single command. But there are two things to be said about this observation. In the first place, the letters may have come from widely separate periods of time (for virtually none of them contain any dates) ranging all the way from 1400 B.C. to the latter part of the reign of Akhnaton. Those references to Ḫabiru activity which seem to imply the operation of smaller bodies of troops may have been written in the latter period after the main campaigns had been completed. Second, it should be observed that some of the letters give the very distinct impression that Ḫabiri have come into the land in great force and are subjugating large tracts of land at a time.

One noteworthy example of the latter type is EA No. 286 from Abdi-Ḫeba: "As truly as the king, my lord, lives, when the commissioners go forth I will say, 'Lost are the lands of the king! Do you not hearken unto me? All the governors are lost; the king, my lord, does not have a [single] governor [left]!' Let the king turn his attention to the archers, and let the king, my lord, send out troops of archers, [for] the king has no lands [left]! The Ḫabiru plunder all the lands of the king. If there are archers [here] in this year, the lands of the king, my lord, will remain [intact], but if there are no archers [here] the lands of the king, my lord, will be lost!" Again in EA No. 288 he pleads, "Let the king care for his land. The land of the king will be lost. All of it will be taken from me; there is hostility to me. As for the lands of Sheeri [Seir] and even to Gintikirmal [i.e., Mount Carmel] there is no peace to all the regions, but to me there is hostility." This obviously refers to the second phase of Joshua's campaign, when he was subduing the central portion of Palestine (although, of course, he never took over Jerusalem itself as a permanent Hebrew possession).

Many excellent scholars who have thoroughly gone over the evidence feel certain that the Ḫabiri of the Amarna correspondence are to be identified with the Hebrews of Joshua's army. Edward Meyer in *Geschichte des Altertums* (1928) states: "The substantial identity of the Hebrews or Israelites with that part of the Ḫabiri of the Amarna tablets-who were invading Palestine in Amarna times is...beyond doubt." As evidence he pointed to the fact that those cities whose governors maintained correspondence with Egypt according to the Amarna archives were Megiddo, Ashkelon, Acco, Gezer, and Jerusalem, precisely those cities which the Israelites were late in capturing.[4] On the other hand, as F. Böhl pointed out in *Kanaanäer und Hebräer* (1911, p. 93), those cities which had already fallen to the Israelite advance or had joined ranks with Joshua's forces are represented by no communications at all—cities like Jericho, Beersheba, Bethel, Gibeon, and Hebron. In connection with the solemnization of the national covenant with Jehovah at Mount Ebal and Mount Gerizim near Shechem (cf. Josh. 8:30-35), it is highly significant that Abdi-Ḫepa of Jerusalem accused that city-state of defecting to the Ḫabiru cause (EA 289): "Or shall we do like Labayu, who gave the land of Shechem to the Ḫabiru?" If there was some informal understanding between Joshua and the Shechemites, there would have been no difficulty about holding this religious assembly near that powerful city.

The objection has also been made that there are few names appearing in the Amarna letters which are also discoverable in the text of Joshua. With the partial exception of Japhia *(Yāpīᵃ)*, king of Lachish,[5] none of the royal names seems to corre-

---

4. Progress in identifying previously unidentified cities attested to in the biblical record has recently been made. "Middin and Nibshan, the second and fourth cities given to Judah in the list recorded in Joshua 15:61-62, can now be identified respectively with archaeological remains at Khirbet Mazin and Ein el-Ghuweir, on the western coast of the Dead Sea. When all these sites are plotted on a plan, it is possible to identify more confidently the five cities, in addition to Ein Gedi, mentioned in Joshua 15:61-62" (BAR 19, no. 4, p. 41).

5. Japhia is probably the same as Yapaḫu, king of Gezer, mentioned in the tablet EA 298. Note that Josh.10:33 indicates that Gezer was confederate with Lachish. Possibly, therefore, Horam of Gezer was a vassal of Japhia.

SHECHEM between Mt. Ebal and Mt. Gerizim (looking west) where Joshua renewed the covenant of Yahweh with the nation.

spond. Ingenious attempts have been made to correlate Abdi-Ḫeba (Abdu-Ḫeba) with Adonizedek,[6] but these involve major improbabilities. On the other hand, this lack of correspondence is not to be wondered at in view of the unsettled nature of the times, when local dynasts were apt to be dethroned or assassinated in swift succession. Most of the royal names given in Joshua pertain to the earliest phases of the conquest, and it may simply be that most of the Amarna letters come from a later period. In this connection it might be mentioned that one letter, EA 256, from Mut-Ba'lu of Megiddo, suggests to the Egyptian regent Yanḫamu that he is on intimate enough terms with Benenima (also read as Benilima) and Yasḫuya to ask them the whereabouts of the prince of Pella, who has absconded to parts unknown. The question arises whether "Benenima is equivalent to Benjamin and "Yashuya" to Joshua. Possibly the remark is ironical and rhetorical in nature and is meant to imply that the Israelite invaders have something to do with the disappearance of Ayab of Pella. Without further knowledge of circumstances, it is impossible to decide this question one way or the other.

At this point, a word should be said about the six known occurrences of the name 'Apiru (or, according to J. A. Wilson, 'Eperu) in the records of the Egyptian empire between 1300 and 1150. In three cases the 'Apiru appear as unskilled workmen in the quarries; once as temple property (in a list of temple serfs at Hieropolis in the reign of Rameses III) and once as workers at a stable. Wilson comes to the conclusion that the term was applied to foreigners in Egyptian service who occupied the status of slaves or serfs.[7] In one remaining reference, however, they are mentioned as foreign mercenary

---

6. Cf. C. R. Conder (trans.), *The Tell el-Amarna Tablets*, 2d ed. (London: A. P. Watt, 1894), p. 143.
7. Wilson, in *American Journal of Semitic Languages* 49 (1933): 275.

troops. Hence we are to understand *Apiru* in the broader nonethnic sense of *Ḥabiru*, just as in the cuneiform records which antedate the Amarna correspondence.

The earliest reference is found in the tomb of Puyemrē in the reign of Thutmose III. Next comes the tomb of Antef, in that same reign; then it appears in a list of booty recorded in the Memphis Stela of Amenhotep II (ANET, p. 247), written at the conclusion of his second Asiatic campaign (which contains an item of 3,600 'Apiru carried off as captives). Next, Seti I in the smaller Beth-shean Stela (cf. ANET, p. 255) records an encounter with the 'Apiru of Mount Yarumtu (i.e., Jarmuth). A Nineteenth-Dynasty story of the capture of Joppa in the reign of Thutmose III refers to the 'Apiru as potential horse stealers (ANET, p. 22). Among the offerings dedicated to the temple of Amon at Heliopolis by Rameses III is a group of slaves referred to as 'Apiru (ANET, p. 261). Rameses IV mentions 800 'Apiru of the bowmen of 'Antiu—in this case apparently mercenaries.

From a survey of the Egyptian references, it will be easily seen that no deductions may be drawn in favor of either the early date or the late date for the Exodus. The 'Apiru of the time of Thutmose III may well have been the Israelites; those mentioned by Rameses II, Rameses III, and Rameses IV may have Hebrews who did not join the Exodus, or who were perhaps taken captive by Egyptian raiders during the time of the Judges. As for the 'Apiru whom Amenhotep II encountered in central Palestine, they could hardly have been the Israelites themselves (who were at that time still confined to the wilderness of Sinai), but wandering freebooters who were called by the term Ḥabiru, used in its larger and more general sense.

In conclusion we may state that while there are many problems and individual details which have yet to be cleared up, there is a sufficient agreement between the data of the Amarna correspondence and the account in the book of Joshua to establish a close connection between the two.

THE LONG DAY OF JOSHUA

The book of Joshua records several miracles, but none perhaps as noteworthy or as widely discussed as that pertaining to the twenty-four hour prolongation of the day in which the battle of Gibeon was fought (10:12-14). It has been objected that if in fact the earth was stopped in its rotation for a period of twenty-four hours, inconceivable catastrophe would have befallen the entire planet and everything on its surface. While those who believe in the omnipotence of God would hardly concede that Jehovah could not have prevented such catastrophe and held in abeyance those physical laws which might have brought it to pass, it does not seem to be absolutely necessary (on the basis of the Hebrew text itself) to hold that the planet was suddenly halted in its rotation. Verse 13 states that the sun "*did not hasten* to set for an entire day." The words *did not hasten* seem to point to a retardation of the movement so that the rotation required forty-eight hours rather than the usual twenty-four. In support of this interpretation, research has brought to light reports from Egyptian, Chinese, and Hindu sources of a long day.[8] Harry Rimmer reports that some astronomers have come to the conclusion that one full day is missing in our astronomical calculation. Rimmer states that Professor Pickering of the Harvard Observatory traced this missing day back to the time of Joshua;[9] likewise Dr. Totten of Yale (cf. Ramm, CVSS, p. 159). Ramm reports, however, that he has been unable to find any documentation to substantiate this report.

Another possibility has been deduced from a slightly different interpretation of the word *dôm* translated in the KJV as "stand thou still." This verb usually signifies "be silent," or "cease, leave off." Dr. E. W. Maunders of Greenwich and Robert Dick Wilson of Princeton Seminary therefore interpreted Joshua's prayer to be a petition that the sun cease pouring down its heat upon his struggling troops so that they might be permitted to press the battle under more favorable conditions. The tremendously destructive hailstorm which accompanied the battle lends some credence to this view, and it has been advocated by men of unquestioned orthodoxy. Nevertheless, it must be admitted that verse 13 seems to favor a prolongation of the day: "And the sun stood in the half [or midway point] of the sky, and it did not hasten to set for about an entire day."

The Keil and Delitzsch *Biblical Commentary on the Old Testament* suggests that a miraculous prolongation of the day would have taken place if it seemed to Joshua and all Israel to be supernaturally prolonged, because they were able to accomplish in it the work of two days. It would have been very difficult for them to make an accurate measurement of time if the sun itself did not move (i.e., the earth did not rotate) at its normal rate. They add another possibility, that God may have produced an optical prolongation of the sunshine, continuing its visibility after the normal setting time by means of a special refraction of the rays.

In the *New Bible Commentary* the commentator Hugh J. Blair suggests that Joshua's prayer was made early in the morning, since the moon was in the West and the sun was in the East. The answer came in the form of a hailstorm which prolonged the darkness and thus facilitated the surprise attack of the Israelites.[10] Hence in the darkness of the storm, the defeat of the enemy was completed. And we should speak of Joshua's "long night" rather than Joshua's "long day." This of course is essentially the same view as that of Maunders and Wilson. Such an interpretation necessitates no stopping of the earth on its axis, but it hardly fits in with the statement of 10:13, and is therefore of dubious validity.

THE EXTERMINATION OF THE CANAANITES

In certain instances such as the capture of Jericho and of Ai, Joshua records that the Israelites completely exterminated the inhabitants according to the command of Jehovah Himself. It needs to be emphasized that the responsibility for this extreme measure rested with God (i.e., if this account is to be trusted) rather than with the

---

8. Cf. Sir Charles Marston, *The Bible is True* (London: Eyre & Spottiswoode, 1936).
9. Rimmer, *The Harmony of Science and Scripture*, 3d ed. (Grand Rapids: Eerdmans, 1937).
10. Blair, in *New Bible Commentary*, p. 231.

HIGH PLACE AT TEL–DAN
Dan and Bethel were the centers of Northern Israel's idolatrous golden-calf worship established by Jeroboam I.

Hebrews. This needs to be emphasized in view of the frequent statement heard in some quarters that the "primitive minded, half savage" Israelites performed this atrocity because of their backward state of religious development. The text makes it very plain that Joshua was simply carrying out divine orders when these inhabitants were indiscriminately put to the sword.

What was the justification for this total destruction? The subsequent history of Israel serves to illustrate very pointedly the grave danger that remained for Israel so long as the Canaanites were permitted to live in their midst. Given over as they were to the most degenerate forms of polytheism and sexual impurity, these depraved inhabitants of the land were sure to exert a baneful influence and spread a deadly contagion among the covenant people of God. Recent archaeological discovery has brought to light concrete testimony to the crass and brutal features of the Canaanite faith as displayed in the literature of the Ras Shamra Tablets. Throughout the region there seems to have been a readiness to incorporate into the indigenous worship all the foreign cults that were practiced by the surrounding heathen nations. Thus we find

THE JUDGES OF ISRAEL

Judges	Enemy Nation	Years of Oppression	Years of Deliverance	Approx. Date B.C.	Reference
Othniel	Mesopotania	8	40	1374-1334	3:9-11
Ehud	Moab Ammon Midian	18	80	1316-1235	3:15-30
Shamgar	Midian			ca. 1230	3:31
Deborah	Canaan	20	40	1216-1176	4:4-5:31
Barak	Canaan	20	40	1216-1176	4:4-5:31
Gideon	Midian	7	40	1169-1129	6:11-8:35
Tola	Amalek		23	1120-1097	10:1-2
Jair	Amalek		22	1120-1097	10:3-5
Jephthah	Ammon	18	6	1085-1079	11:1-12:7
Ibzan	Ammon		7	1079-1072	12: 8-10
Elon	Ammon		10	1072-1062	12: 11-12
Abdon	Ammon		8	1062-1054	12:13-15
Samson	Philistia	40	20	1095-1075	13:2-16:31

a series of hyphenated gods: Teshub-Ḥepa (the Hurrian storm-god and his consort), the Osiris-Isis cult from Egypt; Shamash (the sun-god) and Ishtar (the bloodthirsty goddess of war and love) and Tammuz (a fertility god) from Mesopotamia. Many sites have yielded serpent stelae and Ashtoreth images with sexual symbols. In view of the corrupting influence of the Canaanite religion, especially with its religious prostitution the abomination of Baal-peor (as in Num. 25) and infant sacrifice, it was impossible for pure faith and worship to be maintained in Israel except by the complete elimination of the Canaanites themselves, at least in those areas which the Hebrews were able to occupy. Much of the periodic spiritual decline and apostasy which marked the history of Israel during the time of the Judges is attributable to a toleration of the Canaanite inhabitants and their degenerate religion in the midst of the land.

JUDGES

The Hebrew title for this book is *Shôpheṭîm,* meaning "judges" or "executive leaders." The Septuagint title *Kritai* means the same thing, Judges. This title is derived from the type of government or leadership which dominated the Israelite tribes in the interval between the death of Joshua and the coronation of King Saul. The basic theme of the book is Israel's failure as a theocracy to keep true to the covenant even under the leadership of men chosen of God to deliver them from oppression by the pagan world. The frequent and repeated failures of the twelve tribes to remain true to God and His holy law prepared the way for the institution of a central monarchy.

OUTLINE OF JUDGES

I. Partial conquest of Canaan by Israel, 1:1–2:5

II. Reasons for survival of Canaanite remnants, 2:6–3:6

III. Oppression under Cushan-Rishathaim, deliverance by Othniel, 3:7-11

IV. Oppression under Eglon of Moab, deliverance by Ehud, 3:12-30

V. Exploits of Shamgar, 3:31

VI. Oppression under Jabin of Hazor, deliverance by Deborah and Barak, 4:1-24

VII. Song of Deborah, 5:1-31

VIII. Oppression under Midian, deliverance by Gideon, 6:1–8:35

IX. Career of the tyrant Abimelech, 9:1-57

X. Judgeships of Tola and Jair, 10:1-5

XI. Oppression under Ammonites, deliverance by Jephthah, 10:6–2:7

XII. Judgeships of Ibzan, Elon, and Abdon, 12:8-15

XIII. Oppression under Philistines, the exploits of Samson, 13:1–16:31

XIV. Micah's priest and the Danite migration, 17:1–18:31

XV. Atrocity at Gibeah and the Benjamite war, 19:12–1:25

DATE OF COMPOSITION

Internal evidences point to some period in the early monarchy, but prior to David's capture of Jerusalem (ca. 990 B.C.). The expression occurring in 18:1 and 19:1, "There was at that time no king in Israel," seems to imply composition during the early period of the monarchy, before the unhappy age of the divided kingdom when once again troubles and disasters came to afflict the nation. The greatest likelihood is that the book was completed early in the reign of David; but Judg. 1:21, "The Jebusites dwell with the children of Benjamin in Jerusalem unto this day," is most reasonably construed to refer to the period prior to David's capture of Jerusalem and his appointment of it to be the capital of the Hebrew kingdom. Judg. 1:29 states that the Canaanites were still dwelling in Gezer rather than submitting to Israelite sovereignty. This certainly points to a time before the king of Egypt captured the city of Gezer and bestowed it on Solomon as a dowry for his daughter (ca. 970 B.C.). Some portions of the book maintain a viewpoint antedating the time of David, for 3:3 refers to Sidon as the chief city in Phoenicia rather than Tyre (which began to overshadow Sidon soon after the twelfth century B.C.).

One apparent difficulty with an early date of composition is furnished by Judg. 18:30: "And Jonathan, the son of Gershom...he and his sons were priests to the tribe

THE SITE OF THE OLD JEBUSITE WALL.
THE JEBUSITE CITY OF JERUSALEM OCCUPIED AN AREA OF 10 TO 15 ACRES. THIS LAND RIDGE WAS SOUTH OF THE TEMPLE MOUNT, JUST OUTSIDE THE WALL ENCLOSING THE OLD CITY.

Legend:
- city
- City of Refuge
- mountain peak
- city not captured according to Joshua 17 or Judges 1
- city outside area of Israelite control
- city within area of Israelite control
- city within area of Israelite control (uncertain location)
- area permanently controlled by ancient Israel
- modern boundary of the West Bank of Jordan

PRE-MONARCHIAL ISRAEL ISRAEL DURING THE TIME OF THE JUDGES.

MOUNT TABOR,

RISING 1,600 FEET ABOVE ITS SURROUNDING PLAIN, WAS AN IMPORTANT STRONGHOLD DATING BACK TO DEBORAH (JUDG. 4:6). MOUNT TABOR'S PEAK IS 1,300 YDS. LONG BY 450 YDS. WIDE.

of Dan until the day of the captivity of the land." If this refers to the Assyrian conquest of 732 when Tiglath-pileser III took over the northern territory of the kingdom of Samaria, this verse at least would seem to come from the late eighth century if not later.

Unger (IGOT, p. 292) suggests that this verse might possibly have been inserted by a later editor—a rather questionable proposition. Young and Steinmueller have raised the question as to whether the word for "land" ('ereṣ) was original, and inclined to the view that it should be amended to "ark" ('ārōn), which would involve simply the change of one consonant (final nūn instead of final tsadhe). The amended phrase "the captivity of the ark" would then refer to the disaster which befell the Israelites at the battle of Shiloh in the year that Eli died. Yet it is not easy to see how this would have much relevance to what happened at the northern tip of Israelite territory in the tribe of Dan. Nevertheless Moeller (GATE, p. 150) has pointed out the close relationship between Judg. 18:30 and 1 Sam. 4:21 (The glory is departed from Israel: because the ark of God was taken). In both verses the same verb gālâ ("go into captivity") is used, the verbal form appearing in Samuel and the noun form in Judges. Moreover, a close connection is made in Judg. 18:31 between the institution of the idolatrous worship in Dan and the existence of the legitimate worship of Jehovah in Shiloh. In the light of these data, the substitution of "ark" for "land" may perhaps be justified.

But a third and simpler suggestion would be that "the captivity of the land" might refer to a crushing military defeat and deportation at the hand of Dan which took place some time in the latter period of the judges in the course of bloody border warfare. Standing at the northern flank as it did, the inhabitants of the city of Dan might well have been overwhelmed by foreign invaders just as suddenly as they themselves captured the site from its former inhabitants (cf. Judg. 18:27-28). Thus construed, Judg. 18:30 refers simply to the land of Dan, and does not necessarily indicate any later time of composition than the reign of David.

AUTHORSHIP AND UNITY OF COMPOSITION OF JUDGES

While the approximate time of composition may be deduced from the information furnished above, namely 1000 B.C., there is no clear evidence as to the identity of the author. His standpoint was unmistakably prophetic, for he measures Israel's history by the standard of faithfulness to Jehovah's covenant. (It should be noted that the purpose of this book is not to glorify Israel's ancestors, as some writers have alleged, but rather to glorify the grace of the God of Israel.) It would be natural to suppose that either Samuel himself or else some student or disciple of his might have been responsible for the compilation of this history. Whoever the author was, he seems to have made use of original sources, some of which at least were in the northern Israelite dialect, such as Judg. 5 (the song of Deborah) and the Gideon cycle (chaps. 6-8), where we find several occurrences of the relative pronoun *še* (rather than the usual *'ašer*). Whatever the prior sources, the unity of arrangement and structure is unmistakable. All the author's material has been arranged according to a unitary plan exhibiting a single dominant idea: Israel's welfare depends upon her spiritual relationship to Jehovah. Characteristic formulas are used which introduce or bring to a close each stage in the narrative. A characteristic introduction is, "And the children of Israel did evil in the sight of the Lord" (cf. 3:7, 12; 4:1; 6:1; 10:6; 13:1). Often a section is closed by the comment "and the land had rest [a certain number of years]" as in 3:11, 30; 5:31; 8:28. Moeller (GATE, p. 147) points out that the fourteen judges are so arranged that Othniel and Samson stand alone at the beginning and at the end of the series, but those who come in between are usually connected in pairs. Thus Shamgar (3:31) appears as a brief adjunct to Ehud (3:12-30); Barak is of course paired up with Deborah; and there is a fairly clear connection between Gideon and his natural son, Abimelech.[11]

PROBLEMS OF CHRONOLOGY

If all the terms of service performed by the various judges are added end to end, along with the stated periods of oppression, they form a consecutive total of approximately 410 years. But the long date of 480 years given in 1 Kings 6:1 seems to allow for only 292 years between the judgeship of Othniel and that of Eli. We must therefore conclude that many of these careers of service overlapped or were even contemporane-

11. Cf. Raven, OTI, p. 158, for a list of expressions peculiar to Judges and which characteristically recur in this work.

THE PHILISTINES WERE AN AGGRESSIVE WARRING PEOPLE WHO MAINTAINED A MILITARY ADVANTAGE BY EXERCISING A MONOPOLY ON IRON–MAKING.

ous. The statement in Judg. 10:7, "The Lord...sold them into the hands of the Philistines, and into the hands of the children of Ammon," clearly indicates that Samson and Jephthah must have been almost contemporaneous, since the Ammonite oppression and that of the Philistines occurred at approximately the same time. J. B. Payne has worked out a basic chronology of the six most important judges ranging from Othniel in 1381 B.C. to Samuel whose career ended in 1050 B.C.[12] Confirmation of the soundness of this method of computation is furnished by the remark of Jephthah in Judg. 11:26 where he reckons the interim between the Israelite occupation of Heshbon and the time of the Ammonite war as 300 years. This would allow for a Transjordanian occupation somewhere between 1400 and 1100 B.C. It should be remembered that no long date is given for the whole period of the judges in the book of Judges itself; hence there is no reason why several of the periods of judgeship should not have been contemporaneous.

ARCHAEOLOGICAL CONTRIBUTIONS TO AN UNDERSTANDING OF THIS ERA

Extensive discussion has already been devoted to the relevance of the Tell el-Amarna letters to the period of conquest after General Joshua. It may be fairly said that a survey of the data furnished by these letters indicates that the Hebrew conquest, after the initial successes resulting from combined effort, became greatly slowed down in

12. Payne, OHH, p. 79.

pace. Many of the city-states defeated in battle with Joshua were permitted to reoccupy their respective capitals and continue their struggle to survive. Thus Lachish, for example, was roundly defeated by Joshua some time between 1400 and 1390 (cf. Josh. 10:32), but Tell el-Hesi (now identifed with Eglon, not Lachish) does not seem to have been completely destroyed by fire until around 1230 B.C. (Excavations there have recovered potsherds written in Egyptian hieratic recording the deliveries of wheat up to the "year 4" of some pharaoh, who on the basis of the ceramic series is believed by Albright and others to have been the Pharaoh Merneptah.) Late Bronze remains at Tell Beit Mirsim (which until recently has been identified with Debir) indicate that it was not destroyed until around 1200 B.C. Archaeologists date the fall of Megiddo (see Joshua 12:21) between 1150 and 1050. Of course it was not necessary that the Israelite conquerors make a complete destruction of all the cities which they initially took by storm, but in the course of time, as the Hebrew population increased, they were able to take more effective control over the territory the Lord had granted them.

Another important feature of this period was the persistence of Egyptian authority, at least into the twelfth century B.C. It has already been noted that Joshua and Judges fail to mention the maintenance of Egyptian power along the principal trade routes through Palestine. As stated before, this silence cannot successfully be explained by the late date theory of the Exodus, for no mention is made in the Hebrew record of the successful raid of Merneptah in 1229 B.C., nor of the persistence of Egyptian authority in key centers like Megiddo and Beth-Shean, where inscriptions bearing the name Rameses III (1198-1167) have been discovered. A careful synchronism has been worked out by John Garstang between the various periods of "rest" mentioned in Judges and the establishment of effective control by Egypt in Palestine. The policing of the main arteries of commerce by Egyptian troops would naturally inhibit aggressiveness on the part of the Canaanite nations without necessarily affecting too drastically the life of the Israelites themselves, who largely kept to the hills (cf. Judg. 1:19) in the earlier stage of their occupation. Consequently there would not be too much occasion for mentioning the Egyptians by name, and it may well have been that there was a natural reluctance to refer to them at all.

As for the Philistines, considerable discussion has been devoted to the question of when they first settled in the southwest coast of Palestine. Because of an inscription of Rameses III at Medinet Habu recording a naval victory over the Philistines about 1195 B.C., many critics have assumed that it was their defeat at the hands of the Egyptians which first impelled them to settle along the Palestinian coastline. They therefore conclude that every mention of Philistines prior to 1195 B.C. is necessarily anachronistic, whether in Gen. 21, Josh. 13, or Judg. 3. According to this interpretation, neither Abraham nor Isaac could have found any Philistines at Gerar as they are recorded to have done (cf. Gen. 21:32, 34; 26:1, 8, 14, 15, 18). But the fact that Philistine raiders were driven back by Rameses III to the Palestinian littoral by no means constitutes proof that there could have been no Philistines there before that time. Biblical references show that they were a heterogeneous people including several distinct groups such as the Kaphtorim, the Keftim, the Cherithites, and the Pelethites. The probabilities are that these various groups came in successive waves of migration from the island of Crete. Even in the Minoan period, the inhabitants of Crete were enterprising traders well before Abraham's time. As such they would have had every incentive to establish trading centers on the Palestinian coastline for the purposes of commerce.

THE SACRIFICE OF JEPHTHAH'S DAUGHTER

A final word should be said about an episode in Judges which has occasioned much perplexity and has often led to erroneous conclusions. Apparently Jephthah offered up his daughter as a human sacrifice on the altar, in fulfillment of his "rash" vow (11:30, 31; cf. v. 39). The term for "burnt offering" is 'ôlâ, which everywhere else signifies a blood sacrifice wholly consumed by fire upon the altar. But, as Keil and Delitzsch show, this interpretation as a literal human sacrifice cannot stand in the light of the context.

1. Human sacrifice was always understood, from the days of Abraham (for whose son, Isaac, a ram was substituted by God) to be an offense and an abomination to Yahweh, being expressly denounced and forbidden in Lev. 18:21; 20:2-5; Deut. 12:31; 18:10. There is no evidence that any Israelite ever offered human sacrifice prior to the days of Ahaz (743-728 B.C.). It is inconceivable that God-fearing Jephthah could have supposed he would please the Lord by perpetrating such a crime and abomination.

2. His daughter was allowed two months of mourning, not to bewail her approaching loss of life, but only to bewail her *virginity* (*bᵉtûlîm*) (Judg. 11:37-38).

3. It is stated in verse 39 that after Jephthah had performed his vow and offered her as a "burnt offering," "she knew not a man." This would be a very pointless and inane remark if she had been put to death. But it has perfect relevance if she was devoted to the service of Jehovah at the door of the tabernacle the rest of her life. (For references to the devoted women who performed service in connection with the national cultus, cf. Ex. 38:8 and 1 Sam. 2:22; also Anna in the days of Jesus—Luke 2:36-37.) The pathos of the situation in this instance did not lie in Jephthah's daughter devoting herself to divine service, but rather in the sure extinction of Jephthah's line, since she was his only child. Hence, both he and she bewailed her virginity. There was no human sacrifice here.[13]

RUTH

This book bears as its title the name of the principal character whose biography is related within its pages. The etymology of this name (רות)is uncertain; some have suggested a Moabite modification of the Hebrew *rᵉ'ût*, "friendship, association." The purpose of the book is to relate an episode in the ancestry of King David which accounted

---

13. Cf. Keil and Delitzsch, *Joshua, Judges, Ruth* (Grand Rapids: Eerdmans, 1950), pp. 388-95.

for the introduction of non-Israelite blood into his family line. It also teaches the far-reaching scope of the grace of God who is ready to welcome even Gentile converts to the fellowship of His redeemed people. Perhaps most important of all, this brief narrative is designed to exhibit the function of the *gōʾēl*, or kinsman-redeemer.

OUTLINE OF RUTH

I. Migration and sojourn in Moab, 1:1-5

II. Ruth's choice to return with Naomi to Judah, 1:6-18

III. The mournful homecoming to Bethlehem, 1:19-22

IV. Boaz, a friend in need, 2:1-23

V. Redemption law invoked, 3:1-18

VI. Boaz' acceptance of his responsibility as *gōʾēl*, 4:1-16

VII. Promise and posterity, 4:17-22

DATE OF COMPOSITION

The historical setting of this little book is laid in the time of the Judges (Ruth 1:1), and it seems to have been composed at about the same time as the larger work. It could hardly have been written earlier than the time of King David, since he is mentioned in it by name (4:22). Had it been written as late as the time of Solomon, it is quite likely that David's famous son also would have been listed in the notice of Ruth's descendants.

Critics of the Liberal school insist on a date later than the reign of Josiah, inasmuch as Ruth seems to betray a knowledge of Deut. 25, and Deuteronomy was (according to them) composed just before Josiah's reform. Most critics date it about 550 B.C. during the time of the Exile, but others have looked to a period some one hundred years later, feeling that it was intended as a counterblast to Nehemiah's strict enforcement of the laws against marrying foreign wives. It is interesting to note that W. F. Albright expresses a preference for an earlier date than Josiah's time, regardless of its possible dependence upon Deuteronomy. In the Alleman-Flack *Old Testament Commentary*, he refers to the demonstration by Millar Burrows that the legal usage described in connection with the marriage of Boaz and Ruth represents a stage much earlier than the Pentateuchal laws respecting levirate marriage. On this questionable basis, therefore, Albright says, "We cannot date the bulk of Ruth after the seventh century, and a date as early as the ninth century for the underlying poem is quite possible."[14]

---

14. Albright, in *Old Testament Commentary*, p. 147.

KINSMAN–REDEEMER AS A MESSIANIC TYPE

REQUIREMENT	FULFILLMENT IN CHRIST
Be a blood relative	Christ born of a woman
Be able to purchase forfeited inheritance	Christ had the merit to pay the price for sinners
Be willing to buy back the forfeited inheritance	Christ willingly laid down His life
Be willing to marry the wife of the deceased kinsman	The Church, as the Bride of Christ

In the interests of the later date, some critics have pointed to alleged Aramaisms such as *lāhēn* in 1:13 and *mārā'* in 1:20. It is true that *lāhēn* exists in Aramaic as a word for "therefore," but as a Hebrew term it may be rendered "to them" in the sense of "for those (things)." While it is true that *mārā'*, "bitter," is spelled in an Aramaic way, its Hebrew equivalent for an identical sound is only slightly varied in spelling. Moreover, since inscriptions have been found as early as the ninth century B.C. containing both Canaanite and Aramaic spellings in the same text,[15] these two questionable words furnish very tenuous grounds for a late dating of the book.

As for the historicity of the narrative, Ruth appears to give an accurate account of the customs during the early period.[16] It was perfectly natural at that era (before the Moabites had become embittered by Israelite overlordship) for a Jewish family to take refuge in Moab during a time of drought and famine. Under those conditions it would be natural also for young people to fall in love and get married with the inhabitants of the land. The fact that David was descended from a Moabitess would furnish a ready explanation for his seeking refuge with the king of Moab during the time he was being pursued by Saul. As Young remarks, "The very fact that Ruth, the ancestress of David, was a Moabitess, is in itself an argument for the historicity of the book."[17]

---

15. Cf. the Zakir inscription mentioned in chap. 10, p. 143.

16. The custom of Levirate marriage, as with Boaz and Ruth, is well attested by early documents from the Ancient Near East. From the Nuzi tablets we glean written records of this practice as cited by J. A. Thompson in *Archaeology and the Old Testament*, "One case is well known in Nuzi where a father in obtaining a bride for his son specified that if the son died the girl was to be married to another of the sons," (p. 28). Further verification of the accurate portrayal of ancient customs in the book of Ruth are illuminated by tablets which record the passing of shoes from one person to another during a transaction as a seal of agreement. Thompson states, "By a special transaction involving the passing of a pair of shoes and some other articles of quite inadequate economic worth when compared with the value of the item being transferred, the whole thing was given a legal cloak." We are reminded of later incidents in the Bible where shoes were transferred between parties to cover up the avoidance of certain moral obligations. When Ruth was redeemed by Boaz, the kinsman took off his shoe and gave it to Boaz. This was according to 'the manner in former time in Israel concerning redeeming and concerning changing, for to confirm all things' (Ruth 4:7-8)" (ibid, p. 29).

17. E. J. Young, IOT, p. 340.

BASIC TEACHINGS OF THIS BOOK

The basic teachings of Ruth may be summed up under three headings.

1. It affords a foreshadowing of the enlarged blessing to come: Gentiles are capable of being joined to the commonwealth of Israel upon condition of repentance and of faith in Jehovah.

2. God's marvelous and unexpected providence is exhibited also by the inclusion of a Gentile in the royal lineage of the Messiah (cf. Matt. 1:5).

3. The kinsman-redeemer serves as a Messianic type, the $g\bar{o}'\bar{e}l$ who fulfills the following qualifications and functions of his kinsmen: (*a*) he must be a blood relative (even as Christ became a blood relative of man by the Virgin Birth); (*b*) he must have the money to purchase the forfeited inheritance (4:10—even as Christ alone had the merit to pay the price for sinners); (*c*) he must be willing to buy back that forfeited inheritance (4:9—even as Christ laid down His life on His own volition); (*d*) he must be willing to marry the wife of a deceased kinsman (4:10—typical of the bride and groom relationship between Christ and His Church). From this standpoint, therefore, the little book of Ruth is one of the most instructive in the Old Testament concerning the mediatorial work of the Lord Jesus.

20 1 AND 2 SAMUEL
1 AND 2 KINGS

IN ITS EARLIER form the Hebrew Bible seems to have regarded the two volumes of Samuel as a single book. The same was true of 1 and 2 Kings. It was on this basis that Josephus in the first century A.D. reckoned the books of the Old Testament as twenty-two in number (cf. chap. 5, pp. 76-77). But the Alexandrian Jews brought both Samuel and Kings together as books of "Kingdoms" (*Basileiōn*) and then subdivided each of them so as to form four books of "kingdoms." The Latin Vulgate in the course of time dropped the term *books of kingdoms* (*Libri Regnōrum*) and shifting to the Hebrew division between Samuel and Kings, came out with the titles which the Western church has employed ever since. (But the Eastern church still speaks of 1 and 2 Samuel as 1 and 2 Kingdoms and refers to 1 and 2 Kings as 3 and 4 Kingdoms.) Not until the Bomberg edition of 1517 did the Hebrew Bible make the partition of Samuel and Kings into two books. The purpose of these four books was to record the founding of the Hebrew monarchy, and its varying fortunes and ultimate demise in 587 B.C.

1 AND 2 SAMUEL

First and Second Samuel include (*a*) the career of Samuel, the kingmaker,[1] (*b*) the career of Saul, the unfaithful king who, forsaking the covenant, became a tyrant; (*c*) the career of David, a truly theocratic king who founded the permanent and valid dynasty out of which the Messiah was to come.

OUTLINE OF 1 SAMUEL

I. The career of Samuel and the deliverance from Philistia, 1:1–7:17

A. Samuel's mother and her song, 1:1–2:10
B. Samuel's apprenticeship in the Tabernacle (or temple), 2:11–3:21
C. The disaster of Shiloh and the death of Eli, 4:1-22

---

1. The name *Shᵉmū'ēl* is variously interpreted as "the name of God," "His name is God," or even "heard of God"—if a short form of *Shᵉmū'ēl*.

D. The captivity of the ark in Philistia, 5:1-12

E. The return of the ark to Israel, 6:1-21

F. Samuel drives out Philistine oppressors and leads a revival, 7:1-17

II. The rise of King Saul, 8:1–15:35

A. The Israelites petition for a king, 8:1-22

B. Saul anointed by Samuel and vindicated by victory over the Ammonites 9:1–11:15

C. Samuel's final address, of warning and counsel 12:1-25

D. Victories of Saul and Jonathan over the Philistines, 13:1–14:52

E. The Amalekite campaign and Saul's disobedience, 15:1-35

III. The decline of Saul and the rise of David, 16:1–31:13

A. David anointed by Samuel and introduced to the royal court, 16:1-23

B. David's deliverance of Israel by slaying Goliath, 17:1-58

C. David's flight from Saul's jealousy, 18:1–20:42

D. David's wanderings as an outlaw, 21:1–30:31

E. Saul's final battle and death on Mount Gilboa, 31:1-13

OUTLINE OF 2 SAMUEL

I. David's career as King over Judah and all Israel, 1:1–14:33

A. David's lamentation over the death of Saul and Jonathan, 1:1-27

B. The crowning of David at Hebron; the war with Abner, 2:1-32

C. Abner's defection and murder by Joab, 3:1-39

D. The assassination of Ishbosheth, 4:1-12

E. Establishment of national and religious unity, 5:1–6:23

F. God's covenant with David, the Messianic King, 7:1-29

G. Extension of David's rule to the limits of the Promised Land, 8:1–10:19

H. David's sin with Bathsheba and his ultimate repentance, 11:1–12:31

I. The crime of Amnon and Absalom's revenge, 13:1–14:33

II. The closing phase of David's reign, 15:1–24:25

A. Absalom's rebellion and final defeat, 15:1–18:33

B. David's restoration to power, 19:1–20:26

C. The famine and the Gibeonites' revenge upon Saul's descendants, 21:1-14

D. Later wars with the Philistines, 21:15-22

E. David's psalm of praise and final testimony, 22:1–23:7

F. The list of David's mighty men, 23:8-39

G. David's sin in numbering the people; the subsequent plague stopped at the site of the future temple, 24:1-25 [2]

2. Note that Araunah, who sold his threshing floor to David, bore a Hittite name that is *arawanis* meaning "freeman" or "noble"; cf. F. F. Bruce, *The Hittites and the Old Testament* (Wheaton, Ill.: Tyndale, 1947), p. 18.

DATE OF COMPOSITION

Judging from internal evidences, the books of Samuel could hardly have been written prior to the death of Solomon. In 1 Sam. 27:6 we infer that the divided monarchy had already begun because of the words, "Ziklag pertaineth unto the kings of Judah until this day." Although there is no obituary of David, yet the record of his last words would clearly imply the knowledge of his death. Indications of a precise *terminus ad quem* seem to be lacking, and none of such conservative writers as Steinmueller, Young, or Moeller can come to a more definite conclusion than that the composition took place between 930 and 722. The author seems to be ignorant of the fall of Samaria, and so it is reasonable to date the composition of the work prior to the captivity of the Ten Tribes.

Rationalist critics analyze the book as mainly composed of two documents (Pfeiffer) or else possibly of three (Eissfeldt—who specifies L, J, and E). Some parts of it they hold to be Solomonic, with other installments added until about 550 B.C. by a redactor of the so-called "Deuteronomic school." It is noteworthy that there are sufficient evidences of an early date in some sections of Samuel such that even a divisive critic like R. H. Pfeiffer could assign the earliest stratum of this book to a tenth-century author such as Ahimaaz, the priest.[3] Yet other portions are construed to be as late as the exile, because of the references to Levites to be found in 1 Sam. 6 and 7.[4] The same general technique of analysis is employed as in Pentateuchal criticism, with the endeavor to isolate parallel accounts and doublets which show such "inconsistencies" with each other as to indicate authorship in different periods of Israel's history. For example, there are alleged to be two diametrically opposed attitudes toward the establishment of a monarchy in Israel: that of 1 Sam. 7 and 8 (involving divine condemnation of the people's lack of faith in desiring a king), and that of chapter 9 (especially v. 16), with its gracious promises of blessing to the king whom Samuel is to anoint.

What these critics fail to see is that condemnation of an untheocratic motive on the part of the nation does not preclude God's blessing upon the human instrument He has chosen to lead His people under the new form of government which they have wrongly preferred.[5] We find numerous instances of this type of divine response to human errors in the course of Hebrew history. For example, despite the crimes perpetrated by David in acquiring Bathsheba as his wife, God graciously elected her second son, Solomon, to be David's successor, the most glorious of his descendants. The artificiality of higher-critical stratification is pointed up by the occurrence of interlocking allusions in later parts of the narrative to the earlier sections, for often these allusions cut across all the lines of division which the critics have set up. Certain characteristic

---

3. Pfeiffer, IOT, p. 356.

4. Cf. A. Bentzen, IOT, 2:95.

5. Cf. K. A. Kitchen's comments on Samuel's alleged denunciation of kingship in 1 Sam. 8. He compares this with documents from Alalakh and Ugarit which advert to the regular civil powers (not abuses) that an earthly king would assume in order to govern them. Samuel's purpose was simply to warn his countrymen of the cost of a monarchy. AOOT, p. 158; cf. BASOR no. 143 (1956) for details.

phrases in the supposedly distinct sources recur with such frequency as to render the whole analytical technique highly dubious.[6]

Although division into post-Davidical strata cannot be successfully made out, there is little doubt that the compiler of the books of Samuel employed prior written sources, as for example the *Book of Jasher* referred to in 2 Sam. 1:18. While other written records are not referred to by name, it is quite likely that the official archives were consulted, including the "Acts of David" composed by Samuel, Nathan, and Gad (according to the statement in 1 Chron. 29:29).

PRESERVATION OF THE TEXT

For some reason, the text of 1 and 2 Samuel seems to have been more poorly preserved in the Masoretic recension than any other book in the Bible. A likely explanation is that the official temple text drawn up in the inter-testamentary period relied upon a very ancient *Vorlage* (or earlier manuscript from which it was copied) which contained occasional lacunae (perhaps due to a worm-eaten or frayed condition resulting from overuse).[7] This, for example, would account for the absence of any number preceding the word for "years" in 1 Sam. 13:1 (ASV). But a study of the Septuagint version of Samuel indicates that its *Vorlage* was in somewhat better condition than that of the Masoretic tradition, and hence it is occasionally useful for the textual criticism of these two books. Several important fragments have been discovered in the Qumran caves containing a Hebrew text which is now and then closer to that of the Septuagint than to the MT.[8] (Yet even the Septuagint offers no help in discovering the missing number in 1 Sam. 13:1.) Or again, in 1 Sam. 12:11 a letter *'ayin* apparently dropped out of the name Abdon, one of the twelfth-century judges (cf. Judg. 12:13-15); hence his name comes out as *B-D-N* rather than *'-B-D-N* and is vocalized by the Masoretes as "Bedan."

ALLEGED INCONSISTENCIES IN THE NARRATIVE

Many of the inconsistencies which divisive critics have pointed out in their analysis of the books of Samuel can be made out only by a deliberate policy of artificial dissection. If the text is read and accepted as it stands, a perfectly obvious reconciliation is apparent. Yet there are a few passages where a harmonizing explanation is not quite so ready at hand.

Some have insisted that the tribal background of Samuel himself was variously given in 1 Sam. 1 and 1 Chron. 6:27-28, the latter making Samuel out to have been a Levite of the subtribe of Kohath. Yet 1 Sam. 1:1 asserts that Elkanah was an Ephraimite, since his home was in Ramathaim-zophim. But actually this latter verse says nothing

---

6. Cf. the phrases listed in Raven, OTI, p. 167.

7. Cf. chap. 3, pp. 46-47.

8. Cf. chap. 3, pp. 44-45. Qumran 4 Fragments contain deviations from both the MT and the LXX, and even some details contained by neither. Cf. *Tradition and Testament* (Moody Press, 1991), eds. J. S. Feinberg and P. D. Feinberg. LXX of "1 Samuel in the Light of 4QFragments," G. L. Archer, pp. 232-37.

about Elkanah's tribal affiliation, and only indicates his place of residence. According to the Torah, the Levites had no particular tribal territory of their own, but were to be settled in forty-eight different Levitical cities scattered among the twelve tribes (cf. Num. 35:6). There is no reason why Ramathaim or Ramah may not have been one of the cities in Ephraim set apart for the Levites.

Another difficulty has been found in the twofold introduction of young David to King Saul. In 1 Sam. 16:14-23 he is introduced as a harpist employed to soothe Saul's troubled spirit. In 1 Sam. 17:55-58 Saul apparently has to be introduced to him all over again. But a more careful study of this "second introduction" indicates that Saul's only concern at this point was to learn the name of David's father, or rather what kind of man his father was, in view of Saul's policy of attaching the most valiant warriors in his kingdom to his personal bodyguard (1 Sam. 14:52). It was quite appropriate for him to look into the possibilities of appointing Jesse himself or some of his other sons to his elite corps, after being treated to an example of the prowess of his youngest son in slaying the giant Goliath. First Samuel 18:1 suggests that a lengthy conversation ensued after Saul put his question to Abner concerning David, and we may reasonably infer that much more than mere names would have been discussed at that time.

One interesting problem arises in connection with David's encounter with Goliath. Although 1 Sam. 17 states that Goliath was killed by David, 2 Sam. 21:19 (ASV) indicates that the giant met his death at the hands of Elhanan. Even though the Septuagint follows closely the reading of the MT in this latter verse, it is quite obvious that a scribal error has marred the transmission of the original text. Fortunately 1 Chron. 20:5 affords great assistance in discovering how the error took place. In Chronicles the verse reads: "And Elhanan the son of Jair slew Lahmi the brother of Goliath the Gittite." The copyist of 2 Sam. 21:19 apparently mistook the sign of the direct object (*'et*) for the word *beyt* (probably because the manuscript was smudged or eroded before the final *t*), and thus changed *Lahmi* into "the Bethlehemite" (Hebrew: *B-t-l-h-m-y);* then for a similar reason he misread the word brother (*'-h*) for the sign of the direct object (*'-t*), which meant that Goliath himself became the object of the slaying instead of Goliath's brother. In the fifth century B.C. the Hebrew *het* (*h*) greatly resembled the appearance of the letter *taw* (*t*) and also the letter *yod* had become very tiny. Additional evidence that the verse was poorly copied in 2 Sam. 21 is afforded by the intrusion of the name *Oregim* after *Jaare*. As 1 Chron. 20 shows, this word *'ōrᵉgîm*, meaning "weavers," belonged only after the word for "beam." This transmissional error must have arisen at a time when the letter *het* already resembled *taw* in appearance, but before the Septuagint was translated; that is, between the fifth century and the third century B.C.

Other parallels which are allegedly inconsistent include those two occasions when David had Saul in his power so that he could have killed him in his sleep. (But under the peculiar conditions accompanying the pursuit of guerrillas in mountainous terrain, it is quite possible that this could have happened twice.) Or again, in the several

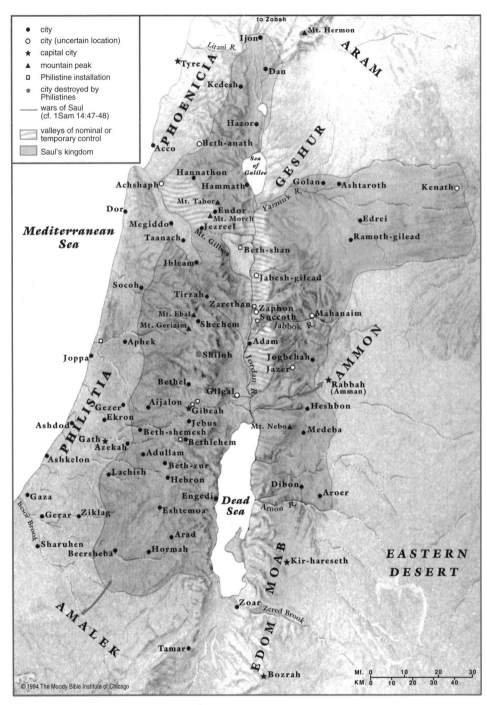

Legend:
- city
- ○ city (uncertain location)
- ★ capital city
- ▲ mountain peak
- ▢ Philistine installation
- city destroyed by Philistines
- — wars of Saul (cf. 1Sam 14:47-48)
- valleys of nominal or temporary control
- Saul's kingdom

© 1994 The Moody Bible Institute of Chicago

THE EARLY MONARCHY OF ISRAEL

episodes of reconciliation and alienation between Saul and David, temporary reestablishment of friendship would be followed by a sudden outbreak of murderous hatred. And yet it should be recognized that in view of Saul's dementia and progressive deterioration under the eroding influence of a besetting envy and a profound sense of insecurity, this sequence of events is altogether true to life. Neither here nor in any of the other less significant examples which Source Critics have brought up are there any genuine discrepancies to be found.

1 AND 2 KINGS

As has already been indicated, these two books were originally counted as one in the Hebrew canon. The title is altogether appropriate in view of the subject matter, for the books contain a record of the careers of the kings of Israel and Judah from the time of Solomon to the downfall of the Jewish monarchy before the armies of Nebuchadnezzar in 587 B.C. As pointed out before, the Septuagint reckons these two books as 3 and 4 Kingdoms (*Basileiōn*).

The theme of these two books was to demonstrate on the basis of Israel's history that the welfare of the nation ultimately depended upon the sincerity of its faithfulness to the covenant with Yahweh, and that the success of any ruler was to be measured by the degree of his adherence to the Mosaic constitution and his maintenance of a pure and God-honoring testimony before the heathen. The purpose of this record was to set forth those events which were important from the standpoint of God and His program of redemption. The author had no intention of glorifying Israel's heroes out of nationalistic motives; hence he omitted even those passing achievements which would have assumed great importance in the eyes of a secular historian. His prime concern was to show how each successive ruler dealt with God in his covenant responsibilities.

OUTLINE OF 1 AND 2 KINGS

I. The reign of Solomon, 1 Kings 1:1–11:43

   A. David's final arrangements and the suppression of Adonijah, 1:1–2:11
   B. The beginning of Solomon's reign, 2:12-46
   C. Solomon's prayer for wisdom after his marriage to Pharaoh's daughter, 3:1-28
   D. Solomon's administration of the kingdom, 4:1-34
   E. Solomon's erection of the temple, 5:1–7:51
   F. Dedication of temple and bestowal of God's promise, 8:1-66
   G. Solomon's wealth and glory; the Queen of Sheba, 9:1–10:29
   H. Solomon's apostasy, decline and death, 11:1-43

II. Early kings of the Divided Monarchy, 12:1–16:28

   A. Rehoboam's folly; the revolt under Jeroboam, 12:1–14:31

B. Abijah and Asa of Judah, 15:1-24
C. Nadab, Baashah, and Elah of Israel, 15:25–16:14
D. Zimri and Omri of Israel, 16:15-28

III. Period of alliance between Judah and Israel, 16:29–2 Kings 9:37

A. Ahab and Elijah, in the test on Mount Carmel, 16:29–18:46
B. Ahab and Elijah until Ahab's death at Ramoth-Gilead, 19:1–22:53
C. Ahaziah of Israel, 2 Kings 1:1-18
D. The anointing of Elisha and death of Elijah, 2:1-25
E. Jehoram and Jehoshaphat against the Moabites, 3:1-27
F. Miracles of Elisha; the cleansing of Naaman, 4:1–5:27
G. Wars with Ben-Hadad and the deliverance of Samaria, 6:1–7:20
H. Edom revolts from Joram of Judah, who is defeated by Hazael of Damascus
    (8:20-29)
I. Elisha's mission to Hazael and Jehu; the death of Jezebel, 9:1–9:37

IV. Decline and fall of Israel, 2 Kings 10:1–17:41

A. Jehu's extermination of the house of Omri and the worshipers of Baal,
    10:1-36
B. Athaliah succeeded byJoash of Judah, 11:1–12:21
C. Jehoahaz and Jehoash of Israel, 13:1-25
D. Amaziah and Azariah (Uzziah) of Judah, 14:1-22; 15:1-7
E. Jeroboam II, 14:23-29
F. Last kings of Israel: Zechariah, Shallum, Menahem, Pekahiah, Pekah,
    Hoshea, 15:8-31
G. Jotham and Ahaz of Judah, 15:32–16:20
H. Fall of Samaria; its resettlement by semiconverted pagans, 17:1-41

V. Jewish monarchy after the fall of Samaria, 18:1–25:30

A. Hezekiah and Sennacherib, 18:1–19:37
B. Hezekiah's illness; his display of wealth to the Chaldean envoys, 20:1-21
C. Wicked King Manasseh; his son Amon, 21:1-26
D. Reforms of Josiah, 22:1–23:30
E. Final kings and the fall of Jerusalem, 23:31–25:21
F. Assassination of Gedaliah; favor shown to Jehoiachin, 25:22-30

DATE OF COMPOSITION

As to the sources of this work, it is obvious that the prophetic author has drawn even more largely upon prior written documents than did the author of Judges or Samuel. Three such documents are actually named: (1) The Book of the Acts of Solomon (1 Kings 11:41); (2) The Book of the Chronicles of the Kings of Judah (*passîm*); (3) The Book of the Chronicles of the Kings of Israel (*passîm*). It may fairly be inferred that these three works largely consisted in the notations of the official court chronicler or recorder, the *mazkîr* mentioned in 2 Sam. 8:16. Also not cited but obviously borrowed is a fourth source, Isaiah 36-39, large sections of which have been taken over almost verbatim in 2 Kings 18-20. (Since the author of 2 Kings carries the narrative of Hebrew history to the fall of Jerusalem and thereafter, it is obvious that he borrowed from Isaiah rather than the other way around. Some critics have argued that the Isaiah chapters were copied from Kings, but the evidence on which they have relied can just as well be interpreted to favor the opposite conclusion.

As to the date of the composition, it is obvious from the foregoing that prior written sources were relied upon, coming from as early a period as the reign of Solomon. Final composition is to be dated after the fall of Jerusalem, probably in the early exile; yet it is possible that only the final chapter comes from exilic times, inasmuch as the frequently recurring phrase "unto this day" throughout the book indicates unmistakably a pre-exilic perspective, 1 Kings 8:61; 9:13, 21; 10:12; 12:7; 22:19; 2 Kings 7:9; 17:34 (8x).

Talmudic tradition asserts that Jeremiah was the author of Kings (*Baba Bathra*, 15*a*), a suggestion which commends itself to Steinmueller. Since the author speaks from a consistently prophetic standpoint and is a man of great literary ability, it is possible that Jeremiah may have composed everything except the final chapter. One very strong consideration in favor of this conjecture is that there is no mention whatever of Jeremiah himself in the chapters dealing with Josiah and his successors. Apart from modesty on the part of the author, it is hard to account for the failure to mention so important a factor in Judah's history as was the ministry of Jeremiah, her last great prophet. As for the final chapter, it seems to have been written by someone dwelling in Babylon, rather than in Egypt, where Jeremiah met his death.

Liberal criticism regards the books of Kings as composed of two main strata, one a pre-exilic source which knows nothing of the fall of Jerusalem and regards worship on the high places outside Jerusalem as perfectly legitimate; the second stratum comes from the work of the Deuteronomic school which flourished about 550 B.C., (according to the theory), which looks back upon the fall of Jerusalem and the judgment of exile as already accomplished facts, and explains them as the result of failing to limit the worship of Jehovah to the temple at Jerusalem. This school of thought allegedly reinterpreted Israelite history so as to imply condemnation even for King Solomon for sacrificing at Gibeah prior to the erection of his temple. It goes without saying that the theory of a Deuteronomic school depends upon the Josianic dating of the book of Deuteronomy, the evidence for which is being increasingly recognized as too slender for successful defense. That the attitude of Deuteronomy frequently emerges in the moral judgments of 1 and 2 Kings may be freely admitted, but this is admirably accounted for by the Mosaic authorship of that book. (The same is true of the Deuteronomic influences which have been noted in the books of Samuel and Judges. Obviously the authors of these earlier works were familiar with Deuteronomy as well as the rest

KINGS OF ASSYRIA

King	Date (b.c.)
Shalmaneser III	858-824
Adad-nirari V	810-758
Assur-dan III	772-754
Assur-nirari V	754-745
Tiglath-pileser III	745-727
Shalmaneser V	727-722
Sargon II	722-705
Sennacherib	705-681
Esarhaddon	680-669
Ashurbanipal	669-626

of the Torah, and considered it to be authoritative as being authored by Moses himself.

PROBLEMS OF CHRONOLOGY

In the earlier days of Old Testament scholarship, considerable difficulty was encountered in harmonizing the numbers given in the books of Kings for the reigns of the various rulers of the Northern and Southern Kingdoms. In the case of the Jewish kings particularly, when all the regnal years were added, they came to a total considerably greater than that which could have elapsed between the death of Solomon and the fall of Jerusalem. Later research, however, demonstrated the fact that in many instances the crown prince or immediate successor to the throne was formally crowned and his reign officially begun even in the lifetime of his father. In the case of Uzziah, to take an extreme example, he seems to have been crowned as secondary king back in 790 after his father, Amaziah, had been reigning but six years. He became sole king in 767 when Amaziah died. In 751 he was smitten with the plague of leprosy and had to be set aside from his governmental responsibilities, for the most part at least. His son Jotham was then crowned (in 751) and reigned until 736; but he apparently did not die until 732 or 731, according to 2 Kings 15:30. In 743 his son Ahaz was crowned as coregent, and reigned until 728 (when he was apparently deposed, although he did not die until 725). Thus it transpired that between 743 and 739 Judah was ruled over by no less than three kings at once: Uzziah, Jotham, and Ahaz.[9]

Much difficulty for the chronology of this period has been occasioned by the statement in 2 Kings 18:13 that Sennacherib's invasion (of 701 B.C.) took place in the fourteenth year of Hezekiah's reign. From this, Edwin Thiele deduced that Hezekiah began ruling in 715, despite the fact that all other references in 2 Kings indicate or

9. Cf. the usage in the Northern Kingdom: 2 Kings 15:1 speaks of the 27th year of Jeroboam II and in the following verse it states he reigned 52 years until 753 B.C., which would include both his years of vice-regency and his sole reign.

imply that he began his joint rule with Ahaz in 728 (2 Kings 15:30; 16:1-2; 17:1; and even 18:1, 9-10). Thiele reluctantly comes to the conclusion concerning the Hebrew author: "He was a man deeply concerned about truth, but who did not understand all the truth."[10] He buttresses this conclusion by attempting to show that Hezekiah's "Great Passover" must have taken place after the fall of Samaria rather than before (even though 2 Chron. 30–31 implies that this took place about the same time as the religious reforms which he enforced in Judah, early in his reign). As the Hebrew text now reads, there is a clear discrepancy between 2 Kings 18:13 and all the other passages cited above. But if "fourteenth year" is amended to "twenty-fourth year,"[11] this points to 725 as the commencement of Hezekiah's sole rule after the death of Ahaz. If the type of numerical notation was used in the *Vorlage* which appears in the Elephantine Papyri, it would require only the smudging of one horizontal stroke to make a twenty-four look like a fourteen. Or if the numbers were spelled out, then it would take only the misreading of one letter (*mēm* miscopied as *hē*) to convert "twenty-four" (*'arba' 'eśrîm*) into "fourteen' (*'arba' 'eśrēh*) according to the earlier orthography. In support of this emendation is the instance of 2 Chron. 36:9, which gives the age of Jehoiachin as eight when he ascended to the throne; whereas 2 Kings 24:8 indicates that he was actually eighteen. Here again we have a type of manuscript error which involves a second-place digit. Even Thiele readily acknowledges that 2 Chron. 36:9 contained such an error, and that *eight* should be corrected to *eighteen*.[12] Quite possibly the scribal error originated in a *Vorlage* of Isa. 36:1, which contained the mistaken *fourteen* instead of *twenty-four*, and had no other chronological check points in context to ensure the accuracy of this numeral. The scribe who copied out 2 Kings 18:13 may have deferred to this statement in Isaiah, remembering that this was what the prophet apparently recorded. Another such example is found in 2 Chron. 2:2, which gives the age of Ahaziah ben Jehoram as forty-two when he began to reign, whereas 2 Kings 8:26 gives it as twenty-two. Perhaps Chronicles read ⇁ as ≡ (or possibly ⇥ because of a streak in the *Vorlage*).

Much light has been thrown upon the chronology of the Hebrew dynasties by the synchronisms (or simultaneous dates) contained in the Assyrian monuments. Of especial importance are the Assyrian eponym lists which cover the history of the empire from 893 to 666 B.C. There is also the Greek *Canon of Ptolemy* (who lived from A.D. 70 to 161), giving the reigns of the kings of Babylon from 747 B.C. onward into the Graeco-Roman period. Astronomical verification of an eclipse which Ptolemy dated as occurring in 522 B.C. has served as a valued reassurance of his accuracy. Contemporary

---

10. Thiele, *Mysterious Numbers of the Hebrew Kings*, 2d ed. (Grand Rapids: Eerdmans, 1965), p. 140.

11. E. J. Young, *Book of Isaiah, New International Commentary on the Old Testament* (Grand Rapids: Eerdmans, 1969), 2:540-42. 2 Kings 18:1 says Hezekiah began as viceroy in the third year of Hoshea (who came to the throne in 732/1), i.e., 729/8. In 18:9 Hezekiah's fourth year equals Hoshea's seventh year (731-7–724). In 18:10 Hezekiah's sixth year equals Hoshea's ninth year (731-9–722). Second Kings 17:1, 3 confirm that Hoshea's reign began in 731. Tiglath-pileser's campaign against Damascus and Samaria was in 732.

12. Thiele, p. 139.

official monuments, such as the Black Stela of Shalmaneser III and the Taylor Cylinder of Sennacherib, occasionally contain dated references to Israelite kings. From such data as these it has been established that there were numerous coregencies in both Judah and Israel, and that the years of the coregency were reckoned in the total figure for the reign of each king involved.

Thiele has also established that there was a difference in calendar reckoning between the Northern and Southern Kingdoms. The "non-accession-year" system of dating counted the remainder of the calendar year in which a king was crowned to be his first year. This meant that even though he was crowned as late as the last day of the previous year, that one day would be counted as year one in his reign, and year two would begin on the next day when the calendar New Year had its commencement. According to the "accession-year" system, however, the year in which the king was crowned was not counted in the numbering at all, but year one of his reign would commence with the following New Year. In the case of Judah, from the time of schism in 930 B.C. until about 850 the accession year system was followed. Then from the reign of Jehoram ben Jehoshaphat to the reign of Joash ben Ahaziah (848 to 796 B.C.), the non-accession year system of the Northern Kingdom was followed. Last, from the time of Amaziah to the fall of Jerusalem (796 to 587 B.C.), Judah reverted to the accession-year system. As for the Northern Kingdom, it began with the non-accession-year system in 930 and continued it till about 800 B.C. From the time of Jehoash ben Jehoahaz to the fall of Samaria (798 to 722 B.C.) it shifted to the accession-year method of computation. Thus it could happen that what was reckoned in Judah as Jehoshaphat's tenth year would be regarded in Israel as Jehoshaphat's eleventh year.

A still further complication was introduced by the fact that the Northern Kingdom began its new year in Nisan or Abib, the first month of the religious year. With equal consistency, the kingdom of Judah throughout its history used the month of Tishri or Ethanim (the seventh month of the religious year) as the first month of its secular year, and computed all dates and reigns on that basis. Why this difference arose, it is impossible to determine; nevertheless it must be taken into account in handling cases where there appears to be a one-year discrepancy in dating.

At this point it should be added that since chronology is a branch of historical science, it is constantly subject to revision. Even among conservative scholars there is some divergence. Thiele computes the time of the schism as 931 B.C., whereas Payne makes it 930. A certain amount of flexibility must always be preserved and appropriate adjustments made as new evidence comes in.

A more recent work on the later history of Judah has come out under the name of D. J. Wiseman, *Chronicles of the Chaldean Kings in the British Museum* (1956), pp. 29-31, 70-71. The tablets published in this work give a series of precise dates between 626 and 566 B.C. They indicate that Nabopolassar, the father of Nebuchadnezzar, was officially crowned November 23, 626, after defeating the Assyrian army at Babylonia. Asshuruballit II, who assumed the Assyrian throne after the fall of Nineveh in 612, was com-

SARGON II

pelled to abandon his defenses in Haran in the year 610. The battle of Megiddo, at which Josiah perished, took place in 609, and in the same year or the following year, 608, Jehoiakim began his reign under the sponsorship of Necho, then shifted allegiance to Nebuchadnezzar after the battle of Carchemish and died in 598 in a state of rebellion against him. The epoch-making battle of Carchemish, in which Nebuchadnezzar defeated the allied armies of Egypt and Assyria, took place in May or June of 605. Nabopolassar died on August 16, 605, and on September 7 Nebuchadnezzar was crowned in Babylon as his successor. In 601 the Babylonian armies were temporarily checked by the Egyptians on the Egyptian border after a fierce battle. (This fact, not previously known, helps to explain why Jehoiakim dared to risk rebellion against Babylon in the last years of his reign.) Jerusalem capitulated to Nebuchadnezzar the first time on March 15 or 16, 597. In that same month Zedekiah received his appointment as king. Last of all, Jerusalem fell in July, 587, during Nebuchadnezzar's third invasion.

These tablets clear up one discrepancy between 2 Kings 24:12, which dates the 597 capture of Jerusalem as the eighth year of Nebuchadnezzar, and Jer. 52:28, which dates it as occurring in his seventh year. It is apparent that at the battle of Carchemish, Nebuchadnezzar was in sole command of the Chaldean troops, and may well have been recognized in the west as *de facto* king already; hence the Jewish historian of 2 Kings regarded 605 or 604 as his first regnal year. But in Babylon, which used the accession-year system, his reign did not officially begin until 604 or 603. Apparently Jeremiah followed the official Babylonian reckoning in this instance.

One thorny problem has arisen in connection with the date of Sennacherib's invasion of Palestine and siege of Jerusalem as recorded in Isa. 36-37 and 2 Kings 18-19. The monuments of Sennacherib report such an invasion as having occurred in 701

SENNACHERIB'S CYLINDER

THE ANNALS OF SENNACHERIB (705–681 B.C.) ARE RECORDED ON A SIX–SIDED CLAY PRISM. IT WAS FOUND AT KUYUNJIK AT NINEVEH BY COLONEL R. TAYLOR IN 1830. ESSENTIALLY THE SAME TEXT IS ALSO ON A PRISM (THE CHICAGO PRISM) AT THE UNIVERSITY OF CHICAGO. THE PRISM DESCRIBES SENNACHERIB'S SEIGE OF 46 FORTIFIED JUDEAN CITIES (DEPORTING 200,150 PEOPLE). ALSO KNOWN AS THE TAYLOR PRISM. BAKED CLAY; HT. 38.5 CM.

B.C., and it has usually been assumed that this was the time of the great crisis recorded in the Hebrew account. But the publication by M. F. L. Macadam of Kawa Stela IV was interpreted by him to mean that Tirhaqa would have been only nine years of age by 701, and therefore hardly competent to lead the Egyptian army that tried unsuccessfully to defeat Sennacherib and raise the siege of Jerusalem. On the basis of this interpretation, many scholars (including Albright) elaborated a theory that the action with Tirhaqa implied a second invasion of Judah by Sennacherib not recorded in extant Assyrian annals, but occurring sometime in the 680s.[13] All of these speculations have been rendered nugatory, however, by a later edition of Kawa Stela IV published by Leclant and Yoyette in 1952. This second examination of the Egyptian text shows that Macadam was guilty of a misinterpretation; it was actually Tirhaqa's father, Piankhy, who died in 713 at the very latest, but far more likely in 717 or 716. This means that Tirhaqa was much older than nine in 701. Macadam mistakenly assumed that there was a coregency of six years involving Tirhaqa and his older brother, Shebitku; he was also mistaken in assigning Tirhaqa's age at twenty, referred to in Kawa Stela V: 17, to the year 690/689 B.C. Actually it pointed to the time just after Shebitku's accession in 702. As correctly interpreted, then, these texts tell us that Tirhaqa was twenty years old in 701, when his brother summoned him to assume leadership of the campaign into Judah. Thus he was old enough to play this responsible role, even though he was not then the reigning king (as he had become by the time the episode was recorded in is 36 and 2 Kings 18). Kawa Stela IV:7-8 records concerning Tirhaqa: "His Majesty was in Nubia, as a goodly youth...amidst the goodly youths whom His Majesty King Shebitku had summoned from Nubia." (Note that here too the later report of the incident refers to Tirhaqa as "His Majesty," even though he was at that time only the crown prince.)[14]

Before leaving this discussion of the Divided Monarchy in the period of Assyrian expansion, some mention should be made of a remarkable discovery made back in

---

13. See also H. Stigers in *Wycliffe Bible Commentary* (Chicago: Moody, 1962), p. 358.
14. Consult Kitchen, AOOT, pp. 82-84, for further details and documentation.

UZZIAH TABLET

UZZIAH'S ACTUAL BURIAL INSCRIPTION HAS BEEN FOUND. IT READS, "HERE WERE BROUGHT THE BONES OF UZZIAH, KING OF JUDAH – NOT TO BE OPENED."

1880 that brought to light an historic Hebrew record from the time of Hezekiah and Isaiah. This consisted of a record carved into the hard lime-stone of the Siloam tunnel which was undertaken in order to insure an adequate water supply for the city of Jerusalem in times of siege. In six lines one of the workmen involved in this operation incised an account of how the two gangs of work-men, digging simultaneous from the east and from the west, finally heard each other when they were three cubits apart, and dug through a jog which united the tunnel bore sufficiently to enable the water from the Siloam Spring outside the city wall to flow into a large retention pool inside the ramparts of the city. The tunnel extended for 1,200 cubits, 100 cubits below the top of the rock. A good translation of this inscription may be found in ANET[3,] p. 321, and a serviceable photograph of it appears on p. 127 of E. Würthwein's *The Text of the Old Testament* translated from the 4th German edition and published by Eerdmans in 1979. From this text we gain a more accurate knowledge of the exact shape of epigraphic Hebrew writing back in the late 700's B.C. This type of information is especially helpful in establishing what letters of the Hebrew alphabet so resembled each other in shape as to lead to possible miscopying on the part of a scribe. Hence it is valuable for textual criticism.

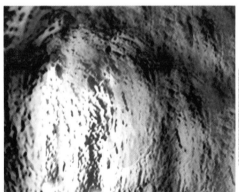

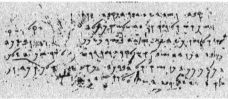

SILOAM CAVE INSCRIPTION

THE SILOAM INSCRIPTION DISCOVERED IN 1880, HAS SIX LINES OF TEXT WHOSE CONTENTS AND SCRIPT INDICATE IT WAS WRITTEN DURING THE REIGN OF HEZEKIAH (728-697 B.C.). IT REPORTS HOW TWO TEAMS OF MEN DUG A TUNNEL UNDER JERUSALEM FROM THE GIHON SPRING (2 KINGS 20:20). HEIGHT, 0.38 M.; LENGTH, 0.72 M.

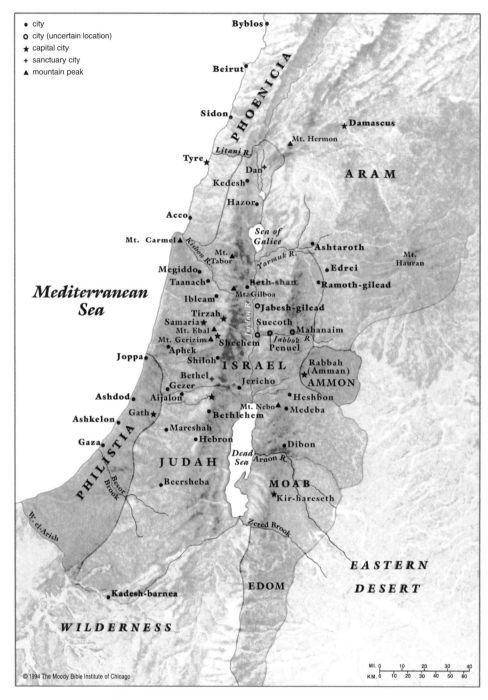

THE DIVIDED MONARCHY AFTER 931 B.C.
THE NORTHERN KINGDOM, SOUTHERN KINGDOM

21 INTRODUCTION TO THE PROPHETS; OBADIAH, JOEL, AND JONAH

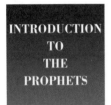

INTRODUCTION TO THE PROPHETS

IT SHOULD BE REMEMBERED that according to the terminology of the Hebrew Bible, the Former Prophets include four books which we have already discussed—Joshua, Judges, Samuel, and Kings. Although these books deal with the history of Israel, they were composed from a prophetic viewpoint and possibly even the authors themselves may have been prophets by profession. But the books considered in this and the next six chapters are classified in the Hebrew Bible as the Latter Prophets. These are subdivided into the Major Prophets (Isaiah, Jeremiah, and Ezekiel), and the twelve Minor Prophets, whose writings could all be included in one large scroll, which came to be known in Greek as the *Dōdecaprophēton* ("the Twelve-Prophet Book").

NATURE OF HEBREW PROPHECY

By way of general definition, a prophecy is an oral or written disclosure in words through a human mouthpiece transmitting the revelation of God and setting forth His will to man. In the broader sense, even events, such as the crossing of the Red Sea or the episode of the brazen serpent, may have a prophetic significance, in that their importance is not exhausted by the historical occurrence itself. They in turn point forward to an antitypical fulfillment in the times of the Messiah. The ordinances of the tabernacle and the priesthood were fraught with prophetic significance, for often they provided types pointing to the person and work of the Lord Jesus. Under this heading may be included the priesthood of Aaron, the tabernacle itself, the various articles of furniture which it contained, and the rituals of sacrifice. In this broader sense, then, a great portion of the Old Testament constitutes prophecy; but in the narrower sense the term is confined to the discourses of those specially chosen and anointed men who occupied the prophetic office.

Even among these men, however, there was a considerable number whose utter-

FOUNTAIN OF ELISHA
THOUGHT TO BE THE LOCATION WHERE ELISHA THREW SALT TO PURIFY THE WATERS (2 KINGS 2:19-21).

ances were never preserved in written form, although their messages are indirectly alluded to in the various historical books. Such was the case with men like Nathan and Gad of David's generation, and in the later period Shemaiah, Ahijah, Elijah, Micaiah, Elisha, Oded, and many others. These are known as the oral prophets, since their messages were transmitted only by word of mouth. In most cases their manifestos were addressed largely to contemporary crises in the life of Israel and did not have a permanent significance for coming generations in the same sense and to the same degree as did the writings of the prophetic canon. But where a revelation of God contained information relevant to the succeeding ages, the Holy Spirit inspired the authors to commit their messages to writing. These, then, are the documents which have been preserved to us as the Major and Minor Prophets.

NATURE OF THE PROPHETIC OFFICE

The responsibility of the Old Testament prophets was not principally to predict the future in the modern sense of the word *prophesy*, but rather to tell forth the will of God which He had communicated by revelation. The Hebrew word "to prophesy" is *nibba'* (the *niphal* stem of *nābā'*), a word whose etymology is much disputed. The most likely derivation, however, seems to relate this root to the Akkadian verb *nabû*, which means to "summon, announce, call." In the prologue of Hammurabi's Code, the Babylonian king asserts that he was *nibit Bêl* ("called of Baal") and that the gods *nibba'* ("called or appointed") him to be their viceroy on earth. Thus the verb *nibba'* would doubtlessly signify one who has been called or appointed to proclaim as a herald the message of God Himself. From this verb comes the characteristic word for prophet, *nābî'* ("one who has been called"). On this interpretation the prophet was not to be regarded as a self-appointed professional whose purpose was to convince others of his own opinions, but rather he was one called by God to proclaim as a herald from the court of heaven the message to be transmitted from God to man.

A second designation often applied to the earlier prophets particularly was *the man of God* (*'îš 'Elōhîm*). This title implied that the prophet must be a man who belonged first and foremost to God, was wholly devoted to His cause, and enjoyed His personal fellowship. Therefore he could be trusted to transmit God's word, because he spoke only as God enlightened him and guided him to speak.

A third term applied to the prophets was that of *seer* (*hōzeh* or *rō'eh*, in Hebrew). The implication of this title was that the prophet would not be deluded by external semblance or the deceitful appearances of the material world, but rather would see the issues as they really were from the perspective of God Himself. As a seer, the prophet might receive special visions and *ab extra* revelations from the Lord and thus be qualified to convey the spiritual realities which other men could not see. As a seer he would avoid evolving ideas or opinions of his own mind and would confine himself to that which God had actually shown him. Related to the term *hōzeh* was *hāzôn* or *hāzût*, a significant word for "prophecy" which appears in the title of Isaiah's prophecies (Isa. 1:1). Or else the verb "to see" (*hāzah*), might be so employed as in Amos 1:1 ("the words of Amos which he saw").

In the earliest period, the prophetic function was assigned to the Levitical priests, who were charged with the responsibility of teaching the implications of the Mosaic law for daily conduct in the practical issues of life. But even the Torah envisioned the possibility of a special class of prophets distinct from the priests and playing a role analogous to that of Moses (cf. Deut. 18—a passage which not only predicts the Messianic Prophet but also establishes the prophetic order as such). As the priesthood became increasingly professionalistic in attitude and lax in practice (as for example Hophni and Phinehas, the sons of Eli), a new teaching order arose to maintain the integrity of the covenant relationship in the heart of Israel. Some of these prophets came from the priestly tribe of Levi, such as Jeremiah and Ezekiel, but the majority

MIRACLES IN THE OLD TESTAMENT

SCRIPTURE	MIRACLE (OR EVENT)
Gen. 19:26	Lot's wife becomes a pillar of salt
Ex. 3:2	Burning bush
Ex. 7:10-12	Aaron's rod changed into a serpent
Ex. 7-11	Plagues of Egypt
Ex. 14:21-31	Red Sea divided
Ex. 15:23-25	Waters of Marah sweetened
Ex. 16:14-35	Manna in the Wilderness
Ex. 17:5-7	Water from the rock at Rephidim
Lev. 10:1, 2	Nadab and Abihu destroyed
Num. 16:32-35	Earth swallows Korah
Num. 17:1-13	Aaron's rod budded
Num. 20:7-11	Water from the rock at Meribah
Num. 22:21-35	Baalam's donkey speaks
Josh. 3:14-17	Israelite passage through the Jordan
Josh. 6:6-20	Destruction of the walls of Jericho
Josh. 10:12-14	Sun and moon delayed the close of the day
1 Sam. 5:1-12	Dagon falls before the Ark of God, worshipers afflicted with hemorrhoids and death
1 Sam. 7:10-12	Thunderstorm in the battle with the Philistines
2 Sam. 6:7	Uzzah killed after touching the Ark
1 Kings 13:4-6	Jeroboam's hand withered before the new altar at Bethel, then suddenly healed
1 Kings 17:14-16	Widow's grain and oil multipled
1 Kings 17:17-24	Widow's son raised from the dead
1 Kings 18:30-38	Elijah's sacrifice on Mt. Carmel consumed by fire; priests of Baal totally failed
1 Kings 18:41-45	Elijah obtains rain after drought
1 Kings 20:30-38	Wall of Aphek
2 Kings 1:10-12	Ahaziah's soldiers consumed by fire
2 Kings 2:7, 8-14	The Jordan divided before Elijah
2 Kings 2:11	Elijah translated
2 Kings 3:16-20	Water provided for Jehoshaphat's army in desert
2 Kings 4:2-7	The cruse of oil does not fail the widow
2 Kings 4:32-37	The Shunammites' son restored to life by Elisha
2 Kings 4:42-44	One hundred men fed with 20 loaves
2 Kings 5:10-14	Naaman healed of leprosy
2 Kings 5:20-27	Gehazi stricken with leprosy
2 Kings 6:5-7	Iron axe-head floats
2 Kings 6:18-20	A Syrian expeditionary force blinded
2 Kings 13:21	Elisha's bones resurrect the dead
2 Kings 19:35	Destruction of Sennacherib's army by plague
2 Kings 20:9-11	The sun goes backward on the dial of Ahaz
2 Chron. 26:16-21	Uzziah is afflicted with leprosy
Dan. 3:19-27	Shadrach, Meshach, and Abednego
Dan. 6:16-23	Daniel in the lion's den
Jonah 2:1-10	Jonah in the belly of the whale

came from the other tribes.

FUNCTION OF HEBREW PROPHECY

As has already been suggested, the function of the prophet went beyond mere prediction of things to come. Four principal elements may be defined in the ministry of the Old Testament prophets.

1. The prophet had the responsibility of encouraging God's people to trust only in Yahweh's mercy and redemptive power, rather than in their own merits or strength, or in the might of human allies. Just as Moses admonished the Israelites to trust God for the impossible at crisis times when they faced the menaces of the Egyptians or Canaanites, so the great eighth-century prophets exhorted their countrymen to put their whole dependence upon the delivering power of the Lord rather than upon the assistance of human allies such as Assyria or Egypt.

2. The prophet was responsible to remind his people that safety and blessedness were conditioned upon their faithful adherence to the covenant, and that this adherence involved not only doctrinal conviction, but also a sincere submission of their will to obey God with their whole heart and to lead a godly life. Apart from such submission, no amount of sacrifice or ritualistic worship could satisfy the Lord. In other words, a saving faith involves a sanctified walk. This is perhaps the foremost emphasis in the prophets: "Bring no more vain oblations...your hands are full of blood....Cease to do evil; learn to do well....Come now, and let us reason together" (Isa. 1:13-18). It is not that the prophets regarded moral living as the essence of religion, but rather they understood a godly walk to be the unfailing product of a genuine saving faith. They recognized that all men were guilty before God and utterly without hope apart from His redeeming grace (cf. 1 Kings 8:46; Ps. 14:2-3; 130:3; Prov. 20:9; Isa. 53:6; 59:4, 12-16; 64:6; Mic. 7:2); no one could be saved by his own virtue or goodness. But on the other hand, Israel needed to be reminded (as does the professing church in modern times) that God would accept no substitute for a sincere faith which expresses itself by a law-honoring life. As various moral issues came up, it was naturally the function of the prophets to interpret and apply the law of Moses to contemporary conditions. They never regarded their teaching prerogative as more than ancillary and interpretive of the uniquely authoritative Torah.

3. The prophet was to encourage Israel in respect to the future. All too often, the efforts at revival sponsored by godly kings or promoted by the prophets on their own initiative, succeeded in reaching only a small percentage of the population. The controlling majority of the nation would remain hardened in disobedience. Such intransigence could only mean an eventual incurring of divine wrath according to the warnings of Lev. 26 and Deut. 28, until the covenant nation would be finally expelled from the land of promise. The question naturally arose, would these divine judgments bring Israel to an end as a holy nation set apart to witness to the heathen of the one true God? God's answer through His prophets was that after devastation and exile would

come the restoration of the believing remnant of Israel to the land. The nation would yet fulfill its destiny as a testimony to the Gentiles under the leadership of the coming Messiah. This assurance of the future, of the ultimate triumph of the true faith, was well calculated to encourage the sincere believers within Israel to keep faith with God and keep on trusting Him in the face of all contrary appearances and hostile circumstances.

4. Hebrew prophecy was to seal the authoritativeness of God's message by the objective verification of fulfilled prophecy. Thus in Deuteronomy 18 the test of a true prophet was stated to be the fulfillment of what he predicted. Sometimes these fulfillment would come in a relatively short time, as in the case of the scoffing nobleman of 2 Kings 7, who derided Elisha's claim that the price of flour would drop to a mere fraction of famine rates within twenty-four hours. On other occasions the fulfillment was so far in the future as to be beyond the experience of the generation living at the time the prophecy was given. In such a case, naturally the verification would be of benefit only to future ages; nevertheless, circumstances might call for this type of confirmation. "Behold, the former things are come to pass, and new things do I declare; before they spring forth I tell you of them" (Isa. 42:9). "And who, as I, shall call, and shall declare it, and set it in order for me, since I appointed the ancient people? And the things that are coming, and shall come, let them show unto them. Fear ye not, neither be ye afraid; have not I told thee from that time, and have declared it? Ye are even my witnesses" (Isa. 44:7-8). This last utterance was connected with a prediction of the liberation of the Jews by Cyrus, an event which was not to take place for 150 years. Again and again the phrase recurs—especially in Jeremiah and Ezekiel—as future events are foretold: "And they shall know that I am Yahweh" (i.e., the covenant-keeping God of Israel). This knowledge was to come to observers after the predicted judgments actually befell the threatened offenders. It was recognized by all that such fulfillment of predictive prophecy would provide objective evidence incapable of any other explanation than that He who imparted the prediction was the same Lord of history who would bring its fulfillment to pass. They rightly saw that any other attempted explanation would involve a surrender of man's reason to an authoritarian demand on the part of the dogmatic rationalist for a blind faith in his logically untenable position.

OBADIAH

This shortest book in the Old Testament, consisting of only twenty-one verses, bears the distinction of being the most difficult of all the prophecies to date. Even Conservative scholars have offered conflicting conjectures which range all the way from the reign of Jehoram ben Jehoshaphat (848-841 B.C.) to 585, soon after the destruction of Jerusalem by the Chaldeans (a date preferred by Luther). Most Liberal scholars prefer 585 as the time of composition, although a few, like Pfeiffer, divide it up into two different sources; the later of which was written at some time during the Exile or soon after the fall of Babylon in 539.

OUTLINE OF OBADIAH

I. Coming destruction of Edom, 1-9

A. The downfall of impregnable Sela, 1-4
B. The city to be plundered, devastated, and forsaken, 5-9

II. Cause of Edom's judgment: her malice against Israel, 10-14

III. Coming day of the Lord, 15-21

A. Impending judgment upon Edom and the rest of the heathen, 15, 16
B. Future deliverance of Israel, 17-20
C. Ultimate messianic kingdom, 21

TIME OF COMPOSITION

As already indicated, some scholars place the authorship of this little book in the period immediately following the fall of Jerusalem. Others, such as J. H. Raven and J. D. Davis, prefer to date it in the reign of Ahaz (742-728 B.C.), and interpret its historical allusions as referring to his defeats at the hands of the Edomites and Philistines. (2 Chron. 28:17-18 records how these two nations attacked Judah from the south and west soon after the northern coalition of Israel and Damascus had inflicted serious reverses on the armies of Ahaz.) A serious difficulty with this view, however, is derived from the fact that no such capture and despoilation of Jerusalem is reported to have taken place during these campaigns as is implied in Obad. 11.

A good majority of the evangelical scholars of the nineteenth and early twentieth centuries have inclined toward a much earlier date, that of Jehoram ben Jehoshaphat, 848–841. This is the view espoused by Delitzsch, Keil, Kleinert, Orelli, and Kirkpatrick. Second Kings 8:20 states concerning Jehoram: "In his days Edom revolted from under the hand of Judah, and made a king over themselves." The succeeding verses speak of Jehoram's unsuccessful campaign against them in which he inflicted much damage but failed to subjugate them once again to Judah's suzerainty. Second Chronicles 21:16-17 adds these details: "And Yahweh stirred up against Jehoram the spirit of the Philistines, and of the Arabians that are beside the Ethiopians: and they came up against Judah, and brake into it, and carried away all the substance that was found in the king's house, and his sons also, and his wives; so that there was never a son left him, save Jehoahaz, the youngest of his sons" (ASV).[1] Piecing these items of information together, we find it quite probable that the Edomites cooperated with the Arabian-Philistine invasion as subordinate allies, and shared in the booty of Jerusalem when that unhappy capital fell to their combined efforts.

In this way we have a plausible historical setting for Obad. 11: "In the day that

---

1. Here the KJV rendering is misleading. Note the correct translation of the NASB for verse 13: "Do not enter the gate of my people in the day of their disaster." NIV: "You should not march through the gates of my people." The original reads אַל־תָּבוֹא בְשַׁעַר־עַמִּי בְּיוֹם אֵידָם—The NASB is clearly the closest in its handling of the negative command.

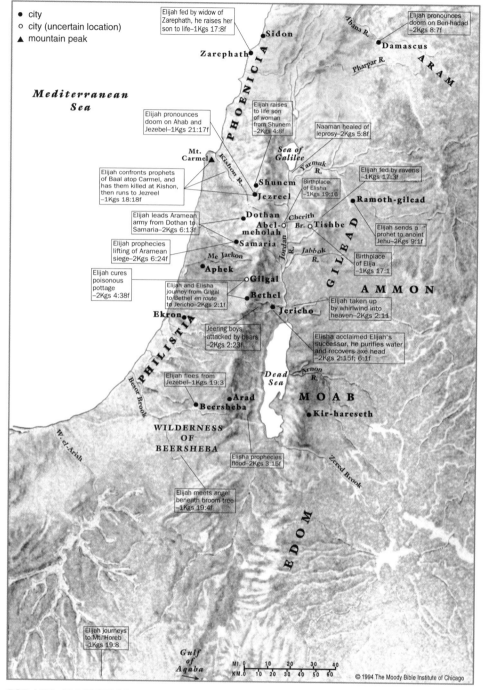

- city
- ○ city (uncertain location)
- ▲ mountain peak

Elijah fed by widow of Zarephath, he raises her son to life–1Kgs 17:8f

Elijah pronounces doom on Ben-hadad –2Kgs 8:7f

Elijah pronounces doom on Ahab and Jezebel–1Kgs 21:17f

Elijah raises to life son of woman from Shunem –2Kgs 4:8f

Naaman healed of leprosy–2Kgs 5:8f

Elijah confronts prophets of Baal atop Carmel, and has them killed at Kishon, then runs to Jezreel –1Kgs 18:18f

Elijah fed by ravens –1Kgs 17:3f

Birthplace of Elisha –1Kgs 19:16

Elijah leads Aramean army from Dothan to Samaria–2Kgs 6:13f

Elijah sends a prophet to anoint Jehu–2Kgs 9:1f

Elijah prophecies lifting of Aramean siege–2Kgs 6:24f

Birthplace of Elija –1Kgs 17:1

Elijah cures poisonous pottage –2Kgs 4:38f

Elijah and Elisha journey from Gilgal to Bethel en route to Jericho–2Kgs 2:1f

Elijah taken up by whirlwind into heaven–2Kgs 2:11

Jeering boys attacked by bears –2Kgs 2:23f

Elisha acclaimed Elijah's successor, he purifies water and recovers axe head –2Kgs 2:15f; 6:1f

Elijah flees from Jezebel–1Kgs 19:3

Elisha prophecies flood–2Kgs 3:15f

Elijah meets angel beneath broom tree –1Kgs 19:4f

Elijah journeys to Mt. Horeb –1Kgs 19:8

Mediterranean Sea

Sidon
Zarephath
Damascus
Abana R.
Pharpar R.
PHOENICIA
ARAM
Mt. Carmel
Kishon R.
Sea of Galilee
Yarmuk R.
Shunem
Jezreel
Ramoth-gilead
Dothan
Cherith Br.
Tishbe
Abel-meholah
Jordan R.
Jabbok R.
GILEAD
Samaria
AMMON
Me Jarkon
Aphek
Gilgal
Bethel
Jericho
Ekron
PHILISTIA
Dead Sea
Arnon R.
Arad
Beersheba
MOAB
Kir-hareseth
WILDERNESS OF BEERSHEBA
Besor Brook
W. el-Arish
EDOM
Zered Brook
Gulf of Aqaba

MI. 0   10   20   30   40
KM. 0 10 20 30 40 50 60

© 1994 The Moody Bible Institute of Chicago

ISRAEL IN THE NINTH CENTURY
DURING THE MINISTRIES OF ELIJAH AND ELISHA.

thou stoodest on the other side, in the day that strangers carried away his substance, and foreigners entered into his gates, and cast lots upon Jerusalem, even thou wast as one of them." This verse implies that the enemies of Judah forced their way into Jerusalem and plundered its treasures. As the city was being looted, lots were cast by the cooperating marauders to decide which quarter of the town would be granted to each contingent for the purposes of plunder. Such a description hardly fits in with the complete and permanent destruction of the city such as was inflicted upon it by Nebuchadnezzar in 587-586. Moreover, as correctly translated in the ASV, verse 13 looks forward to other occasions when this same Jerusalem may again be attacked by invading foes: "Enter not into the gate of my people in the day of their calamity...neither lay ye hands on their substance in the day of their calamity." Such words would hardly be appropriate if Jerusalem were already a desolate heap of ruins, as the 585 date would imply. Hence we must look for some military action which involved the storming of Jerusalem but stopped short of its complete destruction; an engagement, moreover, in which the Edomites might well have played a part (as they probably did not do when the Chaldeans stormed the city in 587). The only recorded episode which fits all these conditions seems to be this invasion in the reign of Jehoram.

The 585 date is also imperiled by the strong evidence that the prophet Jeremiah had read and adapted for his own purposes Obad. 1-9 (see Jer. 49:7-22). Jeremiah's passage is found as one in a series of oracles based to a large extent on the prophecies of earlier messengers of God. (Cf. Jer. 48 with Isa. 15-16, and Jer. 49 with Amos 1:13-15; 8:1-3.) Obadiah could hardly have borrowed from Jeremiah, for he expresses his sentiments more briefly and rapidly than does Jeremiah and in part also more heavily and abruptly. By smoothing down the rugged places in Obadiah's style of expression, Jeremiah shows himself to have been the adapter rather than the original source, and as adapter he has made the whole oracle more lucid and perspicuous.

The later date theory is largely based upon Obad. 20, "And the captivity [$g\bar{a}l\hat{u}t$] of this host of the children of Israel...shall possess that of the Canaanites." Apart from the context this might well refer to the deportation of the total population of Judah into Babylonian Exile, thus substantiating a 585 date; but $g\bar{a}l\hat{u}t$ may also refer to the capture of single individuals or limited groups of people. Thus Amos 1:9 refers to the guilt of the slave traders of Tyre who delivered over an "entire captivity" ($g\bar{a}l\hat{u}t\ sh^{e}l\bar{e}$-mah) to the Edomites composed of kidnapped individuals for use as slaves in the iron mines. In this case "entire captivity" cannot refer to the deportation of the entire population but only to the inhabitants of isolated communities captured in a sudden slave raid. This episode referred to by Amos must, of course, have happened in the eighth century, long before the Babylonian captivity of 586 B.C. In Isa. 20:4 the same term[2] is used of the action of the king of Assyria in leading away Egyptian and Ethiopian prisoners after his victorious campaign in the Nile valley—an incident which was to take place

2. Note Isa. 20:4 is not quite the same, "So the king of Assyria will lead away the captives of Egypt and the exiles of Cush, young and old, naked and barefoot with buttocks uncovered, to the shame of Egypt."

in the early seventh century, in the reign of Essarhaddon. Thus we may conclude that an author who wrote Obad. 20 may have lived one or two centuries before the time of Nebuchadnezzar. The fulfillment of this verse is of course another matter, for it cannot be dated any earlier than the Hasmonean dynasty in the second century B.C., and very probably is to be sought for in the events of the last days of the millennial kingdom.

There is one obscure reference in verse 20, to a distant locality called Sepharad, the identification of which is much disputed. An old rabbinic tradition relates it to the region of Spain; hence the Spanish Jews became known as the Sephardic communion. Other scholars relate it to the capital of Sardis in Asia Minor and cite recently discovered inscriptions in Aramaic referring to that district by the term *S-p-r-d* (these being the consonants of the name *Sepharad*).[3] But since there was no deportation or migration of the Jews to Sardis, so far as is known to us from ancient documents, this is hardly a plausible identification.[4] The most likely identification connects *Sepharad* with a district referred to as Shaparda in southwestern Media mentioned in an inscription of King Sargon of Assyria. It is well known that Sargon deported some of the ten tribes to the "cities of the Medes" (see 2 Kings 18:11). Therefore this locality would have been very appropriate to mention in Obadiah's prediction.

As already mentioned, some critics divide Obadiah into two sources. Lanchester dates section A, verses 1-7, 10-14, soon after 586 B.C. and places section B, verses 8, 9, 15-21, some time during the exile or even later. R. H. Pfeiffer uses a different division: he makes section A include verses 1-14,15*b*, and dates its composition about 460 B.C. (just prior to the time of Ezra). His section B, comprising 15*a*, 16-21, comes from a later period which he does not more closely define. Eissfeldt divides the chapter about the same way as Pfeiffer, but he dates section A as possibly earlier, perhaps soon after 587 B.C. It may seem surprising that so short a work should be parceled out to different authors by these source critics, but their methodology is essentially the same as that employed in the dissection of the larger books of the Old Testament. The effort is made on the basis of a very imperfect knowledge of ancient affairs to link up even the vaguest of references to contemporary affairs with the known historical conditions in each succeeding period, and to operate upon the principle that there is no genuine predictive prophecy but only prophecy after the event. In other words, so-called pre-

---

3. See C. C. Torrey's article, "The Bilingual Inscription from Sardis," *American Journal of Semitic Languages* (Oct. 1917). This contains the Aramaic text of a Lydian-Aramaic funerary inscription, in which the city of Sardis is mentioned twice, and is spelled *S-P-R-D*. Torrey feels certain (p. 190) that this is the city intended by Obad. 20. It carries the date of the tenth year of Artaxerxes, but it is uncertain whether this refers to Artaxerxes I as Torrey thinks (hence 454 B.C.), or Artaxerxes II, as Cook prefers (hence 394 B.C.). It certainly must be conceded that *S-P-R-D* could have referred to Sardis, so far as the spelling of the name goes. But the alternative possibility of *Shaparda* in Media provides exactly the same consonantal spelling, and it fits in much better with the known facts of Hebrew history.

4. It should be noted that it is favored by the *New Bible Commentary* and by Lanchester in the *Cambridge Bible*, whose discussion in "Obadiah and Jonah," pp. 11-20, is both comprehensive and fair minded—although he divides Obadiah into two sources. That there were Jews living in Sardis, Lydia, by the 1st century A.D. is beyond dispute, for they cooperated with the pagan citizenry in the persecution of Christian martyrs there. But by that time, Jewish communities were established in all the major cities of the Near East. Yet there is no record of their having been settled there back in Assyrian times.

THE HIGH PLACE OF PETRA, LOCATED ON TOP OF A MOUNTAIN, WAS ACCESSED BY ROCK-HEWN STAIRS.

dictive prophecy is only a reflection of what has already happened.

As for Obadiah's message of the judgment of God which is to come upon Edom, it should be remembered that the Edomites were regarded by the prophets as typical of the malignant foes of Israel who hated and opposed all that Israel stood for in their witness to the one true God. Thus, Edom became typical of the corrupt, hate-ridden world, ripe for apocalyptic judgment (cf. Isa. 34). But the prediction is made here that despite Edom's opposition, a future day is coming when Israel shall once more be put in sure possession of the promised land, including the surrounding territories of Mount Seir, Philistia, Gilead, and even Phoenicia as far as Zarephath. This future Israelite realm shall belong to Yahweh.

As to the fulfillment of this doom upon Edom, it may be fairly inferred from Mal. 1:3-5 that by Malachi's time (ca. 435 B.C.) the Edomites had already been driven from Sela and Mount Seir by the overwhelming forces of the Nabatean Arabs. Secular sources inform us that as early as the reign of Darius I (522-485), the Nabateans had pushed the Edomites out of their ancestral territory and driven them into the deserted regions of southern Judea. The Nabateans originally came from Nabaioth in the region of Kedar in northern Arabia. Seventh-century Assyrian inscriptions refer to them as the *Nabaitai*. In the course of time the power of this Nabatean kingdom extended up into the Transjordanian region as far as Damascus. By New Testament times Damascus was held for a while at least by King Aretas of the Nabatean dynasty (cf. 2 Cor. 11:32). As for the dispossessed Edomites, the region in which they settled came to be known as Idumea, where they maintained an independent existence for a time, until they were conquered by the Jewish king, John Hyrcanus (135-105 B.C.), and forcibly converted to the Jewish faith. In the following century, the dynasty of Herod the Great, descended from the Idumean stock, came into control of the kingdom of Judea.

JOEL

The name *Joel* means "Yahweh is God" (*Yô'ēl*, Hebrew). The theme of this prophet was a solemn warning of divine judgment to be visited upon Israel in the day of Yahweh. This day of judgment is typified by the devastating locust plague which inflicts staggering economic loss upon the nation. But this plague in turn points forward to a time of final destruction to be meted out to all the forces of unbelief.

OUTLINE OF JOEL

I. Plague of locusts as a type of the day of Yahweh, 1:1–2:11

A. Tremendous devastation by the locust horde, 1:1-7
B. This invasion a prefiguration of the human invaders of the future (Assyrians and Chaldeans), 1:8-20
C. Day of Yahweh as a day of reckoning, 2:1-11

II. Call to repentance, 2:12-19

A. External forms of contrition as well as sincere heart repentance, 2:12-15
B. Repentance on a nationwide scale, including all classes and ages, 2:16-17
C. Promise of the returning mercy of the Lord (apparently fulfilled in the reign of Joash), 2:18-19

III. Promise of showers of blessing, 2:20-32

A. Terrible overthrow of Israel's invaders from the north, 2:20
  1. Sennacherib
  2. The world power of the last days
B. Rain from the Lord after locust plague and drought, 2:21-27
C. This rain a prefiguration of outpouring of the Holy Spirit in the last days (beginning at Pentecost), 2:28-32; meteoric signs the final phase of the last days (cf. Matt. 24:29)

IV. Final triumph of God in the day of Yahweh, 3:1-21

A. Final slaughter of unbelievers; divine judgment upon the final dictator, 3:1-16
  1. Foreshadowing judgment upon Phoenicia and Philistia, now oppressing Judah, 3:1-13
  2. Foreshadowing triumphs of the Maccabean age, 3:14-16
B. Millennial triumph and peace for Jerusalem, including the whole family of the redeemed, 3:17-21

TIME OF COMPOSITION

The prophecy of Joel has been dated all the way from the ninth century to the fourth century B.C. by the various schools of criticism, conservative and liberal. But on the basis of internal evidence, the most reasonable estimate is in the minority of King Joash (835-796 B.C.), during the regency of Jehoida, the high priest, about 830 B.C. For an excellent presentation of the arguments for an early date, see A. F. Kirkpatrick, *The Doctrine of the Prophets* (1890). These evidences may be listed under three categories:

1. The type of government implied by these prophetic utterances best accords with a regency. There is no mention of a king; the elders and priests seem to bear the responsibility of national leadership. This would seem to imply that the king was a minor and that regents ruled in his place. According to 2 Kings 11:4, Joash was crowned at the age of seven, and his uncle, Jehoiada, is said to have exercised a controlling influence in Judah even to the day of his death, in the latter part of Joash's reign.

2. There is distinct evidence of borrowing, as between Amos and Joel. For example, both Joel 3:18 and Amos 9:13 contain the promise, "The mountains shall drop sweet wine." While Joel might possibly have quoted from Amos, the contextual indications are that it was the other way around. Another example is found in Joel 3:16 where in the midst of a prophetic discourse he says, "The Lord also shall roar out of Zion, and utter his voice from Jerusalem." This same verse appears at the beginning of the prophecy of Amos, and it may fairly be inferred that Amos was using it as a sort of sermon text from which he developed his first message. On this basis, then, Joel must have been written earlier than Amos, that is, earlier than 755 B.C.

3. An even more conclusive argument is found in the array of enemies which are mentioned by the author as threatening Judah. There is no reference to the Assyrians or Chaldeans (to say nothing of the Persians), but the foes of Judah are stated to be the Phoenicians, the Philistines, the Egyptians, and the Edomites (cf. Joel 3:4, 19). This points to a period when Assyria and Babylon posed no threat, but Egypt and the surrounding neighbors of Israel were still strong and aggressive. Even in the time of Joash, the power of Egypt was still to be feared; in Rehoboam's time Shishak (identified with Sheshonkh I, 947-925 B.C.) had ravaged the kingdom and sacked the temple at Jerusalem; and in the reign of Asa occurred the dread invasion of Zerah, the general sent by Osorkon I (925-829) of the Ethiopian dynasty (*New Bible Dictionary*, p. 1359). In the time of Joash's grandfather, Jehoram, and even under Jehoshaphat, the Edomites and Philistines made incursions against Judah which were so successful that they even took the city of Jerusalem by storm (cf. 2 Kings 8:20-22; 2 Chron. 21:16-17). At no time after the reign of Joash was the kingdom of Judah faced by this particular assortment of enemies. It should be added that at no time after the Chaldean period could Egypt have been regarded as an aggressive power, for it had all it could do to maintain its own independence. This would seem to eliminate the possibility of a date in the Persian or Greek period.

Among non-Conservative critics of more recent times, there is a tendency to date the prophecy of Joel just after the death of Josiah in 609 B.C. This is the position of A. S. Kapelrud (*Joel Studies*, 1948), who argues that the author was a contemporary of Jeremiah and Zephaniah and composed the entire book more or less as it stands. Usually, however, the critics place Joel after the Exile, in view of his foreknowledge of the Babylonian captivity (2:32–3:1), but more especially because of the mention of the Greeks (*Yāvānîm*) in 3:6. They proceed on the assumption that Greeks could not have been mentioned until after the time of the Alexandrian conquest in 330 B.C. But it should be noted that in this context the Greeks are mentioned as a very distant people, and the enormity of the guilt of the Phoenician slave traders is brought out by the fact that they had no scruples about selling Israelite captives even to regions so remote as those inhabited by the Greeks. It cannot be supposed that the Hellenic peoples were unknown to Israel in the pre-exilic period, since they are found mentioned in Assyrian inscriptions as early as the eighth century B.C.[5] Such a reference is quite incompatible with a situation where the Greeks have already made themselves the masters of the whole Persian empire, for at that later period they could not be considered remote from Palestine, as the text clearly implies. (Partly for this reason Pfeiffer prefers to date Joel around 350 B.C., in the time of Alexander's father, Philip of Macedon.)

These critics also advance the argument that Joel fails to mention the Northern Kingdom or the rule of any king of Judah or even the idolatrous high places (*bāmôt*). And yet it should be pointed out that none of these things are mentioned in Nahum or Zephaniah either, although both of them are admitted by the critics to date from the seventh century, prior to the Babylonian Exile. As Young points out (IOT, p. 249), there was no particular occasion in Joel to mention the Northern Kingdom by name, for these prophetic discourses were directed only against Judah. It should be added that Joel occasionally employs the name Israel (cf. 2:27; 3:2, 16) in such a way that it cannot be demonstrated conclusively whether it refers to the entire twelve tribes or only to the Northern Kingdom; therefore it is by no means certain that he ignored the latter completely. The critics have also pointed to verses like 1:9, 1:13; and 2:14 as indicating the practice of presenting a continual burnt offering before the Lord in the temple (the so-called *tāmîd*). They argue that since there is no mention of the *tāmîd* in the Torah until the P document was added in post-exilic times, Joel must likewise have been post-exilic. But of course this line of reasoning can carry no weight with those who have not already subscribed to the ill-founded Documentary Theory.

Although many critics regard Joel as a single literary unit, there are others like Oesterley and Robinson who hold to a theory of dual authorship. Quite considerable portions of Joel which can be regarded as apocalyptic, they have assigned to 200 B.C. on the ground of its alleged resemblance to inter-testamental apocalyptic productions. Hence they interpret the phrase in 3:6, "the sons of the Grecians" (ASV), to refer to the Seleucid dynasty of Antiochus Epiphanes. Such radical interpretations as these are the

5. J. E. Steinmueller, CSS, 2:281.

outgrowth of an evolutionistic theory, rather than a legitimate deduction from the text itself. According to this view, it was only at a late stage in the history of Israel's religion that the genre of apocalyptic came into vogue. (By the term *apocalyptic* is meant that type of prophetic revelation which envisions the miraculous intervention of God in future history to deliver His people from all their foes and to make them supreme in the earth.) The evolutionary view regards this genre as a product of the despair which gripped the Jewish people after they had failed to achieve political greatness or independence by their own efforts. Not until after the disappointments of the fifth and fourth centuries B.C. could the Jews have fallen into such a mood of despair, and turned so exclusively to God as their last and only hope of achieving a national destiny. But here again the force of the argument depends upon evolutionistic and antisupernatural assumptions. Extensive radical surgery would be needed to excise all such passages from the pre-exilic prophets.[6] Moreover, it should be observed that by no stretch of the imagination can the Hebrew style of Joel's prophecy be regarded as belonging to the Persian or Greek period. Its purity of diction and its grammatical constructions point rather to an early pre-exilic date of composition.

To sum up, then, the internal evidence agrees more closely with the period of 835 B.C. for the composition of this prophecy than with any other. The lack of reference to any reigning king on the throne of Judah, the implication that the responsibility of government rests upon the priests and elders, the allusion to the neighboring nations as the current foes of Judah (rather than Assyria, Babylonia, or Persia)—all these factors point quite conclusively to the period of Joash's minority. The linguistic evidence perfectly accords with this early date and makes a theory of post-exilic composition quite untenable. It is fair to say that the arguments for a late date are largely based upon humanistic philosophical assumptions rather than upon reasonable deduction from the data of the text itself.

JONAH

The name Jonah (*Yōnōh*) means "dove." This prophet is mentioned in 2 Kings 14:25 as having predicted the wide extent of the conquests of Jeroboam II (793-753)—a prediction most congenial to such an earnest patriot as he.[7] His native town was Gath-hepher in the tribe of Zebulon in northern Israel. His prophetic ministry would seem to have begun shortly before the reign of Jeroboam, or at least before that brilliant king had attained his more outstanding military triumphs. The theme of this prophecy (which is really a biography rather than a sermonic discourse) is that God's mercy and compassion extend even to the heathen nations on condition of their repentance. It is therefore Israel's obligation to bear witness to them of the true faith; and a neglect of this task may bring the nation, like Jonah himself, to the deep waters

---

6. Cf. G. E. Ladd, "Why Not Prophetic-Apocalyptic?" in JBL, 76:3 (1957).

7. This context, although it fails to mention the time of prediction, nevertheless implies that it was significantly earlier than the conquests of Jeroboam II, probably before he even came to the throne.

of affliction and chastisement. From the prophetic standpoint, Jonah's experience of the living entombment for three days in the belly of the whale serves as a type of the burial and resurrection of the Lord Jesus (Matt. 12:40). (Incidentally, it should be observed that the Hebrew text of Jonah 2:1 actually reads *dāg gādōl*, or "great fish," rather than a technical term for "whale." But since Hebrew possessed no special word for "whale," and since no true fish—as opposed to a marine mammal—is known to possess a stomach as capacious as a whale's, it is reasonable to adhere to the traditional interpretation at this point. The only other available term, *tannîn*, was too vague to be very serviceable here, since it could also mean shark, sea serpent, or even dragon.)

OUTLINE OF JONAH

| I. God's commission to Jonah rejected, 1:1-3 |
| II. Jonah's flight and Yahweh's pursuit, 1:4-17 |
| III. Jonah's prayer for deliverance, 2:1-10 |
| IV. God's commission renewed and discharged at Nineveh, 3:1-9 |
| V. Jonah's grief at Nineveh's repentance and Yahweh's reply, 3:10–4:11 |

TIME OF COMPOSITION

The text does not specify the author of this biographical account, but it is fair to assume that it was composed by Jonah himself at the latter end of his career as he looked back on the decisive turning point in his ministry. This would account for the use of the past tense הָיְתָה (*hāyᵉtâ*) in referring to Nineveh (3:3), for over a period of decades it might be expected that conditions would have changed in that city since the time of Jonah's visit. This would put the time of composition somewhere in the neighborhood of 760 B.C. Although the author does not speak of himself in the first person, this is no more surprising than the fact that Moses in the Torah always referred to himself in the third person, even as was the case Xenophon in his *Anabasis* and Julius Caesar in his *Gallic Wars*.

Liberal critics date the composition of Jonah about 430 B.C. on the supposition that it was composed as an allegory of a piece of quasi-historical fiction to oppose the "narrow nationalism" of Jewish leaders like Ezra and Nehemiah, at a time when the Samaritans were being excluded from all participation in the worship of Yahweh at Jerusalem, and all the foreign wives were being divorced under the pressure of bigoted exclusivism. It was most timely for some anonymous advocate of a more universalistic ideal to produce a tract for the times that would call the nation back to a more liberal viewpoint. Thus the chief ground for the 430 date is a theory of the sequence of the development of ideas in the history of Israel's religion.

Following through with this concept of Jonah, its allegory is interpreted as follows: Jonah himself represents disobedient Israel; the sea represents the Gentiles; the whale stands for the Babylon of the Chaldean period; and the three days of Jonah's confinement in the whale's belly points to the Babylonian captivity. Just as Jonah was commanded to be true to his evangelistic responsibility to the heathen, so also it was the will of God in fifth-century Judah for the Jews to rise to their opportunities of witness to the one true faith and cast aside the hampering limitations of hidebound exclusivism. As for the miraculous gourd whose sudden demise so grieved Jonah's heart, this has been interpreted by some to refer to Zerubbabel.[8]

A closer examination of the text, however, shows that numerous features of the narrative can scarcely be fitted into the allegorical pattern. If the whale represented Babylon, what did Nineveh represent? As for the ship that set sail from Joppa, it is hard to see what this would correspond to in the allegory; nor is it clear why three days should be selected to represent seventy years of captivity. Furthermore, there is not the slightest historical evidence to show the existence of any such universalistic sentiment among the fifth-century Jews, as this theory predicates. While there were undoubtedly some Jews who believed in maintaining harmonious relations with pagan neighbors, their motives seemed to have been materialistic and commercial rather than missionary in character. For critics to point to the books of Jonah and Ruth as testimonies to this zeal is simply a bit of circular reasoning: these two books must have been written at this period because they fit in with the supposed stage attained by Jewish thought as attested by these two books.

HISTORICAL OBJECTIONS TO AUTHENTICITY

In support of this theory of the quasi-historical character of Jonah, there are at least four main objections which are directed against the credibility of the biblical narrative as it stands. Each of these is now discussed and its weaknesses pointed out.

1. It is said to be hardly conceivable that a king of Assyria would have been referred to merely as the *"king of Nineveh"* by a Hebrew author who lived back in the Assyrian period. Only a writer who lived at a much later age, long after Assyria had passed away, would have employed such terminology. But this explanation for Jonah's use of the title king of Nineveh can scarcely be regarded as satisfactory. No ancient author who ever referred to Nineveh in any of the records preserved to us (whether in Akkadian, Hebrew, Greek, or Latin) seems to have been unaware that Nineveh was the capital of the Assyrian empire. It is therefore naive to suppose that a writer living in 430 B.C. imagined that the king of Nineveh was not also the king of Assyria. Certainly the Greek authors, like Herodotus of the fifth century and Xenophon of the fourth century, were well aware of the Assyrian empire and Herodotus at least of Nineveh as its capital. We must therefore look to some other explanation for this designation "the king of Nineveh" in the third chapter of Jonah. Well-established Hebrew usage in the historical books of the Old Testament provides good analogies for this title. For example, although Ahab was stated to be the king of Israel (i.e., of the entire Northern King-

8. Cf. A. Bentzen, IOT, 2:146.

dom), he is occasionally referred to as the "king of Samaria" (1 Kings 21:1), inasmuch as Samaria was the capital of the realm. Similarly also, Benhadad, who was well known to the chronicler as the king of Syria (Aram), is occasionally referred to as the "king of Damascus" (2 Chron. 24:23). Here again it was the capital city of the kingdom which was employed in this royal title. Jonah's use of the term *king of Nineveh* furnishes a perfect parallel to these examples.

2. It is also urged that Nineveh is spoken of in the past tense "was" (*hāyᵉtâ*) in 3:3. This could only mean that the city had long since ceased to exist; otherwise the author would have said, "And Nineveh was being *[tihyeh]* a great city." It is readily conceded that the author might well have expressed the size of Nineveh by use of the imperfect tense (*tihyeh*) had he chosen to do so; but it was evidently his particular purpose at that point in the narrative to stress the fact that Nineveh had already become a very sizable city (though it had probably become even larger by the time the book was written, i.e., in 760 B.C.). The only way to express this thought, "had become," was by the use of the perfect tense, *hāyᵉtâ*.

3. The enormous size attributed to Nineveh is obviously a fabulous element in the narrative. The author states it required three days to walk through the city because of the vastness of its dimensions (3:3-4). Yet it should be noted that the text does not actually say that Jonah needed three days to walk through Nineveh without stopping.[9] It only states that he took three days to go through it on his preaching mission. Street corner preaching requires a fairly extended stop at each place the message is delivered. Three days was certainly not too long a period to complete this assignment in a city which may well have contained as many as 600,000 inhabitants (judging from the 120,000 infants suggested by Jonah 4:11) in the eighth century.[10] To this should be added the population of the suburbs, which would naturally have been quite considerable. The whole administrative district of Nineveh was thirty to sixty miles in diameter.[11] From the context it is only fair to assume that the phrase "a walk of one day" (*mahalak yôm 'eḥāḏ*) referred to that section of the metropolis which he was able to cover as he paused to preach at many different vantage points where he could catch the attention of the people. For a point of comparison, it was a three day journey for a hiker to travel from Dan to Shiloh, which equated to 60 miles.

4. It is declared to be quite inconceivable that any heathen city such as Nineveh would have repented so quickly and so generally in response to the exhortation of an

---

9. Actually it is quite inconceivable that any ancient author could have supposed that any city on earth was large enough to require three days to walk through. In three days a vigorous man could walk from sixty to seventy miles, or the distance from Jerusalem to the Sea of Galilee. No city in all of human history has ever reached those dimensions, and if it ever did, it would support a population of possibly thirty million, rather than the 600,000 or so implied by Jonah 4:11. We must therefore regard this interpretation of "three days' journey" as an absurd flight of scholarly fancy that never would have occurred to an ancient author or reader.

10. Felix Jones in 1834 estimated the circuit of the walls of Kuyunjik, ancient Nineveh, as seven and three-fourths miles in length, and its probable number of inhabitants as 175,000 or more. See *New Bible Dictionary*, p. 889.

11. Ibid.

unknown foreigner from a small and distant country. The king's decree that all the inhabitants should clothe themselves in sackcloth and even drape their animals in the symbols of mourning, is nothing short of absurd. These too must be regarded as fabulous elements. Well, it must be admitted that such a ready response from a pagan populace was nothing short of miraculous, but the narrative makes it plain that the will and power of God Almighty were behind the whole enterprise. There would have been little point to God's insistence that Jonah go to Nineveh unless He Himself was prepared to make the prophet's preaching effectual. Who can define valid limits to the power of the Holy Spirit in bringing men under conviction when His truth is preached? If the Ninevites became apprehensive of a general destruction which would engulf the whole city, including the livestock as well as the human inhabitants, what could have been more appropriate from their standpoint than to clothe the very beasts with such symbols of contrition?

Apart from such theoretical considerations, moreover, there are also historical evidences that at one or two strategic periods during Jonah's ministry he would have found a congenial atmosphere for a monotheistic message. In all probability the king of Nineveh and Assyria at this time was Adad-Nirari III (810-783 B.C.). It is well known that this king confined his worship to the god Nebo, and thus advanced more definitely in the direction of monolatry than any other occupant of the Assyrian throne. Second, Steinmueller (CSS, 2:289) suggests that if Jonah came to Nineveh somewhat later, in the reign of Assurdan III (771-754), he would have found the populace psychologically prepared to expect a total catastrophe, for a serious plague had befallen the city in 765 and a total eclipse of the sun had taken place on June 15, 763. Another plague had followed in 759.

LINGUISTIC ARGUMENTS

Those who espouse a post-exilic date for Jonah customarily appeal to an assortment of alleged Aramaisms which occur here and there in the text.

1. In 1:5 occurs the word *Sᵉphînâ*, "ship," as a variant of a common Hebrew word, *'oniyyâ*, which also means ship. *Sᵉphînâ* is common in Aramaic; it occurs only here in the Hebrew Bible. Nevertheless it is obviously derived from the root *sāphan*, "to cover," which often occurs in the Old Testament as well as in the Phoenician inscriptions (although this verb never occurs in extant Aramaic). We may conclude that this expression originally signified a covered ship or a boat equipped with a deck, and may well have been borrowed by Aramaic speakers from Canaanite.

2. In Jonah 1:6 occurs the verb *'ašat* (in the *hithpael* stem) meaning "to remember." In Aramaic this verb occurs as early as the Elephantine Papyri. A related noun *'ēšet* appears in Song of Sol. 5:14 with the meaning "artifact"; *ašôt* (or else it is to be pointed as singular, *'aštût*) occurs in Job 12:5 as "thought, opinion." However, the verb does not occur either in Syriac or in Aramaic in the sense in which it is used in Jonah, that is, "to remember."

THE WORLD OF THE PROPHETS

The Prophet	Date of Ministry	Contemporary Prohets
Isaiah	740-680	Hosea, Amos, Micah
Jeremiah	626-580(?)	Habakkuk, Daniel, Ezekiel
Ezekiel	592-570	Daniel, Jeremiah
Daniel	605-530	Jeremiah, Ezekiel, Habakkuk
Hosea	756-725	Amos, Isaiah, Micah
Joel	830-810	Elisha
Amos	ca. 760-757	Hosea
Obadiah	848	Elijah
Jonah	ca. 800	None
Micah	735-690	Isaiah, Hosea
Nahum	ca. 640	Zephaniah
Habakkuk	608-597	Jeremiah
Zephaniah	640-630	Nahum, Jeremiah
Haggai	520	Zechariah
Zechariah	520-475	Haggai,
Malachi	ca. 435	Nehemiah

(I) = Israel   (J) = Judah

Audience	World Power	Contemporary Kings
Judah	Assyria (Tiglath-Pileser III, Sargon II, Sennacherib, Esarhaddon)	(J) Uzziah, Jotham, Ahaz, Hezekiah, Manasseh (I) Pekahiah, Pekah, Hoshea
Judah	Assyria (Sinsharishkun, Ashurbanipal, Ashuraballit II) Babylonia (Nabopolassar, Nebuchadnezzar)	(J) Josiah, Jehoahaz, Jehoiakim, Jehoiachin, Zedekiah
Judah	Babylonia (Nebuchadnezzar)	(J) Zedekiah, Gedaliah–governors
Judah	Babylonia (Nebuchadnezza Nabonidus, Belshazzar) Medo-Persia (Cyrus, Darius I)	(J) Jehoiakim, Jhoiachin, Zerubbabel, Zedekiah, Gedaliah–governors
Israel	Assyria (Tiglath-Pileser III Shalmaneser V)	(I) Jeroboam II, Zechariah, Shallum, Manahem, Pekahiah, Pekah, Hoshea (J) Uzziah, Jotham, Ahaz, Hezekiah
Judah	Assyria (Adad-Nirari III, Shalmaneser III)	(J) Joash (I) Jehu, Jehoahaz
Israel	Assyria (Ashurdan III, Ashur-Nirari V)	(J) Uzziah (I) Jeroboam II
Judah	Assyria (Shalmaneser III)	(J) Jehoram, Ahaziah (I) Jehoram, Jehu
Nineveh	Assyria (Adad-Nirari III)	(J) Joash (I) Jehoahaz
Judah Israel	Assyria (Tiglath-Pileser III, Shalmaneser V, Sargon II, Sennacherib)	(J) Ahaz, Jotham, Hezekiah (I) Pekah, Hoshea
Judah	Assyria (Ashurbanipal)	(J) Amon, Josiah
Judah	Babylonia (Nabopolassar, Nebuchadnezzar)	(J) Jehoahaz, Jehoiakim, Jehoiachin, Zedekiah
Judah	Assyria (Ashurbanipal)	(J) Amon, Josiah
Judah	Medo-Persia (Darius I)	Zerubbabel–governor of Judah
Judah Esther	Medo-Persia (Darius I, Xerxes)	Zerubbabel–governor of Judah
Judah	Medo-Persia (Artaxerxes I)	Nehemiah–governor of Judah

3. The relative pronoun šê ("who, which") appears in its simple form in Jonah 4:10, then appears in two compounds, bᵉshellêmî in 1:7 ("on account of whom?") and in bᵉšellī ("on account of me") in 1:12. Strictly speaking, however, this can hardly be called an Aramaism, since šê is not an Aramaic word at all; and yet in later Hebrew it came to be used very much like an Aramaic particle di. Yet so far as this writer is aware, the particle di never occurs in pre-Christian Aramaic after the preposition bᵉ to mean "on account of." On the other hand, šê occurs as early as the time of the Judges in the Song of Deborah (Judg 5:7), which interestingly enough was composed by a native of northern Galilee (just as Jonah was). It should be noted also that šê quite often occurs in the Phoenician inscriptions (alongside the more frequent '-š) and there is a good possibility that the sailors who manned Jonah's ship were of Phoenician origin; hence there is every likelihood that this particle would have occurred in their conversation.

There are various other alleged Aramaisms which rest on even more tenuous foundations. For example, the verb hēṭîl, to throw (Jonah 1:5, 12), occurs in Job, Psalms, Proverbs, Isaiah, Jeremiah, and Ezekiel, and cannot therefore be regarded as a proof of late authorship. As for qᵉrî'ah ("preaching"), this noun is formed on a root which is as indigenous to Hebrew as it is to Aramaic, even though the noun itself happens to occur only here in the Hebrew Bible. One other word calls for special comment: ṭa'am, meaning "edict, decree." While it is a common Hebrew word with the meaning "taste" or "understanding," it occurs only here in the governmental sense (Jonah 3:7). However, it is obviously related to the Assyrian word ṭēmu, which bears the same meaning, and Jonah's use of it may therefore have been a reminiscence of the actual wording of the Assyrian decree of the king of Nineveh. (It is so used in Ezra 6:14, an Aramaic passage, quoting a decree of the king of Persia.)

In view of the vigorous objections of rationalists to the historicity of Jonah, it is appropriate at this point to refer to the statements of the Lord Jesus as recorded in the gospels. In Matt. 12:40-41 Christ refers to two events which are most forthrightly rejected as fabulous by modern criticism: Jonah's preservation in the belly of the whale, and the effectiveness of his preaching in bringing the Ninevites to repentance. In Matt. 12:40 Christ says: "For as Jonah was three days and three nights in the belly of the whale; so shall the Son of man be three days and three nights in the heart of the earth." If the story of Jonah had been merely fictional, then Christ's own burial from Good Friday to Easter morning would have to be only fictional; otherwise there would be no basis for the comparison ("as–so"). This is especially true where a type and an antitype are involved. Every other instance where an Old Testament typical event is referred to in Scripture (e.g., John 3:14; 1 Cor. 10:1-11), a historical episode is involved. There is no objective evidence whatsoever that Jesus of Nazareth regarded this experience of Jonah's as nonhistorical.

Next we read in Matt. 12:41: "The men of Nineveh shall rise up in judgment with this generation, and shall condemn it; because they repented at the preaching of Jonah; and, behold, a greater than Jonah is here." Nothing could be clearer than the fact that Christ is here reproaching His own contemporaries for their unbelief on the ground that they failed to measure up even to the standard of Bibleless pagans in ancient Nineveh. But if those Ninevites in point of fact never did repent at the preaching of Jonah, then Christ's statement here is untrue and His reproach quite unfounded. Inasmuch as even Conservative scholars like James Orr have conceded the nonhistorical character of Jonah, it is important to come to terms with these clear statements by the Lord Jesus and to realize that one cannot reject the historicity of Jonah without also rejecting the authority of Christ.

COMPARISON OF JONAH AND PSALMS

Jonah	Psalms
2:3*a*	69:14
2:3*b*	42:7
2:4*b*	18:6
2:5	69:1-2
2:6	42:7-8
2:7	5:7

INTEGRITY OF THE TEXT

Liberal scholars regard the book of Jonah as a composite from various sources. In particular, the psalm of thanksgiving (Jonah 2:2-9) is regarded as an alien insertion (1) because 2:1 tells us Jonah prayed (*hitpallēl*), whereas the rest of the composition contains thanksgiving rather than petition; (2) because the thanksgiving was expressed before Jonah had been ejected on dry land and had reason to express gratitude to God. But these objections, as formulated by Wellhausen (*Die kleinen Propheten*, 1898, p. 221), miss the point of this psalm altogether. In the first place, as is readily apparent from numerous examples in the book of Psalms, praise was regarded by the Hebrews as a very legitimate and important part of prayer. Thus this same verb (*hitpallēl*) occurs with its cognate noun for "prayer" (*tᵉpillâ*) in 2 Sam. 7:27, a passage containing adoration and praise to Yahweh as a prayer-answering God. Second, as Young has well pointed out (IOT, p. 257), 2:2-9 does not express thanksgiving for deliverance from the belly of the whale but rather deliverance from drowning, through the agency of the whale. When construed in this way, as it obviously should be, there is no discrepancy at all between Jonah's psalm and the setting in which it is placed by the author. Wilhelm Moeller (GATE, pp. 240-41) calls attention to the fact that there are noteworthy resemblances between this psalm of Jonah and those of David. (See chart above).

Proceeding on rationalistic grounds, Eissfeldt regarded Jonah as a complex of two legends, one of which (chaps. 1-3) treats Jonah's disobedience to God's command, and the other (chap. 4) records Jonah's controversy with God over the application of His grace to the heathen. From the fact that the tale of the fish swallowing a man and spewing him out again is found in other literature, he drew the conclusion that the incident was only legendary and therefore could not have happened.[12] (However Eissfeldt is mistaken in this claim, as footnote 12 demonstrates.)

In reply to this it needs only to be pointed out that no one has ever yet demonstrated that all incidents recorded in legends are incapable of occurrence in actual fact. Fundamentally, of course, Eissfeldt's objection is based upon the premise of the impossibility of miracles. Deductions drawn from this *a priori* cannot be regarded as any more trustworthy than the *a priori* itself. But on the grounds of unbiased literary criticism, no convincing case can be made out for multiple sources underlying the book of Jonah.

12. Several cases have been reported in more recent times of men who have survived the ordeal of being swallowed by a whale. *The Princeton Theological Review* (Oct., 1927) tells of two incidents, one in 1758 and the other in 1771, in which a man was swallowed by a whale and vomited up shortly thereafter with only minor injuries. Still other instances are cited by R. K. Harrison in IOT, p. 907.

One of the most striking instances comes from Francis Fox, *Sixty-three Years of Engineering* (London: J. Murray, 1924), pp. 298-300, who reports that this incident was carefully investigated by two scientists (one of whom was M. de Parville, the scientific editor of the *Journal des Debats* in Paris). In February 1891, the whaling ship *Star of the East* was in the vicinity of the Falkland Islands, and the lookout sighted a large sperm whale three miles away. Two boats were lowered and in a short time one of the harpooners was enabled to spear the creature. The second boat also attacked the whale, but was then upset by a lash of its tail, so that its crew fell into the sea. One of them was drowned, but the other, James Bartley, simply disappeared without trace. After the whale was killed, the crew set to work with axes and spades, removing the blubber. "They worked all day and part of the night. The next day they attached some tackle to the stomach, which was hoisted on deck. The sailors were startled by something in which gave spasmodic signs of life, and inside was found the missing sailor, doubled up and unconscious. He was laid on the deck and treated to a bath of sea water which soon revived him. At the end of the third week he had entirely recovered from the shock and resumed his duties....His face, neck and hands were bleached to a deadly whiteness and took on the appearance of parchment. Bartley affirms that he would probably have lived inside his house of flesh until he starved, for he lost his senses through fright and not through lack of air."

A letter dated November 24, 1906, from Mrs. J. F. Whitney, the wife of the captain of the *Star of the East*, and received by A. Lukyn Williams (who submitted it to the *Expository Times* 18 [Feb. 1907]: 239), categorically denied that any episode of this sort had taken place during the years she had been connected with this ship. Without affirming that she was personally acquainted with James Bartley, or even that Mr. Whitney was in command of the ship in February, 1891, she dismissed the entire account as a mere sailor's yarn. But in view of the previous investigation of this episode by M. de Parvelle, Mrs. Whitney's blanket denial would seem to be hardly credible.

As for Eissfeldt's contention that other ancient traditions speak of a man's being swallowed by a fish and afterwards ejected, he furnishes no documentation whatever to back up this claim. (Cf. his *Einleitung in das A.T.*, p. 547.) He vaguely refers to Perseus as having been swallowed by a fish and expelled. However, he actually was placed in a wooden chest by Acrisius along with his mother Danae and later washed on the shore of the Kingdom of Polydectes without the involvement of any fish or whale. Therefore the adventure of Jonah remains unexampled and unique.

22 AMOS, HOSEA, AND MICAH

IN THE SECOND HALF of the eighth century B.C., Hebrew prophecy attained its golden age of excellence. After the earliest of the writing prophets, Obadiah, Joel, and Jonah, had done their work, the stage was set for the appearance of the four great figures who dominated the scene from 755 to the opening of the seventh century: Amos, Hosea, Micah, and Isaiah. The first three of these are discussed in this chapter; for the work of Isaiah, two additional chapters will be necessary.

The meaning of the name Amos is probably "burden-bearer" (derived from the verb *'āmas,* "to lift a burden, carry"). The central theme of his prophecy was Yawheh's faithfulness to His covenant and to His holy law, and the strict accountability of His people Israel to a practical observance of their covenant obligations. Amos earnestly stressed their duty of cordial compliance with the legal code of the Torah, both in letter and in spirit. Israel's failure to present to the Lord a true and living faith and their attempt to foist upon Him the wretched substitute of mere empty profession could lead only to the utter ruin and destruction of the nation.

OUTLINE OF AMOS

I. Yawheh's judgment upon the nations, 1:1–2:16

A. Prelude: the day of wrath at hand, 1:1-2

B. Judgment of God upon the heathen neighbors for their various crimes of inhumanity (all of these are to suffer fire and destruction), 1:3–2:3

1. Damascus, 1:3-5
2. Gaza, 1:6-8
3. Tyre, 1:9-10
4. Edom, 1:11-12
5. Ammon, 1:13-15
6. Moab, 2:1-3

C. Wrath upon both the covenant nations for neglecting God's Word, 2:4-16
 1. Judah, having turned from God to false teachers, likewise to suffer fire and destruction 2:4-5
 2. Israel also to suffer overpowering destruction for sins of exploiting the poor, and tolerating of incest, showing thanklessness toward God, and persecuting the faithful 2:6-16

II. Offenses of Israel and warnings of God, 3:1–6:14

A. Judgment unavoidable because of Israel's complete depravity, 3:1-15
 1. The greater the privilege, the greater the accountability, 3:1-3
 2. Amos' credentials as God's messenger, 3:4-8
 3. Israel's crimes of oppressing the poor, their luxuries and self-indulgence to be punished by devastation and depopulation, 3:9-15
B. God's challenge to the stiff-necked pleasure seekers, 4:1-13
 1. Their pursuit after pleasure and wealth and their carnal forms of worship to seal their doom, 4:1-5
 2. The unheeded warning of the plagues; judgment will surely come upon them, 4:6-13
C. Lamentation and final appeal, 5:1-27
D. The doom of exile for the pleasure-seeking upper classes, 6:1-14

III. Five visions of Israel's fate, 7:1–9:10

A. Locusts—restrained, 7:1-3
B. Fire—restrained, 7:4-6
C. Plumbline—all to be leveled flat, 7:7-9 (Interlude: the clash with Amaziah; his doom foretold, 7:10-17)
D. Late summer fruit—the end at hand, 8:1-14
E. The smitten temple (of Bethel); Israel to be treated like heathen, 9:1-10

IV. Promises of restoration, 9:11-15

A. Preliminary: the New Testament age, 9:11-12
B. The millennial consummation, 9:13-15

THE AUTHOR

Since the name of his father is not given, it may be assumed that Amos was of humble birth. His native town was Tekoa, situated five miles southeast of Bethlehem in the Judean highlands. By profession Amos was both a herdsman and a cultivator of sycamore figs. He may possibly have tended cattle (as is implied by the term *bōqēr*, "herdsman," in 7:14). Certainly he raised sheep, for he speaks of himself as a *nōqēd* (cf. in 1:1), that is, a shepherd of a small, speckled variety of sheep called *nāqōd*. He also made his living by cultivating sycamore or wild fig trees (*šiqᵉmîm*, 7:14), a tree which exuded a ball of sap, which if nipped at the right season, hardened into a sort of edible fruit which the lower classes were able to afford.

Apparently he was an earnest student of the books of Moses, for his style shows strong Pentateuchal influences. Yet as a farmhand he hardly enjoyed the advantages of a formal education in a "school of the prophets" (such as maintained by Samuel, Elijah, and Elisha), nor was he ever officially anointed for his prophetic ministry. At the call of God he left his home in Judea as a mere layman to proclaim a hostile message in the proud capital of the Northern Kingdom of Israel, without any ecclesiastical authorization. Without any status as a recognized prophet, he nevertheless braved the prejudice of the Ephraimite public to carry out faithfully his commission from God. A man of rugged convictions and iron will, he could not be deflected from his purpose even by the highest functionary of the Samaritan hierarchy.

DATE OF COMPOSITION

There is general agreement among Old Testament scholars that Amos' ministry is to be dated between 760 and 757 B.C., toward the latter part of the reign of Jeroboam II (793-753). This king had enjoyed a brilliant career from the standpoint of military success, for he had accomplished the feat of restoring the boundaries of the Northern Kingdom to the limits with which it had begun in 931 B.C. The result had been a considerable influx of wealth from the booty of war and advantageous trade relations with Damascus and the other principalities to the north and northeast. But along with the increase in wealth, no share of which was granted to the lower classes, there had come a more conspicuous materialism and greed on the part of the rich nobility. They shamelessly victimized the poor and cynically disregarded the rights of those who were socially beneath them. A general disregard for the sanctions of the Seventh Commandment had undermined the sanctity of the family and had rendered offensive their hypocritical attempt to appease God by observance of religious forms.

The text of Amos gives a precise date for his preaching mission to Bethel: "two years before the earthquake" (1:1), that is, the severe earthquake in the reign of Uzziah, which was remembered for centuries afterward (cf. Zech. 14:5, "As ye fled from before the earthquake in the days of Uzziah, king of Judah"). Unfortunately the time of this earthquake cannot be more precisely determined, but at all events it served as a preliminary sign from God. The warnings of doom which Amos conveyed were to be of sure fulfillment. The statement in 1:1 also served to indicate that the book of Amos was not published until at least two years after he had orally delivered his message.

INTEGRITY OF THE TEXT

Liberal critics concede the authenticity of nearly all the text of Amos, whom they regard as "the first of the writing prophets" (for according to the dating of Wellhausen and Driver, Amos would constitute the earliest written portion of the Old Testament, with the single exception of document J). There are, however, fifteen verses which have been classified as later insertions. These include 1:9-12 with its stylized formulae of denunciation ("For three transgressions [the name of the city], and for four, I will not turn away the punishment thereof...but I will send a fire upon [the city], which shall devour the palaces thereof"). For the same reason 2:4-5 is rejected. Expressions of thanksgiving and praise to God, such as 4:13; 5:8-9; 9:5-6, are regarded as foreign to Amos because of their cheerful tone. And the Messianic promise of 9:11-15 is said to represent a type of thinking much later than the eighth century B.C. Oesterley and Robinson interpret 9:11-12 as presupposing the Exile, because of reference to the fall of the "tabernacle of David," interpreted to mean the fall of Jerusalem (IBOT, p. 366). But even Bentzen rejects this inference as ill founded, pointing out that Amos may have regarded the house of David as fallen "because it had lost the position which it had occupied in David's own time." R. H. Pfeiffer regards the historical Amos as capable of only a pessimistic emphasis upon denunciation for sin and quite incapable of the hopeful view toward the future; any passages which disturb this portrait must be explained as later additions (cf. IOT, pp. 583-84). It will be readily seen that all these passages have been objected to from the ground of a special theory of the historical development of Israel's thought, rather than on the basis of the data of the text itself.

POINTS OF CONTACT WITH THE PENTATEUCH

Since Documentarian Critics regard Amos as the earliest of the writing prophets, it is appropriate to point out that there are numerous references even in Amos to the legal provisions of the Torah (including D and P). Observe the cumulative force of the examples which follow.

1. Amos 2:7, "A man and his father go in unto the same maid," is apparently a reference to religious prostitution, which was expressly forbidden in Deut. 23:17-18. Amos' audience could hardly have been expected to know that this practice was a crime unless there had been prior laws which condemned it. It is a fair inference that these laws must have been composed long enough before Amos' time to acquire the weight of a sanction from antiquity.

2. Amos 2:8 condemns the keeping overnight of "garments taken in pledge" (a practice forbidden in Ex. 22:26), an offense which is compounded when the creditor even sleeps on the pawned article overnight (cf. Deut. 24:12-13).

3. Amos 2:12 refers to the consecration of the Nazarites, the sanction for which is found only in Num. 6:1-21 (a P passage according to Driver, ILOT, p. 55).

4. Amos 4:4 (ASV) mentions tithing "after three years," a specification largely unknown to the pagans, and ordained in the Old Testament only in Deuteronomy 14:28 and 26:12, which state that the tithe of the farmer's produce is to be laid up in store for the Lord.

5. Amos 4:5 (ASV), "Offer a sacrifice...of that which is leavened," implies that this practice was forbidden by law—a prohibition contained in Lev. 2:11 and 7:13 (which are, of course, P passages).

6. Amos 5:23 implies that the ritual of sacrifice in Amos' day was accompanied by

AMOS REFLECTS THE TORAH

EXAMPLE	AMOS	TORAH
Religious prostitution forbidden	2:7	Deut. 23:17-18
Condemns overnight pledges	2:8	Ex. 22:26
Consecration of Nazarites	2:12	Num. 6:1-21
Tithing	4:4	Deut. 14:28; 26:12
Unleavened sacrifice	4:5	Lev. 2:11; 7:13
Early sacrificial terms:		
freewill offering	4:5	Lev. 7:16-18; 22:18 Num. 15:3; Deut. 12:6-7
solemn assembly	5:21	Lev. 23:36; Num. 29:35
burnt offering, etc.	5:22	Lev. 7:11-14; 8:1-32

song, an ordinance attributed in the historical books to King David. It is fair to assume that if P had been composed subsequent to the time of Amos, it would have contained some reference to musical accompaniment in the sacrificial ritual in order to invest this practice with Mosaic sanction. But actually there is no reference to music or song as an accompaniment of sacrifice anywhere in the entire Pentateuch.

7. Several terms for sacrifice alleged by many critics to be post-exilic are mentioned quite casually and freely by Amos as if they were commonly practiced in his own time. These include (a) the freewill offering (nᵉdābah) in Amos 4:5 (cf. Lev. 7:16-18; 22:18; Num. 15:3; Deut. 12:67, etc.); (b) "the solemn assembly" (ᵃṣārah) in Amos 5:21 (cf. Lev. 23:36; Num. 29:35); (c) "burnt offering," "meal offering," and "peace offering" all occur in a single clause in Amos 5:22; they are so mentioned in combination and also separately in numerous passages of the Torah (cf. Lev. 7:11-14; 8:1-32).

The only way to evade the impact of this evidence is to label them as insertions by later redactors—a question-begging procedure resorted to by Pfeiffer, Eissfeldt, and others. But any fair handling of the evidence clearly indicates that there was by Amos' day a body of law understood to be ancient and authoritative and labeled by Amos himself as "the Torah of Yahweh" (Amos 2:4). This Torah was evidently accepted by all concerned as an established fact in Amos' time. There is no hint or suggestion of any kind that Amos was pioneering with any new monotheistic message or an enlightened moral code which had not previously been acknowledged as binding.[1] The cumulative impact of this evidence is quite conclusive in favor of a priority of the Torah to Amos.

---

1. A very full discussion of these points of contact with the Pentateuch is included by Moeller in his GATE, pp. 229-36.

HOSEA

The name of this prophet, *Hôšēaʾ*, means "salvation", and is in reality identical with the name of the last king of the Northern Kingdom, Hoshea. For purposes of distinction, however, the English Bible always spells the name of the minor prophet as Hosea (without the second *h*).

The theme of this book is an earnest testimony against the Northern Kingdom because of its apostasy from the covenant and its widespread corruption in public and private morals. The purpose of the author is to convince his fellow countrymen that they need to repent and return in contrition to their patient and ever-loving God. Both threat and promise are presented from the standpoint of Yahweh's love to Israel as His own dear children and as His covenant wife.

OUTLINE OF HOSEA

I. Training of the prophet, 1:1–3:5

A. His homelife symbolic of the nation's punishment and restoration, 1:1–2:1
  1. The marriage with Gomer, a potential adulteress, 1:2
  2. The children: Jezreel, Lo-Ruhamah, Lo-Ammi, 1:3-9
  3. The final triumph of grace, 1:10–2:1
B. His domestic tragedy, a revelation of God's redeeming love, 2:2-23
C. His dealing with Gomer, a command and a revelation, 3:1-5

II. Teaching of the prophet, 4:1–14:9

A. National pollution and its cause, 4:1–6:3
  1. The findings of the Judge and the pronouncement of sentence, 4:1-19
  2. Warning to priest, people, and king: the snare of the idolatrous shrines, 5:1-15
  3. Exhortation to repent, 6:1-3
B. National pollution and its punishment, 6:4–10:15
  1. Statement of God's case against Israel, 6:4–7:16
    a) Fickleness, bloodguiltiness: the bloody harvest, 6:4-11
    b) Mercy prevented by persistent rebellion, adultery, winebibbing, 7:1-16
  2. Judgment pronounced, 8:1–9:17
    a) Reaping the whirlwind, devoured by the world they doted on, 8:1-14
    b) Bondage in exile, the withering away of Israel, 9:1-17
  3. Recapitulation and appeal: the empty vine, 10:1-15
C. The love of Jehovah, 11:1–14:9
  1. His inalienable love in dealing with wayward Israel, 11:1-11
  2. Exile: God's only alternative because of stubborn rebelliousness, 11:12–12:14
  3. Guiding principles and eventual outcome of exile, 13:1-16
  4. Final appeal to repent; promise of ultimate blessing, 14:1-9

AUTHORSHIP AND INTEGRITY OF THE TEXT

The prophet Hosea was apparently a citizen of the Northern Kingdom of Israel, for he refers to the ruler in Samaria as "our king" (7:5). Judah is mentioned only incidentally, whereas the interest is centered on the ten tribes. The author's diction betrays traces of dialect not found in Judah but suggestive of North Israel near the Aramaic-speaking territory of Syria. Hosea's family was of sufficient social standing for his father's name (Beeri) to be mentioned. We have no other biographical details apart from those which he supplies in his own prophecies.

The Liberal critics attribute substantially all this prophecy to the historic Hosea. The only passages that have been challenged as later insertions are those which refer to Judah (so Marti and Nowack); or those sections, like 11:8-11 and 14:2-9 (so Volz and Marti), which predict future blessing or national deliverance. Eissfeldt and Bentzen, however, do not feel disposed to rule out categorically every mention of salvation after punishment, nor even every mention of Judah. Since even in the undoubtedly genuine portions of the book, such as chapters 1-3, the possibility is held out of future deliverance of the nation, those few verses which they label as glosses are denied to Hosea on other grounds. As for the mention of Judah, Young rightly points out (IOT, p. 244) that the prophet regards the government of the Northern Kingdom as a usurpation, implying that only the Davidic dynasty is legitimate.

TIME OF COMPOSITION

Not all the prophecies in this book seem to have been delivered at the same period in the prophet's career. A portion of these must have been given before the death of Jeroboam II (753 B.C.), since chapter 1 interprets the symbolic meaning of Jezreel to signify that the dynasty of Jehu is to be violently ended. This was fulfilled in 752 when Shallum assassinated Zachariah, the son of Jeroboam. On the other hand, chapter 5 seems to have been directed against King Menahem (752-742). Chapter 7 must be dated a decade or two later; it denounces the government's policy of double-dealing whereby Egypt is pitted against Assyria, and this policy is not known to have been followed by Israel prior to the reign of Hoshea (732-723 B.C.). Therefore we are justified in regarding the book as combining excerpts from sermons delivered over a period of at least twenty-five years. Possibly the final compilation was published in 725 B.C., perhaps thirty years after Hosea's preaching ministry had begun.

PROBLEM OF GOMER

Much discussion has been devoted to the difficulty created by God's command to marry an adulterous woman. Would Jehovah have commanded a holy man to do that which was expressly forbidden to the priests and frowned upon for Israel as a whole? In an effort to relieve the moral problem, some conservatives, such as E. J. Young, have suggested that this experience was not real, but only a sort of extended parable. In the interests of this theory, some scholars have even suggested that the name Gomer means "completion," that is, completion of sin; the name of her mother, Diblaim, would then mean "raisin cakes," an idolatrous type of sacrificial offering (cf. 3:1).

The identification of Gomer has been a debated point from the earliest times. Even the ancient commentators in the early Christian period differed as to whether Gomer was really a woman whom Hosea married, or whether she was simply a parable to illustrate the alienation between disobedient Israel and her faithful God. It was argued that this could hardly have been a factual account, since it would be a disgrace for a man of Hosea's priestly and prophetic stature to marry a woman who was of ill repute. For that reason, Jerome and Calvin, from the time of the Reformation, felt that this narrative was to be understood allegorically. Even Hengstenberg, Havernick, Keil, Eichhorn, Rosenmuller and Hitzig favored a parabolic interpretation.

On the other hand, Theodore of Mopsuestia in the older period adhered to the literal interpretation that she was a woman whom Hosea actually married (whether she was immoral previous to the marriage or became so afterward). This is also the view of Franz Delitzsch, Kurtz, Hoffman, Wellhausen, Cheyne, Robertson Smith and George Adams Smith.

In our own century we still have the conflicting interpretations. E. J. Young of Westminster Seminary tended to adhere to the same allegorical view as Calvin rather than an actual biographical episode. Leon Wood felt that it would be doing violence to the credibility of Scripture elsewhere to render it parabolic, in light of the explicit statement in the first chapter of Hosea, which contains the explicit order or encouragement by God to marry this woman. Clearly God's purpose was to teach Hosea what it meant to have an unfaithful wife, even as Yahweh himself had to deal with an unfaithful nation in the case of Israel. Leon Wood in EBC, vol. 7, p. 164, stated, "A woman of adulterous character is really what is implied by the Hebrew phrase "a wife of harlotry." He did not call Gomer an actual $zōnâ$ (which would indicate an already practising prostitute; but rather the "wife of harlotry" is to be understood as proleptic (p. 166). Wood disagreed with Keil in regard to Gomer's status at the time of marriage to Hosea. He rightly points out that this would hardly conform to the analogy of Israel because back in the time of Moses and Joshua the Hebrew race stood in a meaningful covenant relationship with God. Yet it should be recognized that Ex. 32 and Num. 14 show a strong trend towards spiritual infidelity.

William Rainey Harper pointed out that Gomer's first child, Jezreel, was clearly said to have been fathered by Hosea himself, whereas the birth notices for Lo-Ruhamah and Lo-Ammi have no such affirmation, and therfore may have been fathered adulterously. Even Otto Eissfeldt expressed the view that the marriage was literally carried out to serve as an experience through which Hosea went in order understand more fully what God's pain was like in regard to the apostasy of the Northern Kingdom (cf. Pfeiffer's *The Old Testament, an Introduction* [New York: Harper, 1965], p. 390). This agrees with the traditional literalistic view. Interestingly enough, Robert Pfeiffer himself did not feel that the woman in chapter 3 was the same woman as

Gomer in Chapter 1, affirming that chapter 3 had nothing to do with Hosea's personal life, but was a mere symbolic analogy that never actually took place (*Introduction to the Old Testament* [New York: Harper, 1941], p. 569). Wellhausen felt that Hosea became aware of Gomer's unfaithfulness only after the birth of their first child, who was legitimate. Gomer may have been drawn towards an adulterous relationship with some other lover and later went astray after the birth of Jezreel.

LaSor, Hubbard, and Bush in *Old Testament Survey* do not suggest that the marriage of Hosea and Gomer was anything other than an actual occurrence. They espouse the view that Gomer was overtly wicked when she married Hosea (p. 336). There is no real evidence that Hosea (or the Israelites in general) countenanced sexual experience with a stranger prior to marriage. We may conclude therefore that Gomer was not already a prostitute or an adulteress when Hosea married her, because Jezreel was clearly begotten by Hosea (1:3). But, the second and the third children seem to have been fathered out of wedlock.

One very strong objection to a mere figurative type of interpretation is found in the fact that the story of Hosea's marriage is given as a straightforward narrative. There is no evidence in the text itself that it was to be understood as a parable or a purely fictional experience described in order to illustrate a theological teaching. If the transaction did not really take place, even though it is set forth in such a factual manner, then the possibility opens up of questioning the historicity of any number of other episodes which are narrated in Scripture as if they were sober history. A basic hermeneutical principle involved here is that the statements of Scripture are to be interpreted in their plain and obvious sense, unless other Scripture bearing upon the same subject shows that these statements are to be interpreted in some other fashion.

The better solution to this problem is to be found in the supposition that at the time Hosea married Gomer, she was not a woman of overtly loose morals. If Hosea delivered his message in later years, he may well have looked back upon his own domestic tragedy and seen in it the guiding hand of God. Hence the Lord's encouragement to him to marry her in the first place, though her future infidelity was foreknown to God, would have been tantamount to a command: "Go, marry an adulterous woman," even if the command did not come to the prophet in precisely these words.

Micah

The name *Micah* is a shortened form of *Mī-kā-Yāhū*, which means "Who is like Jehovah?" The basic theme of his message is that the necessary product of saving faith is social reform and practical holiness based upon the righteousness and sovereignty of God. Because of the general lack of such saving faith, both the Northern and Southern Kingdoms are destined to experience God's wrath. Yet after the punishment is over, the nation will be restored and the Messiah will eventually come.

OUTLINE OF MICAH

I. Sentence of God upon both idolatrous kingdoms, 1:1-16

A. God to crush Israel's pride because of broken law, 1:1-4

B. Punishment for idolatry: destruction of Samaria, 1:5-7

C. Lament over the coming (Assyrian) invasion; its progress, city by city, 1:8-16

II. Bill of particulars: oppression by upper classes, 2:1–3:12

A. Exploitation of the defenseless lower class as by the idle rich, 2:1-13

B. The government a devourer instead of a defender of its citizens, 3:1-4

C. Contrast between the corrupt state religion and the power and the message of God-fearing preachers, 3:5-8

D. The utter destruction to be meted out on these three evil groups, 3:9-12

III. Ultimate triumph of God's grace, 4:1–5:15

A. Messianic triumph of the kingdom of God over the world, 4:1-8

B. Necessary conditions to be first fulfilled: suffering, exile, restoration, judgment upon heathen neighbors, 4:9-13

C. The divine-human Victor who shall bring this to pass, defending His flock, destroying the world powers, 5:1-6

D. Triumph of Israel after humbling and purging from idolatry, 5:7-15

IV. God's controversy with ungrateful Israel, 6:1-16

A. Summons to the Northern Kingdom to respond to God in view of His exodus mercies, 6:1-5

B. Response of an awakened conscience: holy living must accompany valid worship; yet Israel is still dishonest and oppressive, 6:6-13

C. Failure to repent will be followed by a crop failure; the "clever" policy of alliance with unbelievers is to be discredited, 6:14-16

V. Fulfillment of covenant promise to the faithful remnant, 7:1-20

A. Lament of true Israel over prevalence of barbarous selfishness and shameful corruption in their own land, 7:1-6

B. True Israel's continued trust in God's mercy, 7:7-10

C. Christ's triumph through the church age and the millennium, 7:11-20

AUTHORSHIP OF MICAH

Micah was a citizen of the Southern Kingdom, having been born at Moresheth near Gath, about twenty miles west of Jerusalem. His father's name is not given, and we may conclude that his family was of humble origin. It is significant that his preaching ministry was especially preoccupied with the sufferings of the common people and of the peasants in the agricultural areas who were exploited by rich and unscrupulous, landed nobility. Micah seems to have spent much of his lifetime in the provincial areas rather than at the capital city of Jerusalem. Hence he was not in as close touch with international politics as was his contemporary, Isaiah. Yet he did devote at least one chapter (chap. 6) to the declining career of the Northern Kingdom.

DATE OF COMPOSITION

Micah's ministry was contemporary with the earlier career of Isaiah, that is, during the reigns of Ahaz and Hezekiah. Interestingly enough, the books of these prophets contain one passage in common (Mic. 4:1-3 and Isa. 2:2-4), an oracle relating to the Millennial Kingdom. Since Israel is addressed in Micah 6 as if it were still capable of escaping divine judgment through a last-minute repentance, it may be fairly deduced that Micah commenced his ministry at least before the fall of Samaria in 722 B.C.. The conditions of corruption and immorality in Judah as Micah depicts them correspond well with what is known of the reign of Ahaz (742-728), or else possibly of the earliest years of Hezekiah's reign as co-regent with Ahaz (728-725). Actually Micah's career must have begun even earlier than Ahaz' reign, for 1:1 speaks of his prophesying in the reign of Jotham (751-736). As to the question of when his preaching ministry ceased, there is no certain evidence. From Jer. 26:18-19, we learn that his earnest warnings during the reign of Hezekiah were taken seriously, and made an important contribution to the revival which took place under government sponsorship.

INTEGRITY OF THE TEXT

Some critics have challenged the authenticity of certain portions of chapters 6 and 7 on the ground that they contain thoughts and motifs which occur elsewhere only in passages from a later period of Israel's history. For example, they prophesy the regathering of God's dispersed people after a term of exile, and foretell the destruction of Israel's foes on a catastrophic scale, to be followed by the ultimate triumph of Israel over the heathen under the lordship of the Messiah. Heinrich Ewald assigned chapters 6 and 7 to an unknown author living in the reign of Manasseh (697-642). Julius Wellhausen even regarded 7:7-20 as exilic in origin and contemporary with Deutero-Isaiah; yet some of his more moderate successors like Driver (ILOT, pp. 308-13) question the necessity of so late a date being assigned to it. But all antisupernaturalists unite in denying the genuineness of 4:10: "Thou shalt come even unto Babylon: there shalt thou be rescued; there will Jehovah redeem thee from the hand of thine enemies" (ASV). Such predictions as these are impossible except upon the basis of supernatural revelation. Hence no eighth-century author could have written this verse; it requires a foresight which is more than human. Therefore this verse is denied to Micah on the grounds of antisupernatural bias, just as Isa. 40-66 is denied to an eighth-century author, as we shall presently see.

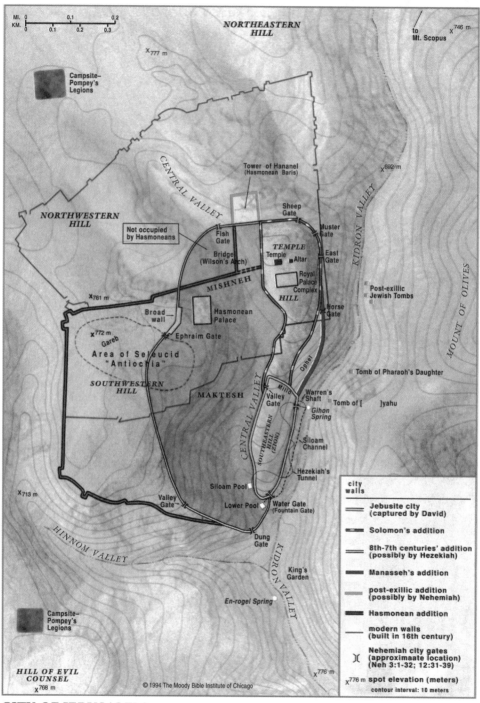

CITY OF JERUSALEM

23 ISAIAH

THE HEBREW NAME of this prophet is *Yᵉšaʻ-Yāhû*, meaning "Yahweh is salvation." Appropriately enough, the basic theme of Isaiah's message is that salvation is bestowed only by grace, by the power of God, the Redeemer, rather than by the strength of man or the good works of the flesh. The holy God will not permit unholiness in His covenant people, and will therefore deal with them in such a way as to chasten and purge them and make them fit to participate in His program of redemption. Isaiah sets forth the doctrine of Christ in such full detail that he has rightly been described as "the evangelical prophet." Deeper Christological insights are to be found in his work than anywhere else in the Old Testament.

OUTLINE OF ISAIAH

I. Volume of rebuke and promise, 1:1–6:13

A. First sermon: rebellion confronted with judgment and grace, 1:1-31
B. Second sermon: present chastisement for future glory, 2:1–4:6
C. Third sermon: judgment and exile for the stubborn nation, 5:1-30
D. Fourth sermon: the prophet cleansed and commissioned by God, 6:1-13

II. Volume of Immanuel, 7:1–12:6

A. First sermon: rejection of Immanuel by worldly wisdom, 7:1-25
B. Second sermon: speedy deliverance foreshadowing the coming Deliverer, 8:1–9:7
C. Third sermon: inexorable doom of exile for proud Samaria, 9:8–10:4
D. Fourth sermon: the future downfall of the false empire (Assyria); the glorious empire to come, 10:5–12:6

III. God's judgment—burdens upon the nations, 13:1–23:18

A. Babylon, 13:1–14:27
B. Philistia, 14:28-32
C. Moab, 15:1–16:14
D. Damascus and Samaria, 17:1-14
E. Ethiopia, 18:1-7

F. Egypt, 19:1–20:6

G. Babylon, second burden, 21:1-10

H. Edom, 21:11-12

I. Arabia, 21:13-17

J. Jerusalem, 22:1-25

K. Tyre, 23:1-18

IV. First volume of general judgment and promise, 24:1–27:13

A. First sermon: universal judgment for universal sin, 24:1-23

B. Second sermon: praise to the Lord as Deliverer, Victor, and Comforter, 25:1-12

C. Third sermon: a song of rejoicing in Judah's consolation, 26:1-21

D. Fourth sermon: punishment for oppressors and preservation in store for God's people, 27:1-13

V. Volume of woes upon the unbelievers of Israel, 28:1–33:24

A. First sermon: God's dealings with drunkards and scoffers in Israel, 28:1-29

B. Second sermon: judgment upon blind souls who try to deceive God, 29:1-24

C. Third sermon: confidence in man versus confidence in God, 30:1-33

D. Fourth sermon: deliverance through God's gracious intervention, 31:1–32:20

E. Fifth sermon: punishment of treacherous deceivers and the triumph of Christ, 33:1-24

VI. Second volume of general judgment and promise, 34:1–35:10

A. First sermon: destruction of the Gentile world power, 34:1-17

B. Second sermon: the ultimate bliss of God's redeemed on the highway of holiness, 35:10

VII. Volume of Hezekiah, 36:1–39:8

A. Destruction of Judah by Assyria averted, 36:1–37:38

B. Destruction of Judah's king averted, 38:1-22

C. Judgment upon the king's pride in his earthly treasures; Babylonian captivity predicted, 39:1-8

VIII. Volume of comfort, 40:1–66:24

A. Purpose of peace, 40:1–48:22

   1. Majesty of Jehovah the Comforter and Sovereign Deliverer of Israel, 40:1-31

   2. Challenge of the God of providence to worldly minded unbelievers, 41:1-29

   3. Servant of Jehovah, individual and national, 42:1-25

   4. Redemption by grace, 43:1–44:5 (deliverance through Cyrus)

   5. Dead idols or the living God? (44:6-23)

   6. The sovereign God employing Cyrus as deliverer and the ultimate conversion of converting the heathen, 44:24–45:25

7. Lessons to be learned from Babylon's downfall and Israel's preservation, 46:1–47:15

8. Judgment upon faithless, hypocritical Israel, 48:1-22

B. Prince of peace, 49:1–57:21

   1. Messiah to bring restoration to Israel and light to Gentiles, 49:1-26

   2. Sinfulness of Israel contrasted with the obedience of the Servant, 50:1-11

   3. Encouragement to trust in God alone, not fearing men, 51:1-16

   4. Summons to Israel to awake and return to God's favor, 51:17–52:12

   5. Divine Servant to triumph through vicarious suffering, 52:13–53: 12

   6. Consequent blessing to Israel and the Church, 54:1-17

   7. Grace for all sinners who trust in Christ, 55:1-13

   8. Inclusion of Gentiles in the blessing of Israel, 56:1-8

   9. Condemnation of the wicked rulers of Israel, 56:9–57:21

C. Program of peace, 58:1–66:24

   1. Contrast between false and true worship, 58:1-14

   2. Confession of Israel's depravity, leading to deliverance by God's intervention, 59:1-21

   3. Glorious prosperity and peace of the redeemed, 60:1-22

   4. The Spirit-filled Christ by whom the kingdom comes, 61:1-11

   5. Zion to be restored and glorified, 62:1–63:6

   6. God's former mercies to cause Israel to plead for deliverance, 63:7–64:12

   7. God's mercy for spiritual Israel alone, 65:1-25

   8. Externalism in worship to be replaced by heart sincerity, 66:1-24

It is important to note in regard to the last section, the Volume of Comfort, that the twenty-seven chapters, 40 through 66, show a remarkable symmetry in the three subdivisions. The end of subdivision A, "The purpose of peace," is virtually identical with the end of subdivision B, "The Prince of Peace"; that is to say, they both conclude with the formula, "There is no peace, saith my God, to the wicked." Each of the three subdivisions sets forth in a systematic way an area of doctrinal emphasis—theology, soteriology, and eschatology. This architectonic structure points to a single author rather than to a collection of heterogeneous sources. What is said about the volume of comfort as to its systematic arrangement may be extended to the first thirty-nine chapters as well, for even the outline as here given indicates a deliberate use of balance or parallelism in structure.

AUTHORSHIP OF ISAIAH

The prophet Isaiah, the son of Amoz (*'āmōṣ*—"strong or courageous"), was apparently a member of a fairly distinguished and influential family. Not only is his father's name given, but he appears to have been on familiar terms with the royal court even in the reign of Ahaz. He must have been a well-educated student of international affairs, who spent most of his time in the city of Jerusalem, where he was in touch with the crosscurrents of national and foreign affairs. Directed by God to oppose with vigor any entangling alliances with foreign powers (whether with Assyria as against Samaria and Damascus, or with Egypt as against Assyria), his cause was foredoomed to failure, for both government and people chose to put their trust in political alliances rather than in the promises of God.

Until the death of Hezekiah (in 697 or 698), Isaiah enjoyed a large measure of respect despite the unpopularity of his political views, and in the period of religious reform carried through by Hezekiah, his influence upon religion was most significant. Yet as God warned him in the temple vision (Isa. 6:9-10), the nation by and large turned a deaf ear even to his spiritual message. Apart from a small minority of earnest believers, his ministry to his contemporaries was little short of a failure. In the reign of Manasseh, the degenerate son of Hezekiah, a strong tide of reaction set in against the strict Jehovah-worship of the previous reign. Isaiah lived to see the undoing of all his own work so far as contemporary politics were concerned. In spiritual matters, his countrymen fell into an even more desperate condition of depravity than they had in the reign of Ahaz. Recognizing the inevitability of God's judgment upon the unrepentant nation, Isaiah's interest during the reign of Manasseh came to be focused increasingly upon the coming overthrow of Jerusalem, the Babylonian Captivity, and the restoration which lay beyond. An old tradition relates that he was martyred at some time in the reign of Manasseh, possibly by being sawed in two inside a hollow log (cf. Heb. 11:37). Since he records the death of Sennacherib in Isa. 37:37-38, it is fair to assume that Isaiah lived until after Sennacherib's death in 681 B.C.

CRITICAL THEORIES OF THE COMPOSITION OF ISAIAH

With the growth of deism in the western world during the late eighteenth century, it was only natural that men of antisupernatural convictions would take exception to those extensive portions of Isaiah which exhibit a foreknowledge of future events. If the book was to be treated as of merely human origin, it was an unavoidable necessity to explain these apparently successful predictions as having been written after the fulfillment had taken place, or at least when it was about to occur. We may distinguish four stages in the history of Isaianic criticism.

1. Johann C. Doederlein (1745-1792), professor of theology at Jena, was the first scholar to publish (in 1789) a systematic argument for a sixth-century date for the composition of Isaiah 40-66. He reasoned that since an eighth-century Isaiah could not have foreseen the fall of Jerusalem (in 587) and the seventy years of captivity, he could never have penned the words of comfort to exiled Judah which appear in chapter 40 onward. Furthermore, from the rationalistic standpoint it was obviously impossible for anyone back in 700 B.C. to foresee the rise of Cyrus the Great, who captured Babylon in 539 and gave permission to the Jewish exiles to return to their homeland. But not only was his work foreseen, Cyrus was even referred to by name in two texts:

CYRUS CYLINDER. THIS INSCRIPTION IS LEGIBLE DESPITE ITS LARGE FRACTURE ON BOTH ENDS. ON IT CYRUS ASCRIBES THE RUIN OF NABONIDUS, KING OF BABYLON, TO THE ANGER OF THE GOD, MARDUK AGAINST HIS OWN SPECIAL CITY. IT RECORDS A PROCLAMATION ALLOWING REPATRIATION OF CAPTIVE PEOPLES TO THEIR HOMELANDS. 6TH C. B.C. BAKED CLAY, 8.1 CM.

Isaiah 44:28 and 45:1. Obviously, therefore, the author of these prophecies must have been some unknown Jew living in Babylon sometime between the first rise of Cyrus as an international figure (around 550 B.C.) and the fall of Babylon to his expanding empire. This spurious author living in Babylon around 540 came to be known to the critics as "Deutero-Isaiah."

These arguments proved so persuasive that the other Old Testament scholars like Professor Eichhorn embraced the same view and expressed their agreement. In 1819, Heinrich F. W. Gesenius (1786-1842) published a commentary, *Jesaja, Zweiter Theil.* A professor of theology at Halle and an eminent Hebrew lexicographer of rationalistic convictions, he made out a very able argument for the unity of the authorship of the last twenty-seven chapters of Isaiah and refuted the attacks of those who had already attempted to separate even Deutero-Isaiah into several different sources, arguing that all the main themes throughout these chapters were treated from a unified standpoint and employed language exhibiting striking affinities in vocabulary and style from chapter 40 to 66. He insisted that they all came from the pen of a single author who lived sometime around 540 B.C.

2. Inasmuch as conservative scholars had objected to the exilic date assigned to Isaiah II on the ground that even in Isaiah I impressive evidences could be found of a foreknowledge of the future importance of Babylon in Israel's history, it became necessary to take a second look at the first thirty-nine chapters of Isaiah. Ernst F. K. Rosenmueller (1768-1835), professor of Arabic at Leipzig, took the next logical step in elaborating the implications of Doederlein's position. If an eighth-century author could not have written the passages in 40-66 which betray a foreknowledge of Babylon's signifi-

cance, then those extensive sections in Isaiah I (such as chaps. 13 and 14) which show a similar foreknowledge must likewise be denied to the historical Isaiah and assigned to the unknown exilic prophet. The removal of such Babylonian sections logically led to the questioning of Isaianic authorship of other passages too, even those in which divine prediction was not a factor. In the process of time, the genuinely eighth-century portions of Isaiah came to be whittled down to a few hundred verses.[1]

3. In the course of this debate it became increasingly apparent that numerous passages in so-called Deutero-Isaiah could hardly be reconciled with a theory of composition in Babylonia. The references to geography, flora, and fauna found in Deutero-Isaiah were far more appropriate to an author living in Syria or Palestine. Arguing from this evidence, Professor Bernard Duhm (1847-1928) of Göttingen came out with a theory of three Isaiahs, none of whom lived in Babylonia. According to his analysis, chapters 40-55 (Deutero-Isaiah) were written about 540 B.C., somewhere in the region of Lebanon, whether in Phoenicia or Syria was not clear. Chapters 56-66 (Trito-Isaiah) were composed in Jerusalem in the time of Ezra, around 450 B.C. Duhm went on to show, however, that in all three Isaiahs there were insertions from still later periods in Judah's history, all the way down to the first century B.C., when the final redaction was worked out.[2] It was this school of criticism which George Adam Smith adhered to, for the most part, in his homiletical commentary on Isaiah in *The Expositor's Bible*. It hardly needs to be pointed out that with the discovery of a second-century B.C. Hebrew manuscript of the complete Isaiah (discovered in the First Qumran cave in 1948) Duhm's theory of first-century insertions becomes impossible to maintain.

Perhaps it should be added that this divisive criticism did not go unanswered, even in Germany, during the nineteenth century. Among the more notable scholars who upheld the Isaianic authorship of all sixty-six chapters were the following: (*a*) Carl Paul Caspari (1814-1892), a convert from Judaism who became a professor at the University of Christiania in Norway. He was a pupil of Ernst Wilhelm Hengstenberg (in Berlin); (*b*) Moritz Drechsler, likewise a pupil of Hengstenberg, who published a commentary on Isa. 1-27, but died before completing the rest of his work; (*c*) Heinrich A. Hahn (1821-1861), who published and supplemented Drechsler's work as far as Isaiah 39; (*d*) Franz Delitzsch (1813-1889), who ably maintained the genuineness of Isaiah's prophecies through all the editions of his celebrated commentary on Isaiah until the final one (when he finally made room for an exilic Deutero-Isaiah); (*e*) Rudolf E. Stier (1800-1862) was another able exponent of the Conservative position. In England, the same position was maintained by Ebenezer Henderson, who taught at the Ministerial College, 1830-1850. In America, Joseph Addison Alexander of Princeton Seminary published a very able commentary in two volumes in which he thoroughly refuted the

---

1. Cf. ISBE, pp. 1504-7.

2. In *Das Buch Jesaia*, 5th ed., Gottingen, 1892, p. 22, Duhm says (in translation), "The Psalms inserted into chapters 24-27 extend to the last decade of the second century, and the epilogues in 16:13f. and 21:16f. may be later yet. The book of Isaiah may have been finished in 70 B.C."

divisive theories of liberal German scholarship.

4. In the twentieth century, the tendency of liberal scholarship has been to lower the date of the non-Isaianic portions of Isaiah rather than to multiply the number of Isaiahs. Thus, Charles Cutler Torrey of Yale argued for a single author for Isa. 34-66 (except 36-39), which were composed by a writer who lived in Palestine, quite probably in Jerusalem itself, near the end of the fifth century. This author, according to Torrey, did not address the exiles at all, but the people to whom he spoke were in his own land of Palestine. The mention of Cyrus and the references to Babylon and Chaldea are all mere interpolations which occurred only in five passages and may therefore be disregarded.

Some more recent scholars, such as W. H. Brownlee, are coming to the view that the entire Isaianic corpus of sixty-six chapters betrays such strong evidences of unity as to suggest an orderly and systematic arrangement by one or more adherents of a so-called Isaianic School. According to this position, a circle of disciples treasured a recollection of the eighth-century prophet's utterances and then gradually added to them with each successive generation until finally an able practitioner of this school, living possibly in the third century, reworked the entire body of material into a well-ordered literary masterpiece.

CRITICAL ARGUMENTS FOR SOURCE DIVISION

Broadly speaking, the grounds adduced for disproving the Isaianic authorship of chapters 40-66 may be classified under three headings: differences in theme and subject matter, differences in language and style, and differences in theological ideas. Each of these criteria is now to be analyzed, with a view to its soundness and tenability.

ALLEGED DIFFERENCES IN THEME AND SUBJECT MATTER

Divisive critics argue that in Isaiah I (1-39) it is contemporary conditions which occupy the center of the author's attention. In Isaiah II (40-66) the center of interest is shifted to the Babylonian Exile and the prospect of a return to the ancestral homeland. It is argued that a futuristic viewpoint could not possibly have been maintained over such a large number of chapters. This has proved to be a persuasive consideration even to those mediating scholars who are not prepared to rule out the theoretical possibility of genuine prediction. By and large, however, the principal architects of the Two-Isaiah theory have simply assumed on rationalistic grounds the impossibility of divine revelation in genuinely predictive prophecy. From this philosophical *a priori* viewpoint they have addressed themselves to the actual data of the text. As J. A. Alexander pointed out in his *Commentary*, the basic assumption of all such critics, however else they may differ among themselves, is that there cannot be such a thing as a distinct prophetic insight of the distant future. He goes on to observe:

"He who rejects a given passage of Isaiah because it contains definite predictions of the future too remote from the times in which he lived to be the object of ordinary human foresight, will of course be led to justify this condemnation by specific proof drawn from the diction, style or idiom of the passage, its historical or archaeological allusions, its rhetorical character, its moral tone, or its religious spirit. On the discovery and presentation of such proofs, the previous assumption, which he intended to sustain, cannot fail to have a warping influence."[3]

This comment contains a valid psychological insight which needs to be borne in mind in any analysis of the structure of the higher critical assault on the genuineness of Isaiah. If there can be no such thing as fulfilled prophecy, it becomes logically necessary to explain all apparent fulfillments as mere *vaticinia ex eventu,* that is, prophecies after the event. The problem for the antisupernaturalist becomes particularly acute in the case of the references to King Cyrus by name (44:28; 45:1). It might be a plausible supposition that some keen political analyst living in the early 540s could have made a successful prediction of the eventual success of the able young king who had already made a name for himself in Media by 550 B.C. But it is quite another thing for an author living in 700 B.C. to foresee events 150 years in advance of their occurrence.

It is usual in this connection to urge that the Scripture seldom predicts a future historical figure by name. Yet it should be pointed out that where the occasion calls for it, the Bible does not hesitate to specify the names of men and places even centuries in advance. For example, the name of King Josiah was, according to 1 Kings 13:2, foretold by a prophet of Judah back in the time of Jeroboam I (930-910), a full three centuries before he appeared in Bethel to destroy the golden calf and idolatrous sanctuary which Jeroboam had erected. This of course may be explained away as a late interpolation in 1 Kings; but there are other instances which cannot be so neatly disposed of. Thus Bethlehem is named by Micah (5:2) as the birthplace of the coming Messiah, seven centuries before the birth of the Lord Jesus. This was a fact well known to the Jewish scribes in the time of Herod the Great.

It is important to observe that the historical situation confronting Isaiah in 690 B.C. gave ample warrant for so unusual a sign as the prediction of Cyrus by name 150 years in advance of the fall of Babylon. Judah had sunk to such a low ebb in matters of religion and morals that the very honor of God demanded a total destruction of the kingdom and a removal of the entire nation into exile (just as had been foretold or forewarned in Lev. 26 and Deut. 28). If God was going to vindicate His holy law, and honor His own promises of disciplinary chastisement, there was no alternative but devastation and captivity. But once a people had been carried off into exile in a distant land, there was virtually no hope that they would ever return to their ancestral soil. Such a thing had never happened before in history, and humanly speaking, there was no prospect that the dispersed Judah of a future generation would ever return to the land of promise. It was therefore altogether appropriate for God to furnish a very definite token or sign to which exiled believers might look as an indication of their coming deliverance and restoration to Palestine. This sign was furnished in the specifying of the very name of their future deliverer.

3. Alexander, *Commentary on Isaiah* (1846-1847), 1:25.

Attempts have been made by C. C. Torrey and others to remove the two references to Cyrus as later insertions which did not truly belong in the text. But the contextual evidence will not permit any such deletion. O. T. Allis in *The Unity of Isaiah* (p. 79) points to the climactic and parallelistic structure of 44:26-28, and shows that this would be quite destroyed or fatally impaired if the name *Kōresh* were removed. In this passage the greatest emphasis is laid on God's ability to foretell the future and to fulfill what He has predicted. The name is then introduced to serve as objective confirmation of the divine authority underlying the entire prophetic utterance.

Allis also points out that the references to Cyrus which begin at 41:2-5 reach a climax in 44:28, and then taper off until the final reference (in which the Persian deliverer is alluded to although not named) in 48:14. Counting all the allusions, there are repeated references to Cyrus through these eight chapters; there is vivid description of his person and work, and his character is set forth as two-sided. On the one hand he is represented as God's "anointed shepherd," and on the other hand he is depicted as a pagan foreigner from "a far country" (46:11) who has not known Jehovah (45:5). It goes without saying that all this would be quite pointless if at the time these passages were composed Cyrus had already become a well-known figure who had made his reputation as the consolidator of the Medo-Persian empire (as the 550-540 date would imply). On the contrary, this future deliverer of captive Israel is always presented as a liberator who will make his appearance in the distant future; and his appearance, in confirmation of this promise, is to furnish an irrefutable demonstration of the divine authority of Isaiah's message.

It should be pointed out that even in the first 39 chapters of Isaiah, the greatest emphasis is laid upon fulfilled prediction, and many future events are foretold. Some of these fulfillments took place within a few years of the prediction; for instance, the deliverance of Jerusalem from the power of Sennacherib by sudden supernatural means in 701 B.C. (37:33-35), the defeat of Damascus within three years by the Assyrian emperor in 732 B.C. (8:4,7), and the destruction of Samaria within twelve years after Isaiah foretold it (7:16). Other events were not to take place until long after Isaiah's death; for instance, the fall of Babylon to the Medes and Persians (13:17), and the eventual desolation of Babylon which should render it an uninhabited and accursed site forever (13:19-20). Also, another long-range prediction was the coming of the glorious Light in a future generation (9:1-2), which was to be fulfilled by the ministry of Christ seven centuries later (cf. Matt. 4:15-16).

As for a foreknowledge of the Babylonian Exile, it should be pointed out that even chapter 6, which is acknowledged by all critics to be authentically Isaianic, points forward to the utter depopulation and devastation of Judah which took place under Nebuchadnezzar. In verses 11 and 12 we read that God's judgment is to be visited upon Judah "until cities be waste without inhabitant, and houses without man, and the land become utterly waste, and Jehovah have removed men far away, and the forsaken places be many in the midst of the land" (ASV). The following verse, when translated according to the indications of the context, clear contains a clear reference to the restoration of the captivity from exile: "Yet in it shall be a tenth, and it shall return, and shall be eaten up." Some interpreters have construed *wašābâ* ("will return") as having the force of the adverb *again*, but in this case such an interpretation is excluded by the appearance of the name of Isaiah's son three verses thereafter. It is obvious that Shear-jashub ("A Remnant will Return") in 7:3, was a name bestowed upon this child as a token of Isaiah's faith that God would fulfill the promise of 6:13, that a remnant would return.[4] To this should be added the clear prediction made by Isaiah himself to Hezekiah (Isa. 39:5-7) after the latter's ill-considered display of all his treasure to the Babylonian envoys, that some day all of this wealth would be carried off to Babylon, along with Hezekiah's own descendants, who would have to serve as slaves there. Since Babylon was only a subject province of the Assyrian empire at the time of this prediction, the same accurate foreknowledge of future Chaldean supremacy must have been revealed to the eighth-century Isaiah as appears in chapters 40-66.

In the latter part of Isaiah, as has already been suggested, the situation confronting Isaiah as a prophet of Yahweh in the midst of the crass idolatry of Manasseh's time demanded a response from the Lord which would be appropriate to the challenge. If God should bring judgment upon disobedient Judah, even to the point of total military defeat and a complete destruction of the land, it might be possible for observers to interpret this as a mere stroke of misfortune such as might happen to any people. Possibly it might even be construed as an expression of displeasure on the part of the national God of Israel toward His unfaithful devotees, for even the pagan religious thinkers were apt to explain national misfortune in this way. (Thus the Babylonian Chronicle explains the subjugation of Babylon by Cyrus on the ground that Marduk was vexed at her for some unspecified offenses. Likewise King Mesha of Moab explained the former subjugation of Moab by Israel on the ground that Chemosh was

NEBUCHADNEZZAR'S BRICKS   A

THOUSANDS OF NEBUCHADNEZZAR'S (605–562 B.C.) BRICKS HAVE BEEN UNCOVERED, EACH STAMPED WITH HIS NAME AND VARIOUS TITLES SUCH AS "KING OF BABYLON" AND "FIRST BORN SON OF NABOPOLASSAR."

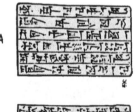
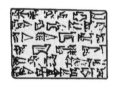

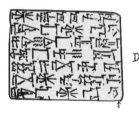

4. It should be understood that *wašābâ* and *yāšûḇ* come from the same verb, *šûḇ* "turn back, return; do again."

MOABITE STONE

THE MOABITE STONE WAS DISCOVERED IN DIBON IN
1868. UNFORTUNATELY, IT WAS LATER BROKEN BY ARABS
AND IN 1873 TAKEN TO THE LOUVRE. IT RECORDS THE
VICTORIES OF KING MESHA OF MOAB, WHO DEFEATED
ISRAEL IN REGAINING THE INDEPENDENCE OF MOAB FROM
THE SONS OF AHAB. MADE OF BLACK BASALT. HEIGHT:
ABOUT 1 M.: WIDTH 0.6 M.

angry with his own devotees.) A decisive testimony to the righteousness and sovereignty of Jehovah as the one true God could be made out only if His acts of punitive judgment and subsequent redemption were solemnly announced by special revelation long before the occurrence of the fulfillment. Only thus could the identity and authority of the Sovereign of the universe be clearly established before the eyes of all mankind. (Cf. Isa. 48:5, where God states that He foretold what He would do, "lest thou shouldst say, Mine idol hath done them, and my graven image, and my molten image, hath commanded them.") So it was that the degenerate age of Manasseh, which threatened to extinguish completely the testimony of Israel, presented a set of circumstances which altogether demanded an extended series of predictive prophecies such as are contained in Isa. 40-66.

Quite clearly this is the intention of the author. In Isa. 41:26 we read: "Who hath declared it from the beginning, that we may know? and beforetime, that we may say, He is right?" (ASV). (There is an allusion here to previous predictions of Isaiah which had already been strikingly fulfilled.) In 42:9, 23: "Behold, the former things are come to pass, and new things do I declare; before they spring forth I tell you of them." And again in 43:9, 12: "Who among them [i.e., the heathen gods] can declare this, and show us former things?...I have declared, and I have saved, and I have showed." Likewise in 44:7-8: "Who, as I, shall call, and shall declare it? And the things that are coming, and that shall come to pass, let them [the idols] declare....Have I not declared unto thee of old, and showed it? And ye are my witnesses."

Such passages as these make it abundantly plain that the extensive and precise predictions of the future contained in these chapters of Isaiah II were intended to achieve a very special purpose. They were to furnish confirmation that the prophet's message was in fact the message of the one true God, who is absolute Sovereign over the affairs of men; that it was by His decree rather than because of the might of Babylon that the covenant nation would be carried off into captivity. Only through the powerful encouragement of fulfilled prediction would the future generation of exiles summon up the courage to return to Palestine, even after the permission of the new Persian government had been granted. In order to sustain the faith of Israel through all these overwhelming reverses—the complete devastation of cities and farmlands, and the destruction of the temple—it was necessary to furnish an absolutely decisive proof that these events had taken place by the permission and plan of the God of Israel, rather than because He was a puny god overcome by the more powerful deities of the Chaldean empire (a conclusion which all heathendom would inevitably draw after the fall of Jerusalem).

It should also be pointed out that the Babylon-centered chapters (40-48) do not appear without some advance preparation in the earlier part of Isaiah. As E. J. Young points out, chapters 1-39 constitute a "staircase, as it were, which gradually leads one from the Assyrian to the Chaldean period. The two belong together, since the former is the preparation for the latter, and the latter is the completion of the former."[5] That is to say, the atmosphere of Isaiah's day was filled with the threat of exile. Samaria had already been carried away captive by the Assyrians in 722; Sennacherib made a supreme attempt to do the same to Jerusalem in 701. With deliberate purpose, Isaiah placed chapters 38 and 39 (even though they narrated earlier events from about 712 B.C.) after chapters 36 and 37, which narrate episodes occurring in 701. (Note Isa. 38:5-6, which quite clearly point forward to the future invasion of Sennacherib in 701.) This is because chapters 38 and 39 lead up to the reason for the coming Babylonian Exile: the pride of Hezekiah in displaying his wealth to the Babylonian envoys sent by Merodach-Baladan. Hence chapter 39 closes with an ominous prediction of the Chaldean captivity.[6] But even in the prior chapters there are numerous intimations of the coming exile of the nation (cf. 3:24-26; 5:5-6; 6:11-13; 24:11-12; 27:13; 32:13-18). Only by the question-begging device of labeling all such references as later interpolations can one evade the impact of this considerable body of evidence that the eighth-century Isaiah foreknew that the Exile was coming. Furthermore, there is the testimony of 2 Chron. 36:23 and Ezra 1:2 that Cyrus's decree of release for the Jewish exiles at Babylon included an affirmation that Yahweh had "charged" him to "build him an house at Jerusalem, which is in Judah." While it is conceivable that recently concocted prophecies were represented to Cyrus as being an authentic prediction from the eighth century, it is far more likely that he was impressed by a genuinely ancient oracle containing his name more than a century before he was born. It is most reasonable to assume that it was this circumstance which convinced him of the reality and power of the God of the Hebrews, and impelled him to take the extraordinary measure of authorizing a mass migration of Yahweh's worshippers to their ancestral homeland. But at the same time it should be recognized that he also restored some other captive peoples to their native cities (ANET, p. 316), possibly to avoid appearing overly partial to the Jews alone.

---

5. E. J. Young, *Who Wrote Isaiah?*, p. 71.
6. Note Isa. 38:5-6, which quite clearly points forward to the future invasion of Sennacherib in 701 B.C. Therefore this illness must have occurred in 713-712 if indeed Hezekiah died in 698.

Finally, it ought to be observed that a Babylonian standpoint does not really prevail as extensively through Isaiah II as advocates of the two Isaiah theory have maintained. Subsequent to chapter 48, clear allusions to the Exile and Restoration are hard to find. Many of the discourses address themselves to conditions known to have prevailed in Judah in the reign of Manasseh.[7] J. A. Alexander appropriately points out: "How seldom, after all, the book mentions Babylon, the Exile, or the Restoration....An exact enumeration of all such cases, made for the first time, might surprise one whose previous impressions had all been derived from the sweeping declarations of interpreters and critics."[8] In other words, the advocates of Deutero-Isaiah have attempted to find many allusions to the late sixth-century situation which are really susceptible to quite other interpretations. It is also a fact that the name of Babylon occurs with less frequency in chapters 40-66 than in 1-39. A statistical count shows that there are only four occurrences in the later section (43:14; 47:1; 48:14, 20), but in chapters 1-39 there are nine occurrences, or more than twice as many.

Internal evidence of the composition of Isaiah II in Palestine. A most important criterion for dating ancient documents is found in those references or allusions to contemporary events or surrounding conditions which it may happen to contain. The geographical setting which it presupposes, the kind of plants and animals which it mentions, the climatic conditions which it implies as prevailing in the author's own environment—all these are important data for determining the place and time for the composition of any document whether ancient or modern. A careful examination of such allusions in Isa. 40-66 points unmistakably to the conclusion that it was composed in Palestine rather than in Babylon. We have already seen that Bernard Duhm, on a rationalistic basis, came to the same conclusion in 1892.

Isaiah 40-66 shows little knowledge of Babylonian geography, but great familiarity with that of Palestine. Thus the trees referred to are not found in Babylonia, but are native to Palestine, such as the cedar, cypress, and oak (cf. 41:19, 44:14: "He heweth him down cedars, and taketh the cypress and the oak...he planteth an ash, and the rain doth nourish it"). The writer's geographical viewpoint is clearly Palestinian. Thus Yahweh is said to send off His decree to Babylon (43:14). Israel is called the seed of Abraham which the Lord has taken from "the ends of the earth" (apparently a reference to Babylonia) in 41:9 and 45:22. The same is true with the phrases "from the east" and "from a far country" as employed in 46:11, and "from thence" rather than "from hence" in 52:11 ("Depart ye, go ye out from thence, touch no unclean thing")—an exhortation to the future exiles to leave Babylon as soon as the invitation has been given them by the coming deliverer, Cyrus.

The author assumes that the cities of Judah are still standing. Compare 40:9: "Say unto the cities of Judah, Behold your God!" This verse implies that Zion and the other cities of Judah are in actual existence at the time of writing, rather than being unin-

---

7. This point is further elaborated in chap. 24, p. 372.
8. Alexander, 1:57-58.

habited sites in the wake of Chaldean devastation. The same is true of 62:6: "I have set watchmen upon thy walls, O Jerusalem." Antisupernaturalists cannot explain this away as an ideal anticipation of cities which are some day to be rebuilt. Such a defense would violate a cardinal maxim of their own, as expressed by Driver, "The prophet speaks always, in the first instance, to his own contemporaries; the message which he brings is intimately related to the circumstances of his own time....The prophet never abandons his own historical position, but speaks from it."[9]

It is only to be expected that if the cities are still standing, the Israelites themselves are assumed to be dwelling in Palestine by the author of these prophecies. Thus in 58:6 we read: "Is not this the fast that I have chosen? to loose the bands of wickedness, to undo the heavy burdens, and to let the oppressed go free, and that ye break every yoke?" This would be very strange language to address to a people who were groaning under the bondage of the Chaldeans as a captive people. It is very evident that the Jews are still dwelling in their own land and are competent to hold their own law courts. Only thus would it be possible for corrupt judges to pervert the administration of the law to the disadvantage of the less privileged classes of society.

Evidence for the pre-exilic composition of Isaiah 11. We have seen there is no good support for a Babylonian origin of Isaiah II. The internal evidence as it has been detailed above has shown how indefensible was this element in the theory of Deutero-Isaiah, as it was propounded by Doederlein, Eichhorn, and Rosenmueller. More recent scholars tend to regard Isaiah II as having been composed either in Palestine or in the region of Lebanon to the north. They nevertheless insist that chapters 40-66 were composed late, either in the exilic or post-exilic period. It remains to be shown that this theory also fails to account for the data of the internal evidence.

In the first place, many of the same evils which prevailed in the time of the eighth-century Isaiah are evidently still current in the generation of the author of Isaiah II. Note for example Isa. 57:7, "Upon a high and lofty mountain you have made your bed. You also went up there to offer sacrifice." Bloodshed and violence are denounced in 1:15: "Yea, when ye make many prayers, I will not hear: your hands are full of blood," and they are still being denounced in 59:3, 7: "For your hands are defiled with blood, and your fingers with iniquity; your lips have spoken lies, your tongue hath muttered perverseness....Their feet run to evil, and they make haste to shed innocent blood." In both parts of the book, the prophet inveighs against the prevalent falsehood, injustice, and oppression which were practiced in Judah. Compare 10:12 "Woe unto them that decree unrighteous decrees, and that write grievousness which they have prescribed; to turn aside the needy from judgment, and to take away the right from the poor of my people, that widows may be their prey, and that they may rob the fatherless" with 59:4-9, where the indictment is very similar: "None calleth for justice, nor any pleadeth for truth: they trust in vanity, and speak lies; they conceive mischief, and bring forth iniquity."

9. Driver, ILOT, p. 224.

Both in Isaiah I and II, a revolting hypocrisy characterizes the religious life of the nation. Compare 29:13: "Forasmuch as this people draw near me with their mouth, and with their lips do honor me, but have removed their heart far from me, and their fear toward me is taught by the precept of men" with 58:2, 4: "Yet they seek me daily, and delight to know my ways, as a nation that did righteousness, and forsook not the ordinance of their God: they ask of me the ordinances of justice; they take delight in approaching to God....Behold, ye fast for strife and debate, and to smite with the fist of wickedness: ye shall not fast as ye do this day, to make your voice to be heard on high." Moreover, in both sections of the book the Jews are assumed to be practicing their orgiastic rites in the sacred groves. (In 1:29: "They shall be ashamed of the oaks which they have desired"; and in 57:5: "Ye that inflame yourselves among the oaks, under every green tree," ASV.)

Although the same types of sin are assumed to be prevalent by the author in both parts of Isaiah, it should be observed that there is a difference. In 40-66 the author refers to an extreme degeneracy and breakdown of morals which accords with no known period of Jewish history so closely as with the age of Manasseh, who "shed innocent blood very much, till he had filled Jerusalem from one end to another" (2 Kings 21:16). One has only to read 2 Kings 21 and Isa. 59 to see the close correspon-

MAẞEBŌTH OR ORTHOSTATS DEDICATED TO BAAL. THE SACRED PILLARS AT GEZER WERE THOUGHT TO HOUSE THE SPIRIT OF BAAL, THE FERTILITY GOD, AND HENCE WOULD BE ERECTED AT THE "HIGH PLACES" AND AMONG THE SACRED ASHERAH TREES (WHICH WERE ASSIGNED THE GODDESS THOUGHT TO BE HIS CONSORT).

dence. Thus 59:10: "We grope for the wall like the blind, and we grope as if we had no eyes: we stumble at noonday as in the night; we are in desolate places as dead men." So also verses 13-14: "In transgressing and lying against the Lord, and departing away from our God, speaking oppression and revolt, conceiving and uttering from the heart words of falsehood. And judgment is turned away backward, and justice standeth afar off: for truth is fallen in the street, and equity cannot enter."

A most decisive objection to a post-exilic date for the composition of Isaiah II is to be found in the numerous passages which refer to idolatry as a wide and prevalent evil in Israel. Isaiah 44:9-20 contains a long diatribe against the folly of making graven images for worship, as if this were a major problem in contemporary Judah. This passage cannot be dismissed as a mere challenge to contemporary pagan nations, for there are too many other passages which speak of idolatry being practiced by the author's own countrymen at that time (cf. 57:4-5, "Against whom do ye sport yourselves?... Enflaming yourselves with idols under every green tree, slaying the children in the valleys under the clifts of the rocks?").

Not only is ritual prostitution here referred to, but also the sacrificing of babies to Molech and Adrammelech, an infamous practice carried on during the reign of Manasseh in the Valley of the Sons of Hinnom (2 Kings 21:6; 2 Chron. 33:6). And again, Isa. 57:7: "Upon a lofty and high mountain hast thou set thy bed; even thither wentest thou up to offer sacrifice." This is an obvious allusion to worship in the high places (bāmôt), a type of worship which flourished in the pre-exilic period, but never thereafter. Again, 65:2-4: "I have spread out my hands all the day unto a rebellious people... a people that provoke me to my face continually, sacrificing in gardens, and burning incense upon bricks; that sit among the graves, and lodge in the secret places; that eat swine's flesh, and broth of abominable things is in their vessels" (ASV). In the very last chapter we find that idolatry is still being practiced. In 66:17: "They that sanctify themselves and purify themselves to go unto the gardens, behind one in the midst [or, one asherah], eating swine's flesh, and the abomination, and the mouse, they shall come to an end together, saith Jehovah" (ASV). Plainly these things represent vicious evils and degenerate pagan abominations which were going on at the time the prophet composed these words.

Let us carefully consider the implications of this prevalence of idolatry in Judah. The hilly or mountainous terrain referred to completely excludes the possibility of idolatrous worship being carried on in Babylonia, which was a flat, alluvial terrain. The types of worship alluded to are precisely those which are described as having been cultivated in the reign of Manasseh. So far as the post-exilic period is concerned, it is agreed by scholars of every persuasion that the returning Jews who resettled Judah from 536 to 450 brought back no idol worship with them. The terrible ordeal of the Babylonian captivity had brought about a complete rejection of graven images on the part of the Jewish remnant. This complete freedom from idolatry in post-exilic Judea is proved beyond all reasonable doubt by the writings of the admittedly post-exilic authors, notably the prophets Haggai, Zechariah, and Malachi, and the historians Ezra and Nehemiah. Many and various were the evils which arose in the Second Commonwealth during the century which elapsed between Zerubbabel and Malachi, and these evils are clearly described and earnestly denounced both by Ezra and Nehemiah. The book of Malachi contains a list of sins into which his countrymen had fallen. Yet none of these suggests the slightest practice of idolatry. There was intermarriage with foreign women of idolatrous background; there was oppression of the poor by the rich; there was desecration of the Sabbath; there was a withholding of tithes—but none of these authors ever mentions the reappearance of idolatry in the land of Judah. There was also acceptance of blemished, defective animals for sacrifice, Mal. 1:12-14. The only possible conclusion to draw is that the worship of graven images there was unknown. Not until the age of Antiochus Epiphanes in the second century B.C. was any real effort made to introduce it once more among the Israelite people. Therefore, in the light of this evidence, it is impossible to hold that Isaiah II was composed at any time after the exile, or indeed after the fall of Jerusalem.

Some Liberal scholars have felt compelled to make slight concessions in this direction and admit the possibility of late pre-exilic strands in Isaiah II. Thus Bentzen notes that "in like manner 63:7–65:25 may be connected with the events of 587 B.C."[10] W. H. Brownlee likewise comments: "It is not impossible that there are some pre-exilic prophecies among the oracles of Volume II. Note especially 56:9–57:13; 58:1-9 as of possible pre-exilic origin."[11] It can easily be seen how damaging to the theory of Isaiah II are such admissions as these. If such considerable passages on the basis of their contemporary allusions are to be dated prior to the fall of Jerusalem, the possibility arises that many other sections which do not happen to contain contemporary allusions may also have been of pre-exilic origin. In other words, if portions of these twenty-seven chapters demand a time of composition prior to the downfall of the Jewish monarchy, and there are no other passages which demand an exilic or post-exilic origin (except upon the basis of a philosophic *a priori* that all fulfilled predictions are *vaticinia ex eventu*), then the only reasonable deduction to draw is that the entire work was composed prior to 587 B.C. This means that the whole case for Deutero- or Trito-Isaiah falls to the ground, simply on the basis of the internal evidence of the text itself.

---

10. A. Bentzen, IOT, 2:109.
11. Brownlee, *The Meaning of the Dead Sea Scrolls for the Bible* (London: Oxford, 1964), p. 5.

24 ISAIAH (CONTINUED)

ALLEGED DIFFERENCES IN LANGUAGE AND STYLE

PROPONENTS OF THE ISAIAH II THEORY affirm that there are very definite and marked contrasts in style between Isaiah I and Isaiah II, and that these can be accounted for only by a difference in authorship. The purpose of the ensuing discussion will be to show that the stylistic similarities between the two parts are even more significant than the alleged differences, and that such differences as there are may easily be accounted for by the change in situation which confronted Isaiah in his later years, and also by the maturing of his literary genius. Numerous parallels to this may be pointed out in the history of world literature. Thus in the case of John Milton, we find far more striking dissimilarities between *Paradise Lost*, which he composed in later years, and the style of *L'Allegro* or *Il Penseroso*, which appeared in his earlier period. A similar contrast is observable between his prose works such as *Christian Doctrine* and *Areopagitica*. Or, to take an example from German literature, Goethe's *Faust Part II* presents striking contrasts in concept, style, and approach as over against *Faust Part I*. These contrasts are far more obvious than those between Isaiah I and Isaiah II. In his *Dictionary of the Bible* (p. 339a), Davis points out that in the twenty-five years of Shakespeare's activity, four distinct periods can be distinguished in his dramatic productions, each period being marked by clear differences in style.

As in the case of Pentateuchal criticism, dissectionists of Isaiah have resorted to lists of rare or unique words or phrases in order to confirm a diversity of authorship. But this type of evidence has to be handled with the greatest care in order to come out to valid results. Mere word lists may prove little or nothing. In the case of the Latin poet Horace, some of the best-known phrases from his *Ars Poetica*, such as *callida junctura, in medias res*, and *ad unguem*,[1] occur nowhere else in the writings of this poet. Yet far from being considered spurious because unique, they are very frequently quoted as

---

1. That it is to say, "*adroit/skillful/linking/joining*"; "into the middle of the action"; "to a hair" (literally–"fingernail"), respectively.

examples of Horace's literary skill. So far as Isaiah is concerned, Nägelsbach points out: "For among the chapters of Isaiah that are acknowledged genuine, there is not a single one which does not contain thoughts and words that are new and peculiar to it alone."[2]

1. The stylistic resemblances between Isaiah I and Isaiah II are numerous and striking. Most distinctive of all is the characteristic title of God which occurs frequently throughout Isaiah and only five times elsewhere in the Old Testament. This title is "the Holy One of Israel" (qeḏôš Yiśrā'ē'l), which expresses a central theological emphasis that dominates all the prophecies contained in this book. A statistical count shows that it occurs twelve times in chapters 1-39 and fourteen times in chapters 40-66. Elsewhere in the Old Testament it only occurs in Pss. 71:22; 89:18 and Jer. 50:29; 51:5: Whether or not Isaiah actually invented this title, it became a sort of authoritative seal for all of his writing. Thus it furnishes very strong evidence of the unity of the entire production. The only alternative possible to advocates of the Deutero-Isaiah theory is to assert that the unknown prophet or prophets who contributed to chapters 40-66 were so dominated by the influence and message of the eighth-century Isaiah that they felt constrained to employ his favorite title of God with even greater frequency than he did himself. But such an explanation does not account for the almost complete absence of this title in the writings of other post-exilic authors who certainly could not have been ignorant of the eighth-century Isaiah. Furthermore, this type of evasion appears to savor of circular reasoning: Isaiah II must have been written by a different author from Isaiah I because of the stylistic differences; but where the most striking stylistic similarities are pointed out, these indicate only that the later author was a pupil or imitator of the original author. Thus the facts are made to conform to the theory, rather than deriving the theory from the facts (i.e., from the textual data).

Conservative scholars have pointed out at least forty or fifty sentences or phrases which appear in both parts of Isaiah, and indicate its common authorship.[3] Of these the following are typical:

"For the mouth of Yahweh hath spoken it" (ASV) occurs in 1:20; 40:5; 58:14.

"I act, and who can reverse it?" (43:13, NASB) is very close to "His hand is stretched out, and who shall turn it back?" (14:27).

"And the ransomed of Yahweh shall return, and come with singing unto Zion; and everlasting joy shall be upon their heads" (ASV) occurs in both 35:10 and 51:11.

"Will assemble the outcasts of Israel" (11:12) is very close to "gathereth the outcasts of Israel" in 56:8.

"For Yahweh hath a day of vengeance, a year of recompense for the cause of Zion" (34:8, ASV) greatly resembles 61:2, "to proclaim the year of Yahweh's favor, and the day of vengeance of our God" (ASV).

"The lion shall eat straw like the ox....They shall not hurt nor destroy in all my holy mountain" appears both in 11:6-9 and 65:25.

2. Nägelsbach, in Lange's *Commentary,* p. 283.
3. Cf. Raven, OTI, pp. 190-91.

"For in the wilderness shall waters break out, and streams in the desert" (35:6) is very close to "I will make the wilderness a pool of water, and the dry land springs of water" (41:18).

"And the Spirit of Yahweh shall rest upon him, the spirit of wisdom and understanding" (11:2, ASV) is quite similar to, "The Spirit of the Lord Yahweh is upon me, because Yahweh has anointed me" (61:1, ASV).

In 35:8 we meet with the figure of the highway of Yahweh which runs through the wilderness or desert; the same thought occurs in 40:3.

"I am full of the burnt-offerings of rams, and the fat of fed beasts....Your new moons and appointed feasts my soul hateth: they are a trouble unto me; I am weary to bear them" (1:11, 14) is very similar to "Thou hast filled me with the fat of thy sacrifices: but thou hast burdened me with thy sins, thou hast wearied me with thine iniquities" (43:24, ASV).

"In that day will Yahweh of hosts become a crown of glory, and a diadem of beauty, unto the residue of his people" (28:5, ASV) greatly resembles, "Thou shalt also be a crown of beauty in the land of Yahweh, and a royal diadem in the hand of thy God" (63:3, ASV).

Even the use of the imperfect tense of 'āmar "to say" with Yahweh as subject (rather than the usual perfect tense 'āmar), namely yō'mar YHWH ("Yahweh is saying") is a peculiarity of Isaiah, and occurs both in I and II (cf. E. J. Young, Who Wrote Isaiah? chap. 8).

In view of these and many other parallels which can be cited, it is difficult to see how an unprejudiced observer could fail to be impressed by such numerous instances of resemblance. These distinctive turns of expression which so obviously bear the stamp of originality and yet which occur in both portions of the book indicate that the same author must have composed the entire production.

2. It should be pointed out that the literary resemblances of Isaiah II to the eighth-century prophet Micah are numerous and striking. This would hardly be expected of a writer who composed in the sixth or fifth century B.C. Here are some examples:

"For ye shall not go out in haste...for Yahweh will go before you" (Isa. 52:12, ASV); "And their king is passed on before them, and Yahweh at the head of them" (Mic. 2:13, ASV).

"Declare unto my people their transgression, and to the house of Jacob their sins" (Isa. 58:1); "I am full of power...to declare unto Jacob his transgression, and to Israel his sin" (Mic. 3:8).

"They shall bow down to thee with their face toward the earth, and lick up the dust of thy feet; and thou shalt know that I am the Lord" (Isa. 49:23); "They shall lick the dust like a serpent, they shall move out of their holes like worms of the earth: they shall be afraid of the Lord our God" (Mic. 7:17).

"Behold, I have made thee to be a new sharp threshing instrument having teeth; thou shalt thresh the mountains...and shalt make the hills as chaff" (Isa. 41:15-16,

ASV); "Arise and thresh, O daughter of Zion; for I will make thy horn iron…and thou shalt beat in pieces many peoples" (Mic. 4:13, ASV).

Whether Isaiah was influenced by Micah or Micah by Isaiah is hard to say; quite possibly they were familiar with each other's preaching. It may also have been that the Holy Spirit moved them both to express God's message to the same generation in similar terms. At any rate, they express the same general mood and viewpoint, and deal very largely with the same issues. In this connection we might mention Hosea 13:4: "Thou shalt know no god but me, and besides me there is no saviour" (ASV). This sentence appears twice in Isaiah II, in 43:11 and 45:21, thus indicating a close relationship. (Since Hosea was slightly earlier than Isaiah, it is quite possible that the younger prophet deliberately borrowed from the older.)

ALLEGED DIFFERENCES IN THEOLOGICAL IDEAS

It is asserted by the advocates of the two-Isaiah theory that Deutero-Isaiah dwells upon the infiniteness of God and His sovereign relationship toward the heathen nations in a way that is far more developed and emphatic than in Isaiah I. On the other hand, Isaiah II makes no mention of the Messianic King nor of the faithful remnant; rather, the dominating concept is that of the suffering Servant. To these allegations it may be replied that no genuine contradictions have ever been pointed out in the theology of the two sections of Isaiah, nor has any critic ever demonstrated that the new emphases which do appear in chapters 40-66 are not sufficiently accounted for by the changed conditions which occurred in the reign of the wicked and idolatrous Manasseh. Actually there is no doctrine set forth in 40-66 which is not already contained, in germ at least, in 1-39. With the influx of idolatry in the kingdom of Judah and the worship of heathen gods, which became fashionable in Manasseh's time, a challenge was presented to the true faith that called for just such an emphasis upon the uniqueness and sovereignty of Yahweh as we find in Isa. 40-48. As for the doctrine of the Messiah, the inevitability of judgment upon apostate Israel quite logically led to the development of the doctrine of vicarious atonement, apart from which there could be no reasonable hope for the spiritual survival of the nation. This accounts for the prominence of the concept of the suffering Servant, or the Servant of Yahweh, in Isaiah II.

Much discussion has been devoted to the question of the identity of the Servant of

JUDEA CAPTA, PICTURES CAPTIVE JUDAH, MOURNING UNDER A PALM TREE GUARDED BY A ROMAN SOLDIER. *OBVERSE:* PORTRAIT OF VESPASIAN UNDER WHOM JERUSALEM WAS DESTROYED IN 70 A.D.

Key Messianic Prophecies in the Old Testament

Gen. 3:15	Messiah to reconcile men to God; fully human, born of woman, He will utterly defeat Satan
22:18	He will be of the family of Abraham
49:10	He will be of the kingly tribe of Judah
Deut. 18:15	He will be a prophet who, like Moses, revealed the word of God
Ps. 2:1-2	He will be tried by Gentile rulers and condemned by His own Jewish people
16:10	Through resurrection, by the Father, Jesus' body will not see corruption
22:1	He will experience the rejection of the Father at His death
22:6-7	He will be mocked at His crucifixion
22:22	Christ will glorify God in His church after His resurrection
40:6-8	Christ delighted in all the Father's will
69:7-12	Christ would be rejected by men
69:21	Christ would drink gall at His crucifixion
89:4	Christ will be of the eternal seed of David
89:26-28	Christ will be God's eternal son, His unique first born
110:1	He will ascend to the right hand of the Father, and be coronated
110:4	His priesthood will be eternal, after the manner of Melchizedek
132:11	He will be of the lineage of David
Isa. 7:14	Christ will have a virgin birth; He will be called Immanuel
7:15-16	He will grow up in a land dominated by a foreign power
9:1-2	He will minister in Galilee
9:7	He will be of the line of David, but His kingship will be eternal and He will be the Son of God.
11:2	He will be anointed with The Holy Spirit
11:4	He will minister perfect justice regarding the poor and the meek
24:16	Christ will offer salvation to the entire world
40:3	He will have a forerunner
42:1	Christ will be the great anointed Servant of Yahweh
42:2	His ministry will be gentle
42:6	Christ will be the fulfillment of God's covenant
49:6	Christ will be a light to the Gentiles
52:14	He would be disfigured by the abuses He suffered prior to crucifixion
53:4	Christ will bear all our diseases
53:5	He will provide atonement for sin
53:9	He will be buried in a rich man's tomb
53:10	The Father will prolong Christ's days by resurrecting Him from the dead
Dan. 9:24	His public ministry to begin in A.D. 26, which would be 483 years after the decree to Ezra to rebuild Jerusalem; 3 1/2 years later (in the middle of the seven year "week") the Messiah would be crucified while atoning for sin as the "Most Holy" One.
Mic. 5:2	Jesus would be born in Bethlehem
Zech. 9:9	He would enter Jerusalem on a donkey's colt
11:12	Christ would be betrayed for 30 pieces of silver
12:10	He would be pierced for our transgressions (Isa. 53:5)

Yahweh, who is referred to in various passages from chapter 41 to 53. Rationalists are compelled by their philosophical presuppositions to deny that the suffering Servant was intended as a prophecy of Jesus Christ. In their search for some more contemporary figure with whom the Servant might be identified, most modern antisupernaturalists resort to the same identification as that favored by modern Judaism that the suffering Servant is equivalent to the Jewish nation. But there can be little doubt that this identification leads to insuperable difficulties in those "Servant songs" which refer to the Messiah. Thus, in Isa. 53:4, 5, 8, 9, this type of exegesis would result in making Israel bear vicariously their own sins; that Israel itself was smitten rather than the Servant; that the nation of Israel did not open its mouth before its judge, and that the whole Jewish race was carried off by a judicial murder and was buried with a certain rich man. Such an interpretation results in self-contradictory nonsense.

The only satisfactory explanation for the Servant concept in Isaiah is that it is of a three-dimensional character. As Delitzsch put it, the Servant may be symbolized by a pyramid. At the base of the pyramid is the Hebrew nation as a whole (as in 41:8 and 42:19). Israel is regarded as God's uniquely chosen people charged with the responsibility of witnessing to the true God before the heathen nations, and serving as custodians of His Word. At the middle level (43:10), the remnant of true believers in Israel will constitute the redeemed people of God and serve as witnesses to their unspiritual countrymen. At the apex of the pyramid stands a single individual, the Lord Jesus

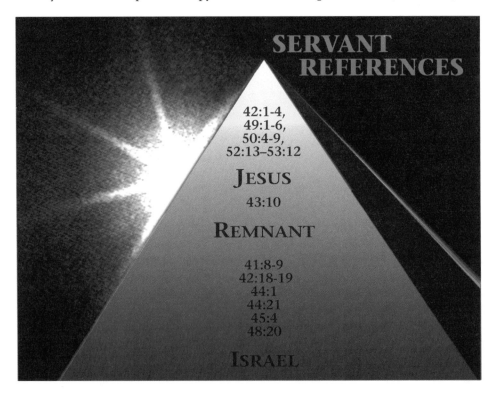

SERVANT
REFERENCES

42:1-4,
49:1-6,
50:4-9,
52:13–53:12

JESUS

43:10

REMNANT

41:8-9
42:18-19
44:1
44:21
45:4
48:20

ISRAEL

Christ, who is set forth as the true Israel (for apart from Him there could not be a covenant nation of Israel, and from Him the nation derives all its standing before God). It is this Servant who will arise as Redeemer and Deliverer from sin by bearing in His own person the death penalty in the place of sinners. There are four main "Servant Songs." (See chart above).

ADDITIONAL PROOFS OF THE GENUINENESS OF ISAIAH 40-66

1. First of all it should be noted that Jesus ben Sirach (48:22-25) clearly assumes that Isaiah wrote chapters 40-66 of the book of Isaiah. E. J. Young notes, "The tradition of Isaianic authorship appears as early as Ecclesiasticus. In 14:17-25 we read, 'He [that is, Isaiah] comforted them that mourned in Zion. He showed the things that should be to the end of time and the hidden things before they ever came to pass'." It is to be observed that the term used for comfort, *parakalein*, is the same as is used in the LXX of Isa. 40:1 and of 61:1-2. The Hebrew original of Ecclesiasticus uses exactly the same word as Isaiah does, the verb *wayyinnahem*. [4]

2. The New Testament writers clearly regard the author of Isaiah I and Isaiah II to be one and the same. Many of the New Testament quotations could be interpreted as referring to the book merely according to its traditional title, but there are other references which clearly imply the personality of the historic Isaiah himself.

Matthew 12:17-18 quotes Isa. 42:1 as "that which was spoken by Isaiah the prophet."

Matthew 3:3 quotes Isa. 40:3 as "spoken of by the prophet Isaiah."

Luke 3:4 quotes Isa. 40:3-5 as "in the book of the words of Isaiah the prophet."

Acts 8:28 states that the Ethiopian eunuch was "reading Isaiah the prophet," specifically, Isa. 53:7-8. In his conversation with Philip (Acts 8:34) he inquired, "Of whom speaketh the prophet [Isaiah] this, of himself, or of some other man?"

Romans 10:16 quotes Isa. 53:1, stating: "Isaiah saith—"

Romans 10:20 quotes Isa. 65:1, stating: "Isaiah is very bold, and saith—"

The most conclusive New Testament citation is John 12:38-41. Verse 38 quotes Isa. 53:1; verse 40 quotes Isa. 6:9-10. Then the inspired apostle comments in verse 41: "These things said Isaiah, when he saw his glory, and spoke of him." Obviously it was the same Isaiah who personally beheld the glory of Christ in the temple vision of Isa. 6 who also made the statement in Isa. 53:1: "Who hath believed our report? and to whom is the arm of the Lord revealed?" If it was not the same author who composed both chapter 6 and chapter 53 (and advocates of the Deutero-Isaiah theory stoutly affirm that it was not), then the inspired apostle himself must have been in error. It therefore follows that advocates of the two-Isaiah theory must by implication concede the existence of errors in the New Testament, even in so vital a matter as the authorship of inspired books of the Old Testament.

3. A most formidable difficulty is presented to the Deutero-Isaiah theory by the

4. Young, E. J., *An Introduction to the Old Testament* [Grand Rapids: Eerdmans, 1958], p. 220.

fact that the author's name was not preserved. It is quite inconceivable that his name should have been forgotten had he been some individual other than the eighth-century Isaiah himself. By the admission of the Dissectionist Critics themselves, no sublimer passages of prophecy are to be found in the entire Old Testament than are contained in Isaiah II. It is commonly conceded that the author of these passages must be regarded as the greatest of all the Old Testament prophets. How could it have come about that such a preeminent genius should have diminished so rapidly in stature that by the third century B.C. when the Septuagint was translated, his name should have been completely forgotten? The earliest extrabiblical reference we have to the writings of Isaiah is found in Ecclesiasticus 49:17-25 (180 B.C.). Here the author (Jesus ben Sirach) refers to the fact that "he [Isaiah] comforted them that mourned in Zion....He showed the things that should be to the end of time, and the hidden things before ever they happened" (this last being an allusion to Isa. 48:6). Here the same word for comfort (*parakalein*) is used as was employed by the Septuagint in translating Isa. 40:1. It is scarcely conceivable that the pupil could have so far surpassed his master and yet remained anonymous. But this is the incredible assumption, hardly to be paralleled in the rest of the world literature, to which the advocates of this divisive theory are driven.

It should be observed in this connection that an almost invariable rule followed by the ancient Hebrews in regard to prophetic writings was that the name of the prophet was essential for the acceptance of any prophetic utterance. This is emphasized by the fact that even so brief a composition as the prophecy of Obadiah bore the name of the author. The Hebrews regarded the identity of the prophet as of utmost importance if his message was to be received as an authoritative declaration of a true spokesman of the Lord. As E. J. Young points out (IOT, p. 205), it is altogether contrary to the genius of biblical teaching to postulate the existence of anonymous writing prophets. And if the shortest, least-gifted of the Minor Prophets was remembered by name in connection with his written messages, it surely follows that the sublimest prophet the nation ever produced should have left his name to posterity. We must therefore conclude that the name of the author of Isa. 40-66 has indeed been preserved and that it was the eighth-century prophet himself.

4. The linguistic evidence is altogether adverse to the composition of Isaiah II in Babylon during the sixth century. In the writings of Ezra and Nehemiah, who came from the region of Babylon or from Susa (if not from the Persian centers of Ecbatana and Persepolis), we have a fair sample of the type of Hebrew spoken by Jews who returned from the Exile to Palestine and settled in their homeland during the fifth century. These writings show a certain amount of linguistic intrusion from Aramaic and are sprinkled with Babylonian terms. But there is complete absence of such influence in the language of Isaiah II. It is written in perfectly pure Hebrew, free from any postexilic characteristics and closely resembles the Hebrew of Isaiah I.

5. Isaiah 13:1 furnishes serious embarrassment to the theory of an exilic Deutero-

THE ISHTAR GATE OF NEBUCHADNEZZAR (605–562 B.C.)
AT BABYLON, ORIGINALLY WAS DECORATED WITH GLAZED TILES DEPICTING LIONS ALTERNATING WITH SERPENT–DRAGONS (OR GRIFFINS) TOTALLING AT LEAST 575 ANIMALS.

Isaiah. Chapter 13 contains a burden of divine judgment upon the city of Babylon, which in Isaiah's day was a mere subject province under the Assyrian empire. Nevertheless, this opening verse states: "The burden of Babylon, which Isaiah the son of Amoz did see." This constitutes the clearest affirmation possible that the eighth-century Isaiah foresaw the coming importance of Babylon, her devastation of Palestine, and her ultimate downfall before the onslaughts of the Medes (cf. v. 17). In view of the often repeated argument that Isaiah's name does not appear in chapters 40-66 and that therefore he is not to be regarded as the author of predictions involving a knowledge of sixth-century events, it is interesting to observe that his name is expressly affixed to this earlier chapter in which such a knowledge is most clearly implied.

It should be noted that chapter 13 occurs in a series of burdens pronounced against foreign nations who posed a threat to Israel (chaps. 13-23). It is quite clear that the eighth-century Isaiah wrote denunciations of this sort, and the language of chapter 13 is altogether similar to that employed in the rest of the chapters in this series. It is only in the interests of salvaging the theory of a Deutero-Isaiah that critics have been compelled to assign a late exilic date to chapter 13. But as E. J. Young points out: "If chapter 13 be denied Isaiah, it is practically impossible to explain its position in the prophecy. Why would a later editor ever have thought that Isaiah had prophesied concerning Babylon?"[5] This point is especially well taken in view of the fact that denunciations of Babylon do occur in other parts of the book (e.g., in chap. 48). It is difficult to

5. E. J. Young, p. 43.

see why chapter 13 would have been placed in close proximity to these other denunciations if in point of fact it was not composed at the same time.

6. Last, we come to the relationship between Isaiah II and the seventh-century pre-exilic prophets. Zephaniah, Nahum, and Jeremiah contain verses which are so similar to Isaiah II as to point to a possible borrowing by one from the other. Thus in Zeph. 2:15 we read: "This is the joyous city that dwelt carelessly, that said in her heart, I am, and there is none besides me" (ASV). This bears a strong resemblance to Isa. 47:8: "Now therefore hear this, thou that art given to pleasures, that sittest securely, that sayest in thy heart, I am, and there is none else besides me" (ASV). Nahum 1:15 reads: "Behold, upon the mountains the feet of him that bringeth good tidings, that publisheth peace!" (ASV). Compare this with Isa. 52:7: "How beautiful upon the mountains are the feet of him that bringeth good tidings, that publisheth peace!" (ASV). Jeremiah 31:35 reads: "Thus saith Yahweh...who stirreth up the sea, so that the waves thereof roar; Yahweh of hosts is his name" (ASV). This is very close to Isa. 51:15: "For I am Yahweh thy God, who stirreth up the sea, so that the waters thereof roar; Yahweh of hosts is his name" (ASV).

In comparing such resemblances as these, it might be argued that Isaiah II was borrowing from the seventh-century prophets rather than the other way around, but in the case of Jer. 30:10-11 (which bears a relationship to Isa. 43:1-6), such an explanation is hardly possible. In the Jeremiah passage, the term My Servant (*'ābdî*) occurs as a Messianic title. Nowhere else does it appear in a Messianic sense in the writings of Jeremiah, and yet it is a frequent term in Isaiah II. There can be no other reasonable conclusion to draw but that Jeremiah did the borrowing and that the Isaiah passage must have been written at an earlier time than his own.[6]

In view of all the foregoing evidence, it may fairly be said that it requires a far greater exercise of credulity to believe that Isa. 40-66 was *not* written by the historical eighth-century Isaiah than to believe that it was. Judging from the internal evidence alone, even apart from the authority of the New Testament authors, a fair handling of the evidence can only lead to the conclusion that the same author was responsible for both sections and that no part of it was composed as late as the Exile.

---

6. Ibid., p. 47, cites at least a dozen other passages in Jeremiah which show a dependence on Isaiah II.

25

NAHUM, ZEPHANIAH, AND HABAKKUK

NAHUM

THE NAME of the prophet (*Nāḥûm*) signifies "consolation" His theme deals with the holiness of God, a holiness which involves both retribution toward rebellious unbelievers and compassion toward His own people, especially those who sincerely believe and trust in Him alone. The believer is represented as rejoicing at the sight of God's righteous vindication of His holiness in the destruction of the God-defying power of Assyria.

OUTLINE OF NAHUM

I. A psalm of God's majesty, 1:1–2:2

A. God's vengeance upon sinners and His goodness toward His own people, 1:2-11
B. The coming restoration of Judah, 1:12–2:2

II. Prophecy of the fall of Nineveh, 2:3–3:19

A. The siege and destruction of the city, 2:3-13
B. Reason for Nineveh's fall, 3:1-19

PLACE OF THE AUTHOR'S ORIGIN

Nahum is stated to have been a native of Elkosh, but the identification of this town is in much dispute. There are four competing theories: (1) Jerome identified it as Elkesi or El Kauze in Galilee. (2) Others identified it as Capernaum, since *Capernaum* (*Kᵉpar-Nāḥûm*) signifies the village of Nahum. According to this theory, Elkosh would have been later renamed after its most celebrated citizen. (3) Some identified it with Alqush near Mosul in Assyria, although the foundation of this conjecture is very slight. (4) Still others have pointed to Elcesei, which according to Pseudepiphanius was a village of Judah below Bet Gabre in the territory of Simeon, midway between Jerusalem and Gaza. Eiselen, Raven, and Young concur in favoring this fourth conjecture, since the internal evidence of the text suggests that the author was a native of the kingdom of Judah, rather than of the Galilean region.

DATE OF COMPOSITION

Since Nahum refers to the fall of Thebes to the armies of Ashurbanipal as a past event, and this event took place in 661 B.C., the prophecy must have been written subsequently to that time. On the other hand, the fall of Nineveh is predicted as a future occurrence; therefore the work must have been produced prior to 612 B.C. Walter Maier in his posthumous *Book of Nahum: A Commentary* (1959) marshals considerable evidence to indicate the 654 date when Nineveh was still in its glory. Other scholars prefer a time closer to the fulfillment, perhaps 625 or 620 B.C. Rationalist critics who explain this fulfilled prediction as a prophecy after the event naturally date it after 612. Some of them, like Robert Pfeiffer, regard only 2:3–3:19 as original and explain chapter 1 as partly original and partly supplemented by a redactor (sometime around 300 B.C.). Pfeiffer alleges that 1:2-10 has nothing to do with Nineveh but is a corrupted piece of acrostic poetry of a type that did not become popular until the fourth century B.C. It should be pointed out, however, that as the text stands, there is virtually nothing acrostic about it. Instead of following along in the order of the letters of the alphabet (as an acrostic poem is supposed to do), the opening letters of verses 2-10 come in the following order in the Hebrew alphabet: 1, 10, 3, 5, 12, 9, 6, 13, and 11. Only by the most radical emendations and reshuffling of verses can the acrostic theory be made out. Furthermore a late origin for acrostic poems has never been proved by any kind of objective evidence. The *Lamentations of Jeremiah* are largely acrostic, and the same is true of Davidic Psalms like 25 and 34, and the post-Davidic Ps. 119 (176 vv.) is entirely acrostic.

MESSAGE OF NAHUM

Nahum 2:6 contains a remarkably exact prediction, for subsequent history records that a vital part of the city walls of Nineveh was carried away by a great flood, and this ruin of the defensive system permitted the besieging Medes and Chaldeans to storm the city without difficulty. Some have objected to the joyous attitude with which Nahum greets the prospect of the fall of Assyria's capital, and regard it as an exhibition of nationalistic fanaticism and vengeful malice. This, however, is a misunderstanding of the

GREAT SPHINX

A COLOSSAL HUMAN–HEADED WINGED BULL THAT GUARDED THE ENTRANCE TO THE PALACE OF SARGON II AT KHORSABAD.

SEVENTH-CENTURY NINEVEH

IN 612 B.C. A COORDINATED ATTACK BY THE BABYLONIANS, MEDES, AND VARIOUS SCYTHIAN GROUPS LAID SIEGE TO NINEVEH. THE BABYLONIAN CHRONICLE OF NEBUCHADNEZZAR DESCRIBES ITS DESTRUCTION: "THE ASSYRIAN KING (PERISHED IN THE FLAMES). THEY (THE VICTORS) CARRIED OFF MUCH SPOIL FROM THE CITY... AND TURNED THE CITY INTO A MOUND OF DEBRIS" (ANET[1], P. 303).

ground which the prophet occupies. Because he is a man of God, he speaks as one who is wholly preoccupied with the Lord's cause on earth. His earnest desire is to see Jehovah vindicate His holiness in the eyes of the heathen, as over against the inhumane and ruthless tyranny of that God-defying empire which had for such a long time trampled upon all its subject nations with heartless brutality. Only by a crushing and exemplary destruction of Assyria could the world be taught that might does not, in the long run, make right, and that even the mightiest infidel is absolutely helpless before the judicial wrath of Yahweh. The fact that the God of Israel could predict with such startling accuracy the fact and the manner of Nineveh's fall was best calculated to prove to the ancient world the sovereignty of the one true God. It was a most remarkable reversal of fortune for the proud pagan capital to fall to its enemies within less than two decades after the reign of the mighty Ashurbanipal. In just fourteen years after his decease in 626 B.C., the apparently invincible empire which he had so successfully maintained toppled in ruins, never to rise again.

ZEPHANIAH

The name of this prophet, S^ephan-Yah, means "Jehovah has hidden (him)." The theme of his message is that Jehovah is still firmly in control of all His world despite any contrary appearances, and that He will prove this in the near future by inflicting terrible chastisement upon disobedient Judah, and complete destruction upon the idolatrous Gentile nations. Only by a timely repentance can this wrath be deferred.

OUTLINE OF ZEPHANIAH

I. Day of the Lord prefigured, 1:1–3:7

A. In judgment upon Judah and Jerusalem, 1:1–2:3

B. In judgment upon the surrounding nations, 2:4-15

C. Woe upon Jerusalem because of her sin, 3:1-7

II. Establishment of the future kingdom, 3:8-20

A. Judgment of the nations, 3:8-13

B. Rejoicing remnant and the Messianic King, 3:14-20

TIME AND AUTHORSHIP OF THE PROPHECY OF ZEPHANIAH

Zephaniah is stated to be the son of Cushi and the great-grandson of a Hezekiah, who might possibly have been King Hezekiah himself. But certain chronological considerations render this virtually impossible.[1] Apparently he lived in Jerusalem, for he refers to it as "this place" (1:4), describing its topography with intimate knowledge. He probably delivered his message in the early part of Josiah's reign, doubtless prior to the revival of 621 B.C. The moral and religious conditions then prevailing were still low, owing to the evil influence of the reigns of Manasseh and Amon (cf. 3:1-3, 7).

Some rationalist critics have challenged the authenticity of 2:4-15 and 3:18-20 and have conjectured that these passages were of post-exilic origin. Their principal criterion for such a dating is a theory of how the Hebrew religious thought developed from stage to stage in evolutionary progression. Eissfeldt and others have preferred a post-exilic date for the judgment against Moab and Ammon (2:8-11) because of their resemblance to Obadiah (who according to them was early exilic). But as Moeller points out, this passage harmonizes very well with the denunciation of Jerusalem and Judah to which it is juxtaposed.

SILVER TETRADRACHMA WITH IMAGE OF PTOLEMY I

FROM THE REIGN OF PTOLEMY V (205–180 B.C.). THE ROSETTA STONE WAS INSCRIBED IN HONOR OF PTOLEMY V.

MESSAGE OF ZEPHANIAH

The prophet seems to make reference (1:10-18) to the sudden and devastating invasion of the Scythians, who swooped down from the Caucasus region about 630 B.C. and swarmed over Media and Assyria. Next they ravaged Syria, and according to Herodotus, so threatened Egypt that Psammetichus I had to buy them off. (It should be mentioned, however, that this account of Herodotus is not

---

1. Manasseh was the oldest surviving son of Hezekiah, and yet he was only twelve at the time of his accession (2 Kings 21:1) in 697 (or, as some prefer, 696). Therefore "Amariah, son of Hezekiah" (Zeph. 1:1) was presumably younger than Manasseh, and hence could not have been born earlier than 708 B.C. If he was twenty-five when he fathered Gedaliah, and Gedaliah was twenty-five when Cushi was born, and Cushi was twenty-five when he begot Zephaniah—using twenty-five as a likely age for fatherhood—this would make Zephaniah's year of birth 634, which would be much too late for a possible ministry in Josiah's reign (Zeph. 1:1). Even if the four generation spans were only twenty years apiece (a most unlikely eventuality), this would make his birth year 649, or only nine years before the beginning of Josiah's reign. Since he was a grown man when he prophesied, he could hardly have served in Josiah's reign.

supported by other ancient evidence, and is moreover embellished with such implausible details as to make it unsafe to accept without some reservation.[2] This scourge of warlike nomads served to warn Israel of the approaching day of Jehovah, when Judah was to be devastated. The prophet states that Philistia also will experience His judgment (2:4-7) and become virtually depopulated; likewise Moab and Ammon (which are to be annihilated like Sodom), Ethiopia, and Assyria. The Assyrian capital of Nineveh is to become a howling wilderness occupied only by wild beasts (2:13).

Along with all this dire warning, there is also an appeal for repentance, addressed primarily to the remnant of Judah, rather than to the nation as a whole: "Seek ye Jehovah, all ye meek of the earth, that have kept his ordinances; seek righteousness, seek [i.e., aim at, practice] meekness [or humility]" (2:3, ASV). This appeal was the one to which Josiah's sympathizers responded, even though they were unable to retain power in Judah after their hero's untimely death in the battle of Megiddo (609 B.C.).

There seems to be a very definite millennial overtone to the promise of the ultimate blessedness of Israel in 3:13: "The remnant of Israel shall not do iniquity, nor speak lies...for they shall feed and lie down, and none shall make them afraid." (Note here the reminiscence of Mic. 4:4 from a previous century). The future age will be one of universal faith, and all nations, even those beyond the rivers of Ethiopia, shall serve Yahweh with one consent and shall speak the same language of faith (3:9-10).

HABAKKUK

The name *Ḥabaqquq* is an unusual one of uncertain meaning; possibly it signified ardent embrace, from *ḥabaq*, "embrace" (Eiselen in ISBE). Some have suggested that it was the name of a garden plant which the Assyrians called *ḥambaqūqu*, but which cannot as yet be identified.

The theme of this prophecy concerns the problems of faith in the face of apparent difficulties hindering the fulfillment of God's promises. These difficulties are grappled with and solved in the light of God's continuing revelation, and the prophet closes in a psalm of joyous trust.

OUTLINE OF HABAKKUK

I. Problems of faith, 1:1–2:20

  A. How can a holy God permit unholiness to go unchecked? 1:1-12

    1. Oppression unchecked in Judah, 1:2-5

    2. The Chaldeans as God's scourge, 1:6-12

  B. How can God permit a wicked nation to triumph over His covenant people? 1:13–2:20

    1. Ruthless cruelty and crass idolatry of the Chaldeans, 1:13-17

2. See Henri Cazelles, RB 1967, 24-44: "Sophonie, Jérémie et les Scythes en Palestine." He equates with Scythians the Esquzay mentioned in texts of Sargon II, and the Umman-Manda of Ashurbanipal's inscriptions.

2. The believer to wait humbly, trustingly for God's answer, 2:1-4
3. Judgment of God will smite the Chaldeans because of their five sins, 2:5-9
4. God's continued sovereignty over His earth, 2:20

II. Doubts all settled: the prayer of faith and unshakable trust, 3:1-19

A. Prayer for revival, 3:1-2
B. Past judgments of the Lord a sure token for the future, 3:3-16
C. The believer's joy in God alone, assured of vindication of God's holiness, 3:17-19

AUTHORSHIP AND TIME OF COMPOSITION

Habakkuk seems to have performed his ministry in the reign of Jehoiakim, since the Chaldeans are mentioned as already well known and of formidable reputation (1:6-10). This would best agree with a time subsequent to the fall of Nineveh in 612, and perhaps even after Nebuchadnezzar had achieved his triumph at the battle of Carchemish in 605. It is fair to conclude that the prediction of the Chaldean subjugation of Palestine was intended for fairly speedy fulfillment. (Whether it referred to Nebuchadnezzar's first invasion in 605 or the second invasion in 597, it is hard to say.) Habakkuk 1:2-4 points to an outbreak of rapacious exploitation of the poor on the part of the Judean nobility; this might imply a time after the death of Josiah (609). It is therefore reasonable to conclude that Habakkuk delivered his message somewhere around 608 or 607 B.C.

Some critics are disinclined to refer 1:2-4 to native Jewish oppressors, but prefer to identify them with the Egyptians (thus dating it at 608, during the brief ascendancy of Necho) or even with the Assyrians (which would make it prior to 612, or perhaps as early as the reign of Ashurbanipal, who died in 626). But there is no good evidence in the text of 1:2-4 that heathen invaders are referred to; the manipulation of the law courts to favor the wealthy points to a domestic evil between Jewish litigants (1:4).

Some critics feel that the material in chapters 1 and 2 has been rearranged by a later editor, even though a pre-exilic Habakkuk may have been the author of each portion. But liberal critics uniformly challenge his authorship of chapter 3 on the ground that it is a psalm rather than a prophetic utterance, and that it mentions musical terms in its first and last verses. On these grounds Pfeiffer dates this chapter in the fourth or third century B.C. But such an argument assumes the validity of the supposition that the musical terms in the Davidic psalms are late, and that despite Amos 6:5 and similar references, King David had nothing to do with music or song, since he was a man of war. But for those who take seriously the biblical tradition that David was very much concerned with the writing and singing of psalms, such musical terms constitute no evidence of late authorship. Nor is there any compelling reason why a prophet would have been incapable of composing a psalm of thanksgiving and praise to the Lord. Large portions of the prophetic writings are highly poetic in character, as the critics themselves are swift to point out.

Some scholars have made much of the fact that the *Habakkuk Commentary* from the First Qumran Cave omits the third chapter. Millar Burrows, however, remarks: "Its absence from the scroll is consistent with this theory, but does not prove it. It does not even prove that the third chapter was unknown to the Judean covenanters. Being a psalm, it does not lend itself to a prophetic *pesher* as readily as the earlier chapters. It is even possible that the Commentary was never finished. The Septuagint has all three chapters, but whether this particular part of the Septuagint is older than the *Habakkuk Commentary* is another question."[3] The Habakkuk pesher from Qumran Cave One does in fact include a sizable space for a column of text which was never written out.

MESSAGE OF HABAKKUK

The rapacious Jewish nobles, allied with corrupt religious leaders, were shamelessly robbing and oppressing the common people in Judah. Therefore they were to be punished through the instrumentality of the Chaldeans. It is interesting to note that it was the upper classes that were first taken into captivity in the two preliminary deportations of 605 and 597. The majority of the lower classes was left in the land until the third deportation of 586.

But the prophet next sees that the conquering Chaldeans will themselves pose a serious problem to reconcile with the doctrine of the holiness of God, for they are a bloody and ruthless people who have no respect for the moral law. But instead of falling into an impatient cynicism, Habakkuk sets a salutary example of waiting upon the Lord for His answer (2:1). In time, the answer comes: the proud, self-confident sinner shall be condemned, his time is ripe, and only the faithful believer shall stand acquitted before God's judgment. Only he will partake of eternal life, or even survive in this life in the onward progress of history (2:4). God has taken notice of the sins of the Chaldeans and will gloriously vindicate Himself in the end as He brings judgment upon them (2:13-14). With all these doubts settled, Habakkuk breaks forth into a psalm of holy rejoicing and harks back to the days of the Exodus, the Conquest, and the times of the Judges, to recall past instances when God similarly vindicated His righteousness and demonstrated His sovereignty to the world.

In many ways the prophecy of Habakkuk is unique. It is especially noteworthy in the style of its approach. Instead of addressing the people directly as a spokesman of the Lord, Habakkuk imparted God's message by telling them how it first came to him and answered the questions that were rising in his soul. With the possible exception of Daniel, no other biblical author employs this particular technique.

3. Burrows, DSS, pp. 321-22.

26 JEREMIAH AND LAMENTATIONS

JEREMIAH

THE NAME JEREMIAH, *Yirme-Yāhū*, apparently means "Jehovah establishes" (Orelli in ISBE), if the verb *rāmâ* ("to throw") is to be understood in the sense of laying a foundation.[1] The theme of this prophet consists largely in a stern warning to Judah to turn from idolatry and sin to avoid the catastrophe of exile. Every class of Hebrew society was condemned as inexcusably guilty. As long as Judah refused to repent, the Babylonian Captivity was inevitable. The Hebrew nation should submit to the Chaldean yoke, rather than to rebel against it, since it was a just chastisement for their unfaithfulness to God's covenant. Nevertheless, the day would come when Israel would be delivered by the Messiah, the righteous Branch; therefore true Israel should always trust in God alone, never in the arm of flesh.

OUTLINE OF JEREMIAH

I. Prophecies under Josiah and Jehoiakim, 1:1–20:18

A. Prophet's call and commission, 1:1-19
B. Sin and ingratitude of the nation, 2:1–3:5
C. Prediction concerning devastation from the north (the Chaldeans), 3:6–6:30
D. Threat of Babylonian exile, 7:1–10:25
E. Broken covenant and the sign of the girdle, 11:1–13:27
F. Drought; the sign of the unmarried prophet; the warning about the Sabbath, 14:1–17:27
G. Sign of the potter's house, 18:1–20:18

II. Later prophecies under Jehoiakim and Zedekiah, 21:1–39:18

A. Nebuchadnezzar, God's instrument to punish Zedekiah and Jerusalem, 21:1–29:32
B. The future Messianic kingdom 30:1–33:26
(The doctrine of individualism, 31:1-40)

---

1. Another possibility involving vowel-point change, *Yārîm-Yāhû*, meaning "He exalts Yahweh" or else "Yahweh exalts."

C. Zedekiah's sin and the loyalty of the Rechabites, 34:1–35:19
D. Jehoiakim's opposition and his destruction of the prophetic scroll, 36:1-32
E. Jeremiah in jail during the siege, 37:1–39:18

III. Prophecies after the fall of Jerusalem, 40:1– 45:5

A. Ministry among the remnant in Judah, 40:1– 42:22
B. Ministry among the fugitives in Egypt, 43:1– 44:30
C. Encouragement to Baruch, 45:1-5

IV. Prophecies against the heathen nations, 46:1–51:64

A. Egypt, 46:1-28
B. Philistia, 47:1-7
C. Moab, 48:1-47
D. Ammon, Edom, Damascus, Arabia, Elam, 49:1-39
E. Babylon, 50:1–51:64

V. Historical appendix, 52:1-34 (events of the fall and captivity of Judah)

BIOGRAPHY OF THE AUTHOR

Jeremiah began his ministry at about twenty years of age in the thirteenth year of Josiah, that is, 626 B.C. For the greater part of his life he lived in his hometown of Anathoth (for he was of a priestly family) and appeared at Jerusalem at the annual feast days of the Jewish religious year. He seems to have been well off financially, since he was able to purchase the forfeited estate of a bankrupt kinsman without apparent difficulty. Under God-fearing Josiah, he remained unmolested by the government and enjoyed such cordial relations with that king that he composed an eloquent lamentation at the time of the king's death at the battle of Megiddo. Yet, even among his fellow priests and relatives, Jeremiah had built up considerable ill will because of his forthright rebuke of their infidelity to the Covenant and his condemnation of their worldly practices.

After Josiah's death, with the rise of the idolatrous faction and the pro-Egyptian party, a serious reaction resulted against Jeremiah and all he stood for. It was only through the interposition of a few God-fearing elders and princes that Jeremiah escaped arrest for his unpalatable arraignment of the nation in the "Temple Sermon" of chapters 7-10. From that time on he seems to have been forbidden to enter the temple precinct, for he had to send aloud his secretary Baruch as his spokesman whenever he had a message of God to proclaim before the people. He therefore dictated his prophecies to Baruch that they might be read aloud to the people of Jerusalem. But soon this copy was turned over to King Jehoiakim, who destroyed it in his fireplace, section by section, as it was read to him by his own secretary. Later, King Zedekiah, a successor of Jehoiakim, permitted the prophet to be incarcerated by the nationalistically minded nobles, who saw Jeremiah as a traitor because he had urged the nation to

KINGS OF BABYLON/CHALDEA

King	Date (B.C.)
Nabopolassar	612-605
Nebuchadnezzar	605-562
Evil-Merodach	561-560
Neriglissar	560-556
Labashi-Marduk	556
Nabonidus	555-539
Belshazzar (co-regency)	553-539

submit to Babylon. Nevertheless, Zedekiah was secretly fearful of God's messenger because of the fulfillment of his past predictions relative to the Chaldean invasion of 598. He therefore had the prophet rescued from death when he was at the point of perishing in his brutal confinement and he kept him hidden from danger until the fall of Jerusalem.

When the forces of Nebuchadnezzar finally stormed the city, it was only natural that Jeremiah was offered by the conquerors a place of honor and a pension in Babylon (since he had constantly urged the Jews to submit to Nebuchadnezzar as God's instrument for chastening them). Yet Jeremiah chose to stay with the remnant of his own people in Palestine and minister to the bands of guerrillas or partisans who had remained behind after the great deportation to Babylonia. But after the treacherous murder of Gedaliah by the treacherous Ishmael he was abducted and carried off to Egypt by the fugitive remnant of the Jews, who preferred to take refuge in the land of the Nile rather than to remain in Palestine and face the wrath of Nebuchadnezzar. In Egypt, Jeremiah prophesied for several years longer, and it was probably there that he died.

By nature, Jeremiah was gentle, tender, and sympathetic; yet he was charged by God to proclaim a stern message of irreversible gloom. Loving his people with a deep affection, he constantly found himself the object of hatred, reproached with charges of treason. Although he was sensitive to the extreme, he was forced to undergo a constant barrage of slander and persecution that would normally have crushed the most callous spirit. Introspective and retiring by nature, he was ever thrust into the limelight. Occasionally, he attempted to throw off his prophetic responsibility as a burden too heavy for him to bear, but again and again he returned to the call of duty, and by the power of the Lord stood indeed as a "tower of bronze" (1:18).

HISTORY OF THE TEXT

There is good evidence to believe that even apart from the original edition of Jeremiah's prophecy, which was destroyed by Jehoiakim, there was a later edition which preceded the final form of the text as we have it in the Masoretic tradition. At least this is a reasonable deduction to draw from the Greek LXX, since it appears to be about one-eighth shorter than the Hebrew text of the MT. It differs also in the arrangement of the chapters, for chapters 46-51 of the MT are placed after chapter 25 in the LXX, and they are arranged in a somewhat different sequence. Jeremiah 33:14-26 of the MT is altogether missing in the LXX. It would seem that this earlier edition was published in the prophet's own lifetime and first disseminated in Egypt. Later, after Jeremiah's death, it appears that his secretary, Baruch, made a more comprehensive collection of his master's sermons and rearranged the material in more logical order. The MT undoubtedly preserves this posthumous edition of Baruch. In this connection, note that 36:32 indicates that a second preliminary edition was published in the reign of Jehoiakim, and it is therefore reasonable to assume that Jeremiah kept adding to these earlier sermons the messages the Lord gave him in the reign of Zedekiah and in the period subsequent to the fall of Jerusalem.

The following table is a correlation between the MT and the LXX in order to facilitate comparison:

MT	LXX
1:1–25:13	1:1–25:13
25:14–46:5	32:1–51:35
46:1–51:64	25:14–31:44

INTEGRITY OF THE TEXT

Most rationalist critics deny certain portions of Jeremiah both to Jeremiah himself and to Baruch his secretary. Passages challenged include (1) 10:1-16, because it warns the Jews in exile against idolatry in terms reminiscent of Deutero-Isaiah; (2) 17:19-27, because of the emphasis upon strict Sabbath keeping, which is reminiscent of Ezekiel or the priestly code and therefore a little too late for Jeremiah; (3) chapters 30 and 31, because of the Messianic expectation which some critics feel was only characteristic of the post-exilic period and also because of the emphasis upon individual responsibility in the mood of Ezekiel 18 (the assumption being that this passage in Jeremiah must have been later than Ezekiel); (4) chapter 51, because in verse 41 Babylon is spoken of by its *Athbash* equivalent, "*Sheshakh*," and the *Athbash* is considered a late artificial device. (*Athbash* is so called because it is a code in which the last letter of the Hebrew alphabet indicates the first, the second to the last indicates the second letter; hence the *B-b-l* of Babel comes out as *Sh-sh-k*, or the code name Sheshach in KJV.)

But it should be noted that all these criteria for later dating depend for their validity upon unproved assumptions such as the post-exilic dating of document P of the Torah and of Isaiah II, and a supposedly late evolutionary hypothesis as to the development of the messianic hope. It is difficult of course, to justify any extensive chronological gap between Jeremiah and Ezekiel, since according to the biblical evidence the two prophets were contemporaneous in their ministries, at least during the latter part of Jeremiah's career. There is a very close resemblance between Jer. 31:29-30 and Ezek.

18:2-3; yet it would appear that what Jeremiah says in passing is taken up by Ezekiel as a sort of text for an extended sermon.

MISCELLANEOUS HISTORICAL MATTERS

In regard to Jeremiah's prediction in 29:10 concerning the seventy years' captivity, there is some question as to how the seven decades are to be computed. The main deportation of the population of Judah did not take place until 586 B.C. In 539, Babylon fell to the Persian conquerors, and within a year or two the Jewish remnant who chose to return resettled in Judah under the leadership of Zerubbabel and Jeshua, possibly in 536. Yet only fifty years elapsed between 586 and 536, and so we must look for other termini. Since the first Palestinian invasion of Nebuchadnezzar took place in 605 B.C., and resulted in the deportation of a considerable number of hostages (including Daniel, Shadrach, Meshach, and Abednego), this date might serve as the *terminus a quo*; thus 536 would be approximately seventy years later. Another possibility is to begin the seventy years at the destruction of the Temple by General Nebuzaradan in 586 and prolong the captivity until the second temple had been completely rebuilt, which took place in 516. Of these two choices, the latter seems to be very definitely favored by Zech. 1:12: "Then the angel of the Lord answered and said, O Jehovah of hosts, how long wilt thou not have mercy on Jerusalem and on the cities of Judah, against which thou hast had indignation, these threescore and ten years?" (ASV). Since this utterance must have been given in 519 B.C., we can only conclude that, from the standpoint of the angel at least, the seventy years were not yet up; and that the gracious promise in Jer. 29:10 was not to be fulfilled until the Temple itself was restored.

Until a few decades ago, considerable skepticism was voiced by many critics as to the fulfillment of the prediction made by Jeremiah in 43:9-13 and 44:30 that northern Egypt would be devastated by an invasion of the Chaldeans under Nebuchadnezzar (cf. also Ezek. 29:19-20, which contains a similar prediction). The pagan Greek historians make no mention of such an invasion, although there is a definite record to be found in Josephus's *Antiquities* 10.9.5-7: "Johanan took those whom he had rescued and came to a certain place called Mandara. On the fifth year (582/81) after the destruction of Jerusalem, which was the twenty-third (582) of the reign of Nebuchadnezzar, he made an expedition against Coele-Syria; and when he had possessed himself of it, he made war against the Ammonites and Moabites; and when he had brought all those nations under subjection, he fell upon Egypt in order to overthrow it, and he slew the king that then reigned and set up another; and he took those Jews that were there captives, and led them away to Babylon; and such was the end of the nation of the Hebrews."

Many authorities tended to discount this testimony of Josephus as merely manufactured in order to support the Hebrew Scriptures. But R. Campbell Thompson of Oxford remarks: "The small fragment of a Babylonian chronicle first published by Pinches shows that Nebuchadnezzar launched an expedition against Egypt in his thir-

LACHISH THE LACHISH LETTERS WERE DISCOVERED AT THIS SITE IN 1933. THESE OSTRACA, CA. 588 B.C., VERIFY THE CONDITIONS THAT PREVAILED DURING NEBUCHADNEZZAR'S SIEGE OF LACHISH AND JERUSALEM.

ty-seventh year, i.e., about 567 B.C....the very distance to which he penetrated is a matter of dispute....We might almost assume from the tradition that certain Babylonian settlers built a 'Babylon' in Egypt near the Pyramids, which appears to have existed as an important fort in the time of Augustus, that his army at all events left some mark there."[2] In ANET[3] (p. 308) appears a translation of a fragmentary Babylonian text in the British Museum containing the following sentence: "In the thirty-seventh year (568/67), Nebuchadnezzar, king of Babylon, marched against Mi-sir [Egypt] to deliver a battle." Additional archaeological confirmation is found in an inscription on the statue of Nes-hor in the Louvre. Nes-hor was a governor of southern Egypt under Hophra (*Uah-ib-Ra*, in Egyptian). In this biographical record he states that an army of Asiatics and northern peoples who had invaded Egypt attempted to advance up the Nile valley to Ethiopia, but this was fortunately averted by the favor of the gods." In view of this evidence, therefore, it is hardly justifiable to deny any longer the historicity of Nebuchadnezzar's invasion of Egypt, or to question that it was a very serious and devastating incursion.

At this point mention should be made of an important archaeological find unearthed at the site of the ancient city of Lachish (Tell ed-Duweir) which brought to light a file of correspondence consisting of about twenty-one ostraca dating from the year 588 B.C. They practically all consist of letters or memoranda written by the captain of a military

SILVER TETRADRACHMA WITH PORTRAIT OF PTOLEMY I (323–285 B.C.)

2. Thompson, "The New Babylonian Empire," in the *Cambridge Ancient History*, vol. 3.

outpost named Hoshaiah to Ya'ush, the district commander of the Jewish forces stationed in Lachish during the third Chaldean invasion. In most of these letters Hoshaiah seems to be defending himself against slanders and misrepresentations concerning his own loyalty or efficiency. In these communications he refers to various people or incidents in such an elusive way that we cannot be sure of their full import. Some scholars have concluded, for example, that a certain prophet mentioned in these letters might either have been Jeremiah himself, or Urijah, who was extradited from Egypt after uttering an adverse prophecy against Jehoiakim (cf. Jer. 26:20-23). A further study of the evidence, however, has led most scholars to conclude that the prophet mentioned in these letters cannot reliably be identified upon the basis of the data at hand. The most significant light cast upon the period of Jeremiah by the Lachish correspondence is to be found in the linguistic field. The type of Hebrew employed in these ostraca bears a very marked similarity to that which appears in the writings of Jeremiah, and serves to confirm the genuineness of his prophecies as stemming from the beginning of the sixth century B.C.

LAMENTATIONS

The Hebrew title of this relatively short work is the word *'ēkâ* ("How!") which appears at the beginning of 1:1. The theme of the book is a lament over the woes that have befallen sinful Judah and the pitiable destruction visited upon the holy city and the temple of the Lord. By implication the prophet appeals to chastened Israel that they recognize the righteousness of God's dealings with them, and that in a spirit of repentance they cast themselves once more upon His mercy.

OUTLINE OF LAMENTATIONS

I. Jerusalem devastated and forsaken, 1:1-22

II. Reasons for God's wrath upon the city; repentance its only hope, 2:1-22

III. The city's lament for its devastation; its repentance at remembrance of God's former mercies, 3:1-66

IV. Zion's ancient glory contrasted with her present misery, 4:1-22

V. Repentant nation casts itself upon God's mercy, 5:1-22

It is interesting to note that the first four chapters are written in the acrostic form. Chapters 1, 2, and 4 are therefore twenty-two verses long, each verse beginning with the successive letter of the Hebrew alphabet. Chapter 3, however, contains sixty-six verses, since three successive verses are allotted to each letter of the alphabet.

AUTHORSHIP AND COMPOSITION OF LAMENTATIONS

The book does not expressly state who its author was, yet there was an early and consistent tradition that Jeremiah composed it. This tradition is reflected in the title of the book in the LXX as well as by the Aramaic Targum of Jonathan. The early church Fathers, such as Origen and Jerome, understood Jeremiah to be the author without any question. Many modern critics, however, have rejected this tradition on the ground of internal evidence; that is, the style is said to be significantly different from that of Jeremiah's prophecies, and two or three historical allusions have been interpreted as referring to much later conditions or events than Jeremiah's time. On the other hand, it is hard to conceive how there could have been a later occasion than the fall of Jerusalem in 586 to serve as the incentive for the composition of such a tragic threnody as this. If Jeremiah was not the composer, whoever wrote it must have been a contemporary of his and witnessed the same pitiless destruction meted out to Zion by its Chaldean conquerors.

In matters of style and phraseology, there are numerous and striking similarities between Lamentations and Jeremiah. Many of these have been acknowledged even by S. R. Driver, who does not accept Jeremiah's authorship; for instance, "the oppressed virgin daughter of Zion" (Lam. 1:15; Jer. 8:21); the prophet's eyes are said to "flow down with tears" (Lam. 1:16a; 2:11; Jer. 9:1, 18b). Compare "Among all her lovers she hath none to comfort her" (Lam. 1:2) with "All thy lovers have forgotten thee; they seek thee not" (Jer. 30:14). Both speak of the winecup of God's judgment: Lam. 4:21 says of Edom, "The cup shall pass through unto thee: thou shalt be drunken, and shalt make thyself naked"; Jer. 49:12, "Behold, they whose judgment was not to drink of the cup have assuredly drunken; and art thou he that shall altogether go unpunished?"

The arguments advanced to indicate a difference in viewpoint between the authors of the two works do not rest upon sound exegesis. Thus it is alleged that unlike Lam. 4:17, Jeremiah did not expect any help for Judah to come from Egypt. But actually this is a misunderstanding, for Lam. 4:17 makes no specific mention of Egypt at all. Moreover, it does not purport to be the utterance of the author personally as much as the attitude of the nation as a whole, which the prophet puts into these words: "As for us, our eyes as yet failed for our vain help: in our watching we have watched for a nation that could not save us." The author does not imply here that he was expressing his own political views. Again, it is alleged that whereas Jeremiah regarded the Babylonians as God's instruments for punishment of His disobedient nation, Lam. 3:59-66 implies that the Chaldeans were wicked enemies who richly deserved God's avenging rod. But it is a mistake to suppose that these two ideas are mutually exclusive. Jeremiah makes it quite obvious that the Babylonians were used by God for the purposes of chastening, and yet were to experience His ultimate vengeance because of the evil motives of their own heart.[3] (Cf. Isa. 10 for a similar treatment of the Assyrians.) We conclude that there are no valid grounds for making out a difference of authorship

---

3. Compare Jer. 50, a prophesy of Babylon's doom.

based upon a difference in viewpoint.

One final observation ought to be made concerning Lam. 3. The first 18 verses of this chapter express mournful lamentation and portray God as cruelly severe, but then verses 19-39 abruptly change to a mood of hope and praise to God for His faithfulness and compassion. This is certainly the type of "discrepancy" which critics have utilized in other books of the Old Testament to demonstrate a difference in authorship. In this particular chapter, however, no theory of multiple sources is possible, for the whole composition is firmly and inescapably locked together by the acrostic pattern in which it is written. Hence this chapter may be taken as irrefutable proof that it was possible for an ancient Hebrew author quite suddenly to shift from one mood to another and express sentiments that markedly contrast with each other (even though they are not actually contradictory).

27 EZEKIEL

THE HEBREW NAME Yeḥezᵉqeʾl means "God strengthens." The theme of Ezekiel's prophecy is that the fall of Jerusalem and the Babylonian captivity are necessary measures for the God of grace to employ if He is to correct His disobedient people and draw them back from complete and permanent apostasy. But the day is coming when Jehovah will restore a repentant remnant of His chastened people and establish them in a glorious latter-day theocracy with a new temple.

OUTLINE OF EZEKIEL

I. The prophet's call and commission, 1:1–3:27

A. The vision of the glory of the Lord 1:1-28
B. God's commission to preach warning and doom 2:1-10
C. The scroll of condemnation upon the apostate nation for their lack of repentance 3:1-27

II. Prophecies against Judah prior to the fall of Jerusalem, 4:1–24:27

A. Messages of the fifth year (593-592 B.C.), 4:1–7:27 (destruction predicted by sign, symbol, and sentence)
B. Messages of the sixth year (592-591 B.C.), 8:1–19:14
   1. Vision of Jerusalem's idolatry and punishment, 8:1–11:25
   2. Punishment necessary because of its universal corruption, 12:1–19:14
C. Messages of the seventh year (591-590 B.C.), 20:1–23:49
   1. Israel's ingratitude since the Exodus; Nebuchadnezzar will turn to besiege Jerusalem; no more Davidic kings until Christ Himself, 20:1–21:32
   2. A catalogue of the sins of adulterous Samaria and Judah, 22:1–23:49
D. Message of the ninth year (589-588 B.C.), 24:1–27
   No mourning for Ezekiel's wife or for Jehovah's fallen Israel

III. Prophecies against the heathen nations, 25:1–32:32

A. Ammon, Moab, Edom, and Philistia (nearest neighbors), 25:1-17
B. Tyre and Sidon, symbols of proud commercial materialism, 26:1–28:26

C. Egypt, the symbol of self-confident idolatry, 29:1–32:32

Like Jeremiah, Ezekiel was of a priestly family. His father's name was Buzi,[1] and he was sufficiently high in rank to warrant inclusion among the hostages whom Nebuchadnezzar took with him to Babylon in 597 B.C. He was settled in a community near Nippur (about fifty miles south of Babylon on the Euphrates River) called Tell-Abib on the Grand Canal (which would be a more accurate translation of "the river Chebar"). This canal, the *Nāru Kabari* of the cuneiform inscriptions, ran from the Euphrates above Babylon sixty miles in a southeasterly direction to Nippur, rejoining the Euphrates below Ur and irrigating the alluvial plain between the Euphrates and the Tigris. Ezekiel was called to his prophetic ministry in 592 B.C. (the fifth year of the captivity of King Jehoiachin) when he himself was about thirty years of age (1:1). His happy marriage was terminated by the death of his wife in 587 (chap. 24). He became a noted preacher among the exiled Jews in Babylonia and was often resorted to both by the elders and the common people, although without much practical response to his message. His last dated discourse (29:17-21) was in the twenty-seventh year of Jehoiachin's captivity, or 570 B.C.

CRITICAL OBJECTIONS TO THE GENUINENESS OF EZEKIEL

As recently as the eighth edition of Driver's ILOT, the genuineness of Ezekiel had been accepted as completely authentic by the majority of rationalist critics. But in 1924 Gustav Hoelscher advanced the thesis that only a small fraction of the book was by the historical sixth-century Ezekiel (i.e., only 143 verses out of 1273) and the rest came from some later author living in Jerusalem and contemporaneous with Nehemiah (440-430 B.C.). In 1930 Professor C. C. Torrey published a discussion of his view that no part of Ezekiel came from the sixth century, or even from the two centuries suc-

---

1. Buzi was a family name which may have been handed down from Buz, son of Nahor, Abraham's older brother (Gen. 22:21). Jer. 25:23 refers to the land of Buz. Buz is located in northern Hejaz.

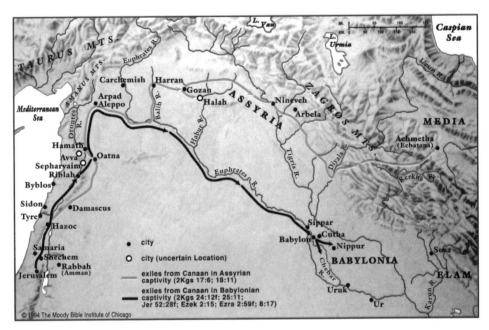

EXILE OF ISRAEL (721 B.C.) AND EXILE OF JUDAH (586 B.C.)

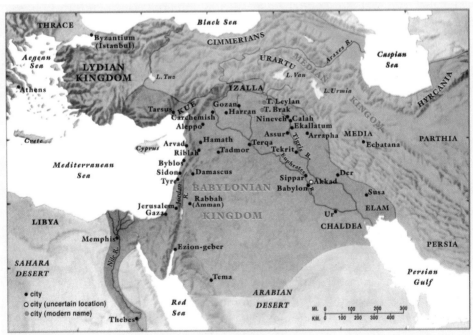

THE KINGDOMS OF BABYLONIA, MEDIA, AND LYDIA

ceeding. He dated the earliest stratum of the book of Ezekiel at 230 B.C. and deduced that it was written in Jerusalem rather than Babylonia. Not long afterward it was re-edited by a redactor who gave it the appearance of having been written in Babylonia by one of the Captivity. It should be mentioned that Torrey did not believe in the historicity of the Chaldean destruction of Judah or the removal of the Jewish population to Babylonia in any sort of national captivity. Few scholars, however, have followed him in this skepticism, and in more recent years the cumulative data of Palestinian archaeology (as interpreted, e.g., by W. F. Albright) point to a complete cessation of Israelite occupation in Palestine during the greater part of the sixth century. G. A. Cooke, who put out the ICC volume on Ezekiel in 1937, still adhered to the view that the historic Ezekiel was the basic author of the book, for he felt it would be just as hard to believe in the supposed late redactor as it would be to accept at face value the statements of the text itself. Nevertheless, the more recent trend in Liberal circles is to deny the genuineness of Ezekiel and to insist that it was really composed in Palestine some time after the restoration from exile. Thus N. Messel in 1945 ventured to date the work at about 400 B.C. Bentzen declared, "The book as it now stands is no authentic work of the prophet Ezekiel."[2]

Two main grounds have been advanced for the denial of this book to the sixth-century prophet Ezekiel.

1. The prophet who pronounced doom upon Israel could not possibly be the same as the one who held forth heartening promises of future blessing. In other words, the historic Ezekiel must have been a preacher of darkness and doom and afforded his nation no ray of light or hope. But it should be pointed out that nearly all the Old Testament prophets who foretell catastrophic judgment also predict subsequent restoration and the ultimate bestowal of covenant grace on the chastened nation of Israel. This observation applies to Amos, Hosea, Micah, Isaiah, and Jeremiah, just to name a few of the outstanding examples. Even Nahum speaks of eventual deliverance and triumph for Israel (2:2) and the destruction of her foes (1:15). The same is true in Zeph. 3:14-20. Only by a rigid dogmatism can these various Old Testament prophets be carved up into different sources and thus preserve the hypothesis that the threatener can only threaten and the promiser can only promise. Even Hugo Gressmann was led by an extensive study of these prophets to this conclusion: "World renewal necessarily follows upon world catastrophe."

2. It is alleged that the author of Ezekiel betrays a Palestinian viewpoint rather than that of an author writing in Babylonia. For example, Ezekiel is portrayed as enacting symbolic prophecies for the benefit of the inhabitants of Jerusalem, which of course they could not have witnessed had he been living in the land of the Chaldeans more than a thousand miles away. In answer to this it should be pointed out that there is no hint or suggestion in the text of Ezekiel itself that the prophet performed his symbolic actions in the presence of Jerusalemites actually living in Jerusalem. On the con-

2. A. Bentzen, IOT, 2:125.

trary, it indicates that his audience was composed of citizens of Jerusalem who shared exile with him in Tell Abib, Babylonia. In 2 Kings 24:14 we read that when King Jehoiachin was taken into captivity in 597 B.C. with his princes and "mighty men of valor," the number of captives deported to Babylon (including the craftsmen and skilled workers) numbered no less than ten thousand. Since the great majority of these must have been residents of Jerusalem, there is no difficulty in supposing that Ezekiel had a very considerable audience of Jerusalemites to whom he might preach, right there in Tel Abib by the Chebar.

Second, it is objected that the author betrays an eyewitness knowledge of such events as took place in Jerusalem itself and which could have been witnessed only by actual bystanders. Thus in chapter 8 the author describes the idolatrous worship of the elders in the Jerusalem temple; in 11:13 he refers to the sudden death of one of their number (Pelatiah, the son of Benaiah). In 12:3-12, he refers to Zedekiah's attempt to escape from Jerusalem by night; in 21:18 he depicts Nebuchadnezzar consulting omens at a crossroads on the way to Jerusalem; and in 24:2 he refers to his encampment outside the city walls. The only reasonable conclusion to draw, according to these critics, is that the author lived in Jerusalem in the last years before the final destruction of 587 B.C. (Most advocates of this theory, however, make the author subsequent to the Exile and understand his work as a mere fictional account pieced together from oral tradition.)

Yet it should be noted that many of these references in Ezekiel are perfectly compatible with the supposition that tidings of the events related might have had opportunity to get to the exiles in Babylon by the time the author wrote what he did. In other cases, an introductory statement is given (e.g., in chap. 8) that what the author relates consists of a vision supernaturally imparted to him by the Lord. Only on the basis of antisupernaturalistic presuppositions can the factor of divine revelation be ruled out as an explanation of how Ezekiel could have had such an exact knowledge of what was going on in the Lord's house back in his native land. Nor can it be successfully maintained that even the assumption of an author living in Jerusalem can satisfactorily explain all the material contained in the text, for some of these visions are obviously of supernatural origin. This is preeminently the case with the vision of the departure of the shekinah glory of the Lord from the temple as set forth in 10:4 and 11:23. Only upon the supposition that Jehovah miraculously conveyed these scenes to His prophet in the form of a spiritual vision can these passages in Ezekiel be intelligently understood.

DISCREPANCIES BETWEEN EZEKIEL AND THE PRIESTLY CODE

Reference has been made in chapter 12 to the role assigned by the Wellhausen school to the sixth-century prophet Ezekiel in laying the foundation for the work of the priestly school. To him or his immediate disciples were attributed the Holiness Code (Lev. 17-26) and the first stages of a new doctrine that the priesthood should be confined to the descendants of Aaron rather than allowed to the tribe of Levi as a whole (cf. Ezek. 44:7-16, which assigns a privileged status to the family of Zadok). But the advocates of this school insisted that document P could not have been in existence before Ezekiel's time; otherwise he would not have ventured to prescribe regulations which markedly differ from those laid down in the Priestly Code. As a matter of fact, there are striking divergences in three general areas: temple dimensions, temple furniture, and the ritual of sacrificial worship. It was for this reason, of course, that some of the ancient Jewish authorities, especially those connected with the school of Shammai, entertained doubts as to the canonicity of Ezekiel—overlooking the possibility that the temple regulations in chapters 40-48 were not intended to be implemented in the period of the old covenant, but rather in the final kingdom of the messianic age.

It should be observed that the theory of post-exilic origin for the Priestly Code does not really furnish an adequate explanation for the divergences just referred to. It is an undeniable fact that the provisions in Ezekiel differ just as much from document D, and even document H, as they do from P. For example, there is absolutely no mention in Ezekiel of the tithes and gifts which are to be presented for the firstborn (such as are prescribed in D and E), nor of the Feast of Pentecost and the regulations pertaining to it, nor of such particular provisions as the avoidance of ascending by steps to an altar. Since all these matters just mentioned are included in Deuteronomy, the same type of logic which makes Ezekiel earlier than P would compel us to make him earlier than D as well.[3] It is noteworthy that Ezekiel presupposes the same general system for sacrificial worship as that set forth in P: burnt offerings, sin offerings, peace offerings, and a clear distinction between the ritually clean and unclean. All these regulations are set forth with the implication that this sacrificial system was well known to its readers and had been practiced from ancient times.

Perhaps the most striking evidence along this line is that the temple dimensions given in the last part of Ezekiel differ not only from those in the Priestly Code but also those of the Solomonic temple as described in 1 Kings 6-7. If Ezekiel's divergence indicates earlier authorship, then a consistent application of this criterion would compel us to understand Ezekiel as earlier than the erection of the Solomonic temple. Here again then we must acknowledge that this whole line of reasoning leads to ridiculous results and cannot be adhered to as a serviceable criterion for comparitive dating.

Another type of divergence which the post-exilic date for P does not explain is found in Ezekiel's vision of the apportionment of the Holy Land among the twelve tribes during the millennial kingdom. As the metes and bounds are given in chapter 48, a geography somewhat different from that which presently exists in Palestine seems to be quite definitely implied. Quite significant extension of the northern tribes into the eastern area beyond the Jordan River seems to be clearly involved (for Dan, Asher, and Naphtali—which includes Damascus and points east). Manasseh and

3. Cf. Koehler, *Biblische Geschichte*, 3:154, containing a survey of evidence that the contents of the entire Torah are presupposed and recognized both by Jeremiah and Ezekiel as dating from ancient times; and that too including not only the book of the covenant (Ex. 21-23, J-E) and Deuteronomy, but also H and various parts of P.

Ephraim likewise extend as far as the Syrian Desert. Below the Sea of Galilee comes Reuben (on the west of the Jordan). Then Judah forms a box above the Jerusalem enclave from the west coast to the Jordan, Benjamin, Simeon, and Issachar all stretch from the

SILVER STATER FROM TYRE UNDER PERSIAN RULE CA. 350 B.C. BEARING THE IMAGE OF BAAL RIDING A MYTHICAL HIPPOCAMP, A TRIPHIBIOUS CREATURE ABLE TO TRAVEL BY LAND, SEA OR AIR.

coast to the Dead Sea. Below them Issachar, Zebulun and Gad have similar horizontal strips from the Wadi el 'Arîš to the Edomite border. This new distribution of tribal territories differs quite markedly from that which was allotted each tribe under Joshua.[4]

Since Ezekiel had been brought up in Judah and must have been thoroughly familiar with the lay of the land in his own generation, he could not have been speaking of an apportionment to be enacted in the near future. He must have had reference to a new state of affairs to be ushered in at the end time. If this is true in regard to geography, there seems to be no reason why it may not also apply to the cultus itself.

PROBLEM OF THE FULFILLMENT OF EZEKIEL 40-48

These chapters contain a long and detailed series of predictions of what the future Palestine is to be like, with its city and temple. To an open-minded reader, it is safe to say the predictions of these nine chapters give the appearance of being as literally intended as those contained in the earlier part of the book (e.g., the judgments upon Tyre and Sidon in 26-28, which found literal fulfillment in subsequent history). The question is whether the plans set forth in chapters 40-48 are ever to be realized. If no temple is ever going to be erected in accordance with these specifications, and if there is to be no such holy city as the prophet describes, and if there is to be no such apportionment of the land among the twelve tribes as he indicates, we are faced with a portion of Scripture containing false prophecy.

The only way to avoid this conclusion, according to many interpreters, is to understand all these provisions as intended in a purely figurative way. These chapters should be understood as referring to the New Testament church, the spiritual Jerusalem. This line of interpretation is widely held even by scholars of undoubted orthodoxy. In the *New Bible Commentary* we read, "The conclusion of Ezekiel's prophecy, therefore, is to be regarded as a true prediction of the kingdom of God given under forms with which the prophet was familiar, viz., those of his own (Jewish) dispensation. Their essential truth will be embodied in the new age under forms suitable to the new (Christian) dispensation. How this is to be done is outlined for us in the book of Revelation (21:1–22:5)."[5]

---

4. For a fuller treatment, cf. Ralph Alexander, *Expositor's Bible Commentary* (Grand Rapids: Zondervan, 1986), 6:979-81.

5. *New Bible Commentary*, ed. Davidson-Stibbs-Kevan, p. 664. Substantially similar views were espoused by C. F. Keil as well as Wilhelm Moeller on "Ezekiel" in ISBE, 2:1071-81.

The application of Ezek. 40-48 to the New Testament church side-steps some of the difficulties attendant upon a more literalistic interpretation. This is especially true of the regulations for blood sacrifice which appear in these chapters and which can hardly be fitted into a post-Calvary economy of salvation, if the sacrifices themselves retain their atoning significance (with which of course they were invested in the law of Moses). In the Epistle to the Hebrews, such passages as 10:4 make it clear that no more animal sacrifices are necessary or efficacious for the atonement of sin. Hebrews announces that the one atoning deed of the Lord Jesus has a permanent efficacy which does away with the Old Testament priesthood of Aaron and the sacrifices of the Levitical code. As H. L. Ellison puts it in *Ezekiel, the Man and His Message,* "In addition they [the opponents of the literalistic interpretation] cannot see why, when water, bread and wine have met the symbolic needs of nearly a thousand generations of

RUINS OF TYRE

Alexander the Great built a 200 ft. wide causeway to the island city of Tyre from the rubble of the mainland city, which was destroyed by Nebuchadnezzar in 580 b.c. After a seven–month siege he successfully took the island, slaughtering thousands and selling more than 30,000 Tyrians into slavery. Top photo: ruins of the old sea wall. (The island city of Tyre sank below water level, providing a series of black reefs offshore, proba- bly at the same time that Caesarea also sank.

Christians, the millennium will need more. The King has returned and the curse on nature has been lifted; why should the animal creation still lay down its life?"[6] It cannot be denied that this is a persuasive line of reasoning, and it is not surprising that a great majority of Conservative scholars are content to dismiss Ezekiel's temple as a mere allegory of the Christian church.

It nevertheless remains true that this matter cannot be so easily disposed of, for the stubborn fact still remains that we have here eight or nine chapters of prophetic Scripture which assure believers that God has a definite plan in the future for Jerusalem, the Temple, and Palestine, all of which give definite and precise measurements and bounds for the temple buildings and precincts and for the division of the tribal territories of the Promised Land. It is also true that the passages referred to in the book of Revelation provide rather dubious support for identification of Ezekiel's temple with the church age. Thus in Rev. 21:22, we learn that in the New Jerusalem there is to be no temple at all, and this appears to be a rather startling type of fulfillment for four chapters (Ezek. 40–43) which describe the future temple in great detail, especially in view of the fact that Ezekiel makes a clear separation between the temple and the city (48:8, 15).

A similarity has been pointed out between the symbolic river in Ezekiel and that in Rev. 22:1, but it should be noted that the river of John's vision flows from beneath the throne of God and of the Lamb, whereas the river in Ezek. 47:1 flows from the threshold of the temple. Undeniably there is a relationship between the Old Testament and the New Testament passages involved, but it seems to be a relationship of the intermediate or typical to the consummate and eternal. In other words, the future millennial kingdom is to be a provisional economy which prepare the way for the new heavens and the new earth announced in Rev. 21 and 22.

It is quite significant that even some who hold that the New Testament church is the fulfillment of Ezekiel's temple feel hesitant to affirm that the church is what Ezekiel had in mind as he composed these chapters. In the *New Bible Commentary* article referred to above, on page 663 we read: "Ezekiel has advanced plans which he expected to be carried out to the letter. To make them a deliberately symbolic description of the worship of the Christian Church is out of the question." This comment of course raises the question, was Ezekiel mistaken in his expectation? If these plans of the temple and Holy City were of his own devising, it is perhaps conceivable that he could have been in error (although such error could hardly have become part of Holy Scripture). But the prophet makes it abundantly plain that he did not devise these plans himself; they were revealed to him by the angel of the Lord who showed him the splendors of the completed temple precinct and measured for him all its metes and bounds. If then there was a mistake in expectation, it must have been shared by the angel of the Lord (unless, of course, Ezekiel has not given us a trustworthy account).

In view of the foregoing considerations, the present writer has come to the view

---

6. Ellison, *Ezekiel, the Man and His Message* (Grand Rapids: Eerdmans, 1956), p. 142.

that a moderately literal interpretation of these chapters is attended by less serious difficulties than a figurative interpretation. Much caution should be exercised in pressing details, but in the broad outline it may be reasonably deduced that in a coming age all the promises conveyed by the angel to Ezekiel will be fulfilled in the glorious earthly kingdom with which the drama of redemption is destined to close. The sacrificial offerings mentioned in these chapters are to be understood as devoid of propitiatory or atoning character, since Christ's sacrifice provided an atonement which was sufficient for all time (Heb. 10:12). Nevertheless, the Lord Jesus ordained the sacrament of holy communion as an ordinance to be practiced even after His crucifixion, and He specified that it was to be observed until His second coming (1 Cor. 11:26: "till he come"). By premillennial definition, the Millennium is to follow His second advent. If, then, there was a sacramental form practiced during the church age, why should there not be a new form of sacrament carried on during the Millennium itself?[7]

We in this age are hardly more competent to judge concerning the new requirements and conditions of the future millennial kingdom than were Old Testament believers competent to judge concerning the new forms and conditions which were to be ushered in in the New Testament age after Christ's first advent.[8]

It should be added that some writers on this subject have introduced questionable precision of detail in their interpretation of what the millennial kingdom will be like, such as the exclusive Jewishness of the citizenry, or the supremacy of the Hebrew race as an ethnic unit over all the nations of the earth. Yet there are many indications in the Old Testament prophets that Jewish and Gentile believers shall be incorporated into one body politic in the coming age. For example, we find it clearly implied in Isa. 11:10-12 that both the Hebrew *'am* ("people," KJV) and the Gentile *gōyîm* ("Gentiles," KJV) will be included under the rule of

MEDIUM BRONZE COIN, the Cleopatra VII, minted about 35 b.c. The reverse bears the inscription "of Cleopatra the Queen."

the same Messiah and enjoy equal standing before Him. The symbol of the good olive tree in Rom. 11 seems to indicate that all Christians, whether Jewish or Gentile in background, are brought into organic relationship as members of the same body, and there is a suggestion that this condition will continue even in the end time (cf. Gal. 6:16, which seems to speak of the Church as the Israel of God).

For these reasons, the sharp dichotomy maintained between Israel and the church

---

7. Erich Sauer, *From Eternity to Eternity* (Grand Rapids: Eerdmans, 1954), pp. 179-84, in which the author makes clear the symbolic and sacramental character of the sacrifices and shows the untenability of both the spiritualizing inerpretation and also of that theory which makes the second temple of Zerubbabel the fulfillment of Ezek. 40-48.

8. For a lucid discussion of this subject from a strict dipensationalist standpoint, see M. F. Unger's articles in *Bibliotheca Sacra*, 103: 312-24.

by Unger seems very difficult to maintain.[9] However, it should be recognized that a belief in the millennial fulfillment of Ezek. 40-48 does not necessarily involve any clear separation between Jewish and Gentile believers, nor does it require any identification between the "prince" (*nāsî'*) or "ruler" of the latter-day commonwealth mentioned in these chapters (44:3; 46:2; etc.) and the person of the Lord Jesus Christ Himself. It is far more likely that this "prince" is to be understood as a vice-regent, ruling under the authority of the Messiah (whose empire, of course, will extend to all the nations of the earth).

It is highly significant that recent evangelical commentaries, such as that by F. F. Bruce in *The New Layman's Bible Commentary* (Zondervan, 1979, pp. 894-99) and by Ralph Alexander in *Expositor's Bible Commentary,* vol. VI (Zondervan, 1986, pp. 942-96) both give serious attention to all the particulars of this Millennial Temple and Holy Land as a sure prophecy certain of future fulfillment. Alexander has this to say about the sacrifices to be maintained during this final stage of history (prior to the lowering of heaven to earth in the New Jerusalem): "The sacrifices in the millennial sacrificial system appear to be only memorials of Christ's finished work and pictorial reminders that mankind by nature is sinful and in need of redemption from sin. The very observances of the Lord's Table is an argument in favor of this memorial view. The Lord's Table is itself a memorial of Christ's death." (EBC, 6:951).

9. Unger, *Great Neglected Bible Prophecies* (Wheaton, Ill.: Scripture Press, 1955), pp. 88-95.

28 DANIEL

THE NAME DANIEL in Hebrew is *Dāniyyē'l*, which means either "God is Judge" or "God is my Judge" (depending upon the force of the medial *-iy-*). The basic theme of this work is the overruling sovereignty of the one true God, who condemns and destroys the rebellious world power and faithfully delivers His covenant people according to their steadfast faith in Him.

OUTLINE OF DANIEL

I. Training and testing of the remnant, 1:1-21

A. Captivity of the hostages by Nebuchadnezzar, 1:1-2
B. Training of the Jewish youths for the king's service, 1:3-7
C. Daniel's first test of obedience, his challenge of faith, 1:8-16
D. Consequent reward: attainment in wisdom, promotion in position, 1:17-21

II. Nebuchadnezzar's dream and God's plan for the ages, 2:1-49

A. Enigma of the dream beyond the wisdom of this world, 2:1-13
B. Daniel's undertaking to interpret it, and his prayer for God's revelation, 2:14-23
C. Daniel's recall and interpretation of the dream, 2:24-45
D. Resultant glory to God and the promotion of Daniel, 2:46-49

III. Golden image and the fiery furnace, 3:1-30

A. Erection of the image and compulsory state religion, 3:1-7
B. Accusation and trial of the steadfast three, 3:8-18
C. Execution of the sentence, 3:19-23
D. God's miracle of deliverance and the Fourth Man, 3:24-27
E. Nebuchadnezzar's second submission to God, 3:28-30

IV. Nebuchadnezzar's warning dream and subsequent humbling, 4:1-37

A. The alarming dream, unexplained by worldly wisdom, 4:1-7
B. Daniel's recognition as interpreter of dreams, 4:8-18
C. Daniel's interpretation and warning to the proud king, 4:19-27

D. The king's great humiliation, in seven years of dementia 4:28-33
E. The king's repentance and acknowledgment of God's sovereignty, 4:34-37

V. Belshazzar's feast: God's judgment upon the profanation of holy items, 5:1-31

A. Belshazzar's arrogant misuse of the holy vessels of God, 5:1-4
B. Handwriting on the wall and the king's terror, 5:5-9
C. Request of the helpless world ruler to the man of God, 5:10-16
D. Judgment of God against the proud king: the pronouncement of doom, 5:17-28
E. The honoring of Daniel and the slaying of Belshazzar, 5:29-31

VI. In the lions' den: the believer's preservation against the malice of the world, 6:1-28

A. Conspiracy of envy: the decree forbidding all prayer except to Darius, 6:1-9
B. Daniel's detection at prayer and the enforcement of the decree, 6:10-17
C. His miraculous deliverance and the punishment of his foes, 6:18-24
D. Darius' testimony to God's sovereignty, 6:25-28

VII. Triumph of the Son of man, 7:1-28

A. The beasts (lion of Babylon, bear of Medo-Persia, leopard of Greece, the terrible beast of Rome), 7:1-8 (the little horn of v.8 and 20 referring to the Beast)
B. Kingdom of God and Messiah's enthronement, 7:9-14
C. Angel's interpretation of the dream to Daniel, 7:15-28

VIII. Conquest of Persia by Greece and the rise of Antiochus Epiphanes, 8:1-27

A. The vision of the ram, the he-goat, and the little horn (Antiochus), 8:1-12
B. The interpretation of the vision by Gabriel, 8:13-27

IX. Vision of the seventy weeks: God's perfect plan for Israel, 9:1-27

A. Daniel's persistent, promise-based prayer, 9:1-19
B. Gabriel's appearance with the answer: seventy heptads of years for Israel, 9:20-27 (an accurate prediction of the interval between the rebuilding of the wall of Jerusalem and the messianic mission of Christ)

X. Triumph of persistent prayer, 10:1-21

A. Angel's appearance with the answer to Daniel's queries, despite satanic opposition, 10:1-14
B. Angel's encouragement of Daniel, promising further revelation, 10:15-21

XI. Prototribulation under Antiochus, typical of the final tribulation, 11:1-45

A. From the Persian empire to the death of Alexander the Great, 323 B.C., 11:1-4
B. Wars between the Ptolemaic and Seleucid empires up to 168 B.C., 11:5-20
C. Persecution of Israel by Antiochus IV, 11:21-39
D. The analogous war of the antitype of Antiochus in the last days, 11:40-45

XII. Tribulation and final triumph of God's people, 12:1-13

A. The Great Tribulation, 12:1

B. Resurrection and judgment, 12:2-3

C. Sealing of these prophecies for future fulfillment, 12:4

D. Angels and the man clothed in linen: prediction of three and a half years, 12:5-7

E. Final commission to Daniel; the 1290 days and the 1335 days, 12:8-13

AUTHORSHIP OF DANIEL

Despite the numerous objections which have been advanced by scholars who regard this as a prophecy written after the event, there is no good reason for denying the sixth-century Daniel the composition of the entire work. This represents a collection of his memoirs made at the end of a long and eventful career which included government service from the reign of Nebuchadnezzar in the 590s to the reign of Cyrus the Great in the 530s. The appearance of Persian technical terms indicates a final recension of these memoirs at a time when Persian terminology had already infiltrated into the vocabulary of Aramaic. The most likely date for the final edition of the book, therefore, would be about 530 B.C., nine years after the Persian conquest of Babylon.

THEORY OF A MACCABEAN PSEUDEPIGRAPH

The great majority of critics regard this book as entirely spurious and composed centuries after the death of the sixth-century Daniel.[1] They understand it to be a work of historical fiction composed about 167 B.C. and intended to encourage the resistance movement against the tyranny of Antiochus Epiphanes. There are a good many scholars, however, who are not completely satisfied with the Maccabean date for the earlier chapters in Daniel. Many, like Eichhorn (in the late eighteenth and early nineteenth centuries), Meinhold, Bertholdt, and (in the twentieth century) Sellin, Hoelscher, and Noth have held that chapters 2-6 (some would include chap. 7) originated in the third century B.C. This multiple-source theory of Daniel will be examined later in this chapter. The arguments for dating the composition of this book in the Greek period may be divided into four general headings: the historical, the literary or linguistic, the theological, and the exegetical.

HISTORICAL ARGUMENTS FOR THE LATE DATE OF DANIEL

1. The Jewish canon places Daniel among the *Kethubhim* or *Hagiographa*, rather than among the prophets. This is interpreted to mean that the book must have been written later than all the canonical prophets, even the post-exilic Malachi and "Trito-

---

1. J. D. Michaelis in 1771 attributed *Daniel* to several different authors and redactors; likewise, L. Berthold, 1806 & 1808. But J. D. Eichhorn in his *Einleitung*, para, 615, separated 1, 7-12 from chapters 2-6. Yet the essential unity of the book (by a Maccabean author) was advocated by F. Bleek in 1822 & A. von Gall in 1895; likewise, J. Wellhausen, K. Marti, C. H. Cornill, W. W. Baudissin, and C. Steuernagel.

Isaiah." But it should be noted that some of the documents in the *Kethubhim* (the third division of the Hebrew Bible) were of great antiquity, such as the book of Job, the Davidic psalms, and the writings of Solomon. Position in the *Kethubhim*, therefore, is no proof of a late date of composition. Furthermore the statement in Josephus (*Contra Apionem.* 1:8) quoted previously in chapter 5 indicates strongly that in the first century A.D., Daniel was included among the prophets in the second division of the Old Testament canon; hence it could not have been assigned to the Kethubim until a later period.[2] The Masoretes may have been influenced in this reassignment by the consideration that Daniel was not appointed or ordained as a prophet, but remained a civil servant under the prevailing government throughout his entire career. Second, a large percentage of his writings does not bear the character of prophecy, but rather of history (chaps. 1-6), such as does not appear in any of the books of the canonical prophets.[3] Little of that which Daniel wrote is couched in the form of a message from God to His people relayed through the mouth of His spokesman. Rather, the predominating element consists of prophetic visions granted personally to the author and interpreted to him by angels. (Here a comparison may be drawn with Zechariah, which likewise features a series of visions. But in Zechariah far more emphasis is laid upon God's communicating His message to Israel through a prophetic mouthpiece.) It was probably because of the mixed character of this book, partaking partly of historical narratives and partly of prophetic vision, that the later Jewish scribes relegated it to the third or miscellaneous category in the canon.

2. It has been pointed out that Jesus ben Sirach (Ecclesiasticus) makes no mention of Daniel even though he refers to all the other prophets (in 170 B.C.). But it should be noted that other important authors like Ezra received no mention earlier. (Nor for that matter did he make mention of such key figures in Hebrew history as Job, or any of the Judges except Samuel, Asa, Jehoshaphat, and Mordecai. How can such omissions furnish any solid ground for the idea that these leaders were unknown to Jesus ben Sirach? See ZPEB ii 19A.[4]) Critics have also pointed to ben Sirach's statement that there never was a man who was like unto Joseph; and yet, it is alleged, Daniel's career greatly resembled that of Joseph. Note, however, that in none of the particulars specified did Daniel resemble Joseph: "Neither was there a man born like unto Joseph, a governor of his brethren, a stay of the people, whose bones were regarded of the Lord" (Ec'us 49:15).

3. It has been alleged that such historical inaccuracies occur in Daniel as to render

2. Cf. the able discussion of Laird Harris on this point in *The Inspiration and Canononicity of the Bible,* pp. 141-42, 184-85.

3. In IOT, p. 276, R. K. Harrison points out that in four instances, the Qumran *Manual of Discipline* (IQS 1:3; 8:13) and the Zadokite Fragment (CDC 5:21; 7:15) refer to the Old Testament simply as "the law and the prophets," and make no mention of a third division in the canon. The same is true of the New Testament references to the Old Testament, except that the psalms are mentioned as separate in Luke 20:44. In the 2d ed. of *The Inspiration and Canonicity of the Bible,* Harris refutes the suggestion of A. C. Sundberg that in all these instances only two-thirds of the Old Testament canon was referred to.

4. As to the Dan'el referred to in the Ugaritic *Tale of Aqhat,* H. H. P. Dressler ("The Identification of Ugaritic Dan'el with the Daniel of Ezekiel" VT29 [1979], pp. 152-61) proves the impossibility of making such an equation. Cf. E B.C. VII, pp. 5-6.

it likely that the author lived much later than the events he describes. For example, in Daniel 1:1, it is stated that Nebuchadnezzar invaded Palestine in the third year of Jehoiakim, whereas Jer. 46:2 says that the first year of Nebuchadnezzar was the fourth year of Jehoiakim. Since the Chaldean conqueror became king upon his father's death in the year that he invaded Judah, there is a discrepancy of one year between Daniel and Jeremiah. More recent investigation, however, has shown that the Jews reckoned their regnal year from the first month preceding the year of accession (reckoning the year as commencing in the month of Tishri, or the seventh month of the religious calendar). This would mean that 605 B.C. would have been the fourth year of Jehoiakim who came to the throne in 608. The Babylonians, however, reckoned the first regnal year from the next succeeding New Year's Day, that is, from the first of Nisan (the first month of the Hebrew religious calendar).Therefore, the year 605 would be only Jehoiakim's third year according to the Chaldean reckoning. Thus in D. J. Wiseman's *Chronicles of the Chaldean Kings* (1956), it is stated that Nebuchadnezzar's first regnal year began in April 604, even though he had been crowned in September 605.

4. Critics point to the fact that one class of wise men or soothsayers in the book of Daniel is referred to as the "Chaldeans" (*Kasdîm*). They allege that this ethnic term for Nebuchadnezzar's race could not have become specialized to indicate a class of soothsayers until a much later time. In Nebuchadnezzar's own time it surely would have carried only a racial connotation. This indicates that the author of Daniel must have written at a time long after the Neo-Babylonian empire had collapsed and had become an almost forgotten memory. This theory, however, fails to fit the data of the text, for the author of this work was certainly aware that *Kasdîm* was the ethnic term for the race of Nebuchadnezzar. Thus in Dan. 5:30 Belshazzar is referred to as "the king of the Chaldeans"; in this case the term certainly could not refer to any class of wise men. Even in 3:8 the accusation against Shadrach, Meshach, and Abednego brought by certain "Chaldean men" seems to refer to high government officials who appear to be "Chaldean by race" (so Brown, Driver, and Briggs, p. 1098), which classifies these officials as Chaldean by race, which means "Chaldean" was used in two senses in this book. Chaldean did not only mean "soothsayer/priest," but also can indicate a specific race of people. Therefore, the theory of late origin fails to explain the facts as we have them. We must look to other explanations for this twofold use of *Kasdîm*. Herodotus (vol. 1, sec. 181-83) refers to the Chaldeans in such a way as to imply that they were speedily put into all the politically strategic offices of Babylonia as soon as they had gained control of the capital. If this was the case, then "Chaldean" may have early come into use as a term for the priests of Bel-Marduk.

Another suggestion has been offered by R. D. Wilson (*Studies in the Book of Daniel*, series one) to the effect that the Akkadian *Kasdu* or *Kaldu*, referring to a type of priest, was derived from an old Sumerian title *Gal-du* (meaning "master builder"), a term alluding to the building of astronomical charts which were used as an aid to astrological prediction. Wilson cites such a use of *Gal-du* in a tablet from the fourteenth year of

Shamash-shumukin of Babylon (668-648 B.C.). It should be noted that a good many Sumerian titles have been found which contain the element *Gal* ("great one, chief, master"). On a single page in Jacobsen's *Copenhagen Texts* (p. 3) we find these titles: *Gal-LU KUR, Gal-UKU, Gal-DAN-QAR,* and *Gal-SUKKAL.* The resemblance between this *Gal-du* or *Kaldu* and the ethnic term *Kaldu* as a by-form of *Kasdu* would be purely accidental.[5] Such an explanation clears up the divergent usages of this term by the author of Daniel. In 3:8, the accusation against Shadrach, Meshach, and Abednego is brought by certain "Chaldean men," who are probably high government officials.

5. The appearance of King Belshazzar in chapter 5 was interpreted by earlier critics to be unhistorical, inasmuch as Nabonidus was known to be the last king of the Chaldean empire. Later discoveries of cuneiform tablets referring to Belshazzar as "the son of the king" serve to discredit that criticism almost completely (one tablet from the twelfth year of Nabonidus calls for oaths in the names of both Nabonidus and Belshazzar [*mar šarri*]).[6] Nevertheless it is still objected that Belshazzar is referred to in chapter 5 as a son of Nebuchadnezzar, whereas his father was actually Nabonidus (*Nabuna'id*) who reigned until the fall of Babylon in 539. It is alleged that only a later author would have supposed that he was Nebuchadnezzar's son. This argument, however, overlooks the fact that by ancient usage the term *son* often referred to a successor in the same office whether or not there was a blood relationship. Thus in the Egyptian story, "King Cheops and the Magicians" (preserved in the Papyrus Westcar from the Hyksos Period), Prince Khephren says to King Khufu (Cheops), "I relate to thy Majesty a wonder that came to pass in the time of thy father, King Neb-ka." Actually Neb-ka belonged to the Third Dynasty, a full century before the time of Khufu in the Fourth Dynasty. In Assyria a similar practice was reflected in the Black Obelisk of Shalmaneser III, which refers to King Jehu (the exterminator of the whole dynasty of Omri) as "the son of Omri." Moreover, it is a distinct possibility that in this case there was an actual genetic relationship between Nebuchadnezzar and Belshazzar. If Nabonidus married a daughter of Nebuchadnezzar[7] in order to legitimize his usurpation of the throne back in 556 B.C., it would follow that his son by her would be the grandson of Nebuchadnezzar. The word for "father" (*'ab* or *'abbā'*) could also mean grandfather (see Gen. 28:13; 32:10; in 1 Kings 15:13 it means "great grandfather").

There is fairly conclusive evidence that Belshazzar was elevated to secondary kingship (*mar šarri*, "son of the king") during his father's lifetime (just as Jotham had been during the lifetime of his father, Uzziah, in the kingdom of Judah—a common practice

---

5. In the later stages of the Babylonian dialect of Akkadian, the sibilants s, š, and ṣ often shifted to *l* before dentals like *t* and *d*; e.g., *a ṣṭur* ("I wrote") appeared as *alṭur* and *ištu* ("out of") as *ultu.* Hence the name *Kasdu* also appeared as *Kaldu,* and in that form came into Greek as *Khaldaioi* ("Chaldeans"). Cf. W. von Soden, *Grundiss der Akkadischen Grammatik* (Rome, 1969).

6. The fragment of the "Prayer of Nabonidus" found in 4Q, published by Milik in 1954, contains a record of Belshazzar. For a full treatment of this subject, cf. EBC, 7:63-64.

7. Possibly Nitocris was originally the wife of Evil-Merodach, son of Nebuchadnezzar, but Nabonidus may have taken her as his wife after she had been widowed (cf. Wood, CD, p. 133). Also cf. R. F. Dougherty, "*Nabonidus and Belshazzar*" (New Haven, 1929), pp. 60-68.

in ancient times in order to secure a peaceful succession). Recent archaeological discoveries indicate that Belshazzar was in charge of the northern frontier of the Babylonian empire while his father Nabonidus maintained his headquarters at Teman in North Arabia. Among the discoveries at the site of Ur is an inscription of

SILVER SIGLOS
OF DARIUS THE GREAT
(522–485 B.C.)
PORTRAYING THE
PERSIAN EMPEROR
DARIUS I.

Nabunaid, dated 530 B.C., containing a prayer for Nabunaid himself followed by a second prayer for his firstborn son, Bel-shar-uṣur (Belshazzar)—such prayers being customarily offered only for the reigning monarch. Among the discoveries at the site of Ur is an inscription of Nabonidus, dated 543 B.C., containing a prayer for Nabonidus and Belshazzar (*mar šarri-* "son of the king") followed by a second prayer for his firstborn son, *Bel-šar-uṣur* (Belshazzar)–such prayers being customarily offered only for the reigning monarch. Still other cuneiform documents attest that Belshazzar presented sheep and oxen at the temples in Sippar as "an offering of the king." The fact that by the time of Herodotus (ca. 450 B.C.) the very name of Belshazzar had been forgotten, at least so far as the informants of the Greek historian were concerned, indicates a far closer acquaintance with the events of the late sixth century on the part of the author of *Daniel* than would have been the case by the second century B.C.

There is an additional detail in this account that makes the theory of late authorship very difficult to maintain, and that is that the writer of chapter 5 quotes Belshazzar as promising to the interpreter of the inscription on the wall promotion to the status of third ruler in the kingdom (5:16). Why could he only promise the third and not the second? Obviously because Belshazzar himself was only the second ruler, inasmuch as Nabonidus his father was still alive.

6. It is alleged that the figure of "Darius the Mede" is an evidence of historical confusion. It is supposed that the author must have confused him with Darius the son of Hystaspes, who was the third successor after King Cyrus, and who was really a Persian instead of a Mede. But this interpretation is impossible to defend in the light of the internal evidence of the text itself. No explanation can be found for calling Darius the son of Hystaspes a Mede, when he was known to be the descendant of an ancient Achaemenid royal line. The author asserts that Darius the Mede was sixty-two years old when he assumed the rule in Babylonia, yet it was well known to the ancients that Darius the Great was a relatively young man when he commenced his reign in 522. In Dan. 9:1 it is asserted that Darius the Mede was *made* king (*homlak*) over the realm of the Chaldeans. This term indicates that he was invested with the kingship by some higher authority than himself, which well agrees with the supposition that he was installed as viceroy in Babylonia by Cyrus the Great. Similarly, in Dan. 5:31 we are told that Darius "received" (*qabbēl*) the "kingdom" (*malkūtā'*). Note

in this connection the reference by Darius I in the Behistun Inscription to his father Hystaspes as having been made a king. Since chronological reckoning shows that he must have been only a sub-king who ruled under the authority of Cyrus, this established that it was Cyrus's policy to permit subordinate rulers to reign under him with the title of king.

It has been objected that a mere viceroy would not have addressed a decree to the inhabitants of "all the earth" (Dan. 6:25). If the word *earth* refers to the whole inhabited Near East, the objection is well taken (since the authority of Darius the Mede would necessarily have been confined to the former dominions of Nebuchadnezzar, which did not include Asia Minor, North Assyria, Media, or Persia). But it should be pointed out that the Aramaic word *'ar'ā* (like its Hebrew cognate *'ereṣ*) may signify only "land or country," rather than having the wider significance. So

DARIUS THE GREAT
(522–485 B.C.) FIRMLY ESTABLISHED PERSIAN WORLD DOMINION WHICH PREVAILED UNTIL THE CONQUEST OF ALEXANDER THE GREAT.

construed, the term presents no difficulty at all. Yet it should also be pointed out that part of the ancient titulary of the king of Babylon ever since the time of Hammurabi was the phrase *šar kiššati* or "king of the universe" ("king of all"). In his decree, therefore, Darius the Mede may simply have been following ancient custom in using terminology which implied a theoretical claim to universal dominion.

The question remains, however, who was this Darius the Mede? No ancient historian refers to him by this name. Nevertheless, there is powerful cumulative evidence to show that he is to be identified with a governor named Gubaru, who is referred to both by the cuneiform records and by the Greek historians as playing a key role in the capture of Babylon and its subsequent administration. For some decades it has been customary to identify this Gubaru ("Gobryas," Greek) with the ruler mentioned by Daniel. Nevertheless, there have been some puzzling discrepancies in the ancient records concerning this personage, and these have encouraged critical scholars like H. H. Rowley to reject the identification between Gubaru and Darius the Mede as altogether untenable.

Rowley's arguments have been superseded, however, by the able work of J. C. Whitcomb in his *Darius the Mede* (1959). Whitcomb has gathered together all the ancient inscriptions referring to Ugbaru, Gubaru, and Gaubaruva, to be found in the

Nabonidus Chronicle, the Contenau Texts, the Pohl Texts, the Tremayne Texts, and the Behistun Inscription. By careful comparison and the process of elimination, Whitcomb shows that the former assumption that Ugbaru and Gubaru were variant spellings of the same name is quite erroneous and has given rise to bewildering confusion. Ugbaru was an elderly general who had been governor of Gutium; it was he who engineered the capture of Babylon by the strategem of deflecting the water of the Euphrates into an artificial channel. While it is true that no cuneiform document yet discovered refers to Ugbaru's role in this, and that the earliest historical record of the strategem of river-diversion comes from Herodotus in the 540s (*Hist* i, 107, 191), nevertheless it is inconceivable that this account was a free invention of his own. It would have served the official propoganda line of Cyrus's government to omit mention of this strategem in the interests of representing that Babylon surrendered to him voluntarily. But according to the cuneiform records, Ugbaru lived only a few weeks after this glorious achievement, apparently being carried off by an untimely illness. It would appear that after his decease, a man named Gubaru was appointed by Cyrus as governor of Babylon and of *Ebir-nāri* ("beyond the river"). He is so mentioned in tablets dating from the fourth, sixth, seventh, and eighth years of Cyrus (i.e., 535, 533, 532, and 531 B.C.) and in the second, third, fourth, and fifth years of Cambyses (528, 527, 526, and 525 B.C.). He seems to have perished during the revolts of Pseudo-Smerdis and Darius I, for by March 21, 520 B.C., the new satrap of Babylonia is said to be Ushtani.

Whitcomb goes on to say, "It is our conviction that Gubaru, the governor of Babylon and the region beyond the river, appears in the book of Daniel as Darius the Mede, the monarch who took charge of the Chaldean kingdom immediately following the death of Belshazzar, and who appointed satraps and presidents (including Daniel) to assist him in the governing of this extensive territory with its many peoples. We believe that this identification is the only one which satisfactorily harmonizes the various lines of evidence which we find in the book of Daniel and in the contemporary cuneiform records."[8]

Whitcomb further cites the statement of W. F. Albright in "The Date and Personality of the Chronicler" (JBL, 40:2: 11): "It seems to me highly probable that Gobryas did actually assume the royal dignity along with the name "Darius," perhaps an old Iranian royal title, while Cyrus was absent on a European campaign....After the cuneiform elucidation of the Belshazzar mystery, showing that the latter was long coregent with his father, the vindication of Darius the Mede for history was to be expected....We may safely expect the Babylonian Jewish author to be acquainted with the main facts of Neo-Babylonian history." As Albright suggests, it is quite possible that the name Darius (*Darayavahush*, in Persian) was a title of honor, just as "Caesar" or "Augustus" became in the Roman empire. In Medieval Persian (Zend) we find the word *dara*, meaning "king." Possibly *Darayavahush* would have meant the "royal one." (The personal name of Darius I was actually Spantadāta, son of Wiʃtāspa [Hys-

---

8. John C. Whitcomb, *Darius the Mede*, p. 24.

taspes]; Darayawuš was his throne-name. Cf. F. W. Konig: *"Relief und Inschrift des König Dareios I"* [Leiden, 1938], p. 1.)

In this connection a word should be said about the remarkable decree referred to in Dan. 6 which forbade worship to be directed toward anyone else except Darius himself during the period of thirty days. Granted that the king later repented of the folly of such a decree when he discovered it was merely part of a plot to eliminate his faithful servant Daniel, it still is necessary to explain why he ever sanctioned the measure in the first place. In view of the intimate connection between religious and political loyalty which governed the attitude of the peoples of that ancient culture, it might well have been considered a statesmanlike maneuver to compel all the diverse inhabitants with their heterogeneous tribal and religious loyalties to acknowledge in a very practical way the supremacy of the new Persian empire which had taken over supreme control of their domains. A temporary suspension of worship (at least in the sense of presenting petitions for blessing and aid) was a measure well calculated to convey to the minds of Darius's subjects the reality of the change in control from the overlordship of the Chaldeans to that of the Medes and Persians. In the light of ancient psychology, therefore, it is unwarrantable to rule out of possibility such a remarkable decree or to condemn it as fabulous or unhistorical, as many critics have done.

LITERARY AND LINGUISTIC ARGUMENTS FOR THE LATE DATE OF DANIEL

1. *Foreign loanwords were found in the Aramaic of Daniel.* It has been alleged that the numerous foreign words in the Aramaic portion of Daniel (and to a lesser extent also in the Hebrew portion) conclusively demonstrate an origin much later than the sixth century B.C. There are no less than fifteen words of probable Persian origin (although not all these have actually been discovered in any known Persian documents), and their presence proves quite conclusively that even the chapters dating back to Nebuchadnezzar and Belshazzar could not have been composed in the Chaldean period. This contention may be freely admitted, but conservative scholars do not maintain that the book of Daniel was composed, in its final form at least, until the establishment of the Persian authority over Babylonia. Since the text indicates that Daniel himself lived to serve, for several years at least, under Persian rule, there is no particular reason why he should not have employed in his language those Persian terms (largely referring to government and administration) which had found currency in the Aramaic spoken in Babylon by 530 B.C. While it is true that the Elephantine Papyri contain fewer Persian loan-words than Daniel (H. H. Rowley in 1929 contended that there were only two—actually there are several more), in the "Aramaic Documents of the 5th Century B.C." published by G. R. Driver (Oxford, 1957) and composed for the most part in Susa or Babylon (*op. cit.* pp. 10-12), there are no less than twenty-six Persian loanwords.

But it is alleged that the presence of at least three Greek words in Daniel 3 indicates that the work must have been composed after the conquest of the Near East by Alexander the Great. These three words (in 3:5) are *qaytᵉrôs* (*kitharis*, Greek), *psantērîn* (*psaltērion*, in Greek), and *sūmpōnyah* (*symphonia*, Greek). The last of these three does not occur in extant Greek literature until the time of Plato (ca. 370 B.C.), at least in the sense of a musical instrument.⁹ From this it has been argued that the word itself must be as late as the fourth century in Greek usage. But since we now possess less than one-tenth of the significant Greek literature of the classical period, we lack sufficient data for timing the precise origin of any particular word or usage in the development of the Greek vocabulary.

It should carefully be observed that these three words are names of musical instruments and that such names have always circulated beyond national boundaries as the instruments themselves have become available to the foreign market. These three were undoubtedly of Greek origin and circulated with their Greek names in Near Eastern markets, just as foreign musical terms have made their way into our own language, like the Italian *piano* and *viola*. We know that as early as the reign of Sargon (722-705 B.C.) there were, according to the Assyrian records, Greek captives who were sold into slavery from Cyprus, Ionia, Lydia, and Cilicia. The Greek poet Alcaeus of Lesbos (fl. 600 B.C.) mentions that his brother Antimenidas served in the Babylonian army. It is therefore evident that Greek mercenaries, Greek slaves, and Greek musical instruments were current in the Semitic Near East long before the time of Daniel. It is also significant that in the Neo-Babylonian ration tablets published by E. F. Weidner, Ionian carpenters and shipbuilders are mentioned among the recipients of rations from Nebuchadnezzar's commissary—along with musicians from Ashkelon and elsewhere (cf. "Jojachin König von Juda" in *Mélanges Syriens*, vol. 2, 1939, pp. 923-35).

Two or three other words have been mistakenly assigned by some authors to a Greek origin, but these have now been thoroughly discredited. One of them was *kārôz* ("herald") which was supposedly derived from the Greek *kēryx* (Brown-Driver-Briggs *Lexicon*). But in more recent works, like Koehler-Baumgartner's *Hebrew Lexicon*, this derivation is explicitly rejected in favor of the old Persian *khrausa*, meaning "caller." Kitchen suggests that the word ultimately came from the Hurrian *Kirenze* or *kirezzi*, "proclamation."¹⁰ C. C. Torrey and A. Cowley regarded *pathgām* as derived from Greek, but Kutscher, in *Kedem* (2:74) published a leather roll of Arsames from about 410 B.C. in which this term occurs more than once. Needless to say, this renders a Greek deriva-

---

9. The true meaning of *sumponyah* (*symphonia*) is by no means certain, and some scholars have suggested that even in Dan. 3:5, it is to be taken as "musical ensemble" rather than as a specific instrument. E. Yamauchi (*Greece and Babylon* [Grand Rapids: Baker, 1967], p. 19) considers the specific interpretation of the word here somewhat dubious but points out that the related adjective *symphonos* appears as a term for "harmony" in Pindar's *Pythian Ode* 1:70 (ca. 430 B.C.). T. C. Mitchell and R. Joyce suggest that *sumponyah* might actually have been borrowed from an Eastern Greek dialectical form of *tympanon* ("tambourine, drum"), since a percussion instrument would have been more appropriate at this point in the listing (cf. *Notes on Some Problems in the Book of Daniel*, ed. D. J. Wiseman [London: Tyndale,1965], p. 26).

10. K. A. Kitchen, AOOT, p. 144.

tion impossible. In all probability it was derived from the Old Persian *pratigama*, which meant originally something which has arrived, hence a "communication" or "order."[11] Actually, the argument based upon the presence of Greek words turns out to be one of the most compelling evidences of all that Daniel could not have been composed as late as the Greek period. By 170 B.C. a Greek-speaking government had been in control of Palestine for 160 years, and Greek political or administrative terms would surely have found their way into the language of the subject populace. The books of Maccabees testify to the very extensive intrusion of Greek culture and Greek customs into the life of the Jews by the first half of the second century, particularly in the big cities.

Furthermore it should be observed that even in the Septuagint translation of Daniel, which dates presumably from 100 B.C., or sixty-five years after Judas Maccabeus, the rendition of several of the Aramaic technical terms for state officials was mere conjecture. For example, in Dan. 3:2 *ʾᵃḏargāzᵉrayyā*, ("counselors") is rendered *hypatous* ("grandees"); *gᵉḏobrayyāʾ* ("treasurers") by *dioikētēs* ("administrators, governors"); and *tiptayyē*, or *dᵉtāberayyā*, ("magistrates," or "judges") by the one general phrase *tous 'ep'exousiōn* ("those in authority"). (Theodotion uses still other translations, such as *hēgoumenous* and *tyrannous*, for the first two officials just mentioned.) It is impossible to explain how within five or six decades after Daniel was first composed (according to the Maccabean date hypothesis) the meaning of these terms could have been so completely forgotten even by the Jews in Egypt, who remained quite conversant in Aramaic as well as in Greek. (Cf. D. J. Wiseman, *Some Problems in the Book of Daniel*, p. 43.)

This is especially significant in view of the fact that the Aramaic of Daniel was a linguistic medium which readily absorbed foreign terminology. It includes approximately fifteen words of Persian origin, almost all of which relate to government and politics. It is hard to conceive, therefore, how after Greek had been the language of government for over 160 years, no single Greek term pertaining to politics or administration had ever intruded into Palestinian Aramaic. The same generalization holds good for the Hebrew portions of Daniel as well. It contains such Persian terms as palace (*appeden* in 11:45, from *apadāna*), noblemen (*partᵉmîn* 1:3, from *fratama*) and king's portion (*paṯbāg* in 1:5, from *patibaga*). Yet the Hebrew chapters contain not a single word of Greek origin (even though, according to some critics, Daniel's Hebrew is later than his Aramaic sections).

It was formerly asserted that the Aramaic of Daniel is of the Western dialect and hence could not have been composed in Babylon, as would have been the case if the sixth-century Daniel was its real author. Recent discoveries of fifth-century Aramaic documents, however, have shown quite conclusively that Daniel was, like Ezra, written in a form of Imperial Aramaic (*Reichsaramäisch*), an official or literary dialect which had currency in all parts of the Near East. Thus the relationship to the Aramaic of the

---

11. Cf. W. F. Albright, *The Biblical Period from Abraham to Ezra* (New York: Harper Torchbooks, 1963), p. 65.

Elephantine Papyri from southern Egypt is a very close one, inasmuch as they too were written in the Imperial Aramaic.[12] E. Y. Kutscher, in a review of G. D. Driver's *Aramaic Documents of the Fifth Century* B.C. (1954), comments upon linguistic peculiarities of these letters which were sent from Babylon and Susa in the Eastern Aramaic area. He states: "With regard to Biblical Aramaic, which in word order and other traits is of the Eastern type (i.e., freer and more flexible in word order) and has scarcely any Western characteristics at all, it is plausible to conclude that it originated in the East. A final verdict on this matter, however, must await the publication of all the Aramaic texts from Qumran."[13] (Noteworthy is the uniform tendency to put the verb late in the clause.)

2. *Grammatical evidences for early date of Daniel's Aramaic.* One noteworthy characteristic in the Aramaic of Daniel which marks it as of early origin is to be found in the fairly frequent interval-vowel-change passives. That is to say, instead of adhering exclusively to the standard method of expressing the passive (by the prefix *hit-* or *'et-*), the biblical Aramaic used a *hophal* formation (e.g., *honhat* from *neḥat*, *hussaq* from *seliq*, *hūbad* from *'abad* and *hu'al* from *'âlal*). Note than an occasional *hophal* appears also in a 420 B.C. Elephantine papyrus (CAP #20, line 7) "they were entrusted." No such examples of *hophal* forms have as yet been discovered in any of the Aramaic documents published from the Dead Sea caves (some of which, like the Genesis Apocryphon, date from scarcely a century later than the Maccabean wars). Such forms cannot be dismissed as mere Hebraisms employed by the Jewish author of Daniel, since even the Jewish scribes of the Targums never used such forms; but only the *'et-* type of passive. If Hebrew influence could have produced internal-vowel passives it might reasonably be expected to have shown itself even in the Targums.

Largely because of the close relationship of biblical Aramaic to the Elephantine Papyri (which date from the fifth and fourth centuries B.C.), many scholars have been forced to date chapters 2-7 of the book of Daniel as no later than the third century B.C. Even H. H. Rowley concedes that the evidence is conclusive that biblical Aramaic stands somewhere between the Elephantine Papyri and the Aramaic of the Nabatean and Palmyrene Inscriptions. Sachau states quite plainly that the language of the Papyri is in all essential respects identical with biblical Aramaic.

C. C. Torrey and Montgomery came to the conclusion that Dan. 1-6 was written between 245 and 225 B.C., and that a later editor translated chapter 1 into Hebrew around 165 B.C.[14] Eissfeldt (*Einleitung*, 1934) likewise indicated that the first six chapters came from the third century B.C. and the last six were from the Maccabean period and were intended as a continuation of the older work. Gustav Hoelscher in *Die Entstehung des Buches Daniel* (1919) followed the view of Ernst Sellin, who stated that an older Ara-

---

12. Incidentally, it is interesting to observe that these Elephantine Papyri contain the name *Abednego*, which was formerly interpreted as a late corruption of "Abed-Nebo" ("servant of Nebo") such as might be expected in a second-century production. But it turns out to be a current name as "Abednego" in the fifth century B.C. Egypt. (cf. E. Sachau, *Aramaic Papyri and Ostraca*, 1911. Cf. also E. Yamauchi: "Slaves of God" in *Bulletin of the Evangelical Theological Society* [Winter 1966], p. 33).

13. Kutscher, in JBL (Dec. 1957), p. 338.

14. See Rowley, *The Aramaic of the Old Testament* (London: Oxford, 1929), p. 9.

maic Daniel apocalyptic or biography comprised chapters 1-7 (chap. 1 being later translated into Hebrew, and Maccabean insertions having been made in chaps. 2 and 7), whereas chapters 8–12 were truly Maccabean in date. Hoelscher states that it might have been possible that the author of the collection of legends (chaps. 2-6) took them directly from oral tradition or found them already in older written form. Yet he points out that they show unmistakably the hand of a single author running throughout the text because of a certain uniformity in style and method of treatment. Both Hoelscher and Martin Noth (*Zur Komposition des Buches Daniel*,[15] 1926) attempted to date the origin of certain elements and motifs by a correlation with current events of Hellenistic history insofar as they were known to them.

The mere fact that chapters 2-7 of Daniel were written in Aramaic and the remainder in Hebrew has been adduced by some writers as a ground for a late dating of the document. Some have argued that Aramaic would hardly have been favored over the traditionally sacred Hebrew until a period so late in Jewish history that Hebrew had become almost unintelligible and forgotten by all except the rabbis themselves. (This position is impossible to maintain, however, if the Hebrew chapters were composed even later than the Aramaic—a clear self-contradiction.) It should be understood, however, that the claim of the sacrosanctity of Hebrew is a mere theory which rests on slender foundations. The Jews apparently took no exception to the Aramaic sections in the book of Ezra, most of which consist of copies of correspondence carried on in Aramaic between the local governments of Palestine and the Persian imperial court from approximately 520 to 460 B.C. If Ezra can be accepted as an authentic document from the middle of the fifth century, when so many of its chapters were largely composed in Aramaic, it is hard to see why the six Aramaic chapters of Daniel must be dated two centuries later than that. It should be carefully observed that in the Babylon of the late sixth century, in which Daniel purportedly lived, the predominant language spoken by the heterogeneous population of this metropolis was Aramaic. It is therefore not surprising that an inhabitant of that city should have resorted to Aramaic in composing a portion of his memoirs.

As to the question of why half the book was written in Aramaic and half in Hebrew, the reason for the choice is fairly obvious. Those portions of Daniel's prophecy which deal generally with Gentile affairs (the four kingdoms of Nebuchadnezzar's dream, the humiliation of that king in the episode of the fiery furnace and by his seven years of insanity, and also the experiences of Belshazzar and Darius the Mede) were put into a linguistic medium which all the public could appreciate whether Jew or Gentile. But those portions which were of particularly Jewish interest (chaps. 1, 8-12) were put into Hebrew in order that they might be understood by the Jews alone. This was peculiarly appropriate because of the command in chapter 12 to keep these later predictions more or less secret and seal them

---

15. This position is impossible to maintain, however, if the Hebrew chapters were composed even later than the Aramaic—a clear self-contradiction.

up until the time of fulfillment (12:9).

So far as the Hebrew of Daniel is concerned, we have already seen that it contains a significant number of Persian governmental terms, indicating its origin during the period of Persian domination. There is no trace whatsoever of Greek influence on the language. It is interesting to observe that the Hebrew text of Ecclesiasticus, dating from about 200-180 B.C., shortly before the Maccabean period, furnishes us with a fair sample of the type of Hebrew which would have been current at the time Daniel was written—according to the late-date theorists. Since Ecclesiasticus is a document of the wisdom literature, it is to be expected that it would bear no great stylistic resemblances to the later chapters of Daniel. Nevertheless, it is quite striking that Ecclesiasticus exhibits later linguistic characteristics than Daniel, being somewhat rabbinical in tendency. Israel Lévi in his *Introduction to the Hebrew Text of Ecclesiasticus* (1904) lists the following: (*a*) new verbal forms borrowed mainly from Aramaic, (*b*) excessive use of the *hiphil* and *hithpael* conjugations, and (*c*) peculiarities of various sorts heralding the approach of Mishnaic Hebrew.

So far as the Qumran material is concerned, none of the sectarian documents composed in Hebrew (*The Manual of Discipline, The War of the Children of Light Against the Children of Darkness, The Thanksgiving Psalms*) in that collection show any distinctive characteristics in common with the Hebrew chapters of Daniel. Cf. J. H. Skilton, ed., *The Law and the Prophets* (Nutley, N.J.: Presbyterian & Reformed), chap. 41: "The Hebrew of *Daniel* Compared with the Qumran Sectarian Documents," by G. L. Archer, pp. 470-81. Nor is there the slightest resemblance between the Aramaic of the *Genesis Apocryphon* and the Aramaic chapters of Daniel.

Dated in the first century B.C., this copy of the *Genesis Apocryphon* presents us with at least five legible columns of Aramaic composed within a century of the alleged date of Daniel, according to the Maccabean date hypothesis. As such it surely should have exhibited many striking points of resemblance to the Aramaic of Dan. 2-7, in grammar, style, and vocabulary. This is especially true since the editors of this manuscript, N. Avigad and Y. Yadin, suggest that the original was composed as early as the third century B.C. Kutscher describes ("The Language of the Genesis-Apocryphon" in *Scripta Hierosolymita* [Jerusalem, 1958], p. 3) the language of the Apocryphon as neither Imperial Aramaic in general nor biblical Aramaic in particular. It should be noted that in contrast to the Eastern dialectical traits of Daniel, the Apocryphon shows distinctly Western traits, such as the prior position of the verb in its clause, the use of *kaman* instead of *kᵉmah* for "how much, how great?" and of *tammān* instead of *tammah* for "there." Note also the appearance of a *mif'ōl* instead of a *mif'al* for the *peal* infinitive; for instance, *misbōq* ("to leave"), instead of the biblical *misbaq*, a form which hitherto had been classed as peculiar to the Palestinian Targumic or Midrashic dialect. If Daniel then was composed in Eastern Aramaic, it could not possibly have been written in second-century Palestine, as the Maccabean theory demands.

At this point mention should be made of one phonetic characteristic of Daniel's

Aramaic to which appeal has been made by H. H. Rowley, J. A. Montgomery, and others, as an evidence for a later date of composition. In the earlier Aramaic inscriptions, as well as in the Elephantine Papyri of the fifth century, a certain phoneme appears as *z*, which in biblical Aramaic almost always appears as *d*. It is urged that if Daniel had been written as early as the fifth century B.C. (to say nothing of the sixth century) the older spelling with *z* should have been retained.

In answer to this, it ought to be pointed out that up to the present time no Aramaic documents from any region have been discovered from the sixth century B.C., much less from the eastern or Babylonian section of the Aramaic-speaking world. Until such documents are discovered, it is premature to say whether the shift from *z* to *d* had taken place by that period. It certainly ought to be recognized that this shift had consistently taken place in the Aramaic chapters of Ezra (at least so far as the text has come down to us), which presumably reflected the pronunciation of Aramaic in Persia, from which Ezra came. It would therefore appear that the shift from *z* to *d* took place earlier in the East than it did in the West (since the Elephantine Papyri show this shift only in four or five examples: *'-,h-d* for *'h-z* ["take"], *d-y l-k-y* for *z-y l-k-y* ["yours"] in A. Cowley's *Aramaic Papyri of the Fifth Century* B.C. (London: Oxford, 1923), (hereafter CAP), 13:7, 11, 16; *d-k-'* for *z-k-'* ["clean"] CAP 14:6, 9; *d-k-y* for *z-k-y* ["that"] CAP 21:6; 27:12; *d-n-h* for *z-n-h* ["this"] CAP 16:9). See also CAP 30 *m-d-b-h-'* ("altar") and *d-b-ḥ-n* ("sacrificing") instead of *m-z-b-ḥ* and *z-b-ḥ-n*. It is by no means necessary to suppose all the consonantal shifts took place simultaneously in Aramaic throughout the whole area of the Near East where this language was current.[16] (For example, in the history of Medieval German it may be verified from documentary evidence that the High German consonantal shifts took place earlier in some regions of Germany than they did in others.)

Moreover, many grammatical traits mark the Apocryphon as centuries later than the Aramaic of Daniel, Ezra, or the Elephantine Papyri, such as *-hā'* for the femine third person possessive pronoun, instead of *-āh*; *dēn* for "this" instead of *dᵉnah*; the ending *-iyat* for third feminine singular of *lamed-aleph* verbs instead of *-āt*—and many other examples. As for the vocabulary, a considerable number of words occur in the Apocryphon which have hitherto not been discovered in Aramaic documents prior to the Targum and Talmud. (A full account of these distinctives in grammar and vocabulary will be found in the author's article [chap. 11] in *New Perspectives on the Old Testament*, ed. B. Payne [Waco, Tex.: Word, 1969]. Neither in morphology, nor syntax, nor style of expression can any evidence be found in Daniel for a date of composition approaching the period of these sectarian documents. According to the Maccabean Date Theory, the entire corpus of Daniel had to have been composed in Judea in the second century B.C., only a few decades before these documents from Qumran. In the light of this newly discovered linguistic evidence, therefore, it would seem impossible to maintain any longer a second-century date for the book of Daniel.

---

16. H. G. Asmussen has come to the conclusion that the Aramaic portions of Daniel have been translated from an Akkadian record. ("*Daniel, Prophet oder Fälscher Heide,*" 1981 (cited in "*Wat is er Gebeurth?*" in Telos, 1982, Stichting Evangelische Hogeschool).

29 DANIEL (CONTINUED)

THEOLOGICAL ARGUMENTS ADVANCED TO SHOW
THE LATE DATE OF DANIEL

ADHERENTS OF THE MACCABEAN THEORY customarily lay great emphasis upon the supposed development or evolution of religious thought of the Israelite nation. They point to motifs and emphases in Daniel which they believe to be akin to those characterizing the apocryphal literature of the Inter-testamental Period (such works as the *Book of Enoch* and the *Testament of the Twelve Patriarchs*, or even such books of the *Apocrypha* as *Tobit and Susanna*). These emphases include the prominence of angels, the stress upon the last judgment, the resurrection of the dead, and the establishment of the final kingdom of God upon earth with the Messiah as the supreme ruler of the world. It is conceded that there are occasional references to angels and judgment, the kingship of God, and the Messiah in some earlier books of the Old Testament, but it is felt that these teachings have achieved a far more developed form in Daniel than in Ezekiel or Zechariah. The angelology in particular is thought to resemble that of the *Book of Enoch* (first century B.C.).

This, however, is a very difficult statement to substantiate. Any reader may easily verify the fact that Zechariah also mentions the Messiah and angels on several occasions in his prophecies, which date from 519 to approximately 470 B.C. (2:3; 3:1; 6:12; 9:9; 13:1; 14:5). Furthermore, angels play a very similar role in *Zechariah* to that in *Daniel*, namely, that of interpreting the significance of visions which were presented to the prophet. The affinity is close enough to warrant the deduction that either Zechariah had influenced Daniel or Daniel had influenced Zechariah.[1] There are two significant references to the Messiah in Malachi as well (Mal. 3:1 and 4:2) and to the last judgment also in chapter 3. On the other hand, works which are admittedly of the second century B.C., such as 1 Maccabees and the Greek additions to Daniel, Baruch, and Judith, show none of these four elements (angelology, resurrection, last judgment, and

---

1. Cornill and Farrar are therefore unjustified in their contention that Hebrew literature prior to 200 B.C. shows no trace of Daniel's influence; cf. Robert Dick Wilson's article "The Influence of Daniel" in *Princeton Theological Review* 21 (July and Oct. 1923).

Messiah) which are asserted to be so characteristic of this period that they betray the second-century origin of Daniel. Even the Jewish apocryphal literature from the first century A.D. contains only two works (out of a possible sixteen) having all four characteristics, namely, the *Vision of Isaiah* and the *Ascension of Isaiah.*

Perhaps it would be well at this point to review the occurrence of these four elements in the earlier books of the Old Testament. Concerning the ranks of angels, Genesis mentions cherubim, Joshua refers to a prince of the angels. Their function was said to be the delivery of messages to Abraham, Moses, Joshua, Gideon, and various prophets such as Isaiah, Zechariah, and Ezekiel. Thus as early as the Torah we find the angels revealing the will of God, furnishing protection for God's people, and destroying the forces of the enemy. So far as the resurrection is concerned, there is the famous affirmation of Job in Job 19:25-26 (although another interpretation of this passage is possible); Isaiah's affirmation in 26:19 ("Thy dead shall live; my dead bodies shall arise," ASV); Ezekiel's vision of the valley of dry bones, and possibly the resuscitation of the dead by Elijah and Elisha. On the other hand, of the large number of postcanonical works, only the *Book of the Twelve Patriarchs* refers to a resurrection of both the righteous and the wicked as is found in Dan. 12:2. The doctrine of the last judgment is mentioned in Isaiah, Zephaniah, Haggai, Zechariah, Malachi, and in many of the psalms. In many instances this judgment pertains to the nations of the world as well as to Israel. References to the book of life or a book of remembrance go back as far as Ex. 32:32-33 and Isa. 4:3 (cf. Isa. 65:6; Ps. 69:28; and Mal. 3:16). The concept of the Messiah appears as early as Gen. 3:15 and 49:10 (cf. Num. 24:17; Deut. 18:15; Isa. 9:6-7; 11:1; Jer. 23:5-6; 33:11-17; Ezek. 34:23-31; Mic. 5:2).

Doubtless it is possible to make out some kind of progression in the development of these doctrines during the history of God's revelation to Israel, but it is a mistake to suppose that Daniel contains anything radically new in any of the four areas under dispute. Moreover, these precise doctrines were most appropriate for Israel's comfort and encouragement during the time of captivity and on the threshold of their return to the promised land.

EXEGETICAL ARGUMENTS FOR THE LATE DATE OF DANIEL

Champions of the Maccabean Date Theory allege that it was impossible for a sixth-century author to have composed such detailed predictions concerning coming events in the history of Israel as are contained in the prophetic chapters of the book of Daniel. They also allege that it is a suspicious circumstance that such accurate predictions only extend to the reign of Antiochus IV (175-164 B.C.) but nothing beyond this time. The obvious conclusion to draw, therefore, is that the entire work was composed by one who lived in the reign of Antiochus IV and who composed this literary fiction in order to encourage the Jewish patriots of his own generation to join with the Maccabees in throwing off the Syrian yoke. Thus, all of the fulfilled predictions can be explained as *vaticinia ex eventu.*

This explanation of the data in Daniel, which is as old as the neo-Platonic polemicist Porphyry (who died in A.D. 303), depends for its validity on the soundness of the premise that there are no accurate predictions fulfilled subsequently to 165 B.C. This proposition, however, cannot successfully be maintained in the light of the internal evidence of the text and its correlation with the known facts of ancient history. Yet it should be recognized that considerable attention in Daniel is devoted to the coming events of the reign of Anti-

TETRADRACHMA OF THE SELEUCID EMPIRE OF ANTIOCHUS IV EPHIPHANES (175–164 B.C.) — THE "LITTLE HORN" OF DANIEL 11. THIS COIN PORTRAYS ZEUS ENTHRONED; THE OBVERSE BEARS THE PORTRAIT OF ANTIOCHUS IV WITH THE INSCRIPTION "OF KING ANTIOCHUS GOD MANIFEST" DAN. 11:21–34.

ochus, for the very good reason that this period was to present the greatest threat in all of subsequent history (apart, of course, from the plot of Haman in the time of Esther) to the survival of the faith and nation of Israel. Assuming that these predictions were given by divine inspiration and that God had a concern for the preservation of His covenant people, it was to be expected that revelations in Daniel would make it clear to coming generations that He had not only foreseen but had well provided for the threat of extinction which was to be posed by Antiochus Epiphanes.

This prophetic emphasis was all the more warranted in view of the fact that Antiochus and his persecution were to serve as types of the final Antichrist and the great tribulation which is yet to come in the end time (according to Christ's Olivet discourse, recorded in Matt. 24 and Mark 13). This is made evident from the startling way in which the figure of the Greek emperor Antiochus suddenly blends into the figure of the latter day Antichrist in Dan. 11, beginning with verse 40. (Note that the Little Horn is said in 11:45 to meet his death in Palestine, whereas Antiochus IV actually died in Tabae, Persia.) It is interesting to note that even S. R. Driver admits that these last mentioned verses do not correspond with what is known of the final stages of Antiochus' career; actually he met his end at Tabae in Persia after a vain attempt to plunder the rich temple of Elymais in Elam.

It is fair to say that the weakest spot in the whole structure of the Maccabean theory is to be found in the identification of the fourth empire predicted in chapter 2. In order to maintain their position, the late-date theorists have to interpret this fourth empire as referring to the kingdom of the Macedonians or Greeks founded by Alexander the Great around 330 B.C. This means that the third empire must be identified with the Persian realm established by Cyrus the Great, and the second empire has to be the short-lived Median power, briefly maintained by the legendary Darius the Mede. According to this interpretation, then, the head of gold in chapter 2 represents the

Chaldean empire, the breast of silver the Median empire, the belly and the thighs of brass the Persian empire, and the legs of iron the Greek empire. Although this identification of the four empires is widely held by scholars today, it is scarcely tenable in the light of internal evidence. That is to say, the text of Daniel itself gives the strongest indications that the author considered the Medes and Persians as components of the one and same empire, and that despite his designation of King Darius as "the Mede," he never entertained the notion that there was at any time a separate and distinct Median empire previous to the Persian Empire.

In the first place, the symbolism of Dan. 7 precludes the possibility of identifying the second empire as Media and the third empire as Persia. In this chapter, the first kingdom is represented by a lion. (All scholars agree that this represents the Chaldean or Babylonian realm.) The second kingdom appears as a bear devouring three ribs. This would well correspond to the three major conquests of the Medo-Persian empire: Lydia, Babylon, and Egypt (under Cyrus the Great and Cambyses).[2] The third empire is represented as a leopard with four wings and four heads. There is no record that the Persian empire was divided into four parts, but it is well known that the empire of Alexander the Great separated into four parts subsequent to his death, namely, Macedon–Greece, Thrace–Asia Minor, the Seleucid empire (including Syria, Babylonia, and Persia), and Egypt. The natural inference, therefore, would be that the leopard represented the Greek empire. The fourth kingdom is presented as a fearsome ten-horned beast, incomparably more powerful than the others and able to devour the whole earth. The ten horns strongly suggest the ten toes of the image described in chapter 2, and it should be noted that these toes are described in chapter 2 as having a close connection with the two legs of iron. The two legs can easily be identified with the Roman empire, which in the time of Diocletian divided into the Eastern and the Western Roman empires. But there is no way in which they can be reconciled with the history of the Greek empire which followed upon Alexander's death.

In Dan. 8 we have further symbolism to aid us in this identification of empires two and three. There a two-horned ram (one horn of which is higher than the other, just as Persia overshadowed Media in Cyrus's empire) is finally overthrown by a he-goat, who at first shows but one horn (easily identified with Alexander the Great) but subsequently sprouts four horns (i.e., Macedon, Asia Minor, Syria, and Egypt), out of which there finally develops a little horn, that is, Antiochus Epiphanes.

From the standpoint of the symbolism of chapters 2, 7, and 8, therefore, the identification of the four empires with Babylon, Medo-Persia, Greece, and Rome presents a perfect correspondence, whereas the identifications involved in the Maccabean Date Theory present the most formidable discrepancies.

In this connection it ought to be noted that the strongest argument for identifying Daniel's fourth empire with that of Alexander and his Greek successors is derived from

2. The succesive advances of Persian Empire: 550 B.C. Media merged with Persia; 546 B.C. Lydia was conquered; 539 B.C. Babylon was taken; 525 B.C. Egypt was conquered (Psamtik III, 526-525) by Cambyses.

the appearance of the little horn in chapters 7 and 8. That is to say, in chapter 7 the little horn admittedly develops from the fourth empire, that is, from the fearsome ten-horned beast who overthrows the four-winged leopard. But in chapter 8, the little horn develops from the head of the he-goat, who plainly represents the Greek empire. As we have already mentioned, this goat commenced its career with one horn (Alexander the Great), but then produced four others in its place. There can be no question that the little horn in chapter 8 points to a ruler of the Greek empire, that is, Antiochus

HISTORY OF KINGDOMS

Diadochi (i.e. "Successors"):

Antipater, reigned as regent 321-319 B.C.

Cassander, his son, ruled 319-317 B.C. and secured Macedonia and Greece. He assumed the title of king in 305 after he had murdered Alexander IV in 310.

Lycimachus received custody of Thrace in 323 B.C., and Asia Minor in 301, assuming the title of king in 305 B.C.

Ptolemy took over Egypt in 323 B.C.; after 301 B.C. he also took over Phoenicia and re-conquered Cyprus in 294 B.C. He also assumed the title of king in 305, expelling Demetrius Poliorcetes from Macedonia in 288, and died in 281 B.C.

Seleucus I independent king of Babylon in 311 B.C., conquered all the way to the Indus River in 302 B.C.—died in 281.

Perdiccas served earlier as regent of the empire from 323 to 321 B.C.

Antigonus I assumed position of regent in 320, fought Eumenes, killing him in 316 B.C. and then claimed all Asia under his control. He died in 301 at the Battle of Ipsus.

Demetrius Poliorcetes defeated Ptolemy at Cyprus in 306 B.C. (although Ptolemy later conquered it). Demetrius narrowly escaped from his own defeat at the Battle of Ipsus in 301 B.C.

To sum up, then, it should be understood that prior to the development of these four realms an effort was made to keep the Alexandrian empire together. First Perdiccas was chosen as regent, but he passed away in 321 B.C. After him came Antigonus I who defeated King Eumenes of Pergamum, slaying him in 316 B.C., and subsequently claimed all of Asia under his control. Eventually, however, Antigonus and his son, Demetrius Poliorcetes, were defeated by the armies of Antipater, Lycimachus, and Seleucus at the Battle of Ipsus in 301 B.C. Then, along with Ptolemy, the way was clear for each of them to claim the title of king and maintain a separate realm.

THE IMAGE OF XERXES OR AHASUERUS (485–464 B.C.) THIS RELIEF FROM HIS PALACE IN PERSEPOLIS IS SCULPTURED IN STONE AND PORTRAYS THE KING SEATED ON HIS THRONE. IN HIS RIGHT HAND IS THE ROYAL SCEPTER, IN HIS LEFT HE HOLDS A LOTUS FLOWER. IN FRONT OF HIM IS A MEDE DIGNITARY, WHO PRESSES HIS HAND OVER HIS LIPS AS SIGN OF VENERATION FOR HIS ROYAL MASTER. BEHIND THE KING STAND THE HOLDER OF HIS FAN AND HIS BODYGUARDS.

Epiphanes (cf. 8:9). The critics therefore assume that since the same term is used, the little horn in chapter 7 must refer to the same individual. This, however, can hardly be the case, since the four-winged leopard of chapter 7 (i.e., 7:24) clearly corresponds to the four-horned goat of chapter 8; that is, both represent the Greek empire which divided into four after Alexander's death. The only reasonable deduction to draw is that there are *two* little horns involved in the symbolic visions of Daniel. One of them emerges from the third empire, and the other is to emerge from the fourth. It would seem that the relationship is that of type (Antiochus IV of the third kingdom) and antitype (the Antichrist who is to arise from the latter-day form of the fourth empire). This is the only explanation which satisfies all the data and which throws light upon 11:4-45, where the figure of the historic Antiochus suddenly blends into the figure of an Antichrist who is yet to come in the end time.

Two other considerations should be adduced to show that the author regarded the Medes and Persians as constituting the one and same empire. In Dan. 6, Darius is said to be bound by "the law of the Medes and Persians," so that he could not revoke the decree consigning Daniel to the lions' den. If the author regarded Darius as ruler of an independent

TETRADRACHMA, LYSIM-ACHUS (297–281 B.C.), BEARING THE HEAD OF ALEXANDER THE GREAT DEIFIED. THE OBVERSE BEARS THE IMAGE OF ATHENA.

Median empire earlier in time than the Persian, it is impossible to explain why he would have been bound by the laws of the Persians. Second, we have the evidence of the handwriting on the wall as interpreted by Daniel in 5:28. There Daniel is represented as interpreting the inscription to Belshazzar, the last king of the first empire, that is, the kingdom of the Chaldeans. He says in interpreting the third word, *peres*, "Thy kingdom is divided, and given to the Medes and Persians." This is obviously a word play in which the term *parsîn*, or rather its singular *peres*, is derived from the verb *p^eras*, meaning "to divide or separate." But it is also explained as pointing to *pārās*, or "Persian." This can only mean that according to the author, the Chaldean empire was removed from Belshazzar as the last representative of the first empire and given to the Medes *and Persians* who constituted the second empire. This cannot mean that the rule was first given to the Medes and only later to be transmitted to the Persians, because the significant word which appeared in the handwriting on the wall was quite specifically the word "Persia." The sequence, therefore, is clear: the empire passed from the Chaldeans to the Persians. There can be no legitimate doubt that the author regarded the Persians as masters of the second empire. This being the case, we must conclude that the fourth empire indeed represented Rome.[3]

If, then, the fourth empire of chapter 2, as corroborated by the other symbolic representations of chapter 7, clearly pointed forward to the establishment of the Roman empire, it can only follow that we are dealing here with genuine predictive prophecy and not a mere *vaticinium ex eventu*. According to the Maccabean Date Theory, Daniel was composed between 168 and 165 B.C., whereas the Roman empire did not commence (for the Jews at least) until 63 B.C., when Pompey the Great took over that part of the Near East which included Palestine. To be sure, Hannibal had already been defeated by Scipio at Zama in 202 B.C., and Antiochus III had been crushed at Magnesia in 190, but the Romans had still not advanced beyond the limits of Europe by 165, except to establish a vassal kingdom in Asia Minor and a protectorate over Egypt. But certainly, as things stood in 165 B.C., no human being could have predicted with any assurance that the Hellenic monarchies of the Near East would be engulfed by the new power which had arisen in the West. No man then living could have foreseen that this Italian republic would have exerted a sway more ruthless and widespread than any

---

3. One alternative has been suggested by Zoeckler in Lange's *Commentary*, and while it has little to commend it, it is worthy of mention. Zoeckler suggests that the third empire represented that of Alexander the Great, and the fourth empire, that of the Seleucids. That is to say, one of the four main subdivisions into which the Alexandrian empire fell, namely, that established by Seleucus I, ca. 311 B.C., is construed to be the final empire in Daniel's scheme. This would mean that the third empire lasted only from 334 to 323, when Alexander died, plus twelve more years of transition. Thus it was from the fourth empire, or the dynasty of Seleucus, that Antiochus Epiphanes came in the year 175 B.C. But this identification of the fourth empire runs afoul of the fact that our author plainly states that the fourth empire was greater, stronger, and more extensive than the third (cf. Dan. 7:7). It is hardly conceivable that a mere fraction of Alexander's empire which occupied less territory and often experienced defeat on the battlefield could be considered as more fierce and powerful than the irresistible Alexander whose domain stretched from Yugoslavia to India, and who never tasted military defeat during his entire career. In the light of subsequent history, it must be conceded that the portrait of the fourth empire clearly corresponds to that of Rome and to Rome only.

empire that had ever preceded it. This one circumstance alone, then, that Daniel predicts the Roman empire, is sufficient to overthrow the entire Maccabean Date Hypothesis (which of course was an attempt to explain away the supernatural element of prediction and fulfillment). As we shall presently see, there are other remarkable predictions in this book which mark it as of divine inspiration and not a mere historical novel written in the time of Maccabees.

It should also be pointed out that the Maccabean Date Theory fails to explain how the book of Daniel ever came to be accepted by the later Jews as Holy Scripture. In Deut. 18:22 the principle was laid down: "If the thing follow not, nor come to pass, that is the thing which the Lord hath not spoken." That is to say, any person claiming to be a genuine prophet of the Lord, whose predictions of coming events do not come to pass, is to be utterly rejected. There can be no doubt that the description given in Dan. 11:40-45 relative to the latter end of the little horn does not at all correspond to the manner in which Antiochus Epiphanes met his death; there is a definite break in the prophetic revelation beginning at 11:40. This break is indicated by the words, "and at the time of the end." Those who espouse the Liberal theory can only allege that the

Maccabean author of Daniel was unsuccessful in his effort to predict the manner of Antiochus's downfall. He did his best, but it simply did not come out that way. Yet if this was actually the case, it is impossible to conceive how the Jews could have continued to regard this writing as canonical or authoritative, since it

SILVER DENARIUS, PORTRAYING THE HEAD OF POMPEY THE GREAT, (42–38 B.C.), CONQUEROR OF PALESTINE IN 63 B.C. MINTED BY HIS SON SEXTUS AFTER HIS DEATH.

contained false prophecy. If, however, the work was composed by the historic Daniel, it is easy to see how this work would have been preserved as the genuine Word of God. The fact that so many events in subsequent history were accurately predicted back in the sixth century by the historic Daniel would serve as an authentication of its trustworthiness as a divine revelation.

ADDITIONAL PROOFS OF DANIEL'S AUTHORSHIP

First of all, we have the clear testimony of the Lord Jesus Himself in the Olivet discourse. In Matt. 24:15, He refers to "the abomination of desolation, spoken of through [*dia*] Daniel the prophet." The phrase "abomination of desolation" occurs three times in Daniel (9:27; 11:31; 12:11). If these words of Christ are reliably reported, we can only conclude that He believed the historic Daniel to be the personal author of the prophecies containing this phrase. No other interpretation is possible in the light of the preposition *dia*, which refers to personal agency. It is significant that Jesus regarded this "abomination" as something to be brought to pass in a future age rather than being simply the idol of Zeus set up by Antiochus in the temple, as the Maccabean theorists insist.

Second, the author of Daniel shows such an accurate knowledge of sixth-century events as would not have been open to a second-century writer; for example, in 8:2, the city of Shushan is described as being in the province of Elam back in the time of the Chaldeans. But from the Greek and Roman historians we learn that in the Persian period Shushan, or Susa, was assigned to a new province which was named after it, Susiana, and the formerly more extensive province of Elam was restricted to the territory west of the Eulaeus River.[4] It is reasonable to conclude that only a very early author would have known that Susa was once considered part of the province of Elam.

Third, we have in chapter 9 a series of remarkable predictions which defy any other interpretation but that they point to the coming of Christ and His crucifixion ca. A.D. 30, followed by the destruction of the city of Jerusalem within the ensuing decades. In Dan. 9:25-26, it is stated that sixty-nine heptads of years (i.e., 483 years) will ensue between a "decree" to rebuild the walls of Jerusalem, and the cutting off of Messiah the Prince. In 9:25-26, we read: "Know therefore and understand, that from the going forth of the commandment to restore and to build Jerusalem unto the Messiah the Prince shall be seven weeks, and threescore and two weeks....And after threescore and two weeks shall Messiah be cut off, but not for himself: and the people of the prince that shall come shall destroy the city and the sanctuary."

There are two ways of computing these sixty-nine heptads (or 483 years). First, by starting from the decree of Artaxerxes issued to Nehemiah in 445 B.C. (cf. Neh. 2:4, 8) and reckoning the 483 years as lunar years of 360 days each,[5] which would be equivalent to 471 solar years and would result in the date A.D. 26 for the appearance of the Messiah and His "cutting off" (or crucifixion).[6] Or, more reasonably, the starting point may be identified with the decree of Artaxerxes in his seventh year, issued for the benefit of Ezra in 457 B.C. This apparently included authority for Ezra to restore and build the city of Jerusalem (as we may deduce from Ezra 7:6-7, and also 9:9, which states, "God...hath extended lovingkindness unto us in the sight of the kings of Persia, to give us a reviving, to set up the house of our God, and to repair the ruins thereof, and to give us a *wall in Judea and in Jerusalem*," ASV). Even though Ezra did not actually succeed in accomplishing the rebuilding of the walls until Nehemiah arrived eleven or twelve years later, it is logical to understand 457 B.C. as the *terminus a quo* for the decree predicted in Dan. 9:25; 483 solar years from 457 B.C. would come out to A.D. 26 as the time of Christ's ministry (or A.D. 27, since a year is gained when passing from 1 B.C. to

4. Cf. Strabo. 15:3, 12; 16:1, 17; Pliny, *Natural History*, 6:27.

5. In his *Commentary on Daniel* (sec. 683), Jerome records this tradition from Africanus, who in his *Tempora* says: "On the other hand, the interval from the twentieth year of Artaxerxes to the time of Christ completes the figure of seventy weeks, if we reckon according to the lunar computation of the Hebrews, who did not number their months according to the movement of the sun, but rather according to the moon....For according to their computation, these years can be made up of months of twenty-nine and one-half days each."

6. Note that John Davis in his *Bible Dictionary* proceeds on the basis of a lunar year of 358 days 8 5/6 hours, and thus interprets the 483 as equivalent to 469 lunar years, coming to the result A.D. 24. Yet this is two or three years before Jesus' appearance as the Messiah.

A.D. 1). Note that the wording of verse 26, "And after threescore and two weeks shall Messiah be cut off," does not compel us to understand the 483 as pinpointing the time of the actual crucifixion; it is simply that after the appearance of the Messiah, He was going to be cut off. It should be noted that in Neh. 1:3-4 Nehemiah was shocked and disheartened by the news that the walls and gates of Jerusalem had recently been destroyed (presumably by the same hostile neighboring nations as later tried to frustrate Nehemiah himself—(Neh. 2:19-20, 4:1-3; 7-23). This strongly suggests that Ezra himself had earlier attempted to rebuild but had been overcome by these malicious raiders. (It is out of the question to understand that in 446...Nehemiah could have been shocked with the news that the walls of Jerusalem had just been destroyed in 587, 140 years ago!)

Theory of Diverse Sources for the Origin of Daniel

Mention has already been made of the concessions by Hoelscher and Torrey that the Aramaic portions of the book of Dan. originated from the third century B.C., although they feel that the chapters in Hebrew were quite definitely composed by an unknown Maccabean novelist. Since the allowance of such earlier components would seem to undermine the supporting structure for the Maccabean date as a whole, it is appropriate to summarize the suggestions made by proponents of this earlier source theory and to append a few pertinent comments.

In 1909 C. C. Torrey published his view that the first half of Daniel was composed about the middle of the third century B.C., whereas the second half originated with a Maccabean author who translated chapter 1 into Hebrew and then composed chapter 7 in Aramaic in order to make it dovetail more closely with chapters 2-6. Montgomery in the ICC accepted this suggestion with this exception: he regarded chapter 7 as a composition distinct from the other two sections. Otto Eissfeldt in his *Einleitung* (1934) espoused the same view: that the first six chapters were from the third century, and the last six were from the Maccabean period and composed as a continuation of the older work.

Gustav Hoelscher in *Die Entstehung des Buches Daniel* (1919) had strongly supported the pre-Maccabean origin of chapters 1-7, demonstrating very convincingly that Nebuchadnezzar as portrayed in chapters 2-4 represented a far more enlightened and tolerant attitude toward the Jewish religion (generally speaking) than did the Greek tyrant Antiochus Epiphanes, and therefore could not have served as a type of the latter. Martin Noth in *Zur Komposition des Buches Daniel* (1926) went so far as to date the original portions of chapters 2 and 7 from the time of Alexander the Great; then, during the third century, the legends of chapters 1-6 were collected and the vision of the four kingdoms was included in a remolded form.

H. L. Ginsburg in his *"Studies in Daniel"* (cf. pp. 5ff., 27ff.) in 1948 undertook to isolate six different authors who contributed to the corpus of Daniel: chapters 1-6 were composed between 292 and 261 B.C.; chapter 2 was then subjected to reworking and insertions between 246 and 220 B.C.; chapter 7 came from the Maccabean period generally; chapter 8 was composed between 166 and 165; chapters 10-12 came from a different author from the same period; and chapter 9 came from a slightly later period than 165. H. H. Rowley in *The Unity of Daniel* (1952) conceded the earlier existence in oral form of some of the materials composing chapters 1-6, but nevertheless undertook to defend quite vigorously the essential unity of the composition of Daniel in its present literary form—that is, in the time of the Maccabees.

It should be noticed that the assignment of considerable sections of Daniel to a century or more before the time of the Maccabean revolt serves to endanger the whole hypothesis of a second-century origin as propounded by advocates of the late-date theory. Thus, if the portrait of Nebuchadnezzar greatly contrasts with the character and attitude of Antiochus Epiphanes, his relevance to the Maccabean situation becomes rather obscure. The same is true with the rest of the historical episodes in which the heathen government seems to treat the Jews with toleration and respect. Moreover it should be observed that the whole concept of *vaticinium ex eventu* is fatally compromised if Dan. 1-7 was in fact composed before the fulfilment of the political developments so explicitly foretold in those seven chapters.

30

POST-EXILIC HISTORICAL BOOKS: 1 AND 2 CHRONICLES, EZRA, NEHEMIAH, ESTHER

1 AND 2 CHRONICLES

THE HEBREW TITLE of these books is *Diḇᵉrê hāyyāmîm* or, "the accounts of the days," or, more literally, "the words of the days." The purpose of these two volumes is to review the history of Israel from the dawn of the human race to the Babylonian captivity and Cyrus's edict of restoration. This review is composed with a very definite purpose in mind, to remind the Jews of the Second Commonwealth of their great spiritual heritage and foster a deeper appreciation of the divinely ordained foundations of their theocracy as the covenant people of Jehovah. This historian's purpose is to show that the true glory of the Hebrew nation was found in its covenant relationship to God, as safeguarded by the prescribed forms of worship in the temple and administered by the divinely ordained priesthood and the divinely authorized dynasty of David. Always the emphasis is upon that which is sound and valid in Israel's past, as furnishing a reliable basis for the task of national reconstruction which lay before them. Great stress is placed upon the rich heritage of Israel and its unbroken connection with the patriarchal beginnings (hence the prominence accorded to genealogical lists).

OUTLINE OF 1 AND 2 CHRONICLES

It is to be noted that 1 Chronicles carries the narrative up to the death of David; 2 Chronicles continues with the reign of Solomon, the temple builder, and finishes with the Exile and Cyrus's decree of restoration. Originally the two books were accounted as one, but as early as the Septuagint (which gives them the title *Paraleipomenōn*, "of things omitted") there seems to have been a division into two parts. We follow here the brief outline of M. F. Unger (in IGOT, p. 407).

I. Genealogies from Adam to David, 1 Chron. 1:1–9:44

A. From Adam to Jacob, 1:1–2:2
B. Jacob's generations, 2:2–9:44

II. History of King David, 10:1–29:30

A. The death of Saul, 10:1-14
B. Capture of Zion, and David's heroes, 11:1–12:40
C. David's prosperous reign, 13:1–22:1
D. David's accomplishments on behalf of ritualistic worship, 22:2– 29:30

III. History of King Solomon, 2 Chron. 1:1–9:31

A. Solomon's wealth and wisdom, 1:1-17
B. His building and dedication of the temple, 2:1–7:22
C. His various activities and death, 8:1–9:31

IV. History of the Kings of Judah, 10:1–36:23

A. From Rehoboam to Zedekiah, 10:1–36:21
B. The edict of Cyrus, 36:22-23

AUTHORSHIP AND DATE OF CHRONICLES

Like the other historical books, Chronicles does not specify the name of its author. Internal evidence points to a period between 450 and 425 B.C. as its time of composition. It is quite possible that the Talmudic tradition (*Baba Bathra*, 15*a*) is correct in assigning the authorship to Ezra. As the chief architect of the spiritual and moral revival of the Second Commonwealth, he would have had every incentive to produce a historical survey of this sort. As a Levite from the priestly line, his viewpoint would have been in perfect agreement with that of the author of this work, and he would be very apt to lay the stress just where the Chronicler has. It is pertinent to note that there was embodied in 2 Macc. 2:13-15 a tradition that Governor Nehemiah owned a considerable library: "He, founding a library, gathered together the books about the kings and prophets, and the books of David and letters of the kings about sacred gifts." If Nehemiah did possess such a sizable collection of reference works, it might very well be that his close collaborator, Ezra, would have had ready access to these reference works and used them in the compilation of Chronicles.

E. J. Young favors the theory of Ezra's authorship, although he has some reservations about the last two verses of the book (containing Cyrus's decree) which give indications of being earlier than the first chapter of Ezra. M. F. Unger inclines to the same view, although he seems to entertain the possibility that the books were not written until the first half of the fourth century (IGOT, p. 407). J. E. Steinmueller discounts the Talmudic tradition and regards the author as unknown.[1] D. N. Freedman espouses the

---

1. *Catholic Bible Quarterly*, 23:436-42.

view that the basic work of the Chronicler, starting with 1 Chron. 10, dates from about 515, when the second temple had just been completed. He was doubtless a colaborer with the prophets Haggai and Zechariah, who regarded Zerubbabel as the legitimate heir of the divine promise to the Davidic dynasty.[2]

Among Liberal scholars there is no unanimity as to the time of composition. W. F. Albright was earlier inclined to the view that the Ezra who composed the work lived in the reign of Artaxerxes II in the first half of the fourth century.[3] Many others place the time of the composition in the second half; that is, 350-300 B.C. Still others, like Pfeiffer, make it as late as 250 or even 200 B.C. Supposing that the testimony of 1 Chron. 3 (according to a variant attested by the Septuagint, Vulgate, and Syriac) points to eleven generations after the time of Zerubbabel, W. Rudolph assigned the nucleus of Chronicles to a period around 400-380 B.C. This was later supplemented by material too varied and contradictory to have proceeded from a single editor (Wilhelm Rudolph, *Chronikbücher*, 1955).

As already suggested, one of the most frequently used arguments in favor of the late authorship of Chronicles is to be found in 1 Chron. 3:19-24, which according to the MT indicates six generations after Zerubbabel. But actually, as Young points out, the listings in Chronicles do not always give straight series of successive generations from father to son, but some of them include several sons born to the parent previously named.[4] In this particular instance it is possible that the genealogy is carried on only to the second generation after Zerubbabel. The text indicates that Hananiah was the son of Zerubbabel, and that Pelatiah and Jeshaiah were merely his grandsons. None of the names following these (from v. 21 and thereafter) have anything to do with the genealogy of Zerubbabel; hence this verse can hardly be regarded as furnishing real support for a late date of composition.

For some reason, another verse which is often referred to as proving a late date is 1 Chron. 29:7, which mentions a sum of money in darics (*adarkōnim*). Since the daric apparently received its name from Darius I (522-485 B.C.), its mention in connection with the time of King David must be regarded as anachronistic. At the same time it must be conceded that darics had for many decades been in circulation before Ezra's

---

2. The most persuasive evidence that Freedman advances for this position is to be found in the remarkable gap in the record of Ezra between the work of Zerubbabel and Joshua and the advent of Ezra himself. If the Chronicler composed his original work shortly after the completion of the temple, this gap admits of easy explanation. The Chronicler's work came to an end with Ezra 3. The Aramaic documents of Ezra 4-6 constitute a later supplement. From chapter 7 to the end of the book we have the personal memoirs of Ezra himself, who, according to Freedman was roughly contemporaneous with Nehemiah. Ezra's own emphasis, as gathered from his long prayer recorded in Neh. 9:6-37, was upon the tradition of Moses and the Exodus; he scarcely mentioned the dynasty of David at all. This furnishes a sharp contrast with the Chronicler, who showed the keenest interest in the Davidic dynasty and the Davidic promise (2 Sam. 7). It is therefore inconceivable, according to Freedman, that Ezra himself could have been the author of the books of Chronicles (*Catholic Biblical Quarterly* 23: 441).

3. But cf. last paragraph under "The Authorship and Date of Ezra-Nehemiah" in this chapter.

4. E. J. Young, IOT, p. 383.

time, and there would be no difficulty in his referring to them as a current unit of exchange. Since the daric represented a well-known weight in gold, there is no particular reason why Ezra could not have computed the amount of bullion actually contributed by the Israelite princes for the service of the temple and then have converted the sum into an equivalent number of darics as more meaningful to the public of Ezra's own generation.[5]

SOURCES OF CHRONICLES

Well over half the material contained in Chronicles is paralleled by other books in the Old Testament, especially Genesis, Samuel, and Kings. The author mentions many of his extracanonical sources by name: It is much disputed whether the Chronicler actually copied from Samuel and Kings; most authorities assume that he did so (cf. *New Bible Commentary*). Others, like Zoeckler (in Lange's *Commentary*, pp. 18-20) and E. J. Young (IOT, pp. 384-85), believe that he copied from common earlier sources, but that differences in detail and arrangement preclude the possibility of any direct borrowing.

HISTORICAL RELIABILITY OF CHRONICLES

There has been a tendency among Liberal critics to challenge the reliability of nearly every statement in Chronicles which is not also found in Samuel or Kings.[6] Such skepticism is altogether unjustified, inasmuch as the Chronicler cites many

EXTRACANONICAL SOURCES OF CHRONICLES

Source	Scripture
Book of the Kings of Judah and Israel	2 Chron. 16:11; 35:27
Story of the Book of the Kings	1 Chron. 9:1
Words of Uzziah composed by Isaiah	2 Chron. 32:32
Words of Shemaiah the Prophet	2 Chron. 12:15
and of Iddo the Seer	2 Chron. 13:22
Midrash of the Prophet Iddo	2 Chron. 9:29; 13:22
Words of Jehu the son of Hanani	2 Chron. 20:34
Words of Hozai (or the seer)	2 Chron. 33:18,19
Book of Nathan the prophet	1 Chron. 29:29

5. The more recent evidence points to the possible identification of this term *adarkōnim*, as well as the *darkᵉmōnim* of Neh. 7:70, with Greek drachmae rather than Persian darics. Cf. point 6 on p. 462.

6. Recent archaeological evidence, however, tends to support the accuracy of the biblical text in 2 Chronicles, "The fortified coastal settlements, together with fortresses on the routes to the hill settlements, reflect a state-organized strategic plan probably undertaken during the reign of Uzziah, who, according to the Bible, built towers in the wilderness." (BAR, vol. 19, no. 4, p. 41). DeVaux's finds fit nicely with the Biblical description of the reign of Uzziah (770-739 B.C.). In 2 Chronicles 26:10 we learn that Uzziah "built towers in the wilderness" (BAR, vol. 19, no. 4, p. 38).

sources which are not mentioned in Samuel or Kings and which therefore would be apt to include information not discoverable in the latter. It is noteworthy also that these additional items by and large conform to the basic purposes of the book as outlined in the opening paragraph of this chapter. Thus the concern for religious institutions, as essential for the perpetuating of a true theocracy, leads to a mention of the temple musicians and singers, the priestly genealogies, and cultic developments of various sorts. So also the concern for great decisions of faith leads to inclusion of additional information about kings and prophets who had these decisions to confront. Thus there is also mention of Rehoboam facing Shishak's invasion and Asa confronting Zerah the Ethiopian; the attempt of Uzziah to attain security by a large standing army and ambitious mercantile enterprises; the latter-day repentance of Mannasseh;[7] the great national Passover of Josiah, and so on. Additional information is given concerning the prophets Samuel, Gad, Nathan, Ahijah, Shemaiah, Hanani, Jehu, and even Elijah. Other prophets are referred to who do not appear elsewhere in Scripture: Asaph, Heman, Jeduthun, Iddo, the two prophets named Oded, and also Jehaziel and Eliezer.

True to his basic principles, the Chronicler omits from the time of David onward all that is not strictly connected with the Davidic dynasty, inasmuch as that was the only valid line for the theocracy. Thus the crimes of David, Amnon, Absalom, Adonijah, and Solomon are largely omitted because they contributed nothing of significance to the upbuilding or preservation of the theocracy. So also the Northern Kingdom is alluded to only as it came in contact with the kingdom of Judah, because the Ten Tribes had no valid king ruling over them by God's authority, and because they upheld a heretical schism which largely cut them off from worship at the Jerusalem temple.

If it is true that the genealogies in this book are often sketchy and incomplete, it may well be that the author assumed other sources of knowledge (both Samuel and Kings and the noncanonical books) were usually accessible and well known to his public. Thus in 2 Chron. 26:17 and 31:10 Jehoiada and two Azariahs are omitted. Of course we cannot rule out completely the possibility that subsequent copyists of Ezra's manuscript inadvertently omitted some of these names. W. J. Beecher (in ISBE) suggested that perhaps the Chronicler had recourse to fragmentary clay tablets, ostraca, and papyri, and that in some cases he copied them just as they were, failing to indicate the gaps or lacunae by dots and dashes as modern copyists would have done.

There are several indications of careless transmission of the text of Chronicles. Thus we find a goodly number of differences in the spelling of names, as compared with the spelling found in Genesis, Samuel, and Kings. Some of these errors are easily explained by the mistaking of similar letters for each other such as *daleth* (the letter *d*) and *rēsh* (the letter *r*). "Dodanim" in Gen. 10:4 appears as "Rodanim" in 1 Chron. 1:7

---

7. The account in 2 Chron. 33 concerning Manasseh's imprisonment in Babylon has been treated by many scholars as late and apocryphal. But it receives confirmation from a text of Essarhaddon which states: "I summoned the kings of Syria and those across the sea—Baal king of Tyre, Manasseh king of Judah...Musuri king of Moab...twenty kings in all; I gave them their orders" (D. D. Luckenbill, *Ancient Records of Assyria and Babylonia* [Chicago: U. Chicago, 1927] vol. 2, sec. 690).

(ASV). (In this particular instance the spelling in Chronicles seems superior, since the probable reference is to the inhabitants of Rhodes.) Or again, *mēm* is confused with *hē* in "Abijah," the Chronicler's spelling for "Abijam" (although in this case the two letters never resembled each other in appearance). Since the vowel points were not supplied by Jewish scribes until A.D. 600 or later, we should not be surprised at discrepancies in the vowels contained by these divergent proper names.

Inferiority in textual transmission also appears in the numerals given in statistical statements. Liberal critics have tried to show a consistent tendency on the part of the Chronicler to exaggerate the numbers wherever a discrepancy occurs between Chronicles and Kings. This is alleged to represent a consistent policy of glorifying the past by deliberate exaggeration. Actual check of the textual data, however, indicates the unsoundness of these conclusions. In the vast number of instances where numerical values are given in Chronicles, Kings, and Samuel, they are in perfect agreement. There are only eighteen or twenty examples of discrepancy. Of these about one-third involving precisely the same statistics display a larger number in Samuel or Kings than in Chronicles (cf. 1 Chron. 11:11 and 2 Sam. 23:8; 1 Chron. 21:5*b* and 2 Sam. 24:9*b*; 2 Chron. 3:16*b* and 1 Kings 7:20*b*, cf. v. 42; 2 Chron. 8:10 and 1 Kings 9:23; 2 Chron. 36:9 and 2 Kings 24:8). Often the discrepancy is of a very minor character in so far as numbers are concerned, and the great majority of them are explainable as not referring to precisely the same group of people or things at precisely the same time or in precisely the same category. Occasionally the figure given in Chronicles is lower and more

SOLOMON'S GATE, THE WALL AT HAZOR

Solomon built a casemate wall structure in his fortifications at Hazor. These parallel walls were from 5 to 7 ft. apart and were each 3 to 5 ft. thick, forming rooms between the walls.

credible than that in the parallel passage. For example, the number of horse stalls Solomon built is stated by 1 Kings 4:26 to have been 40,000, but the number appears as 4,000 in 2 Chron. 9:25. Or again, the number of enemies the battle hero Jashobeam slew in a single engagement is given as 300 in 1 Chron. 11:11 but 800 in 2 Sam. 23:8 (ASV, marg.).

In dealing with this matter of numerical discrepancy, we must take account of the type of notation used in ancient times. Keil points out that practically all the suspiciously high numbers are expressed in thousands as if they were round numbers based upon the approximate estimate of contemporaries. He suggests that the numbers themselves were undoubtedly expressed by alphabetic letters and in that form were most liable to corruption by later copyists, especially where they had to deal with a manuscript that was worn and smudged. (It is interesting to note that the earliest Jewish currency, certainly from the time of the First Revolt in A.D. 67, if not from the Hasmonean period in the second century B.C., employed alphabetic letters for numbers, especially in the recording of dates.) Thus exaggerated figures like 50,070 recorded by 1 Samuel 6:19 as the number slain by the Lord at Beth-shemesh are to be explained by a garbling of the digits. Note that the alphabetic system of numerical notation needed only a few dots above or below to multiply by one thousand; thus the letter *nun* with two dots above it would signify 50,000 (cf. Gesenius-Kautzsch, *Hebrew Grammar*, 5:1).[8]

The discovery of the Elephantine Papyri, however, gives rise to the possibility that while the Hebrews used a numerical notation system to indicate large numbers, they may have used vertical or horizontal strokes rather than alphabetic letters. In these papyri, for example, the digits up to ten are indicated by vertical strokes with a special sign for the number five. The numbers ten and above are indicated by horizontal strokes; and there are special signs for hundreds and thousands derived from the initial letter of names of these numbers.[9] In the light of all this evidence it is impossible to construct an airtight case proving any original discrepancy between the autograph manuscript of Chronicles and the relevant passages in the other canonical books. It is safe to say that all the so-called discrepancies that have been alleged are capable of resolution either by textual criticism or by contextual exegesis.

We should not close this discussion without mentioning one interesting observation from W. F. Albright. He states that the critics were mistaken in regarding the Chronicler to be in error in tracing the musical guilds of the temple back to King David. "We can now

FIRST REVOLT SHEKEL (68 A.D.) IMPRESSION OF POMEGRANATES; A CHALICE WITH A DATE OR AARON'S BUDDING ROD ON THE REVERSE (INSCRIPTION IN HEBREW, "JERUSALEM THE HOLY").

8. C. F. Keil discusses this problem at some length in his commentary on Chronicles, pp. 43-45.

9. A good discussion of these numbers and their bearing upon numerical discrepancies in Nehemiah and Ezra is to be found in the article by H. L. Allrik, "The Lists of Zerubbabel and the Hebrew Numeral Notation" in BASOR, no. 136 (Dec. 1954), pp. 21-27.

say with entire confidence that the principal musical guilds traced their origin back to Canaanite times long before David. The Canaanites of the second millennium had developed music to a high point, as we know from Egyptian sources, which often refer to Canaanite musical instruments and portray Canaanite musicians. The names of the putative founders of these guilds, Heman, Ethan (Jeduthun), Asaph, are demonstrably of the Canaanite type, and the proverbial wise men, Calcol (ASV) and Darda, associated with them in 1 Kings 4:31, bear names of a type particularly common among musicians."[10] Thus, Calcol appears in a thirteenth-century Egyptian inscription recently discovered at Megiddo, as the name of a great Canaanite musician at Ashkelon.

EZRA AND NEHEMIAH

The name *Ezra* seems to be an Aramaic form of the Hebrew *'ezer,* "help." The name *Nehemiah,* Hebrew *Neḥem-Yah,* means "The Comfort of Yahweh." These two books are treated as one by the Hebrew scribes; there is no gap in the MT between the end of Ezra 10 and the commencement of Neh. 1, and the verse statistics are given for both at the end of Nehemiah. The theme of this composite book is a record of the reconstruction of the Hebrew theocracy upon the physical and spiritual foundations of the past. As God protected His remnant from the hatred of external foes, so also He delivered them from the insidious corruption of the false brethren within the commonwealth.

OUTLINE OF EZRA AND NEHEMIAH

I. First return of the exiles, Ezra 1:1–2:70

II. Restoration of the worship of Jehovah, 3:1–6:22

III. Second return under Ezra, 7:1–10:44

IV. Restoration of the city walls, Neh 1:1–7:73

V. Reforms of Ezra and Nehemiah, 8:1–13:31

As was mentioned in the chapter on the canon, Ezra and Nehemiah were regarded as a single book by the earliest authorities, such as Josephus, who gave the number of the Old Testament books as twenty-two. Christian authorities like Melito of Sardis (quoted by Eusebius) and Jerome followed this same tradition. The LXX also grouped the two books as one, calling the canonical Ezra-Nehemiah Esdras B or 2 Esdras, in contradistinction to the apocryphal 1 Esdras. The Vulgate, however, divided them into 1 Ezra and 2 Ezra. The soundness of this division appears from the duplicate list of returning Jews as recorded in Ezra 2 and Neh. 7, for it is difficult to imagine why the same list should have been given twice in the same original work.

10. Albright, "The Old Testament and Archaeology," in *Old Testament Commentary,* ed. Alleman and Flack, p. 63.

AUTHORSHIP AND DATE OF EZRA AND NEHEMIAH

On the assumption that Artaxerxes mentioned in Ezra 7:1 was Artaxerxes I Longimanus, Ezra's arrival at Jerusalem must have occurred in 457 B.C. (the seventh year of the king, Ezra 7:8). Thus Ezra's career at Jerusalem commenced twelve years before that of Nehemiah, who did not come until the twentieth year, or 445 B.C. Ezra himself undoubtedly wrote most of the book named after him. (Note the use of *I* in Ezra 7-10.) But he evidently incorporated into the final edition the personal memoirs of Nehemiah (i.e., the book of Nehemiah) including even his form of the list of returnees. Using Nehemiah's library facilities, Ezra probably composed Chronicles during this same period.

As already suggested, Albright formerly placed Ezra in the reign of Artaxerxes II Mnemon, 404-359; but this theory would render passages like Neh. 8:2 quite spurious, since they mention Ezra as Nehemiah's contemporary. It would also conflict with the evidence of the Elephantine Papyri, which mention the high priest Johanan and Sanballat, the governor of Samaria. This Johanan was a grandson of the Eliashib mentioned in Neh. 3:1 and 20, and Nehemiah was a contemporary of Eliashib.[11] It therefore follows that when the biblical record speaks of Nehemiah going to Jerusalem in the twentieth year of Artaxerxes (Neh. 1:1) and again in his thirty-second year (Neh. 13:6), the reference must be to Artaxerxes I (yielding the date 445 and 433 respectively) rather than the reign of Artaxerxes II (which would result in the dates 384 and 372 respectively—far too late for the high priesthood of Johanan).

It is interesting to note that in his most recent pronouncement on the subject, Albright receded somewhat from his earlier position. He said: "We are very unsatisfactorily informed about the date of Ezra. The most recent evidence favors a date for Ezra's mission in or about the thirty-seventh year of Artaxerxes; that is, about 428 B.C.E. It is not clear whether Nehemiah was in Jerusalem at the time; he is not specifically mentioned in the Ezra memoirs proper; the evidence is conflicting. There can, however, be little doubt that his influence was directly responsible for the royal rescript giving Ezra extensive powers in connection with his plan to reform the religious organization at Jerusalem."[12]

More recently John Bright has defended this "thirty-seventh year" theory on the following grounds.[13]

1. If Ezra had really arrived in the seventh year of Artaxerxes, it would have meant that thirteen years had elapsed before he, whose express purpose in coming to

11. "Evidently, the Sanballat referred to [in the Elephantine Papyri] is the same man as we meet in the days of Nehemiah, but now grown older. We are led to the conclusion that Nehemiah lived before 407 B.C. Since he went to Jerusalem in the twentieth year of King Artaxerxes, we look for a king of this name who ruled prior to 407 B.C. This is, of course, Artaxerxes I, who reigned from 465 to 425 B.C., which means that Nehemiah's arrival in Jerusalem is to be dated in 445 B.C. In a most exciting way, the discovery of some Aramaic papyri in Egypt, hundreds of miles away from Palestine, enables us to give an exact date to an important Bible character." (See J. A. Thompson, *Archaeology and the Old Testament*, p. 78, for further discussion.)

12. Albright, quoted in L. Finkelstein, *The Jews* (New York: Harper, 1955), p. 53.

13. Bright, *A History of Israel*, pp. 377-78.

Jerusalem had been to teach the Torah (Ezra 7:10), got around to reading the Torah to the people (as recorded in Neh. 8:1-8). Yet Neh. 8 only records a solemn reading of the law in a public meeting on the occasion of the Feast of Tabernacles. It by no means implies that Ezra had not been diligently teaching the law to smaller groups of disciples and Levites during the preceding twelve years.

2. If Ezra's reforms, as listed in Ezra 9 and 10, really preceded those of Nehemiah, then we are forced to "the conclusion that Ezra in one way or another failed." Presumably, therefore, these reforms of Ezra (regarding intermarriage with the heathen) must have been contemporaneous with those of Nehemiah (who took corrective measures regarding to usury in chap. 5, and in chap. 13 regarding the temple quarters improperly granted to Tobiah the Ammonite, the neglect of the payment of tithes, the desecration of the sabbath, and intermarriage with foreign women). But it should be noted that it is only the evil of mixed marriages which was dealt with by both Ezra (ca. 457 B.C.) and Nehemiah (ca. 434). It is naive to suppose that in an interval of twenty-three years, this abuse could not have normally arisen again, so as to require renewed attention on Nehemiah's part. It is altogether unwarranted, therefore, to describe this as a "failure."

3. When Ezra first came to Jerusalem, it is alleged, he found the city "inhabited and relatively secure," whereas Nehemiah found it "largely in ruins." Nowhere does Nehemiah state that Jerusalem was not inhabited or that it was largely in ruins. What it does explain is that the walls of the city had not been successfully restored and that the gates had been burned with fire (Neh. 1:3-4). The same was true of both Berlin and London after the Second World War; yet who would deduce from this that those cities were not inhabited?

The unhappy tidings concerning the walls and gates came to Nehemiah as a sore disappointment (Neh. 1:3-4) and could have had no reference to the Chaldean destruction way back in 587 B.C. 141 years earlier. It seems clear therefore, an effort must have been made, undoubtedly under the leadership of Ezra, to rebuild the walls and the gates and it had been thwarted by the hostile action of Judah's enemies who lived nearby and later who threatened Nehemiah himself when he came back to do the job.

Nehemiah had to bring pressure upon the outlying cities to contribute more population for the proper maintenance and defense of the newly fortified capital (chap. 11), but this was a measure dictated by military considerations. The record in the book of Ezra nowhere implies that the old city limits of Jerusalem were completely repopulated in his day. It seems altogether likely that the hostile neighbors — the Samaritans, Amonites, Edomites, etc.—had been responsible for the destruction of the efforts of rebuilding which had begun under Ezra's leadership. Ezra apparently had received permission to rebuild the walls and gates, (cf. Ezra 9:9). Ezra, of course, had no adequate army troops to ward off aggression—such as Nehemiah was later

NEHEMIAH'S WALL
EXCAVATIONS AT THE CITY OF DAVID HAVE
REVEALED A SECTION OF NEHEMIAH'S WALL
(NEH. 4:6, 6:15).

able to field against the enemy. [14]

4. The fact that Neh. 12:26 lists the name of Nehemiah before that of Ezra is supposed to prove that he preceded Ezra in point of time. But quite obviously the reason his name was mentioned first is that he was the head of the state, as governor appointed by Artaxerxes, and therefore outranked Ezra, who was only the spiritual leader of the community.

5. It should be observed that the supposition that "seventh year" in Ezra 7:7 was an error for "thirty-seventh year" is greatly embarrassed by the fact that Nehemiah's reforms of chapter 13 were apparently carried out in the "thirty-second year" of Artaxerxes (Neh 13:6). It seems far more improbable that the measures against intermarriage with idolaters would have to be repeated by Ezra within the short space of five years after Nehemiah had dealt with this problem in 445-444, than that Nehemiah should have faced the issue anew twenty-three years after Ezra's reform.

The only reasonable conclusion which remains, therefore, is that Ezra returned in 458 or 457 B.C., and that Nehemiah's first governorship came in 445, and his second in 433. This alone does justice to all the testimony of the biblical texts themselves.

CRITICAL OBJECTIONS TO THE HISTORICITY AND AUTHENTICITY OF EZRA AND NEHEMIAH

1. In order to show a late third-century date (or even later), many critics have made use of two names mentioned incidentally in these books, that of Johanan (Ezra 10:6) and of Jaddua (Neh. 12:11). As has been suggested, Johanan was the "son" of the Eliashib who was mentioned as Nehemiah's contemporary in Neh. 3:1.[15] Now the Elephantine Papyri mention a high priest Johanan who was the grandson of Eliashib and who lived somewhat later than Nehemiah's time. E. J. Young raises some question (IOT, p. 375) as to whether the Johanan of Ezra 10:6 (into whose apartment Ezra went in order to mourn and fast) was the same one as the grandson of Eliashib. He feels it more likely that he was the son of the Eliashib mentioned in Neh. 13:4 and 7, rather than a grandson (although the Hebrew *ben* can indicate the third generation as well as

---

14. For a full discussion, cf. EBD, p. 290.
15. A fine recent discussion is contributed by Edwin M. Yamauchi in "The Reverse Order of Ezra/Nehemiah Reconsidered," in *Themelios*, vol. 5, no. 3 (1980), pp. 7-13. Note especially p. 9 and F. M. Cross's geneological table showing 2 Eliashibs, 3 Johanans, and 2 Jadduas.

the second). On the other hand, Young concedes, he might have been the grandson who in his younger years had not yet attained the high priestly status; nevertheless as a member of the high priestly family he might have been expected to have an apartment assigned to him in the temple precincts.

GOLD STATER
WITH A PORTRAIT OF
APOLLO DURING THE
REIGN OF PHILIP II
OF MACEDON
(CA. 345 B.C.)

More serious objections to the historical accuracy of Nehemiah arise from the mention of Jaddua. Josephus (*Antiquities* 11.8.4) states that the name of the high priest at the time of Alexander the Great in 330 B.C. was Jaddua, and the inference has therefore been drawn that the mention of him in Neh. 12:11 betrays the fact that Nehemiah must have been composed long after the time of the historical Nehemiah himself. The facts are as follows. The high priestly line beginning with the time of the return from exile in 536 B.C. included the following succession: Jeshua, the father of Joiakim, the father of Eliashib, the father of Jehoiada or Joiada, the father of Jonathan and Johanan (younger contemporaries of Nehemiah, Neh. 13:28) and then Jaddua, the son of Jonathan (Neh. 12:11). If Johanan was twenty years of age in 456, he would have been sixty-eight by the time Elephantine Letter No. 30 (the Cowley edition) was written.[16] If Eliashib was twenty-five when Jehoiada was born and fifty when Johanan was born, then he would have been eighty by 446 and still have been able to furnish leadership in the building of the priests' section of the Jerusalem wall. It follows that Jaddua could hardly have been born later than 420 or 410 B.C., and he would therefore have been anywhere from eighty to ninety by the time of Alexander the Great. E. J. Young therefore suggests that Nehemiah may have lived to see Jaddua in his youth. On the other hand, it is quite possible, as R. D. Wilson points out (ISBE, p. 1084a), that

KINGS OF MEDO-PERSIA

King	Date (b.c.)
Cyrus II	558-529
Cambyses II	529-523
Pseudo-Smerids	523-522
Darius I	522-485
Xerxes I	485-464
Artaxerxes I	464-424
Darius II	423-406
Artaxerxes II	404-359

16. Letter No. 30 was addressed by Jedoniah, religious leader of the Elephantine Jews, to Gov. Bagohi (also vocalized as Bigvai) of Judea, complaining that Johanan, the high priest at Jerusalem, had ignored the need for rebuilding the recently destroyed temple in Elephantine.

Josephus's account is not altogether trustworthy. In the same chapter Josephus speaks of the demonstrably fifth-century characters Sanballat[17] and Manasseh as being with Jaddua, and this leads to the suspicion that Josephus somehow garbled his sources and involved himself in anachronisms. It may therefore have been a descendant of Jaddua who actually greeted Alexander the Great when he entered Jerusalem. In any event, the evidence above cited is by no means strong enough to overthrow the historical credibility of the books of Ezra and Nehemiah.

2. Some critics have pointed to another expression as a betrayal of a late date of composition: "Darius the Persian" (Neh. 12:22). The argument runs that since Darius was described as a Persian, this would indicate an author living in the Greek period, after Alexander's conquest of Asia. This however is by no means a necessary conclusion. He may well have been so designated to distinguish him from the earlier Darius the Mede referred to in Dan. 6.

Similarly, the title "the king of Persia," which is found in Ezra 1:1 and other passages, has been condemned by some authorities as unhistorical for the Persian period. More recent investigation, however, has shown that the title "the king of Persia" was employed by at least eighteen different authors in nineteen different documents and in thirty eight different references dating from the Persian period, and that, too, in reference to at least six different Persian kings. There are few other "scholarly" objections which have been so thoroughly refuted by archaeology as this one.

3. Objections have been raised on the ground of variations discoverable in the two copies of the decree of Cyrus, the Hebrew version in Ezra 1 and the Aramaic version in Ezra 6. But it should be observed that the edict recorded in Ezra 6 was found in Ecbatana in Persia, whereas that of Ezra 1 was promulgated in Babylon. It is legitimate to infer that the Aramaic copy was a file abstract of the edict for preservation in the archives; the Hebrew form doubtless represented the actual wording as it was delivered to the Jews themselves. It is interesting to observe that it shows a deference to the God of the Jews quite similar to that deference which Cyrus expressed to Marduk of the Babylonians when he promulgated an edict of religious freedom for the Babylonian populace (cf. Pritchard, ANET, p. 316).

4. It was formerly thought that the Aramaic portions of Ezra (i.e., the correspondence and decrees recorded in chaps. 4-7) reflected a later period of Aramaic than that which a fifth-century author would have used. But as Albright points out (in Alleman and Flack, p. 154), the Elephantine Papyri demonstrate that the Aramaic of Ezra is indeed characteristic of the fifth century (apart from the few modernized spellings) and that the letters which Ezra quotes are very similar in style and language to those emanating from fifth-century Egypt. He goes on to say, "The still unpublished letters in Mittwoch's hands will add substantially to the number of parallels and will deal the

17. Note, however, that an Aramaic papyrus published in 1962 and dating from 375-335 B.C., makes it clear that there were *three* Sanballats: one contemporary with Nehemiah, another contemporary with the Elephantine Papyri (ca. 400 B.C.), and a third contemporary with Alexander the Great (ca. 330 B.C.) (Cf. E. Yamauchi, "Stones, Scripts and Scholars," in *Christianity Today*, Feb. 14, 1970).

coup de grâce to Torrey's view that there are numerous Greek words in the Aramaic of Ezra."

5. Objection has been raised to apparent anachronisms in Ezra 4, which passes from a reference to Cyrus the Great (558-529) to Xerxes (485-464) to Artaxerxes I (464-424), and then to Darius I (522-485). It is urged that such confusion in the order of monarchs could only arise

TETRADRACHMA (SHEKEL) MINTED BY PTOLEMY I KING OF EGYPT (AND PALESTINE) WITH PORTRAIT OF ALEXANDER THE GREAT IN AN ELEPHANT HEAD-DRESS (CA. 300 B.C.)

in a late production in which the author had forgotten the true succession of kings. But this conclusion cannot successfully be maintained in the light of internal evidence. It is perfectly apparent from Ezra 4:5 that the author was aware that King Darius reigned between Cyrus and Xerxes "to frustrate their purpose, all the days of Cyrus...even until the reign of Darius king of Persia. And in the reign of Ahasuerus, in the beginning of his reign, wrote they an accusation against the inhabitants of Judah and Jerusalem" (ASV). A careful study of the chapter reveals that verses 5-23 constitute a long parenthesis dealing not with the building of the temple but rather with the erection of the walls of the city. This material is introduced at this point simply to indicate the malignity of Judah's adversaries.[18] We are not to understand the opposition of Rehum and Shimshai as arising in the 520s, but rather in the late 460s, early in the reign of Artaxerxes I. In 4:24 the narrative is brought back to the point at which verse 3 had left it, that is, at the time when the temple had not yet been rebuilt. In other words, we are not to understand Ezra's purpose here as a strictly chronological account, but rather a history of the opposition to the building of the city walls from the time of Cyrus to the reign of Artaxerxes. He follows a topical order rather than chronological. Since the letter quoted in 4:11-16 makes no reference at all to the rebuilding of the temple, but only to the erection of the walls, it is quite evident that the temple had already been completed (an event which took place in 516 B.C.) and that the reference here is to an attempt made in the beginning of Artaxerxes' reign to hinder the repair of the fortifications of Jerusalem itself.

6. Some writers hold that the reference to Greek drachmas in Neh. 7:71 (*dark°mōnîm*, Hebrew) is evidence of authorship during the Greek period. But as J. P. Free points out (ABH, p. 253), Greek drachmas have been discovered at the Persian level of the excavations at Beth-zur. Apparently the enterprising merchantmen of Hellas had extended trade relations even to the Near East by the fifth century B.C. W. F. Albright (IBL, [June 1942], p. 126) refers to the evidence of the Elephantine Papyri for the existence of the drachma standard even in Egypt at that period.

18. As for one of Judah's most determined opponents, Gashmu (mentioned in Neh. 2:19; 6:1-2, 6) the Arabian, note the recent discovery of some silver bowls at an Egyptian shrine in the northeast Delta region which bear the name of "Qaynu, son of Geshem, king of Qedar." Thus we know from what capital in Arabia this princeling ruled, namely Qedar in the northwest. (Cf. I. Rabinowitz, *Journal of Near Eastern Studies*, 15 [1956]:2-9; and K. A. Kitchen, AOOT, p. l59.)

ESTHER

The name *'Estēr* is apparently derived from the Persian word for star, *stara*. Esther's Hebrew name was *Hᵃdassâ (from hâdassâ,* meaning "myrtle." The theme of this short book is an illustration of the overruling providence of the sovereign God who delivers and preserves His peo-

TETRADRACHMA MINTED BY LYSI-MACHUS OF THRACE, OBVERSE BEARING THE IMAGE OF ALEXANDER THE GREAT WITH A RAM'S HORN HEAD-DRESS (CA. 300 B.C.)

ple from the malice of the heathen who would plot their destruction. Although there is no explicit mention of the name of God, in this book, nothing could be clearer than the irresistible power of His omnipotent rule, watching over His covenant people, preserving them from the malignity of Satan in his vain attempt to work through Haman and accomplish the annihilation of the Jewish nation.

While it is not easy to account for the absence of God's name in this narrative; the best explanation available is that the account deals principally with those Jews who had passed up their opportunity of returning to the land of promise and chose to remain among the Gentiles after the return of the faithful remnant in 536 B.C. It is certain that all the acts of this gripping drama take place in Gentile territory; it is also certain that the overruling providence of God is definitely implied in 4:14: "For if thou altogether holdest thy peace at this time, then will relief and deliverance arise to the Jews from another place...and who knoweth whether thou art not come to the kingdom for such a time as this?" (ASV).

OUTLINE OF ESTHER

I. The feast of Ahasuerus and the divorce of Vashti, 1:1-22

II. Choice of Esther as queen, 2:1-23

III. Haman's plot to destroy Mordecai and the Jews, 3:1-15

IV. Mordecai's persuasion of Esther to intervene, 4:1-17

V. Esther's successful petition to the king, 5:1–7:10

VI. Downfall of Haman and deliverance of the Jews, 8:1–9:16

VII. Feast of Purim, 9:17-32

VIII. Conclusion: the prominence of Mordecai, 10:1-3

ESTHER'S PALACE This harem palace of Xerxes was completely rebuilt by the University of Chicago and, hence, now looks much as it did before it was destroyed.

AUTHORSHIP AND DATE

The text itself fails to indicate either the author or the date of composition. The Jewish authorities record the tradition (as old as Josephus and repeated by Ibn Ezra) that Mordecai was the author of the book, but the way in which Mordecai is referred to in 10:2-3 suggests that his career was already finished. Other possible authors might be Ezra or Nehemiah, but for either of these there is no good linguistic evidence, judging from the style or diction of the three books concerned.

As to the date, *the terminus a quo* is the death of Xerxes (464 B.C.), since 10:2 seems to imply that his reign is finished. The latest *terminus ad quem* is prior to 330 B.C. since there are no traces of Greek influence either in language or in thought to be discovered in Esther. The most likely date of composition is somewhere in the latter half of the fifth century (so E. J. Young). Whoever the author may have been, he shows such intimate knowledge of Persian customs and of the fifth-century historical situation that he may well have lived in Persia and been an eyewitness of the events recorded.

OPPOSITION TO THE HISTORICITY OF ESTHER

1. Rationalist critics have made much of the failure of secular records to contain any mention of Queen Esther. According to Herodotus, Xerxes's queen during this period, that is, from the seventh year of his reign (Est. 2:16), was named Amestris, the daughter of a Persian named Otanes (7.61). It is stated that she brutally mutilated the mother of Artaynta, a paramour of Xerxes (9.112) and that also upon one occasion she

had fourteen noble Persian youths buried alive as a thank offering to a god of the netherworld (7.113). Certainly the Persian origin of Amestris and her sadistic brutality exclude any possibility of her being identified with Esther—unless Herodotus has preserved a very garbled and erroneous tradition.[19] It should be recognized that in the following details there is satisfactory agreement between the accounts of Esther and Herodotus: (*a*) it was in the third year of his reign, 483 B.C., that Xerxes convoked an assembly of his nobles to plan an expedition against Greece—an occasion which might well have given rise to the feast mentioned in Est. 1:3 (cf. Herodotus 7.7); (*b*) it was in his seventh year (479 B.C.) that Esther was made queen (Est. 2:16), which would correspond to the year Xerxes returned from his defeat at Salamis and sought consolation in his harem (Herodotus 9.108). After the violent clash with Amestris over the Artaynta affair, Xerxes may well have chosen a new favorite as his acting queen. So far as Vashti is concerned, it is true that Herodotus makes no mention of her; yet it should be borne in mind that Herodotus omitted many important people and events in his account. (It should be remembered, for example, that on the basis of Herodotus's omission, modern scholars used to deny the existence of Belshazzar, until subsequent archaeological discovery verified the historicity of Dan. 5.)

2. On the basis of Est. 2:5-6 some critics have alleged that the author must have regarded Xerxes as a near successor to King Nebuchadnezzar, since he implies that Mordecai was carried off in the deportation of Jehoiachin in 597 and yet was still very much alive in the reign of Xerxes (485-464 B.C.). But this deduction is founded upon a mistaken interpretation of the Hebrew text; the true antecedent of the relative pronoun *who* in verse 6 is not Mordecai himself but rather Kish, his great-grandfather. If it was Kish who was Jehoiachin's contemporary, as the author implies, three generations would have elapsed by the time of Mordecai—a proper interval between 597 and 483.

3. An objection has been raised to Est. 1:1 on the ground that 127 was a number much too high for the provinces under Xerxes's rule, since Herodotus states that the empire was then divided into twenty satrapies. But it is by no means certain that the Hebrew term *mᵉdînah* ("province") represented the same administrative unit as the Greek *satrapeia*; in all probability the *mᵉdînah* was a mere subdivision of it. Thus in Ezra 2:1 Judah is referred to as *mᵉdînah* or "subdivision" of what Herodotus itemizes as the fifth satrapy, Syria. Even the number of satrapies was by no means stable, for in the Behistun Rock inscription the empire is said to be composed of twenty-one satrapies, and then later in the same inscription, twenty-three, and later still, twenty-nine. Herodotus himself states that there were about sixty nations under the Persian rule. In view of all this evidence, it is premature for anyone to state categorically that the Persian empire could not have been divided into 127 *mᵉdînôt* in the time of Xerxes.

---

19. John Urquhart in the ISBE article on Esther feels hesitant about dismissing as impossible Scaliger's identification of Esther with Herodotus's Amestris. He suggests that in a world of merciless intrigue, she may have had to take measures which formed the basis of Herodotus's lurid account. Yet this would leave unexplained the Persian name and nationality of her father Otanes.

4. It has also been objected that the armed Jews could not possibly have killed as many as 75,000 enemies in the Persian empire in so short a time as a single day (as Est. 9:16-17 asserts), nor would the Persian government ever have permitted such slaughter. It is, however, most precarious reasoning to insist that the unusual is equivalent to the impossible. In the light of the peculiar situation brought about by Haman's plot to destroy the entire Jewish nation, and the careful equipping of the Jews with arms to destroy their foes, it is by no means incredible that the Jews could have encountered and overcome such a large number of foes. Moreover, the ancient historians abundantly testify that the Persian government had a remarkably callous attitude toward human life and that where a member of the royal family was involved, they were known to be altogether unsparing in their severity.

5. Doubts have been raised by many authors as to the historicity of Mordecai, and advocates of the late-date theory have labeled Esther as a mere romance intended to bolster nationalistic self-esteem and improve the morale of the oppressed and downtrodden Jewish people. But more recently those scholars who formerly rejected the entire account as fictitious have been forced to revise their conclusions in the light of an inscription published by Ungnad mentioning a certain *Marduk-ai-a* as an official in Susa during the reign of Xerxes. In fact, the name *Mardukai* has been found frequently in Late Babylonian inscriptions (as might well be expected of a name signifying "Man of Marduk"—the tutelary god of Babylon itself).

6. As for doubts concerning the historicity of Haman the Agagite, it is significant that an inscription of Sargon has been published by Oppert which mentions Agag as a district in the Persian empire. In the light of this evidence, it is apparent that Haman was a native of this province (rather than a descendant of the Amalekite king, Agag, as late Jewish tradition has supposed; cf. ISBE, p. 1008a).

POST-EXILIC FEASTS

Feast	Date	Significance	Source
Purim	Adar 13-15	Deliverance of Jewish race from genocide (Plotted by Haman in the reign of Xerxes)	Est. 9:24-32
Feast of Dedication	Kislev 25	Rededication of the Jerusalem Temple cleansed by Maccabean patriots in 165 B.C.	1 Macc. 4:52-59 2 Macc. 10:5-8

Impressive confirmation of the historical accuracy of the author of Esther has been found in an inscription of Artaxerxes II which states that the palace of Xerxes was destroyed by fire in the reign of Artaxerxes I. This would mean that within thirty years of the time of Esther, the palace in which she lived would have been destroyed, and in the natural course of events, a recollection of it would have passed away. It is difficult to suppose that any late romancer would have had any knowledge of a building which had been destroyed so long before his own time. Excavations of French archaeologists have uncovered the remains of this palace and show that it agrees perfectly in ground plan with the structure presupposed in the book of Esther (cf. ISBE, p. 1009*a*).

In conclusion, it should be observed that there is no other reasonable explanation for the historic fact of the Feast of Purim as observed among the Jews except that such a remarkable deliverance of the nation from extinction actually took place in history. There would have been absolutely no motive for manufacturing such a story as this unless it was based upon an actual occurrence. The name Purim is unimpeachably authentic, for the term *puru*, meaning "lot," has been discovered in Assyrian inscriptions.

31 POST-EXILIC PROPHETS: HAGGAI, ZECHARIAH, MALACHI

HAGGAI

THE NAME ḥaggay means "festal" derived from ḥag, "festival." Possibly the prophet received this name because he was born on the Feast of the Passover or some other major feast. The theme of his prophecy is that if God's people will put first His program, His house, and His worship, then their present poverty and failure will give way to a blessed prosperity commensurate with their covenant faithfulness.

OUTLINE OF HAGGAI

I. First message: neglect of the temple is the cause of economic depression, 1:1-15

II. Second message: though less pretentious, the second temple will be more glorious than the first, 2:1-9

III. Third message: unholiness vitiates sacrifice, selfishness leads to crop failure, 2:10-19

IV. Fourth message: God will finally triumph, 2:20-23

DATE AND AUTHORSHIP OF HAGGAI

Of all the books of the Old Testament, this one enjoys the unusual status of being uncontested by all critics of every persuasion. It is acknowledged to be the work of the prophet Haggai himself, and the date it assigns to each message is accepted as reliable. The first message was delivered on the first of Elul (Aug-Sept) in the second year of Darius, or 520 B.C.; the second message came on the twenty-first of Tishri (Sept-Oct) in the same year; the third and fourth messages were both given on the twenty-fourth of Chislev (Dec-Jan) in the same year. All four sermons, then, were delivered within three months of each other.

HISTORICAL BACKGROUND OF HAGGAI

This was a time of severe testing of faith for the remnant that had recently returned from Babylon. The hostile intrigues of Judah's adversaries during the reign of Cyrus had arrested the rebuilding of the temple fourteen years before. Nothing had been done on the project since that time, even though a new king, Darius, the son of Hystaspes, had ascended the throne in 522. The influential members of the Jewish community were content to leave the expensive undertaking incomplete while they spent their money on building comfortable mansions for themselves. But repeated crop failure had come as a warning to them all that they had sinned in using political opposition as an excuse for neglecting the sanctuary of the Lord. In Ezra 5:1-2, we read: "Now the prophets, Haggai the prophet, and Zechariah the son of Iddo, prophesied unto the Jews that were in Judah and in Jerusalem; in the name of the God of Israel prophesied they unto them" (ASV). Alongside this should be placed Ezra 6:14-15: "And the elders of the Jews builded, and they prospered through the prophesying of Haggai the prophet and Zechariah the son of Iddo....And this house was finished on the third day of the month Adar, which was in the sixth year of the reign of Darius the king" (516 B.C.). As Marcus Dods comments: "No prophet ever appeared at a more critical juncture in the history of a people, and it may be added, no prophet was more successful."[1]

From the perspective of our own time, it may be questioned whether the issue of completing the temple was as vital as these prophets represented it to be; in the Christian era we are accustomed to having no central sanctuary. But it should be remembered that much of the Mosaic constitution presupposed the carrying on of worship in such a sanctuary, and the failure to complete a suitable house of worship could lead to a paralyzing of the religious life of the Jewish community. It should also be understood that the second temple was to play a very important role in the history of redemption, for it was in this temple (as remodeled and beautified by Herod the Great) that the Lord Jesus Christ was to carry on His Jerusalem ministry. It was, of course, His advent that fulfilled the promise of Hag. 2:9, "The glory of this latter house shall be greater than of the former."

ZECHARIAH

The name Z^ekar-Yah means "Jehovah has remembered" (i.e., presumably, the Lord has remembered the prayers of his parents for a baby boy). The theme of his prophecy was: God is going to preserve His remnant from all the world powers which oppress them and threaten their extinction; these Gentile empires shall be destroyed, but Israel shall survive every ordeal to come, because they are the people of the Messiah. It is He who shall some day establish the kingdom and rule over all the earth after vanquishing all heathen opposition.

---

1. Marcus Dods, *The Post-Exilian Prophets: Haggai, Zechariah, Malachi* (Edinburgh: T. & T. Clark, 1879), p. 44.

OUTLINE OF ZECHARIAH

I. Messages during building of the temple, 1:1–8:23

A. First message: call for national repentance, 1:1-6

B. Second message: the eight visions, 1:7–6:15

    1. Horseman among the myrtles, 1:7-17 (the sovereign God ready to intervene in the peaceful world scene in order to bless His city and people)

    2. Four horns and four smiths, 1:18-21 (Israel's oppressors to be successively crushed: Assyria, Babylon, Greece, Rome)

    3. Measuring line, 2:1-13 (half desolate Jerusalem is someday to become large and populous)

    4. Joshua, symbol of the priestly nation, 3:1-10 (Israel is to be forgiven and purged by the grace of God)

    5. Candelabrum: Israel as the lamp of witness, 4:1-14 (Israel to be fed with the oil of the Spirit by the Priest-King, Christ)

    6. Flying scroll of divine judgment, 5:1-4 (a curse upon all who reject the Law and Covenant)

    7. Removal of the ephah of iniquity to Babylon, 5:5-11 (ungodliness removed from Judah and consigned to the degenerate world from whence it came and where it belongs)

    8. Four chariots of divine judgment, 6:1-8 (death, conquest, famine and pestilence meted out to the surrounding heathen powers)

    9. Sequel: the symbolic crown of Joshua as type of the Messianic Branch, 6:9-15

C. Third message, 7:1–8:23

    1. The query about extra fasts, 7:1-3

    2. The fourfold answer (godliness and obedience more important than fasts), 7:4–8:23

II. Messages after the building of the temple, 9:1–14:21

A. Burden of Hadrach (the anointed King rejected but triumphant), 9:1–11:17

    1. The king announced: (the Palm Sunday entrance), 9:1-10

    2. The king's program set forth, 9:11–10:12

    3. The king rejected (the good shepherd and the foolish shepherd), 11:1-17

B. The burden of Israel (the rejected King enthroned), 12:1–14:21

    1. Final victories of Israel: her conflict, triumph, conversion, and sanctification, 12:1–13:6

        a) Downfall of the heathen who attack Jerusalem, 12:1-4

        b) Miraculous strength of Israel to vanquish all their foes, 12:5-9

        c) Repentance of latter-day Israel for the crucifixion of Christ, 12:10-14

        d) Spring of cleansing water for the repentant, 13:1

      e) Permanent removal of idolatry from Israel and the silencing of all
         false prophets, 13:2-6
    2. Final victories of the King, 13:7–14:21
      a) His rejection, and the purging of Israel, 13:7-9
      b) Assault upon Jerusalem, and deliverance by the Lord, 14:1-8
      c) Establishment of the supremacy of Judah and her King over the earth,
         14:9-15
      d) Millennial subjection of the nations to Christ and the holy status of
         millennial Israel, 14:16-21

AUTHORSHIP AND DATE OF ZECHARIAH

The first verse presents Zechariah as the son of Berechiah and the grandson of Iddo, who was undoubtedly the same priest as the one mentioned in Neh. 12:4 as a contemporary of Zerubbabel. In Zech. 2:4 the prophet is spoken of as a youth (*na'ar*). He would probably have been a young man at the time he cooperated with Haggai in the rebuilding campaign of 520 B.C. His last dated prophecy (chap. 7) was given two years later, in 518; yet chapters 9-14 show every appearance of having been composed some decades after that, possibly after 480 B.C. in view of the reference to Greece (9:13). As Unger points out (IGOT, p. 355), the successful resistance of the Greek nation to the invasion of Xerxes would naturally have brought them into a new prominence in the eyes of all the peoples of the Near East. We have no further information concerning Zechariah's personal career, except the reference in Matt. 23:35, which seems to indicate that he was martyred by mob action in the temple grounds (since the Zechariah that Christ mentions is said to be the son of Berechiah rather than of Jehoiada, who however met his end in a like manner back in the days of King Joash, according to 2 Chron. 24:20-21).

CRITICAL OBJECTIONS TO THE UNITY OF ZECHARIAH

Since the rise of nineteenth-century criticism, two competing views have arisen concerning the origin of chapters 9-14: the pre-exilic theory and the post-Alexandrian theory.

The pre-exilic theory is based upon the following considerations:

1. Since Zech. 11:12-13 is quoted in Matt. 27:9-10 as a prophecy by Jeremiah, chapter 11 as a whole has been assigned to the time of Jeremiah or some pre-exilic contemporary of his (so Joseph Mede in 1653). Yet we should observe that it is not quite accurate to say that Matt. 27 quotes exclusively from Zech. 11, for in certain important respects it deviates from both the MT and the LXX form of that passage. The fulfillment to which Matthew refers pertains to the purchasing of the potter's field; this points to Jer. 32:6-9, which records the purchase of a field for a certain number of shekels. Compare also Jer. 18:2, which speaks of the prophet's watching a potter fashion earthenware vessels in his house. Likewise Jer. 19:2 speaks of a potter employed

about the temple and having his workshop in the valley of Hinnom. In Jer. 19:11 we read: "Thus saith the Lord of hosts: Even so will I break this people and this city, as one breaketh a potter's vessel, that cannot be made whole again: and they shall bury them in Tophet." Therefore, we

BRONZE LEPTON OF THE JUDEAN KINGDOM, JOHN HYRCANUS I (135–104 B.C.), IMPRINTED WITH 2 HORNS OF PLENTY WITH POMEGRANATES. POCAMP, A TRIPHIBIOUS CREATURE ABLE TO TRAVEL BY LAND, SEA OR AIR.

are to understand Zechariah's casting of the money to the potter as simply the renewal of an old symbol dating back to the time of Jeremiah. Since Matt. 27 combines both Jeremiah (from whom the word *field* has been borrowed) and Zechariah, it is only Jeremiah who is mentioned, because he was the older and the more important of the two prophets.[2] A direct parallel for this procedure is found in Mark 1:2-3, where the quotation begins with Mal. 3:1 and follows with Isa. 40:3; yet Mark refers (ASV) only to Isaiah as the source of the citation.

2. Since Zech. 9:1-2 mentions Hadrach,[3] Damascus, and Hamath as independent countries (so the argument runs), this passage must be dated prior to the conquest of Syria by Tiglath-pileser in 732. Actually, however, there is no necessary implication in these verses that the three Syrian principalities mentioned were free and independent, any more than the three Philistine cities referred to in 9:5. There is no particular reason why they could not have had a predictable future even during the reign of Xerxes, when they were subject to the Persian empire. In the light of subsequent history it is quite obvious that this passage contains a revelation of a judgment to come upon these principalities at the time of the invasion by Alexander the Great in 332 B.C.

3. Zechariah 11:14 envisions the possibility of establishing brotherhood between Judah and Israel. This has been taken to imply a time of composition prior to the fall of Samaria in 722, and probably even prior to Pekah's alliance with Rezin of Damascus in 734. But this line of reasoning is based upon tenuous evidence, for the northern and southern tribes were considered by postexilic authors as reunited at the time of the restoration in 536. Thus Ezra 6:17 and 8:35 imply that many of the descendants of the Northern Kingdom returned with the remnant of Judah, inasmuch as offerings were presented to the Lord on behalf of all twelve tribes. Moreover, there was even in

---

2. Cf. Hengstenberg on this passage and also Basil Atkinson in Davidson-Stibbs-Kevan, *New Bible Commentary*, p. 804a.

3. Until recent times, there has been considerable uncertainty as to the identification of Hadrach in Zech. 9:1, but the Zakir Stele discovered at Hamath refers to the city of Hazrek (or Hadrach) as the capital of the principality of Lu'ash. It lay southwest of Aleppo and north of Hamath. It seems that Lu'ash contracted an alliance with Hamath and succeeded in defeating Benhadad II of Damascus. On the other hand, Assyrian records mention a city called Hatankka located on the Orontes River south of Hamath and north of Damascus. From the fact that both Hamath and Damascus fought over Hadrach, some authorities like Lidzbarski have inferred that it lay to the south or southeast of Hamath rather than to the north. Lidzbarski suggests that it was probably near the city of Homs (*Ephemeris für semitische Epigraphik*, 8:175).

TETRADRACHMA UNDER SELEUCUS I, FOUNDER OF THE SELEUCID EMPIRE THE "LION OF BABYLON ON THE OBVERSE"

Zechariah's time (the early fifth century) a need for the reunification of the whole territory of the twelve tribes as a spiritual and geographical unity. The hostile attitude of the Samaritans (who were largely the descendants of foreign settlers) presented an obstacle toward the realization of this ideal. Zechariah 11:14 therefore looks forward to the later unification of the whole area by the descendants of the Maccabees during the Hasmonean dynasty.

4. Zechariah 10:10-11 refers to Assyria as an independent power; therefore, the passage must have been written prior to 612 B.C., when Assyria fell. But actually this is an unwarranted deduction. As the term is used here, *Assyria* is not intended to refer to a contemporary kingdom; rather, it is a geographical designation employed in a futuristic, predictive context. It apparently stands for the world power which shall be in control in the Near East during the last days, and as such is contrasted with the southern world power of Egypt. Compare Ezra 6:22 which speaks of Assyria as a geographical entity, without any implication that it continued to be an independent kingdom in his time.[4]

5. Zechariah 10:1-4 is thought to indicate a pre-exilic date because it refers to teraphim and diviners, and post-exilic Judah witnessed no revival of idolatrous worship. But actually the context shows that this mention of the vanity of idols and diviners refers to the experience of Israel in ages past;[5] by God's providences He showed the nation the folly of trusting in idols back in the days of Jehoiakim and Zedekiah, and demonstrated that He Himself was the one true God. Because of the encroachments of the pagan or half-pagan neighboring countries, this lesson needed to be mentioned even in Zechariah's day, that the Jews might be discouraged from taking foreign wives. Ezra's prayer of confession in Ezra 9 likewise shows a most vivid recollection of the lessons of the past concerning the vanity of idol worship in Israel.

The pre-exilic theory was defended by the following eminent nineteenth-century scholars: Rosenmueller, Hitzig, Baudissin, and Strack. In the twentieth century, however, this theory has become largely discarded as obsolete in favor of a much later date of composition.

The post-Alexandrian theory, which now enjoys the widest support, rests upon the following principal arguments:

4. "They observed the Feast of Unleavened Bread seven days with joy, for the Lord...had turned the heart of Assyria toward them." Clearly "Assyria" here means Persia rather than the empire that had perished back in 612 B.C.

5. Note that the MT verbs in Zech. 10:2 are in the perfect tense (*dibberu, ḥāzū*) which indicates that the third verb, *yᵉdabbērû* ("they were speaking") is to be understood as continued action in past time. The same is true of the fourth verb, *yᵉnaḥēmûn* ("they were offering comfort in vain"). The rest of this verse states that "they have wandered like sheep; they are afflicted because they have no shepherd."

1. Zechariah 9:13 mentions the sons of Javan, or Greece: "For I have bent Judah for me, I have filled the bow with Ephraim; and I will stir up thy sons, O Zion, against thy sons, O Greece, and will make thee as the sword of a mighty man" (ASV). It is argued that this reference indicates a date

SILVER TETRADRACHMA FROM THE SELEUCID EMPIRE OF ANTIOCHUS III THE GREAT (223–187 B.C.) DAN. 11:15.

when the Greeks had already entered upon the scene of Near Eastern politics, that is to say, after the conquest of the Near East by Alexander the Great (ca. 330 B.C.). While this passage purports to be a prediction of coming defeat (i.e., the defeat of the Seleucids at the hands of the Maccabean patriots), it is most reasonably to be understood as a *vaticinium ex eventu*. Such a deduction, of course, has greatest appeal for those who occupy an antisupernaturalistic position in their philosophy. But as far as the situation in Zechariah's own time is concerned, the defeats recently administered by the Greeks to Xerxes at the battles of Salamis, Plataea, and Mycale in 480-479 would furnish ample cause to bring them to the attention of all the inhabitants of the Persian empire. Therefore, unless one is prepared to rule out the possibility of predictive prophecy on dogmatic grounds, there is no particular reason why Zechariah could not have penned these words in the 470s.

2. Since Zech. 9:1-2 admittedly refers to provinces which were conquered by Alexander, this naturally indicates to the rationalist school of thought that his invasion was already a matter of history. The same line of reasoning has been applied to Zech. 11:14, with its vision of the reunification of Judah and Israel. This would make the composition of the passage Maccabean (e.g., around 150 B.C.). It should, however, be borne in mind that Ezra 6:17 and 8:35 establish the fact that a theoretical reunion had already been consummated at the time of the dedication of the second temple in 516 B.C. It was only natural, therefore, to look for the implementation of this new unity as a future political event.

3. The references to the "good shepherd" in Zech. 11 have led advocates of the Late Date Theory to attempt various historical identifications. According to E. Sellin, this good shepherd was the high priest Onias III, who held office during the reign of Seleucus IV (187-175 B.C.). But according to K. Marti, he was Onias IV (apparently the same as that brother of Onias III who held the high priestly office for ten years and was finally put to death in the time of Judas Maccabeus, according to 2 Macc. 13:1-8. So far as the "evil shepherd" is concerned (Zech. 11:17), he has been identified with Menelaus (apparently the same as Onias IV) by Sellin, and by others with Alcimus, or Jakim, who was installed as high priest by King Demetrius in 161 B.C. and who died in 159. (Alcimus is also Marti's candidate.) As for the three shepherds of Zech. 11:8, they

have been identified as Lysimachus, Jason, and Menelaus, according to Marti; or according to Sellin, they were Simon II, Menelaus, and Lysimachus.

These highly conjectural identifications, which greatly vary among themselves, would imply a date of composition in the neighborhood of 150 B.C. All of this procedure involves, of course, the naive assumption that Hebrew experienced no linguistic changes whatever between the fifth century and the second century B.C. The style and diction of Zechariah, even in chapters 9-14, give no indication of being any later in time than Haggai or Malachi. We may now contrast with this supposedly second-century Hebrew document the recently discovered sectarian literature from the Qumran caves dating from the second and first centuries B.C. Linguistically they furnish great contrasts with the Hebrew of Zechariah, which bears a much stronger affinity with the other early fifth-century prophets.

4. In dependence upon the dogmatic theory of evolutionary development, as formulated by Wellhausen, the advocates of the second-century date stress the apocalyptic tendency in these chapters of Zechariah which laid a distinct emphasis upon eschatology. (According to the evolutionary scheme, apocalypticism is regarded as the final stage of Jewish religion, a product of the desperation to which the Jews were driven when they saw their hopes of worldly empire disappointed and their nation kept under bondage by Gentile empires.)[6] On these theoretical grounds, therefore, much of the content of chapters 12-14 is assigned a very late date, because it contains a hope of a catastrophic judgment to be visited upon the Gentiles. Yet because of supposedly inconsistent views concerning the coming defeats and victories of Israel, even these chapters are regarded as a composite from various late sources.

5. The literary style of Zech. 9-14 is allegedly so different from that of chapters 1-8 as to indicate a different author. For instance, Zechariah II (chaps. 9-14) employs the phrase "thus saith Jehovah" just once, whereas it occurs with great frequency in Zechariah I (chaps. 1-8). On the other hand, Zechariah II uses the expression "in that day" eighteen times or more, whereas Zechariah I employs it only three times. Moreover, the style of Zechariah II is regarded as more poetic and full of parallelism than is the case of Zechariah I.

In refutation of these alleged evidences of diverse authorship, it may easily be shown that there are even more significant traits of style which are possessed in common by both sections of the book. Of course it should be understood that no author's style remains completely static over a period of three or four decades. If the last six chapters of Zechariah were composed between 480 and 470 B.C., this would adequately account for the variations and contrasts listed in the previous paragraph. The difference of mood and situation prevailing between the early period of his ministry, when Zechariah was emphasizing that the summons to rebuild the temple really came from God (hence the frequency of "thus says Yahweh"), and the state of affairs prevailing

---

6. For an effective critique of this dogma of the late date of all apocalyptic, see G. E. Ladd's article, "Why Not Prophetic-Apocalyptic?" in JBL 76 (1957), pp. 192-200.

thirty or forty years later, when Zechariah's authority as a spokesman of the Lord was already well accepted, quite adequately explains the differing frequency of the quotation formula. On the other hand, the prophecies of Zechariah II are directed toward a much more distant future than those of Zechariah I. It is only natural, therefore, that the eschatological phrase "in that day" would appear more frequently in the later chapters. The earlier chapters, 1-8, deal with the more immediate judgments upon the world powers of Persia, Greece, and Rome, rather than with the end time.

Conservative scholars, in demonstration of the unity of authorship in Zechariah, point out the persistence of such stylistic traits as the following:

a) "Saith Jehovah" (*ne'ūm Yahweh*) occurs fourteen times in Zechariah I and six times in Zechariah II (10:12; 12:1, 4; 13:2, 7, 8).

b) "The eyes of Yahweh," a peculiar designation referring to God's providence, is found twice in Zechariah I (4:10; 8:6) and once in Zechariah II (9:8; perhaps add 12:4, "mine eyes").

c) The divine title "Yahweh of hosts" is found three times in Zechariah I and three times in *Zechariah II*.

d) The verb *yāšab*, "to sit, to dwell," in the special sense of "be inhabited" is found twice in *Zechariah I* and twice in *Zechariah II*. (Very seldom does this verb have that meaning outside of Zechariah.)

e) There is a peculiar five-member type of parallelism which is scarcely found outside of Zechariah, but which occurs once in *Zechariah I* and three times in *Zechariah II* (6:13; 9:5, 7; 12:4). (Cf. Young, IOT, p. 273.)

So far as the style is concerned, all scholars admit that Zechariah is remarkably free of so-called Aramaisms; it is written in good, pure Hebrew. This is scarcely what one would expect of a work composed in the second century B.C as the Liberal critics maintain. As we have already pointed out, the grammatical and stylistic peculiarities of the prose documents of the Qumran sectarians are completely missing from Zechariah's work.

One more observation should be made concerning the modern advocates of the post-Alexandrian theory; that is, they markedly disagree among themselves as to the precise dating of Zechariah II in its various component parts. Speculations range all the way from 280 to 140 B.C., depending upon what correlations they attempt to make with episodes and historical characters connected with Hellenistic history. This does not inspire confidence in the soundness of their methodology.

MALACHI

The most reasonable explanation for the meaning of *Malachi* (*Mal'ākī*, Hebrew) is that it is hypocoristic for the full form *Mal'ak-Yah*, or "Messenger of Jehovah." In its abbreviated form, the name could only mean "my messenger," or possibly, if an adjective, "one charged with a message." It should be noted that many authorities have expressed uncertainty as to whether the real name of the author has been preserved. Such doubt is grounded upon the fact that the LXX translates 1:1 as "by the hand of his messenger" (rather than by the hand of Malachi). This discrepancy would indicate a textual variation; the LXX must have read the final letter as *w* (*waw*), meaning "his," rather than the final *y* (*yod*) of the MT. On the other hand, it should be noted that the LXX entitles the book Malakhias, or Malachi. The Targumic tradition indicates uncertainty, since it paraphrases the first verse as "by the hand of my messenger, whose name is called Ezra the scribe." It should be observed that every other prophetic book in the Old Testament bears the name of its author. It would be strange if this one were left anonymous. Moreover, if the archetype or previous manuscript used by the LXX spelled Malachi's name with a longtailed *yod*, it could easily have been misunderstood as signifying His messenger. Even if *yod* were read (as apparently the Targum of Jonathan did so read), it might well be misconstrued as a common noun followed by the suffix *my*. Of course it was true that any of the numerous Hebrew names that ended in *i* (such as Palti, Bukki, Buzi, etc.) could be misconstrued as "my," since the gentilic ending *i* happens to resemble the suffix pronoun *my*.

The theme of Malachi is that sincerity toward God and a holy manner of life are absolutely essential in the Lord's eyes, if His favor is to be bestowed upon the crops and the nation's economic welfare. Israel must live up to her high calling as a holy nation and wait for the coming of the Messiah, who by a ministry of healing as well as judgment will lead the nation to a realization of all her fondest hopes.

OUTLINE OF MALACHI

I. Introductory appeal: God's love for Israel, 1:1-5

II. Oracle against the priests for dishonoring the Lord, 1:6-2:9

    A. Neglect in liturgical functions, 1:6-2:4

    B. Insincere, corrupt teaching of the law, 2:5-9

III. Oracles against the laity, 2:10-4:3

    A. Treachery toward God in divorce and mixed marriage, 2:10-16

    B. Warning of judgment by the coming Lord, 2:17-3:6

    C. Repentance in tithing will bring blessed prosperity, 3:7-12

    D. Vindication of the godly against sneers of cynics in the day of the Lord, 3:13-4:3

IV. Concluding admonitions: to keep the law and wait for Christ's coming, 4:4-6

AUTHORSHIP AND DATE OF COMPOSITION

As indicated above, the name of the author was probably Malachi or Malachijah (the Targumic tradition that he was Ezra is hardly worthy of consideration), and apart from that we have no knowledge of his background or circumstances. Judging from internal evidence, it seems clear that his prophecies were given in the second half of the fifth century, probably around 435 B.C. We come to this conclusion from the following indications: (1) The temple had already been rebuilt and Mosaic sacrifice reinstituted (1:7,10; 3:1). (2) A Persian governor (or *pe ̣hah* mentioned in 1:8) was in authority at that time; hence it could not have been during either of Nehemiah's governorships (in 445 and 433).[7] (3) The sins which Malachi denounces are the same as those Nehemiah had to correct during his second term, namely, (*a*) priestly laxity (1:6; Neh. 13:4-9), (*b*) neglect of tithes, to the impoverishment of the Levites (3:7-12; cf. Neh. 13:10-13), (*c*) much intermarriage with foreign women (2:10-16; cf. Neh. 13:23-28). It is reasonable to assume that Malachi had already protested against these abuses in the years just preceding Nehemiah's return; hence a fair estimate would be about 435 B.C.

Even rationalist critics, for the most part, find no objection to this date, although a few, like Pfeiffer, prefer to date him somewhat earlier, about 460 (Pfeiffer, IOT, p. 614). Nor do they question the integrity of the book either on stylistic or ideological grounds, since they concede that a messianic hope may have been cherished by the Jews as early as the late fifth century.

---

7. Note that Nehemiah himself was never referred to as *pe ̣hah* while he was in office, but only as *tirshatha* (a Persian term probably meaning "the revered one," comparable to Persian *tarsta*, "the feared one")—a title occurring in Ezra 2:63 and Neh. 7:65.

32 INTRODUCTION TO HEBREW POETRY

MANY NINETEENTH-CENTURY CRITICS assumed that the Hebrews were incapable of cultivating hymnic, lyric, or didactic poetry until a fairly late period, and then only under the influence of their more cultured neighbors. The more radical representatives of the Rationalist School felt confident in ruling out not only Davidic authorship of any and all of the Psalms, but even the composition of any of them prior to the Babylonian Exile. They did not hesitate to assign a substantial number of them to the Maccabean period (ca. 160 B.C.). The same is true of the other poetical books; Job, Proverbs, Ecclesiastes, and the Song of Solomon were all considered definitely post-exilic.

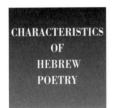

CHARACTERISTICS OF HEBREW POETRY

In the twentieth century there has been a trend toward moderating this view and conceding that at least some of the Hebrew productions went back to an early period, especially in their original oral form. The discovery of an increasing number of Akkadian and Egyptian hymns has clearly confirmed the early cultivation of this genre by Israel's neighbors in the second millennium B.C. More recently this has been supplemented by the Ugaritic poetry composed in a Canaanite language very close to Hebrew and dating from the fifteenth century B.C.[1] Most modern critics, therefore, now concede the possibility of early elements going back to the time of David or before, even though the finished production may not have been finally committed to writing until the late monarchy or the post-exilic period. The increasing amount of religious and didactic poetry recovered from almost every culture with which Israel had contact prior to the Exile makes it increasingly difficult to defend the post-exilic thesis for these books. In fact, we may say that these non-Israelite productions of Semitic poetry compel us to conclude that even the Hebrews must have committed their verse to written form, unless they were very backward culturally by comparison with their neighbors.

The most noteworthy characteristic of Hebrew poetry is its parallelism. This term

1. Cf. pp. 175-76, 484-85.

refers to the practice of balancing one thought or phrase by a corresponding thought or phrase containing approximately the same number of words, or at least a correspondence in ideas. In modern times the earliest systematic treatment of Hebrew parallelism was made by Bishop Robert Lowth in his work, *De Sacra Poesi Hebraeorum Praelectiones Academicae* ("Lectures on the Sacred Poetry of the Hebrews"), published in 1753. There he defined the three basic types of *parallelismus membrorum* as synonymous, antithetic, and synthetic. More recent authors like S. R. Driver have added a fourth and fifth type, the climactic and the emblematic. We may illustrate these various types by the following examples:

SYNONOMOUS PARALLELISM:
Identical
Psalm 24:1:
> "The earth is the Lord's, and the fullness thereof;
> The world, and they that dwell therein."

Similar
Psalm 19:2:
> "Day unto day uttereth speech,
> And night unto night showeth knowledge."

ANTITHETIC PARALLELISM:
Psalm 1:6:
> "For the Lord knoweth the way of the righteous;
> But the way of the ungodly shall perish."

(This type is particularly common in the book of Proverbs.)

SYNTHETIC OR CONSTRUCTIVE PARALLELISM:
Completion type (which is largely a parallelism of rhythm rather than of sense)
Psalm 2:6:
> "Yet have I set my king
> Upon Zion my holy hill."
> (*Wa 'ânî' nāsāḵtî malkî 'al Ṣiyyôn har-qoḏšî*)

Comparison type
Proverbs 15: 17:
> "Better is a dinner of herbs where love is,
> Than a stalled ox and hatred therewith."

Reason type
Proverbs 26:4:
> "Answer not a fool according to his folly,
> Lest thou also be like unto him."

CLIMACTIC PARALLELISM:

Psalm 29:1:

> "Ascribe unto Yahweh, O ye sons of the mighty,
> Ascribe unto Yahweh glory and strength"

(Observe the first line is itself incomplete, and the second line takes up some of its words anew and then completes the thought.)

EMBLEMATIC PARALLELISM:

(In the emblematic parallelism the second line gives a figurative illustration but does so without any words of contrast, simply by placing the two ideas loosely together. In such a case the first line serves as an emblem to illustrate the second.)

Proverbs 25:25:

> "Cold water to a thirsty soul,
> And good news from a far country" (literal rendering).

Or, without a connective,

Proverbs 11:22:

> "A gold ring in a swine's snout—
> A fair woman and without understanding" (literal rendering).

There are other types of parallelism which are discussed by some authorities, but those listed represent all the really significant types. A *chiastic* parallelism is a subtype of the synonymous parallelism, but instead of giving the parallel ideas in the same order (a-b, a^1-b^1) it is presented in the opposite order (i.e., a-b, b^1-a^1) as in Ps. 51:1. (KJV, "Have mercy upon me, O God according to thy lovingkindness: according unto the multitude of thy tender mercies blot out my transgressions.")

Unger (IGOT, p. 365) describes the *stairlike* parallelism in which the second line takes up again and carries on further a portion of the first line (as in Ps. 139:5-7); but this is very similar to the climactic. (A thorough and adequate treatment of Hebrew parallelism may be found in G. B. Gray's *Forms of Hebrew Poetry*, 1915.)

QUESTION OF RHYTHM

A much disputed point in connection with Hebrew poetry in the Old Testament pertains to the rhythmic pattern. A certain cadence is often observable in Hebrew verse; sometimes for several lines at a time a uniform number of stresses can successfully be made out. Thus in Ps. 23 the first few verses present a 2:2 pattern; that is to say, each half-verse is characterized by two accentual stresses. Sometimes we may even discover a group of verses which show a fair uniformity in the number of unaccented syllables which fall between the stressed syllables.

Many nineteenth-century and early twentieth-century critics have proceeded on the assumption that in its pure, original form, each of these poetic texts in the Old Testament must have conformed to a systematic and predictable pattern. Even in ancient times authorities like Josephus, influenced by Greek poetical theory, attempted to classify passages like Ex. 15:1-8 and Deut. 32:1-43 as a species of hexameter (or poetry containing six-foot verses). Modern adherents to such theories, like Hoelscher, attempted to make out an iambic (short-long, short-long) basis. Julius Ley thought he detected a frequent anapestic 3:2 meter (an anapest being a short-short-long foot). Budde gave this poetry the label of *Qinah* ("lamentation") meter. Eduard Sievers (1901) tried to establish a 4:4-time basis for Hebrew poetry, with a long or accented syllable counting as two beats (as in Greek poetry). He also catalogued the various stress sequences as 2:2, 3:3, 4:4, 4:3, 3:4, 2:2:2, and so forth. Once having established what the dominant metrical pattern was for each particular passage, these theorists believed that they could amend the Received Text of the Hebrew wherever it did not conform to the ideal rhythm.

Many of the Liberal commentaries on the poetical books (and especially Psalms) are filled with large numbers of such conjectural emendations based on the attempt to compel the Received Text to conform to their preferred metrical pattern.[2] Since the actual texts as transmitted very often do not follow a consistent or regular metrical pattern, it was necessary to amend quite frequently—even drastically. In some cases this process of emendation was carried out to such an extent that the critics felt free to rearrange entire verses or groups of verses in a new order so that they might conform to some imagined strophic pattern. (A strophic pattern implies a division into stanzas in which a later stanza is supposed to correspond in rhythm and number of feet with the preceding stanza.) It is only in very exceptional instances that identifiable stanzas can be made out in the Received Text of the poetical books.

With the discovery and evaluation of the Ras Shamra Tablets, the unsoundness of this metrical approach has been exposed. The Ugaritic poetry is of utmost relevance, because (1) it is written in a Canaanite dialect quite closely related to Hebrew; (2) it contains many poetic cliches and turns of expression which occur in the Hebrew psalms; (3) it dates back to the age of Moses, and is therefore contemporaneous with Moses' own poetry (as preserved in Ex. 15; Deut. 32, 33; Ps. 90). Certainly, then, if meter was observed in the original Hebrew poetry, it would have been operative in the Canaanite verse of Ras Shamra.

G. D. Young has reported the results of a thorough study of Ugaritic poetry under every category known to metrical science. He defines as possible manifestations of meter: (1) a stich series (i.e., the appearance of a uniform pattern of verse units); (2) the number of stresses per stich (or line); (3) consistency of strophic pattern. After tabulat-

---

2. Very signifiicant is the statement made by Marvin Pope in the *Anchor Bible Commentary* on Job (p. xlviii): "To achieve rigidly regular patterns of meter and of strophes in any of the longer poems of the O.T. almost inevitably requires too much cutting and patching to be convincing. The counting of syllables, unstressed and stressed, in lines where the text is above suspicion, shows such irregularity as to cast doubt upon emendations made purely upon the ground of metrical theory." D. N. Freedman in "Pottery, Poetry and Prophecy," (JBL, 77 [March], pp. 5-26), deplores the rigid systems of metrical or strophic patterns imposed by modern scholars on ancient Semitic poetry. Those simply do not work with the extensive emendation of the text. Better than trying to find a key to Hebrew metrics is to provide an adequate description of the phenomena. He opts for a syllable-counting system.

ing the results, and after a careful study of the fifty or more cases of parallel accounts and repeated statements in the Ugaritic verse, he comes to this conclusion: "At none of these levels can any definable metrical pattern be demonstrated in the poetry of Ugarit. The repetition required for poetic expression is here not accentual or syllabic, but is simply the very beautiful repetition of ideas in parallel form....The idea that meter is found in this poetry is, we feel, an illusion resulting from the observable facts of parallelism and the Semitic morphology. A poetry whose one outstanding feature is the paralleling of thoughts, which is necessarily accompanied by lines approximating each other in length, a poetry written in a language in which almost any clause can be couched in from two to three words, is a poetry which naturally lends itself to the creation of an impression of lines of uniform metric length....The facts, however, show a complete lack of pattern at any of the levels noted."[3] This basic lack of meter was long ago recognized by Franz Delitzsch: "Old Hebrew poetry has neither rhyme nor meter; not till the seventh century after Christ did Jewish poetry adopt either."[4]

THE WISDOM LITERATURE

The so-called *ḥokmâ* literature (*ḥokmâ* being the Hebrew word for "wisdom") was extensively cultivated among all the ancient Near Eastern peoples. Pritchard's ANET contains translations of some of the more outstanding Egyptian examples, such as: "The Instruction of Ptaḥḥotep," "The Instruction for King Mer-ka-Re," "The Instruction of King Amen-em-ḥet," "The Instruction of Prince Ḥor-dedef," "The Instruction of Ani," and "The Instruction of Amen-em-Opet." There are also collections of Akkadian proverbs and counsels of wisdom which have been discovered, and in the Aramaic literature, "The Words of Aḥiqar."

It is against the background of this widely cultivated genre as practiced among Israel's neighbors that we are to understand the wisdom literature of the Hebrews themselves. Most characteristic of the Semitic *ḥokmâ* are the practical precepts based upon a canny observation of the laws of human nature and of the rules for success in social, business, and political life. In general it may be said that the "wisdom" with which these ancient sages were concerned was of a practical rather than a theoretical nature. Like the *sophoi* ("wise men") of the early Greek culture, the Hebrew *ḥākām* originally was a person who knew how to do things well which the average person could only do indifferently or not at all. In this sense the master craftsman Bezaleel is referred to in Ex. 31:3 as *ḥākām*. From this usage it came to be applied to the art of getting along successfully with God and with men. As a necessary involvement it also brought in the moral law which governs both human relationships and relationships with God, and which determines the degree of success to which a man may attain. As Driver points out (ILOT, p. 392-93), the quality of *ḥokmâ* was imputed especially to per-

---

3. G. D. Young, "Semitic Metrics and the Ugaritic Evidence," in *The Bible Today* (Feb. 1949), pp. 150-55.
4. Delitzsch, *Commentary on Psalms*, trans. Rev. Francis Bolton (Grand Rapids: Eerdmans, 1949), p. 28.

sons who were able to come up with the right answer in critical situations.[5] Thus Joseph is described as *ḥākām* because of his ability to interpret Pharaoh's dream (Gen. 41:39). The same is true of the wise woman of Tekoa who engineered a reconciliation between David and his son Absalom (2 Sam. 14); likewise also Solomon in his clever stratagem for deciding which of two claimants to a single baby was its true mother (1 Kings 3).

There actually seems to have been a prominent class or school of wise men in ancient Hebrew society, and, as Driver puts it, "They applied themselves rather to the observation of human character as such, seeking to analyze conduct, studying action in its consequences, and establishing morality upon the basis of principles common to humanity at large" (ILOT, p. 393). In its highest form, Hebrew *ḥokmâ* sought to look into the essence of God's truth and grasp the general ideas which gave the Israelite faith dimensions fitting it to become a world religion. From this perspective all natural and moral phenomena and experiences were reflected upon in order to apprehend more perfectly the final ground of life and the principles by which it is governed.

---

5. Cf. chap. 34, pp. 496-97

33 PSALMS

THE HEBREW TITLE for this book is *T^ehillîm,* or "Praise Songs"; the Greek rendering *Psalmoi* in the LXX means literally "songs to the accompaniment of a stringed instrument." *Psalmos* comes from *psallein,* "to pluck a stringed instrument" as an accompaniment to song. The 150 psalms composing this collection cover a great variety of themes, and it is difficult to make any valid generalizations. Probably it is safe to say that they all embody at least an element of personal response on the part of the believer toward the goodness and grace of God. Often they include a record of the psalmist's own inner emotions of discouragement, anxiety, or thankful joy in the face of the opposition of God's enemies or in view of God's varied providences. But whether the psalmist is occupied with a mournful or a joyous theme, he always is expressing himself as in the presence of the living God. There are a few psalms, of course, which mostly contain the thoughts and revelations of God Himself, such as Ps. 2, but these are most exceptional.

From ancient times the Psalter seems to have been divided into five books, perhaps to correspond to the five books of the Torah. Each of these divisions ends with a doxology. The divisions are as follows:

DIVISION OF THE PSALTER

Book I: Psalms 1-41

Book II: Psalms 42-72

Book III: Psalms 73-89

Book IV: Psalms 90-106

Book V: Psalms 107-150

AUTHORSHIP AND DATE OF COMPOSITION OF THE PSALMS

In most cases, the texts of the psalms themselves do not indicate the author by name. Psalm 72:20 forms an apparent exception to this rule; and yet it is possible to explain it as an editorial addition to the original collection of all of the Davidic psalms, of which Ps. 72 was the last unit in the collection. For the most part, the only definite information about authorship is found in the psalm titles. Not all of the titles contain the author's name, but those which do present us with the following tradition: one by Moses (Ps. 90); seventy-three by David (mostly in Book I and Book II); twelve by Asaph (50, 73-83); ten by descendants of Korah (42, 44-49, 84, 87-88); one or two by Solomon (72, 127); one by Heman the Ezrahite (88); one by Ethan the Ezrahite (89).

Of these, the earliest would naturally be Ps. 90, by Moses, presumably composed about 1405 B.C. The Davidic psalms would have originated between 1020 and 975 B.C.; those of Asaph from approximately the same period; Ps. 127 from the period of Solomon's reign, possibly 950. It is hard to date the descendants of Korah and the two Ezrahites who are mentioned; presumably they were pre-exilic. Of the psalms not carrying titles, some were undoubtedly Davidic (e.g., 2 and 33) and the others date from later periods all the way up to the return from exile (such as 126 and 137, the latter of which is at least as late as the Exile). No convincing evidence, however, has been offered for the dating of any of the psalms later than approximately 500 B.C.

AUTHORSHIP OF THE DAVIDIC PSALMS

As we shall presently see, the rationalist critics take a very skeptical view of the reliability of the psalm titles and largely disregard their value as mere speculations of later rabbis. Having thus disposed of the evidence of the titles, the critics tend to reject the possibility, on theoretical grounds, that David could have composed any of the psalms in the Psalter. (Eissfeldt allows him only one or two.) These are the principal arguments advanced in rejecting the claims of Davidic authorship:

1. Some of the psalms attributed to David speak of the king in the third person rather than in the first person (e.g., 20, 21, 61, 63, 72, 110). One would expect an author to refer to himself as *I* or *thou* rather than *he*. There is, however, abundant evidence that ancient authors referred to themselves frequently in the third person. In classical literature, for instance, there can be no doubt that Xenophon was the author of *The Anabasis*; nevertheless, he refers to himself almost always in the third person. The same is true of Julius Caesar in his *Gallic Wars*. Repeatedly in the Old Testament we find Jehovah quoted as speaking of Himself in the third person. Even in the Ten Commandments which begin in the first person ("I am Yahweh thy God, who brought thee out of the land of Egypt"), there is an occasional shift to the third person ("for Yahweh will not hold him guiltless who takes his name in vain"). It is therefore out of the question to use this matter of the third person as a criterion for ruling out authorship.

2. Some of the psalms attributed to David allegedly refer to Israel's sanctuary as a temple structure already built (e.g., 5, 27, 28, 63, 68, 69, 101, 138), even though this edifice was not erected until the reign of Solomon, David's successor. This argument, however, rests upon a misunderstanding of the terms *the house of Jehovah*, *the sanctuary*, or *the temple* (*hēykāl*). We occasionally meet with all of these terms in literature which purports to have been composed before the time of David; for instance, *sanctuary* (*qōdeš*) is used of the tabernacle in Ex. 28:43; *house of the Lord* (*bēyt Yahweh*) in Joshua 6:24; *the house of God* (*bēyt Elôhîm*) in Judg. 18:31; and even *temple* (*hēykāl*) in 1 Sam. 1:9; 3:3. At the same time it should be observed that the sanctuary mentioned in the psalms attributed to David is often referred to in terms that never could be used in connection with Solomon's temple. Thus, in Ps. 27, the sanctuary is referred to not only as "temple" (*hēykāl*) and the "house of Jehovah" (*bēyt Yahweh*) but also as *sukkah* or "booth" and *'ōhel* or "tent." Judging then from the internal evidence of the psalms themselves, the Hebrews sometimes referred to the tent of the tabernacle as "sanctuary," or "house of the Lord," or "house of God," or "temple." No structure of wood or stone was necessarily implied by any of these expressions.

3. It is objected that some of the psalms attributed to David show telltale Aramaisms which indicate late post-exilic authorship. An example of this would be Psalm 139, where verse 2 shows the preposition *le* ("to") as a sign of the direct object (rather than *'ēt*); verse 4 uses *millah* for "word" rather than the regular Hebrew term, *dābār* or *'imrâ*; and verse 8 employs the verb *sālaq* for "ascend," rather than the usual *'ālâ*. Some critics have even objected to poetical forms of the pronominal suffix such as *-aiki* as a variant for the usual Hebrew *-ayik* for "thy." It should be remembered, however, that David had extensive contact with the Aramaic-speaking principalities to the north of Israel, and that many of his reading public from the ten tribes would be quite familiar with words borrowed from across the border in Damascus. The poetry of many nations shows a tendency to incorporate rare or dialectic forms in order to enrich the vocabulary, and there is no reason why Hebrew poetry should have been an exception. It cannot be denied that the fifteenth-century Canaanite poetry of the Ras Shamra (Ugarit) shows a very strong Aramaic coloring. The presence of occasional Aramaisms, therefore, is not by itself conclusive evidence of authorship later than the time of David. Thus, while Ps. 139 may not be properly attributed to David (for we cannot maintain the inerrancy of the Hebrew psalm titles as such), much more extensive proof must be adduced to prove this than the mere presence of Aramaisms here and there.

4. The historical David, according to many critics like Sellin, could hardly have found leisure to compose poetry, because his life was so filled with practical affairs; nor would he have had the inclination to such a refined, cultural pursuit.[1] In answer to this, we should recognize that not only the psalm titles themselves but also abundant evidences from other Old Testament records point to the importance of music and

---

1. But compare the literary interests of King Alfred the Great of England, who was much involved in warfare with Viking invaders during most of his reign.

poetry in David's career. The book of 1 Samuel presents him as a skilled harpist at the court of Saul. In 2 Sam. 22 we find in slightly different form the entire substance of Ps. 18 quoted as a composition of King David. The passage in 2 Sam. 1:19-27 contains a poetical lamentation composed by David on the occasion of the death of Saul and Jonathan at the battle of Mount Gilboa. Since this latter composition does not appear in the Psalms, it could not have been borrowed from them. The fact that it actually names Saul and Jonathan as such indicates that it cannot be explained away as a later composition wrongly attributed to David; it could only have been composed by a contemporary living around 1010 B.C.

If David could have composed so highly artistic an elegy as this, he certainly had the capacity for the other psalms attributed to him by the psalm titles. In 1 Samuel 16:18 we see clearly that according to the ancient Hebrew author, it was possible for a really talented man to combine the professions of war and music: "Behold, I have seen a son of Jesse the Bethlehemite, that is cunning in playing, and a mighty valiant man, and a man of war, and prudent in matters, and a comely person, and the Lord is with him." In 2 Sam. 23:1, after a full account of David's prowess in war and effectiveness in governmental administration, he is referred to as "the sweet psalmist of Israel." He apparently was interested in the improvement of musical instruments and designed innovations of his own. Amos 6:5 (ca. 755 B.C.) refers to him as an inventor or player of musical instruments. But he was known not only as a soloist but also as an organizer of choirs or singing guilds. This is attested by 2 Sam. 6:5: "And David and all the house of Israel played before the Lord with all manner of instruments...harps ... psalteries... timbrels, and on cornets and on cymbals"; and also verse 15: "So David and all the house of Israel brought up the ark of the Lord with shouting, and with the sound of the trumpet." In 1 Chron. 16:4-5; 2 Chron. 7:6; and 29:25 we find explicit reference to David's activity in organizing the guilds of singing Levites, who were to play such a large role in the liturgy of the Jerusalem temple.

In this connection it is worth noting that the New Testament repeatedly refers to David as the author of the psalms quoted by Christ and the apostles. In no case is a psalm so cited attributed by the Hebrew psalm title to someone other than David (although a few, like Ps. 2, lack any Hebrew title at all). Critics often assert that the book of Psalms was simply known by the title of David in New Testament times and that references to the Psalter which employ his name do not necessarily indicate a belief in his personal authorship. A careful study, however, of the numerous instances in point leads almost unavoidably to the conclusion that both Jesus and His disciples assumed without question that David was the personal author. Otherwise there is no point to Christ's query in Matt. 22:45: "If David then call him Lord, how is he his son?" The question at issue was whether the Messiah was to be a mere human being or someone divine; only if divine was it appropriate for the mighty king David to refer to him as his Lord. In Mark 12:36, Jesus says very explicitly, "David himself said by the Holy Spirit—" (Ps. 110:1). The apostolic testimony occurs in passages like Acts 4:24-25:

"Lord...who by the mouth of thy servant David hast said"—and then they proceed to quote Psalm 2:1-2. Other New Testament citations include Luke 20:42-44 (Ps. 110); Acts 1:20 (Ps. 69); Acts 2:25-28 (Ps. 16); Acts 2:34 (Ps. 110); and Rom. 4:6-8 (Ps. 32).

RELIABILITY OF THE HEBREW PSALM TITLES

The critics generally regard the Hebrew psalm titles as very late and unreliable, usually being derived by inference from the internal evidence of the psalms themselves. This conclusion is often based upon two lines of evidence: the occasional discrepancies between the psalm titles in the MT and those in the LXX, and the lack of correspondence between statements of historical background and the situation presupposed in the psalms themselves. An example of this supposed discrepancy is found in Ps. 7, the title of which states that David sang this psalm to the Lord "concerning the words of Cush the Benjamite"; or again, the title of Ps. 34 is thought to accord very poorly with the mood and sentiments conveyed by the text.

Mature reflection, however, should lead the investigator to quite an opposite conclusion. It is impossible to explain how any "later rabbis" would have ventured to attach titles of this sort to psalms whose text does not clearly reflect the situations in David's life which are assigned as settings for the compositions. Many of the titles contain allusions to incidents in David's career of which we have no other knowledge. For example, in Ps. 60 biographical details appear concerning battles fought with Aram-naharaim, Aram-zobah, and Edom which are not recorded at all in the books of Samuel. As Wilhelm Moeller points out (GATE, p. 273), the supplemental details constitute a powerful argument for the antiquity of the psalm title itself. A later editor would never have ventured to manufacture new details not contained in the books of Samuel or Chronicles. It is also significant that several of the "orphan" psalms (i.e., psalms that bear no title) teem with historical allusions and references to recent events or contemporary situations which would have furnished ample ground for later rabbinical conjecture.

The LXX furnishes conclusive evidence that the titles were added to the Hebrew Psalter at a date long before Hellenistic times. That is to say, there are several technical terms appearing in the Hebrew titles the meanings of which had been completely forgotten by the time the Alexandrian translation was made (ca. 150-100 B.C.). For example, the expression "to the choir leader" *(lam-mᵉnaṣṣēaḥ)* is nonsensically rendered by the LXX translator "unto the end" *(eis to telos).*[2] (Cf., e.g., Ps. 44, equivalent to the LXX Ps. 43). Apparently the Alexandrian scholar conjectured the vocalization to be *lᵉ-min-*

---

2. It can hardly be doubted that the Greek reader would understand the phrase *eis to telos* as meaning "to the end." However, it should be conceded that the word *telos* when not preceded by the preposition *eis* may occasionally mean "ceremony or rite of initiation" (cf. Aeschylus, Eum. 799; Sophocles, Ant. 1226, Plato, Rep. 8:560c). The Targum renders *lam-mᵉnaṣṣēaḥ*, for "praise" *(liš^ebāḥā)*. The Hebrew *mᵉnaṣṣēaḥ* is a participle derived from the verb *nāṣaḥ*, ("to shine, to surpass"). In the Piel, this verb was used for a liturgical presentation of music, as it appears in 1 Chron. 15:21. The noun *nēṣaḥ* could mean "brilliance, glory," or "long continuance, eternity." In a derived sense, this root could also be a term for "victory." Hence the choir leader would serve as the most prominent member of the entire group as they performed before the public.

nēṣaḥ—"to from the end." Jerome in his commentary on Daniel (par. 620) suggests that the proper translation of this Hebrew expression should be "to the victor"; he was probably influenced in this by the rendering of Theodotion, *eis to nikos*, "to the victory"; or else by Aquila's *tō nikopoiō*, "to the victory winner"; or possibly even by Symmachus's *epinikion*, "song of triumph." Another example is the title of Ps. 80, which contains *el-šōšannîm*, "to the lilies," which is rendered by the Septuagint, "For those who will suffer alteration" *(hyper tōn alloiōthēsomenōn)* as if it had come from *el-šeššōnîm* ("to those who change")—a mistaken interpretation followed by Jerome's *Commentary on Daniel* (par. 653). A third example is *'al-'alāmôṯ* (Ps. 46), which probably means "According to maidens," that is, to be sung at a soprano pitch. The LXX renders it, "Concerning the hidden things" *(hyper tōn kryphiōn)* as if derived from the verb *'ālam*, "to hide."

The fact that these Hebrew technical terms were no longer understood can only lead to the conclusion that these particular words had fallen out of use so long before the second century B.C.; that the true meaning had been completely forgotten. In view of the fact that many scholars like Duhm, Eissfeldt, and Pfeiffer have confidently assigned many of the psalms to the Maccabean period (i.e., 165 B.C. or thereabouts), it is important to understand the significance of this evidence from the Greek version. Admittedly the psalm titles were added after the composition of the psalms to which they were attached; yet the titles themselves—at least those that contain the phrases above mentioned—must have been added so long before the Septuagint translation that their meaning was already forgotten. It necessarily follows that such psalms themselves must have been written long before the Greek period.

In regard to the once favored theory of Maccabean origin of the Psalms, it is interesting to note that in 1 Macc. 7:17 a passage from Ps. 79:3 is quoted as Holy Scripture. This would indicate that there was already a canonical collection of psalms in the Hebrew Bible by the time of the Maccabees.[3] The more recent trend among rationalist critics has been away from the extremes of late dating. Bentzen states: "The result of the investigations carried on since the beginning of the twentieth century must however be that we have to leave behind us the *a priori* presupposition that the Psalms were post-exilic. Psalmody was known in Israel from its earliest days. The oldest Israelite poem which we are able to date approximately, the Song of Deborah (Judg. 5), is a psalm, and psalms were composed in the Old Testament style in other parts of the Near East before we know anything of Israel" (IOT, 2:167). Engnell adds, "Speaking candidly, there is merely one psalm in the whole Psalter of which I am quite convinced that it is post-Exilic: number 137. And as far as I can determine, no other psalm is com-

---

3. W. Staerk and R. Kittel insist that Ps. 79 dates from the Maccabean period despite the fact that it is quoted in Maccabees as sacred Scripture included in an already established canon (cf. Rowley, OTMS, p. 185). R. H. Pfeiffer also (IOT, p. 63) blandly labels Ps. 79 as Maccabean, even while he acknowledges its citation in 1 Macc. 7:17. It seems to be his naive assumption that this particular psalm had just been completed in time for quotation by the author of Maccabees, as though the quotation formula, "according to the word which he had written," could have been used by a Hebrew writer of a mere contemporary production.

parable with it in contents and style. Should this be a mere coincidence?"[4] In his *Fresh Approach to the Psalms* (1957) Oesterley cites numerous Babylonian and Egyptian parallels to the Psalms as indicating the necessity of finding a pre-exilic origin for much of the Psalter.

The most significant evidence of the antiquity of the Psalms as a literary genre comes from the poetry of ancient Ugarit. Perhaps the most reliable listing of their parallels in poetic phraseology and verse structure is to be found in the footnotes of the Ugaritic portion of Pritchard's ANET. Typical examples are:

Psalm 104:3: "Who maketh the clouds his chariot"; cf. the common Ugaritic title of Aleyan Baal: *rkb 'rpt* (i.e., *rākib 'urpāti* or "Rider upon the clouds").

Psalm 6:6: "I water my couch with my tears" resembles Krt 28-30: "His tears are shed like shekels earthward, like fifth-shekels on the bed as he weeps."

The Ugaritic "Thou wilt take thine everlasting kingdom, thy sovereignty of generation (after) generation (*d-r-k-t d-t d-r-d-r-k*)" (Text 68:10) is quite similar to Ps. 145:13: "Thy kingdom is an everlasting kingdom, and thy dominion endureth throughout all generations."

"O El, haste thee, O El, come to my help" is very similar to Ps. 40:13: "Make haste to help me, O Yahweh."

These are but samples of the very large number of striking parallels in Ugarit poetry and they lead to the conclusion that the Hebrews adapted a poetic genre which they found already highly developed among the Canaanite peoples whom they conquered.

HISTORY OF THE COMPILATION OF PSALMS

In addition to seventy-three psalms which are by their titles attributed to David, there are, as we have already seen, many others which are assigned to contemporary authors or those who were slightly later than his time. Psalm 90 is attributed to Moses; twelve psalms are assigned to Asaph; ten others to the descendants of Korah; one (Ps. 127) to Solomon; one to Heman the Ezrahite[5] (Ps. 88), and one to Ethan the Ezrahite (Ps. 89). Of the "orphan" or anonymous psalms there is little doubt that some of them indicate a date of composition during or after the Exile. We may regard Ps. 137, "By the waters of Babylon," as exilic and Ps. 126, "When the Lord turned again the captivity of Zion," as early post-exilic, perhaps 500 B.C. (But it should be noted that 50 percent of the Psalms are anonymous).

It was therefore inevitable that the Psalter should be accumulated by stages over a long period of time. Apparently the grouping into books dated from an early period. Thus Ps. 72:20 states, "The prayers [*tᵉpillôt*] of David the son of Jesse are ended"; this

---

4. I. Engnell, *Studies in Divine Kingship* (Stockholm: Almqvist & Wiksells Boktryckeri, 1943), p. 176, n. 2.

5. The term *Ezrahite* seems to indicate a descendant of Zerach of the tribe of Judah. Apparently a Levitical family stationed in Judah was incorporated into the family of Zerach, both because of living in a Jewish community and also possibly by intermarriage.

notation doubtless marks the end of an earlier smaller edition of the Psalter which contained largely the Davidic psalms and those alone. At least three collections can be distinguished.

1. Book I (Pss. 1-41) was probably arranged by David, or else by some collaborator under his direction. Although it bears no title, Ps. 1 serves as a logical introduction to the whole collection and may well have been composed either by David himself or by Solomon his son. Psalm 2, which likewise lacks a title, is definitely ascribed to David in Acts 4:25. The reason Ps. 10 has no title is probably to be found in the original unity of Pss. 9 and 10 (they are regarded by the LXX as a single composition). Psalm 33, which has no title in the MT, is ascribed by the LXX likewise to David. It thus appears that the entire contents of Book I is to be assigned to David. Yet it is hard to tell why only a partial collection should have been made of David's poetry and incorporated into this first volume. It would be difficult to show that these psalms were composed earlier in his career and that the Davidic psalms of the later books came from his old age, for in some cases (notably Ps. 32 and Ps. 51), some of those appearing in the later books are quite possibly as early as those in Book I. It has been suggested by Ewald and others that possibly the earliest edition of the Psalter contained not only Pss. 1-41, but also 51-72, and that it was only at a later period that the psalms of Asaph and the sons of Korah were inserted (i.e., Pss. 42-50). It certainly is true that none of Pss. 51-72 is assigned by title to any other author besides David, and the last verse of Ps. 72 would then constitute an appropriate *finis* to the entire collection as it was originally published.

2. Book II (Pss. 42-72) and Book III (Pss. 73-89) may well have been collected and published at a later period, possibly in the reign of Josiah, to furnish additional material for devotional expression during his revival movement. On the other hand, it is just as likely that this compilation took place earlier, in the reign of Hezekiah (ca. 710 B.C.). It is well known that Hezekiah had an active Bible committee ("the men of Hezekiah," Prov. 25:1) as part of his reform program. These two books then could have been prepared for publication and certainly for liturgical use in the temple under Hezekiah's sponsorship.

3. The remaining books, IV (90-106) and V, (107-150) are largely a collection of a miscellaneous sort, the date of which is uncertain. Some of them may have been as early as David or even Moses, and some as late as the return from the Exile. No doubt, this compilation was made in the time of Ezra and Nehemiah, when the reconstruction of the political and religious life of the second commonwealth was vigorously carried through. It is fair to say that there are no historical allusions or situations presupposed in Pss. 90-150 which do not accord with events in Hebrew history prior to 430 B.C.

Rationalist higher criticism has come to no significant measure of agreement as to the time when the various individual psalms were composed. Scholars of the late nineteenth and early twentieth centuries tended to deal with each individual psalm on its merits, and conjecturing its age by that stage in the development of Israel's religious thought which it seemed to reflect, they could arrive at an approximate date on evolutionistic principles. Or else the critic might search for possible historical allusions and then look for a set of circumstances in Israelite history to which those allusions might be appropriate. Those who espoused the Maccabean Theory for the composition of many of the psalms often followed this latter methodology.

With the advent of Hermann Gunkel, an entirely new approach came into favor. Beginning with his *Ausgewählte Psalmen* (1904) he started to use the principles of Form Criticism in analyzing the corpus of the Psalter. He classified the psalms into various categories or types (*Gattungen*) and sought to identify the general situation in life (*Sitz im Leben*) which brought them into existence. By a careful study of similar material from the early civilizations of Egypt and Mesopotamia, Gunkel sought to recapture the ancient Hebrew viewpoint and to analyze the psalms in a much more valid and appropriate way than had been possible by the earlier method. (Cf. Rowley, OTMS, p. 163.) The great majority of the psalms he was able to divide into five main types:

1. The hymns intended for purposes of communal worship expressing the author's own personal adoration and devotion toward Jehovah.

2. The communal laments in the face of some major catastrophe or disaster which had befallen the community (e.g., Pss. 44; 74; 79; 80; 83).

3. Royal psalms which focus particular attention upon the Israelite king as a servant of Jehovah.

4. The individual lament—a type which formed the backbone of the Psalter—in which the individual author finds himself in distress, threatened by his foes, and unjustly persecuted; and yet by an upsurge of faith he expresses a certainty that he will be heard, and often makes a vow of tangible expression for his gratitude in response to the confidently expected deliverance.

5. Individual songs of thanksgiving (such as Pss. 18, 30, 32, 34, 41, 66, 92, etc.) in which a grateful recital is made of the deliverances and blessings the worshiper has received as he approaches the altar of thanksgiving. Gunkel's principal concern was not chronological, but his tendency was to place the major part of the Psalter in the time prior to the Exile (especially in the case of the "royal" psalms).

This Form Critical approach was taken up and extended by many of the more recent scholars such as Eissfeldt, Bentzen, Engnell, Oesterley, Robinson, and E. A. Leslie (*The Psalms*, 1949). Sigmund Mowinckel (*Psalmen Studiën*, 1921-24) also followed the Form Critical approach, with the important modification, however, that virtually none of the psalms was genuinely personal in an individualistic sense but all pertained to the worshiping community. A great many of the "enthronement psalms" are believed to have originated in connection with the yearly celebration of the enthronement of Yahweh which Mowinckel supposed took place at the New Year festival (on the analogy of the Babylonian enthronement of Marduk at the time of each new year). He even understood the "day of Yahweh" as referring originally to the cultic day of God's enthronement, but projected into the future as the time when Yahweh would come with power to assert Himself as King over all the earth. Many of these "enthronement psalms" he regarded as dating back to the time of the Jewish monarchy. Norman Snaith vigorously opposed the theory that the psalms of this type were actually composed for the celebration of the Sabbath or that the majority of them were post-exilic in origin. (These ingenious speculations will be taken seriously only by those who accept the humanistic presuppositions of those who devise them.)

Numeration of the Psalms

Both the MT and the LXX contain a total of 150 psalms. Whether this was the original number is not completely certain. The Talmud (*Sabbath* 16) speaks of 147, one for each year of life of the patriarch Jacob. Nor is it certain how the psalms were originally divided. The Talmud (*Berachoth 9b*) speaks of Pss. 1 and 2 as constituting a single composition. On the other hand, Acts 13:33 explicitly refers to Ps. 2:7 as coming from "the second psalm."

The English version follows the division of the MT so far as psalm numbers are concerned. Unlike the Hebrew practice, however, it does not count the psalm titles as constituting a verse. Hence there is usually a divergence in verse numbering between the English Bible and the Hebrew Bible whenever the psalm in question has a title. (I.e., the Hebrew number will be one higher than the English number; in the case of Ps. 51 and a few others, it will be two higher.) As indicated, the psalm numbering of the LXX differs from that of the MT (and therefore of the English Bible) because: (1) it counts Ps. 10 as part of Ps. 9; (2) it counts Ps. 115 as part of Ps. 114; (3) it divides Ps. 116 into two separate psalms; and (4) it divides Ps. 147 into two separate psalms. The LXX also adds Ps. 151, with the notation, "outside of the number."[6] Since the Vulgate follows the numeration of the LXX, naturally the Catholic English translations follow suit.

Contents of the Psalm Titles

It is not altogether certain that the present arrangement of the psalm titles in the MT accurately reflects their original position. J. W. Thirtle in *The Titles of the Psalms* (1905) has very convincingly argued that many of the psalms possess not only a prescript but also a postscript. At a later period, however, the postscripts of some psalms were mistakenly attached by the scribes to the prescripts of the succeeding psalms. He assigned to the postscript (or notation at the end of the composition) the following types of material: (1) the notation "To the choirmaster"; (2) musical directions indicating what kind of instrument was to be played (such as *neĝînôt*, or "stringed instruments;" *neḥîlôt* or "wind instruments"); and (3) the occasion (or melody tune) which applied to the psalm in question, for instance, *'al mût lab-bēn* in Ps. 9 and *'al-'ayyelet*

---

6. The Hebrew original of Ps. 151 has recently been discovered in Qumran Cave 11.

haš-šaḥar in Ps. 22. In other words, if elements of this sort appear in a psalm title, according to Thirtle, they have been incorrectly transferred from the original postscript at the end of the preceding psalm. When such elements are removed, it then appears that a proper prescript or initial title contains only these three elements: (1) the genre label, such as *mizmōr* or "psalm"; *maskîl* or "instruction"; *shîr* or "song"; *mikhtām*, or "atonement song"; (2) the ascription of authorship, of David, of Asaph, et cetera; (3) the occasion (e.g., "when he fled from Absalom," or "which he sang to Jehovah concerning the words of Cush," etc.). Thirtle pointed out that some of the Egyptian and Akkadian hymns ended with a final notation including even "to the end"—which may have been a factor influencing the LXX to render *lam-mᵉnaṣṣēaḥ* as *eis to telos* ("to

TECHNICAL TERMS IN THE PSALMS

TYPES OF PSALMS

Term	Meaning	Psalm
Mizmōr	Musical accompaniment	57
Shîr	Vocal music	27
Maskîl	Didactic or contemplative	13
Mikhtām	Song of covering, atonement	6
Tᵉpillah	Prayer	5
Tᵉhillah	Song of praise	5
Šiggāyôn	Wandering or irregular song	1

Musical Terms

Term	Meaning	Psalm
Lam-mᵉnaṣṣēaḥ	To the choir leader	55
Negînôt	With string instruments	13
Neḥillôt	With wind instruments	1
Šemīnît	With an eight-stringed lute or an octave lower than soprano	2
ʿalamot	Soprano or high pitched	2
Maḥalat	Song of lament	2

Melody Indicators

Term	Meaning	Psalm
'al mût lab-bēn	Death of a son	1
'al 'ayyelet haš-šaḥar	According to the hind of the morning	1
Šūšān or `al šošnnîm	To the lilies	3
'al tašḥêt	Do not destroy or corrupt	4
'al Yônat 'ēlem rᵉḥōqîm	According to a dove of silence those who are afar off	1

the end"). (In this connection it should be mentioned that in the case of Thirtle's prescripts there are about twenty-five discrepancies in the psalm titles between the LXX and the MT. For example, seven have *psalmos* where the MT does not read *mizmōr*; seven have *ōdē* where the MT lacks *shîr*; and five in the LXX have *allēlouia* where the Hebrew has no *hallelûyah*.)

TECHNICAL TERMS IN THE PSALM TITLES

1. *Mizmōr*, or "psalm," meant a song rendered to the accompaniment of instrumental music, originally a stringed instrument, from *zāmar*, "to pluck" (but cf. also *zamara*, Arabic, "to play on the reed"). Fifty-seven of the psalms are so labeled.

2. *Shîr*, or "song," implies nothing concerning a musical accompaniment. It is simply a general term for vocal music. Twenty-seven psalms are so labeled; fifteen of these are called *shîr ham-ma'alôth* or "the song of ascents."

3. *Maskîl*, or "didactic poem," or "contemplative poem" (the verb from which it comes, *hiskîl*, may mean "give attention to, consider, ponder; or give insight to, teach someone"). It appears as a title for thirteen psalms. Since the contents of these psalms are by no means uniformly didactic, we should probably prefer the interpretation "contemplative."

4. *Miktām* is a disputed term. If it derives from a root meaning "to cover" (cf. *katama*, Arabic, and *katāmu*, Akkadian, both of which mean "to cover"), it might signify a song of covering or atoning for sin (so Mowinckel). Later Hebrew construed this word to mean "epigram" (hence the LXX *stēlographia*), or "engraving," as if referring to a composition intended to record memorable thoughts, pithy sayings, or eloquent refrains. Six psalms bear this title.

5. *Tᵉpillah* simply means a "prayer." Five psalms are so designated.

6. *Tᵉhillah* means a "song of praise" and is found in five psalm titles. Note that this word in the plural, *Tᵉhillîm*, furnishes the Hebrew title for the whole book of Psalms.

7. *Šiggāyôn* may perhaps mean an "irregular" or "wandering" song (from *šāgâ*, "to wander"); hence, an irregular dithyrambic ode. (Only Ps. 7 bears this term, but so also does the psalm in Hab. 3.)

MUSICAL TERMS IN THE TITLES

1. *Lam-mᵉnaṣṣēaḥ*, as explained above, probably means "to the choir leader." It has plausibly been suggested that this term was affixed to those psalms which were included in a special anthology made by the temple choir leader for the convenience of his singers—rather than including the entire group of 150 in the complete repertoire of the Psalter. Fifty-five psalms are so labeled.

2. *Nᵉgînôt* means "stringed instruments" or "songs to be sung to the accompaniment of stringed instruments." (Pss. 4:1, 6:1, 54:1, 55:1, 61:1, 67:1, 69:18, 76:1; also Job 30:9; Isa. 38:20; Lam 3:14, 5:14; Hab 3:19)

3. *Nᵉhillôt* means "wind instruments" (cf. *hālîl*, flute). (Ps. 5)

4. *Šĕmînît* seems to mean either an "eight-stringed lute", or possibly an "octave" (i.e., an octave lower than the soprano or *ʿalamôt*). (Pss. 6, 12)

5. *ʿalamôt*, or "maidens," may mean "soprano" or "high pitch" (cf. 1 Chron. 15:20; Ps. 46).

6. *Maḥalat* means "sickness" and/or "grief" and may imply therefore a song of lament (Pss. 53, 88). Alternatively, it may have been the name of a woman singer, as R. K. Harrison suggests (IOT, p. 979).

MELODY INDICATORS

Some of the cryptic words in the psalm titles may indicate either the occasion on which the psalm was originally composed; or, as is more likely, the opening words of a well-known melody, according to which the psalm was to be sung (just as we might say, "Sing to the tune of the 'The Battle Hymn of the Republic'").

1. *ʿal m t lab-bēn* in Ps. 9 may indicate some well-known song beginning with the words, *The death of a son* (the preposition *ʿal* being construed as "according to").

2. *ʿal ʿayyelet haš-šaḥar means* "according to the hind of the morning" (Ps. 22).

3. *Šūšān* or *ʿal šôšannîm* would refer to the lily and perhaps signified "to the lilies."(Pss. 60, 69, 80).

4. *ʿal tašḥēt* seems to mean "do not destroy" or "do not corrupt." Apparently a well-known song began with these words, and its melody was to be followed here (Pss. 57, 58, 59, 75).

5. *ʿal Yônat ʾēlem rᵉḥōqîm* apparently means "according to a dove of silence those who are afar off." Some have suggested that it should be repointed to read *ʾēlîm rᵉḥōqîm*, or, "terebinths afar off" (Ps. 56).

A technical term which does not occur in the psalm titles is the perplexing *selah.*, which appears often in the body of the text. While many explanations have been given for this word the most plausible is that which derives it from the root *sālal* meaning "to lift up." The LXX renders it *diapsalma*, which means "musical interlude." *Selah* then is not a word to be read aloud, but simply a notice to the reciter that at this point he should pause in his utterance and permit the musical accompaniment to strike up; or else it is a direction for him to lift up his voice to a higher intensity or pitch, or possibly even to lift up his heart to pious contemplation or meditation. Psalm 67:1-2 contains *selah* in the middle of the sentence, and this makes it difficult to construe as pause for musical interlude. However, in most other instances this interpretation seems quite appropriate.

Psalms 120-134 bear in their titles the expression "the song of the ascents" ("degrees," KJV; *šîr hammaʿᵃlôt*, Hebrew). An old Jewish tradition explains this as referring to a semicircular flight of steps leading up to the court of men in the temple (Mishnah: *Middoth* 2:5). A more likely explanation is that these "ascents" referred to the stages of pilgrimage up to Jerusalem (the word *maʿᵃlôt* being derived from the verb *ʿālâ*, "go up," i.e., to Jerusalem). Some prefer to interpret as "processions" (of pilgrims), by metonymy from "ascent." Thus these would be pilgrim songs, to be sung on the way to Jerusalem for the annual feast days. This explanation also seems preferable to that of Gesenius and Delitzsch, who refer it to the steplike, progressive movement of the thoughts expressed in the psalms themselves; unfortunately for this theory, some of this group do not show this characteristic at all (e.g., Pss. 125 and 133).

MESSIANIC PSALMS

One of the most remarkable features of the Psalter is its frequent allusion to the coming Messiah. The chart below lists a few of the many examples of Messianic psalms.

Christ's Ascension ....Ps. 68:18 (Eph. 4:8)
Christ's Betrayal..Ps. 41:9 (Luke 22:48)
Christ's Death ....Ps. 22:1-21 (Matt. 27)
Christ's Deity.. Ps. 45:6-7 (Heb. 1:8-9)
Christ's Exaltation .... Ps. 8:5-6 (Heb. 2:6-9)
Christ's Kingship..Ps. 2:6; 89:18-19 (Acts 5:31)
Christ's Lordship ....Ps. 8:2 (Matt. 21:15-16)
                                                    Ps. 110:1 (Matt. 22:44; Acts 2:34)
Christ's Obedience ....Ps. 40:6-8 (Heb. 10:5-7)
Christ's Priesthood..Ps. 110:4 (Heb. 5:6)
Christ's Resurrection ....Ps. 2:7; 16:10 (Acts 2:25-28, 13:33-35)
Christ's Sonship...Ps. 2:7 (Matt. 3:17, Heb. 1:5)
Christ's Sufferings...........Ps. 69:9 (John 2:17, Rom. 15:3) Ps. 69:4 (John 15:25)
Christ's Supremacy ....Ps. 118:22-23 (Matt. 21:42)
Examples of other Messianic Psalms include: 72, 102, 109.

IMPRECATORY PSALMS

Various psalms contain appeals to God to pour out His wrath upon the psalmist's enemies. These seem to contradict the Christian stance of love toward one's enemies. Nevertheless, it is a mistake to explain away these expressions as degenerate and sub-Christian sentiments which have been permitted in the sacred canon by the principle of "progressive revelation." Progressive revelation is not to be thought of as a progress from error to truth, but rather as a progress from the partial and obscure to the complete and clear. A consistent Evangelical will hold that all portions of the Word of God are true in the sense intended by the original author under the inspiration of the Holy Spirit, even though couched in terms which may perhaps have been more comprehensible and relevant to God's people at the time of composition than in later ages.

It is important to realize that prior to the first advent of Christ, the only tangible way in which the truth of the Scripture could be demonstrated to an unbelieving world was by the pragmatic test of disaster befalling those who were in error and deliverance being granted to those who held to the truth. As long as the wicked continued to triumph on earth, their temporal prosperity seemed to refute the holiness and sovereignty of the God of Israel. A Hebrew believer in the Old Testament age could only chafe in deep affliction of soul as long as such a state of affairs continued. Identifying himself completely with God's cause, he could only regard God's enemies as his own, and implore God to uphold His own honor and justify His own righteousness by inflicting a crushing destruction upon those who either in theory or in practice denied His sovereignty and His law. Not until the supreme exhibition of God's displeasure at sin, demonstrated by the death of His Son upon the cross, was it possible for the believer to wait patiently while God's longsuffering permitted the wicked to enjoy his temporary success. Nor was the longsuffering of God properly understood until Jesus came to earth to teach His love to men.

34 THE BOOKS OF WISDOM: JOB AND PROVERBS

JOB

AS TO THE MEANING of the name Job (*'Iyyôḇ*, in Hebrew), it probably comes from a root meaning "come back," or "repent," and hence may signify "one who turns back" (to God). This interpretation is based upon the Arabic *'āba*, "repent" or "go back" (often followed by the phrase *'ila 'llāhi*, "to God"). The older Arabic spelling of the name seems to have been *'Awwābun* in the *Arabic Bible* (as translated by Cornelius Van Dyck) *it is 'ayyûbu*. It is found in Akkadian inscriptions as *Ayyabum*, for instance, in the Mari documents of the eighteenth century B.C. In the Amarna Letters the name appears as *Ayab* (a prince of Pella). Interestingly enough, this name even occurs in the Berlin Execration Texts (written in Egyptian hieratic) as the appellation of a prince in the region of Damascus during the nineteenth century (cf. BASOR no. 82 [1941], p. 36). Another possible etymology for *'Iyyôḇ* is "the assailed one," from the Hebrew *'āyēb*, "to hate, be at enmity" (so Koehler-Baumgartner), or else, "object of enmity" (so Brown-Driver-Briggs, *Lexicon*). But it is worth noting, in favor of the Arabic etymology, that Job was a native of North Arabia, and the whole setting of the story is Arabic rather than Hebrew.

THE THEME OF JOB

This book deals with the theoretical problem of pain and disaster in the life of the godly. It undertakes to answer the question, Why do the righteous suffer? This answer comes in a threefold form: (1) God is worthy of love even apart from the blessings He bestows; (2) God may permit suffering as a means of purifying and strengthening the soul in godliness; (3) God's thoughts and ways are moved by considerations too vast for the puny mind of man to comprehend. Even though man is unable to see the issues of life with the breadth and vision of the Almighty; nevertheless God really knows what is best for His own glory and for our ultimate good. This answer is given against the background of the stereotyped views of Job's three "comforters," Eliphaz, Bildad, and Zophar.

An adequate psychological motive for their persistence in carrying on the controversy with Job over so many chapters is to be found in the dilemma into which his catastrophic disaster had placed them. If a man of such high reputation for godliness could suffer so devastating a misfortune, their own security was imperiled by the possibility that the same thing could happen to themselves. Their basic motive in attempting to elicit from Job a confession of sin was to bolster their own sense of security. If in point of fact Job had been guilty of some grievous sin of which the public had no knowledge, his overwhelming disasters could be easily understood as the retribution of the righteous God from whom no secrets could be hidden. Failing to secure from him any such confession despite all their diligent efforts to compel from him an admission of guilt, they felt unable to return home relieved and reassured that calamity would be kept from their door if they only "lived a good life." Hence they stayed with him in a continuing effort to extract from him the admission of some well-hidden but heinous transgression.

OUTLINE OF JOB

I. Prologue: Job's test, 1:1–2:13

II. False comfort by the three friends, 3:1–31:40

    A. First cycle of speeches, 3:1–14:22
        1. Job's lament, 3:1-26
        2. Eliphaz' reply, 4:1–5:27; and Job's rejoinder, 6:1–7:21
        3. Bildad's reply, 8:1-22; and Job's rejoinder, 9:1–10:22
        4. Zophar's reply, 11:1-20; and Job's rejoinder, 12:1–14:22
    B. Second cycle of speeches, 15:1–21:34
        1. Eliphaz' reply, 15:1-35; and Job's rejoinder, 16:1–17:16
        2. Bildad's reply, 18:1-21; and Job's rejoinder, 19:1-29
        3. Zophar's reply, 20:1-29; and Job's rejoinder, 21:1-34
    C. Third cycle of speeches, 22:1–31:40
        1. Eliphaz' reply, 22:1-30; and Job's rejoinder, 23:1–24:25
        2. Bildad's reply, 25:1-6; and Job's rejoinder, 26:1–31:40

III. The speeches of Elihu, 32:1–37:24

    A. First speech: God's instruction to man through affliction, 32:1–33:33
    B. Second speech: God's justice and prudence vindicated, 34:1-37
    C. Third speech: the advantages of pure and consistent piety, 35:1-16
    D. Fourth speech: God's greatness and Job's guilt in accusing God of unfairness, 36:1–37:24

IV. God's speeches from the whirlwind 38:1–42:6

    A. First speech: God's omnipotence proclaimed in creation; Job's self-con demning confession, 38:1–40:5

B. Second speech: God's power and man's frailty; Job's humble re-response, 40:6–42:6

V. Epilogue: God's rebuke of the three comforters; Job's restoration, and reward of a long and blessed prolongation of life 42:7-17

AUTHORSHIP OF JOB

The text of this book does not indicate its author, and there is no consistent tradition even in rabbinic circles as to who the composer of this work might have been. The Talmud ventures only to suggest that the writer must have been someone who lived prior to the time of Moses. There seems to be nothing in the internal evidence of the text itself to furnish a clue as to the author's identity. The commentator Jacques Bolduc (1637) suggested that it may have been secondarily the work of Moses himself, who found it in an original Aramaic form and felt it worthwhile to translate into Hebrew. While it can scarcely be said that there is anything Mosaic about the style of Job, this theory would at least account for (1) its being possessed by the Hebrews, (2) its attaining a canonical status, (3) its patriarchal flavor and setting, and (4) the Aramaic flavor in some of the terminology and modes of expression exhibited by the text.

DATE OF THE EVENTS

Inasmuch as Job contains no references to historical events and reflects a non-Hebraic cultural background concerning which we possess little or no information, it is not easy to assign a probable date for the lifetime and career of Job. The district of Uz, in which the action took place, was located in northern Arabia; the Septuagint refers to it as the land of the Aisitai, a people whom Ptolemy the geographer locates in the Arabian desert adjacent to the Edomites of Mount Seir. Job's friend Eliphaz came from Teman, a well known locality in Edom. Elihu came from the Buzites, who probably lived adjacent to the Chaldeans in northeast Arabia. It is important to bear this in mind when weighing the force of arguments based upon absence of Mosaic influence.

J. H. Raven inclines to a pre-Mosaic date because (1) Job indicates a patriarchal family-clan type of organization far more reminiscent of Abraham's time than of post-Exodus conditions; (2) the offering of sacrifice by the head of the family rather than by an official priesthood would also be pre-Mosaic; (3) the mention of qᵉsîṭâ as a piece of money (Job 42:11) suggests a date at least as early as Joshua (cf. Josh. 24:32), if not the patriarchal period (cf. Gen. 33:19). But if the scene was laid in North Arabia near Edom, a clan type of society may well have persisted there as late as the time of the Hebrew monarchy. Possibly private sacrifices by the heads of families persisted alongside the official tribal priesthood.

This foreign locale would also account for the comparative rarity of the name *Yahweh* in most chapters of the book. Job shows a distinct preference for the pan-Semitic term, *'Elōah* or *'Elōhîm*, for God. ("Yahweh" occurs twice in chap. 1, once in chap. 2, once in chap. 12, once in chap. 38, three times in chap. 40, and five times in chap. 42.) Interestingly enough, the title *Shaddai* ("the Almighty") occurs no less than thirty-one times in Job as against its sixteen occurrences in the rest of the Old Testament. This evidence from the use of the divine names certainly tends to confirm the theory of a non-Israelite background.

And yet it remains true, apart from the absence of Mosaic influence, that the background of the story of Job points to a setting in the early second millennium B.C. W. F. Albright in his chapter on the "Old Testament and Archaeology" in the Alleman and Flack *Commentary* indicates that the historical Job may well have been contemporary with the patriarchs. His basis for this conclusion rests partly upon the dubious ground that Ezek. 14:14 couples the names of Job and Daniel. Albright understands this Daniel to be the ancient Canaanite hero Dan'el, who appears as a prominent figure in one of the Ugaritic epics, that is, as the idol-worshiping father of Aqhat.[1] Thus he rejects the possibility that Ezekiel could be referring to his own contemporary, Daniel, in Babylon. He also points out the fact that the other names in the narrative are authentic for the second millennium B.C. Thus Bildad was probably shortened from Yabil-Dadum, a name found in cuneiform sources dating from that period. He also traces a noteworthy resemblance to the account of the "Babylonian Job," a cuneiform composition translated in Barton's AB (i.e., *Archeology of the Bible*). This is the story of a righteous man who underwent the bitterest agony of body and spirit, even though he was conscious of having lived an upright life, and nevertheless remained steadfast in the midst of his affliction. Ultimately he was granted a happier life than ever, to the glory of Marduk, the god of Babylon. This Babylonian account may go back to 1200 B.C., and may rest upon materials even earlier.

DATE OF THE COMPOSITION OF JOB

A distinction must be drawn between the historical period when Job actually lived and the time when this record of his ordeal was composed. It might naturally be supposed to have been written soon after the events themselves. Nevertheless there is the widest divergence of opinion on this point, some estimates, as we shall see, deferring the time of authorship until after the Babylonian Exile. In general there are five main views maintained by biblical scholars today: (1) in the patriarchal age; (2) in the reign of Solomon; (3) in the reign of Manasseh; (4) in the generation of Jeremiah; (5) during or after the Exile.

1. *Before the time of Moses, in the patriarchal age.* If the contents of Job are to be

---

1. But, Dan'el, father of Aqhat in that document is portrayed as a dedicated idol-worshipper devoting blood sacrifices to El, Baal, and the other gods for weeks at a time. He got so drunk at a banquet that he had to be helped home. He spent seven years weeping and mourning for his dead son and persuaded his daughter to murder a warrior named Yatpan, who had been implicated in the death of his son seven years previously. No more implausible correspondent to the character and nobility of Daniel could be imagined than this pagan hero.

regarded as historically accurate and a faithful transcript of the actual conversations of the five men involved, it would be natural to assume that this record was composed soon after Job's restoration to prosperity, the final addition, 42:16-17, having been completed not long after his decease. If therefore Job's career took place before the time of Moses, the book itself must date back to that same approximate era. This was the view of the Talmud and was widely held by Christian scholars until modern times.

In our present century there are rather few scholars even among leading Conservatives who would venture to insist upon a pre-Mosaic date. As has already been pointed out, the fact that the events take place on non-Israelite soil, that is, in North Arabia, makes the period of composition difficult to date with any precision. There is no compelling reason why the influence of the Mosaic Torah should have been felt in Uz or Teman even as late as 1000 B.C. In the absence of any literature from the same locality it is impossible to do more than conjecture what allusions to history or law or local custom might have been present in any artistic composition of North Arabia. If, moreover, the work was composed in the pre-Mosaic period prior to the Hebrew conquest, it gives rise to the possibility that it was originally composed in some language other than Hebrew, whether in a North Arabian dialect or possibly in Aramaic, as some have suggested.

Some critics have pointed to the mention of the worship of the sun and moon in Job 31:26, feeling that this would exclude a period of composition earlier than the rise of Mesopotamian cults in the latter days of the Jewish monarchy. It should be remembered, however, that the worship of the sun and moon had been carried on by Sumerians, Akkadians, and Egyptians from time immemorial, and the earliest Old South Arabic inscriptions which have survived indicate vigorous cults of this type flourishing in the southern part of the Arabian peninsula.

There is no evidence of the pre-Mosaic dating of Job due to a total ignorance of the Torah, of Abraham, Moses, or the nation of Israel in the texts of Job. This is impossible to explain in the light of total commitment to monotheism which is apparent from all of the conversations between Job, his three counselors, and Elihu. It is difficult to imagine that they could have totally ignored the existence of a fairly nearby nation (cf. Hebrews) who were also committed to a monotheistic concept of God. Therefore, the only reasonable conclusion to draw is that the experience of Job must have taken place prior to the Israelite conquest of Canaan.

Some critics have uncovered what they feel to be traces of the influence of the Mosaic law, especially in Job 24:2-11. This passage mentions (*a*) the wickedness of keeping pawned clothes overnight (forbidden in Ex. 22:25); (*b*) the custom of reserving for the poor the gleaning of the fields of the rich (prescribed in Lev. 19:9); (*c*) the wickedness of moving the boundary marker of a farm (cf. Deut. 19:14). However, a second reading of this passage in Job reveals that it amounts to only a statement that the poor have been reduced to gleaning the fields of the rich, and that having pawned their clothes to the wealthy they are forced to sleep naked overnight. This falls short of invoking any legal sanctions in either case. As for denouncing the moving of a boundary marker, this was a commonplace sentiment throughout the Fertile Crescent, from Sumeria to the Nile. Numerous boundary stones have been found from the time of Hammurabi and earlier invoking divine wrath upon any miscreants who should venture to shift them from position. It turns out, therefore, that the case for an acquaintance with the Mosaic code cannot be sustained for the book of Job.

The absence of any demonstrable knowledge of the existence of the Mosaic code is of utmost significance. Furthermore there is a complete unawareness of any other monotheistic culture to be found in any adjacent region of western Asia than that represented by Uz, Teman, Shuah on the Euphrates and Naamah (from which the three comforters had come). Surely if the Hebrew nation, devoted to the exclusive worship of the same God (El, Eloah, Elyah, Shaddai and Yahweh) had already settled in nearby Canaan, some allusion to them would surely be expected in the conversations between Job and his counselors. Why is there no awareness whatever of Abraham, Isaac or Jacob or Moses or Joshua? Every other book in the Old Testament presupposes Abraham and the Torah and God's covenant with Israel. How can Job center attention upon God and the basic principles of theology without any cognizance of Israel and God's Lordship over this monotheistic nation? The only reasonable explanation for this is that the episode of Job's trial and the written record of his experience was written down before the conquest of Canaan by Joshua and before the departure of Israel from Egyptian bondage. This implies that the original composition was written in a language other than Hebrew, even though it was later translated into the form which has been preserved in the Hebrew Bible. If so, it turns out that Job is actually the earliest book in the Bible, and that it was included in a Hebrew translation as a part of Scripture because of its perceived value as solving the age-long problem of how undeserved suffering can befall even sincere and godly believers.

2. *In the reign of Solomon.* This view was advocated as early as the time of Gregory Nazianzen (fourth century A.D.) and also by Martin Luther, Haevernick, Keil, and Franz Delitzsch. In the conservative handbooks on Old Testament introduction, it is favored by Raven, Young, and Unger. The grounds adduced for this dating fall generally under these heads: (*a*) Solomon's age was one of prosperous leisure in which literary pursuits were practiced against a background of national self-realization; (*b*) the age of Solomon devoted particular interest to *hokmâ* and pondered the deepest practical problems of life; (*c*) there is a similar exaltation of godly wisdom in Proverbs 8 to that which appears in Job 28; (*d*) a fairly extensive knowledge of foreign countries, or at least of conditions which existed throughout the Near East generally, indicates a wider acquaintance with the contemporary world than North Arabian conditions would presuppose. In Solomon's time, of course, there was the widest acquaintance with the foreign nations even as remote as India, which enjoyed commercial relations with the Hebrew empire. It cannot be denied that these considerations possess a certain cumulative force; yet it is questionable whether they can be regarded as really conclusive, for most of the four fea-

tures above mentioned are reconcilable with an earlier date as well, particularly if the account was composed by a non-Israelite author on non-Israelite soil.

A problem immediately presents itself to the conservative scholar as soon as he settles upon a Solomonic date for the composition of this book. If the events themselves took place four centuries or more before Job was written—and most of these writers consider Job to have lived at least as early as the time of Moses—then it is difficult to see how an accurate record could have been maintained of the actual remarks expressed by Job and his four counselors. Delitzsch therefore suggests that the book was not meant to be a historically accurate transcript of words actually spoken in the patriarchal period, but that it was probably intended as a drama for which the dialogue had been composed by the author. Such a drama would be historically accurate only as a play based, for example, upon the life of Abraham Lincoln might artistically represent the man's character and what he stood for without purporting to be a reporter's transcript of remarks that he actually voiced. Delitzsch contends that no Hebrew reader would have understood the speeches in Job as a verbatim report, since the narrative was put into a poetic, dramatic form. Yet even as drama, Job is not to be dismissed as mere fiction, for the author may well have composed it under the inspiration of the Holy Spirit and accurately represented the sentiments and theological opinions historically expressed by the parties concerned. It was simply that the dramatic or poetic form in which they were composed was the product of the literary artist. If, then, the book did not purport really to be a reporter's transcript and would not have been so understood by the ancient reader, it should be understood and interpreted by the modern reader in the light of the author's original intention.

In support of this interpretation it certainly must be conceded that the text of Job does not read like an ordinary conversation such as would be carried on under usual circumstances. Apart from the introductory and the concluding chapters, the main body of the text reads like a poetic and highly artistic composition, employing language which would not normally be used by persons speaking extemporaneously in a real life situation. In this respect Job may be put in a different category from the other books in the Old Testament which purport to give a narrative of historical events, particularly if the original speakers were expressing themselves in a language other than Hebrew—as indeed they must have. Thus the ancient reader for whose spiritual benefit the book was composed would naturally expect a certain amount of artistic license in the literary form in which the speakers' sentiments and opinions were expressed.

3. *In the reign of Manasseh, seventh century B.C.* This was an age of moral degeneracy and social injustice, a time when questions concerning divine providence would call for anxious scrutiny, with error on the throne and truth on the scaffold. Therefore the prominence given to the suffering of the innocent and the prevalence of misfortune and calamity, "The earth is given into the hands of the wicked" (Job 9:24), accords well with the time of King Manasseh.

Ewald and Hitzig were outstanding proponents of this view. But as Raven points out (OTI, p. 277), these allusions in Job do not indicate any more widespread misfortune than could be found in many periods in Hebrew history, or indeed in human experience generally. The author quite clearly is referring to the hardships of individuals here and there as exemplified by Job himself, who in his despondency over private disasters naturally tended to emphasize these darker aspects of calamity which can befall any man in this life. There is no suggestion whatsoever that national misfortunes are referred to or that what is afflicting Job is intended to be parabolic for the distress of Israel generally.

4. *The period of Jeremiah in the late seventh century B.C.* This is the view of J. E. Steinmueller (CSS, 2:165), who feels that there is a striking similarity in both contents and language between Job and the writings of Jeremiah (cf. Jer. 12:1-3 and Job 21:7; Jer. 20:14-18 and Job 3:3). He thinks it significant that the land of Uz is mentioned outside of Job only in Jer. 25:20 and Lam. 4:21. Yet this evidence can scarcely be called compelling; the similarities referred to are quite vague in character and consist of commonplace sentiments which can be found in the writings of many ancient authors.[2] The problem of the prosperity of the wicked (Job 21:7-15) was more thoroughly discussed in Ps. 37 (which was presumably Davidic and therefore early tenth century) than in the Jeremiah passage (Jer. 12:1-3). While it is true that the curse which Jeremiah invokes upon the day he was born (Jer. 20:14) bears a close similarity to Job 3:3, it is far more likely that Jeremiah borrowed from Job than the other way around. If in Jeremiah's time the book of Job was known and acknowledged as Holy Scripture, it is altogether likely that the unhappy prophet would have found in it many a sentiment which accorded with his own mood. The fact that Uz is mentioned in Jer. 25:20 is hardly of pivotal significance, unless it can be proved by other evidence that the name had not arisen until the age of Jeremiah or else was completely unknown to the Hebrews before his time.

5. *The Babylonian Exile, sixth century B.C.* This view is advocated by Genung in ISBE, who classifies the book of Job as mere legend if not outright fiction. He interprets it as reflecting at least indirectly the long imprisonment and eventual release of King Jehoiachin. (It should be noted, however, that Jehoiachin's career bears little analogy to that of Job; there is no evidence that Jehoiachin was any more godly than his wicked father, Jehoiakim, nor was he restored to his kingdom at any time prior to his death. He was simply granted more pleasant conditions during his confinement in Babylon.) Genung regards Job 12:17-25 as suggesting the wholesale deportation of eminent persons or even of whole nations, as if the author had actually witnessed the tragic events of 587 B.C. Thus Job 12:17-19, 23 reads: "He leadeth counselors away stripped, and judges maketh he fools. He looseth the bond of kings, and bindeth their loins with a girdle. He leadeth priests away stripped, and overthroweth the mighty....

---

2. Consult, for example, the Egyptian "Admonitions of Ipuwer," probably composed during the Second Intermediate Period (as Van Seters has convincingly argued) or even in the earlier First Intermediate Period (2300-2050 B.C.) according to J. A. Wilson in ANET³, p. 441.

He enlargeth the nations, and he leadeth them captive" (ASV). Yet it should be pointed out that generalizations of this sort would be appropriate to almost every normal period of Near Eastern history; such scenes as these were repeated every time a fortified city was stormed. Therefore this passage would be perfectly appropriate even in the time of Abraham in the violent age in which he lived (cf. Gen. 14).

Driver, Budde, and Cheyne seek to buttress the argument for an exilic or post-exilic date of Job by pointing out resemblances with Deutero-Isaiah (which they would date about 550-540 B.C.). These resemblances include: (*a*) the extraordinarily developed form of morality and of the doctrine of God discoverable in Job; (*b*) the basic analogy between the suffering of the innocent Job and that of the Servant of the Lord in Isaiah II; (*c*) the points of contact between Job and Jeremiah already discussed in connection with Steinmueller's theory.

As to (*a*), it should be observed that neither the ethical standards nor the portrait of God can be regarded as any more "advanced" (if this question-begging term may be used) than that displayed in what critics have assigned to document D or in the Davidic psalms. This type of argument can appeal only to those who are committed to the presuppositions of Wellhausen's theory of the evolutionary development of Israel's religion. As far as (*b*) is concerned, the resemblance between Job and the suffering Servant is superficial indeed. While it is true that both suffered innocently—a commonplace in world literature—yet there was nothing redemptive or vicarious about the afflictions of Job as there was in the case of the suffering Servant. These arguments therefore seem to be quite weak and inconclusive except to those who are committed to the Development Hypothesis of Israel's religion.

INTEGRITY OF THE TEXT

From the time of Eichhorn there has been a growing tendency among rationalist critics to deny the single authorship of Job. There has been a general trend toward regarding the speeches of Job and his three comforters as being the earliest portion of the work, and to regard as later additions the four sections which are described below.

1. *The prologue and the epilogue.* From the obvious ground that the first and last chapters of the book are composed in prose, it has been argued that they must have been composed by a different author from the artist who produced the poetic chapters. As Steinmueller points out (CSS, 2:166), however, the literature of neighboring nations exhibited the same phenomenon. Thus the Twelfth Dynasty Egyptian "Tale of the Eloquent Peasant" dating from around 1900 B.C. likewise possessed a prose prologue and a prose epilogue as a framework for the long, poetic text which made up the body of the work. So also the Aramaic *Wisdom of Ahikar* has a prose introduction to its poetic proverbs.

It has also been argued that the mood and viewpoint of the prologue and epilogue of Job differ from those of the rest of the book. However, if we consider the particular purpose of the prologue and epilogue, it would be very strange if their mood and viewpoint did not differ from that prevailing in the dialogue between Job and his friends. It is the basic purpose of the introductory chapter to present Job's situation from the divine perspective as a contest between God and Satan, in which the issue at stake is whether a man is capable of loving God for His own sake rather than merely for the blessings He bestows. The final chapter presents the eventual outcome of Job's period of testing. After the situation of agonizing trial has given way to a new prosperity and success, it would have been highly unrealistic on the part of the author had he attempted to maintain the same viewpoint and mood throughout the entire book. Moreover, as an increasing number of critics are coming to see, the dialogue of Job would be lacking in any adequate motivation if the prologue had not introduced it right from the beginning. Likewise also the epilogue is absolutely essential for the final vindication of Job's righteousness, and it is therefore hard to believe that the dialogue could have originally circulated without the final chapter. Even Aage Bentzen concedes: "The dialogue cannot have had any independent existence. In 8:4–29:1 it presupposes the description of Job's illness as given in the narrative" (IOT, 2:175).

2. *Chapters 27 and 28.* Adherents to the multiple-source theory often single out chapter 27 as an interpolation, because it contains a denunciation of the wicked far more in harmony with what the three comforters have been saying in the earlier chapters than with the defensive position Job has maintained. Repeatedly Eliphaz, Bildad, and Zophar have been discoursing upon the inevitable punishment of the wicked and have been urging Job to come out with a confession of secret sin. But on the other hand it should be recognized that Job himself at no point offers any defense for the sinner or holds out any hope for him that he would escape God's judgment in the final outcome. Actually what he does in chapter 27 is skillfully turn the tables on his unjust accusers who have dogmatically insisted that his calamity must be a consequence of hidden and unconfessed sin. Then, insisting on his own unqualified adherence to the cause of righteousness, decency, and justice, Job very logically passes on to express his expectation that his slanderous accusers will themselves taste the fruit of their injustice in blackening his character (v. 7: "Let mine enemy be as the wicked, and he that riseth up against me as the unrighteous").

As for chapter 28, it is urged that this constitutes a unit by itself which is not logically related to what precedes or what follows. But this criticism is not well taken, for Job's analysis of what constitutes true wisdom is evidently intended as a rebuke and a rebuttal to the narrow-minded and shortsighted "wisdom" on which his so-called comforters had preened themselves. Job's testimony here is eminently appropriate as a summary of his basic theological conviction and abiding trust in God, even when His ways were hard for man to understand. In this chapter, therefore, Job shows that true and valid wisdom does not reside in them nor indeed in any man, but only in the Lord Himself and what He has revealed. Even his final axiom, "The fear of the Lord is the beginning of wisdom," carries the connotation that his three accusers had gone astray at the very outset of their thinking because they lacked a genuine fear of the

Lord in their attitude toward Job's divinely permitted calamities.

3. *The speeches of Elihu* (chaps. 32-37). Many critics object that this young disputant is not mentioned in the prologue (2:11) when the other three are introduced, nor is he alluded to either in the speeches of Jehovah (chaps. 38-42), or in the epilogue itself. It is therefore deduced that he must have been an invention of a later contributor to the Job legend, inserted into the account in order to present a more satisfactory theological viewpoint than could be found in the speeches of the other four speakers. Some critics have even argued that Elihu adds nothing new to the discussion, but either repeats what the three friends have already said or else anticipates what God is going to say.

In reply to these objections, it may be pointed out that chapter 32 makes it perfectly clear that Elihu was not one of the original participants in the discussion when it first began back in chapter 2, but that he happened in on the conversation at a later time after it had already well begun. If this was the case, it is hard to see why he should have been mentioned in the prologue at all.[3] So far as the speeches of Jehovah in the epilogue are concerned, there is no particular reason for Elihu to be mentioned in either section if he had uttered nothing that was worthy of correction. It was because the three comforters had misrepresented God's nature and providence that they received the divine rebuke. Nor is it accurate to allege that Elihu simply repeated what the other three had already said; otherwise he would not be represented by the author as chiding them. It is true that Elihu had to repeat much of what they had already brought out in order to evaluate that measure of truth which they had on their side, but this was intended only as a groundwork for making his own position clear. Elihu's contribution was to rebuke their pharisaic explanation of all misfortune as necessarily a punishment for personal sin. In fact, it may be fairly said that Elihu's remarks serve admirably to prepare the way for the theophany of the final chapters.

It is also alleged that from the linguistic standpoint, Elihu's speeches contain so many Aramaisms as to indicate a different author from the one who composed the rest of the book.[4] But this assertion is difficult to maintain on a statistical basis. As Stein-

---

3. As D. N. Freedman points out, Elihu quotes some of Job's earlier remarks in order to refute him (cf. 13:24 and 33:10, 13:27 in 33:11, and 27:2 in 34:5). This can only mean that Elihu was present for most of the discussion, just as 32:2-4 affirms. Freedman goes on to suggest that Elihu's speeches were originally intended to be inserted earlier in the discussion, but were then discarded in favor of the more dramatic speech of Yahweh from the whirlwind. He imagines these discarded speeches of Elihu as being inserted all in a group by some later editor (*Harvard Theological Review* 61 [1968], pp. 53, 59). There is no solid evidence for this theory, but the demonstration of Elihu's earlier presence at the discussion is quite conclusive.

4. A. Guillaume insists that there are really no demonstrable Aramaisms at all in Elihu's speeches, but all of the cited examples can be explained as Arabisms. Thus, *'illēp* ("teach") is cognate with Arabic *'allafa*, ("to tame, form, unite"); *ḥiwwâ* ("show, declare") is related to *waḥay* ("suggest, indicate") with a metathesis of the first two radicals; *millâ* ("word") is related to *'amalla* ("dictate"); and *sāḡā'* ("grow, get big") is cognate with *sagwā* ("thick and tall"). He discusses twenty other examples and reinterprets several of them, as having been previously mistranslated, and relates them to Arabic cognates rather than Aramaic. Guillaume is perhaps extreme in his bias against Aramaism here, but this interpretation at least does justice to the North Arabian setting of Uz—which according to certain Thamudian inscrip-

mueller points out (CSS, 2:1–7), there are only twelve Aramaisms to be found in these chapters (32-37), whereas there are a good twenty-six in the rest of the book. The most that can be said is that the percentage of Aramaisms is slightly higher, but not enough to indicate the necessity of a different author. Also it is alleged that Elihu's style and language markedly differ from those of the other speakers in Job. Even if this point be granted, it is difficult to see why, when the author presents a distinct and different personality, he should not show that distinctiveness even in his style of speech. On the other hand, the alleged differences cannot be pressed too far, for the general vocabulary of Elihu's remarks is about the same as that of all the other speakers. Some of the favorite words of the author scarcely found in the rest of the Old Testament are shared by both Elihu and the three comforters.

4. *The speeches of Jehovah* (38:1–42:6). It is alleged that these pronouncements of God bear little connection with the remarks of Job and his visitors in the earlier part of the book, and their style and mood present very marked contrasts. But it should be recognized that it is the very purpose of the author to present marked contrasts between God and mankind. It would be very strange if the contrasts were any less pronounced than they are. God reminds Job that he cannot be competent to administer providence until he could show an intelligent understanding of the management of the physical universe at the level of meteorology and of the birds of the air and the beasts of the field. He could not do valid "exegesis" if he could not even read the elementary alphabet of God's physical universe.

As for the distinctive motifs featuring Behemoth and Leviathan (generally equated with the hippopotamus and the crocodile), it should be noted that Leviathan is also mentioned in 3:8, and that several other distinctive ideas occur in these chapters which have already made their appearance in the earlier speeches. If these pronouncements by God were removed from the book, it is safe to say that it would be left without a climax, the sublimest sections would be missing from this literary masterpiece, and the basic problem of pain would remain altogether unsolved. We therefore conclude that each portion and division of Job is necessary to make up the architectonic structure which the author has so skillfully employed.

A final word should be said concerning the divergent interpretations of Job 19:26. The KJV seems to indicate that Job entertained a hope of the resurrection of the body. There are, however, many critics who insist that the correct interpretation of the original Hebrew indicates no more than a vindication of the soul after death in a perfectly disembodied state; thus the RSV, "And after my skin has been thus destroyed, then *without* my flesh I shall see God." (This is to be contrasted with the KJV: "Yet *in* my flesh shall I see God.") Here the interpretation hinges upon the meaning of the preposition *min*, which sometimes does signify "without"; yet it is fair to say that in connection with the verb *to see*, (ḥāzâ) *min* in its usage elsewhere almost always indicates the

tions is located near the oases of Medina and Khaybar in Hejaz. ("The Unity of the Book of Job," in *Annual of Leeds University*, Oriental Sec. 14 [1962-63]: pp. 26-27.)

vantage point from which the observer looks. It is fair to conclude that a Hebrew listener would have understood this statement to mean, "And from the vantage point of my flesh, I shall see God."

PROVERBS

The Hebrew title of this book is *Mišᵉlê Šᵉlōmōh*—"The Proverbs of Solomon." The term for "proverb" is *māšāl* which comes from a root idea meaning "parallel" or "similar," and hence signifies "a description by way of comparison." The term is then applied to figurative speech of an epigrammatic or prophetic character, such as the oracles of Balaam (Num. 23:7).

OUTLINE OF PROVERBS

I. Title and purpose, 1:1-6

The object of this book is to be practical, bearing upon moral edification (vv. 3-5) and intellectual truth (v. 6).

II. Fifteen lessons on wisdom, 1:7–9:18

A book of admonition for youth. The prevailing form is the extended *māšāl* song.

1. 1:7-19	6. 3:27-35	11. 6:12-19
2. 1:20-33	7. 4:1-5:6	12. 6:20-35
3. 2:1-22	8. 5:7-23	13. 7:1-27
4. 3:1-18	9. 6:1-5	14. 8:1-36
5. 3:19-26	10. 6:6-11	15. 9:1-18

Not all these songs possess internal coherence, yet they somehow compose an internal unity, with a well-arranged multiformity.

III. Additional proverbs of Solomon, 10:1–22:16

A series of approximately 375 short maxims. They are not grouped according to a comprehensive plan, except for certain sections which contain a series linked together by common characteristics or analogies. All these *mᵉšālîm* are distichs predominantly antithetic in nature, although there are some synonymous parallelisms as well (cf. 11:7, 25, 30; 12:14, 28; 14:19). There are quite a few which are synthetic or integral, especially those with the *min* of comparison (e.g., 12:9; 15:16, 17; 16:8, 19; 17:10, etc.) or with the phrase *'aphkî*, much more (11:31; 15:11; 17:7; 19:7, etc.).

IV. The sayings of the wise, first series, 22:17–24:22 (apparently edited by Solomon).

This section includes all types of *māšāl* distichs (22:18; 23:9; 24:7, 8, 9, 10), tetrastichs (22:22, 24, 26; 23:10; 23:15, 17; 24:1, 3, etc.), pentastichs (23:4; 24:13), and hexastichs (23:1-3, 12-14, 19-21, 26-28; 24:11).

The "wise men" perhaps refer to those mentioned in 1 Kings 4:31 as background sources for what was composed by King Solomon.

V. The sayings of the wise, second series, 24:23-34

This section contains one hexastich (24:23b-25), one distich (24:26), a tristich (24:27), a tetrastich (24:28), and a māšāl ode (24:30-34) dealing with the slugard.

VI. Proverbs of Solomon, recorded by the committee of Hezekiah, 25:1—29:27

This section is not arranged according to any observable plan, yet it contains occasional series of related proverbs (e.g., 26:1-12, 13-16, 20-22). In chapters 25-27 the prevailing type of parallelism is not the antithetic, but rather the parabolic (the "as—so" type, such as 26:1) and the emblematic (where the "as—so" particles are omitted; cf. 25:4). Antithetic parallelisms are more frequent in chapters 28 and 29; yet there are also a good many of the comparative and figurative type as well. It is noteworthy that several proverbs or portions of proverbs are repeated from section III. Some are perfectly identical (25:24 = 21:9; 26:22 = 18:8; 27:12 = 22:3; etc.), while others are identical in meaning although with slightly changed phraseology (26:13 = 22:13; 26:15 = 19:24; 28:6 = 19:1, etc.).

VII. The sayings of Agur ben Jakeh, 30:1-33

This chapter has an unusual number of the *middah type* (*middah* means "measure or allotted number") such as verses 15-17; "There are three things that are never satisfied, yea, four things say not, It is enough," etc.

VIII. The sayings of Lemuel, 31:1-9

A warning to rulers against the use of liquor, and an exhortation to integrity in judgment.

IX. The perfect wife, 31:10-31

The standards of virtue and accomplishment by which a godly wife may evaluate her life.

TERMS FOR "WISDOM" IN PROVERBS

The purpose of a book of proverbs is to instruct in the principles of wisdom. There are three major terms for wisdom employed throughout this work: *ḥokmâ*, *bînâ*, and *tûšiyyâ*.

1. *Ḥokmâ* ("wisdom") the term most frequently used, pertains not so much to the realm of theoretical knowledge or philosophy as to a proper grasp of the basic issues of life and of the relationship of God to man as a moral agent.[5] This kind of "wisdom" involves a proper discernment between good and evil, between virtue and vice,

---

5. Cf. chap. 32, pp. 485-86.

between duty and self-indulgence. It also includes prudence in secular matters and a skill in the accomplishment of business affairs as well as in interpersonal relationships. It implies an ability to apply theory to practice in real-life situations, consistently applying that which we know to that which we have to do.

2. *Bînâ* ("understanding") connotes the ability to discern intelligently the difference between sham and reality, between truth and error, between the specious attraction of the moment and the long-range values that govern a truly successful life. The root idea of this term is found in the related preposition *bên*, meaning "between;" hence there is always an analytical or judgmental factor involved and the ability to distinguish between the valid and the invalid, the false and the true.

3. *Tûšiyyâ* ("sound wisdom, efficient wisdom," or, in a derived sense, "abiding success"). This term conceives of wisdom as an authentic insight into, or intuition of, spiritual or psychological truth. It focuses upon the ability of the human mind to rise from below to a grasp of divine reality above, so to speak, rather than the wisdom of a prophetic revelation that comes down supernaturally from heaven. It points to the activity of the believer's mind by which he is able to deduce from what God has revealed the manner in which these principles are to be applied in everyday situations of life (cf. Prov. 3:21; 8:14; 18:1; and also in the sense of help or deliverance, Prov. 2:7).

It should be noted that the characteristic type of *māšāl* or proverb in this book is the balanced antithesis which incisively contrasts the wise man and the fool, the good man and the wicked, true value and false appearance, in such a way as to set forth the two sides of the truth in clearest opposition to each other and thus perform an incisive didactic function. The constant preoccupation of the book is with the elemental antinomies of obedience versus rebellion, industry versus laziness, prudence versus presumption, and so on. These are so presented as to put before the reader a clear-cut choice, leaving him no ground for wretched compromise or vacillating indecision.

AUTHORSHIP AND DATE OF COMPOSITION OF PROVERBS

1. The following sections of Proverbs seem to be attributed to Solomon the son of David: (*a*) 1:1–9:18, according to 1:1; (*b*) 10:1–22:16, according to 10:1; (*c*) 25:1–29:27, according to 25:1, although selected and published by a committee under the appoint-

TERMS FOR WISDOM

Ḥokmâ ....practical ability to apply theory to practice
Bînâ ....ability to discern intellectually between truth and error
Tûšiyyâ ....sound wisdom, efficient wisdom as an authentic intuition
                   of the spirital or psychological

ment of King Hezekiah (728–697 B.C.). It should be remembered that according to 1 Kings 4:32, Solomon's original collection of Proverbs numbered no less than three thousand. Since canonical Proverbs contains only 800 verses, it is obvious that the original Solomonic writings (secs. I, II, III) contained ample material for later excerpters.

2. Two sections (chaps. 22-24, IV and V in outline) are attributed to the "wise men" (ḥakāmîm), who are not otherwise specified but who probably belonged to the same class referred to in 1 Kings 4:31. There is every reason to believe that they antedated Solomon himself and that he was responsible for assembling this anthology under his own editorship.

3. The sayings of Agur the son of Jakeh (chap. 30) are of uncertain origin, inasmuch as we have no information whatever as to Jakeh's historical, geographical, or even ethnic background.

4. The sayings of King Lemuel are certainly of non-Israelite origin, but it is reasonable to suppose that he was a North Arabian prince, living possibly in an area not far from Uz, who still cherished a faith in the one true God. So far as Prov. 31:10-31 is concerned, it is ambiguous whether this beautiful description of the perfect wife is attributed to King Lemuel or to some other. The fact, however, that it is composed as an acrostic or alphabetic poem of twenty-two lines shows that it is a separate composition and its style bears little resemblance to the first nine verses of chapter 31.

CRITICAL THEORIES OF AUTHORSHIP AND DATE OF PROVERBS

Using as their principal criterion an evolutionary theory of the development of Hebrew thought, the Liberal critics have tended to deny to the Solomonic period a large portion if not all of the material attributed by the text to King Solomon himself. Thus Driver, Nowack, and A. B. Davidson regard chapters 1-9 as composed shortly before the Exile, about three and a half centuries later than Solomon's reign. These critics concede that Solomon may have written some portions of chapters 10-22, which they regard as the oldest nucleus of the book, but the whole collection reached its present form only in the seventh century B.C. The section 22:17–24:34 is thought to have originated in the post-exilic period (on the supposition of its being derived from the *Wisdom of Amenemope*, which will be discussed later). Possibly chapters 25-29 were composed at about the same time. Last of all, chapters 30 and 31 were added at a substantially later period. In this connection it should be noted that some moderate conservative critics, like Genung in the ISBE, put chapters 22-24 at an earlier period than chapters 1-9. But they see no reason for postponing the substantial completion of Proverbs beyond the reign of Hezekiah. Even chapters 30 and 31 may have been added at that same period, since their foreign origin would sufficiently account for differences in language and tone as compared with the rest of the book.

More radical critics such as C. H. Toy, the author of the ICC commentary on Proverbs (1899), come to the conclusion that nothing in Proverbs dates from a period earlier than 350 B.C., and that the later material was contributed some time in the second century. Toy advances the following six arguments to support this view:

1. Since Solomon was said by Jewish tradition to be the author of Proverbs, Song of Solomon (cf. 1 Kings 4:30-34), Ecclesiastes, and two of the Psalms, it is apparent that he had become the symbol of wisdom and the patron saint of all philosophical or nonliturgical poetry (just as Moses, e.g., had become the symbol of Hebrew law). In the course of time it became conventional to attribute such compositions to Solomon, even though they were of late manufacture, in order that they might gain wider acceptance with the credulous Jewish public. This certainly must have been the motivation for attributing the apocryphal book, the *Wisdom of Solomon*, which was quite obviously composed in Greek, to the ancient paragon of Hebrew philosophy.

It is of course perfectly apparent that in the intertestamental period it became fashionable to compose didactic or apocalyptic works which were attributed, ostensibly at least, to ancient patriarchs like Enoch or the twelve sons of Jacob. But there is no good evidence that such a procedure was ever followed in pre-Hellenistic Israel. The primary question to settle would seem to be, How did Solomon ever get this reputation for proverbial and wisdom literature if in fact he never composed any? It is far more logical to conclude that he gained the reputation because he was the first to compose this type of literature on a classical standard rather than assuming that the tradition was utterly without foundation. Thus in Greek literature the existence of the later epic poetry falsely attributed to Homer by no means demonstrates that Homer never composed any epic poetry of his own (i.e., the *Iliad* and the *Odyssey*). The same is true of the large body of lyric poetry attributed to Anacreon. The existence of such productions does not prove there never was such a person as Anacreon who composed the earlier poetry attributed to his name. It is therefore difficult to see how the tenth-century Solomon could have acquired such a high reputation as a classical model for *ḥokmâ* literature if he never composed any of his own.

2. Toy also deduces a post-exilic origin from the assumption of pure monotheism which seems to be applied throughout Proverbs. (Liberal higher critics have held in the past that by a process of religious evolution, true monotheism appeared late in Israel.) This approach necessarily involves a complete ignoring of the abundant textual evidence of the Old Testament records that the Israelite people were strictly monotheistic from the days of the patriarchs and always regarded idolatry as a heretical or apostate deviation from their covenant relationship to Jehovah.

3. There is a noteworthy lack of distinctive national traits observable in the text of Proverbs. From this, Toy deduces that the nation was already scattered to foreign regions, as was the case after the fall of Jerusalem. On the other hand, however, it is far more probable that this lack of distinctive national traits is to be explained (a) as part of the genius of the *ḥokmâ* genre itself, which is concerned with individuals as such, rather than with nations, and deals with the laws of human behavior as observable among almost all the ancient Near Eastern peoples; (b) as resulting from the central

location of Israel between the cultures of Mesopotamia, Syria, Phoenicia, North Arabia, and Egypt. It was inevitable that there should be extensive cultural interplay from the earliest stages of Israel's career as a nation.

4. Proverbs is said to reflect the social manners and vices which are known to have existed after the Exile, especially in the urban centers of Judah. This, however, must be regarded as a very dubious generalization. No proof has been adduced that a single custom or vice mentioned in Proverbs was unknown to the culture of Jerusalem or the other large cities of Israel during Solomon's reign.

5. The constant assumption in Proverbs that virtue is to be identified with knowledge and wickedness is equivalent to ignorance is supposed by Liberal critics to reflect the Hellenic approach to moral philosophy as exemplified by Plato in his *Dialogues* (ca. 370 B.C.). It argued out that knowledge of this Greek approach to the problems of ethics would have come to the Near East only after the Alexandrian conquest (ca. 330 B.C.). However, this interpretation involves a basic misunderstanding of the fundamental distinction between Greek *sophia* and Hebrew *ḥokmâ*. Greek philosophy tended to be speculative and concerned with cosmogony and the underlying constituent principles of the universe. Hebrew philosophy, however, as formulated in the Old Testament, was concerned rather with understanding the implications of the revealed will of God for the problems and choices of daily life. Whereas Greek philosophy tended toward a dialectical deduction from first principles arrived at by purely intellectual induction, Hebrew philosophy was more intuitive and analogical, endeavoring to interpret the moral order in the light of a personal, omniscient, and omnipotent God, who had revealed His will for ethical living.

As for the relationship between ignorance and sin, the Platonic concept of moral ignorance was intellectual and mental, whereas the Solomonic concept in Proverbs recognized in man a certain darkness of the soul resulting from an immoral prior choice of heart. Moral philosophy among the Greeks did not really come to grips with the problem of radical evil in man or his capacity to acknowledge in theory the truth of righteousness, and yet to choose evil out of a perverse self-interest.[6] One of the characteristic terms for "folly" in Proverbs is *nᵉbālâ'* which suggests the example of Nabal, whose story is related in 1 Sam. 25. Verse 25 of that chapter judges him a "fool" (*nābāl*), not because he was not intelligent enough to figure out that virtue is a more successful means to attain personal happiness than wickedness can possibly be, but rather because he made a wrong choice in the moral realm: to requite David's friendliness with a miserly and vilifying ingratitude.

6. Toy dismisses the book of Proverbs as the product of a professional caste of wise men, who also were responsible for *Ecclesiastes*, the *Wisdom of Solomon*, and *Ecclesiasti-*

---

6. A few scholars have attempted to buttress this theory of late origin by pointing to a few Hebrew words supposedly derived from Greek. Thus, Eissfeldt has suggested that *'ēṭûn* ("linen") in Prov. 7:16 is borrowed from the Greek *othonē* ("fine linen"). Yet this derivation is really not tenable. The K-B *Lexicon* does not even mention this derivation as possible, but links it rather with the Egyptian *'idmj*, a red-colored linen manufactured in Egypt and ultimately derived from the Semitic root *'-d-m* ("red").

cus. But as we have previously pointed out, the existence of a later caste presupposes a founder. Just as the prophets would be incomprehensible without a prior Moses, whose law they interpreted and applied to the problems of their own generation, so also there must have been a classical model for written proverbial literature before any caste of practitioners could have arisen. Compare Jer. 18:18, which speaks of the wise men as a class of experts on a par with priests and prophets in the pre-exilic generation. There can be no question that wisdom literature had a very early origin in the history of Egypt, going back at least to Ipuwer in the Sixth Dynasty (ca. 2500 B.C.) or the Second Intermediate Period (1780-1550 B.C.). It is also evident from 1 Kings 4:30 that there was a long tradition of pre-Solomonic sages in Israel, and it is quite unwarranted to hold that the tenth century was too early for this kind of literature to have arisen among the Hebrew people.

In this connection it is appropriate to quote the remarks of W. F. Albright (*Wisdom in Israel and in the Ancient Near East*, 1955, p. 4):

In the course of the past century a curious myth has arisen that the Age of Wise Men, who are supposed to have flourished in the Achaemenian and early Hellenistic periods, dates to about the fifth to third centuries B.C. We may freely admit that the Book of Proverbs was not edited in approximately its present form until about the fifth century B.C. without assuming that any material of post-Exilic date is included in the book. But the content of Proverbs is considerably older, and it is entirely possible that aphorisms and even longer sections go back into the Bronze Age in substantially their present form. Cullen I. K. Story has shown in a Johns Hopkins study [cf. *Journal of Biblical Literature*, 64, 1945, pp. 319-337] that the metric style of Proverbs often agrees entirely with that of the Ugaritic epics as analyzed by C. H. Gordon. Story has given numerous examples of different categories; the number might easily be increased several times.[7]

Albright goes on to cite a series of significant parallels, for instance, Proverbs 10:26 ("As vinegar to the teeth, /And as smoke to the eyes, /So is the sluggard to them that send him") and the Baal Epic I Ab, Gordon No. 49 ("Like the feeling of a wild cow for her calf, /like the feeling of a wild ewe for her lamb, /So was the feeling of Anath for Baal"). Here we have in each case a tricolon whose third member differs from the two preceding in such a way as to produce a climactic effect. Another type is the bicolon, which omits a word parallel to an outstanding word in the first column, as for instance, Prov. 27:2 ("Let a stranger praise thee, and not thy mouth; /A foreigner and not thy lips") and I Aqhat I, 1:13 ("From his mouth let the message go forth, /From his lips the word").

It should be mentioned that in this same article Albright notes that these poetic forms common to Proverbs and the Ugaritic literature are totally absent from the Aramaic wisdom literature of the seventh century B.C. as represented by the *Sayings of*

---

7. Albright, in *Wisdom in Israel and in the Ancient Near East,* ed. M. Noth and D. Winton Thomas (Leiden, Netherlands: E. J. Brill, 1960), p. 4.

Aḥiqar. He states, "We must accordingly date the content of Proverbs as a whole well before *Aḥiqar* and look to the earliest Canaanite sources for its metrical stylistic structure as well as for direct Canaanite prototypes of many individual proverbs and bodies of material."[8] He then goes on to mention that Umberto Cassuto isolated forty pairs of words in parallelism which appear both in Hebrew wisdom literature and in the Ugaritic texts. These were augmented by thirty more examples pointed out by Cassuto's pupil, Moshe Held.

Albright asserts that Prov. 8-9 is full of Canaanite words and expressions, including the description of the origin of Wisdom in 8:22-31. Thus verse 22 begins with four words which apparently reflect a Canaanite influence: "El created me (at) the beginning of his dominion." Here we have the verb *qānâ* with the unusual meaning of "create" (a meaning well known" however, in Canaanite), and the noun *derek* used in a way suggesting the Canaanite *drkt* meaning "dominion." Albright closes with this judgment: "In a nutshell, my opinion with regard to the provenience and date of Proverbs is that its entire contents is probably pre-Exilic, but that much of the book was handed down orally until the fifth century B.C., when we know from Elephantine that Jews were interested in literature of a different kind."[9]

THE RELATIONSHIP OF CHAPTERS 22-24 TO THE WISDOM OF AMENEMOPE

A hieratic manuscript of the late Egyptian work, *The Wisdom of Amenemope* (or *Amen-em-apt*) was discovered by E. A. Wallis Budge in 1888 and provisionally dated by him as Eighteenth Dynasty in origin. So dated, of course, there would be no difficulty in supposing that Solomon was familiar with this Egyptian work and adapted it for his purposes in Prov. 22:17–24:34. But subsequent study by Erman, Spiegelberg, Griffith, and Lange brought down the date for *Amenemope* to 1000 B.C., then Dynasty XXII, and finally Dynasty XXIV, or even the Persian or Greek period. The majority of critics assumed that the demonstrably close relationship between the Hebrew and the Egyptian texts was to be explained as only a dependence of the former upon the latter; that is to say, while the Hebrews might borrow from Egyptian lore, the Egyptians would never borrow from Palestine. By this reasoning, then, these chapters in Proverbs must stem from the Persian or even the Greek period. Although the majority of Liberal scholars are still of this opinion, a close examination of the linguistic data indicates quite conclusively that the borrowing must have been the other way around in this particular case. In 1930, R. O. Kevin (following the lead of Oesterley in his *Commentary on Proverbs*, 1929) adduced the following considerations:

1. There are proportionately far more Semitisms in Amenemope's Egyptian text than in any other Egyptian work on morality; at least nineteen of these Semitisms are indisputable and sixteen more are highly probable.

2. Numerous cases of Egyptian words garbled or otherwise unknown can be suc-

---

8. Ibid, p. 6.
9. Ibid., p. 13.

cessfully explained as textual corruptions from an earlier text which translated the Hebrew terms employed in the corresponding passage in Proverbs.

3. There are several instances where the Egyptian translator has misunderstood the corresponding Hebrew word; thus the word *t-ḥ-š-w-k* ("hold back from or rescue") in Prov. 24:11 has been rendered in *Amenemope* XI. 7 as if it were *t-ḥ-š-y-k*, meaning "to hide" (hence the Egyptian *ḥ'pw*, "to hide"). Or again, the Hebrew *šā'ar* ("to think" or "to reckon") in *Amenemope* XIII. 1. 2 has been misunderstood as the Hebrew *š-'-r (šā'ar)* or "storm" (the Egyptian *sn'*) in a nonsensical connection, even though the Hebrew original is perfectly clear and coherent in its own context. Or else the Egyptian author has grappled with the difficulty of an obscure Hebrew phase by resorting to a banal paraphrase. For example, Prov. 23:4 says, "Do not toil to acquire wealth, cease from thine own wisdom"; this comes out in *Amenemope* IX. 14-15: "Do not strain to seek an excess when thy needs are safe for thee." In other words, the un-Egyptian sentiment "from thy wisdom desist" has been altered to "when thy needs are safe for thee," or "when your property is intact," as Kevin renders it. The important thing is to observe that while satisfactory reconstructions of the Egyptian can be made on the basis of the Hebrew original, it is never possible to reconstruct the Hebrew text on the basis of the Egyptian original.

4. It should also be noted that the word *š-l-š-w-m* in Prov. 22:20, which probably means "adjutant" (third man in the chariot), has been misinterpreted as the more common word *š-l-š-y-m* which means "thirty." So construed, this would be a statement that thirty proverbs are included in this section (Prov. 22:17–23:12), although there are actually only twenty-seven separate units that can be made out in this section. Quite evidently *Amenemope* interpreted the word as "thirty," saying in XXVII. 7, "Behold these thirty chapters," and therefore was careful to come out with that number of proverbs. (Note that the Hebrew text of Prov. 22:20 yields the meaning, "Have I not written to thee *excellent* things in counsels of knowledge?"—the word *excellent* being vocalized as *šālišîm*. The consonantal text, as indicated above, ends the word in *w-m*. Many modern scholars follow Amenemope's amendment and construe the word as "thirty." Among these are Erman, Eissfeldt, and the RSV: "Have I not written for you thirty sayings of admonition and knowledge?") Perhaps it should be added that only one-third of the material in Proverbs 22-24 shows any relationship to the text of *Amenemope*; the latter seems to have drawn much of his material from non-Hebrew sources (although Kevin sees traces of Ps. 1 also).[10]

10. Kevin, in *Journal of the Society of Oriental Research* (Nov. 1930), pp. 123-25, 144, 150.

35

ECCLESIASTES AND SONG OF SOLOMON

THE HEBREW TITLE for this book is *Qōhelet*, which apparently meant the preacher's office, and then became a term for the preacher himself. It is derived from the root *qāhal*, meaning "to convoke an assembly," hence, "to address an assembly." The author of this work so refers to himself in numerous passages, and therefore this is a fitting designation. The Greek term *ecclēsiastēs* is a good translation of this term, for it too means "preacher" and is derived from *ekklēsia*, meaning "assembly."

PURPOSE AND THEME OF ECCLESIASTES

The purpose of Ecclesiastes was to convince men of the uselessness of any world view which does not rise above the horizon of man himself. It pronounces the verdict of "vanity of vanities" upon any philosophy of life which regards the created world or human enjoyment as an end in itself. To view personal happiness as the highest good in life is sheer folly in view of the preeminent value of God Himself as over against His created universe. Nor can happiness ever be attained by pursuing after it, since such a pursuit involves the foolishness of self-deification. Having shown the vanity of living for worldly goals, the author clears the way for a truly adequate world view which recognizes God Himself as the highest value of all, and the meaningful life as the one which is lived in His service. Only as a vehicle for the expression of divine wisdom, goodness, and truth, does the world itself possess any real significance. It is only God's work that endures, and only He can impart abiding value to the life and activity of man. "I know that, whatsoever God doeth, it shall be forever: nothing can be put to it, nor anything taken from it" (Eccl. 3:14).

OUTLINE OF ECCLESIASTES

I. First discourse: the vanity of human wisdom, 1:1–2:26

A. Basic theme: vanity of all merely human effort and experience, 1:1-3

B. Demonstration of the theme, 1:4–2:26
1. Meaningless cycle of human life and history, 1:4-11
2. Ultimate uselessness of human wisdom and philosophy, 1:12-18
3. Emptiness of the enjoyments of pleasure and wealth, 2:1-11
4. Ultimate death of even the wise, 2:12-17
5. Futility of leaving fruits of hard work to undeserving heirs, 2:18-23
6. Necessity of contentment with God's providences, 2:24-26

II. Second discourse: coming to terms with the laws which govern life, 3:1–5:20

A. The prudent attitude in view of the facts of life and death, 3:1-22
1. A proper time must be recognized for each activity and experience, 3:1-9
2. God is the only guarantor of abiding values, 3:10-15
3. God will punish the unrighteous, visiting death upon all, 3:16-18
4. Man must share physical death with animals, 3:19-20
5. Unsure of the life beyond, man must make the best of this present life, 3:21-22
B. The disappointments of earthly life, 4:1-16
1. Cruelty and misery make life a dubious blessing, 4:1-3
2. Disadvantages are cited for materialistic success, laziness, and insatiable covetousness, 4:4-8
3. Life's trials are better faced by partners than alone, 4:9-12
4. Political success is temporary and unstable, 4:13-16
C. Futility of the self-seeking life, 5:1-20
1. Presenting to God false sacrifices, vain words, unkept promises is folly, 5:1-7
2. Retribution overtakes oppressors and disappointment is in store for the covetous, 5:8-17
3. Thankful enjoyment of God's gifts brings contentment, 5:18-20

III. Third discourse: no satisfaction in earthly goods and treasures, 6:1– 8:17

A. Inadequacy of attainments esteemed by the world, 6:1-12
1. Neither wealth nor large family can bring final satisfaction to the soul, 6:1-6
2. Neither the wise nor the foolish attain satisfaction in their heart, 6:7-9
3. Apart from God, man cannot even discern the real reason for life, 6:10-12
B. Counsels of prudence in this sin-corrupted world, 7:1-29
1. True values are best gauged from the perspective of sorrow and death, 7:1-4
2. Cheap gaiety, dishonest gain, and shortness of temper are but pitfalls, 7:5-9
3. Wisdom is a greater asset than financial wealth in coping with life, 7:10-12
4. God is the author of both good fortune and ill, 7:13-14
5. Both self-righteousness and immorality lead to disaster, 7:15-18
6. Wisdom has surpassing power, but sin is universal, 7:19-20
7. Be heedless of base malice toward yourself, 7:21-22

8. Man's quest for wisdom cannot by itself attain profound spiritual truth, 7:23-25

9. A wicked woman is the worst of evils a man can encounter, 7:26

10. But all human beings, male and female have fallen from original goodness, 7:27-29

C. Coming to terms with an imperfect world, 8:1-17

1. The wise man reverences the authority of the government, 8:1-5

2. Divine law operates in our life despite woes and wrongs and inevitable death, 8:6-9

3. Though esteemed and unpunished, the wicked will finally be judged by God, 8:10-13

4. Injustices in this life falsely encourage a shallow hedonism, 8:14-15

5. But God's ways are inscrutable to human wisdom, 8:16-17

IV. Fourth discourse: God will deal with the injustices of this life, 9:1–12:8

A. Death inevitable to all; make the best use of this life, 9:1-18

1. Death is inevitable to both the good and the evil; moral insanity grips them all, 9:1-3

2. Moral choice and the knowledge of this life are cut off at death, 9:4-6

3. Let the godly use to the full life's opportunities and blessings, 9:7-10

4. Even to the worthy, success is uncertain and life span unpredictable, 9:11-12

5. Wisdom, though unappreciated, succeeds much better than force, 9:13-18

B. The uncertainties of life and the baneful effects of folly, 10:1-20

1. Even a little folly can ruin a man's life; be prudent before princes, 10:1-4

2. Life provides reversals in fortune and strokes of retribution, 10:5-11

3. A fool is marked by his empty talk and misdirected effort, 10:12-15

4. The welfare of nations and men depends on accepting responsibility, 10:16-19

5. Contempt of authority brings sure retribution, 10:20

C. How best to invest a life, 11:1–12:8

1. Kindness returns with blessings to the benefactor, 11:1-2

2. Man's wisdom cannot change or fathom God's laws of nature, 11:3-5

3. The wisest course is lifelong diligence and cheerful industry, 11:6-8

4. A youth misspent in pleasure brings later retribution, 11:9-10

5. Start living for God while young, before afflictions and senility come upon you, 12:1-8

V. Conclusion: life in the light of eternity, 12:9-14

A. Solomon's purpose was to teach his people wisely about life, 12:9-10

B. These trenchant admonitions are of more practical value than all literature, 12:11-12

C. Put God's will first, for His judgment is final, 12:13-14

AUTHORSHIP AND DATE OF COMPOSITION OF ECCLESIASTES

The author of this work identifies himself as the son of David, king in Jerusalem. While he does not specify that his name is Solomon, it is fair to assume that the direct successor of David is meant rather than some later descendant. This assumption is confirmed by numerous internal evidences, such as the references to his unrivaled wisdom (1:16), his unequaled wealth (2:8), his large retinue of servants (2:7), his opportunities for carnal pleasure (2:3), and his extensive building activities (2:4-6). No other descendant of David measures up to these specifications but Solomon himself. It has therefore been the traditional view, accepted by Jewish and Christian scholars alike, that Solomon, the son of David, wrote the book in its entirety. The Jewish tradition in *Baba Bathra* 15*a* to the effect that "Hezekiah and his company wrote Ecclesiastes" probably means no more than that Hezekiah and his company simply edited and published the text for public use (cf. Young, IOT, p. 369). Elsewhere Jewish tradition is quite explicit that Solomon was the author (cf. *Megilla* 7*a* and *Shabbath* 30). Until the rise of nineteenth-century criticism, it was generally accepted by both the synagogue and the Church that this book was a genuine work of Solomon's.

In more recent times, however, there are some Conservative critics who join with Liberal scholars in regarding this work as post-exilic. They understand the figure of Solomon as intended to be a mere artistic device designed to present more effectively the message of the unknown late author. Since Solomon was known to have experienced the satisfaction of every human ambition and had drunk to the full every possibility of earthly pleasure, he would serve as an admirable test case in evaluating hedonistic enjoyment and intellectual achievement as over against a life entirely devoted to God. Among the Conservatives who have adopted this view of the book are Hengstenberg, Delitzsch, W. J. Beecher (in ISBE), Zoeckler in the *Lange Commentary*, Steinmueller, Raven, E. J. Young, and H. C. Leupold. Davis's *Dictionary of the Bible* is noncommittal. In the *New Bible Commentary* of Davidson, Stibbs, and Kevan, Solomonic authorship is not even discussed as a serious option. There is, however, a significant number of modern Conservative scholars who still uphold Solomonic authorship, at least in a modified form. For the late nineteenth century, we may include A. R. Fausset in the Jamieson, Fausset, and Brown Commentary; W. T. Bullock in *The Speaker's Commentary*; Wilhelm Moeller (*Einleitung in das Alte Testament*, p. 210); Dean Milman (*History of the Jews*, 1881); and A. Cohen (*The Five Megilloth*, p. 106). In the twentieth century, we may add the names of L. Wogue and M. F. Unger. Among the Catholic scholars favoring Solomonic authorship are Gietmann (whose article in the *Catholic Encyclopedia* [5:244-248] is very helpful), Schumacher, Vigoroux, and Cornely-Hagen.

The most significant evidence advanced in demonstration of the late date of composition of Ecclesiastes is said to be derived from the linguistic data of the text itself. It is undeniably true that the language of this work is markedly different from that of the other tenth-century Hebrew texts which have been preserved in the Bible. For that matter, it is different from all the other books in the Old Testament of whatever age, with the partial exception of the Song of Solomon. In support of the fifth-century date, Franz Delitzsch listed no less than ninety-six words, forms, and expressions found nowhere else in the Bible except in exilic and post-exilic works like Ezra, Esther, Nehemiah, Chronicles, Malachi—or else in the *Mishnah*. He describes many of these as Aramaisms largely on the ground of demonstrable noun endings in *-ût, -ôn* or *-ān*.[1] Hengstenberg, however, acknowledged only ten demonstrable Aramaisms in the book; at the other extreme is the claim of Zoeckler that Aramaisms were to be found in almost every verse. The most frequently cited Aramaic or late Hebrew terms are *pardēs*, "park" (found also in Nehemiah and Song of Solomon); *shālaṭ*, "to rule" (found only in post-exilic books); *tāqan*, "be straight" (found only in Daniel and the *Talmud*); *zᵉmān*, "definite time" (found only in Nehemiah and Esther); *pithgām*, "official decision" (only in Esther and the Aramaic of Daniel); *mᵉdînâ*, in the sense of "province" (a word found in 1 Kings, Esther, Ezra, Nehemiah, Ezekiel, and Lamentations); and *kāshēr*, "be correct" (found otherwise only in Esther). The obvious inference is that Ecclesiastes comes from a time when the Jews made very large use of Aramaic, which presumably was not the case until after the Exile.

Apart from vocabulary, it is argued that there are evidences of grammatical structure which place the book at a late date. For example, the independent pronoun (especially *hû'*, *hî'*, and *hēm*) is used as a copular verb with a greater frequency than in the pre-exilic books. Again it is argued that the imperfect conversive is rare in Ecclesiastes, since it is generally replaced by *waw*-connective plus the perfect. Since the latter construction is the prevailing one in the *Talmud*, its frequency in Ecclesiastes is thought to be evidence of a late date. In answer to this, however, it should be pointed out that *waw*-connective plus the perfect occurs only five times in Daniel (which according to the critics is mid–second century B.C.) and only five times in the extant Hebrew text of *Ecclesiasticus*, dating from about 180 B.C.). If this construction is a sign of lateness, Ecclesiastes must be later than the second century B.C., since the works from that period do not yet use it with any frequency.

This latter possibility is, however, completely ruled out by the discovery of four fragments of Ecclesiastes in the Fourth Qumran Cave, dated on paleographic grounds from the middle of the second century B.C. As Muilenberg remarks in BASOR, no. 135: "This gives the *coup de grace* to earlier views such as those of Graetz, Renan, Leimdorfer, König, and others, and makes unlikely a dating in the second century." R. H. Pfeiffer back in 1941 (IOT, p. 731) suggested that the period 170-160 B.C. was most in harmony with the characteristics of the thought and language of Ecclesiastes. But in the light of this Qumran evidence, one can only conclude that here again is an example of demonstrable fallacy in the higher critical method practiced by rationalists of Pfeiffer's persuasion.

In the above mentioned article, Muilenberg goes on to remark: "Linguistically the

---

1. It has already been pointed out in chap. 10 that these endings constitute very slender ground for establishing of genuine Aramaisms.

book is unique. There is no question that its language has many striking peculiarities; these have been explained by some to be late Hebrew (discussed by Margoliouth and Gordis) for which the language of the *Mishnah* is said to offer more than adequate support (a contention effectively answered by Margoliouth in the *Jewish Encyclopedia* V, 33, where he points out the linguistic affinities of Qohelet with the Phoenician inscriptions, e.g., Eshmunazar, Tabnith). The Aramaic cast of the language has long been recognized, but only within recent years has its Aramaic provenance been claimed and supported in any detail (F. Zimmermann, C. C. Torrey, H. L. Ginsburg)....Dahood has written on Canaanite-Phoenician influences in Qohelet, defending the thesis that the book of Ecclesiastes was originally composed by an author who wrote in Hebrew but was influenced by Phoenician spelling, grammar and vocabulary, and who shows heavy Canaanite-Phoenician literary influence (*Biblica* 33, 1952, pp. 35-52, 191-221)."[2] At this point it should be noted that neither a Phoenician background nor an Aramaic background would necessarily preclude Solomonic authorship, inasmuch as the political and commercial ties with both the Phoenician-speaking and the Aramaean peoples of the Syrian areas during Solomon's reign were closer than any other period in Israel's history (with the possible exception of of Ahab in the ninth century or possibly the time of Jeroboam II and his successors in the eighth century).

In weighing the force of the linguistic argument, it should be carefully observed that a comprehensive survey of all the data, including vocabulary, morphology, syntax, and style, yields the result that the text of Ecclesiastes fits into no known period in the history of the Hebrew language. No significant affinities may be traced between this work and any of those canonical books which rationalist higher criticism has assigned to the Greek period (such as Daniel, Zechariah II, and portions of "Deutero-Isaiah"). So far as the early post-exilic period is concerned, the Hebrew of Ecclesiastes is quite as dissimilar to that of Malachi, Nehemiah, and Esther as to any of the pre-exilic books. This raises an insuperable difficulty for the theory of Delitzsch and Young, who date it around 430 B.C., and of Beecher in ISBE, who makes it 400. If Ecclesiastes came from the same period, how could there be such a total lack of similarity in vocabulary,

---

2. Cf. G. L. Archer, "The Linguistic Evidence for the Date of Ecclesiastes," in *Journal of the Evangelical Theological Society* (Summer 1969), pp. 167-81. This reviews and amplifies Dahood's arguments for a Phoenician background, showing the tendency toward a Phoenician orthography (which lacked vowel letters even for inflectional sufformatives), distinctively Phoenician inflections, pronouns and participles, Phoenician syntax, lexical borrowings and analogies, including a score of mercantile terms suggestive of the commercialistic emphasis of emporia like Sidon, Tyre and Byblos. This Phoenician influence is best explained by understanding this genre of the philosophical discourse as having been earlier developed in Phoenician circles and then adopted by Solomon for his own literary and theological purposes. This article also discusses the weaknesses and fallacies of Robert Gordis's attack against Dahood's treatment, as set forth in his *Koheleth: The Man and His World* (New York: Schocken, 1988), p. 416. Dahood's own suggestion that Qohelet emerged from some otherwise unknown Jewish refugee colony in Phoenicia in the sixth century or later is hardly credible in view of the absolute control maintained by Nebuchadnezzar over the Phoenician mainland after the fall of Jerusalem in 587. In view of his pursuit and massacre of the refugee Jews in Egypt, it is inconceivable that he would have permitted any Jewish colony to remain in Phoenicia either. Thus the only reasonable alternative is to place the composition of Ecclesiastes in the reign of Solomon, when commercial and cultural relations with Phoenicia were closer between Tyre and Jerusalem than they ever were again.

syntax, and style? Nor can the linguistic problem be solved by moving the date up into the late intertestamental period. We have already seen that Qohelet fragments from the Fourth Qumran Cave make a date any later than 150 B.C. absolutely impossible and furnish the strong probability of the third century or earlier as the time of composition. There are absolutely no affinities between the vocabulary or style of Ecclesiastes and that of the sectarian literature of the Qumran community. Older authors like Kenyon (BAM, pp. 94-95) spoke in generalities of the so-called rabbinical element discoverable in this text. But an actual comparison with the Hebrew of the *Talmud* and *Midrash* shows fully as great a dissimilarity to Ecclesiastes as to any other book in the Old Testament canon.

It is true that the relative pronoun *še* occurs frequently throughout Qohelet (sixty-eight times) alongside the more usual *ašer*[3] (which occurs eighty-nine times). Although *še* appears several times in Judges, quite frequently in the later psalms, and occasionally in Lamentations, Ezekiel, Job, and Joshua, the fact remains that in Ecclesiastes this is the relative pronoun used in sixty-eight instances out of one hundred fifty-seven. Yet it is noteworthy that this is the characteristic relative for the Song of Solomon also (i.e., in thirty-two instances out of thirty-three)—a fact which furnishes greatest embarrassment to those who, like Delitzsch and Young, place Canticles back in the tenth century and Ecclesiastes in the fifth. If in this stylistic peculiarity there is such a close resemblance between the two, it is only reasonable to attribute them to the same period, if not indeed to the same author. Hence, if the Song of Solomon is tenth century and composed by Solomon, it is hard to resist the conclusion that Ecclesiastes is of the same period and origin.

If it is true that the language and style of Ecclesiastes do not correspond to any literature known to us from any stage of Hebrew history, but present radical contrasts to every other book in the Old Testament canon (with the possible exception of Canticles) and to all extant intertestamental Hebrew literature, then it follows that there is at present no sure foundation for dating this book upon linguistic grounds (although it is no more dissimilar to tenth-century Hebrew than it is to fifth century or second century). What then shall we say of this peculiarity?

It seems fairly obvious that we are dealing here with a conventional style peculiar to the particular genre to which Ecclesiastes belonged. Just as in Akkadian literature, legal codes and contract tablets present a great contrast to each other in technique and

---

3. In his *Grammar of Mishnaic Hebrew*, M. H. Segal has this illuminating comment to make: "Now, whatever the relationship of the two forms to each other, there can be no doubt that *še* is as old as *ašer*, if not older. Its confinement in the earlier books of the Bible to North Israelitish documents would prove that its use must have been common in the colloquial speech of northern Palestine, under the influence, to some extent at least, of the Phoenician '*-sh, sh*, the Assyrian *sha*, and perhaps also the Aramaic *zi, di*. The scarcity of its occurrence even in these documents must be explained by the assumption that it was regarded as a vulgarism which the literary language had to avoid. Its use gradually extended to southern Palestine, and being the shorter and more pliable form, it must in the course of time have entirely supplanted the longer *ašer* in the language of the common people, and from this it descended directly to Middle Hebrew. But the literary prejudice against it seems to have remained even after biblical Hebrew had ceased to be a living speech" (London: Oxford, 1927), p. 43.

style, and these too in turn differ greatly from the epistolary or historical prose from this same period, so also there grew up in Hebrew culture a conventional language in style which was felt to be peculiarly fitting for each literary genre. In the case of Greek literature, where we have much more literary data than we do from Palestine, we find that once a genre developed on a particular soil in a particular city-state, the dialect and vocabulary type of the original practitioner who exalted this genre to a classical status would then prevail throughout the rest of the history of Greek literature (until the triumph of *Koinē* in the Greek or Roman period). For example, since Homer was the first to develop the epic, from his time on, all epic poetry had to be written in the Old Ionic dialect which he had used, even though the more modern poet spoke a quite different dialect, such as Attic, Doric, or Aeolic. Correspondingly, since the Dorians were the first to develop choral poetry, convention demanded that whenever an Attic-speaking tragedian (like Sophocles or Aeschylus) moved into a choral passage in his play, the actors abruptly shifted from Attic Greek to Doric Greek (or at least a Doricizing type of Attic) with particular clichés and turns of expression conventional for that particular genre. It so happens that in the case of the precise genre to which Ecclesiastes belongs, we have nothing else which has survived from Hebrew literature. Otherwise we would doubtless find abundant parallels for all the peculiar phenomena of Qohelet in the compositions which belong to the same genre. If this type of philosophical discourse was first practiced in North Israel before Solomon's time, this would explain the Aramaic and Phoenician traits and influences of which modern critics have made so much. It would also explain the infrequency of the name Yahweh in this text.

In this connection it may be well to mention the theory of L. Wogue, that we have in our present text of Ecclesiastes a modernized recension. That is to say, the original version of this work as composed by Solomon was written in an older Hebrew which eventually became too obscure for ready comprehension by post-exilic generations of Jews. For this reason, says the theory, it was published anew in a more up-to-date vocabulary and style that it might be more widely enjoyed. To take an analogy, most English readers read Chaucer's *Canterbury Tales* in a modernized version, since Chaucer's fourteenth-century English contains so many obsolete terms and expressions as to require a glossary for intelligibility. The weakness of this theory, however, derives from the incorrect assumption that the Hebrew of Ecclesiastes can be clearly identified as a post-exilic product. Since in point of fact it resembles no known document from the post-exilic period, there does not seem to be much point to this suggestion. Moreover the Hebrew text itself is so difficult to understand that it would hardly serve as a popularization intended for ready comprehension.

Apart from linguistic considerations, the objection is often raised to the Solomonic authorship of Qohelet that the author seems to speak, occasionally at least, from the standpoint of a third party or observer, rather than as the king himself. He may even be said to cherish a critical attitude toward kings, which would scarcely be compatible with the viewpoint of the historic Solomon. As an oppressive exactor of taxes whose kingdom upon his decease fell apart over the issue of excessive taxation, it would be out of character for him to say: "Blessed art thou, O land, when thy king is the son of nobles, and thy princes eat in due season, for strength, and not for drunkenness" (10:17); or again: "Curse not the king, no not in thy thought" (10:20, which critics understand to imply that the king is so objectionable that his subjects are strongly tempted to curse him); and again: "Better is a poor and a wise child than an old and foolish king, who will not be admonished" (4:13).

To this it may be replied that none of these passages is really decisive against royal authorship. Solomon was composing a discourse upon government in general from the standpoint of a philosopher and not as a progovernment propagandist. It would be naive to suppose that he could have been ignorant of the existence of gluttonous, bibulous, cantankerous, or stubborn-minded kings, or of the unhappy consequences incurred by their subjects in having such men rule over them. Ecclesiastes 10:17 may even be interpreted as a bit of self-congratulation on the part of the royal author; 10:20 may simply have been an admonition to malcontents to show a proper respect for the government; 4:13 may have been meant as a wholesome reminder to himself. But at any rate, the whole composition is written from the standpoint of a philosophical observer of political and social life rather than as a partisan of royalty. The *Meditations of Marcus Aurelius* furnishes a good parallel to Qohelet in this respect, for the Roman emperor wrote this work from the standpoint of a philosopher rather than as a propagandist for his own government.

Many modern critics such as R. H. Pfeiffer allege that Ecclesiastes betrays the influence of Greek philosophy. The skeptical attitude toward Judaism, the occasional expressions of eudaemonism or Epicureanism, the notion of time as cosmic flow, and the attempt to understand the world as a whole—all these are thought to be of Hellenic origin (so F. C. Grant in *Encyclopaedia Americana*; likewise Cornill). But G. A. Barton has shown that the asserted resemblances between Ecclesiastes and the Stoics are merely superficial, and their two viewpoints are in fundamental opposition. Moreover the indeterminism of Epicureanism contrasts sharply with the rigid, deterministic thought of Qohelet. But the often cited commendations of the general enjoyment of eating and drinking were a commonplace found as early as in the *Gilgamesh Epic*.[4] In this latter connection, Oswald Loretz (*Qohelet und der alte Orient, Herder*, 1964) points to a specific parallel, where Gilgamesh says to Enkidu: "Mankind, its days are counted; all that it can do is of wind." R. Gordis is disposed to concede some Greek influence, but he insists, "Efforts to prove Ecclesiastes an Aristotelian, a Stoic, an Epicurean, a Cynic, or a Cyrenaic have not been successful. The alleged Grecisms in style have also shown it to be authentically Hebrew or Semitic."[5] Pedersen shows that the estimates of mankind in Greek philosophy are entirely different from those in Ecclesiastes. Galling

---

4. Barton, *Commentary on Ecclesiastes*, ICC (Edinburgh: T. & T. Clark, 1959), pp. 34-40.
5. Gordis, in *Twentieth Century Encyclopedia*, 1:361.

demonstrates that the supposed dependence upon Greek gnomists is only a superficial resemblance. Dornseiff points out the possibility that some Greek apothegms may themselves be of oriental extraction and imported into Greek thought (cf. W. Baumgartner, "The Wisdom Literature" in OTMS, p. 226).

Attempts have been made to show a post-Solomonic authorship by various telltale anachronisms. Thus in 1:16 the preacher speaks of having attained "more wisdom than all they that have been before me in Jerusalem." This is construed by critics to mean, more than all kings who were before him, which would of course be a rather strange statement for one who was preceded by only one Israelite king in Jerusalem, namely David. It is interesting to observe that while E. J. Young feels the force of this argument in the case of Ecclesiastes, he resorts to an alternative explanation in an exactly similar situation at 1 Kings 14:9. In this latter passage a denunciatory prophet from Judah rebukes Jeroboam I, comparing him "with all that were before thee." Rather than conceding this to be an anachronism, Young comments, "Those who preceded him were probably elders and judges" (IOT, p. 189). In a similar way we can confidently assert that there were many more kings before Solomon in Jerusalem than just his father David. Jerusalem had been a royal city for pre-Hebrew inhabitants many hundreds of years, even back to the time of Melchizedek, Abraham's contemporary.

Yet there is another explanation of the phrase in 1:16. The text does not specify all *kings*, but only *all*. In the context it is fair to say that the author implies "all wise men who were before me in Jerusalem." The statement in 1 Kings 4:31 concerning Solomon's superiority draws the comparison with Heman, Chalcol, and Darda, who may very well have been sages in pre-Davidic Jerusalem. Melchizedek himself certainly would have rated highly as a wise man, in view of his encounter with Abraham in Gen. 14.

Another supposed anachronism is found in Eccl. 1:12: "I...was [*hāyîtî*] king...in Jerusalem." This perfect tense is thought to betray the fact that Solomon was already a figure of the past, possibly of the remote past, by the time this composition was written. It is urged that this one word would suffice for the Hebrew reader to show him that Solomonic authorship was only intended to be fictional. To this it may be answered that the form in question may more properly be rendered: "I became king over Israel." This would be a very natural statement for Solomon to make in his old age as he looked back on the important turning points in his life's career. It is difficult to imagine what other verb form would have been more appropriate in this connection; the imperfect *'ehyeh* might have been construed by the reader to mean either "I was being king," or "I am king," or "I will be king." Torczyner and Galling have pointed to Egyptian parallels in which "I was king" occurs as the statement made by a dying king as he composes his final testament for a funerary inscription (cf. OTMS, p. 222).

It is interesting in this connection to point to the similar use of this same verb in Jonah 3:3: "Now Nineveh was [*hāyᵉtâ*] a great city," which Young explains as follows: "Furthermore, 3:3 does not describe Nineveh as a city that had existed long ago in the past, but simply indicates the condition or size as Jonah found it" (IOT, p. 279). In the light of this clear and appropriate explanation, it is strange that the same author (E. J. Young) should insist that the clear implication of *hāyîtî* in Eccl. 1:12 "is that the writer had been and no longer is king" (IOT, p. 368). On the contrary, it is altogether natural for a man in his old age to make reference to the commencement of his career by the use of this perfect tense in Hebrew.

Last, it is contended by advocates of a late date that the contemporary age implied by the text of Ecclesiastes is one of misfortune, misery, and oppression, rather than of the unexampled prosperity which characterized the reign of Solomon (cf. 1 Kings 4:25). For example, we meet verses like these: Ecclesiastes 4:3: "Better is he....[that] hath not yet been, who hath not seen the evil work that is done under the sun," and 7:10: "Say not thou, What is the cause that the former days were better than these?" To this it may be replied that a proper interpretation of these verses can only be made in the light of the context. Thus 4:3 occurs in a passage which describes oppression and hardship as vicissitudes entering into human experience generally, despite intervals of comparative prosperity and security such as Israel passed through in the tenth century. Solomon would not have been unmindful of the fact that the experience both of nations and of individuals normally includes times of hardship and testing which challenge an optimistic concept of life. Surely with his vast knowledge of history and world affairs, as well as of the dark era of Saul's reign in Israel, Solomon would have been aware of the bitter aspects of human life. He certainly had the wit to realize that much evil was carried on "under the sun" even in his own kingdom and during his own reign. As for 7:10, it should be pointed out that the "better days" spoken of may well have had reference to the life of an individual complainer who had fallen upon some personal misfortune. There is nothing whatever in the context to imply that he was talking about the current situation of his country as a whole.

In view of the foregoing discussion, it is fair to assert that the so-called anachronisms are all capable of an interpretation reconcilable with Solomonic authorship. We have already seen that the linguistic data do not permit any certainty in dating, whether early or late, and that the most plausible explanation is that Ecclesiastes is written in a particular style conventional for its own genre.

Perhaps it should be added that words of so-called Persian origin, like *pardēs* ("park") and *pitgām* ("official decision") are also derivable from Sanskrit (*paridhis* and *pratigāma*, respectively), a language of ancient India closely related to Persian. Although there is no explicit record in Scripture that Solomon's merchant marine operating from the port of Elath on the Red Sea made voyages to India, there is every likelihood that they did so in quest of choice spices and fabrics. There exists, therefore, the possibility that these words might have found their way into currency at an era when Israelite commercial relations were more extensive than at any other time in history. In other words, it is fair to say that until we discover more Hebrew literature of the same genre and from the age of Solomon himself, we simply do not know enough to assert positively that Solomon could not have been the author of the book. Inasmuch as the plain implication of the text is that he was indeed the composer and left this work as a final testament to his people, on the basis of his own life's experience, it seems best to hold to the traditional view of the synagogue and the church that this work is an authentic production of his pen. This view is strengthened by the fact that there are some remarkable similarities between such passages in Ecclesiastes as 10:8, 9, 12, 13, 18 and the corresponding sections in Proverbs.

A word should be said concerning the so-called pessimism of Ecclesiastes with regard to the life to come. There are, for instance, frequent reminders of the inevitability of death for all creatures, man, and beast (3:19)—although it is recognized that the spirit of man "goes upward" and the spirit of the beast "goes downward to the earth" (3:21). The worthwhileness of life seems to be questioned by such passages as 4:2: "Wherefore I praised the dead which are already dead more than the living which are yet alive." But this statement has to be construed in context. The previous verse makes it clear that if life is going to consist in oppression, calamity, and sorrow, then it is better never to have been born. In 6:8 the preacher asks, "For what hath the wise more than the fool? What hath the poor, that knoweth to walk before the living?" This comment is to be understood in the light of the basic purpose of the book, which is to demonstrate that apart from God and His holy will, life lacks any ultimate meaning, and amounts to no more than vanity. This is true of the life of the well-educated, the rich, and the healthy, as well as that of the less fortunate members of the human race. But when a man's relationship to the Lord is right, it will be well with him (8:12). Apart from the fear of God and a dedicated purpose to do His will, even the most favored of men lead a wretched and depraved existence. Hence, "This is an evil among all things that are done under the sun, that there is one event unto all: yea, also the heart of the sons of men is full of evil, and madness is in their heart while they live, and after that they go to the dead" (9:3).

Great stress, however, is laid upon the importance of this life as the only arena of opportunity and significant accomplishment available to man before he steps out into eternity. Hence, "For to him that is joined to all the living there is hope: for a living dog is better than a dead lion" (9:4). From 9:5 some have mistakenly derived a teaching of soul sleep for the dead: "For the living know that they shall die: but the dead know not anything, neither have they any more a reward; for the memory of them is forgotten." But taken in context, this verse simply means that the dead have no more knowledge of a personal future with its opportunities of choice for or against God, and between life and good, and death and evil, such as they had prior to the grave. Nor do they have any more knowledge of what goes on under the sun, that is upon earth, while they await in Sheol the day of judgment. At this stage of revelation back in Solomon's time, it was premature for anything to be revealed about the glories of heaven, since of course they were not yet open to deceased believers until the resurrection of Christ.

In conclusion, then, those who interpret the position of Ecclesiastes to be skeptical agnosticism grossly misconstrue the message of this book. They are compelled to classify as later additions the numerous sentiments of reverent faith and trust in God with which the twelve chapters of Ecclesiastes abound. In the interests of their theory, they must exclude from the original text the conclusion of the final chapter: "Let us hear the conclusion of the whole matter: Fear God, and keep his commandments: for this is the whole duty of man" (12:13).

SONG OF SOLOMON

The Hebrew title of this book is *Šîr haš-šîrîm*, that is, "The Song of the Songs," or "The Best of Songs." The LXX rendered this title literally as *asrna asmatōn*, and the Vulgate as *Canticum Canticorum*, both of which mean the "song of songs." It is from the Latin title that the term Canticles is derived as a designation of this book.

The theme of Canticles is the love of Solomon for his Shulamite bride and her deep affection for him. This love affair is understood to typify the warm, personal relationship which God desires with His spiritual bride, composed of all redeemed believers who have given their hearts to Him. From the Christian perspective, this points to the mutual commitment between Christ and His church and the fullness of fellowship which ought to subsist between them.

OUTLINE OF THE SONG OF SOLOMON

A simple and adequate outline is furnished by Delitzsch, who divides the book into six acts:

I. Mutual affection of the lovers, 1:2–2:7

II. Mutual seeking and finding of the lovers, 2:8–3:5

III. Fetching of the bride, and the marriage, 3:6–5:1

IV. Love scorned but won again, 5:2–6:9

V. The Shulamite as the attractively fair but humble princess, 6:10–8:4

VI. Ratification of the love covenant in her home, 8:5-14

AUTHORSHIP AND DATE OF COMPOSITION OF THE SONG OF SOLOMON

The opening verse of the book attributes authorship to King Solomon, using the formula "which is of Solomon" (*'ªšer li-Šªlomoh*). Some scholars have interpreted this phrase as a formula of dedication rather than a true attribution of authorship (essentially the same issue involved as in the *lª-Dāwîd* of the psalm titles), but it should be understood that this preposition *lª*, "to," is the only convenient way of expressing possession or authorship in Hebrew where the same author may have composed many

SONG OF SOLOMON

THEORIES OF INTERPRETATION

Allegorical	Christ and His church
Literal	Secular love song
Typical	Historical incident elevating love to a holy level

other works. It has been the uniform tradition of the Christian church until modern times that Canticles is a genuine Solomonic production. Even in more recent times, Delitzsch, Raven, Steinmueller, and Young have shown little hesitation is assigning the authorship of Canticles to Solomon.

This all the more noteworthy because, as we have already pointed out, there is a considerable similarity in vocabulary and syntax between the Song of Solomon and Ecclesiastes (the Solomonic authorship of which all the above named have denied). Liberal scholars have usually classed these two works together as representing approximately the same period of Hebrew literature. Certainly this relationship is favored by the standard Hebrew dictionaries, which tend to group the two together lexically. It is a striking fact that neither of them refers to God as Yahweh; the Tetragrammaton does not appear in either of them. There is a significant number of words which occur only in these two books, so far as the Hebrew Scriptures are concerned. There would seem to be, therefore, a basic inconsistency in denying authenticity to Ecclesiastes on linguistic grounds and yet affirming it for the Song of Solomon despite linguistic factors. Liberal scholars uniformly deny Solomonic authorship of Canticles and assign the composition of the books to a period considerably later than the tenth century B.C. Moderates like W. R. Smith and S. R. Driver favored a pre-exilic date, that is, before 600 B.C.; such radicals as Kuenen, Cornill, Cheyne, Budde, Kautzsch, and Eissfeldt confidently dated it in the post-exilic or even in the Hellenistic period. W. Baumgartner assigns it to the late third century (cf. OTMS, p. 223).

It is principally on linguistic grounds that the case for late composition is based. The following phenomena are most conspicuous:

1. The prevalence of *še-* instead of *ᵃšer* as the relative pronoun. But as we have seen in the discussion of Ecclesiastes, the relative *še* is not per se a proof of late authorship. A cognate of the Akkadian relative *ša*, which is as old as the third millennium, it appears in the song of Deborah (Judg. 5) and elsewhere in Judges; also in Job 19:29; 2 Kings 6:11; once in Jonah; in Lamentations, and various psalms. It seems to have been a very acceptable substitute for *ᵃšer* in Hebrew poetic style. It was probably characteristic of the dialect of northern Israel. The abundant use of *še-* in later Hebrew may simply reflect a common use in the vernacular which literary Hebrew shied away from

until the post-exilic period. In the intertestamental age, of course, the frequent use of the corresponding particle *dî* in Aramaic tended to encourage the Jews, who were naturally well versed in Aramaic as their colloquial tongue, to employ *še-* in their Hebrew compositions.

2. The presence of various Aramaisms like *nāṭar* (cognate with *nāṣar*, Hebrew, "guard, watch over"), *berōṭ* (cognate with *berōš*, Hebrew, "cypress") and *setāw* ("winter") is taken to indicate post-exilic authorship. Yet, as has already been observed in chapter 7 of this work, they may have been brought into the Hebrew language at an early date, or else they may indicate a North Israelite coloring. (Note that if the Shulamite came from Shunem, as the LXX transliteration *Sounamitis* indicates, then the bride would have come from the territory of the northern tribe of Issachar.) Significantly enough, even the *Brown-Driver-Briggs* Lexicon labels *berōṭ* as North Palestinian rather than as an Aramaism.

3. It is alleged that the book contains two words derived from Greek, *'appiryôn* (3:9) or *palanquin,* from the Greek *phoreion,* and *pardēs* (4:13) meaning "orchard," from either the Greek *paradeisos* or the Persian *pairideca,* meaning "enclosure." Yet as already pointed out in connection with Ecclesiastes, such words as these could have come to Solomon from his trade contacts with India, since the Sanskrit word for palanquin is *paryama* or the diminutive *parynka,* and the Sanskrit for "enclosure" is *paridhis* (cf. *pardīsu,* "park, preserve," late Assyrian).

POSITIVE EVIDENCES OF SOLOMONIC AUTHORSHIP

The author shows a noteworthy interest in natural history, corresponding to the historical notices about Solomon's encyclopedic knowledge in this field (1 Kings 4:33). Thus the flora mentioned in Canticles include twenty-one varieties of plant life (such as henna flowers in 1:14, rose of Sharon, lily of the valley in 2:1, apple trees, pomegranates, saffron, calamus, cinnamon, and mandrakes). Among the fauna are no less than fifteen species of animals (roes, hinds, harts, doves, foxes, goats, ewes, etc.). There is also prominent mention of Pharaoh's cavalry in 1:9, which accords with the statement in 1 Kings 10:28, where the cavalry appears as an important item in Solomon's army as well as in his trade relations. The book shows many evidences of royal luxury and the abundance of costly imported products, such as spikenard in 1:12; myrrh in 1:13; frankincense in 3:6; palanquins in 3:9; cosmetic powders, silver, gold, purple, ivory, and beryl.[6]

The geographical references unmistakably favor a date prior to 930 B.C. The author mentions quite indiscriminately localities to be found in both the Northern and Southern Kingdoms: Engedi, Hermon, Carmel, Lebanon, Heshbon, and Jerusalem. These are spoken of as if they all belonged to the same political realm. Note that Tirzah

---

6. H. R. Hall makes the interesting suggestion that Solomon's imports of apes and peacocks point to the Cochin coast as the location of "Ophir," rather than to Punt in Africa, as is usually assumed (*The Ancient History of the Near East,* 11th ed. [London: Methuen, 1960], p. 434).

Silver Shekel of Tyre (160 B.C.) portraying the head of Baal–Melkarth. Similar to the coin received by Judas Iscariot. The obverse bears the inscription, "Tyre, the Holy City of Refuge."

is mentioned as a city of particular glory and beauty, and that too in the same breath with Jerusalem itself (6:4). If this had been written after the time when Tirzah was chosen as the earliest capital of the breakaway Northern Kingdom in rejection of the authority of the dynasty of David, it is scarcely conceivable that it would have been referred to in such favorable terms. On the other hand, it is highly significant that Samaria, the city founded by Omri sometime between 885 and 874, is never mentioned in the Song of Solomon.

Judging from internal evidence, then, the author was totally unaware of any division of the Hebrew monarchy into North and South. This can only be reconciled with a date of composition in the tenth century, prior to 931 B.C. Even after the return from exile, no Jew of the province of Judea would have referred so indiscriminately to prominent localities in the non-Jewish areas of Palestine which were by this time under Gentile or Samaritan overlordship. It is true that this whole area was reunited under the rule of the Hasmonean kings, John Hyrcanus and Alexander Jannaeus, but the evidence of the Qumran fragments from Cave IV indicates that Canticles was already in written form at least as early as the outbreak of the Maccabean revolt in 168 B.C. It is interesting to note that even a Liberal scholar like R. Gordis feels warranted in asserting that Canticles 3:6-11 is "the oldest poem in the whole collection and was composed on the occasion of one of Solomon's marriages to a foreign princess."[7]

CANONICITY OF THE SONG OF SOLOMON

It has already been noted in chapter 5 that this book (along with Ecclesiastes) was listed with the five Antilegomena, not so much on the ground that Solomon did not compose it, but on the ground that it lacked religious value. The Alexandrian Jew Philo, who quoted so extensively from the Old Testament, failed to mention Canticles in any of his extant writings. It does not seem to be referred to in the New Testament. The earliest identifiable reference to it is found in 4 Esdras 5:24-26; 7:26 (a book composed between A.D. 70 and 130), and in Ta'anith 4:8 (a tractate in the *Mishnah*), which states that certain portions of Canticles were used in festivals celebrated in the temple prior to A.D. 70. The question of whether the book had been rightly admitted to the Hebrew canon was warmly debated by the scholars of Jamnia around A.D. 90, but the

7. Gordis, in JBL 63 (1944): 262-70.

tradition of divine inspiration was successfully upheld by Rabbi Akiba, who used allegorical interpretation to justify its spiritual value.

THEORIES OF INTERPRETATION OF THE SONG OF SOLOMON

1. *Allegorical.* The allegorical interpretation prevailed from ancient times until the rise of modern scholarship. It identified Solomon with Jehovah (or else, according to the Christians, with Christ) and the Shulamite as Israel (or the Church). The historicity of Solomon's love affair is of small importance to the exponents of this theory. They tend to interpret each detail in a symbolic manner; thus Solomon's eighty concubines, according to some, represent the eighty heresies destined to plague the Church. Broadly speaking, even the nineteenth-century conservatives Hengstenberg and Keil tended to favor an allegorical line of interpretation (without, of course, advocating any fanciful identifications) and pointed to the allegorical overtones of Ps. 45 and Isa. 51:1-17 (which contains several different allegories) for justification. There is no question that the marriage relationship was viewed by the prophets as bearing an analogy to Jehovah's position toward Israel (cf. Isa. 54:6; 61:10). Correspondingly, they regarded apostasy as constituting adultery or whoredom (cf. Jer. 3:1; Ezek. 16, 23; Hos. 1-3). Compare in the Torah, Ex. 34:14-16, which refers to idolatry as whoredom; and likewise Lev. 20:5-6.

It must be admitted that these passages establish at least a typical relationship between human love and marriage and the covenant relationship between God and His people. Nevertheless, the allegorical view faces certain difficulties, not the least of which is that the book seems to speak of a historical episode in Solomon's life and accords well with Solomon's situation, at least in the earlier part of his reign (judging from the comparatively small number of his concubines). Moreover, the allegorical method if consistently carried out requires a spiritual counterpart for every physical detail. Certainly it is objectionable to equate Solomon and his enormous harem with the figure of the Lord Jesus Christ, at least upon an allegorical basis.

2. *Literal.* This literal theory regards the poem as a secular love song not intended to convey a spiritual message or theological overtone, but simply a lyric expression of human love on a high romantic plane. Advocates of this theory, such as E. J. Young and H. H. Rowley, defend the canonicity of the book on the ground that it implies a divine sanction for the relationship of marital love as over against the degenerate or polygamous perversions of marriage which were current in Solomon's time (cf. Rowley, *Servant of the Lord and Other Essays,* p. 233; Young, IOT, p. 354). Young goes on to comment, "The eye of faith, as it beholds this picture of exalted human love, will be reminded of the one love that is above all earthly and human affections—even the love of the Son of God for lost humanity" (IOT, p. 355).

Yet it must be admitted that on the supposition that the lover here is Solomon, the husband of seven hundred wives and three hundred concubines (1 Kings 11:3), it is difficult to see how this poem taken as an expression of mere human love can be said to furnish a very high standard of marital devotion and affection. At best it can be regarded as the one experience that Solomon ever enjoyed of pure romance, and yet one which was destined to exert little influence upon his subsequent conduct. (Franz Delitzsch advocated the view that the Song is a drama in which King Solomon falls in love with a Shulamite girl, and after taking her to his harem in Jerusalem, is purified in his affection from a sensual lust to pure love. Zoeckler shared essentially this same view.)

This literal theory assumes various specialized forms, of which the two most important are the shepherd hypothesis and the erotic hypothesis. The shepherd hypothesis introduces a new male figure who is not the same person as the king, but rather is the Shulamite's fiance back in the hometown of Shunem (so Jacobi, Umbreit, and Ewald). By dint of arbitrarily assigning the sentiments of warm affection to the shepherd and the more stiff and formal speeches to the king, a distinction may be made out, even though it results in very unnatural parceling up of the dialogue. Thus in chapter 4 verses 1-7 are assigned to Solomon, and verses 8-15 to the shepherd, even though there is absolutely nothing in the text to indicate that the speaker has changed. Some passages highly inappropriate to a bucolic lover are interpreted as refer-ring to the shepherd, such as: "My beloved has gone down to his garden, to the beds of spices, to feed in the gardens, and to gather lilies" (6:2). It is at least unlikely that Israelite shepherds would have had the means, the time, or the inclination for such luxuries as spice gardens or the gathering of lilies.

The erotic hypothesis is advocated by such scholars as Budde, Eissfeldt, Pfeiffer, and Dussaud, who understand Canticles as an anthology of love songs of the so-called *wasf* type. The *wasf* or "description" was a type of song sung by guests at a Syrian wed-ding feast in which the beauty of the bride and the excellencies of the wedding couple would be glowingly described. This custom is practiced in the Near East even in mod-ern times, according to J. G. Wetstein. On the other hand, there is no literary evidence of the existence of the *wasf* genre in Hebrew Palestine in any age (apart from Canticles itself), and the closely connected structure of the whole poem certainly discourages the theory of its being an anthology of originally independent lyrics.

3. *Typical view.* In many ways this seems to be the most satisfactory of the theories (though Young dismisses it with a single deprecatory sentence—IOT, p. 353). This interpretation is defended by Raven and Unger, who understand the poem as based upon an actual historical incident in Solomon's life. In contrast to some of the more glamorous wives of Solomon, such as Pharaoh's daughter, the Shulamite was a country girl who possessed a beautiful soul as well as a fair body. By her radiant sincerity and personal charms she taught Solomon, temporarily at least, to know the meaning of true, monogamous love—a love for which he gladly exchanged the corrupt splendor of his court. This song transfigures natural love by elevating it to a holy level. And yet (in opposition to the literalists) the author intends this couple to stand in a typical rela-tionship reflecting Jehovah's love for His people and foreshadowing the mutual affec-

tion of Christ and His Church. According to the typical view, the lines of analogy are found not in all the subordinate details (as in the allegorical view) but only in the main outlines. Despite his gross personal failures, King Solomon is represented else-where in Scripture (2 Sam. 7:12-17; 23:1-7; Ps. 72; cf. Matt. 12:42) as a type of Christ as the King of the millennial age sitting upon David's throne. Understood in this way, the Song is rich in spiritual overtones which have proved a comfort and an encourage-ment to devout students of Scripture throughout the ages of church history. And yet it requires a really mature soul to appreciate the spiritual beauties which are latent in this book. Not without justification is the old rabbinical requirement that no Jew should read the Song of Songs until he had attained the age of thirty.

APPENDIX 1

OLD TESTAMENT CHRONOLOGY

The dates marked with an asterisk are especially important for Old Testament introduction. Essentially this list follows the chronology of J. B. Payne's *Outline of Hebrew History*. Some minor adjustments may be warranted in the light of more recent discovery, but the dates given below are at least approximately correct.

EGYPTIAN KINGS		PATRIARCHS AND ISRAELITES	
Egyptian Dynasties I and II (3100-2700, Vos, ABS, p. 222)	3000-2600		
*Egyptian Old Kingdom (Dyn. III-VI) III-IV 2660-2500 (Pfeiffer & Vos, HGBL, p. 68) Dyn IV 2723-2563 (ZPEB ii, p. 231, K. A. Kitchen) 2613-2494 (Encyclopedia Britannica, 8;38, '59)	2600-2250		
First Intermediate Period (Dyn. VII-XI)	2250-2000	*Birth of Abraham	2166
*Egypt's dynasty XII (Middle Kingdom)	2000-1780	*Jacob's migration to Egypt	1876
Second Intermediate Period (Dyn. XII-XVII)	1780-1546		
Hammurabi (Rowton) (Finegan) (Hyksos Period, Dyn. XV-XVI)	1792-1750 1728-1686		
*Egyptian New Kingdom	1546-1085		
Dynasty XVIII			
Ahmose I	1584-1860		
Amenhotep I	1560-1539		
Thutmose I	1539-1514	*Birth of Moses	ca. 1527
Thutmose II	1514-1501		
Queen Hatshepsut	1501-1482		
*Thutmose III	(1501-) 1482-1447		

*Amenhotep II	1447-1421	
Thutmose IV	1421-1410	
*Amenhotep III	1410-1376	
Amenhotep IV (Akhnaton)	1376-1362	
Tutankhamen	1361-1352	

Dynasty XIX

Horemhab	1349-1319
Seti I	1320-1300
*Rameses II	1300-1234
Merneptah	1234-1224
(Vos, p. 210)	1224-1214

Dynasty XX

Rameses III	1204-1172

*The Exodus   1446
(Late Date Theory: 1290)

*Conquest of Jericho   1406
*Period of the judges 1389-1050

UNITED MONARCHY

*Saul	1050-1010
*David	1010-970
*Solomon	970-931
*Temple begun	ca. 966

DIVIDED MONARCHY

KINGS OF JUDAH		KINGS OF DAMASCUS		KINGS OF ISRAEL	
*Rehoboam	931-913				
Abijam	913-910	Rezon	940-880	*Jeroboam I	930-910
*Asa	910-869	Ben-Hadad I	880-842	Nadab	910-909
		Hazael	842-806	Baasha	909-886
		Ben-Hadad II	806-770	Elah	886-885
		Rezin	750-732	Zimri	885
				Omri	885-874
*Jehoshaphat	872-848			*Ahab	874-853
Jehoram	848-841	**PROPHETS**		Ahaziah	853-852
(coregent already in 853)		Obadiah	ca. 845	Jehoram	852-841
Ahaziah	841			*Jehu	841-814
Athaliah	841-835				
*Joash	835-796	Joel	830-810	Jehoahaz	814-798
Amaziah	796-767	Jonah	ca. 800	Jehoash	798-782
*Uzziah	790-739	Amos	ca. 760-757	*Jeroboam II	793-753
				Zechariah	753-752
				Shallum	752
				Menahem	752-742
Jotham	751-736	Hosea	756-725	Pekahiah	742-740
Ahaz	742-728	*Isaiah	740-680	Pekah (752)	740-732
*Hezekiah	728-697			Hoshea	732-723
		Micah	735-690	Fall of Samaria	721
*Manasseh	697-642				
*Amon	642-640				
*Josiah	640-609				
		Nahum	640		
		Zephaniah	640-630		
		*Jeremiah	626-570		

KINGS OF ASSYRIA

Shalmaneser III	858-824
Adad Nirari III	810-783
Asshur-Dan	771-754
Tiglath-pileser III	744-727
Shalmaneser V	727-722
Sargon II	722-705
Sennacherib	705-681
Essarhaddon	680-669
Ashurbanipal	669-626
Fall of Nineveh	612

Egyptian Dynasty XXVI

Psamtik I	663-610
Neco	610-595
Psamtik II	595-589
Hophra (Apries)	588-569
Ahmose II (Amasis)	569-526
Psamtik III	526-525
Habakkuk	608-597
*Ezekiel	592-570

Jehoahaz	609-608
Jehoiakim	608-597
Jehoiachin	597
Zedekiah	597-587
*Fall of Jerusalem	587
Gedaliah	ca. 586-585
Fourth Deportation	ca. 583

CAPTIVITY

KINGS OF CHALDEA

Nebucadnezzar	605-562
(invasion of Egypt)	568/7
Evil-Merodach	561-560
Nabonidus	555-530
*Fall of Babylon	539

*Daniel	600-530

KINGS OF PERSIA

Cyrus the Great	558-529
(defeat of Medes)	550
Cabyses	529-523
(conquest of Egypt)	
*Darius I	522-485
*Xerxes (Ahashuerus)	485-464
Artaxerxes	464-424
Darius II	423-406
*Artaxerxes II	404-359

*Haggai	520-519

*Second temple rebuilt	520-516
Zechariah	519-475
*Ezra's return	457
*Nehemiah's return	445
Malachi	ca. 435
Nehemiah's second governorship	433-430

INTERTESTAMENTAL PERIOD

KINGS OF GREECE
*Alexander the Great	336-323
*Antiochus IV (Epiphanes)	175-164

HASMONAEAN DYNASTY
John Hyrcanus	135-105
Alexander Jannaeus	104-78

ROMAN RULE
*Pompey's conquest of Syria Palestine	63

* Rededication of the temple by Judas Maccabaeus (Hanukkah) Dec. 165

ANACHRONISMS AND HISTORICAL INACCURACIES IN THE KORAN

SURA 11-HOUD

:42-43. Noah's (unnamed) son is said to have refused to take refuge in the ark while the flood waters were rising, and despite his father's plea, chose rather to flee to a mountaintop, from which he was swept away by a wave. (Gen. 6-7 indicates that Noah had only three sons, and that they all entered the ark. Gen. 10 gives the line of descendants from each.)

SURA 12-JOSEPH, PEACE BE ON HIM

:11-20. Joseph did not go seeking his brother up at Dothan (as Gen. 37 records), but rather the brothers, having already plotted his death, persuaded Jacob to let him go with them simply for fun and sport. Having gotten him into their power, they put him down into a well with water in it (rather than a dry pit). Nor was it they who sold him to the passing merchantmen, but rather a chance wayfarer who had come to the well to draw water. He sold the boy to the merchants "for a few dirhams" (rather than the substantial price of twenty shekels of silver, as Gen. 37:28 states).

:21-32. His Egyptian owner's wife (Potiphar's name is not given), in her attempt to seduce him, tore his shirt from behind (rather than from in front) in her pursuit of him—a fact observed by Potiphar's canny servant, and which served to expose the falsity of her charge. Later she admitted to her women friends that this was the case, yet in some unexplained way she managed to get Joseph into jail all the same.

:36-55. In jail, Joseph tried to convert the two "youths" (i.e., Pharaoh's butler and baker) to "Islam" and away from idolatry. Years later, the surviving youth (the butler) remembered Joseph's dream-interpreting ability, went to him in jail with a report of the substance of the king's dream (rather than the king's relating it to him directly in the palace), and got an interpretation from him which he then relayed to Pharaoh. As a result the king placed Joseph in charge of the nation's grain supply. (The rest of the story, with disclosure to the ten brothers, etc., closely follows the account in Gen. 40-45.)

Sura 26-The Poets

:55-60. In Egypt, the Israelites were stated by Pharaoh to be but "a scanty band" (in contrast to Ex. 1:9). As they are permitted to leave Egypt, they are said to be forsaking "their gardens and fountains and splendid dwellings." Apparently they had not been subjected to slavery at all (for no mention is made of it), but rather had enjoyed wealth and luxury while in Egypt. (This renders the whole motive for deliverance of God's covenant people from Egypt rather obscure.)

Sura 2-The Cow

:57, 61. During the Exodus, the Israelites became tired of manna and demanded vegetables from the soil. After scolding them, Moses said, "Get down to Egypt, for you shall have what you asked." They proceeded to do so: "And they returned with wrath from God." (The record in Exodus-Numbers makes it clear that while discontented Israelites spoke of returning to Egypt, none of them actually did so.)

In this connection, it is stated in v. 61: "They disbelieved the signs of God, and slew the Prophets unjustly; this, for they rebelled and transgressed." On this passage, see Rodwell's footnote: "This passage (cf. 26:59) is one of the numerous anachronisms which abound in the Koran and prove the gross ignorance of the Arabian prophet" (*Koran*, trans. J. M. Rodwell, Everyman's Library [New York: Dutton, 1909], p. 344).

:249. When King Saul of Israel (called Ṭalût in Sura 2:247) marched forth with his forces, he said, "God will test you by a river. He who drinks of it shall not be of my band; but he who shall not taste of it, drinking a drink out of the hand excepted, shall be of my band." (Rodwell's footnote here calls attention to Muhammed's confusion here between Saul and Gideon. Cf. Judg. 7:5-8.)

Sura 3-The Family of Imran

Rodwell's introductory note to this Sura points out that Muhammed supposed that Imran (or Amram) was the father of the Virgin Mary—"Mary" being "Maryam" or Miriam, in Arabic. Cf. Sura 66:12, "Mary the daughter of Imran," who remained a virgin after marriage and motherhood. He also supposed that Mary and Elizabeth were sisters, and along with Zecharias, John the Baptist, and Jesus, they made up the family of Imran. It is just possible, as some Muslim authors assert, that Muhammed thought that Miriam's soul and body were miraculously preserved until the time of Jesus (1400 years!), in order that she might become His mother, Mary. This he may have gotten from the Talmudists, who fabled that the Angel of Death and the worm of corruption had no power over the body of Miriam (cf. *Babba Bathra* 17, and *Josephus, Antiquities*, 4.4.6). Another source for this account may have been the *Protevangelium* of *James*, iv, which states: "And Anna said, 'As the Lord my God lives, he shall be a minister to Him all his days,'" referring to the future career of her offspring. Thus the wife of Imran says here (Sura 3:31): "O my Lord, I vow to Thee what is in my womb, for Thy special service; accept it from me, for Thou hearest, knowest!"

:41. Zacharias said to the angel, "Lord, give me a token." He said, "Thy token shall be that for *three days* thou shalt speak to no man but by signs." (Luke 1:18-20 makes it clear that he was to remain speechless until the promised child should be born, or about nine or ten *months*.)

:55. "Remember when God said, 'O Jesus, verily I will cause thee to die [or, this *mutawwafika* may also be rendered: "take thee unto Myself"], and "will take thee up to Myself, and deliver thee from those who believe not." (Rodwell's footnote here: "Muhammed apparently believed that God took the dead body of Jesus to heaven—for three hours, according to some—while the Jews crucified a man who resembled him. Cf. Sura 4:156; Sura 19:34. Muhammed supposed Jesus to have died a natural death, though it is nowhere stated how long He remained in this state.")

Sura 61-Battle Array

:6. "And remember when Jesus the son of Mary said, 'O children of Israel, of a truth I am God's apostle to you to confirm the law which was given before me, and to announce an apostle that shall come after me whose name shall be Aḥmad.'" (Rodwell notes: "This apparently Muhammed got from the title *Parakletos* which Jesus assigned to the Holy Spirit in John 16:7 et al., which Muhammed confused with *perikytos* ("famous, praised"), for which the Arabic would be Aḥmad or Muhammad.")

Sura 5-The Table

:119. "And when God shall say, 'O Jesus, son of Mary, hast thou said to mankind, "Take me and my mother as two Gods beside God,"' he shall say, 'Glory be to Thee! It is not for me to say that which I know to be not the truth. Had I said that, verily Thou wouldst have known it; Thou knowest what is in me.'" (This involves a complete misunderstanding of the Trinity, with Mary as a third person, rather than the Holy Spirit. It also implies that Jesus denied He was the Son of God; cf. Mark 14:61-62 and related passages.)

Sura 21 - The Prophets

:68-69 claims that Nimrod threw Abraham into the fire in an act of bitter hostility. But according to the Torah, Gen. 10:8-11 tells us that Nimrod came in the *third* generation after Noah, whereas Abraham came *ten* generations after Noah (Gen. 10:22-25; 11:13-25). Therefore it is highly unlikely that Nimrod was still alive when Abraham was born to Terah.

One of the most perplexing puzzles in the Koran has to do with the Virgin Mary. In 3:35 she is said to be the wife of 'Imran. Admittedly 'Imran is the same as the Hebrew Amram, who was the father of Moses. Yusuf Ali explains this as meaning that Mary was descended from 'Imran and married to a man named 'Imran (p. 131, n. 375). But this interpretation runs counter to the clear statement in Matthew 1:6 that Jesus' foster father, Joseph, was descended from David, of the tribe of Judah rather than of Levi, and Mary seems to have descended from David as well, by a collateral line (Luke 3:31). Hebrews 7:14 states: "For it is very evident that our Lord arose from Judah, a tribe about which Moses said nothing concerning priestly office." Therefore, Jesus' mother and father both descended from Judah and not from Levi (as Amram and Miriam did). As for the name of Mary's husband, it was unquestionably Joseph, not 'Imran, who took her in marriage. Therefore the reference to 'Imran must be an error in the Qur'an.

SURA 19 – MARYAM

:22 states that Mary gave birth to Jesus under a palm tree, rather than in a stable in the town of Bethlehem as foretold in Mic. 5:2 and recorded in Matthew 2:1 and Luke 2:4-7, as taking place in a stable connected with an inn. The three Magi who came looking for the recently born King of the Jews, were directed by Herod's Bible experts to look for Him down in Bethlehem, and it was this information which soon afterward prompted Herod himself to send down a platoon of butchers to Bethlehem in order to massacre all the baby boys in that town who were two years old or younger. The birth under a palm tree is in complete variance with Old Testament prophecy and New Testament records. The Coptic Church cherishes many traditions of the Holy Family taking refuge in Egypt to escape from the murderous Herod until he died a year or two later.

SURA 20 – TA NA

:87, 94 inform us that when the Israelites set up their idolatrous golden calf in Ex. 32, they did so at the instigation of a *Samaritan*: "And that was what the Samari/Samarian suggested." Yusef Ali suggests that *Samariyyu* may have been an Egyptian name meaning "stranger, foreigner," or possibly a Hebrew term derived from *Shomer* ("watchman")—in a valiant effort to avoid the charge of anachronism. Samaritans did not come into being as a race until after the 6th century B.C., and so there could have been no Samaritan around as early as 1445 B.C.! But unhappily for Ali's explanation, the word "Samaritan" appears in standard Arabic dictionaries as *Samariyyun*, spelled exactly the same as it is in this verse of Sura 20. There is no word or name like Samiriyyu in the Egyptian lexicon.

ANACHRONISMS AND HISTORICAL INACCURACIES IN THE MORMON SCRIPTURES

APPENDIX **3**

1. In 1 Nephi 2:5-8, it is stated that the river Laman emptied into the Red Sea. Yet neither in historic nor prehistoric times has there ever been any river in Arabia at all that emptied into the Red Sea. Apart from an ancient canal which once connected the Nile with the coast of the Gulf of Suez, and certain wadis which showed occasional rainfall in ancient times, there were no streams of any kind emptying into the Red Sea on the western shore above the southern border of Egypt.

2. Second, Nephi states that only the family of Lehi, Ishmael, and Zoram were left in Jerusalem in 600 B.C. to migrate to the New World. These totaled fifteen persons, plus three or four girls, or no more than twenty in all. Yet in less than thirty years, according to 2 Nephi 5:28, they had multiplied so startlingly that they divided up into two nations (2 Nephi 5:5-6, 21). Indeed, after arriving in America in 589 B.C., they are stated to have built a temple like Solomon's. Now Solomon's temple required no less than 153,000 workers and 30,000 overseers (1 Kings 5:13, 15; 6:1, 38; 9:20-21; 2 Chron. 2:2, 17-18) to complete its erection in seven and a half years. It is difficult to see how a few dozen unskilled workers (most of whom must have been children) could have duplicated this feat even in the nineteen years they allegedly did the work. Nor is it clear how all kinds of iron, copper, brass, silver, and gold could have been found in great abundance (2 Nephi 5:15) for the erection of this structure back in the sixth-century B.C. America.

3. According to Alma 7:10, Jesus was to be born at Jerusalem (rather than in Bethlehem, as recorded in Luke 2:4 and predicted in Mic. 5:2).

4. Helamen 14:20, 29 states that darkness covered the whole earth for three days at the time of Christ's death (rather than three hours, as recorded in Matt. 27:45 and Mark 15:33), or beyond Easter morning, which would have made it impossible for the woman at the tomb to tell whether the stone had been rolled away from its mouth.

5. Alma 46:15 indicates that believers were called "Christians" back in 73 B.C. rather than at Antioch, as Acts 11:26 informs us. It is difficult to imagine how anyone could have been labeled Christian so many decades before Christ was even born.

6. Helamen 12:25-26, allegedly written in 6 B.C., quotes John 5:29 as a prior written source, introducing it by the words "We read." It is difficult to see how a quotation could be cited from a written source not composed until eight or nine decades after 6 B.C.

7. Quite numerous are the instances in which the Mormon scriptures, said to have been in the possession of the Nephites back in 600 B.C., quote from or allude to passages or episodes found only in exilic or post-exilic books of the Old Testament. Several examples follow.

(*i*) First Nephi 22:15 states: "For behold, saith the prophet, the time cometh speedily that Satan shall have no more power over the hearts of the children of men; for the day soon cometh that all the proud and they who do wickedly shall be as stubble; and the day cometh that they must be burned." Compare this with Mal. 4:1 (ca. 435 B.C.): "For, behold, the day cometh, that shall burn as an oven; and all the proud, yea, and all that do wickedly, shall be stubble: and the day that cometh shall burn them up, saith the LORD of hosts, that it shall leave them neither root nor branch."

(*ii*) Second Nephi 26:9: "But the Son of righteousness shall appear unto them; and he shall heal them, and they shall have peace with him, until three generations shall have passed away." Compare this with Mal. 4:2: "But unto you that fear my name shall the Sun of righteousness arise with healing in his wings; and ye shall go forth and grow up as calves of the stall." Note the confusion between Son and Sun, which could only have originated from their similar sound in the English language.

(*iii*) Third Nephi 28:21-22: "And thrice they were cast into a furnace and received no harm. And twice they were cast into a den of wild beasts; and behold they did play with the beasts as a child with a suckling lamb, and received no harm." Compare this with Dan. 3 and 6 where such adventures befell Shadrach, Meshach, and Abednego, along with Daniel himself. It is difficult to understand how these Mormon believers could have had experiences just like those related in the book of Daniel, which was not even composed until several decades after their alleged departure for the New World in 589 B.C. (Daniel could have found written form only after the fall of Babylon to the Persians in 539 B.C., since it contains at least fifteen Persian loanwords.)

(*iv*) Alma 10:2 states that Aminadi "interpreted the writing which was upon the wall of the temple, which was written by the finger of God." Surely this is a reminiscence of Daniel's feat in reading the divine handwriting upon the wall of Belshazzar's banquet hall in 539 B.C.

8. Even more remarkable is the abundance of parallels or word-for-word quotations from the New Testament which are found in the *Book of Mormon*, which was allegedly in the possession of the Nephites back in 600 B.C. Jerald and Sandra Tanner (*The Case Against Mormonism*, vol. 2 [Salt Lake City, 1967], pp. 87-102) have listed no less than 400 clear examples out of a much larger number that could be adduced; and these serve to establish beyond all question that the author of the *Book of Mormon* was actually well acquainted with the New Testament, and specifically with the KJV of 1611. A few examples follow:

(*i*) First Nephi 4:13: "That one man should perish than that a nation should...perish in unbelief." Compare this with John 11:50: "That one man should die for the people, and that the whole nation perish not."

(*ii*) 1 Nephi 10:8: "Whose shoe's latchet I am not worthy to unloose." Compare this with John 1:27: "Whose shoe's latchet I am not worthy to unloose."

(*iii*) 1 Nephi 10:9: "In Bethabara beyond Jordan...he should baptize." Compare this with John 1:28: "In Bethabara beyond Jordan, where John was baptizing."

(*iv*) 1 Nephi 11:22: "The love of God, which sheddeth itself abroad in the hearts of the children of men." Compare this with Rom. 5:5: "The love of God is shed abroad in our hearts by the Holy Ghost."

(*v*) 1 Nephi 11:27: "The Holy Ghost come down out of heaven and abide upon him in the form of a dove." Compare this with Luke 3:22: "The Holy Ghost descended in bodily shape like a dove upon him."

(*vi*) 1 Nephi 14:11: "The whore of all the earth, and she sat upon many waters; and she had dominion over all the earth, among all nations, kindreds, tongues, and people." Compare this with Rev. 17:1,15: "The great whore sitteth upon many waters... The waters which thou sawest, where the whore sitteth, are peoples, and multitudes, and nations, and tongues."

9. Most interesting is the recently exposed fraud of the so-called "*Book of Abraham*," part of the Mormon scripture known as *The Pearl of Great Price*. This was assertedly translated from an ancient Egyptian papyrus found in the mummy wrappings of certain mummies which had been acquired by a certain Michael H. Chandler. In 1835 Joseph Smith became very much interested in these papyrus leaves, which he first saw in Kirtland, Ohio, on July 3, and arranged for the purchase of both mummies and manuscripts. Believing he had divinely received the gift of interpreting ancient Egyptian, he was delighted to find that one of the rolls contained the writings of Abraham himself, whose signature he had personally inscribed in the Egyptian language. In 1842, Smith published his translation under the title, "The Book of Abraham" in *Times and Seasons*. He even included three drawings of the pictures or vignettes appearing in the manuscript, and interpreted the meaning of these illustrations: Abraham sitting upon the throne of Pharaoh, the serpent with walking legs who tempted Eve in Eden. For many years this collection of papyri was lost, but somehow they (or else a duplicate set of them from ancient times) were presented to the Mormon Church by the Metropolitan Art Museum of New York City on November 27, 1967. This made the translation skill of Joseph Smith susceptible of objective verification. The unhappy result was that earlier negative verdicts of scholars like Theodule Devaria of the Louvre, and Samuel A. B. Mercer of Western Theological Seminary, and James H. Breasted of the University of Chicago, and W. M. Flinders Petrie of London University (who had all been shown Smith's facsimiles) were clearly upheld by a multitude of present-day Egyptologists.

Their finding was that not a single word of Joseph Smith's alleged translation bore any resemblance to the contents of this document. It turned out to be a late, even Ptolemaic, copy in hieratic script of the *Sensen Papyrus*, which belongs to the same genre as the *Egyptian Book of the Dead*. As John A. Wilson, professor of Egyptology at the University of Chicago, described it in a published letter written on March 16, 1966, it contains vignettes familiar from the *Book of the Dead*. The first illustration shows the god of embalming named Anubis preparing the body of the deceased for burial, with the soul hovering over his head in the form of a bird, and the canopic jars containing the dead man's inwards set beneath his bier. The third picture shows the deceased led into the presence of Osiris, the infernal deity who judged the souls of the dead. (This is what Smith had identified as Abraham sitting on Pharaoh's throne!). Figure 2 was a round disc made of cloth and jesso and customarily placed as a pillow under the head of a corpse in the Late Egyptian period. The accompanying text, as can be ascertained from other copies of this not uncommon document, deals with magical spells intended to open the mouth of the deceased and to prepare him for his audience before Osiris in the judgment hall of the dead (as set forth in detail in chapter 125 of the *Book of the Dead*, the Egyptian title of which is *P-r m h-r-w*, or "The Going Forth by Day"). Needless to say, the completely mistaken concept of Joseph Smith as to his competence in ancient Egyptian is now clearly demonstrated to be beyond debate.

APPENDIX 4

INVENTORY OF THE BIBLICAL MANUSCRIPTS FROM THE DEAD SEA CAVES

One of the chief concerns of the Qumran sect was the diligent study of the Hebrew Scriptures. This was considered to be essential to the devoted service of God, to which these pious believers were committed. At all times, night and day, there was to be continuous Bible study and meditation, in groups of ten or more, each one of which was presided over by a priest. Apparently the installation at Khirbet Qumran, the headquarters of the order, was erected during the reign of Simon Maccabaeus (143-135 B.C.), whose assumption of power as both priest and king over the Judaean commonwealth was felt to be clearly contrary to Scripture. (As Levites, the family of the Maccabees, for all of their great prowess in throwing off the tyranny of Antiochus Epiphanes and the Seleucid empire, could not serve on the throne, since that was reserved for the descendants of King David.) If Frank M. Cross (*The Ancient Library of Qumran* [New York: Doubleday, 1961]) is correct in his interpretation of the allusions in the Habakkuk Pesher and other *pᵉsharim*, the "Wicked Priest" these refer to as the persecutor of the "Righteous Teacher" (who founded the sect) was none other than Simon Maccabaeus himself, whose sons perished along with him in an assassination perpetrated by his own son-in-law at Jericho (regarded as the antitypical fulfillment of the curse upon the rebuilder of Jericho, according to Josh. 6:26). We may thus account for the abundance of manuscript material datable on paleographic grounds to the second century B.C. Apparently their truck-gardening and manufacturing installation at 'Ain Feshka, a few miles south of Khirbet Qumran, was the place where many of these leather scrolls were prepared from carefully tanned hides. (Cross contains a list of published texts already available by 1957.)

CAVE ONE

1QIsᵃ. The complete copy of all sixty-six chapters of Isaiah, dating from about 150 B.C. (the St. Mark's Monastery Isaiah Scroll).

1QIsᵇ. An incomplete copy of the last half of Isaiah, with a portion of many of the pages missing due to deterioration. But the text preserved closely approximates the consonantal text of the MT (the Hebrew University Isaiah Scroll), ca. 50 B.C.

1QpHab. A verse-by verse commentary on the first two chapters of Habakkuk in a text very close to that of the MT. Each quoted verse is followed by a *pesher* indicating how it has been fulfilled or will be fulfilled very shortly. This *pesher* refers to the "Teacher of Righteousness" and "The Wicked Priest" and therefore has a historical value for the inter-testamental period. (M. Burrows, et al., *The Dead Sea Scrolls of St. Mark's Monastery*, 1 [1950], 2:2 [1951].)

1QM. (for *Milḥāmā*, "War"). The "War of the Sons of Light against the Sons of Darkness" scroll; a sectarian document containing plans for organization as a fighting force for God in the soon expected "end time." First century B.C.

1QS. (*Sereḵ*, "Order"). "The Manual of Discipline" or "Rule of the Congregation," as it is variously called; the constitution and by-laws of the Qumran sect, with rules for membership, service, communal activities, and discipline to maintain purity of faith and conduct. First century B.C.

1QH. (*Hôdayôt*, "Praises"). Four sheets containing twenty noncanonical psalms of praise, with some notable differences from the Psalter in language, speech, and theology. First century B.C.

1QpMic. (commentary or *pesher* on Micah). A fragment dealing with a portion of chapter 1 and chapter 6; uses old epigraphic spelling for YHWH.

Pentateuch fragments. Some of these small scraps are in epigraphic script, and some (like the Leviticus fragments *BASOR* 118 [Apr. 1950]: 21; cf. 28-30. DJD 1Q, 1955) may be as early as fourth century B.C.

1QpPs. 68. A *pesher* fragment on Ps. 68.

1QJub. A fragment of the pseudepigraphical Book of Jubilees.

1QDan. A few fragments of Daniel in a second-century B.C. hand; one fragment shows where the Hebrew leaves off and the Aramaic begins in chapter 2. (Pub. by John Trever in RQ no. 19 [1965]: 323-26, plates i-vi. DJD I: 150-52 (1:10-17; 2:2-6; MS-B; 3:22-28; 3:27-30).

1QApoc. The Genesis Apocryphon, a midrashic type of enlargement upon the biographies of Noah and Abraham (possibly others in the lost columns). Only five columns legible out of twenty-two. All in Aramaic. "Documents of Jewish Sectaries," 1(1910). S. Zetlin, "The Zadokite Fragments," (1952), photographs. C. Rabin, "The Zadokite Fragments" (1958), transcription.

CAVE TWO

2QEx. Portions of Ex. 1, 7, 9, 11-12, 21, 26, 30; there is also a second MS represented containing Ex. 18, 21, 34.

2QJer. Portions of Jeremiah chapters 42-46, 48-49.

2QLev. Portions of Lev. 11:22-28 in epigraphic script.

2QNum. Portions of Num. 3-4, 7, 18, 33.

2QDeu. Portions of Deut. 1, 10, 17.

2QRu. A fragment of Ruth 2:13–3:8, 14-18

2QPs. Portions of Pss. 103 (:6-8) and 104 (:6-11).

2QJub. A portion in Hebrew of Jubilees 46:1-2.

Fragments of liturgy in Aramaic, referring to a ceremony involving the use of bread.

Miscellaneous nonbiblical MS fragments, about forty in all.

CAVE THREE

3QIs. A tiny scrap of Isaiah 1:1, possibly with a *pesher*.

3QInv. The celebrated Copper Scroll, containing an inventory in Mishnaic Hebrew of three strips 8´ x 1´ containing twelve columns listing sixty treasure caches belonging to the temple. Associated with first-century A.D. pottery fragments.

CAVE FOUR

4QSam^A. Portions of 1 Sam. 1:22–2:6; 2:16-25. Twenty-seven fragments on leather in first-century hand. Favors the LXX variants as over against the MT quite consistently. BASOR 132 (Dec. 53): 17. BA 17 (1959): 19. BA 36 (Dec. 73): 141. One fragment in Cross. ALQ 141 (plate).

4QSam^B. In third-century B.C. hand. Uses more "defective" spelling than the MT (i.e., fewer vowel letters); portions of 1 Sam. 19-21. Agrees with the LXX against the MT five times, but with MT against LXX two times. F.M. Cross in JBL 74 (1955): 147-72. It also contains verses found in neither the LXX nor the MT.

4QIs. Twelve different MSS represented, containing portions of Isa. 12-13, 22-23, in a late first-century B.C. hand. Some loss of text through homoeoteleuton. Never favors the LXX against the MT. (BASOR 135 (Oct. 54): 29, 31).

4QJer^B. Verses 9:22–10:18, showing omissions of text similar to LXX. (See Cross, ALQ: 187.)

4QXII. A third-century B.C. cursive handwriting; seven different MSS represented from various portions of the twelve Minor Prophets.

4QDeu. A fragment of Deut. 32, one scrap containing 32:41-43 written as poetry in hemistichs, with some lacunae. There are thirteen different MSS of Deuteronomy represented in this cave.

4QEc. One fragment of Ecclesiastes in a third-century B.C. cursive, another ca. 150 B.C. greatly resembling 1QIs^a in style. (Cross: ALQ, 141 [plate], BASOR 135 [Oct. 54]:22).

4QDan. A late second-century B.C. hand preserving both Dan. 2:4 and 8:1, the two transitional passages (Hebrew to Aramaic and Aramaic to Hebrew, respectively).

4QEx. Portions of Ex. 6-18 in columns of thirty-two lines each. In narrative of the plagues, tends to favor Samaritan as against the MT and the LXX. 4QEx^a—one fragment in Cross: ALQ, 141 (plate). 4QEx.–4QEx^a, F. M. Cross, ALQ: 184-85; transliteration. 4QEx^c, F. M. Cross, JTC 5 (1968): 13-16. 4QpaleoEx^m, P. W. Skehan, JBL 74 (1955): 182-87. Cf. SWDS 16, 26. 4QEx^f, F. M. Cross in SWDS 14: 23.

4QJob. In paleo-Hebrew epigraphic script, yet with Hasmonaean type proliferation of vowel-letters (proving that paleo-Hebrew script was still used occasionally in second century B.C.).

4QCh. Six lines containing only four complete words from Chronicles.

4QPs. Ten different MSS of the Psalms represented. 4QPs[f], J. Starcky, RB 73 (1966): 352-71: apocryphal psalms. 4QPs[q], J. T. Milik, "Biblica" 38 (1957): 245-55. 4QPs[89] J. T. Milik, RB 73 (1966): 94-106.

4QLXX. Two fragments in Greek from the Septuagint (F. M. Cross does not specify which passages in his "Report on the Biblical Fragments of Cave Four at Wadi Qumran" in BASOR no. 141 [Feb 1956].)

4QLXX Lev. (QHBT, 221-25—photographed and transcribed) 26:2-16. Skehan, VT suppl. 4 (1957): 159-60, cf. SWDS 15, 25.

4QLXX Num. (QHBT, 219-20) 3:40-42; 4:6-9 (QHBT, 268 photo). P. W. Skehan, VT suppl. 4 (1957): 155-56; photo in BA 28 (1965): 191.

4QNum. A fragment combining variants favoring LXX at times, the Samaritan Pentateuch at other times, or combining the two together.

4QNab. The purported prayer of King Nabonidus of Babylon, after he was afflicted with a severe inflammation (not insanity) in the city of Teman, Arabia (not in Babylon), and was delivered by an unnamed Jewish exorcist. He acknowledges the impotence of idols and the power of the God of the Hebrews. Written in Aramaic. RB 63 [1956] (Xerox), plate 2, (J. T. Milik).

4Q158-186. P[e]sharim ("prophetic commentary") J. M. Allegro with A. A. Anderson, DJD-5 (1968).

4QpIs. J. M. Allegro, JBL 75 (1956): 174-87, Document III; DJD-5, 11-15, Plates 4-5. J. M. Allegro, JBL 77 (1958:) 215-21; DJD-5, 15-28, Plates 6-9. DJD-5, 28-30, Plate 9.

4QpHos. (4Q166,167) J. M. Allegro, JBL75 (1956): 89-95; DJD-5, 32-36, Plate X. J. M. Allegro, JBL 78 (1959): 142-47; DJD-5, 31-32, Plate X.

4QpNah. J. M. Allegro, JBL 75 (1956): 89-95; J. M. Allegro, JSS 7 (1962): 304-8; DJD-5, 37-42, plates 12-14. cf. SWDS 17: 26-27. Y. Yadin, IEJ 21 (1971): 1-12.

4QpZeph. DJD-5, 42, Plate 14.

4QpPs[a]. J. M. Allegro, PEQ 86 (1954): 69-75, plate 18. J. M. Allegro, "The People of the Dead Sea Scrolls," plates 48 and 50 (86-87); DJD-5, 42-49. H. Stegemann, RQ 14 (1963): 235-70, RQ 22 (1967): 193-210.

4QpPs[60]. DJD-5, 49-50, plate 17.

4QpPs[b]. A Commentary on Pss. 127, 129, and 118. DJD-5, 51-53, plate 18. CD Fragments of the Damascus Covenant.

Cave Five

Fragments of Tobit (both Hebrew fragment and Aramaic fragment). Fragments of the Zadokite Work (Damascus Covenant). RB 63 (1956 Xerox) pl. 1 (J. Milik).

Cave Six

Fragments of the Zadokite Work. 6QDan. pap (cf. DJD-1, p. 150).

CAVE SEVEN

This cave is unique in that it contained no documents in Hebrew or Aramaic, but only in Greek. 7Q1 and 7Q2 were identified as Septuagintal in the original publication of these nineteen fragments, but not until 1972 did Jose O'Callaghan in his "Papiros neotestamentarios en la cueva 7 de Qumran?" (in *Biblica* 7:1 [Rome: Pontifical Biblical Institute, 1972], pp. 91-104) identify several of the smaller fragments as belonging to the *New* Testament. Note that only Christians used papyrus for their Scriptures, whereas the Jews preferred parchment or leather.

7Q1. Exodus 28:4-7 in a script known as *Zierstil*, used from about 100 B.C. to A.D. 50.

7Q2. Epistle of Jeremiah 43-44, likewise in *Zierstil*.

7Q4. 1 Timothy 3:16; 4:1, 3.

7Q5. Mark 6:52-53, also in *Zierstil*, apparently copied in Egypt (judging from a letter *tau* erroneously substituted for a *delta* in the word *diaparasantes*), and featured by the omission of a phrase (*eis tēn gēn*) which normally appears in this verse.

7Q6[1]. Mark 4:28, in Herculanean script (used by scribes from A.D. 50 to 80).

7Q6[2]. Acts 27:38, in Herculanean script (probable).

7Q7. Mark 12:17 in *Zierstil* (probable).

7Q8. James 1:23-24, in Herculanean script; implies omission of *gar auton* after the verb *katenoesēn*.

7Q9. Romans 5:11-12 (probably), perhaps late first century A.D. copy.

7Q10. 2 Peter 1:15 (possibly); not enough text to establish date of copying.

7Q15. Mark 6:48 (possibly); date uncertain.

CAVE ELEVEN

These documents seem to be from the first century A.D.

11QPs. Fairly complete texts of Pss. 93-150, but in a somewhat different order than that of the MT. There are also eight additional, noncanonical psalms, including the "Psalm 151" of the Septuagint. (BA [Dec. 73]: 139.)

11Qtarg Job. Fragments which are distinctly different from the later standard Targums.

11Q Melchiz. The fragment of a prose commentary in Hebrew concerning Melchizedek (cf. Gen. 14:17-20), presenting him as a superhuman personage who will be involved in bringing about God's victory over His foes on earth at the end of the age (cf. M. de Jonge and A. S. van der Woude: "Melchizedek and the New Testament" in *New Testament Studies*, no. 12, pp. 301-26; first published in *Oudtestamentlische Studien*, no. 14, [Leiden, Netherlands, 1965], pp. 354-73).

11QLev. Lev 9:23–10:2 is written in Hebrew with LXX readings. A. S. Van der Woude, *Bibel und Qumran* (H. Bartke Fest. 1968): pp. 153-55. Cf. J. Strugnell, RB 77 (1970): 268.

11QEz. W. H. Brownlee, RQ 13 (1963) 11-28.

11QPs. J. A. Sanders, DJD-4 (1965); J. A. Sanders, "The Dead Sea Psalms Scroll" (1967).

11QT. The Temple Scroll. A late third century list of regulations concerning the conduct of public worship in the Second Temple. Presumably composed at Qumran.

WADY MURABBA'AT (EIGHTEEN MILES SOUTH OF QUMRAN)

1. Biblical fragments from Gen. 2:4; 32-35; Ex. 4 and 6; Deut. 10-12, 15; Isa. 1:4-14.
2. A Greek MS of the Minor Prophets, and such nonbiblical documents as:
   (a) two personal letters from Simon ben Kosebah (Bar Kochba)
   (b) two contracts in Aramaic
   (c) some long MSS in Nabatean Aramaic, difficult to decipher
   (d) a palimpsest in old epigraphic characters, containing a list of names, probably originating in seventh century B.C.
   (e) a fragment in Latin from second century A.D., apparently legal in character
   (f) a letter from the administrators of Beit Mashbo.

1 PREDICTION AND FULFILLMENT AS PROOF OF DIVINE INSPIRATION

As was pointed out in chapter 2, the presence of predictions uttered by God, according to the Biblical record, furnishes an infallible proof of the divine inspiration of the Scriptures themselves. The previous announcement of events which are to occur in the future is admittedly beyond the ability of any human being, except as he has received that prediction from the Lord Himself. The test of fulfilled prophecy is clearly set forth in Deut. 18:20-22: "But the prophet who shall speak a word presumptuously in My name which I have not commanded him to speak, or which he shall speak in the name of other gods, that prophet shall die. And you may say in your heart, 'How shall we know the word which LORD has not spoken?' When a prophet speaks in the name of the LORD, if the thing does not come about or come true, that is the thing which the LORD has not spoken."

The frequent occurrence of prophecy in the Holy Scriptures is unique among all the purported scriptures of non-Christian religions. False and unfulfilled predictions abound even among deviant Christian sects, such as the Seventh Day Adventists, the Jehovah's Witnesses, and the Mormons (if they can be classed as Christian at all, in view of their polytheism). The dates these groups have set for the return of Christ and the advent of the Tribulation or the Kingdom of God on earth have completely failed every time. But even in Old Testament times there were false prophets like Hananiah, whom Jeremiah sternly denounced for predicting the defeat of Nebuchadnezzar and the restoration of the holy vessels he had taken from the temple of Yahweh (Jer. 28:2-4). In reply the true prophet, Jeremiah, predicted that not only would Hananiah's prediction prove utterly false, but that he himself would die within the current year—which he did.

Throughout the pages of the Old Testament, approximately, 200 Scripture texts (not individual verses) are predictive, many of which explicitly foretell with astounding accuracy major events such as the fall of the Northern Kingdom to Assyria in 722 B.C., the fall of Jerusalem and deportation of the Jews under Nebuchadnezzar in 586 B.C., and most prominently, the coming of Messiah, along with details of His life, ministry, death, and resurrection. Psalm 22 and Isa. 53 graphically detail the events and

effects of Christ's sacrifice on Calvary with a clarity that surpasses even the gospel narratives in intensity, pathos, and descriptive detail.

The accuracy and specificity of biblical prophecy is uncompromisingly unique and
breathes with the evidence of divine revelation recorded in the written oracles of the
Old Testament. First Kings 13:2 prophecies that Josiah, from the lineage of David,
would arise to obliterate the idolatrous worship Jeroboam I had instituted in Bethel.
Three hundred years later, as recorded in 2 Kings 23:15-16, King Josiah of Judah fulfilled this prophecy explicitly, even to the matter of burning of human bones upon
that altar, in order to totally wipe out every matter of trace of idolatry from the land.

A very comprehensive collection and analysis of nearly 600 topics of prediction in
Holy Scripture has been assembled by J. Barton Payne in his 754-page volume, *Encyclopedia of Biblical Prophecy* (Harper & Row, 1973), which pertain to the era of the Old Testament and of the New Testament as well, up to the present century. (He lists 127
more topics of predictions pertaining to the Last Days and the Millennial Kingdom.)
This immense body of evidence renders all claim to uninspired human origin of the
Bible totally absurd. Such a denial amounts to a hide-bound fideism unworthy of any
scholar who claims to be an intelligent thinker. There is no possibility of explaining
away 600 topics of fulfilled prophecies as within the competence of uninspired human
authorship.

The evidence of fulfilled prophecy lies not only in the realm of historical accuracy,
but also in volume. According to J. Barton Payne, 8,352 verses of the Bible are predictive; a total of 27 percent of the entire Bible. Of the total Old Testament Scripture texts
that are predictive, 70 percent find fulfillment within the confines of the biblical narrative itself. The 30 percent that remain unfulfilled are primarily eschatological in
nature, i.e., the second coming of Christ, the Millennial Kingdom, and the consummation of the Church Age. Virtually no prophetic utterance recorded in Scripture pertaining to any event through to the advent of the Church in New Testament narrative has
failed to be fulfilled. Biblical prophecy is precise, explicit, and accurate with a record of
proven fulfillment that stands as its own testimony of conclusive evidence as to the
veracity of Scripture.

Those who wish to examine this evidence are invited to examine *Encyclopedia of
Biblical Prophecy*. But for the purposes of this excursus it will be sufficient to set forth a
few striking examples. Some of these prophecies were fulfilled before the completion
of the Old Testament canon, and therefore they may conceivably be explained away as
vaticinia ex eventu (prophecies invented after they had already been fulfilled). To treat
them in this way betrays more of fideistic closed-mindedness than of truly objective
scholarship. It is most significant that there are prophecies both in the Old Testament
and the New Testament which were not fulfilled until a period after the composition
of all 66 books of the Bible had been completed.

But before discussing individual predictions, a few general observations are in
order. Although there are many specific events foretold, ranging over a broad field of
interest and concern, involving not only the fate of individual actors upon the stage of

history, but also the fortunes of cities, nations and empires, yet through them all there appears to be a unitary master plan. This is no hodgepodge of isolated events, such as students of Nostradamus attempt to identify with later events or the fortunes of various scoundrels or leaders, but what we find in Holy Scripture is a concatenated series of developments relating to heroes of the faith and leaders of the people of God. In other words, there is a marvelously crafted program of redemption, beginning with the first promise of the Messiah in Gen. 3:15 and concluding with the complete triumph of the divine-human Redeemer in the ultimate Millennial Kingdom and the union of heaven and earth in the last two chapters of the Apocalypse. The final proclamation of victory in Revelation 22:13 is: "I am the Alpha and the Omega, the first and the last, the beginning and the end." In other words, the Bible sets forth the drama of human redemption and the total defeat of the Prince of Evil and all his works. We must take note of the fact that the Almighty Creator has a master plan moving inexorably towards a predetermined goal, to the glory of the divine Redeemer whose sacrificial death and glorious resurrection brought about the fulfillment of the purpose of the Triune God in creating the human race.

1. *Genesis 3:15* contains the first indication of this plan, as God affirms to the Satanic serpent: "And I will put enmity between you and the woman, and between your seed and her seed. He shall bruise you on the head, and you shall bruise Him on the heel." Obviously this Messianic descendant of Eve will suffer injury at Satan's hand, but a bruised heel is capable of healing, whereas a bruised or crushed skull is an injury of fatal consequence. This means that Jesus Christ will be the final victor over all the forces of evil, and the earth will become completely subject to His rule.

2. *Genesis 15:13-16* sets forth God's plan to produce a great and numerous race of believers from a man like Abraham whose wife proved to be incapable of pregnancy until the age of ninety. Not only did he have a son by her, but that son engendered a nation as numerous as the stars in heaven. "And God said to Abram, 'Know for certain that your descendants will be strangers in a land that is not theirs, where they will be enslaved and oppressed four hundred years. But I will also judge the nation whom they will serve, and afterward they will come out with many possessions. And as for you, you shall go to your fathers in peace; you shall be buried at a good old age. Then in the fourth generation they will return here.'" The fulfillment of these promises is unfolded step by step in the remainder of the Pentateuch. The people among whom the descendants of Abraham are to multiply turns out to be Egypt, where their initial acceptance under Joseph turned into degrading oppression under a new dynasty (probably Hyksos) who had no regard for him. This slavery went on for four centuries (for Abram the interval between his birth and the birth of his son was a hundred years) until finally they were be enabled by God's providence to return to the Promised Land.

3. *Leviticus 26:44* contains the prediction that after the descendants of Abraham have taken possession of the Holy Land, they will fall into such spiritual defection and apostasy that God will have to consign them to the severe discipline of the Babylonian Exile, which occurred between 605 and 536 B.C. But in their humiliating captivity they

will repent of their disobedience and unbelief and will be allowed to return to their native land in Canaan. Leviticus 26:44 reads: "Yet in spite of this, when they are in the land of their enemies, I will not reject them, nor will I so abhor them as to destroy them, breaking My covenant with them, for I am Yahweh their God."

This same warning appears again in Deut. 28:36: "Yahweh will bring you and your king whom you shall set over you, to a nation which neither you nor your fathers have known, and there you shall serve other gods, wood and stone." Further on in this same chapter at verse 49 we read: "Yahweh will bring against you a nation from afar, from the end of the earth, as the eagle swoops down, a nation whose language you shall not understand." It becomes apparent that this passage predicts a second captivity or exile from Palestine, for the invaders in this case come from a region remote from the Middle East, speaking a language not at all Semitic (as was the language of Babylon) and having an eagle for their military symbol. This strongly suggests the Roman invasion and the dreadful events of the First Revolt (A.D. 67-70). Quite decisive for this identification is verse 68: "And Yahweh will bring you back to Egypt in ships, by the way about which I spoke to you, 'You will never see it again!' And there you shall be offered for sale to your enemies as male and female slaves, but there will be no buyer." Josephus records that (*Wars* 6.9) when Titus finally stormed Jerusalem in A.D. 70, he had the 97,000 survivors dragged down to Joppa and put aboard cargo ships, to be sold in Alexandria, Egypt (which was the largest slave market in the Roman Empire) in order to be offered at bargain prices to whoever wanted to buy them. But such an enormous number of slaves proved to be a glut on the market, and so finally there were no bidders left to purchase them. All of the details of this prediction point so strongly to the events of A.D. 70 as to make any other interpretation incapable of successful defense. It should be noticed that this fulfillment could not have been a mere *vaticinium ex eventu*, for this would postpone the composition of Deuteronomy until the late first century A.D., and we have many fragments of Deuteronomy preserved in the Qumran caves dating from the second century B.C. or earlier.

4. *Isaiah 13:19* reads: "And Babylon, the beauty of kingdoms, the glory of the Chaldeans' pride, will be as when God overthrew Sodom and Gomorrah." Verse 20 continues: "It will never be inhabited or lived in from generation to generation; nor will the Arab pitch his tent there, nor will shepherds make their flocks lie down there." Note that at the time this prophecy was written down by Isaiah in the early seventh century B.C., Babylon was the most wealthy and prosperous city of the ancient world. If any capital in all of the Middle East had a prospect of indefinite survival, surely Babylon would seem the most likely of them all. Isaiah's prediction must have seemed just as absurd as if some pundit of our present century would predict that Manhattan, New York, would some day become a deserted wasteland without a building still standing. And yet the time came when Babylon was not only conquered and overthrown by foreign enemies, but even became uninhabitable because of the extreme salinization of its surrounding farmlands after more than two millennia of irrigation from the salt-bearing waters of the Euphrates. It was later avoided as a site accursed by Allah after

the Muslim conquest.

The reference to Arab shepherds is highly significant in this passage, especially in view of the fact that there were no Arabs at all in this Mesopotamian region until the eighth century A.D. Here again the resort to *vaticinium ex eventu* proves to be untenable. For many centuries the location of Babylon was largely conjectural, and its *tell* known as Birs Nemroud. Not until the 19th century and the extensive excavation carried on by Koldewey was it confirmed as the true location of the ancient megalopolis, and even to this day it remains without any residential population, apart from the tourist-trap motivation of the Hussein regime, somewhat like the ghost towns of our Far West.

5. *Isaiah 52:13-15; 53:1-12.* This celebrated passage concerning the suffering, death and resurrection of the Servant of the Lord, composed during the reign of King Manasseh, sets forth the role and experience of Jesus of Nazareth with amazing accuracy. Isaiah 52:13-25 predicts both the amazing exaltation of Christ and His equally amazing humiliation in terms anticipatory of Phil. 2:6-11. Isaiah 53:1 foretells the incredulity of the Jewish public towards Jesus after He began His three years of preaching ministry. Isaiah 53:2 predicts the humble circumstances of His birth and childhood rearing up in Nazareth of Galilee. Isaiah 53:3 indicates that His countrymen would despise and reject Him, and that he would be a man of sorrows, acquainted with grief. Isaiah 53:4-5 affirms that He would be smitten and pierced for the sins of His people, rather than for any wickedness of His own. Isaiah 53:6 declares that all mankind has gone astray in sin, but that the Servant of the Lord would suffer death in their place and on their behalf. Verse 7 foretells His refusal to speak up in His own defense when He would be unjustly accused in court—a court procedure conducted with injustice and oppression. Verse 9 predicts that He would be buried in a rich man's tomb, and verse 10 states that His death would serve as a guilt-offering (*asham*) that would atone for the sins of mankind, and indicates that after His death He would behold His spiritual offspring, His disciples, and that He would "prolong His days"—a statement that unmistakably implies His resurrection after death and His fellowship with His believers on earth after He had risen from the dead.[1] Verse 12 proclaims His final triumph over the forces of evil as the blessed result of His substitutionary atonement and His intercession for all those who repent and put their trust in Him. Every one of these predictions is clearly pointed out in the New Testament record.

Skeptical critics are completely unable to come up with any other candidate as the fulfiller of this prophetic portrait of the Servant of Yahweh. Hezekiah, Josiah, and Isaiah himself, have all been proposed, but none of them even approaches the fulfillment of all these specifications. Most unsatisfactory of all is the suggestion that Israel itself is the fulfillment of Isa. 53. For nowhere in Isaiah or any of the prophets of Israel is there the slightest intimation that the Hebrew nation, or any more spiritual segment of it,

---

1. It should be noted that the Hebrew idiom יַאֲרִיךְ יָמִים (*Yaᵃrîk yāmîm*) always in the Old Testament refers to life on earth prior to death and burial. For this reason this prediction of prolonging days must refer to Messiah's post-resurrection ministry on earth 40 days prior to his ascension to heaven.

has maintained the absolute sinlessness predicated of the Servant in 53:9. On the contrary the prophets all unite in indicting their countrymen as inexcusably guilty sinners deserving of God's judgment. Even apart from that, no one has ever explained how, if the Servant is really the nation Israel, it could be said to have borne the punishment and death of Israel in the place of Israel instead of Israel! Such an argument borders on total irrationality.

6. *Daniel 9:25-26* records the angelic revelation that there is going to be a word or decree granted by the king (the Persian king, that is) to authorize the rebuilding of post-exilic Jerusalem. A span of 69 heptads of years will intervene between that decree and the appearance of Messiah the Prince. Since the decree of Cyrus issued in 537 B.C. pertained only to the successful rebuilding of the Temple rather than the walls of the city, it could hardly be the intended *terminus a quo*. Some have supposed that the permission granted to Nehemiah by Artaxerxes I which resulted in the rebuilding of the city walls must be the correct starting-point for the 483 years, but Neh. 1:3-4 clearly indicates that an earlier attempt had already been made to rebuild the walls and gates of Jerusalem. However it appears that some hostile forces had burned up and broken down the structures which had been attempted. Therefore upon hearing these tidings from Hanani, Nehemiah was grievously disappointed, and prayed that God would intervene on his behalf and on behalf of the Holy City. This leaves only the return of Ezra in the seventh year of Artaxerxes (or 457 B.C.) as the correct terminus. Ezra 9:9 clearly refers to such a royal permission, for there Ezra prays about the boon granted by "the kings of Persia,...to give us a *wall* in Judah and Jerusalem." It is fair to assume that the same hostile neighboring nations which later threatened Nehemiah himself were responsible for the violence done to Ezra's earlier building efforts. If this was indeed what happened (as the evidence strongly suggest) this means that the 69 heptads should be reckoned from 457 B.C. This means that 457 subtracted from 483 comes out to A.D. 26. But since we actually gain a year when moving from 1 B.C. to A.D. 1, it really come out to A.D. 27. This means that Messiah the Prince would begin his ministry in A.D. 27, or three years before A.D. 30 when Jesus was crucified. How can we explain this amazingly accurate prediction? Certainly not on the basis of *vaticinium ex eventu!*

No other explanation will account for this pattern of prediction and fulfillment except authentic revelation by God Himself as the Lord of history and providence. It is logically impossible to explain the Bible as a book of mere human composition. To reject such an overwhelming body of evidence as this and to hold to a theory of mere human authorship is to forsake all reason and logic in the interests of fideistic subjectivism, scarcely worthy of honest scholarship.

2 ADDITIONAL DATA FROM EBLA

A fine summary of the discoveries of Ebla may be found in the appendix to the French Edition of this *Survey of Old Testament Introduction*, published by Editions Emmaüs in Saint-Legier, Switzerland in 1978. This is Appendix 4, pp. 585, consisting of a French translation of an excellent article by Heinrich von Siebenthal of Basel composed in German. This is perhaps the finest short discussion of the discoveries and language of Ebla. But a much fuller discussion is found in The *Archives of Ebla* written by Giovanni Pettinato himself, with a supplemental section composed by Dr. Mitchell Dahood (Doubleday: Garden City, N.Y., 1981). As the primary decipherer and translator of the Eblaite tablets, Pettinato furnishes a wealth of information, replete with charts and translations of various significant documents in that language. On page 43 he presents a copy of the cuneiform text of TM.74.G.120. The formation of the cuneiform characters greatly resembles that of the *Code of Hammurabi* from the 18th century B.C., and it contains a large list of theophoric personal names.

As he analyzes the native language of the Eblaites (in contradistinction to the Sumerian in which most of their records were composed), he notes that the verbal stems of this dialect resemble the Akkadian system, with the patterns *qatal*, the *qi'til* for intensive, and *šiqtil* for the causative, while *niqtal* furnishes the passive voice. Even the Akkadian use of the prefix conjugation for past time appears in Eblaite, as in *ištama* (the Gt of *šama'* (although no *'ayin* could be expressed in any cuneiform language except Ugaritic), meaning "he heard" (rather than "he hears" or "will hear" of NW Semitic). For the most part the verbal prefixes and sufformatives correspond to those of Akkadian, yet there is an occasional *t* - prefix which is used with a masculine subject — contrary to all the other Semitic languages. Nevertheless, despite this conformity to East Semitic in the morphology of the verb, the vocabulary choice is so strongly on the side of Canaanite that he links it more closely with NW Semitic than with Akkadian. He is not comfortable with identifying it as Old Amorite, as Ignace Gelb and others have suggested, yet he makes no really satisfactory identification with any other language group known to Semitic scholarship.

As to the history of Ebla (which, by the way, reveals an era of North Syrian power in the late Third Millennium B.C. of which we had almost no knowledge previously), the foundation for which was King Igrish Halam, who raised City II to a strong military power. He was followed by Irkab-Damu, Ar-Ennum (contemporary with Sargon of Agade, who for a time held domination over him), then Ebrium (a very successful and powerful king), Ibbi-Sippiš, and Dubaha-Ada (in whose reign Naram-Sin of Agade succeeded in totally destroying the city around 2250 B.C.). But by 2000 City III was built by the surviving Eblaites, who restored it to a certain measure of recovery, although not to what it had been before. It was the discovery of a statue base of King Ibbiṭ-Lim of this dynasty that first revealed that Tell Mardikh was indeed the site of Ebla, for it bore the words: "The King of Ebla." In its heyday, City II had numbered at least 260,000 inhabitants according to its own documentation. (Cf. Pettinato, op. cit. 44.) (This size population serves to substantiate the historical accuracy of the figure of 120,000 infants in Nineveh specified in Jonah 4:11— a figure which some critics had dismissed as perfectly legendary, prior to this decade.)

As to the religion of the Eblaites, their pantheon consisted mostly of Canaanite deities. They seem to have counted up to 500 gods (Pettinato, p. 245), although the most prominent of them were Dagan (Philistine Dagon), Rasap (Akkadian Nergal), Sipis (god of the sun, Sumerian Utu, Akkadian Shamash), Astar (god of the planet Venus, later known as the goddess Istar or Ashtoreth), Kamish (perhaps related to the Moabite Chemosh), Il (the Ugaritic king-god El) and Yau or Ya (which resembles the short form of Yahu or Yahweh in Hebrew, even though not conceived of as a supreme god, by any means.)

One intriguing feature that so far denies explanation is that during the reign of Ebrium there was a tendency to shift from the use of *-il* at the end of proper names to the ending *-ia* or *-ya*. Thus the former *En-na-il* was replaced by or favored over, *En-na-ia; Iš-ra-il* became *Iš-ra-ia; Iš-ma-il* appears as *Iš-ma-ia, Mi-ka-il* becomes *Mi-ka-ia,* and so forth (Pettinato, op, cit., p. 249). It is amazing to see such Hebrew names as Israel, Ishmael and Michael employed in pagan Syria as early as 2500 B.C., well before the birth of Abraham, not to mention the period of Moses and the Hebrew monarchy. There are other names referred to which had formerly been dismissed as unhistorical by 19th-century scholarship which are now confirmed by their appearance in Ebla documents. Thus King Tudiya was formerly regarded as merely legendary, even though he was referred to as the first king of Assyria. But in an Eblaite manifesto dealing with taxation obligations of the Assyrians to pay taxes to the government or merchants of Ebla, a threatening malediction is invoked upon Tudiya if he ever fails to comply (Pettinato, pp. 104-5).

It is quite significant that we have such evidence of international treaties in the Middle East as early as the third millennium B.C. But there are at least ten international treaties recorded or referred to in the documents of Ebla. In fact there are no less than seventeen kingdoms listed as subject to Ebla according to a schoolboy's text datable to the period of King Ebrium (op. cit., pp. 106-7).

The end result of all of these new data from Ebla is that much more history was taking place back in the time of Abraham and his successors than the Documentarian scholars knew anything about as they condemned the Genesis records as unreliable. What they really must recognize at this end of the 20th century is that arguments *e silentio* are far from trustworthy.

EXCURSUS ③ LIBERAL SCHOLARSHIP IN THE 20TH CENTURY

As indicated at the end of chapter 7, the present excursus is intended to inform the student concerning the contributions made by some of the leading rationalistic scholars of the second half of this 20th century. In pursuing this discussion and analysis of the Pentateuch and the Prophets we have chosen to center our review on such leading figures such as Gerhard von Rad and Brevard Childs along with others who occupy the same Liberal position.

GERHARD VON RAD

Von Rad's basic presupposition is that the Hexateuch represents Israel's developed confession of faith that already had attained a fixed form in terms of both structure and proclamation at an early time. In the centuries which followed, additional layers of tradition were superimposed upon these simple confessional statements. Von Rad assumes the validity of the Documentary analysis of the Graf/Kuenen/Wellhausen school. Therefore he assumes that Yahweh was not "venerated as creator of the world" (*Old Testament Theology*, vol. 1, p. 136), until the 7th or 6th c. B.C. Von Rad states "the lateness of the emergence of the doctrine of creation was that it took Israel a fairly long time to bring the older beliefs they already possessed into proper theological relationship with the tradition that was their very own, that is, what they believed about the saving acts done by Yahweh in history. In the old cultic credo there was nothing about creation" (p. 136).

In this connection we should observe the religious writings of all Israel's neighbors had very definite statements about creation very early. The Egyptian traditions, although difficult to date, trace to a time long before the age of Moses. In a text carved in the inside of the pyramid of Mer-ne-Re or Pepi II of Dynasty VI (24th c. B.C.), Atum-Kheprer is credited with having spit out Shu, the god of air, and the goddess Tefnut, the goddess of moisture. This speaks of the creation of the first elements of nature which were a prelude to the creation of other things (ANET², p. 3). But the Shabaka Stone inscription from Memphis, dating from 2700 B.C. says Shu and Tefnut were the first deities created. "There came into being as the heart and there came into being as the tongue (something) in the form of Atum. The mighty Great One is Ptah, who transmitted [life to all gods], as well as (to) their kás, through this heart, by which Horus became Ptah, and through this tongue, by which Toth became Ptah" (ANET², p. 5).

The Mesopotamian creation myth ("Enuma Elish") on tablet I states, "When on high heaven had not been named, firm ground below had not been called by name, naught but primordial Apsu, their begetter, (and) Mummu-Tiamat, she who bore them all, their waters commingling as a single body; no reed hut had been matted, no marsh land had appeared. When no gods whatever had been brought into being, uncalled by name, their destinies undetermined—Then it was that the gods were formed within them. Laḥmu and Laḥamu were brought forth, by name they were called" (ANET², p. 61). This Akkadian myth from Ashurbanipal's library originated prior to the time of Hammurabi, centuries prior to Moses. Pritchard states "The extant form of this document dates only to 700 B.C., but linguistic, philological, and geopolitic evidence is conclusive in support of its derivation from an original text more than 2000 years earlier" (ANET², p. 4).

Pritchard further notes, "None of the extant texts antedates the first millennium B.C. On the internal evidence, however, of the context and linguistic criteria, the majority of the scholars would assign the epic to the Old Babylonian period, i.e., the early part of the Second Millennium B.C. There does not seem to be any convincing reason against this earlier dating" (ANET², p. 60).

The fallacy von Rad follows is that if there is no surviving record dating back to a specific period, then you have proof-positive that creation was never conceived of prior to that document, i.e., document E in the 8th or 9th c. B.C. Of the literature that survived from the time of Moses, apart from Egyptian and Akkadian, no more than 3% is extant. If over 90% of the documents have disappeared, to reason that the ancient Hebrews never entertained belief in a monotheistic Creator God is a complete fallacy.

It is very strange that von Rad, being aware of the much earlier literature of the Egyptians and Babylonians, could assume that even though they had theories of creation in their literature, the Hebrews never formulated their own view of creation until the theoretical "Deutero-Isaiah" or the so-called Priestly document period around the time of Ezra. It is certainly a fallacy of logic to say that the Hebrews had no theory of how creation came to pass, in view of abundant literature from the Nile and Mesopotamian Valley that speculates about creation well before 2000 B.C.

Von Rad assumes that we have in the Bible an account of God's reaching out with redemptive grace to lead a specific people to a stage of religious maturity that specifically is monotheistic. Therefore, he brings in a pre-history, whether fictional or factual, that would be part of the development of his theory of God's saving grace. But it is difficult to imagine how the Psalms that speak in great detail of how God delivered His people out of Egyptian bondage and brought them safely through the Red Sea and over the Jordan, could have been making up sheer fiction out of whole cloth. This is not the way national traditions are built up in any culture; they go back to actual world events.

What we have in von Rad is an eclecting and choosing of elements of thought or religion, as suggested by Hegelian dialectic. Yehezkel Kaufmann, however, presents strong evidence to show that there is no truly demonstrable element in any part of the Torah that allows the legitimacy of faith in the existence of more than one God so far as the early Hebrews were concerned, even back in patriarchal times. This well-proven conclusion on Kaufmann's part was overlooked completely by German scholarship and most unjustifiably so, especially in view of the fact that Kaufmann himself affirmed adherence to the JEPD hypothesis, even though he insisted P was not by any means the only source that committed itself to monotheism. But actually, he insisted, the very earliest levels of Torah tradition, even prior to document J, cherished a concept of the unity of God and His sole legitimacy as a deity to be worshiped.

Von Rad states, "Previous historical research nevertheless still believed it possible to grasp the actual historical course of events, in its basic features at any rate, by a more or less immediate penetration behind the literary presentation. But this has turned out to be mistaken, since what lies at the back of the picture offered in the Hexateuch is still far from being the actual course of events, but is again only certain interpretations of conceptions of older tradition which originate in *milieux* very different from one another which must be judged from the view of form criticism, as completely diverse" (*Old Testament Theology*, vol. 1, pp. 3-4).

It should be added that "historical intuition" on the part of a modern critic characteristically assumes that unique events could never have taken place at all, since factual history can consist only of repeatable episodes. But this is a complete fallacy, for the progress of mankind through the ages has been marked by many unique events which have controlled subsequent history in a most decisive way. By the likelihood criterion Alexander the Great, for instance, could never have built up an enormous empire extending from Yugoslavia to Pakistan in only four or five years of warfare. Or again, only one successful invasion of England has ever taken place, and that was under William the Conqueror in 1066 A.D. Even in our present generation what analogue can be found to the sudden collapse of the whole Marxist empire (apart from China and North Korea) can be discovered in the annals of history? The dogma of probability proves utterly untenable at this point and should be discarded as a controlling criterion for the history of the Bible. After all, what could be more improbable than the unique event of the crucifixion and resurrection of Jesus of Nazareth in its effect upon all of subsequent history?

BREVARD CHILDS

One interesting observation that Brevard Childs brings into his treatment of the Old Testament canon is that there seems to have been a policy of purposeful arrangement of the Old Testament books into a logical pattern that was hardly feasible before the completion of the Hebrew Scriptures. Childs suggests that in the final composition and arrangement of the thirty-nine Old Testament books there was an artistic balancing out of type and antitype in the final disposition of the text (e.g., the Garden of Eden serves as a sort of prototype of Jerusalem).

It should be understood Brevard Childs embraces the Documentary Hypothesis as valid in the matter of explaining how the text of Scripture actually came into being; he accepts the basic postulate that the Bible is simply a piece of human literature composed perhaps by gifted people, but by no means supernatural in origin or divine in its authority or inspiration.

But on the other hand, Childs devotes his attention to the Scripture as it has come down to us in its canonical form and tries to focus attention upon what the human authors (whoever they were) believed and were trying to communicate to those who studied their works. Thus we may say that Childs treats the Hebrew Scripture as a valuable and useful piece of literature, but not essentially different from any other piece of great literature from the past. In other words, we are to deal with the Bible in the same respectful way we would deal with the epics of Homer or Virgil, or the Socratic dialogues of Plato. Childs, then, studies the Bible to come to grips with the message conveyed by this literary masterpiece, rather than belaboring the higher critical questions of origin and the historic development of the Hebrew text as it has come down to us. His concern in his canonical or structural approach is to come to terms with what the Bible, as we have it, has to say, so that we may properly interpret each book or passage in the light of the literary genre to which it belongs.

Dennis Olson observes, "Childs, however, objects to the Enlightenment's claim to confine the Bible solely to the arena of human experience (historical, sociological, or psychological explanations). Biblical theology must take seriously a dimension of scripture that historical criticism often excludes, namely, the function of the Bible as a witness or testimony pointing beyond itself to a divine reality external to the text. The canonical approach seeks to move beyond the location of biblical texts in specific ancient times and places as the goal of interpretation. The canonical approach seeks to uncover the various ways in which biblical texts have been shaped so that they may address and confront succeeding generations in witness to the ongoing reality of the living God" (*The Princeton Seminary Bulletin* XIV, no. 3 [1993]: 297).

Childs also seems to imply that it is possible for a careful student to come up with intuitive insights that could possibly emanate from God through the Scripture. But discriminating judgment is required if we are to figure out what is from God, what is nationalistic, what is rationalistic, or what is mere human tradition.

It should be added that a similar approach is observable in the writings of his predecessors, Barth and Brunner. In Barth's *Church Dogmatics*, we find that he does his best to examine each passage of Scripture with great respect, with a view to an intelligent interpretation of what it is saying and what it implies. Yet, he also indicates we can not equate any written document in the entire Scripture as being the written Word of God. What Scripture does do is to point to the living Word of God, which is Christ. There seems to be a clear desire on his part to accept Christ as true God, which gives neoorthodoxy its specific character as Crisis Theology. (This Barthian approach came out as a revolutionary development on the heels of World War I.)

Barth and Brunner were both preachers in Switzerland and Germany who went through the tragedy of defeat in 1918 and the humiliating disappointment of German imperialistic hopes. Yet it was this very frustration which led to abandonment of the triumphal rationalism of the Documentarian School and drove Neo-orthodox scholars to search for the meaning and role of man in the presence of God. They went back to the Scripture with the feeling that if one has a sense of personal confrontation between God the Holy Spirit and the human reader, there might be a life changing heart-response to the message which could very well be accepted as an authentic insight or revelation from God. This Neo-orthodox approach requires a high level of intuition and one which is beyond objective verification. The Bible student must then somehow trust the infallibility of his own subjective judgment as being inerrant as he comes to an understanding of Scripture.

Martin Noth

Of the Old Testament Liberal establishment, Martin Noth is perhaps the most extreme critic of the whole fraternity. In his *Commentary On Numbers*, Noth offers his criticisms about the lack of unity and the inconsistencies that he claims to have found in the text. For example he points to Edom's refusal to allow the Israelites to pass through their land. Noth concludes that the language is so inconsistent, as to be unable to determine who is speaking in the various sections. This leads him to believe that there was conflation[1] from several sources.

He assumes that an ancient author has to follow the same rules of consistency and style that he would in the European culture of the 20th century A.D. This of course is a highly questionable assumption, but it is more than doubtful that a truly unbiased reader would perceive these alleged inconsistencies with which he charges the Hebrew author of Numbers. Only by a kind of hostile desire to discover discrepancies that would never occur to an ordinary reader can Noth come out to this judgment. For example, to say that the series of prophecies given by Balaam do not lead to any definite result is to overlook the obvious thrust of these successive oracles. Most readers would come to the conclusion they did indeed lead to a definite result; namely the survival and the triumph of the followers of Moses as they took over possession of the land of Canaan which God had promised from the time of Abraham. Furthermore, they indicate the futility of attempting to resist the will and plan of God by the use of the occult or of hostile magic such as King Balak desired to have Balaam per-

---

1. The approach of the Documentary School assumed that the history of biblical texts involved not only the discovery of the original sources, such as J or E or D or P, but also the redactive activities of later generations who reshaped or further developed the texts handed down from the original authors. Gable and Wheeler in *The Bible as Literature* (Oxford, 1990), p. 11 make this observation: "Unfortunately the redactors are just as mysterious as most of the authors are. Not one of them is identified in any manner in the Bible and the evidences of redaction are all inferential. Still redaction did take place, for there is no other way to explain the condition of the texts as we have them."

It is very significant that both the hypothetical original sources and the later people who were alleged to have manipulated them are impossible to identify and are to be found in the realm of mystery. For those of us who are reading the biblical record from an unbiased standpoint and desiring to be informed, there is no convincing evidence for redaction. The asserted contradictions or inconsistencies seem to be the invention of critics who are determined to find discrepancies in what they assume to be the uninspired invention of ancient pseudepigraphers.

form. In fact, the passage is a magnificent testimony to the faithfulness and the sovereignty of God, both of which may be of no scholarly interest to Martin Noth. The bias here is so obvious as to make his analysis altogether tendentious rather than the objective scholarly type of analysis that one should expect of a well trained *Alttestamentler*. The fact of the matter is that even a child may read through the text of Numbers without perceiving any of these dreadful inconsistencies and confusions which Dr. Noth feels he has discovered. Apparently the presuppositions of the reader have a profound effect upon one's analysis.

MEDIATING CRITICS

Terrance Keegan states, "What is most important is the text which is accepted by the Church as canonical. This canonically accepted text is the starting point of all biblical exegesis."[2] Randolph Tate further elaborates, "Canonical criticism is more concerned with the text as accepted by the believing community than what lies behind the text itself"[3]

Keegan agrees with Childs in commending the approach of canonical criticism in dealing with the Bible and by that term they understand what was accepted by the historic church as canonical. Therefore interest must be centered on the text that has come down to us as canonical and authoritative, and we are to endeavor to catch the meaning of what the text is saying in the form in which it has come to us, rather than confining ourselves to theories as to how those texts historically came into being. Canonical criticism therefore deals with what we actually have in our hands as Scripture which contains a message for us in our day. Therefore it is a matter of accepting this religious document as having a bearing on the life of modern man for him to follow and to believe according to his own personal choice. This mediating view, however, fails to take into account that a book classified as canonical cannot be accepted as final unless the reader is given to understand that it is a faithful document in all it affirms concerning the history of revelation and the gracious dealings of God. If it is to be treated as a message from God, then it won't suffice to say that it arose as a series of pseudepigraphs in the way the Documentarian School maintains.

In other words, the quality of historical trustworthiness is indispensable for a book in the Canon to exercise a meaningful religious function. Randolph Tate writes, "Exegetical concern is not primarily centered on what lies behind the text but on the text itself. Also important within canonical criticism is the situation of the reader. Readers produce meaning in their present situation. This idea of reader produced meaning however holds true only for members of the believing community" (p. 183). In response to this we must observe that reader-produced meaning is only possible if

---

2. Terrance Keegan, O. P., *Interpreting the Bible: A Popular Introduction to Biblical Hermeneutics* (New York: Paulist, 1985), p. 30.

3. Randolph Tate, *Biblical Interpretation: An Integrated Approach* (Hendrickson, 1991), p. 183. Tate should be commended for simplifying and clarifying the issues at stake. This book should be consulted for a convenient review of these various options. This is a very helpful survey for understanding the broad scope of interpretive methods.

the reader himself believes that the meaning he derives is actually conveyed by the text as the revealed word of God.

GENERAL REFLECTIONS ON THE METHODOLOGY OF LIBERAL HIGHER CRITICISM

Now that we have completed a survey of the history and development of modern higher criticism, it seems appropriate to point out certain basic presuppositions which fatally vitiate the Liberal methodology of handling evidences on anything better than a subjective basis and renders their scholarly endeavors a mere exercise in futility. This may sound like a harsh judgment, but for one who has been trained in the laws of legal evidence and who observes how grossly these guidelines observed in a law court are basically ignored in practice from Astruc to von Rad, we can hardly come to any other conclusion.

The Holy Bible is assumed to be a mere piece of religious literature to liberal scholars, purely human in origin and reflective of an evolution of religious thought, a product of Hegelian dialectic process (thesis, antithesis and synthesis). Far from being an authentic revelation of a personal God and His will for the human race, it is assumed to be a mere invention of human minds, devoid of any demonstrable trustworthiness or authority whatever, except insofar as the modern critic personally approves of it and endorses it as valid. No serious account is taken of the many infallible proofs of divine inspiration with which the sixty-six books of the Bible abound. Even to suggest an investigation of these evidences is absolutely unthinkable in the minds of the Liberal establishment. To propose any kind of objective examination is to invite ridicule and scorn from the practitioners of the Documentary Hypothesis or Form Criticism or Canonical Criticism who maintain a rigid control of the Biblical studies department in most of our present day universities and state-supported seminaries throughout the Western World.

The amazing feature about this Bible-denigrating procedure is its flagrant violation of the rule against circular reasoning which underlies all evidential logic. To the rationalistic mind-set of the *Aufklärung* and the Encyclopedistes of the mid-eighteenth century it was well-nigh inconceivable for any educated thinker to take seriously the truth-claims of Holy Scripture, and those who undertook to do so were ridiculed as benighted and naive, no matter what scholarly attainments they had achieved in their education. If they really believed that the Bible was the Word of God, they were *ipso facto* outdated traditionalists who could be safely ignored.

From the standpoint of legal evidence, such a cavalier trampling upon the rights of a defendant in a criminal court proceeding would be completely disallowed. Yet the Scriptures are treated to the same procedure as that practiced by the Spanish Inquisition. Confined in a dungeon without a possibility of contact by any friend or relative or legal counsel, the hapless prisoner was confronted only by stern inquisitors who announced to him, "We know you are guilty already, and no testimony in your defense will be allowed." In this case, then, the Bible is assumed to be of mere human origin, and therefore no evidence of divine authorship can be seriously entertained. There is little possibility for one who has gone through Liberal training to learn how to understand and preach the Bible as the Word of God or to come through that training with any measure of religious conviction. He may learn how to pick and choose elements in the Scriptures that appeal to him as being valid, but since the validation has to come from the human critic, it ends up with no greater measure of authority than that possessed by the human judge, thus the doctrinaire specialists fall into many fallacies that essentially go back to a naive belief in their own superior judgment.

One of the most amazing features of the modern Liberal scholarship is its complete ignoring of the overwhelming evidence afforded by the multitude of fulfilled predictions with which the Bible abounds. The whole idea of fulfilled prophecy is absolutely unanswerable on humanistic grounds. It is beyond the ability of any man to foretell with accuracy what is going to happen in advance. It is still more impossible for us to predict an entire series of events according to a coordinated plan extending over thousands of years. Yet the Bible record indicates God's amazing plan of redemption for the race descended from Adam and Eve as early as Gen. 3:15. A descendant of Eve is destined to crush the head of the Satanic serpent after it has bruised the heel of the Redeemer. The rest of the Bible unfolds the execution of this program of redemption, relating the atoning death of the God-Man on the cross, His subsequent rising from the dead on Easter morning, and His ultimate triumph upon His return to crush the rebellious world at Armageddon, and after a thousand-year reign upon earth, to bring about the merger of heaven and earth in the New Jerusalem.

Skeptics may attempt to dismiss this redemptive scenario by supposing that Jesus was mistaken about His messianic role on Golgotha, and that the bodily resurrection of Christ never really took place. But they can never explain why the craven, panicked disciples of Jesus were transformed into death-defying proclaimers of the Resurrection triumph over death—unless they knew that it really happened, and that they really did see Him and touch His wounds and eat food with Him as the Conqueror over sin and death. No disciple would ever be willing to lay down his own life in faithfulness to a leader who actually died and never rose again. Skeptics may discount these records in the four Gospels and in the New Testament epistles, but they cannot cite any ancient written records from the same period as the First Century apostles to furnish justification for their rejection of the resurrection testimony. All they can argue is they do not believe in miracles, and therefore no miracle could ever have taken place.

But for a modern scholar, living over nineteen centuries after the fact, to reject all testimony of the miraculous is to betray an irrational fideism which could hardly be received as evidence in court. In the last analysis there is no thinker alive, not even an atheist, who does not assume the occurrence of miracle. That is to say, he who does not believe that creation came into being through a Creator is forced to resort to a dogma of the eternity of matter—a completely untenable position to hold, in view of the discoveries of nuclear fission. The only alternative left is the supposition that matter was created by Nothing! It will not do to say that everything fell into its present shape by the operation of chance, because chance is not and cannot be a creative force. Chance is only a calculation of observed occurrences of phenomena under study. But chance can no more create or arrange matter than a clock can create time. Therefore we can only conclude that the person who supposes creation could have come into being without a creator holds to a theory of total impossibility rather than a more reasonable theory that for every effect there must be a cause. Thus such a rationale becomes a dismal form of irrationality which can have no credibility or standing either in theology or in science.

The fulfilled predictions contained in the Old Testament number more than 800—and all of them beyond the ability of mortal man to foretell. We may start with the promise of God to Abraham and Sarah that they would produce a family which would grow into a great nation (Gen. 12:1-3) which would bring blessing to all other nations, whose converts would far outnumber the lineal descendants of Abraham in the age to come. Customarily the rationalist higher critic tries to explain away all fulfilled prophecy as mere pious fraud, as *vaticinium ex eventu* (prophecy forged after the fulfillment itself). But this cannot possibly explain the great multiplication of the early Christian Church in the second half of the First Century A.D. In line with this we find in Isa. 49:6 (composed at a time when the mere survival of Mosaic religion was gravely in doubt even for the Jews themselves) that the promised Servant of the Lord would not only "raise up the tribes of Jacob and restore the preserved of Israel," but he would also "Make you a light of the Gentiles, so that My Salvation may reach to the end of the earth." No prediction could have seemed less likely of fulfillment back in Isaiah's day, yet we see today a worldwide Christian church established on every continent of Planet Earth. No human insight could ever have foreseen such an amazing extension of the covenant promises to the national and spiritual descendants of Abraham. No escape is possible from the conclusion that predictions like this could never have been successfully made by merely uninspired human authors, whether J or D or E or P, or even Isaiah I, II, or III.

The description of what our Lord Jesus Christ suffered on the day He was crucified is found in its most moving and eloquent form in the 53rd chapter of Isaiah. The Servant's characteristics and experiences as set forth in Isa. 52 :13–53 :12 cannot be fitted to the career of Hezekiah or Josiah or the nation Israel—even though such theories have been advanced by those who are desperate for an alternative to Jesus of Nazareth. Israel was never described as sinless and blameless by any of Israel's own prophets. The Servant of the Lord is so described in this chapter. Nor could Israel have been punished by God in the place of Israel, as Liberals argue today, for this amounts to a self-contradictory absurdity. You simply cannot explain away Isaiah's prediction on the basis of humanism and rationalism as has been pursued by the Liberal establishment. The attempt to explain away fulfilled prophecy by saying the biblical book itself must have been written after the fulfillment had taken place can be easily refuted by those prophecies which were fulfilled after the last line in the Old Testament was written. Therefore we are driven to the conclusion that only a personal, almighty, covenant-keeping God, sovereign over history, could have originated such predictions as these and brought them to pass.

We could adduce hundreds of other predictions, many of which must have seemed very unlikely of fulfillment, but those above mentioned amply suffice to prove the point that the Bible was not of mere human origin, but rather (as 2 Peter 1:21 puts it) "No prophecy was ever made by an act of human will, but men moved by the Holy Spirit spoke from God" (NASB). No other conclusion is possible for any honest investigator whose mind has not been warped by a stubborn bias which self-defensively repels all contrary evidence. No judge or jury operating according to the laws of evidence could come to any other conclusion but that there are irrefutable proofs of divine origin to be found in Scripture which defy all possibility of mere human invention.

It may be argued at this point that while fulfilled predictions made far in advance of their realization are to be found in Holy Scripture, yet there seem to be numerous discrepancies and contradictions discoverable in the Bible which could hardly have been inspired by a God of truth. To this we respond that no error has ever been adduced which can be proven to have arisen in the autographs (the original manuscripts) of Scripture. There may be a few discrepancies in the spelling of names or in the citing of statistics which appear even in the earliest of manuscripts which have come down to us. But with the responsible use of the rules of textual criticism, there is no unanswerable objection which robs the Bible of inerrancy—when properly exegeted in the light of what the original Hebrew, Aramaic, and Greek reader would have understood as the meaning of the sacred authors themselves. (See G. L. Archer's *Encyclopedia of Bible Difficulties*, pp. 15-44). This of course presupposes a thorough acquaintance with the vocabulary and grammar of these three languages, along with a control of the data furnished by comparative linguistics (Ugaritic, Phoenician, Akkadian, Egyptian) which shed light upon the meaning and implications of the idioms and connotations that appear in the Scripture text. Over half of the difficulties found in Scripture are readily solvable by adequate knowledge of the original languages and of the relevant data from archaeology.

Many of the most discussed difficulties in the Bible are theological, such as the nature of the Triune God Himself, the hypostatic union of Jesus Christ as the God-Man, and the tensions between divine predestination and man's free will. These deep and basic questions are also dealt with in that volume, although they are not on the agenda of Higher Criticism as such. But just let me say that after forty years of study and investigation I have encountered no difficulties or apparent discrepancies which cannot be dealt with satisfactorily by a proper use of the laws of legal evidence.

Before concluding this chapter I would like to point out the grave consequences of espousing a theory of non-inerrant Scripture. If indeed there are errors to be found in the Bible record which still remain after careful, objective exegesis of the text, the only possible recourse would have to be a judgment passed upon this error that would necessitate a competent critic who is somehow better informed as to the truth than was the author of Holy Scripture Himself. But as was pointed out in chapter 2, this results in setting a human judgment over what purports to be the Word of God. If an error in the autograph can be conclusively proven in one passage, it opens up the possibility of error in other passages as well. The subjective preference of the modern critic may intervene at this point, and essentially the Bible is demoted to the status of any other human-composed book on religion—a combination of truth and error that demands an inerrant critic to discern between what is wrong and what is right – one who is wiser and better informed than the original prophet or apostle who composed the book in question. Thus the modern scholar becomes an arbiter of truth on a superior level to those whom God allegedly inspired. It then follows that the text of theological truth rests upon the infallibility of the present-day savant. And unhappily, such savants have been known to disagree with one another, and so there is no positive certainty possible to know what was really contained in the text or even whether it spoke the truth. Thus the initial spot of cancer tends to spread throughout the rest of the body, as it were, and the seeker is ultimately left to his own opinion rather than resting on the certainty of an objective revelation from God, a God who really cares about man and who has made provision for him to be saved from his guilty, fallen condition. The end result is apt to be a resignation to agnosticism which leads to a feeling of personal meaninglessness and despair, similar to that of H. G. Wells in "The Mind at the End of its Tether" or the final reproach against Nature or the Universe which came from the pen of Bertrand Russell. The honored savant who has bet his life on the verity of Liberalism goes out into the night that awaits him, unforgiven and unrepentant, to face his Maker and a divine judgment which lies beyond the competence of man to alter or to mitigate.

Before concluding this chapter it would be good to listen to the recent (1990) testimony of Dr. Eta Linneman, who first rose to prominence in the University of Marburg, Germany, as an accomplished disciple of Rudolf Bultmann and Ernst Fuchs, Friedrich Gogarten and Gerhard Ebeling. In other words she had the finest professors in the area of historical-critical theology that Germany could produce. As a professor of theology and religious education at Braunschweig Technical University, she was very highly regarded by faculty and student body wherever she came to speak. But to her dismay she began to notice that she was falling into a state of profound disillusionment and failed to find any real relief in an alcoholic addiction. But when she found herself at lowest ebb, she came in contact with a group of women who met weekly for Bible study and prayer, and who impressed her as believers who really knew and loved God and who had a meaningful relationship with Him. After listening to the testimony of a converted Nepalese who had been imprisoned and beaten for turning from Buddha to Christ, she turned with her whole heart back to the personal faith in which she had been brought up as a girl. She felt the influence of the Holy Spirit taking over her whole being and surrendered her life to her Redeemer.

The scientific approach of the rationalist higher critics could not enable her to understand the Bible better and turned out to be utterly false and debasing. The very foundations of the Documentary Theory were faulted through antitheistic presuppositions which were nothing more than an exercise in subjectivism that had nothing to do with true science. The little volume featuring this story, translated by R. W. Yarbrough, as *Historical Criticism of the Bible (Grand Rapids: Baker, 1990),* is an amazingly powerful and convincing treatment that every student should read before surrendering his mind to the fallacies of Wellhausen's developmental hypothesis or the vagaries of *Formgeschichte.*

SELECTED BIBLIOGRAPHY

Aalders, G. C. *A Short Introduction to the Pentateuch*. London: Tyndale, 1949.

Adams, J. M. *Ancient Records and the Bible*. Nashville: Broadman, 1946.

Aharoni, Yohanan. *The Land of the Bible*. Philadelphia: Westminster, 1967.

Albright, W. F. *The Archaeology of Palestine*. Rev. ed. Harmondsworth, Middlesex: Pelican, 1960.

————. *From the Stone Age to Christianity*. Baltimore: Johns Hopkins, 1957.

Alleman, H. C., and Flack, E. E., eds. *Old Testament Commentary*. Philadelphia: Muhlenberg, 1948.

Allis, O. T. *The Five Books of Moses*. Philadelphia: Presb. & Reformed, 1943.

————. *The Unity of Isaiah*. Philadelphia: Presb. & Ref., 1950.

Archer, G. L. *Encyclopedia of Bible Difficulties*. Grand Rapids: Zondervan, 1992

Barton, G. A. *Archaeology and the Bible*. 7th ed. Philadelphia: American Sunday School Union, 1941.

Barton, John. *Reading the Old Testament*. Philadelphia: Westminster, 1984.

Bentzen, Aage. *Introduction to the Old Testament*. 2 vols. Copenhagen: G. E. C. Gad, 1949.

Biblical Archaeology Today (Proceedings of the International Congress on Biblical Archaeology). Israel Exploration Society, 1984.

Bimson, J. J. *Redating the Exodus and Conquest*. JSOT. Sheffield: Almond, 1978.

Bright, J. M. *History of Israel*. Philadelphia: Westminster, 1959.

Brown, Driver, and Briggs, eds. *Hebrew and English Lexicon of the Old Testament*. Oxford: Clarendon, 1907.

Brown, Raymond D. *Recent Discoveries and the Biblical Word*. Wilmington, Del.: Michael Glazier, 1983.

Burrows, Millar. *The Dead Sea Scrolls*. New York: Viking, 1955.

————. *More Light on the Dead Sea Scrolls*. New York: Viking, 1958.

Cassuto, Umberto. *The Documentary Hypothesis*. Jerusalem: Magnes, 1961.

Childs, Brevard. *Introduction to the Old Testament as Scripture*, vol 2. Philadelphia: Fortress, 1979.

————. *The Book of Exodus*. Philadelphia: Westminster, 1974.

Clark, R. E. D. *Darwin Before and After*. Grand Rapids: Eerdmans, 1958.

Cross, F. M. *The Ancient Library of Qumran*. New York: Doubleday, Anchor, 1961.

Cross, F. M. and Talman, S. *Qumran and the History of the Biblical Text*. Cambridge, Mass.: Harvard U. Press, 1975.

DeVaux, Roland. *Ancient Israel*. New York: McGraw-Hill, 1961.

Dowley, Tim, ed. *Discovering the Bible*. Grand Rapids: Marshall Pickering/Eerdmans, 1986.

Driver, S. R. *Introduction to the Literature of the Old Testament*. New York: Scribner, 1891.

Eissfeldt, O. *The Old Testament, an Introduction*. Translated by Ackroyd. New York: Harper, 1965.

Erman, Adolf, and Grapow, Herman. *Wörterbuch der Aegyptischen Sprache*. Berlin, 1955.

Finegan, Jack. *Handbook of Biblical Chronology*. Princeton: Princeton U. Press, 1964.

————. *Light from the Ancient Past*. 2d. ed. Princeton: Princeton U. Press, 1959.

Flack, E. E., and Metzger, B. M. *The Text, Canon and Principal Versions of the Bible*. Grand Rapids: Baker, 1956.

Free, Joseph P. *Archaeology and Bible History*. Wheaton: Scripture, 1956.

Garstang, J., and J. B. E. *The Story of Jericho*. Rev. ed. London: Marshall, Morgan, and Scott, 1948.

Hahn, H. F. *The Old Testament and Modern Research*. Philadelphia: Muhlenberg, 1954.

Harris, R. L. *The Inspiration and Canonicity of the Bible.* Grand Rapids: Zondervan, 1957.

Harrison, R. K. *Old Testament Introduction.* Grand Rapids: Eerdmans, 1979.

———. *Old Testament Times.* Grand Rapids: Eerdmans, 1970.

———. *Introduction to the Old Testament.* Grand Rapids: Eerdmans, 1969.

Harrison, R. K.; Waltke, B. K.; Guthrie, D.; and Fee, G. D. *Biblical Criticism: Historical, Literary, and Textual.* Grand Rapids: Zondervan, 1978.

Hayes, W. C. *The Scepter of Egypt: A background for the study of the Egyptian.* New York: Metropolitan Museum of Art.

Henry, C. F. H., ed. *Revelation and the Bible.* Grand Rapids: Baker, 1958.

———. *International Standard Bible Encyclopedia.* Rev. ed. 5 vols. Grand Rapids: Eerdmans, 1946.

Kaufmann, Yehezkel. *The Religion of Israel.* Chicago: U. Chicago Press, 1960.

Keller, Werner. *The Bible as History.* New York: Morrow, 1964.

Kenyon, Frederic. *Our Bible and the Ancient Manuscripts.* 5th ed. New York: Harper, 1958.

Kitchen, Kenneth A. *Ancient Orient and the Old Testament.* Chicago: InterVarsity, 1966.

———. *The Bible and Archaeology.* Chicago: InterVarsity, 1977.

Kittel, Rudolph ed. *Biblia Hebraica.* 3d. ed. Stuttgart: Württembergische Bibelanstalt, 1950.

Kline, M. G. *Treaty of the Great King.* Grand Rapids: Eerdmans, 1963.

LaSor, William; Hubbard, David A.; Bush, Frederick. *Old Testament Survey.* Grand Rapids: Eerdmans, 1982.

Linneman, Eta. *Historical Criticism of the Bible: Methodology or Ideal?* Translated by R. W. Yarbrough. Grand Rapids: Baker, 1992.

Livingston, George H. *The Pentateuch in its Cultural Environment.* Grand Rapids: Baker, 1974.

Longmann III, Tremper. *Literary Approaches to Biblical Interpretation. Foundations of Contemporary Interpretation.* Vol 3. Edited by Moises Silva. Grand Rapids: Zondervan, 1987.

Maier, Gerhard. *The End of the Historical Critical Method.* Edited by E. Leverenz, R. Norden. St. Louis: Concordia Publishing House, 1977.

Mixter, R. L., ed. *Evolution and Christian Thought Today.* Grand Rapids: Eerdmans, 1959.

Manley, G. T. *Deuteronomy—the Book of the Law.* Grand Rapids: Eerdmans, 1957.

Moeller, Wilhelm E. *Grundriss für Alttestamentliche Einleitung.* Berlin: Evangelische Verlagsanstalt, 1958.

New Bible Commentary. Edited by Francis Davidson, A. M. Stibbs, and E. F. Kevan. Grand Rapids: Eerdmans, 1953.

New Bible Commentary, The: Revised. Edited by Donald Guthrie. Rev. ed. Grand Rapids: Eerdmans, 1970.

Noth, Martin. *Numbers, The Old Testament Library.* Edited by G. Wright, J. Bright, James Barr, Peter Ackroyd. Philadelphia: Westminster, 1968.

Oesterley, W. O. E., and Robinson, T. H. *Introduction to the Books of the Old Testament.* London: SPCK, 1931.

Olmstead, Albert T. *History of Assyria.* New York, London: Scribner, 1923.

Orr, James. *The Problem of the Old Testament.* New York: Scribner, 1906.

Ottley, R. R. *A Handbook to the Septuagint.* London: Methuen, 1920.

Payne, J. B. *An Outline of Hebrew History.* Grand Rapids: Baker, 1954.

———. *Encyclopedia of Biblical Prophecy.* New York: Harper & Row, 1973.

———. ed. *New Perspectives on the Old Testament.* Waco, Tex.: Word, 1970.

Pettinato, Giovanni. *Archives From Ebla.* Garden City, NY: Doubleday, 1981.

Pfeiffer, Robert H. *Introduction to the Old Testament.* New York: Harper, 1941.

Pfeiffer, Charles F. *Baker's Bible Atlas*. Grand Rapids: Baker, 1972.

Pritchard, J. B., ed. *Ancient Near Eastern Texts*. Princeton: Princeton U. Press, 1950.

Rahlfs, A., ed. *Septuaginta*. 2 vols. 3d. ed. Stuttgart: Württembergische Bibelanstalt, 1949.

Ramm, Bernard. *The Christian View of Science and Scripture*. Grand Rapids: Eerdmans, 1954.

Raven, J. H. *Old Testament Introduction*. New York: Revell, 1910.

Rehwinkel, A. M. *The Flood in the Light of the Bible, Geology and Archaeology*. St. Louis: Concordia, 1951.

Robinson, G. L. *The Bearing of Archaeology on the Old Testament*. 2d. ed. New York: American Tract Society, 1944.

Rowley, H. H., ed. *The Old Testament and Modern Study*. Oxford: Clarendon, 1951.

Rypins, Stanley. *The Book of Thirty Centuries*. New York: Macmillan, 1951.

Silva, Moises, ed. *Literary Approaches to Biblical Interpretation: Foundations of Contemporary Interpretation*, vol. 3. Grand Rapids: Zondervan, 1987.

Smith, W. Robertson. *The Religion of the Semites*. New York: Meridian, 1956.

Sproul, R.C. *The Holiness of God*. Wheaton: Tyndale, 1985.

Steinmueller, J. E. *Companion to Scripture Studies*. 2 vols. New York: Joseph F. Wagner, 1942.

Tate, Randolph. *Biblical Interpretation: An Integrated Approach*. New York: Hendrickson, 1991.

Thompson, J. A. *Archaeology and the Old Testament*. Grand Rapids: Eerdmans, 1959.

Unger, Merrill F. *Archaeology and the Old Testament*. Grand Rapids: Zondervan, 1954.

———. *Introductory Guide to the Old Testament*. Grand Rapids: Zondervan, 1952.

Urquhart, John. *The Wonders of Prophecy*. London: Pickering & Inglis, 1939.

von Rad, Gerhard. *Old Testament Theology*, vol 1. Stalker, D. M. G. New York: Harper & Row, 1962.

Walvoord, John W., ed. *Inspiration and Interpretation*. Grand Rapids: Eerdmans, 1957.

Whitcomb, John C. *Darius the Mede*. Grand Rapids: Eerdmans, 1959.

Whitcomb, John C., and Morris, Henry M. *The Genesis Flood*. Philadelphia: Presb. & Ref., 1962.

Wilson, Robert Dick. *A Scientific Investigation of the Old Testament*. Chicago: Moody, 1959.

———. *Studies in the Book of Daniel*. New York: Putnam. Ser. 1, 1911; ser. 2, 1938.

Wiseman, D. J., et al. *Notes on Problems in the Book of Daniel*. London: Tyndale, 1965.

Wood, Leon. *A Survey of Israel's History*. Grand Rapids: Zondervan, 1970.

Wright, G. E. *The Old Testament Against Its Environment*. Chicago: H. Regnery, 1950.

Würthwein, Ernst. *The Text of the Old Testament*. 4th ed. Translated by Rhodes. Grand Rapids: Eerdmans, 1979.

Young, E. J. *Introduction to the Old Testament*. Grand Rapids: Eerdmans, 1958.

———. *Thy Word Is Truth*. Grand Rapids: Eerdmans, 1957.

———. *Who Wrote Isaiah?* Grand Rapids: Eerdmans, 1958.

AUTHOR INDEX

SUBJECT INDEX

SCRIPTURE INDEX